BATTLE FOR THE SOUL

BATTLE
FOR THE
SOUL

INSIDE THE
DEMOCRATS'
CAMPAIGNS TO
DEFEAT TRUMP

Edward-Isaac Dovere

VIKING

VIKING
An imprint of Penguin Random House LLC
penguinrandomhouse.com

ISBN 9781984878076 (hardcover)
ISBN 9781984878083 (ebook)

Printed in the United States of America
1st Printing

Book design by Daniel Lagin

To Sarah and the boys who make every day happiness,
no matter what else the days may hold. There is more day to dawn.

CONTENTS

BATTLE FOR THE SOUL

PROLOGUE

November 8, 2016
Election Day

H ow do you feel?"

Hillary Clinton's campaign manager, Robby Mook, was headed out of the Javits Center as the sun set, hours before the polls closed, when excited people were still showing up to get a good spot for the party. He looked up, trying to find who'd called out to him.

"I feel nothing," he said back.

They knew in the White House by the afternoon that they had a problem. The early vote from Florida could not have been better, but when they started seeing the numbers for the people actually showing up on Election Day, panic quickly spread. By quarter to eight, they realized that the state was probably gone.

Barack Obama spent the afternoon and the evening mostly alone, up in the residence. David Simas, Obama's political director, who'd been assuring everyone in the White House every morning that Clinton was going to win, would check in every forty-five minutes by phone, telling him where things stood. He listened quietly, not asking many questions, and waited for the next update.

The Wisconsin results ended it. Wisconsin, where Obama had been scheduled to make his debut on the trail with her in June, before the Pulse nightclub shooting led them to scrap the trip. Where he'd always won easily. Where the last Democrat to have lost the state in a presidential election had been Walter Mondale in 1984. Where Clinton had never gone for the whole campaign. Simas called Mook, holding a printout of the preliminary results from the state. "What am I missing?" he asked. Mook said something about more votes being out, but Simas wasn't buying it. Making up the margin in one state would be a historic shift. Then to replicate that in two or three states?

"Donald Trump," Simas said when he next called Obama, "is going to be the president."

There was silence for a few seconds. Obama asked them to get Trump's phone number. The closest contact they had was Chris Christie, from work the White House had done with the New Jersey governor during Hurricane Sandy. They started tracking down the ever more likely to be president-elect. Obama asked what the Clinton campaign's plan was for what was now unavoidable. They didn't seem to have one, Simas told him. They seemed to be buying time. "Well," Obama said. "That's a problem."

Obama had never understood why people disliked Clinton so much. He could also never get over how bad a campaigner she was. When they had finally hit the trail together at the beginning of July in North Carolina and made the obligatory surprise stop at a barbecue restaurant, she'd quickly slipped out—Jim Comey had announced the end of the FBI investigation into her email server that morning, and she was ducking reporters waiting to shout questions at her. Obama had been working the crowd so intently, shaking so many hands and buying so much food, that he hadn't realized she'd gone until he was outside and looking for her to say goodbye. "Where did she go?" he asked aides, confused.

He liked that story. He has told it over and over again in the years since.

Obama shouldn't have been surprised. She was a pioneering force for feminism, an icon of America's shift into the twenty-first century, and the most successful woman in the history of American politics, but she was also the frozen-faced embodiment of Democrats as "Democrats"—all the good and bad qualities of government, all the promises it had made that hadn't addressed what was actually happening in the country. There was racism and sexism and xenophobia and nativist paranoia particular to Trump, the overnight pop culture icon who'd wheedled his way into the public consciousness to the point of becoming an easy joke on sitcoms. But the core of Trump's campaign was the same as the core of Bernie Sanders's campaign, and it was the same as what had been the core of Obama's campaign against her: "Change You Can Believe In." That 2008 slogan was just a shorter way of saying what Trump had charged her with in their first debate—"Secretary Clinton and other politicians should have been doing this for years, not right now, because of the fact that we've created a movement."

Voters went with the outsider they hated over the insider they despised.

Obama would have been able to make more sense of Clinton's losing if it hadn't been to a man he thought of as a moronic carnival barker, who brought out the worst in people, and whom he'd never forgive for turning a fringe obsession with his birth certificate into an issue he'd had to address from the White House briefing room in 2011.

At the beginning of September, after a briefing to discuss how Trump was apparently bouncing back from yet another scandal—at that point, it was the outrage of insulting Khizr Khan's Gold Star military family—and how Clinton could never seem to make up any ground, Obama was starting to get exasperated. His order: *fix it.* "Do you really want a psychopath sitting at that desk?" he'd asked. Find a way to break through to voters. "Get someone to listen."

But of course she was going to win. If he'd had any doubts about it, he never would have appeared on Jimmy Kimmel's show just a few weeks before the election and done Kimmel's standard bit of having a guest respond to mean tweets. He read an infamous one from Trump—"President Obama will go down as perhaps the worst president in the history of the United States!"—and replied, "Well, @realDonaldTrump, at least I will go down as a *president*," and then glared right into the camera and dropped the prop iPhone. He never really even considered Clinton could lose.

Until those last few days. The crowds didn't feel right. The previous Friday in North Carolina, they were into him in Fayetteville, but they were more into booing an old man in what might have been an old army jacket who'd gotten up and started waving a Trump lawn sign. He couldn't get them to stop, to listen, shouting, "Hold up!" into the microphone over and over. "I told you to be focused, and you're not focused right now," he said. A couple of hours later in Charlotte, the rally hadn't been interrupted, but it didn't feel right to him.

They wanted to see him, they wanted to beat Trump, but they didn't seem to be thinking much about her.

At first he, like Clinton, blamed the lingering legacy of the long, brutal primary she'd been through in the spring. "Bernie hurt her more than I realized," he'd told an aide that day. The only response from the Clinton campaign was all their data, their voter turnout models, their polls, and data, and data, and data. It was going to be a crappy, bitter win, especially after the Comey letter, but they'd done the math, and it was going to be a win. Like everything else she'd ever done, she was going to have to grind it out, aim to be less hated, not loved. Trump would turn out his votes; she'd turn out hers. It would be fine. "I don't know," Obama would respond, hesitantly.

With Wisconsin, he knew.

———

Joe Biden spent most of that night watching the results for the House and Senate candidates for whom he'd campaigned. As each race was called, he got each one of them on the phone. Winners, losers all got the same line: "You ran a hell of a race."

Only late into the night did he start paying attention to the presidential election. He'd always been concerned that people simply didn't like Clinton, and the lack of enthusiasm he'd sensed during those last few appearances for her made him nervous—on a trip to Madison, Wisconsin, the previous Friday, he'd warned the audience, "The arc of history has always been forward, and what these guys want to do is literally move it backward," and then he included his now familiar routine about how America could be defined in "one word: possibilities." But when he returned to Washington, he told aides, "It doesn't feel right there." Not off enough to really consider that Trump could win, though.

He listened while Mike Donilon, one of his closest advisers, insisted that Clinton would be all right. He listened as his younger aide, Greg Schultz, presented the same rundown from Florida that had spooked Simas.

Jill Biden headed upstairs early with a book and a bottle of wine.

Close to eleven that night, Biden stepped out to call his buddy Mike Duggan, the mayor of Detroit, to check in. Duggan had been fighting with the Clinton campaign for months about trying to take control of the turnout operation in the city. Three weeks earlier he had gone to their headquarters in Brooklyn, making one last push, getting one last brush-off from top aides, who assured him that the statistical model they had built off their polling showed her 5 points ahead in Michigan. "What if your model," Duggan asked them, "doesn't match the world?" Well, he told Biden that night, it hadn't. "What's going to happen?" Biden said. Duggan guessed she was going to lose the state by about 10,000 votes.

"Oh, Lord," Biden replied.

They talked for a moment about why Biden hadn't run. Duggan was regretful. Biden was emotional.

"I want to be the first person to sign up for the 2020 campaign," Duggan told him, "because this never would have happened if you were the candidate."

Biden, quiet, deflected.

Michigan wound up going to Trump by 10,704 votes.

Biden walked into the next room to call the White House, waiting for Obama to get on. That conversation didn't last long. There wasn't much to say.

———

Obama phoned Clinton. He was just as level with her as he'd been with everyone else. Democrats couldn't be the ones to fight the results. She resisted. He then called John Podesta, Clinton's campaign chairman and his own former senior adviser, catching him after Podesta had given his speech back at the Javits Center trying to buy time, now riding back to Clinton's hotel in a van full of depressed top campaign staffers. "You've got to make her concede," Obama told him.

The president was looking at the numbers as he spoke. *It can't come back. Don't fight it anymore.* Podesta listened, finally agreeing.

"I feel like I really let you down, Mr. President," he said. "I feel like I really let her down."

While they were speaking, Clinton's closest aide, Huma Abedin, called Jennifer Palmieri, who was sitting in the van next to Podesta. "Well," Abedin said. "She did it." Clinton had called Trump to concede. She didn't call Obama back that night to tell him she had done so.

She never got over how he'd rushed her to quit. "It was a very tough call for him, and obviously for me. But we didn't know very much. We didn't have a lot of insight into what had gone on. I certainly didn't. I learned much, much more after the election," Clinton said in late 2020. She was trying to avoid saying directly that she felt Obama had pushed her to concede too soon, so she used a lot of words that added up to the simple answer she meant: yes. "I think knowing much more that we know now about how voters were treated in Milwaukee, for example, you would be more cautious," she said. "You would want to really do the kind of careful auditing of the vote that we didn't do in 2016." It ate at her. "You don't win by three million votes and have all these other shenanigans and stuff going on and not come away with an idea like, 'Whoa, something's not right here.'"

After Obama himself phoned to congratulate Trump, he called over to two of his closest aides, his deputy national security adviser, Ben Rhodes, and his speechwriter Cody Keenan, well into a bottle of whiskey at Keenan's apartment, to talk through what he was going to say in the Rose Garden in the morning. "I have to do this the right way," he insisted. He dictated most of the text. They were deep into their scotch by then, but not so much that they missed that Obama's heart wasn't in it. "Do you want to put any reassurance in there for our allies around the world?" Rhodes asked. "I can't give it to them." They left that part out.

━━━

The next few days were full of tears and *West Wing* moments of Obama's saying how proud he was of everyone and urged them to "run through the tape" and keep focused on their work, as he told them at the senior staff meeting he'd popped in to one morning. No one really could. Denis McDonough, Obama's chief of staff, pulled top aides into the Roosevelt Room. "The United States is resilient," he told them. "And we have, and will, overcome challenges and divisions. We are going to take this transition very seriously. We owe it to America." Aides who used to spend their days being snarky and tough had tears streaming down their faces. They waited for Clinton to finally give her concession speech up in New York. Then Obama came out into the Rose Garden, Joe Biden at his side, saying something about how the sun would rise tomorrow. There'd never been so many staff gathered there. They did not look as if they believed the sun would rise tomorrow. They could barely see it then.

Simas and a few others took a quiet trip to Iowa in early December to try to make sense of what had happened. The Obama crew was rational and data driven and serious minded, but they were also superstitious and completely immersed in their own mythology. White House meetings tended to feature someone's knocking on wood, or being screamed at for forgetting to knock on wood. There were special shirts, Election Day routines. Simas kept a betta fish in a tank in his office on the first floor of the West Wing because he liked to joke that it was beautiful and small and seemingly sweet, but if you put another betta fish in the tank, they'd try to kill each other.

There was nowhere more wrapped in Obama superstition and mythology than Iowa, the magical place that took a chance on the Black guy with the funny name. Where the podium that he spoke at on the night he won the caucuses is in a museum. Where he'd become so well known that when he called a high school senior to ask for her support a few days before the 2008 caucuses, she'd replied, "Oh, hi, Barack," and told him she had to call him back because she was in the middle of a yearbook meeting. The feeling people had for him there was different, his staff believed, and they always went there for what they thought was a reliable reflection of reality. They'd always wanted to do the last focus group of his presidency there, as a tie-the-ribbon gut check. Now they changed the criteria for who was invited to the focus group: only people who'd voted for Obama twice, approved of the job he was doing on the day of the election, and *still* voted for Trump. Iowa was the biggest Trump win of any state that had voted for Obama.

They landed the Wednesday after Thanksgiving. "What were the things about Hillary Clinton that prevented you from voting for her?" was the first question, and they dug in from there: "Did you see any election-related items on social media or Facebook that caught your eye?" They asked about Obamacare. They asked what Trump would have to do to be a successful president, and what they would be most turned off by.

Then: What about the current president? "The thing I will most miss about President Obama," they were asked, "is ____."

This wasn't getting them enough information. What are the similarities between Obama and Trump, and what are the differences? asked David Binder, the longtime Democratic pollster. The two presidents wanted different directions for the country, came back the responses, with Obama more inclusive and a believer in the power of government, and Trump more selective and concerned with putting people in a position to help themselves. Obama, one pointed out, is more soft-spoken. "Family is important to both," another answered. Both are passionate, said a third, and both are intelligent: "They both took on the system in their own way—both wanted change."

Obama, observed one, "did a much better job than people give him credit for. People will recognize that down the road. He was good with world leaders. He didn't make enemies." "He was someone you can look up to. A family person. And a deep thinker," another said.

One woman stood out. She seemed to be the quintessential Obama voter: late fifties, a mom, independent, who said she thought both parties were terrible. They locked in on her. "Hope and change" and "drain the swamp," she said, were the same thing, as far as she could see. "We'd sent this young man to Washington hoping to make change, and they stopped him every time. And I'm angry about it, and I want somebody to get in there now and drain the swamp."

Back from Iowa, Simas and a few other aides stood in the Oval Office, summarizing the results that were written up in the report of their findings: "Voters who chose Obama in 2012 and Trump in 2016 were not sending a signal nor repudiating the president in any way. Rather, many felt those choices were consistent by voting for a candidate who promised to shake up the political system and bring change to Washington. Many were highly conflicted in their 2016 decision, but ultimately chose Trump because they concluded that Hillary Clinton was too flawed as a candidate and would not deliver on promises to move the country forward."

Obama took it in quietly. They waited for him to say something profound.

"I get it," he finally replied.

CHAPTER ONE

BENIGN NEGLECT

Talk to me if he wins. Then we'll have a conversation about how responsible I feel about him.

—BARACK OBAMA, JANUARY 12, 2016

April 2015–November 7, 2016

They spent hours at the dining room table in Chappaqua, with Hillary Clinton doing most of the talking. Donald Trump had delivered his first State of the Union the night before. Seeing him up there hurt, she said. It hurt on a personal level, but it was also about taking in that first month—the Muslim ban, Michael Flynn stomping into the White House briefing room in his first appearance as national security adviser to declare that "we are officially putting Iran on notice," and all the chaos and infighting in the new West Wing, which had already become a worn-out joke. Thinking back on Mitch McConnell's refusal to sign on to a public statement the previous summer harshly calling out the Russians for election interference. . . . That hurt, but it also made her angry.

None of that was why she had invited Tom Perez over. He'd been elected Democratic National Committee chair a few days earlier in Atlanta, and she wanted to give him some advice. That was another part of the job of being president that she'd been looking forward to. The Clintons were party people. Institutionalists. They liked the horse-trading and the bench building and the favor collecting. WELCOME TO DNC HQ, read a sign that appeared over the summer of 2016 at the reception desk in her Brooklyn campaign office, at once mocking the old operation and bragging about how much they had taken control of it.

Now, instead of a state dinner in the White House, Hillary and Bill Clinton were having fish with Perez and Jaime Harrison—the new DNC associate chair and before that the Democratic Party chairman in South Carolina—in the house they'd bought so that she could justify snapping up a Senate seat in New York on her way to running for president.

They talked for hours, sitting around the table. "The Democratic Party now is left literally at zero—zero dollars in the bank, zero infrastructure as the Clinton campaign closes up shop," wrote a consultant for the DNC in a postmortem ordered up after the 2016 race, "and, most importantly, zero majority control in Washington and in thirty-three of the states."

"You have to rebuild the party," Hillary said. "That's one of the things I was going to do if I was president." She recommended staff and made operational suggestions, such as how much work needed to be done on building out the data and technological capacities. She was only insistent on one point: don't let Bernie Sanders and his progressives take over the party. She didn't like their politics, and anyway, she felt sure they couldn't win.

Bill Clinton chimed in every few minutes. He had been raging for months, frustrated at everything—at her smarmy, data-obsessed campaign aides who had been ignoring his warnings about losing white men, at Jim Comey, at Democratic officials, at Obama for not doing more about the Russians, at Sanders for how much he'd wounded her, at America, at Donald Trump, at himself.

Ultimately every question came back to the same one from him: "Why didn't we do more?"

—————

There was a moment when it all seemed to be coming together—the promise of Obama, the idea that the system could actually start to change, and that Republican resistance was getting outpaced; that "the twenty-first century" was more than just a phrase from a slogan.

The fourth week of June 2015 had started in tears. So much of America was wrapped up in what had taken place in the basement of the Mother Emanuel

Church in Charleston the previous Wednesday. A white supremacist pulled up in a black car, sat for forty minutes in a bible study about the Parable of the Sower, and then—just a few miles from where a white police officer had shot a Black man in the back two months earlier—took out a semiautomatic .45 Glock with hollow-point rounds and killed nine people. The wife of the reverend, himself an up-and-coming state senator, hid under the desk in his office with their young daughter, listening to the sounds of the massacre, the bullets, the screams. The shooter believed he could spark a race war. He hoped that police would be waiting for him outside, and he'd take a couple of them out too, then kill himself. Instead, he just got in his car and drove away.

America felt as if it hadn't worked. As if none of it had worked. As if, certainly, the promise of the first Black president and the future he was supposed to have promised hadn't borne out. Guns, hate—the nation was stuck, living out the same Faulkner novel. Whatever had been sown was coming up thorns.

Nowhere did the Mother Emanuel murders hit harder than in the Obama White House itself, a place where corny optimism was wrapped in superstition—constantly knocking on wood, constantly believing the knocking actually helped. There were going to be dark days ahead.

Then, on June 25, the Supreme Court upheld Obamacare. The majority opinion, written by Chief Justice John Roberts, seemed a little incoherent, but so did the challenge itself: trying to unravel the entire plan on a technicality. Seven years of congressional fighting over a health care law after seventy years of failing to deliver one, and it was suddenly over. Obama—who for the first moments of Roberts reading the decision had thought that the law was about to be overturned—came to the Rose Garden for a serious statement, declaring the health care fight over. "My greatest hope," he said, "is that rather than keep refighting battles that have been settled again and again and again, I can work with Republicans and Democrats to move forward."

The gay marriage decision came the next morning, sooner than the White House had been expecting. Despite his own labored, calculated history of avoiding getting pinned down on gay marriage until he absolutely had to, the president saw this win as embodying what he was talking about when he had said on Super Tuesday 2008, nearly wrapping up the nomination, "We are the ones we've been waiting for. We are the change that we seek."

He went back to the Rose Garden. This speech was a fist-pumper. "Our nation was founded on a bedrock principle that we are all created equal," Obama said. "Sometimes, there are days like this, when that slow, steady effort is rewarded with justice that arrives like a thunderbolt."

A few minutes, later he was in a helicopter on his way to Air Force One for the memorial service in Charleston. The shooter was proud of what he had done, but the church congregants had come together, weeping, saying they forgave him. The Republican governor—a woman born to Indian immigrants who seemed part of a new future for the GOP itself—had spoken of her state looking "evil in the eye" and that she knew now that the Confederate flag had to come down from the state capitol in Columbia. As the helicopter lifted, Obama looked down at the White House, holding the binder with the speech for the memorial service he had been up late rewriting, thinking about the stanzas of "Amazing Grace." Maybe, he told the aides who were with him, he would sing.

When he did, six thousand people were suddenly on their feet with goose-bumps, singing along with him.

That evening at the airport, waiting for her flight to be cleared after Air Force One took off, one of the bishops who had been onstage with the president joked that in Black congregations, when someone starts singing, if the congre-gants are not with him, they'll just stare, but if they are with him, they'll join in the song, clapping in. That afternoon, she said, they were *with* him.

Obama returned to a White House that had been lit up in rainbow colors. The last time so many people had gathered there was the night Osama bin Laden was killed, but that was more a patriotic exorcism, a decade of hate and PTSD screamed into the sky at the man whose body was sinking to the bottom of an ocean. This was pure party. Less whooping, more dancing. Less victory, more success.

In hindsight it's hard not to see delusion in the self-assurance and the cel-ebration and the sense of moving forward of those two weeks in America. That period, Obama's 2008 campaign manager, David Plouffe, said then, was "an exclamation point on already historic and satisfying paragraphs."

American politics in the Obama years had in fact been consumed by the larger instability rippling through the country, with late-stage American cap-italism no longer working for many citizens, the consolidation and gamifica-tion of media, and the destabilization of society. Neighborhoods were being bulldozed to make way for big-box stores. Cliff Huxtable was revealed to be a sociopathic rapist. Lance Armstrong doped. The guy who lost all the weight in the Subway ads was into child porn.

It's also hard to see how Obama, despite his beatification among Democrats, didn't inadvertently help usher in what followed him.

———

Before every State of the Union, Obama would sit at his desk, looking over charts of economic growth, the number of jobs added. He pored over the wage numbers each month, well aware of what a problem his administration had, and worried that stagnation was going to erode any confidence in the economy and everything else. Americans were being squeezed. Every run-up to the State of the Union, there would be a debate at the White House about going in hard on economic growth, to make people feel better, to grab some of the credit. Every time they'd back off, worried he'd appear wrong, or insensitive.

Polls measuring approval of the economy have always been partisan—voters will say they feel better about the economy if the guy they voted for is in the White House, and worse if he isn't. Like everything else, those views were getting more polarized. Since before Obama's reelection, his aides had been going over "ethnographic" studies by pollster Joel Benenson, asking a select group to keep diaries of how they were keeping up, because obviously the Dow Jones and the GDP weren't of much use as indicators.

Obama alumni now argue about whether they should have tried to be bolder earlier out, fought Obama's negotiate-with-himself-to-make-a-deal instincts, rather than reinforce them, as his first chief of staff, Rahm Emanuel, and others did. By 2014, any dreams of Obama going big were long gone, and the best they'd come up with to address the still recovering economy was proposing to raise the minimum wage. That was quickly abandoned, after operatives overseeing House and Senate campaigns complained they weren't eager to give the country another reminder that Democrats wanted to give money to poor people instead of doing something for them. Dan Pfeiffer, an adviser who started as a junior aide back when Obama was a long shot in Iowa and quickly became one of his main sounding boards for politics, saw wages as their entry into talking about the economy, how to make middle-class voters think that they were talking about them too. They never cracked it.

That was the long rot of the Obama years. Saving the economy felt to many like an abstract achievement, especially because a depression never came after the 2008 collapse. The world was changing, but even the people who weren't as scared about their jobs disappearing, or America seeming less American, knew how hard everything felt—making mortgage payments, taking a vacation, wrapping their heads around how the hell they were supposed to send their kids to college. The cost of everything was going up. Wages were flat. Each family felt that differently, but each family felt it.

Millennials started families only to discover they were left with fumes of the lives they were supposed to have. They'd been shaped by the "nothing is safe or secure" aftermath of 9/11, and now they didn't even get health care, or a job that let them keep up with the student loan payments that were more than the rent that they could barely pay, even with their degrees. Worse, they were being told they were being taken care of.

Obama's election was supposed to demonstrate that anything was possible, that the world could change. Instead, every flash of panic about paying a bill, every sneaking sense that *other* people were getting by or being helped along was like trying to fall back into a good dream on a bad pillow. In the richest country on earth, pretty much everyone but the billionaires felt as if they were getting fucked over by someone else.

Inside the Obama White House they knew they were losing this battle. Obama talked about his frustration constantly and continued to do so as he watched the gaps grow even wider after he was out of office. "We didn't fix some of the core structure stuff that is part of making people feel insecure. The wages still don't go up as fast as profits do. Inequality continues to rise," he acknowledged in the spring of 2019 in a small gathering with the new House freshmen who had given Democrats the majority in the midterms a few months earlier. "These are global phenomena, there's all sorts of reasons for it, but some have to do with policy. Some of them have to do with globalization, some of them have to do with technology. Our institutions haven't adapted."

Obama's frustration about not getting credit for saving the economy ran up against not taking enough responsibility for people being left behind, said Deval Patrick, the former Massachusetts governor and one of Obama's few actual friends in politics.

"You know, we're pretty good in this country historically at innovation, right?" he said. "But we're not as good at transition, which is to say we get around to the impact on people later, if at all. People know we have that pattern, so they say, 'OK, clean tech is coming.' What's that mean in coal country except 'a threat to me'? 'Driverless cars are coming'—what's that mean if I'm a truck driver except 'a threat to me'? We don't bring people along."

———

"Benign neglect" is how Obama aides privately described his abandonment of the party while he was in the White House. "Negligence" might be more accurate. The numbers are hard to ignore: during his eight years in office, Obama oversaw a net loss of 947 state legislative seats, 63 House seats, 11 senators, and 13 governors. Some of this was beyond his control. After the Bush backlash, history was now working against Democrats, given voters' tendency to flip back and forth between parties. So was their own success in the years leading up to Obama's win: they had effectively hit the high-water mark for Democratic victories, so there were many marginal seats to lose in swing districts. Pile that on top of a larger party realignment—there were seats in the South that the Democrats would have lost even if Obama's approval rating had been in the eighties, just as there were seats in the Northeast that were going Democratic no matter what— and the blame for the losses is less clear. Is Republican control of the governor's mansion in Oklahoma really on Obama? Both senators from Arkansas were Democrats at the time of Obama's inauguration, a situation that obviously wasn't going to last. (One lost in 2010, the other in 2014.) And though Obama himself grappled with how to admit and acknowledge it, every analysis has always underestimated the racial backlash, which ran from the Tea Partiers protesting health care outside the Capitol in their costume-store tricorn hats straight through to the famous ride down the golden escalator in Trump Tower.

The fact that Obama's first midterms were in the census year of 2010 only amplified the problem, with smart and ready Republicans rushing to take advantage of their wins to gerrymander Democrats into all but assured permanent minorities in many states, often paired with new voting restrictions as insurance.

"It is very unfortunate timing that that election—which was going to snap back, because it was after two wave elections and a global recession—happened at the census election," Pfeiffer said. "And we paid a price for it."

"You can't change history: You go back and look at midterm elections over the last hundred years, these things happen. They're uncontrollable," said Harry Reid in defense of Obama. But that was Reid's defense after four years of Trump.

"Everybody thought his election would lead to a postracial society, that somehow the normal rules would not apply to him, that all things negative in America were gone as a result of his election. That clearly did not prove to be the case," said Eric Holder, his friend and first attorney general, later recruited to run the redistricting-focused group that Obama tried to use in his post-presidency to finally deal with what had been exposed. "The 2008 election was one where hopes were certainly raised. And the pushback was not anticipated. And so 2010, maybe you expect to lose some seats, but given the magnitude of his victory in 2008 and the spirit that his victory unleashed, there was a huge step back in 2010 that then set the tone for the rest of his presidency."

Defenders like to argue that Obama's approach to governing was a reflection of his unwillingness to taint his presidency by mucking about in fundraising. Or because he didn't want to spoil the image that many 2008 voters had had of him as an independent-minded politician who could appeal to independents. Or that if faced with the choice between campaigning and governing, he was always going to opt for governing. They admit now those were excuses. Obama never built a Democratic bench and never cared to, aside from a few scattered candidates who interested him. He appointed his buddy Tim Kaine as Democratic National Committee chair, even though Kaine was still governor of Virginia for the entire first year he was on the job, commuting two days a week to oversee the pilfering of talent, money, resources, and purpose for the Obama reelection effort that was already under way.

In his first term, Obama used the party structure as a host for his campaign. In his second term, he cared about what happened to the husk as much as any parasite does. Obama aides tend not to admit they're wrong about anything, including the late 2012 decision to stick the DNC with a $2.4 million debt from the reelection campaign. That amount was enormous for the committee, but a drop to a reelection campaign that raised $400 million.

Debbie Wasserman Schultz's time as DNC chair is the exception to the Obama self-assured self-regard. Wasserman Schultz is a Jewish congresswoman from Florida, which is why she was picked to replace Kaine when he quit the

DNC in 2011 to run for the Senate. Obama aides wanted to win Florida in 2012, which meant they wanted to win women and they wanted to win Jews. In Wasserman Schultz they had an eagerly performing politician who'd broadcast on TV, with her name and her accent, a not-at-all subliminal message for the reelection campaign.

They were not expecting that Wasserman Schultz would interpret her appointment as a mandate to turn the DNC into a platform for promoting herself on Sunday shows, or that she'd be scheduling meetings with DNC donors to pitch them on giving to her personal PAC, or on one occasion, using what was supposed to be a phone call with Biden to request the sitting vice president headline a fundraiser to instead invite him to her daughter's bat mitzvah. (Instead, he recorded a congratulatory video, which she played for everyone at the event.) State parties rebelled, and her colleagues in Congress wanted her removed from the job, but Obama was so uninterested in the party organization that he didn't care enough to have the fight she was suggesting if he fired her, threatening to imply that the White House had problems with women and with Jews. Through years of Obama rolling his eyes at her always asking for another photo at fundraisers ("You need another picture, Debbie?" he'd ask) and years of the nascent Clinton political operation getting anxious that she wasn't building up the party operations as they needed, the president and his aides left her in place. No one, aides would eventually admit, had the energy to really do anything about the situation—as if they were talking about getting a roommate to do the dishes, and not taking responsibility for what was happening to their party. Obama remained focused on his agenda, he would say, as if his agenda ever had any hope of succeeding in a country where he got elected arguing that there were no red states and blue states.

Wasserman Schultz only left when she was forced to resign under pressure after the first big WikiLeaks dump of 2016. On the eve of the Democratic convention in July, the site released internal emails showing her and top DNC staff being dismissive of Bernie Sanders and tilted toward Clinton. Even then, Obama stayed out of the situation, with the White House political operation acting more as biased mediator than direction setter.

By the time Obama wrapped his arms around Clinton onstage at the Democratic convention in Philadelphia in the summer of 2016 and handed her back the nomination she felt he had taken from her eight years earlier, the

Democratic Party was hopped up on delusion. *Everything* had changed, they had persuaded themselves to believe. Obama had fused a new kind of progressivism out of the party's traditional liberal base and demographic cores, and that cosmopolitan, twenty-first century approach was redefining what politics was about, from health care to reopening relations with Cuba. He had said over and over during the 2012 campaign that "the fever" in the country of partisan obstructionism would break if he was reelected, and Republicans would stop fighting him for the sake of fighting. He never really believed that.

By 2016, though, he was starting to believe that the fever was going to kill the patient, who had never actually recovered. The Republican Party, after all, was nominating a bright-orange cartoon of what Obama would have been roasted for suggesting it was: imagine the outraged segments on Fox News if he had ever contended that Republicans were on their way to calling Mexicans rapists. He had "reshaped the American electorate for Democrats at the national level" and had "provided a road map for Democrats on the state level," Simas, his political director, had said the day before the convention speech. "Once you extend the electorate, not only are you extending the people, you are extending the issue set that you can talk about."

That is not at all what happened.

They only thought they saw and understood the threats from what Republicans weren't even bothering to go into the shadows to build. While the Democrats complained about the Supreme Court's *Citizens United* decision and clicked on preciously worded essays about the subversion of the democratic process on their favorite websites, Republicans were constructing a war machine the size of Greenland's GDP.

As his 2020 run took shape, Biden and a few of his how-ya-like-us-now? aides tripped into revisionist mythologizing about how he would have run in 2016, if only Obama hadn't gotten in the way and steered the nomination toward Clinton. In fact, Biden hadn't even been preparing to run, and if he had tried to go up against the Clintons, even with the kind of campaign operation he finally managed to put together at the beginning of 2019, he would have been vaporized by her team. Back in 2015, Biden's pseudocampaign headquarters was located at whichever table happened to be open at the coffee shop across the street from the White House.

Biden told himself that he hadn't started a PAC as vice president because he didn't want to seem as if he had his eyes on anything other than helping Obama. The truth was that he knew he wasn't going to do it. He didn't want to risk embarrassing himself for a Joe Quixote campaign. He wanted to be Joe Panza, not missing out on meetings at the White House, not getting cornered by reporters into explaining where he differed from Obama, not giving up the best job he'd ever had for a run at one he probably wouldn't get. He would let the 2016 campaign come and go, keeping the idea of his run dangling long enough until everyone suddenly realized that he'd never actually gone through with it.

Obama, for his part, went from assuring his aides not to worry, that his vice president was just working out his grief at his son's death by entertaining the fantasy of running for president, to becoming worried that Biden was actually getting lost in his fantasy. In June, weeks after Beau Biden died, Obama was telling aides to give his vice president some space. By September, he was ordering them to go and meet with Biden to jolt some sense into him, to stop him from getting himself hurt and embarrassing Obama as he did so. "Mr. Vice President, you've had a great career, you've been such an asset to this administration—and we love you," Plouffe told Biden at the end of a conversation that was meant to force the ending of the campaign, but which clearly wasn't breaking through. "Do you really want it to end in a hotel room in Des Moines, coming in third to Bernie Sanders?"

With a little more encouragement, or at least a little less discouragement, could Obama have given Biden the room to try his idea that he could go all in on a big South Carolina primary win and slingshot into nabbing the nomination on Super Tuesday? It was less about the politics at that point than it was seeing how unprepared logistically and emotionally Biden was for a presidential campaign: in those months after his son died, Biden was constantly breaking down in tears, his attention wandering, getting mixed up in his memories and in his grief.

The way his inner circle sometimes likes to tell the story, Obama's plan had always been to do nothing while the 2016 Democratic primaries played out, and lo and behold, his doing just that played right into Clinton's becoming the nominee. Very soon after Obama won his second term, the hunger in the party for a female candidate—and Clinton in particular—was intense. A PAC called

Ready for Hillary was launched in January 2013, and the then Missouri senator Claire McCaskill, who had endorsed Obama early in 2007, endorsed the
group that June. Clinton quickly became the gravitational force that the rest
of the Democratic space began to orbit around.

Obama's protestations of neutrality are hard to take seriously. He made
Clinton secretary of state not only to give himself a boost but also with an eye
toward her political future, and the party's. He thought it was generally understood that Biden wouldn't run in 2016 because of his age, and so she would
be the implicit heir. For a few brief weeks in 2011, when his aides considered
shaking up the reelection race by swapping her and Biden to make an Obama–
Clinton ticket, she almost became the obvious one. Obama genuinely did warm
to Clinton over the years, and there were a few dinners at the White House that
helped the bitter spouses get over the 2008 race too.

Obama had Bill Clinton ride in to vouch for and validate him at his own
reelection convention in 2012. Obama repaid him by helping rehabilitate the
former president's image in return, tagging him as the "secretary of explaining
stuff" in a joke that made him fun in the present and helped overshadow his
leching past. He gave Hillary a send-off from his administration with a very
public embrace by sitting for a joint *60 Minutes* interview with her in January
2013, then kept in touch as she got ready to run. In December 2014, while
Obama aides were rushing to do one final reboot of his presidency after the
Republican rout in the midterms, Clinton aides were already in preliminary
interviews for campaign staff. Insisting that she still hadn't made up her mind
about running, she just happened to show up in the Oval Office for a long
meeting with Obama. Both kept deliberately cagey at first—"It was an hour to
catch up and enjoy an informal discussion on a wide range of issues," is how
an Obama aide, staying anonymous, worded the official statement when news
of the visit just happened to leak. The next day at a women's conference in
Boston, Clinton coquettishly mentioned the hour she had just spent with
Obama. "And I was thinking, sitting there in the Oval Office talking, that I've
known a lot of presidents over the course of the last many decades," she said,
"and it is such a hard job. . . . It is such a challenging job." None of this was
subtle. Nor were all the Obama aides who either went to work for Clinton or
stayed in close touch with the ones who did. Obama had Plouffe, his own
campaign mastermind, sit down with Clinton at her house in Washington to

go over his own plan with her and then come back to Obama with his assessment of whether she was ready.

Obama wasn't naive about Clinton's political weaknesses—he had beaten her because of them. Still, he believed she would win. He thought she would do a good job, and he would say privately at the time, she seemed to him to be the only plausible option to succeed him, which was in itself a pretty clear comment on what he made of his own party's bench under his presidency. While Obama liked her as the candidate, creating the impression that he loved her was a tactic—a way to protect her, but also a way to preserve the impression that he was in control. He and aides look back and wonder if they took the exact opposite lesson from the 2008 race that they said they were going to: avoiding a tough primary rather than using one to get hardened up to run against the Republican. If Biden had run, then would having him in the race with Clinton and Sanders have "led to a more robust debate?" said Denis McDonough, his friend and chief of staff in those years, looking back. "I just don't know."

But the way the race was already taking shape, Obama and Clinton aides at the time agree, to stop her from becoming the nominee would probably have required Obama's campaigning against her directly. He would have had to take her out, and make it clear to anyone who was listening—while making sure that everyone was listening—that he definitely did not want to see her in the White House. Who knows if that could have even worked. It might have blown back on him, leading to charges of petty grudge holding, misogyny, intraparty immolation, and to a weird undermining of his own judgment for having picked someone as his secretary of state whom he would now be saying he wanted nowhere near power.

———

Like most Democrats, Obama completely underestimated Sanders's appeal in the primaries, and was flabbergasted at how to wind down the challenge the socialist senator presented without doing more damage to the fabric of the party. He considered endorsing Clinton early but then pulled back after Sanders won the Michigan primary in mid-March to begin what became a weeks' long rally of wins against Clinton.

The bigger problem started over a lunch in the White House private dining room: CIA director John Brennan arrived with a package of classified material that could have been a James Bond script. The Russians weren't just coming. They were already here.

Aides in the West Wing started to notice the long blocks of time that kept getting added to the schedule. The meetings were held in McDonough's office, with Brennan, Susan Rice, and Director of National Intelligence Jim Clapper. Attorney General Loretta Lynch often joined; Defense Secretary Ash Carter didn't. There were no assistants present, and no one without top security clearance. Brennan had brought the intel to Rice at the end of July, and she'd immediately taken it to Obama and McDonough. McDonough is always do-it-by-the-book, and Obama was with him: it couldn't leak, it couldn't get sucked into the race. Treat it like a national security issue, not a polarizing campaign issue. Clinton was going to win anyway, and they needed to protect the intelligence community from getting pulled into all of this.

"Obama's view, which I fully supported and would defend to this day, is that this was a national security threat—a threat not just to one party, not to one candidate," Rice remembered. "At that point, we knew that this was a threat to our democracy, and it was potentially going to affect candidates up and down the ballot in every state and every party. The most important thing we were trying to do was not politicize it."

There were elements of the interference that everyone could see—Trump's reigniting the chatter over Clinton's computer server one morning during the week of the Democratic convention, "Russia, if you're listening, I hope you're able to find the 30,000 emails that are missing." Other intelligence was being pushed around privately, between operatives, and then between operatives and reporters, trying to string together the pieces—was Guccifer 2.0 part of the GRU Russian intelligence service? Why did WikiLeaks just happen to drop hacked emails in one particular race in South Florida, in which Trump's buddy Roger Stone seemed to have an interest? By the time Biden was spending an August afternoon back home in Scranton endorsing Clinton, one of her top aides was puzzling to reporters about why the Trump campaign had focused on watering down the language in the official Republican Party platform about assistance to Ukraine. That had to be the Russian misunderstanding about the American system, that is, their belief that the party platform mattered, the aide insisted. The first time one top aide on the National Security

Council staff at the White House saw the Steele dossier, the famous mishmash of rumors compiled by a British former espionage expert, it was sent by a reporter.

Word began moving through the West Wing that there was even more going on. It was all just guesses at that point. "This isn't complicated," Rice recalled. "What we knew about Russian interference was some of the most sensitive information that we ever dealt with and the sourcing was some of the most sensitive. The implications of it leaking or getting out in a fashion that wasn't thoughtfully coordinated was huge." Keeping the circle tight, she added, wasn't something to regret, or reconsider. "To have done otherwise would have been irresponsible."

One of the first orders Obama gave in response to the intelligence was to alert the congressional leadership. But it was August, and with Congress in recess, Obama called Brennan and told him to get to wherever they were and give them the classified briefing. Nancy Pelosi and Harry Reid, the two Democratic minority leaders, met with him right away, as did House Speaker Paul Ryan, whom, Brennan recalled, "was very honest with me in the discussion. He said, 'As you know, I'm not a fan of Trump.' I said, 'Yeah, I have noticed that.' And so he was very interested in it."

Mitch McConnell, the Republican Senate majority leader, dawdled on his briefing until after Labor Day, and then told Brennan that the report seemed as if it might just be an effort by the CIA to undermine Trump. In the Oval Office soon after with the other congressional leaders, he made clear that he hadn't been swayed. Obama asked them to sign on to a joint statement condemning the Russians, and McConnell refused. Obama walked out of the meeting unable to comprehend the pushback.

"Even Speaker Ryan was characterizing his exasperation with McConnell," McDonough recalled.

By then Obama had been in China for the G-20 summit, his final meeting with the international group and the last time he would encounter Vladimir Putin face-to-face before the election. The way Obama would eventually recount the meeting, he portrayed himself as acting in a way that had always led Republicans to characterize him as feckless. He wanted to make sure that Putin didn't get involved in "potential hacking that could hamper vote counting," Obama said, so he went "to talk to him directly and tell him to cut it out and there were going to be serious consequences if he didn't."

The reality was less of intimidation than of fear. They had seen so much evidence. Putin was so brazen. They knew it was him, and they knew he didn't care that they knew it was him. They could see how much more direct damage he'd be able to do. They assumed he'd do it.

Obama and Putin had a first conversation accompanied by Rice and an interpreter, huddled in a corner. Well, what about the Americans and the Rose Revolution in Georgia or the Orange Revolution in Ukraine? Putin asked in response. What about the way Americans had landed in Kyiv after he'd invaded Crimea and were propping up its weak government?

They weren't getting anywhere. They stood up as Obama sent the others away and then turned back to Putin. At six foot one, he towered over the Russian leader, looking down on him and pointing at him as he spoke. Rice watched from a distance, struck by Obama's forcefulness. Don't touch the voting machines. Don't touch the data. Stay out of the systems. The CIA could see they were trying to get in.

"He wanted response options at the ready so that he could decide at whatever point to deploy them. He was all over it, but he was also sober and calm," Rice recalled, "and very focused on not doing the Russians' job for them."

Putin didn't say much but only listened, his face fixed in a bemused, KGB-trained smirk. Obama broke off, hoping he'd had some impact, having made it clear that the Americans had considered what Brennan will only describe as "some options that would have responded more tangibly to what the Russians were doing." They convinced themselves that with that threat, Obama may have headed off the bigger attack, because the bigger attack never came.

"I think Putin had to do his calculus," Brennan said, "take into account that 'I can do these things and maybe I'll even try to affect the vote tallies, but if she does win, we're probably going to have a rough time of it.' So if I were Putin at that time, I think my calculation would have been 'OK, I'm not going to do the stuff on the technical front, because if we do something on the technical front, they're probably eventually going to find out that. But if we do things on the information front, that's basically propaganda.' That's the type of stuff that intelligence services have been doing forever."

At the time, however, they publicly underplayed the threat, and their concerns about it. "We did talk about cybersecurity, generally," Obama said at his press conference before leaving the summit. "I'm not going to comment on specific investigations that are still live and active," he added, when asked about what he described as the "candid, blunt, businesslike" conversation with Putin, "but I will tell you that we've had problems with cyber-intrusions from Russia in the past, from other countries in the past."

Clinton was going to win. He wasn't about to let the Justice Department and American intelligence get muddied by Putin to stop a Trump win that wasn't going to happen. She'd have enough problems without this hanging over her too.

They flew back to Washington, still waiting on McConnell. Reid had confronted the majority leader directly, insisting that they had to do more, but all he got in return was an argument that elections should be left to the states. Finally, McConnell agreed to sign on to an open letter to the president of the National Association of State Election Directors. The White House figured this would be a workable way to get the warning out into the air, and were satisfied with the draft Ryan put together. McConnell, however, rejected that draft and wrote his own. The result was a perfunctory write-up that left out most of the relevant details, obscurely referring to "the challenge of malefactors" rather than to Russia's mounting an attack. "We got a letter, but it was just—it was so watered down, it was worthless. It was meaningless," Reid recalled.

Reid blames Comey directly for the lack of more action from the FBI, accusing him of letting his Republican leanings get in the way of his duty of investigating Trump, and more important, of not publicizing that investigation as much as he did that of Clinton's email server. "Obama did the best he could without some strength from Comey," Reid explained. "He couldn't do it. He couldn't just go out on his own doing this. He needed support from his FBI director." In January 2018, when Biden bumbled into being the first one to tell the story during a talk at the Council of Foreign Relations, he justified Comey's reticence by saying, "Can you imagine if the president called a press conference in October, with this fella, Bannon, and company, and said, 'Tell you what: Russians are trying to interfere in our elections and we have to do something about it.' What do you think would have happened? Would things have gotten better, or would it further look like we were trying to delegitimize the electoral process, because of our opponent?"

Facing no consequences, the Russians went on interfering and getting away with it.

Brennan thinks hindsight judgment doesn't make much sense in this. Beyond the political considerations, there was the threat of a potential cyberwar if the American response had been escalation. "What might the Russians have decided to do?" Brennan wondered. "What did they already have loaded in the chamber that they could have went forward with? And what could have been the implications of that?"

A few days after the letter went out, McDonough expanded the circle in his office to include some of the top press aides to prepare them for how they would talk about the letter once it was released. Internally, the debate was whether to condemn Putin by name, or go with where they had landed, that "only Russia's senior-most officials could have authorized these activities." Press Secretary Josh Earnest had developed a close relationship with Rice from checking in with her constantly about what he could and couldn't say, and how, from the White House podium at his briefings. McDonough liked him. He had gotten his job because of his relationships with the press corps, how good he was at predicting the questions the administration would be hit with. This one wasn't hard: What were they supposed to say, he asked, when reporters asked if Russia was trying to help Trump?

McDonough and Rice, as other people in the room remember it, looked at each other as if they hadn't considered the possibility that question would be posed.

"The fact is," Rice said, "they are. We know that." But both agreed that they had to avoid saying so.

The statement came out on Friday afternoon, October 7. An hour later the *Access Hollywood* tape dropped, with Trump bragging about how he liked to "grab 'em by the pussy." That night the first batch of John Podesta's emails showed up on WikiLeaks.

———

Obama has never been weighed down by self-doubt. Sometimes aides or people who have leveraged their political and donor relationships into face time with him try to draw out his anxieties, mostly looking for some validation of their own. They never get it. He doesn't have many, but what he does, he saves for his closest friends. He knows that everyone else is intimidated by him, or that they might leak. He also has a sense of himself as a leader, no matter where he is. He can't afford to be the guy taking swings or freaking out, so he won't be. He certainly won't be the guy looking back, wondering what could have been done differently, or more pointedly, what *he* could have done differently.

"It's perfectly human to say, 'Was I a participating factor in this?' But I think in the long arc of history, he appreciates the fact that disruptors shake things up, and he was a disruptor and he shook up the establishment and the status quo," said his friend and closest adviser, Valerie Jarrett. "And I think as we have seen it play out, what they are willing to do to hold on to power is quite something."

Obama knows that he came up short on wrapping his hands around the economy, but he sees Republicans bearing blame for having performed for their base over what are supposed to be procedural issues like passing a budget or raising the debt limit. After years of manufactured drama over fiscal cliffs and sequestration, he would say, it's a marvel that he was able to oversee the economic recovery that he did. He was inaugurated during a global meltdown, and he left with unemployment under the historical average, average weekly earnings up, and stock prices and corporate profits breaking records.

He takes no blame for the deterioration of the DNC infrastructure. He raised more money for the party, and for individual candidates, than anyone in history. Maybe he could have been more invested in thinking about leadership or strategy, but with the limited amount of time he had, he believes, wasn't everyone happier that he stayed focused on managing the government—especially with what has happened since? When he left office, America was more prepared for a pandemic than any country on earth, he was saying by the summer of 2020, and since then it had fallen far behind. Clinton had $1 billion and the entire party establishment behind her for a year. Whatever problems there may have been, his defense is that she should have been able to put together a functional campaign in twelve swing states against the weakest major party candidate in modern history, who didn't even have the support of many in his own party.

Obama's decisions on how to deal with Russia were a gamble. Even if Mc-Connell had been more cooperative, his options were limited. He had to focus on protecting the country from an attack, and to preserve national security in a nonpartisan and effective way.

Between the Mueller report and the bipartisan Senate Intelligence Committee report, Obama's national security team feels vindicated that they had their facts right. Even with what has happened since, given how close Clinton was to winning despite all the mistakes she made, they feel vindicated as well that they had been trying to do what seemed right for the country in that moment.

Ultimately Obama's math comes down to a simple calculation: he has suggested in conversations with people close to him that he thinks he would have won had he been able to be a candidate in 2016. The economy, the Democratic debris, Russia—if he could have run for a third term, even confronted with all these issues, he believes, he would have figured out how to pull a victory off anyway.

"If you asked him, 'Would he have beaten Trump?' I don't think he thinks it would be close. So for him to take fault," a friend of his said, "that doesn't hold water with him."

CHAPTER TWO

BREAKING THE GLASS

You don't remember what it's like when there wasn't someone in charge. You've been part of this movement since 2007, jumping from one fight to the next, the most talented, brilliant, and dedicated group I've ever been a part of. But you are used to having someone to tell you where to jump. Those people aren't in charge now—you are. Take the idea you have, and get it started. You don't need anyone's permission.

—JON CARSON, EXECUTIVE DIRECTOR OF OBAMA'S ORGANIZING
FOR ACTION GROUP, FACEBOOK POST, NOVEMBER 10, 2016

November 9, 2016–September 2017

A few days before the 2016 election, one of Hillary Clinton's top advisers sat at a diner a few blocks from her campaign headquarters in Brooklyn, summing up the race over breakfast. "We realized this was going to be a change election," the adviser said. "But she was never going to be the change candidate."

And so, the adviser said, with that glorious smile of remembering triumphing in the meeting, "we decided to change the *question*."

By then, the mood on the Clinton campaign had gone from *They're actually going to nominate Trump; can you believe this luck?* in the spring to *She's going to cream him, but dark forces have been unleashed* around the time of the conventions, then to *We will grind this out and deal with the wreckage once she's in* by the fall, then to her stopping in the hall on the way into the first debate and saying, "I have to win this—he can't be president," to *He's falling apart and she's even going to win Arizona* after the *Access Hollywood* tape, and then to *Oh my god, she was right that THEY were always going to try to stop her and it's Comey and Anthony Weiner's sexting.* By that final week they'd settled in to *They came at us with everything, this is going to be awful, but she's going to pull through.*

Big donors already had their ambassadorships lined up by the time they arrived at the VIP reception at the Javits Center on election night. A couple of hours later, aides who'd been ambling around, ready to party, had all been quickly pulled away from access to reporters, the room with the glass ceiling and glass stage in the shape of America seemed a monument to naivete, and backstage was full of scenes like Billy Eichner sitting on the floor screaming and throwing up as the Florida returns came in.

The 2016 election was supposed to cement the Democrats' claim on the future. Instead, it scrambled their brains and left them constantly on edge from their worst nightmare now in the White House, who continued to outmaneuver them in the media and throw up more targets than they could ever hope to shoot at. As the shockwaves rolled over and over them during the Trump transition, Democrats weren't so much going through the five stages of grief as being chronically punch drunk. Any chance at political recovery meant either a cold break from the past, or a concession to the new reality. "A lot of Democrats laughed at Bernie Sanders when he proposed free college. First of all, that's not impossible," said Connecticut senator Chris Murphy, sitting in his office on Capitol Hill that December. He added, "It's a way to communicate a really important issue in terms that people will understand." In his early forties, Murphy was rocketing through a career in which he had started young but was already massively successful, and starting to think about how to be part of the bridge to whatever was supposed to be next, to translate the youthful energy he still felt into the establishment world of which he was now part.

Chuck Schumer, the new Democratic leader in the Senate, thought he understood Trump as a fellow New Yorker, one he'd known for years, and had a forever faith in his own ability to out-connive. "You ran against both the Democratic and Republican establishments—if you do that as president, you could get some things done. But if you just let the hard right capture your presidency, like with the Cabinet appointments," Schumer would say he told Trump in one of their early phone calls during the transition, "it could well be a flop."

Democrats definitely had to acknowledge the country was different, Schumer would say, they had to adjust. Trump wanted to talk infrastructure? They could talk infrastructure. Everyone loved infrastructure. "If he comes much closer to where we are, we could work with him," Schumer said, his voice insisting on his canniness, "and that kind of issue unites our caucus and divides theirs."

Those were the early days, when Schumer was saying privately that Obamacare was finished, telling donors not to bother throwing their money at the lost cause of fighting its repeal. Those were the days when Democratic leaders talked themselves into thinking that maybe Trump was going to be like a normal politician, or maybe an abnormal one, in that he wouldn't believe in anything, and they could play off his promote-a-win dealmaking until he got bored and probably didn't run for a second term, or maybe didn't even finish out the first one. What a wacky chapter in American history this was going to be, but hey, America had had hiccups before and survived those.

Robby Mook, Clinton's campaign manager, combed through the campaign's numbers for a study delivered to the Democratic National Committee called the *Retrospective Polling Project*, which proposed a simpler answer to what had happened: They'd misread the data, they admitted, and that had led them to bad strategic decisions. "Was there last-minute movement?" was the title of one of its charts, showing a tightening of the race when Jim Comey's letter landed, and both the red and blue trend lines heading to a gray box with a question mark around Election Day. In fancy clip art infographics, they said that Comey's letter wasn't enough to account for what they'd gotten wrong. The reasonable response, they concluded, was that "a majority of the forecast error can be attributed to 'hidden' response bias that none of the voter file variables could control for." This was the essence of the Clinton campaign's postmortem and Clinton's own hardened bitterness from her life in politics: half the country was a lost cause. They were never going to be convinced. They were never going to be persuaded. Trump voters were Trump voters. All Democrats could hope for, according to this theory, was to get better at mobilizing the voters who were already theirs.

Human nature is to not confront our worst fears. We push them aside and try to cope. Sherrod Brown, the Ohio senator, started by reading a biography of Hitler. Cory Booker, the New Jersey senator, asked staff to dig in on how far the president could go just by issuing executive orders. Brendan Boyle, a congressman from Pennsylvania, ordered twenty copies of the *Federalist Papers* for his staff.

One week after the election, Harry Reid stood on the Senate floor for one of his last speeches before his retirement. He was furious but not surprised that Trump had appointed Steve Bannon to a top job at the White House, and annoyed at the Democrats who were arguing that the party had to accept the new reality.

"Democrats want to work with Trump when we can. I understand and respect that impulse, because Democrats like to get things done," Reid said. "We have a responsibility to prevent Trump's bullying, aggressive behavior from becoming normalized in the eyes of Americans—especially the millions of young people who are watching and wondering, for example, if sexual assault is now a laughing matter. We have a responsibility to say that it is not normal for the KKK to celebrate the election of a president they view as their champion with a victory parade. They have one scheduled."

"In other words," Reid said, "we have a responsibility to lead."

Schumer asked Reid to stop causing problems. He was leaving Washington. They were the ones who had to figure out how to make this work, how to protect the ten Democratic senators in states that Trump won who were going to have to run in 2018, while he'd be back home in retirement in Vegas.

"It would be hard to challenge the veracity of what I was saying," Reid noted in July 2020, his quiet voice sometimes making people think he was being humble, when in fact he was usually just calmly tearing apart those he has deemed bad, wrong, or hapless. "That's what I believed. And time has proven me correct."

———

In the middle of the night after the election, about an hour after Trump gave his acceptance speech, Neera Tanden got on an Amtrak train back home to Washington. A former Clinton aide herself, Tanden was a protégé of Clinton campaign chairman John Podesta's, and she was now president of the Democrats-in-exile think tank, the Center for American Progress, which Podesta had founded during the Bush years. Tanden had just come off a month of insanity, courtesy of being swept up in the WikiLeaks dump of Podesta's hacked emails, and anyone who wanted could now read all her private doubts about Clinton's instincts and sneers at Sanders. Trump supporters came after her, Sanders supporters came after her even more intensely, and reporters yipped around the great revelatory Shakespearean schadenfreude over what Clinton insiders *really* thought of her.

For months Tanden, disappointed in advance, had been mapping out the ways that Clinton would manage to mess up in the White House. Trump's win, though, elicited genuine fear. Tanden had always been a nervously wary type, but she could see that Trump was well aware of his superpower to drive the worst instincts in his followers. Early that morning as the train headed down the Northeast corridor, she emailed Podesta: *We have to move to opposition.*

So many meetings followed—group therapy for the traumatized Clinton supporters. Some organizations hired staffs just to attend all of them to keep up. Tanden had the Center for American Progress start working on an analysis of how democracy had fallen apart in Viktor Orbán's Hungary, then emailed the finished paper to every top Democrat in her contacts. Cecile Richards, then running Planned Parenthood, brought progressive leaders into her office every two weeks, trying to come up with some kind of strategy. "Everyone had their own break-the-glass plan for a Trump victory," Richards recalled, "but we had never talked seriously, collectively about how we would organize ourselves as the resistance."

First, though, came philosophical debate over how much to negotiate, and how much to fight. Some of the leaders in the meetings pushed back at using *resist,* arguing that the word was too negative, too defined by being in reaction to Trump.

"It's just like in World War II," Tanden responded. "This transcends normal politics. You can't look for a happy word." The group eventually landed on coordinating around each of them taking on a single cabinet nominee, rather than going scattershot after the whole list.

Protesters were marching, and Facebook posts were popping. Every frustrated Democratic operative and disillusioned liberal was posting about the new organizations they were going to start. There was a parody-level Slack channel for coordinating activists who were coordinating the resistance. Existing organizations like the ACLU and the LGBTQ-advocacy Human Rights

Campaign were seeing a massive spike in their memberships and donations. They didn't know what to do with all the new interest.

Podesta decided to make some risotto for dinner.

The former Bill Clinton chief of staff, Obama adviser, and Hillary Clinton campaign chairman had planned to take a trip out of the country for Trump's inauguration. His own Clinton campaign–scarred psychology aside, he decided there was no time to wait. Invitations went out to like-minded Democratic leaders, the type of people who never ran for office themselves, but controlled many of the strings.

Assembled around the table in December at Podesta's home in northwest Washington were Randi Weingarten, the president of the American Federation of Teachers; Mary Kay Henry, the president of the Service Employees International Union (SEIU); Lee Saunders, the president of the American Federation of State, County and Municipal Employees; John Stocks, a top official at the National Education Association; Guy Cecil, the 2008 Hillary Clinton political director who was by then running the Democratic super PAC Priorities USA; and Tom Steyer, the venture capitalist billionaire who had become the Democrats' biggest donor and youth organizer (before deciding the following summer that he was going to run for president himself).

The first twenty minutes were, as one attendee recalled, "Holy Fuck"—a collective unloading. There was some discussion about Russia. Then they started to talk about what to do now. The Democratic infrastructure wasn't ready for what was coming, Podesta told the group. They needed to start building up resources, and quickly, triaging priorities and projects among them.

Podesta had intentionally invited only allies he knew were already on the same page about Trump: he was massively dangerous and had to be stopped. This wasn't going to be another of those ideological debates, or another rehash of all the things that Clinton had done wrong. This was operational: How would they push back, what would they invest in, where would the money come from, what would they need to build what they started to think of as a platform of resistance? Did they need a new setup to take on Trump? Or would they coordinate better within the existing groups? Could the new groups popping up do more than protest, and actually help with the midterms in 2018— or was it too premature to even have that discussion?

Some of the labor leaders present looked over the numbers and warned that they would have to sit out the fight, or at least sit back. Many of their members had clearly voted for Trump. Even without going against them, the leadership had to look ahead to what they assumed would be the new administration's following the lead of Wisconsin and North Carolina and other states where Republican governors had come in prioritizing slashing union protections. If this was going to be a war against Trump, they said, don't count on all their members being the ground troops.

Randi Weingarten was not one of the cautious ones. Like Schumer, she viewed Trump through a New Yorker's perspective—before she became the national teachers union president, she had led the New York City chapter. What she drew from that experience was different from Schumer's: Trump would be a dealmaker, sure, but a corrupt one who would sell out the people he said he was trying to help. Schumer, she thought, was mistaking Trump for other New York real estate moguls who were more of the honest crook variety. She said at the table that night what she had been warning in meetings with her own executive council, in preparation for repositioning the union: this was going to be a dark presidency, based on fear and division. And they needed to think seriously about not letting him draw them into traps of polarization and xenophobia.

"How do we recognize the world that is in front of us, and how do we combat it?" Weingarten recalled asking. "The Trump Party had turned into a cult, and we had to rekindle real alliances that were based on trust and affinity, and being in solidarity and unity with our values, not just do a critique of Trump." This wasn't just about high-minded pronouncements. This was about tactics. Democrats weren't playing the same game as Trump, she said. They were getting lapped online with active disinformation from at home and abroad. "The art form of disinformation to move distrust into trusting that he alone could fix it, that they had the strategy and enough people had bought into it—that's what I thought we had to deconstruct," Weingarten said.

The first fight, they decided, was going to be stopping the repeal of Obamacare. Paul Ryan and Mitch McConnell wanted to start the new Republican administration by getting rid of the signature health care law, and Obama had long been Trump's obsession. The people around that table knew Trump was going to make it a target before he himself did. They had to quickly dissuade Democrats in and out of Congress from considering any compromise position, and persuade them to see Trump as a bully who would respond to negotiations by threatening to add cuts to Medicaid.

All four of the unions represented at the table that night joined a new organizing coalition called Protect Our Care. John Stocks, who was soon to be the chairman of the secretive elite Democratic donor group Democracy Alliance, focused on preparing to move on the state level. The Center for American Progress began churning out more research to add to the critiques, and convened a separate meeting to bring together aligned unions, interest groups, and staff from Schumer's office.

Meanwhile, in an office in Chicago that most of the political world had forgotten about, a few Obama alumni descended. Organizing for Action (OFA)—a cute filching of the acronym from Obama for America—was the product of Obama's deciding to keep his reelection campaign structure active but pulling all its top talent, support, and donors. Obama for America had been founded as a nonprofit with a grand mission of generating interest around the country in his second-term agenda. That never happened. Instead of spending any time in his second term rebuilding the DNC, Obama created another group to do some of what the DNC already did, but even less effectively, and only for his own promotion. Organizing for Action was a shapeless monument to the most cynical view of the president: do-goodish dreams of hope and change without any direction or understanding of how to get anything done toward achieving those goals. Obama would always say that his campaigns weren't about him. This was direct proof that his campaigns were.

A plan was already in place to wind down OFA if Clinton won, maybe shift some of the organizer training over to the Obama Foundation. As with everywhere else, there was no plan for what to do if Trump won. All they knew was that Obama would be even less involved with the group in his postpresidency, and that he was taking back the rising sun "O" logo for the Obama Foundation, along with control of his Twitter account and the barackobama.com address. From new offices that opened on to a broad street with Trump's downtown Chicago tower looming at the end of it, they tried to find their footing.

For most of the year, OFA heard nothing from Obama. The group was like an abandoned religious sect, trying to guess what its leader would have wanted based on interpreting his past statements. The only clear direction they had was not to embarrass him. Dozens of additional staff were hired. Leaders reached out to some of the newer groups, offering guidance on organizing training. A few said they were interested, to be polite, but also because many of them had no idea what to do now. OFA had its own donor base, and what had become a huge email list, including everyone who had signed up for the Obama campaigns, and it had continued to build since. Over the next six months, as bewildered Democrats tried to figure out what to do, and as Obama became their totem, OFA benefited: by the time Senator John McCain killed Obamacare repeal at the end of July, 1.1 million people had signed up to take some action, and forty thousand people had participated in trainings in person or online. Connect beyond politics, OFA leaders would advise organizers it was coordinating. Host movie screenings about global warming. Focus the opposition. Don't be screaming all the time or risk burning out the less committed. It was Obama-style politics that even Obama was moving past.

What OFA still had in common with Obama was that it, too, wasn't going to be the Democrats' savior.

═══

No one was expecting the enormity of the Women's March the morning after Trump's inauguration—not on the scale of streets too packed to move in Washington, and not all the companion protests around the country and around the world. Trump hadn't been president for twenty-four hours, and he had already inspired the largest protests in history, with crowds clearly larger than the scattered one that had shown up for his inauguration.

This was going to be their Tea Party, progressives insisted, not their Occupy Wall Street. A movement that would redefine politics, not aimless pseudo-protesting that was mostly about sleeping on the sidewalks in tents. Clinton supporters came, Sanders supporters came, each angry that the other group was there. The Clinton supporters were convinced that she would have been a day into her own presidency already if the Sanders supporters had shown as much enthusiasm for voting for her as they had for coming up with their clever homemade signs. The Sanders supporters were certain that the Clinton crowd didn't get why she hadn't been able to inspire their degree of enthusiasm, and that mainstream Democrats would need the Sanders base's help keeping activity going now that Trump was in office.

It became less a march than a stand-around. Police cars parked on the streets for crowd control couldn't have moved far if they'd needed to. So many people. So many signs. GOT EMPATHY? with a drawing of Trump with a milk mustache. KEEP YOUR TINY HANDS OFF MY HUMAN RIGHTS. WE ARE NOT AFRAID. MAKE PERIODS GREAT AGAIN. I SPENT MORE TIME ON THIS SIGN THAN YOU DID PREPARING FOR OFFICE. In a bunch of different scripts and a bunch of different colors, WE WILL HOLD YOU ACCOUNTABLE TO ALL AMERICANS. One of the simpler ones, held over her head by a woman in a gray pom-pom cap with a heart on it, read: CTRL+ALT+DEL, in black letters against a light-blue background.

On the stage, which almost no one ever got near, the 2020 race was already under way. "We want to be counted. We want to be heard. And we are going to fight for what we believe in," said Kirsten Gillibrand, the New York senator who had found her voice as an advocate for women, LGBTQ rights, and 9/11 first responders.

Kamala Harris, who'd been a senator for only two weeks, delivered what was her first speech in Washington. "Even if you are not sitting in the White House, even if you don't run a corporate super PAC, you have the power—and we the people have the power," she said. "It's going to be harder before it gets easier. I know we will rise to the challenge, and I know we will keep fighting no matter what."

John Kerry, fresh from being secretary of state, showed up with his dog, Ben—as in Ben Franklin—as if he just happened to be taking his yellow Lab out for a walk in downtown DC and stumbled into the event. Kerry had come of age in the Vietnam War protests. He wanted to be connected to these. He wanted to feel as if he were the official messenger from then, giving his blessing to the crowd as he cut through it, far from the stage. "What we have to do is make sure it becomes an activist, everyday movement that keeps politicians accountable. The key is to turn it into work that leads to elections," Kerry said to a reporter, caught just before he disappeared from the Mall. "A lot of people are going to be working on that."

Many of the Democrats' experienced operatives were initially aghast at the disorganization. No one was getting names and phone numbers on clipboards, assembling lists for the future. Some leaders, though, were starting to realize was that organizing wasn't happening that way anymore. "No organization could have 'planned' the March," Cecile Richards said. "Seriously, it would have taken ten years and $50 million for the established organizations to organize a four-million-person march—and even then I don't think it would have been possible."

The following Tuesday Trump invited the congressional leaders to the White House. For every new president, this first joint meeting is steeped in protocol, down to the speaking order. Nancy Pelosi had taken part in this initial gathering in George W. Bush's term and in Obama's. Now she wasn't sure what to expect. Would Trump start by quoting the Bible? The Founders? Cite the Constitution? Tell a family story?

Jared Kushner sidled up to her at the start of the event, strutting now that all of a sudden people like the Speaker of the House had to talk to him. "Aren't you excited about all the wonderful new things that are happening?" he asked earnestly.

"You know what I'm excited about?" she replied. "I'm excited about the Women's March."

A few minutes later, when Trump began the meeting by announcing that *actually*, he had won the popular vote, Pelosi looked around and realized no one else was going to speak up. "Mr. President, that's not true," she said, and if they were going to have meetings over budgets and bills, they were going to need to stick to reality. "If we cannot have a discussion based on data, evidence, truth, or fact, there's no use."

Trump responded by goading her San Francisco district in his popular vote nonsense. "I'm not even counting California."

Pelosi left the room early, as she had to get back for votes in the House. In any case, she had had enough. "This guy is really the worst I-don't-know-what that you ever could think," she remembers concluding, in her very Pelosi way. She started holding her own weekly organizing calls and meetings with progressive groups, hoping to capture their energy toward looking ahead to the midterms.

———

Leah Greenberg and Ezra Levin were a pretty standard liberal political couple, both former Hill staffers, both working at nonprofits. She focused on human trafficking. He focused on poverty. The gathering they had at their house the weekend after the election featured fewer bold-faced names, but it was full of people who were just as determined not to bend to Trump.

There were so many new groups those days. So many Google docs of groups stating their goals, such as how to fight fascism in your community. The one they launched, Indivisible, hit a nerve, and so many people logged on to the Google doc that it started crashing. Maybe because George Takei, the *Star Trek* actor, and Robert Reich, the former labor secretary, shared it on Twitter for easy guidance on what to do with all the anger and tears. "Trump is not popular," they wrote. "He does not have a mandate. He does not have large congressional majorities. If a small minority in the Tea Party could stop President Obama, then we the majority can stop a petty tyrant named Trump."

The secret of Indivisible's success, Levin argued, was the combination of distributed organizing and group-based organizing, powered by Facebook groups and Twitter promotion. It was one thing to think of yourself as a quiet liberal in a red state or red county, and to understand why the prospect of Hillary Clinton in the Oval Office could be a little nauseating to your neighbors. It was another to think that it was a viable option to send Trump there instead. A deep-red county could have thousands of such bewildered Democrats. Most of the people who joined Indivisible groups hadn't been involved in politics before. They were disproportionately white college-educated women. They were all looking for leadership, purpose, agency.

"We didn't set out to start an organization," Levin said. "We didn't set out to start a movement. That's part of what made it powerful. We said, 'Here's a structure. Here's a platform. Here's some ideas of what you can do with it, but ultimately you've got to own it.' And that allowed it to just take off like a rocket because it meant that we didn't have to Johnny Appleseed around the country planting seeds for Indivisible groups."

On January 3, Robert Goodlatte, a House Republican, announced that the new Congress's first act would be getting rid of its own ethics office. The following day Indivisible Roanoke, from the congressman's Virginia district, showed up at his office to protest. He backed off. Rachel Maddow's producers called Levin and asked to fly him to New York to be on MSNBC that night, which she introduced with a twenty-minute segment waving a printout of the Google document on the air.

Outside groups soon began looking to connect with Indivisible. Priorities USA, the super PAC, had gone through its own existential moment after Trump won. Over a dinner with the top staff and consultants during the transition, Guy Cecil—who had wanted to be Clinton's campaign manager in 2016, but didn't get the job—had asked a simple question: Should we exist? Priorities USA had been conceived of as a tool for presidential elections. There wasn't a clear enough place for it in the 2018 midterms, when there would be all sorts of House and Senate candidates, rather than a single presidential candidate for whom to flood ads with unlimited money. They decided yes, Priorities USA should exist—but only if it could integrate successfully into the growing universe of organizations, pumping in money and connections to more money. Indivisible was leading efforts to flood town halls that members of Congress were holding back in their districts, and Cecil offered to have the super PAC pay for the online ads rustling up support. Priorities USA worked out deals with the House Majority PAC and the Senate Majority PAC, the two well-funded groups committed to winning the midterms, and asked them to match the money they were putting into design, targeting, and placement.

Indivisible lived up to some of its Tea Party promise. By the end of June, as Congress barreled toward what looked like Obamacare repeal, they were demanding that Schumer pull a procedural move to "withhold consent," twisting the rules of the Senate to buy them more time to whip up more of the opposition they had mobilized at town halls all through the spring. When Schumer's staff pushed back, Levin informed them that their local groups had die-in protests scheduled for his district offices back in New York at the end of that week. The following day the Senate Democrats announced they were pulling consent.

Amanda Litman took a simpler approach than Levin and Greenberg. A midlevel operative on Clinton's 2016 campaign, in November she was on a group vacation with seven other depressed alums in Costa Rica, reading Ellen

Malcolm's book about starting the Democratic women's fundraising group EMILY's List, mulling over a Facebook message from an old college acquaintance who was a public school teacher complaining about budget cuts: "If Trump can be president, why can't I be?"

So many people suddenly wanted to get involved, but there wasn't really a place to figure out what to do for those who weren't rich, white, male, or part of a political network, Litman thought. And if Clinton's loss was supposed to have revealed, in part, how desolate the Democratic bench was, the problem wasn't going to be fixed by trying to line up candidates for just governorships or the Senate.

She started reaching out. Litman was introduced to another operative, Ross Morales Rocketto, by his wife, Jess Morales Rocketto. They came up with the idea for Run for Something—so long as the "something" was no higher than state legislature. School board, city council, town offices were all good targets. If first-time candidates signed up for their program and pledged to support its "values criteria" on abortion rights, gun control, climate change, and women's and LGBTQ equality, they would have their credibility and campaign plans vetted by local leaders and in-state experts. Those who passed would get endorsements, which they hoped might make other groups on the ground pay attention.

The more experienced Democrats who heard about it thought it was a great if unworkable idea, as no one actually wanted to run for these boring low-level offices. Others warned that they'd never be able to scale up to reach enough people. After the election in 2008, the Obama campaign had taken a survey of two million supporters, which included a question asking how many were interested in running for office themselves. More than thirty thousand people raised their hands, digitally. The information went to the DNC, and while other data from the survey was used over the years to mobilize help in Obama's push for Obamacare, basic climate change legislation, and his reelection campaign, no one ever followed up with the respondents who said they might want to get involved themselves.

Run for Something launched officially on Trump's Inauguration Day. Litman and Morales thought that maybe one hundred people would be interested. The number rose quickly to one thousand.

Clinton surprised them by getting on board almost immediately, inviting

Litman and Morales to her office in Manhattan for two hours in the spring of 2017. She ran through their plans, their ambitions. She asked about their legal structure and who their lawyers were, and when she found out that it was the same firm that had been on retainer for her campaign, she made a joke about how they'd kept her out of jail, despite all of Trump's "Lock her up!" chants. Not long afterward she wrote the group a check for $100,000 from her own new PAC. A year later she gave another $100,000. Then she wrote the forward for Litman's book, which laid out the Run for Something mission.

Several state parties told Run for Something to keep out, as they liked non-competitive down-ballot races and worried that its involvement would only help Republicans to start calling attention to more of them. Several big donors were wary, wanting to see clearer returns on their investments—or in political consultant terms, cost per vote. The world was burning, and they were supposed to donate a couple thousand bucks to help train people to run for school board?

Cory Booker immediately bought in, as did Gillibrand. Harris was non-committal, her staff saying in those early days that she was trying to avoid national politics. They could never get Sanders or his team interested, then or over the next four years, no matter how many times they asked. On May 9, 2017, Litman was the youngest person in a group seated around a table with Joe Biden, who wanted a briefing to get him up to speed with the resistance. Kelly Ward was there from the new Obama–Holder redistricting group, as was Jason Kander, who had turned his Senate loss in Missouri into a win by becoming a new Democratic celebrity, and had translated that into a state-level voting rights group—"There are a lot of Scrantons in Missouri," Biden observed at one point. Cristobal Alex represented the Latino Victory Fund. Nick Rathod came from State Innovation Exchange, which was working to write and promote progressive bills in state legislatures. Quentin James came from the Collective PAC, which sought to elect more Black local officials. Brad Lander, a city councilman from Brooklyn, ran a group called Local Progress. Arisha Hatch came from Color of Change. Levin came from Indivisible.

They each gave presentations, laid out their plans. Biden told Litman how he'd gotten his own start, back in 1970, as a member of the New Castle County Council. How he'd been the young buck who no one gave much of a chance, but who had won and started changing politics in Delaware. He'd had to sit through so many boring meetings about water tables and leeching, but there was a lesson in that, he said: it turned out that those meetings were actually about cancer rates. While they were sitting there, their phones started buzzing with the news alerts that Trump had fired FBI director Jim Comey.

In November 2017, thirty-five Run for Something candidates won—including six of the fifteen Democrats who came within one seat of flipping the Virginia House of Delegates. They had demonstrably established themselves. More than eleven thousand people had applied that first year, and by the time Biden was elected, sixty-two thousand people had signed on, with twenty thousand in 2020 alone. Many of those were gearing up to run in 2021 and 2022.

The Women's March turned the idea of spontaneous protests into a phenomenon. Nine days later, when Trump signed his first Muslim travel ban, Democratic officials and protesters rushed to the airports, many of them alerted that the actions were springing up via tweets and Facebook posts. Members of Congress arrived to assert that they had standing to see anyone who had been detained in the airports, confusing TSA and border control agents who hadn't been given instructions about what to do, and let them through.

The action had come at the local level, as Democratic mayors and governors were already building a new kind of federalism. One result was the Climate Alliance, which aimed to put in place by local regulation what Trump had abandoned when he said America would pull out of the Paris climate accords. Sometimes that was symbolic—Rahm Emanuel, now the mayor of Chicago, copied the scientific data on climate change from the federal government's website to a city government website, where it would be preserved—but often it led to real action in the form of renewable energy and emission standards. "We don't have to argue states' rights," said Jay Inslee, the Washington governor, who'd become friendly with Al Gore from talking about climate change since the 1990s. Inslee was one of the first governors who signed on to the alliance, reflecting on the evolution of thinking already popular in early 2018. "There is no argument about this, that Donald Trump cannot stop us from taking action individually. So in my state he cannot stop us from adapting to common sense."

Republicans started to falter. Just mentioning the infrastructure plan Trump never came up with became a running joke. His White House was one looping palace intrigue story, like a combination of *Henry IV* and *The Benny Hill Show*. In late March, on Trump's sixty-third day in office, Speaker Paul Ryan had to cancel a planned vote to repeal Obamacare in the House. The flood of activists and volunteers appearing in town halls into the spring meant that when the House finally did pass the bill in May, Trump's declaration at the celebration rally he held for Republican members in the Rose Garden that "this has brought the Republican Party together" became yet another joke. Republicans in the Senate, seeing the opposition and staring into the reality of actually getting rid of the popular law, whiffed over and over in coming up with a plan, and ultimately, with a way to vote for the plan.

Two weeks after the Obamacare vote, the Nazis took their tiki torches into Charlottesville. They chanted "You will not replace us!" a slogan Jews knew in their guts. They didn't hide their faces with hoods, and the light of the torch flames flicked on their features. This was what Trump had inspired, and he made sure to sustain the inspiration over the following week, as he talked about the "very fine people on both sides." He did what he had always done when being attacked, lashing out and praising the people who were standing up for him, no matter who they were.

The largest new organization that sprang up was also the most idiosyncratic—and like Trump's campaign, it began as one rich man's obsession with Trump. Tom Steyer, a hedge fund investor who'd retired at fifty-three after earning a few billion dollars and becoming the biggest donor in Democratic politics, had been looking for a new way in for a while. He'd started a massive youth turn-out group called NextGen America and pumped money into other groups and candidates, anyone who fit with his increasingly particular and increasingly hands-on view of what a candidate should be. He'd complained that he hadn't been given a speaking spot at the Democratic conventions in 2012 or 2016, apparently oblivious to how odd it would have looked to put someone onstage simply because he'd given a lot of money. He had toyed with running for governor or senator in California, only to abandon the idea at the last minute, after staff and consultants had begun being hired. When the party was on the rocks, his group and his checkbook became ever more important.

To him, the answer was never the Obama–Biden voters. "You know, is it possible to flip 10,000 Trump voters? Definitely," he said. "But think about turnout. Think about how many people who voted for Obama didn't show up in '16. Multiple, multiple, multiple of 10,000."

In October 2017, Steyer launched Need to Impeach. Out of the same San Francisco office building that housed NextGen and his foundation, he poured money into TV and Facebook ads. Millions of people started signing up, tracked in real time on a counter on the group's website, eventually reaching eight million and forming the largest list in politics—outstripping the National Rifle Association by about three million.

"We decided this guy is a total crook and we have to stand up to him, and there was a huge response to that, that had nothing to do with insider politics," Steyer said, looking back. "Those people were just like, 'This stinks. This is corrupt. This is wrong. We have to take back our country.'"

CHAPTER THREE

I HOPE _____

Obama's election revealed a fundamental truth about our country. And so does Donald Trump's. One is a fundamental truth I really like, and one is a fundamental truth that pains me. But they're both true.

—TIM KAINE

February 2017–December 2017

He was always more relaxed on the plane. Obama hadn't flown commercial since his presidential campaign had gotten serious in 2007, and he liked that he was never going to have to do so again. The guy who used to complain that he didn't get to take walks in the park anymore had no interest in being patted down by the TSA.

The holiday party for the Obama Foundation back in Chicago had been a relief, a welcome break from reality after a year that had been one pile of shit after another, with the exception of saving Obamacare, thanks to, of all people, John McCain, with his middle of the night thumbs down on repeal.

It was getting late. Obama and his staff were kicking back. Usually there was only a short window to throw questions at him between the small talk at takeoff, with Words with Friends or some *SportsCenter* clip playing on his iPad. They had to catch him before he popped in his earbuds and started tapping at his memoir on his laptop. (They could usually tell what section he was working on based on which stories he would begin reminiscing about.) They got him going by asking what it was like, after coming in working with Jamie Dimon and Lloyd Blankfein and the other big bankers, to be made out as an anticapitalist by the Republicans. Obama gave a long, reasoned answer. As for the Tea Party, Obama said, well, they were "racist motherfuckers."

But enough looking back. Obama started the latest round of his favorite game, Who Do You Want to Be the Democratic Nominee? This time he had a new format: Who do you want in your head? Who do you want in your heart? Who could win?

A few aides threw out their suggestions. Obama listened, tossed the ideas around. He was interested in some, less so in others. He ragged Cory Booker. He listened as staff expressed doubts about Kamala Harris. She'd been good, he thought, at key moments, like turning Jeff Sessions into blinking blubber at a Senate Judiciary Committee hearing. They joked about the meme, which had been popular around the office when it had started a few months earlier, that NBA coaches Gregg Popovich and Steve Kerr should run for president—basketball coaches get leadership, and they get race, he'd say, and they were certainly outsiders . . .

Obama's head choice was Bill McRaven, the commander of the Navy SEAL raid that had killed bin Laden, and at the time, the chancellor at the University of Texas who kept putting himself out, defending the media and talking about keeping democracy together.

From his heart, Obama picked Biden, because of course. He loved Biden. Part of the reason he'd picked him as his running mate in 2008 was because he thought Biden was already old enough that he'd never run for president, and by the end of their time in the White House together—with Biden in politics so long, and with so many examples of either making deals that would leave the left suspicious or flubbing deals that would have Republicans mocking him—Obama was doubtful about his prospects. He didn't think Biden could be a disciplined enough candidate. "He undervalued Biden's political abilities because they had such different styles," observed Jen Psaki, Obama's communications director (and later Biden's White House press secretary), over the summer of 2020. Still, he and Biden were brothers. No one else was going to have his heart.

But who could actually win? Obama struggled. Biden? Maybe. Obama had been spending a lot of time those days talking about how physically exhausting running for president is, how difficult it actually was for someone older to do it. He'd say it was unfortunate that voters tended to like taller candidates more than shorter ones. He saw the party changing, wondered whether Biden could fit into what it was becoming. He'd seen for himself back in 2008, and had gotten reports confirming his observations, how much trouble Biden had connecting with crowds. "I've never seen a man who's better at talking to a thousand people than to one," Biden himself once marveled about his boss while flying on Air Force Two at one point. Obama's view was essentially the reverse: he'd never seen a thousand people show up to hear Biden talk about anything. "Americans like their presidents to have some swagger," Obama would say in private. "It's a primal thing, the way voters react." Biden had the strut, and he had the aviator sunglasses. But swagger? He worried it was more of a stumble.

Obama's postpresidency was supposed to be fun. He had hired a small caretaker staff. Nothing big was on his plate. He'd hand the White House over to Hillary Clinton, build a library, and figure out how to establish his foundation while she ran the world and everyone left him alone. He'd get his thoughts together to write his book. Go on long vacations. Make a lot of money.

There was no political model for what lay before him. For all the party changes and bitter races from White House to White House—George H. W. Bush at first regarding Bill Clinton as a hillbilly interloper who'd kept him from a second term, Obama campaigning against George W. Bush as a fool who bumbled the country into a war and a recession—there'd never been a president whose political existence was so much a function of the hatred for his predecessor as Trump, or one who spent his days and nights obsessing about his predecessor the way Trump mashed his Obama hate-tweets into his phone.

Trump was literally a 2012 article in *The Onion* from the week after Obama's reelection come to life: AFTER OBAMA VICTORY, SHRIEKING WHITE-HOT SPHERE OF PURE RAGE EARLY GOP FRONT-RUNNER FOR 2016. Obama thought he recognized that anger, thought he could take it apart. But he never really understood it and could never make sense of its appeal.

The night before the 2016 election Obama had come for a final campaign rally in Philadelphia in front of Independence Hall. No other Clinton event during the entire campaign had been this packed, with fumes that cold night of the movement that had been there at every Obama rally in 2008. Bon Jovi performed. Bruce Springsteen came out solo in a scarf and denim shirt, talked about how Clinton was going to put an end to what Trump had brought out in the country, and what a relief it would be to be rid of "somebody who would be willing to damage our long-cherished and admired system rather than look to himself for the reasons behind his own epic failure." The three songs he played, though, were downbeat, as if he knew he was at a wake. "It's gonna be a long walk home," he sang, closing out the set. "Hey pretty darling, don't wait up for me, gonna be a long walk home."

But the crowd stayed with him. And with Michelle Obama. And then with Barack Obama, up at the podium with the presidential seal on it, so that Clinton could follow him up and just happen to get the perfect shot of her looking the part for the Election Day front pages and local news B-roll.

"Donald Trump is uniquely unqualified to be our chief executive," Obama said. "On foreign policy, Donald Trump is temperamentally unfit to be commander in chief."

"I'm betting that America will reject a politics of resentment and a politics of blame, and choose a politics that says we are stronger together. I am betting that tomorrow, you will reject fear and you'll choose hope. I'm betting that the wisdom and decency and generosity of the American people will once again win the day," Obama said, closing it out. "And that is a bet I have never, ever lost."

He lost.

For all their mutual sniping over the years, and all the time they spent talking about each other, they'd never actually spoken until Obama called to congratulate Trump on winning, at two a.m. on election night. About thirty hours later, on Thursday morning, Obama welcomed him into the Oval Office.

Down the hall in the West Wing, Trump's incoming communications director, Hope Hicks, was meeting with her counterparts in the Obama press office. She arrived saying how proud she was of "Mr. Trump." They asked her where she was going to live in DC, if they could help suggest a place or neighborhood, but it seemed as if she hadn't considered that she was actually going to be living in DC now. She was focused on other matters, like what Obama's approval process was for reviewing statements out of the White House. When they told her that they didn't show most statements to him, she seemed confused. "Mr. Trump will want to see everything and sign off on it," she said.

"Imagine if we asked Obama to approve the Botswana Independence Day declaration," Ben Rhodes joked to other aides later.

Other aides took Jared Kushner on a tour of the West Wing, down the stairs from the press offices, toward the White House Mess and the hallway leading to the Situation Room and the National Security Council offices, where the walls and carpet are done in beige on beige on beige, with a touch of wood paneling. "Oh, Mr. Trump is going to love this," Kushner told his guides. "It's going to remind him of one of his golf clubhouses."

They dropped Kushner off for a walk around the South Lawn with Denis McDonough, who had spent the summer and fall having transition conversations with Chris Christie, who made sense as a counterpart. McDonough was a round-the-clock national security wonk who would talk about getting "rat fucked" by holdouts in Congress and use expressions like "busman's holiday," who'd order a beer just because the menu said it was from his home state of Minnesota. Kushner was a wannabe wunderkind, a rich kid who'd been bought into Harvard and NYU Law with millions of dollars and sweetheart real estate deals, then ran his family real estate business while his father was in prison for hiring a prostitute to seduce his brother-in-law. Kushner's big achievement had been overleveraging himself into the most expensive commercial real estate deal in New York City history. By then he was already chasing foreign money to cover the debt.

Obama had spent the day between the election and the meeting trying to place Trump in history. Maybe he was just a con man, and it wouldn't be so bad. Maybe if he just walked Trump through why he'd done what he'd done, he'd convince him how difficult and damaging it would be to start unraveling all the work. He planned his strategy: start by buttering up Trump by talking about how they'd both beaten Clinton; how they both drew big, crazy crowds; how they both were better politicians than any of the people who hadn't taken them seriously. He would run through some of the perks—Air Force One is *great*. Then he'd move in and save the undocumented children known as Dreamers by saying, *Think what it will look like on TV, seeing all those kids rounded up.*

Obama thought the plan was working while they were sitting there. When the Cuba reopening came up and Trump talked about the market opportunity for new hotels, Obama encouraged it. He'd laid it on thick about the Iran deal, walked him through provisions. "I didn't know that," Trump had said. "I'll get you a briefing," Obama offered. Rebrand it the Trump Anti-Nuclear Deal, Obama suggested. Make a few patches to Obamacare and call it Trumpcare. He'd warned him about North Korea, that they hadn't been able to crack it, and that it was going to be an enduring problem. He'd offered to keep talking, giving advice. Don't hire Michael Flynn, Obama warned, as the retired general was unstable and his contacts with foreign officials kept showing up in their intelligence reports. In that moment Trump seemed to take his advice seriously. Trump asked for a list of people to consider for national security jobs, and Obama promised to follow through. At one point Trump asked him how he'd spend his time out of office. Maybe they would see more of each other? Trump told him he'd be welcome anytime at Mar-a-Lago.

Trump and Obama had been scheduled to meet for half an hour. Their conversation went on for ninety minutes. By the time reporters were called into the Oval Office, Kushner and Hicks were at the back, by the Resolute desk. She still had on her tan trench coat, while he stood taking pictures on his iPhone. Obama leaned forward in his chair, arms on his legs, full-on alpha male. Trump was visibly nervous, fidgeting, his eyes wandering around the room. In that moment, in that room, he came off as an unsettling combination of swooning and fearful, more impressed that the president was being so gracious to him than that he was now the president-elect himself. Trump wasn't as much focused on Obama's policy agenda as he was on how to become a popular president, how to attract public attention and get approval, all of which was obvious in his mostly incoherent remarks: "I very much look forward to dealing with the president in the future, including counsel, to explain some of the difficulties, some of the high-flying assets, and some of the really great things that have been achieved." It was a nice moment and met with lots of smiles.

Then the questions started getting shouted, mostly at Obama: What did you two discuss? Do you think he's going to uproot your legacy?

Then, pointing first at Obama, and then at Trump: "Do *you* still think that *he* is a threat to the republic?"

Obama had been through enough of these back and forths with the press, and he wasn't going to respond to any of the baiting. He leaned over and shared a chummy joke with Trump about how this was what the press corps always did, and that they had to ignore the White House reporters calling out questions like this.

A few hours later, at the daily press briefing, Josh Earnest tried to hold to the official line, ducking a question about whether, given all that the president had said on the campaign trail, he was still concerned for the future of the country and the world with Trump's election.

"Those are authentic views that haven't changed. That's not just rhetoric. Those aren't just slogans. Those represent the president's actual views and preferences about the direction that he'd like to see the country go," Earnest said. "But that's not what the American people voted for."

"Coming out of it, [Obama's] view was that it had gone pretty well: Maybe Trump is such a wild card, he's not going to rip up the Iran deal; maybe he's going to see it's not in his interest to rip up the ACA because it'll be so much trouble," recalled Jen Psaki.

Still, the conversation had been bizarre, Obama told aides afterward. He couldn't hold Trump's attention on anything and saw how nervous he was. "This guy has no idea and doesn't give a shit," he said. He hoped, though, that he had gotten through. He thought there was a glimmer of a chance that maybe the Trump presidency wouldn't be what he feared, that he had done what he could to try to rein in some of the chaos.

The next day, Trump announced he was bringing Steve Bannon into the White House. Obama flew to Europe on his final overseas trip, to Greece and then to Germany, where his geopolitical soul mate, Angela Merkel, told him how anxious she was, how she did not believe as he did that everything would be all right.

Then Trump announced he was hiring Flynn as his national security adviser. New intelligence reports about the Russian hacking came in. Whatever sigh of relief there had been, whatever bemusement at Trump's ignorance, was gone.

The rest of the West Wing had been panicked from the start. Obama could feel secure about his own place in history and cling to the Martin Luther King Jr. line he loved about the long arc of the moral universe bending toward justice, but the people who worked for him had missed best friends' weddings or plans to get pregnant or Christmases or birthday parties, or just sacrificed ten years of normal life. All the research into regulations, all the negotiations, the phone calls when they should have been eating dinner. Election night was going to prove that they'd actually changed the country, that it had all been worth it.

And then the Trump aides started showing up for the transition process, few of whom seemed to know much about anything. Then Trump replaced Christie with Mike Pence as the head of the transition, and another group of aides appeared, as uninformed as the first group. Some were certainly respectful; others irritated Obama aides by wearing their Trump campaign lanyards and not paying much attention to their briefings, clearly not caring to listen to people they hated, and were obviously going to ignore. Some seemed as if they were making secret recordings, trying to eavesdrop on conversations that they could leak or mine for intel back at headquarters. Some never showed up at meetings or responded to emails. "We were all extraordinarily underwhelmed with our successors, if we heard from them at all," remembered one aide. Obama's staff proudly touted the transition iPads that they'd stocked with detailed information about each agency and about operations—a step forward in how any previous White House administration had managed the handover. The Trump team didn't spend much time swiping through them.

Aides started running "red team" meetings in McDonough's office, brainstorming on his whiteboard about what mischief Trump aides could stir up once he was president. What if they went through archived email accounts and searched for embarrassing or undermining information they could weaponize? What if they tried to get Congress to launch retroactive investigations? What could they find? What could they protect against at that point? What kind of response could be mounted from the outside? They were terrified. Any planning for the postpresidency and the Obama Foundation went on alert, now with a lawyer part of every conversation.

When they weren't in McDonough's office, top aides were back at their desks, reading through the Russia reports, which had gone public. Anger replaced depression. "We were all extremely pissed off," said Psaki. "Then you start to question whether you could have done more." The national security team had thought they knew what they were doing, and any hindsight about the 2016 election already felt played out by then. But White House aides outside of the tight circle that Obama and McDonough had insisted on still

couldn't get over feeling that the national security experts should have con-
sulted some of the aides with more political experience about propaganda,
public opinion, and unexpected turns. Could they still convince people Trump
wasn't their fault? Could they convince themselves?

They had another problem. Clinton would have been responsible for naming the new Democratic National Committee chair had she been president,
and now Keith Ellison, a Minnesota congressman running from the left and
promising to turn the DNC into a mass organizing apparatus, was the only
viable candidate to be chair. Obama hadn't cared who the DNC chair was when it
was his decision. Now he found himself fighting a proxy war on Clinton's behalf against a junior congressman who'd always annoyed him, getting knocked
by panicked and angry progressives who believed he was only proving his
corporatism and centrism by standing in Ellison's way. After ten years of being
called a socialist Muslim, he didn't want to hand Trump the gift of an actual
socialism-minded Muslim and wasn't going to turn the party over to Bernie
Sanders's pick, given that he viewed Sanders as contributing to Clinton's loss.

Fortunately for Obama, someone had come up with another idea. Tom Perez
was then undergoing his own crisis. After a brief moment during the summer
when he seemed to actually be in consideration as Clinton's running mate, the
fiery-behind-a-rally-microphone-but-dorkily-awkward-in-just-about-
any-other-situation outgoing labor secretary had been expecting her call the
morning after the election asking him to be her attorney general. He felt disillusioned. Scared. Powerless, pointless. He cried that night on the phone, worrying about what Trump in the White House would mean for immigrants, like
his parents decades ago, like the Dreamers now.

Two days later, Perez left on a prescheduled government trip to Argentina
to talk about apprenticeships at Global Entrepreneurship Week. Sam Cornale,
a lanky and wily young political operative who had attached himself to Perez
at the Labor Department, headed to South Dakota for a wedding. They had
planned that if Perez didn't get picked to be Clinton's attorney general, he
would run for governor of Maryland in 2018. Now one of those options wasn't
real, and the other seemed ridiculous because the incumbent governor's polling was so high there was little point in chasing a likely lost cause. Cornale got
Perez's permission to float an idea to a reporter for the new scheme they'd
cooked up: though the extent of the secretary's political experience had been

getting elected to a term on a county council in Maryland and then being disqualified from his 2006 state attorney general race on a technicality, he was going to run for DNC chair. They argued that Perez had successfully rebuilt the voting rights section at the Justice Department in Obama's first term, after the Bush years, and then in the second, he'd rebuilt the Labor Department after it fell apart under Obama's first secretary. The DNC clearly needed its own rescue repair. Perez was also a progressive and as labor secretary, he had developed, at least theoretically, good relationships with labor leaders. He was Dominican, which would mitigate the awkwardness of the first Black president standing in the way of a Black DNC chair as his final political act in office.

Through David Simas, Cornale's idea quickly percolated up to Obama. After the story floating the idea ran, other potential chair candidates, like former Michigan governor Jennifer Granholm, called Perez to tell him they were all in with him. Debbie Wasserman Schultz, still bitter about how Obama and his aides had kept her on the job until her own self-absorbed incompetence and the Russian hack had forced her out, had warned Ellison not to trust the White House. "They might let you come close, but they'll never let you win." He wouldn't accept that. For weeks, Ellison kept calling the White House to at least have a conversation with Obama, to try to work through his resistance. Obama never called back. Instead, he brought Perez into the Oval Office and left his labor secretary with no choice but to agree to run. He even threw in some implied promises of staying involved himself.

Calls started to go out. This was happening. Really, aides told DNC members who were like high school rom-com characters consumed with hate and jealousy after years of being ignored but still desperate to be liked by the cool kid. This is Obama's choice, they would say. He wanted them all in line for it.

The calls inspired some laughter, some exasperation. *Now he cares?* Even the Obama orbit wasn't in alignment: as Simas was helping manufacture the Perez campaign, David Axelrod—who'd been Obama's political guru and Simas's mentor—was working his next project: pushing a South Bend, Indiana, mayor named Pete Buttigieg into the race for the chair as his springboard into national politics.

Where does all this leave us? Obama was asked at his penultimate press conference in mid-December, a few days after meeting with Perez.

He interrupted the question.

"What 'leaves us'? Where my presidency leaves us?" he replied.

"The election—"

"It leaves us in a really good spot," Obama said, "if we make some good decisions going forward."

The question was really about the Electoral College about to officially vote on a president that Obama knew had been helped by Russian interference, and the decimation of the Democratic Party over the years that he led it.

Obama wasn't biting on any of that. He called the election "a clarifying moment," a reminder that voting and politics mattered. He acknowledged that he hadn't been able to make the Democrats about more than him, or in Obama-speak, that "the coalition I put together didn't always turn out to be transferable."

He returned, as he so often did, to the speech that had defined him. "I still believe what I said in 2004, which is this red state/blue thing is a construct. Now, it is a construct that has gotten more and more powerful for a whole lot of reasons, from gerrymandering to big money to the way that media has splintered," he said. "But outside of the realm of electoral politics, I still see people the way I saw them when I made that speech—full of contradictions, and there are some regional differences, but basically folks care about their families, they care about having meaningful work, they care about making sure their kids have more opportunity than they did. They want to be safe, they want to feel like things are fair."

Obama knew that came across as a little absurd by then. He knew that he sounded as if he'd failed. The red states were still red, the blue states were still blue, and the guy who'd said they didn't exist was being rejected. "What the president-elect is going to be doing is going to be very different than what I was doing," he added, "and I think people will be able to compare and contrast and make judgments about what worked for the American people."

And then he left for his annual two weeks in Hawaii, one last vacation before spending the rest of his life on vacation. He wouldn't let Trump mess that up too. "Mele Kalikimaka" on the way out the door.

"Doing my best to disregard the many inflammatory President O statements and roadblocks," Trump tweeted the following week. "Thought it was going to be a smooth transition—NOT!"

They had a phone call that afternoon, checking in about the transition. Six hours after sending the tweet, Trump was asked how he was getting on with Obama. "Oh, I think very, very smoothly," he said. "Very good. You don't think so?"

Other than riding together to the inauguration and a brief handshake at George H. W. Bush's funeral at the end of 2018, they never spoke again.

═══

Some national security staff focused on rushing to get the intelligence assessments made public. Others began preparing the sanctions they wanted to hit Putin with while they still had time. The rest went through panicked moments of wondering what they might have been able to do with one more push on a minimum wage policy, one more trip into Michigan or Pennsylvania without the Clinton campaign having asked for it.

The night before the inauguration, Obama invited some of his closest staffers up to the residence in the White House. It was lower-key than the big goodbye bash he'd hosted for himself a few weeks earlier—Oprah and George Lucas and Dave Chapelle and David Letterman wandering around, Bruce Springsteen sliding by Paul McCartney on the buffet line. That final night was only for aides who had shown up to work every day in the building but had never been upstairs. They'd spent that final day checking every desk drawer and open space for any scrap of a document or forgotten item that could be used against them. McDonough made it into a scavenger hunt, which included their signing their names on the old tiles from FDR's pool under the briefing room floor. There were many hugs and awkward goodbyes. These were people who spent eight years together in that White House, and on that night, walking around, it felt like their home.

Only a few top staff showed up at the White House on the following morning. Most woke up and headed straight to a hangar at Andrews Air Force Base for one last goodbye ceremony. There were no TVs there to watch what was taking place back at the Capitol. When Trump took the oath of office, a few gathered around an iPhone to watch the moment. One last half-hearted chant of "Yes We Can!" went around. Before Trump got to the "American carnage" line in his inaugural address, they were singing the National Anthem, led by a man who'd climbed up on the small stage to conduct, shouting at one point,

"Louder!" One final Obama production—orchestrated and stage-managed with a precious sense of pride and patriotism.

Obama still bore his frustration with Clinton for having blown the election, at how a better candidate would have won, at how the hell she hadn't gone to Wisconsin, at how she had managed to lose Michigan, but his Clinton critique was fading. He thought about the labor leader who'd confided to him that it was easier to get his guys to vote for a Black man than a woman. He agreed with the broader anger that Comey's handling of the politics around the investigations was unacceptable.

By that day, though, deeper anger was building. He was angry at the country and trying to hold it in, even to himself. For eight years, he thought, no one was more attuned to race and racism in America than he had been. He had believed that America was better than this, or that at least enough of America was better to make up for the parts that were worse—the parts that Mitch McConnell spoke to when he never recognized Obama as legitimate, or that had turned his criticizing a cop for arresting Henry Louis Gates Jr. on his own front porch into his lowest point in the polls of his entire presidency.

"He had to pretend like he didn't notice in the same way that Jackie Robinson had to pretend that he wasn't being heckled," said Ben Rhodes, thinking back on his boss's shift during the transition. "Trump made him reconsider all of that."

The helicopter landed with the Obamas, fresh from Trump's sending them on their way at the back side of the Capitol. The new president was already at the desk in the quickly redecorated Oval Office, getting ready to sign an executive order with his first swing at Obamacare. The rundown on the music stands for the Air Force band identified Obama as FPOTUS. They didn't play "Hail to the Chief." He walked right up onto the little platform being used as a stage without taking off his coat. "This is just a little pit stop," Obama said. "This is not a period, this is a comma in the continuing story of building America." The doors to the hangar slowly opened, another perfectly stage-managed moment, the reveal of the red carpet for one last flight on the plane that, because he wasn't president anymore, was technically no longer Air Force One. He threw himself into the crowd, with most of his cabinet secretaries up front, posing for photos, saying hi to the kids. To end it, he had one last hug for McDonough. More cheers. Then, holding hands with his wife, he walked to the plane, joined by a few friends.

"Gut-wrenching," is how Valerie Jarrett remembers the flight to California. "We knew we were leaving behind a disaster. By that time, we all had a pretty good appreciation for the fact that [Trump] would govern just as he had campaigned. His inauguration speech was atrocious. Stunningly so. There was a beginning of an unease." Jarrett hadn't gone to the inaugural ceremony—she remained committed to a pledge she'd made years earlier to be the last one to turn off the lights in her office.

When the plane landed—it had been headed to Palm Springs, but bad weather redirected it to another airport nearby—Obama got into a smaller motorcade, in an SUV instead of the presidential limos he had been driven around in all over the world for the past eight years. In what became a favorite story, he would tell people afterward that as he sat in the back, he kept hearing a noise. He was trying to kick back, his first few hours of no longer being responsible for the world, but he was worried there was something wrong with the car. No one else seemed to notice. Then it hit him: the noise was the turn signal clicking. He hadn't been in a car that needed to wait for a light in ten years.

—————

March 4 used to be Inauguration Day, back through FDR's first. March 4, 2017, was the day Obama completely lost hope in Trump, when an aide called to tell him about his early morning tweet: "Terrible! Just found out that Obama had my 'wires tapped' in Trump Tower just before the victory. Nothing found."

The idea was totally absurd; the scare quotes were nonsensical. Still, to have been accused of misusing power in a way he never would have, to have one president say this about another president, offended and enraged him. "That was when I think everybody went, 'What the . . . ?'" recalled Susan Rice. All morning he was back and forth on the phone with aides, trying to decide how to respond. Why was anyone caring about this? he wanted to know. It's not serious, why does it need to be treated that way? McDonough called Reince Priebus, his successor as Trump's chief of staff, and got nowhere. "Should I just call Trump?" Obama offered at one point. Rhodes, burning in person and on Twitter, pitched going on the Sunday shows the next day to shoot it all down. Obama stopped him. What was the point?

They decided to answer the accusation with a dismissive statement. His press secretary's name was on it, but Obama edited the final version himself.

"At that point," a person who spoke with him that day said later, "we hadn't realized Trump could make stuff up."

A month passed before the next incident, when Trump mused in an Oval Office interview with *The New York Times* at the beginning of April that Obama's national security adviser, Susan Rice, should be prosecuted for seeking to discover the identities of the Americans whom intelligence had been tracking for contact with the Russians (the first time he'd landed on this particular theme). He said he had more information on the matter, and he'd reveal it eventually, but he never did. A mile away at his own office, Obama asked again if he should call Trump, or if his chief of staff should call Trump's. There were check-in strategy calls among senior aides who'd worked for him over the years, and though Obama never got involved directly himself, he wanted to make sure the network was being activated to defend Rice.

"We have now entered the realm of the insane," is how another aide remembers those days. "Something that is totally dishonest, complete fiction—but you still have to deal with it."

In 2016, when the Republican primaries had narrowed down to Trump and Ted Cruz, Obama had said privately that he'd take a Trump presidency over a Cruz one. Cruz was smart, he observed. He'd know what to do, how to turn on the power centers in the White House and make them all work. Trump was a fool, and his presidency would just be a mess.

In the early months of the Trump administration he was still convinced of that. The incompetence, he said, was saving the country. If Trump and his team were better, they could do much more damage. That opinion didn't last long either.

"He's a madman," Obama would occasionally concede to big donors looking to squeeze a reaction out of him in exchange for the big checks they were writing to his foundation. More often: "I didn't think it would be this bad." Sometimes: "I didn't think we'd have a racist, sexist pig." Depending on the outrage of the day, a "Can you believe this?" email with a link in the morning, or a passing "that fucking lunatic" with a shake of his head through the end of a conversation.

Aides and donors would try to get him going on Trump, just to see what he'd say. Usually he'd deflect, or he'd start in and then stop himself—"I'm not getting worked up about this," he'd say. Sometimes enough would slip out anyway, like when he was once asked about Trump's speaking with foreign leaders without having aides on the line to listen in on the conversations. "That corrupt motherfucker," he remarked.

Obama had been hoping to have some fun with his return to public life, start out by popping up somewhere in southern Illinois to show that he was laid back and returning to his roots—and at the same time not so subtly grind in the point he'd been making since right after the election, that Democrats needed to at least compete in parts of states they'd never win. Every week there was some new incident that sent reporters calling to ask for his response. The southern Illinois stop was scrapped, along with any other playful ideas. His official return was set as a relaxed discussion with young activists back at the University of Chicago in April—small audience, mostly students. Only a few reporters attended. He wasn't president anymore, so there were no security checks to get in the door, no motorcade, no police cars with the flashers in the distance blocking off traffic for blocks.

"So . . . uh, what's been going on while I've been gone?" he asked wryly after stepping onto the stage.

He tried not to be the center of attention, instead drawing out each of the people onstage as if he were practicing to be a podcast host. Along the way, he did a little revisionism around the 2004 Democratic convention keynote that had started it all. "When I said in 2004 that there were no red states or blue states, there are United States of America," he explained, "that was an aspirational comment."

─────────

Obama wanted his postpresidency to be as important a part of his life, and as important to the world, as his presidency had been. There was no one else in American politics who had his combination of moral authority and a following. He'd transcended politics—like John Lewis in America, like Nelson Mandela in the world. "I could somehow see myself in his story and he could see himself in mine," he'd said on a hilltop in Jerusalem for Shimon Peres's funeral, five weeks before Trump's election, reflecting on another political leader who'd become bigger than his politics, or his country. "One thing that he said to me initially in the early days of the foundation was, 'Imagine the good that comes out of us finding ten thousand, one hundred thousand, a million of these young folks and connecting them together. Can you imagine the good that flows from there?'" recalled David Simas, who had become the Obama Foundation CEO after leaving the White House. "That's exponentially greater than anything, even with the highest position in the country, in terms of impact." What this meant in terms of what the foundation was actually supposed to accomplish, no one really knew, including Obama.

Obama's postpresidency office is on the ground floor, and his foundation offices are downstairs, about a mile from the White House, with a big panda World Wildlife Fund logo on its front door. When the black SUVs are parked outside, that's the giveaway that Obama is in the building. They would hear him roll in before they'd see him—"Hey, people!"—rarely before noon, and often after a golf game. Never quite as detached as he was made out to be, he would still occasionally check in by phone with Pelosi and Schumer. Usually he was the one initiating the calls that happened. Once, when Pelosi tried to track him down to talk Obamacare strategy and didn't hear back, she asked her aides to track him down, and they were left searching the web until they found an article from the *Daily Mail* that he was at a resort on Marlon Brando's island in the South Pacific, trying to write his book.

He'd pop into aides' offices, ask about some article he'd read, what they made of the latest news, or the latest crazy thing Trump had said. Everyone in the office had been there at the end in the West Wing, though nowhere near the entire staff had come over. While Obama's bare, wood-paneled office with his prized Muhammad Ali boxing gloves displayed at the center was hard to get into, it wasn't the Oval Office, and he wasn't on a minute-by-minute schedule to stop him from just wandering around between meetings, or whenever he wanted to procrastinate writing his book. For a couple of weeks in the spring of 2014, he tried to break through a stagnating patch in his presidency with occasional lighthearted surprise walks from the White House to the nearby Starbucks or by ditching his motorcade to walk a few blocks to a meeting, for which he'd coined the phrase "the bear is loose." Now his staff would joke in quick heads-up internal emails, "The bear is on the prowl."

In the White House, they'd been religious about referring to him only as POTUS, and it took them awhile to shake that habit after January 20. They knew "the president," wasn't right, and they wanted to make sure that it was clear they weren't talking about Trump. "Ex-POTUS" sounded off, and it was too awkward to always say "former president." While the wider Obama world simply took to just referring to him as 44, to show off how seemingly in the inner circle they were, around the office he was always the Boss. To his face, like high school students talking to their friends' parents, they figured out ways to not call him anything at all.

They knew in the office to watch the Boss's eyes after Trump outrages. He was so level most of the time, so forcibly cool around everyone but his closest friends. They could see his expression the morning after Trump's speech at the Boy Scout Jamboree in West Virginia, when Trump had turned the crowd into a writhing rally of booing and shouting—"By the way, just a question, did President Obama ever come to a Jamboree?" To Obama, it was unforgivable: "Those are kids!"

Then again, Obamacare was saved in the middle of the night at the end of July. Republicans had voted to repeal it more than sixty times when he was president, complaining that only his veto was standing in the way. And now, as he carefully kept from getting mixed up in the fight, they had failed first to get it through the House, and then when they did, failed to get it through the Senate. He laughed about the fact that the vote that saved the bill was cast by John McCain. He called McCain the next day to thank him, and they laughed together about the ridiculous irony of the situation: the guy who tried to keep him out of the White House and then kept beating him up for eight years had now single-handedly preserved his legacy.

Then—Charlottesville. Seven months out from the departure of the first Black president, Nazis were on the march in America. More racism. More disappointment. America wasn't living up to what he had thought it was.

Later that summer Obama was bragging on the golf course about having what for years was the most liked tweet of all time: a picture of him meeting with children of different races, accompanied by a Nelson Mandela quote. His staff had been struggling to figure out the right kind of statement in reaction to Charlottesville. Although Obama would tell people that he didn't really get Twitter, and swore he didn't have a secret account, it was he who had come up with the idea to respond with a tweet, selected the quote, and told aides the specific photo to pick. He loved that he had outperformed any of Trump's tweets, outperformed every other tweet, while worrying that this was the world he had now chosen to inhabit too.

One of Obama's strengths and weaknesses is always taking the metahistorical long view, paying less attention to more immediate problems. He saw his presidency as both the product of major forces shaping the country and the world, and the catalyst for many more. It would define what would happen afterward, including a Trump presidency that he accounted for as being an unanticipated, but perhaps necessary, response. It wouldn't last; it couldn't. People would rise up, make up for this stumble. He could see the historical sense in that.

This belief became harder to sustain with each day. Obama always had an agenda—one of the things that used to drive Republicans in Congress like Paul Ryan nuts was when he'd tell them to take their politics out of it and see the situation rationally, by which he really meant that if they were just as smart as he was and had read as much as he had, they'd agree with him. But what was he supposed to do with Democrats' daily outrage at Trump? Every small remark that he made about decency and democracy, or how he didn't think people should spend all day watching TV, came off as if he were going out of his way to poke Trump.

Most days he was torn: fluctuating between saying "I tried to warn you" or "We need to do something" and a center-of-gravity determination not to get pulled in. He'd make a passing comment to an aide about an article he'd read. He'd interrupt a foundation donor griping and let his frustration show, though careful enough that he wouldn't get in too much trouble if it leaked. To close friends, he'd let loose a little more, but even then, he held himself back.

Another thing he wasn't about to do was feel guilty about hanging out on Richard Branson's boat or in his own new $12 million fifteen-bedroom compound on Martha's Vineyard. He felt that he'd put in his time, and now he was entitled to ring up pricey speaking fees like all former presidents did, plus the cost of his private jet travel. Aides were on guard for anything that might make his brand less commercially marketable or might spoil, for example, the Netflix production deal the Obamas signed in 2018. He gave clear instructions that he wanted the Clinton Global Initiative to be a lesson in what *not* to do in aligning the moneymaking with the foundation work and thus running up massive and mind-bending foreign entanglements along the way. (Doug Band, an aide who became rich by helping set up Clinton's postpresidency and then famously showed up all over Hillary Clinton's State Department emails, reached out early on, but his help was politely declined, then laughed about.) They were so worried Trump would target him that a lawyer sat in on even mundane planning meetings to gauge their exposure, and they were so concerned about what petty vengeance Trump might seek that they gamed what to do if he mucked around in Obama's continuing care by the White House Medical Unit or if he tried to cut off the Obama daughters' Secret Service protection.

What Obama and his postpresidency staff weren't worrying about was internal Democratic politics.

"You think he cares about what Ruth Marcus writes?" an aide said in April 2017, when word got out that Obama would speak that fall at a health care conference hosted by Cantor Fitzgerald, and *The Washington Post* columnist had asked, referring to their joint book deal, "Is $60 million really not enough for the Obamas?" The answer was that he did not care what Marcus wrote—except that he kind of did. And when Elizabeth Warren reached out after she realized she might have gone too far by telling reporters she was "troubled" that he was making the speech—"I describe it as a snake that slithers through Washington, and that it shows up in so many different ways here," she'd said about the influence of money—that hadn't stopped him from making the speech.

Part of what the Cantor Fitzgerald incident revealed was how unprepared Obama was for the politics of the postpresidency. His staff had accepted the speech invitation not with the intention of making a statement but as an opportunity to talk about health care, though they had neglected to do the vetting that would have revealed that this was an invitation to be avoided. The other part of what it revealed was that they were not at all ready for Obama to keep getting dragged into fights the Democratic Party was going to keep having about what it was supposed to be. He was annoyed that Warren had come at him, but he was also annoyed that he had blundered into a position to be criticized at all.

Obama and Warren sat for about forty-five minutes. He kept waiting for her to apologize for taking the shot at him in public. She didn't. She kept waiting for him to say it might have been a bad move, but at least he understood why she'd criticized it. He didn't. They met again the following spring, trying to build up a better relationship.

Most of his other meetings with politicians who came to see him went better. Of course they did: most of his other meetings were with politicians asking his advice, coming to tell him he was the smartest man in the party—the one who'd figured it all out. He liked that. Even when it was Cory Booker, a man who had spent his life before he met Obama thinking that he was going to be the first Black president—and if not for Obama, he very well might have been. For years already, since Obama was a new senator and before Booker was mayor of Newark, Obama had felt as if Booker were trying to nudge a closeness that wasn't there, and tended to get annoyed with how much he had to humor him. Now Booker was the first of the 2020 hopefuls who came looking for a spiritual boost and an implicit blessing. This was nice. And interesting. He could get interested in the role of party elder, helping shape the future of the party with all of the trappings and deference—but none of the responsibilities.

That summer in Martha's Vineyard, he expanded that portfolio. Jason Kander had lost a Senate race in Missouri by a shockingly narrow margin the same night Trump was elected, becoming a national phenomenon along the way—mostly thanks to a viral ad that featured him assembling an old army assault rifle while blindfolded and talking about supporting gun control. Despite losing, he had become an overnight star of the Democratic Party circuit. He'd gotten people chattering about how he might leapfrog everything and just run for president. Even though he was just a former Missouri secretary of state without a job or clear lane in the race, he had already made his first trips to Iowa and New Hampshire. And here Kander was with an invite to the most exclusive party that night in the Vineyard.

Obama had heard the presidential talk. He was intrigued, if only to figure out what this guy was all about. "Come see me sometime in DC," he had told Kander. Obama gave him some thoughts about running for president, asked what he was thinking, told Kander he wanted major donors and party bigwigs to pay attention. He offered to put out a few calls of his own to make sure that happened and cautioned Kander about how hard being a long shot presidential candidate could be.

Word of the Obama meetings started to get around. Calls came in from eager Democrats around Washington, gently inquiring if there might be a window on the schedule to get in. Most of the prospective presidential candidates got the standard spiel: running sucks, and you have to really want it. Think about what it will do to you. Speaking in Malaysia at an Obama Foundation event in December 2019, with the primary race finally cresting and very much on his mind, he reflected on the advice he'd been giving to the candidates, acknowledging, "It wasn't as if I had to run for president for Democrats to do well.

"I asked myself 'Why me?' How was it going to affect my family, and could I actually win?" he said of his own experience. "The hardest question was, 'Why you?' other than just your ego." He has a big ego; everyone who came to see him had a big ego. "I concluded that given the time, the moment it might be, that if I was successful as someone from a historically discriminated against group that was able to rise to the most powerful office in the world, in addition to me advancing a policy agenda, that I might send a signal to people about what was possible—to young people and to children and to help people imagine themselves and their society, and that might be the best window for me to do it."

He would give advice, guidance, talk about the future of the party and different leaders' places in it. He'd sometimes veer philosophical, then quickly turn back to campaign mechanics. Some got extra flavor, depending on Obama's mood or an article he had just been reading. To one prospective candidate, he went on about how annoying political journalism could be. He was described as "aloof," he complained. Well, "Motherfuckers, I'm aloof with you because I don't want to talk to you."

Sanders reached out and came in for his meeting in March 2018. The mood of the office was so relaxed that Obama wandered out to meet him himself. There was some small talk, which neither are much good at: immigration, how to talk about Trump. Obama finally stopped him. "Let's cut to the chase," he said, looking straight at Sanders. "You're here because you're thinking about running."

"I'm undecided," Sanders replied, but would love to hear Obama's thoughts.

Obama had come out of the left, and the way he saw it, his twenty-five-year-old self, working those housing projects on the South Side as a community organizer, would probably have been walking around in a Bernie T-shirt. He didn't believe there was any way to really dispute Sanders's fundamental criticisms of the system, but there was a reality to what could get done. Sanders had to take a hard look at precisely what he was going to run on, at what he was going to be promising, if he was actually planning to be the nominee. The political reality, Obama said, is that voters don't give Democrats much leeway on big price tags for their proposals. Medicare for All and free college might seem popular with the base, Obama warned, but they were going to look detached from political reality. There's a difference between idealism and practicality, Obama said. There certainly is, Sanders agreed and tried a joke at one point. Obama didn't laugh.

Sanders wanted respect, feeling he'd earned the deference. Obama committed to giving it to him. They would talk again, he said.

Obama never had one of those set meetings with Biden. Though they weren't talking then nearly as much as would have been expected, given the close friendship they advertised, there were occasional check-ins on the phone. Obama always assumed Biden would run against Trump, that his theory of his own candidacy made sense and that Biden might just be the right antidote. Remembering how Biden had internalized their 2015 conversations and his own doubts about trying to shape the field again, when they did chat, Obama talked through his concerns as if they should be Biden's. He spoke about the pace of the campaign. He warned Biden about the scrutiny that running would bring on, how hard a 2020 campaign was going to be on both him and his family.

Obama remained skeptical about Biden's chances. With decades of presidents winning by running against Washington, with the demographics of the Democratic Party shifting far away from the Biden memories of its old core in Scranton, and with the world a long way from those dinners around the kitchen table with his grandfather that Biden would always talk about, it seemed like a stretch. Obama knew Trump would try to turn a campaign against Biden into a run against his legacy, and he wasn't keen on leaving that fight to Biden to handle.

His friend Deval Patrick, meanwhile, was the rare person whose political skills actually impressed Obama, and who seemed to him to be a possibly credible uniter of the country. In May 2017, a friend sent Obama the transcript of the speech that New Orleans mayor Mitch Landrieu had given about removing three Confederate monuments, and he soon had Landrieu in the office, and was left impressed with how he thought and how he was able to talk about race. After the phenomenon of the Texas Senate campaign the following year, he'd see himself in Beto O'Rourke. During their meeting a month after the race, Obama encouraged him to talk to Plouffe, and kept on it afterward, urging another of his campaign masterminds, Paul Tewes, to sit with him for hours in his living room in El Paso, and urging O'Rourke to hire his former deputy campaign manager Jen O'Malley Dillon.

Obama's take on the candidates didn't change much over time, and eventually only O'Rourke became the rare case of Obama's interest fading. Buttigieg, in turn, became the rare case of his interest increasing. He had walked out of their first meeting convinced that there was no chance the South Bend mayor could be president. By the time they met again, Obama was starting to see why his campaign was catching fire.

———

Nothing did more for Obama's popularity than Trump. Democrats forgot all his stumbles, forgave all his betrayals. No one could seem to get enough of him, and he was so unprepared for staying involved in politics after leaving the White House that he didn't even have the staff for doing so. In his final weeks on the job, he had asked his deputy press secretary, Eric Schultz, to come on as an adviser. Then he invited Paulette Aniskoff, a lower-profile White House aide who'd been with him since the '08 campaign, to run his political activities through an LLC she incorporated called Citizen 44. They were the only political staff he had, and he paid them out of his own pocket.

Everyone wanted him back in the fray except for him. Besides, he would insist, the more he was the focus, the less chance new leaders in the party would have to emerge. But after consulting with Pfeiffer and Plouffe and a few others on and off the official payroll, Aniskoff developed a plan centered on all the elements Obama had never cared about as president: fundraising, redistricting, local races, building a Democratic bench. Calls came in urging him to get out and join the marches, to swing at Trump every chance he could. The core principle they landed on was to keep him relatively quiet, that anything he would say would be devalued the more exposure he had. He needed to add something when only he could. And he could not, must not, be put in a position to lose any fight he might end up having with Trump.

They made it just a few months before asking him to risk all three for Ralph Northam, whom he barely knew, wasn't much impressed by, and who'd won the primary in the Virginia governor's race by running against Tom Perriello, an Obama favorite ever since he gambled his seat (and lost) in the 2010 wipeout after voting for Obamacare.

This was before anyone knew about Northam's blackface picture in an old yearbook, back when he was the Democrats' first experiment in winning in the Trump era by tapping not into their diversity or energy or progressivism but by going with a bland, moderate white guy. He seemed like the kind of throwback Democrat with whom Obama might not want to be connected, and his team tried to determine whether Northam could pull it off, or whether going to Richmond to campaign for him would only embarrass Obama. After a few weeks of debate and scouring of polling data, they brought it all to Obama. He wavered, until two more calls of his own with Perez finally persuaded him to go to Richmond.

Obama had a much easier time agreeing to the first stop of the day that they'd bundled together in October. Phil Murphy, the Democratic candidate for governor in New Jersey, was a big donor whom he'd made his ambassador to Germany. Murphy was up by double digits in the polls and obviously going to win. Standing with him, Obama made a mostly relaxed case about rebutting the "politics of division," where the standout line was, "The world is going to be looking to New Jersey . . . to see what kind of politics we believe in."

While Obama was on the private jet from Newark, George W. Bush had given a rare speech across the river in Manhattan. The two presidents hadn't talked much in the months since Obama left office, though their staffs, along with Clinton's and George H. W. Bush's, were on email chains that featured rapid-fire Trump mocking and consoling one another over the state of the republic. The speech was a surprise. Aside from a few appearances for his brother in the 2016 Republican primaries, Bush had largely avoided any public politics, and in a way that meant a lot to Obama, hadn't said a critical word about him through all his eight years in office.

"Bigotry seems emboldened. Our politics seems more vulnerable to conspiracy theories and outright fabrication," Bush had said at the end of a half-day conference at the Time Warner Center in New York, reading from pages he'd written himself the day before in Texas.

Obama is the most gifted political performer of his generation, but only if he's feeding off the crowd. If they're not with him, if they don't want to see him, he can't fake it. There was no problem that night in Richmond. He came out to U2's "City of Blinding Lights," as he had at every campaign event in 2008. He could hear seven thousand people, many of them in new Obama

T-shirts, lose it as he took the stage. He returned to the theme of unity, but with Bush's words in his head, he went much further than he had in New Jersey: "Our democracy is at stake," he said, touching as close to Trump as he had since the night before the election at a final rally for Clinton in Philadelphia.

"Folks don't feel good right now about what they see. Maybe they don't feel as if our public life reflects our best," he said. It was met with an odd cheer in the convention center hall: A cheer for nostalgia, a cheer for hearing a leader articulate the anger they were all feeling, a cheer mostly for allowing the members of the crowd to close their eyes for a second and believe that it would all be over soon. Obama knew he'd hit it, smacking the podium twice with his left hand after his final shout into the microphone, his own familiar private tic of congratulating himself.

Two days after Richmond he flew to Houston, heart of Bush country, for the Hurricane Harvey relief concert, which featured all the former living presidents (their staffs had negotiated to have Trump appear only by video). Onstage, while Bill Clinton was speaking about the recovery, Bush leaned in to Obama to share a fast joke, and Obama started laughing, crossing his arms and looking down to hold himself in. Bush had the glee of a triumphant class clown at having made Obama crack. Backstage the five presidents took their seats for a photo with Lady Gaga, decked out in a Hillary-style white pantsuit, standing behind them with her hands on the two Bushes, both of them smiling. They all knew exactly what message they were sending.

At the end of the month, back in Chicago, Obama hosted the first summit for his foundation. "It's hard, but you can't help but be optimistic," Simas said there, though for the people who attended, that sentiment was believable only within the bubble of those two days. There was a morning meditation and yoga session, a dinner catered by celebrity activist chef José Andrés, a blackboard with pastel chalk for attendees to fill in "I hope _____" with answers like "Americans will see each other." A closing concert included Lin-Manuel Miranda and Chance the Rapper singing a duet of "Dear Theodosia" from *Hamilton*.

"The moment we're in right now, politics is the tail and not the dog," Obama said, interpolating his line from the Northam rally into the officially nonpartisan setting. "What we need to do is think about our civic culture, because what's wrong with our politics is a reflection of something that's wrong with the civic culture, not just in the United States but around the world."

"Hope does not mean that tomorrow everything's going to be better," Obama had said in his closing remarks. "Where hope comes in handy is when you've put everything you have into something and it hasn't worked yet—and it hasn't worked the week after that, and the week after that, and six months later and a year."

Northam won by 9 points, and Murphy won. Simas was so excited that he started emailing political contacts with whom he'd mostly gone silent for the past year, forgetting for a few bubbly hours that he, like Obama, had been trying to make himself move on from caring about politics.

Still hesitant to become involved, Obama saw tackling gerrymandering as a way to do something without doing much. A little attention, a little fundraising and he could have an outsize effect. Even before Clinton lost, he had asked his friend Eric Holder to lead a new organization committed to redistricting reform. Obama and Holder called this a fight for fairness, and given how Republicans had used this to increase their power—in 2012, the first election year after the 2010 redistricting, Democratic candidates won a combined 1.4 million more votes, but Republicans finished with a thirty-three-seat majority in the House—they were right. But it was also politics, because the changes they were pushing for would claw back power for Democrats in exactly the way Obama hoped: that if more people voted, and the more the system was responsive to those votes, the more the country would inherently tilt to his point of view.

"He's a little bit like a father who's put his hand back on the back of the bike and is wondering when he can let go again. There's an eagerness to let go again," said one person who spoke with him regularly as he was figuring out his postpresidency. "He wants to be the grandfather, not the father figure."

Aniskoff arranged the effort to begin very quietly, and then focus on state legislature races, so that Obama could make a splash just by being the former president endorsing some state assemblyman by email, and maybe even get to claim credit for helping move a chamber one way or the other. By the end of the year, he wanted to do more. "We are *going* to take back the House," Obama told Aniskoff. "I will do whatever it takes."

CHAPTER FOUR

FATE AND PLANNING

This is the way I wanted to go home, the way I came.

—JOE BIDEN, SPEAKING TO REPORTERS ON HIS WAY ONTO AN
AMTRAK TRAIN SHORTLY AFTER DONALD TRUMP'S INAUGURATION

January 2017–October 2018

A week before Trump's inauguration, Joe Biden was sitting in his office in the West Wing, down the hall from the Oval Office. He had more space across the way in the Eisenhower Executive Office Building, but he liked being only a few steps from Obama, closer to the action.

"Everything's good and happy and rosy," he joked, "and nothing to worry about. Everything's going great, and, uh, so I don't think there's much to talk about."

Two days earlier, Trump had compared the intelligence community to Nazis for investigating him. The president-elect was holding a press conference in the lobby of Trump Tower with giant stacks of paper behind him, supposedly full of disclosures that would seal himself off from his business interests. His staff wouldn't let anyone look inside to check. Meanwhile, he was facing questions put to him by reporters trying to look serious about rumors that the Russians were blackmailing him with a video of hookers in his room at a Moscow hotel. Donald Trump's America was now just America.

Biden was kicking back, trying to correct the record on the intelligence, loose enough that at one point he waved his passcode-protected Presidential Daily Briefing iPad in the air. Yes, he acknowledged, the dossier with the pee tape had been included in the official intelligence reports, a subject on which he didn't want to dwell. Politics, he said, wasn't so complicated. And outgoing Senate majority leader Harry Reid had been wrong in the interview he'd just given, complaining that Democrats' prospective 2020 field looked like a retirement home. Biden didn't think the party was in crisis at all.

"Honest to God, I don't, because it's just the nature of the way parties develop and evolve," he said. Obama, he pointed out, had skipped a generation forward for the Democrats. "There's also," he said, "been times where it'll look like there are a lot of qualified people younger, and all of a sudden we turn to the older folks in the party and, you know, go back."

There was not, in fact, a time when Democrats had gone back a generation.

Biden's time in public life was finished, but he wasn't done. How to channel that made so little sense that before the election, Clinton was toying with naming him secretary of state, and after the election, there was speculation that he might run for DNC chairman. Those were the days in early January when Biden was pretending, to himself and to anyone who asked, that he wasn't going to run.

Of Democrats, Biden said, "I don't think they're in a crisis. I think the party has to just remember who the hell they are." By contrast, he observed, "The Republican Party's in enormous crisis. The Republican Party, they're, I mean, what the hell's the party? What do they stand for?" He said he'd had a little epiphany a few days earlier, going to speak to what was left of the House Democrats. He wandered off into a tangent about telling some Republicans to imagine they were back in the Continental Congress, and whether they would have included a requirement for a minimum education level to vote. He said something about being in a group of senators in the late 1970s with Bill Bradley and Gary Hart, who'd seen a presentation centered on the move away from the Saint Lawrence Seaway and the need for new infrastructure. He looped back around and around again. There was some mention of a more recent presentation from Columbia professor Jeffrey Sachs. "I thought about it, and all of the extracurricular malarkey that's going on now between the parties, don't go to the core of the beliefs of either party very much now."

So what, then, *was* a Democrat? Two things, as far as he could tell: everyone was entitled to be treated with dignity, and government existed to prevent abuses of power.

To Biden, there was no conflict in the hearts of Americans, just the idea of conflict, frustration that had been cynically mined for conflict. White working-class men in Youngstown who'd voted for Trump wanted their wives to get equal pay, he insisted, and they might be spooked by gay people, but they could be engaged in a conversation about just letting gay people live their lives, if politicians tried. A few days earlier, Obama had given a fanfare-filled fare-well address in Chicago talking about "the middle-aged white man who, from the outside, may seem like he's got all the advantages, but who's seen his world upended by economic, cultural, and technological change," and said that white Americans needed to acknowledge "that the effects of slavery and Jim Crow didn't suddenly vanish in the sixties." Biden mentioned how much he'd loved that.

"What I've learned in my entire career in politics, you can do anything with somebody and get them to move as long as you don't change their standard of living downward," he said. To him, the problem was simple: Democrats hadn't figured out how to tell people what to do about the effects of globalization. Neither had Republicans. He said he'd been frustrated watching the 2016 campaign, as he'd hoped it could have been an idealized competition of ideas. Instead, "a guy says it's all right to go and grab a woman's private parts and at the same time someone says, 'I've got a plan for college.' What are you going to cover?" he said. "You gotta cover that."

No, he insisted, he wasn't workshopping a stump speech, though he did acknowledge that it sounded like one. And in that funny limbo Biden occupies between insecure humility and prideful faux humility, he said other people should pick up what he was saying: "I hope it becomes a stump speech."

"Remember when you're in school you studied about the Luddites? Well that's kind of where we are. There are people going on saying the answer is smashing machinery. Return to the social order we had before. Well, this is just a new version of smashing machinery," he said. Stop trade. Keep the high-sulfur coal plants burning. Vote for making America great again, because whatever that meant, it was better than this. Turn away from the Democrats because they're just talking ideals and principles.

A few hours later Obama surprised Biden in the East Room with a cere-mony awarding him the Medal of Freedom, the commander-in-chief version of a gold watch. Biden was already looking forward to settling into a life cen-tered around his wife and grandchildren. He was going to write a book, make speeches, put money away for Beau's family, keep up his cancer initiative, set up his institutes at the University of Pennsylvania and the University of Del-aware.

"They'll pay me what I think is more money than I'm making now as vice president," Biden said, referring to the two universities, "which surprised me."

———

Think about the moment in *Anchorman* in which Will Ferrell, playing the '70s man's man with the caring and collapsible core, is banging on the walls of a phone booth, screaming, "I'm in a glass cage of emotion!" Biden is always in his own glass cage of emotion, echoing with the Irish poems he recited to overcome his stutter that have stuck with him like a background narrator for his whole life.

Like any good Irish poetry, everything becomes wrapped around fate and grief. And for Biden, there was so much grief, with him all the time. Being the star twenty-nine-year-old who'd taken out a powerful incumbent in his first statewide race—he was the first senator he'd ever known, Biden likes to say—and then weeks later, while being briefed on his new life down in Washington, getting the call that his wife had taken the children shopping for a Christmas tree and their car had been hit by a truck, that she and their baby daughter had been killed in the accident, and that his two boys were in the hospital. Then, having been elected vice president, forty-three years after the accident, he was now watching one of those boys, who'd been on a glide path to becoming governor and probably much more, slowly dying of brain cancer after a year of treatments they knew wouldn't work.

For Beau Biden's funeral, his father had led his family up the hill in Wil-mington to St. Anthony of Padua in a moving huddle, one giant family hug. The entire Democratic world was already crammed into the church's pews. Obama delayed a trip to Germany for the G-7 for a few hours so he could deliver a eulogy. Biden held his daughter-in-law's hand in his right one, she held her son's hand. In his left, he held Beau's daughter's hand, and Jill Biden held it on the other side. The group stopped briefly between the doors of the church and the hearse. For a moment, as aides stood ready to open the rear doors of the vehicle to remove the coffin, Biden looked up at the sky, his eyes hidden behind the aviators. Holding himself that one moment before seeing the coffin taken out of the hearse. One last chance to believe it wasn't true, to wonder why, to think of Beau before everyone talked about his boy in the past tense. As the coffin was lifted out, the flag over it bright, he cast his eyes down, then kissed his daughter-in-law on the head, placed his hand on his grandson's back. "Bring Him Home" from *Les Misérables* began to play. He crossed himself, exhaled, and led the family in.

"They were the last surviving remnants of that part of his life," Ron Klain, his friend and aide said two days after Beau died. "To then lose one of the two of them, just takes a painful and immeasurable tragedy and then compounds it a second time."

Obama had told him in 2008 to see being vice president as a career capstone, and he had. He let it redefine his entire sense of himself: as the wingman, *The Onion* punchline, America's Uncle Joe. He could accept that he didn't have a mind and political talent like Obama's. He could accept that he had a role to play in helping the first Black president. He could rationalize not being good enough to get to the Oval Office himself if he got his amazing adopted kid brother there, then helped pave the way for his beloved son to get there too. Fate.

He had spent fifty years dreaming of being president—more, actually. In 1968, he quit the law firm where he'd been practicing to work as a public defender, and a secretary offered to give him back the goofy donkey-shaped stapler he had leant her. "No, no, keep it," she remembers him telling her. "Someday you'll be able to tell people the future president of the United States gave you a stapler." Fifty years of dreaming, transferred to his son. That would be his legacy: not President Joe Biden but President Beau Biden.

Beau knew that was what was expected of him too, and had learned to deflect in a way that now comes off humble and haunting. "At 43, I've come to the conclusion: focus on what's immediately in front of you," he said in a 2012 interview at the Riverfront Market in Wilmington, flicking away a question about his political future. "I do not look past that. Anytime I've looked past that—life has a different plan for me."

Not that Joe Biden's longing for the presidency or sense that he deserved it ever fully went away. There was a day in 2009 when Obama got the call that Arlen Specter, the Pennsylvania senator, had finally bent to Biden's lobbying to switch parties and given Democrats the sixtieth vote to stop a filibuster. He sat down in his chair behind the Resolute desk and smiled. "Joe Biden," he said, "employee of the month."

In his head, Biden had come close to running during the summer of 2015. Everywhere except in his head, though, he wasn't ready, and he wouldn't have been ready even if Beau hadn't needed to see a doctor. Clinton had launched her campaign six weeks before Beau died, and Biden hadn't raised a dollar, hadn't hired any campaign staff. Beau's dying ripped reality out from him, so that flirting with a presidential campaign became a way to cope, to keep his son alive. He was distracted from the grief when he was talking up plans. "Let's say I was going to start a company: would you be a stockholder in it?" was his subtle way of pitching donors who totally got the joke. He rambled to potential staffers that he was worried how his support for the Trans-Pacific Partnership trade deal would play out in the primaries.

Was it real? That depends on the definitions of "it" and "real." He invited Elizabeth Warren over for lunch on a Saturday in August and explicitly pitched her on becoming his running mate. If he got into the race, he told her, she'd be the secret weapon to pulling Clinton's support out from under her. Warren asked a lot of questions, but didn't commit. He kept after her on the phone for months, so invested in the idea that even after he dropped out, he'd continue to muse in conversations how he *would have* asked her to run with him. He obsessed over polling data that his small team put together—"No one trusts her!" he often said about Clinton, and remarked that he didn't see how she could win. He called the fees that she had taken for speaking at Goldman Sachs "disgusting," said she had integrity issues, and pointed out that she hadn't even been brought in on the intelligence about the bin Laden raid until the very end. Toxic, is how one of the people he spoke with several times described his opinion of Clinton. By the fall, he had mapped out the hypotheticals sufficiently to be confiding in people that he was worried about how the Clintons might exact revenge if he ran against her.

He talked himself into seeing a campaign, into believing that here was fate again, that it didn't matter that he hadn't actually done anything to prepare for it. The people who were with him day to day, even those who were theoretically trying to build an overnight campaign for him during lunch-break meetings and strategy sessions at the coffee shop across the street from the White House, could see he wasn't really ready to commit.

The morning before Biden pulled out, he threw one last curveball, changing his story to say he had, in fact, secretly supported the raid that killed Osama bin Laden, trying to neutralize an issue where Clinton had seen an advantage: she had supported the raid in front of a group at a national security cabinet meeting, while Biden waited until he was alone in the Oval Office with Obama to say that he did too, but just hadn't wanted to box in the president. That night at the Naval Observatory residence, he was host to a procession of visits and phone calls and aides all getting ready to go.

Late that night, he walked an aide to the door. "Are you going to do it?" the aide asked. His wife, Jill, looked up at him, expectantly. "No," he said, looking up again as he had in front of Beau's hearse. "I can't."

When he called Obama the next morning to say he'd been up late and had decided he wasn't going to do it, Obama told him that they should make the announcement in the Rose Garden together. An act of love, of making the acceptance that he'd been defeated by circumstances that had moved on without him seem like a sort of victory on his own terms. But also important is that it locked Biden into a decision he'd kept so much in the air that the top aides trying to map a campaign for him had already started locking in staff, only to find out that he wasn't actually running by watching the announcement live on TV.

And that was supposed to be it. Except it never was, and Clinton's loss cemented that.

"I'm NOT running," Biden was insisting to people by the spring of 2017. But then to others he'd say, "If I'm walking, I'm running."

The evening after the first White House Correspondents' Dinner under Trump (with Trump boycotting the event) at the end of April, Biden flew to New Hampshire for the big state Democratic Party dinner at a ballroom in the back of the main hotel in Manchester. The speech was familiar—what it meant to be a Democrat, how the country was more united than its politics suggested—but this time he delivered it with more of the political edge that he'd been laying out privately. The Clinton campaign screwed up, he said, which gave

Trump only tiny margins in Pennsylvania, Wisconsin, and Michigan. "Those 172,000 people we needed"—he more than doubled the actual number—"a lot of them wondered whether it'd been forgotten they'd been abused by the system," he said. "They wondered whether or not we remembered." He viewed that narrow loss, which could have been avoided, not as reflecting a massive change in the country, but as the result of political malpractice that let a sliver of the population simply slip away.

"How, how do we unite America again?" he asked. "How do we unite this country? How do we end this bitter, bitter political division?"

Biden's story about his candidacy was already changing. In the new version, he had never intended to get into the 2016 race against his friend Hillary Clinton, no matter how much that account stretched the definitions of *never* and *friend*. And he definitely wasn't going to enter the 2020 race.

"Guys, I'm not running," he said to the crowd, looking toward a few national reporters seated at folding tables in the back because, come on, he was in Manchester.

He couldn't get through the line without smiling. His adviser Mike Donilon had already brushed quickly through the crowd to the back to find a good place to watch, to see how the scene was playing to the audience.

"Remember the core reason why you're a Democrat—we abhor the abuse of power, whether it is financial power, psychological power, physical power," Biden reminded them. "Think about what made you a Democrat. It's the abuse of power. We've got to remember who we are."

―――――

Donilon had written a strategy memo for Biden when he was deciding in 2015. As soon as Biden had finished the Rose Garden speech with Obama, Donilon and his chief of staff, Steve Ricchetti, started using that as a framework for building his post–vice presidency. "I just want to keep doing what I've always done," Biden told them. He'd been in bigger and bigger political jobs for fifty years, and that career was now ending abruptly. He still had two university jobs, a Biden Foundation to keep up his work on veterans and on protecting abused and assaulted women, the book, his Cancer Moonshot project to increase research and funding. In a WeWork office space a few blocks from the

White House and during trips back and forth to Delaware—Ricchetti did all the driving because Donilon is famously idiosyncratic and gets more caught up in thinking about how to break through on American ideals than things like lane dividers and traffic laws—they recalibrated the original thinking about how Biden could fit in amid a Clinton presidency.

That involved a new factor because what Biden did not want Democrats to be was Bernie Sanders. He liked Sanders personally—there aren't many people Biden doesn't like personally—but he also didn't agree with the senator's politics and thought it was a sure way to lose, so he wasn't going to let Sanders become the party's standard bearer. So watching Sanders get invited to fly around the country with Tom Perez for a very unsubtle DNC "unity tour" that spring, Biden told aides that it was finally time to start a PAC. He had to make sure Sanders's view of the party wasn't the only option, he explained, asking them to suggest presidential candidates to support in the order of (1) who was good for America, (2) who was good for the Democratic Party, and (3) who was good for Joe Biden. No one was pretending not to notice that 1 and 2 always seemed to match up with 3.

In typical Biden form, he hobbled himself at first by getting too much in his own head. To prove that this effort wasn't about him, he insisted that he wasn't going to do much fundraising and would only go to existing friendly donors and people he thought of as part of the extended family. That meant he would only be able to write small checks to candidates, and couldn't use the PAC to build up logistical operations that could help him down the road. He'd end up spending about $2 million over eighteen months, $1.3 million of which went into salaries for his staff and other administrative costs, and only about $600,000 into contributions to candidates. He spent half as much on traveling around to campaign as he did to support House and Senate candidates.

In the middle of June, Biden headlined the Florida Democrats' big annual dinner at the Diplomat Hotel in Hollywood. His operation was still enough of a mess that a staffer had accepted the invitation without realizing that the event was on the night of Biden's fortieth wedding anniversary, and though he felt guilty, he loved it that 1,300 people had bought tickets to see him. He schmoozed all the biggest donors who had paid extra to get a shot with him on the photo line, leaned down to talk to their kids.

Onstage he was smiling, emotional, thinking out loud in front of the crowd, trying out new lines ranging from community colleges to opioids. He spoke for almost an hour. Trump—who in New Hampshire had been just "the new guy" and was now "the other guy"—had won by "stoking some of the darkest emotions in this nation," appealing to lesser instincts, lesser angels, and he was keeping at it as president, like no one had before. The problem was, Biden said, that it had worked. People feel forgotten, then they want a scapegoat. Pundits feel uncertain; they wanted to redefine politics to insist on a new reality. Biden was pushing back on both, the stump speech starting to come together.

"The Hobson's choice we've been given is: Do we become less progressive and focus on working folk, or forget about working folk and become more progressive?" he said. This was a "phony" distinction and a dangerous one, like cutting out your heart to save your soul. "There is no need to choose. They are not inconsistent."

Biden has a routine of dropping to a stage whisper, then suddenly starting to shout as if in indignant surprise at a line he'd said dozens of times before. The shouting part is usually how to know the speech has about ninety seconds left. Generally he trails off after the crescendo, and the actual endings seem like afterthoughts. That night he got lost in thought as he talked, "notwithstanding the guy who says he's had the greatest legislative success," he said, sarcastically referring to Trump's constant bragging that he had gotten more done in his first hundred days than any president ever.

"God almighty," he finally exhaled. "I should stop. Thank you."

Then the Nazis marched through Charlottesville. Biden watched the coverage at home. Walking around the office the next few days, he talked about the people who lived in the houses around the Nazi concentration camps, pretending they couldn't see or smell what was going on. He could sound hokey at times, but Biden has been baked so long in politics that he often comes across that way, and aides remember him actually saying, "We have to speak up—this isn't who we are." He started writing down thoughts, trading paragraphs with the small group of aides and advisers. Once he had a draft that satisfied him, he would begin calling up friends to read sections of it aloud, his voice rising to a shout as he went. "Battle for the soul of the nation" was the key phrase they'd landed on. It felt like a mission. A calling. Beyond politics. Fate.

"We are living through a battle for the soul of this nation," he wrote in *The Atlantic* a few days after the Nazi march in Charlottesville in August 2017. "The crazed, angry faces illuminated by torches. The chants echoing the same anti-Semitic bile heard across Europe in the 1930s," was a line he landed on that he would carry with him into his campaign kickoff video a year and a half later and all through nearly every speech he made in the primary campaign. It stayed so consistent that when he gave his acceptance speech at the pandemic-emptied room at the Democratic convention three years later, it was almost exactly intact: "Remember seeing those neo-Nazis and Klansmen and white supremacists coming out of the fields with lighted torches? Veins bulging? Spewing the same anti-Semitic bile heard across Europe in the '30s?"

"It so inflamed Joe. Maybe as much as anything," said his old friend Tom Carper, a senator and former governor from Delaware, whose career had overlapped with Biden's in the small state since the 1970s. "That's it. That's the straw that breaks the camel's back."

No one runs for president without a huge ego. No one runs for president six times without lots of ego to spare. Biden ran for Senate at twenty-nine—he'd been honing and building that ego his entire life. He'd gladly step aside from running, is how he started talking about it in 2017, if he believed there was anyone else he was sure could beat Trump. "He's a great respecter of fate," a person close to him said in the summer of 2017. "At some point, it may turn into fate and planning."

Whatever one thinks of Biden's other skills, he had always been bad at running for president. He could make speeches, connect with voters. He never focused on the basic mechanics, and never surrounded himself with operatives who could. Decades of dominating in Delaware had led him to believe that the world worked as it did in the small state, where every voter was at most the cousin's neighbor's high school classmate's great uncle of whomever he was talking to, where fundraising was basically irrelevant, and where campaigns were simple enough to be run by a family member or friend. The years with Obama had warped him even more, as he tried to convince himself that he was a crucial part of the 2008 and 2012 wins, that the youth and diversity and excitement had been for the Obama–Biden *ticket*.

His circle had calcified around him: Donilon; Valerie Biden Owens, his sister and forever shadow campaign manager; Ted Kaufman, his friend and former chief of staff; and Steve Ricchetti, the former Clinton hand and lobbyist who'd worked up to be his chief of staff as vice president, and then stayed in control. Biden seemed like such a political dead end to many of the younger operatives in the party that few were interested in working for him. It ate at him, that feeling that he wasn't good enough, that the fancy people in the party weren't signing on. Why shouldn't he get what Obama did, what Clinton did?

But he didn't. And he'd gripe about that all the way through to Super Tuesday, tapping into his forever feeling of not being good enough, bitter about not getting the respect he thought he deserved while still always wondering if he actually did deserve it. "He knows he didn't get the A-team," an aide said, deep into the campaign. Biden never hid that feeling; the aide who shared that comment was among those who felt Biden's disappointment directly.

———

Biden's book, *Promise Me, Dad*, was published in November 2017, and was about Beau. His book tour was about seeing if he could live up to the mission he'd taken on from Beau. Could he hold to what he thought that promise was?

The answer, for now, seemed to be no. Biden told close supporters about a month into the tour that he was exhausted from the pace and the travel, and knew a presidential campaign would be at least twice as intense. Biden processes grief by immediately placing himself back in the original moment of the grief. Now he was living out Beau's dying over and over, multiple times a week.

But the book tour had been a success. He'd call one of his granddaughters on the way out of events, brag about how many people showed up, how diverse the crowd was. So many young people! The publisher had picked the stops for where he'd sell the greatest number of copies, but conveniently for him, most were in prime Biden territory in swing states, and he was taking notes.

With Trump's policy of separating children from their parents at the border rocking the administration, the White House bursting with leaks, and the president declaring himself a very stable genius, Biden made himself into a high school civics teacher, talking about the balances of power, the role of institutions. Obama had given him Steven Levitzky and Daniel Ziblatt's *How Democracies Die*, and he started sending copies of it to almost everyone with whom he spoke. He'd also talk up Joan Williams's *White Working Class: Overcoming Class Cluelessness in America*. Or, as soon as he read it, Jon Meacham's *The Soul of America*. It was not a coincidence that he'd called Charlottesville a *battle* for the soul of America, given all the conversations he had with Meacham. Biden would carry that book around with him, read passages aloud in meetings. He also began talking often about *New York Times* columnist David Brooks and the "invisible moral fabric."

But aides could see him aging, whether that was the result of hitting the wall that was Beau's death finally catching up with him, or of not having a marathon job for the first time since he was twenty-nine, or just from being seventy-six. They could hear the loudest and smartest voices bucking the idea of his candidacy in 2020, of his politics, of an old-white-man throwback being the answer to a party that wanted to see itself as the voice of a new America. Biden was being written off as the guy whom Obama needed to reassure the racists that he wasn't a socialist Muslim Kenyan determined to outlaw God and round up their guns. His favorite ice-cream flavor is chocolate chip. His first Senate campaign had run ads with the slogan, "He understands what's happening today," *in 1972*. The majority of Democrats had been born after he was already a senator.

Ricchetti was always cooking up his version of clever political schemes for Biden, stirring the pot, keeping secret about what he was up to. He'd done so in 2015 with the lunch invitation to Elizabeth Warren, and then leaked out that they'd discussed her being his running mate! Maybe Biden would pledge to serve one term! Taking stock of a party that wasn't going to stand for another Clinton-style coronation and a candidate who didn't look as if he were up to a full campaign, Ricchetti updated his playbook for 2020. Maybe Biden could get in early, shrink the field by having candidates opt out due to honoring personal relationships with him or a concern that he'd take up too much of the oxygen. Maybe he could enter really late—like September 2019 late—letting all the smaller candidates blow each other up before he rode in as a savior. Maybe he could come back to that one-term pledge, or the announce-the-running-mate-out-of-the-gate idea.

They started by getting him back on the trail. Biden had been flooded with requests for months, but he deliberately began the campaign at the Pittsburgh Labor Day parade. If Joe Biden's psyche were terraformed, Pittsburgh is what would come out—the Catholics, the union guys, the assertively tough but warm sensibility he imagined onto the residents, the throwback feeling of a city a little past its prime but refusing to give in. The Labor Day parade had been the first and final retail politics stop of his 2015 almost-campaign, back when the Secret Service had all the scrap-frenzied reporters loaded onto the back of a flatbed truck that he jogged along behind, pointing up at them and teasing them for not getting down and walking the route with him. He'd gone back the following year to try to sell them on Tim Kaine, but it wasn't the same.

This time he landed in Pittsburgh straight from attending the burial of his friend John McCain on a hill overlooking Annapolis. Even before checking into his room that night at the William Penn Hotel, which faced Mellon Square, he was telling his staff that he could feel how much harder this was going to be without a government plane.

Walking out of church after the pre-parade Mass that morning, Biden was asked what was on the line in the midterms. "Everything," he said. He kissed foreheads, and repeated stories about his father's and grandfather's working-class roots. He talked about unity, decency, and an America that had to re-assert what it used to stand for. He batted back a reporter who tried to ask him about the risk of socialism by replying, "I'm a Democrat," knocked back each attempt to tee him up about Trump by saying, "Everyone knows who the president is." He stopped to speak to a woman seated along the route who told him that she'd been dreaming of a Biden–Warren ticket since she saw him march in 2015. "Maybe," he said, smiling.

A few blocks in, he connected with Conor Lamb, a freshman congressman he'd helped win in a special election that spring, out in the suburbs just over the city line. Biden had started to politically adopt a few proto-Beaus in the years since his son died—young, handsome veterans pushing their way up through white working-class politics. Lamb even had a chin jut like Beau's, and had the same hair color and was parted on the same side. He'd also been an assistant U.S. attorney (AUSA) the first time he had met Biden, at the 2015 parade, when he had been assigned to be the accompanying federal prosecu-tor, just in case the Secret Service detail had to arrest anyone. Lamb had also come from a political family. His win in this corner of Pennsylvania was supposed to be the beginning of a revival for Democrats, and with Biden the only national Democratic figure who had been invited to campaign for him, it was the first proof of concept for the Biden future.

Biden had been so excited at the start of the race that he again took off in a jog, trailed by aides and the clump of reporters chasing him for clues about 2020. Soon he was seeing all the empty spaces between the lawn chairs set up along the sidewalk, thinking about what that meant for him, and his sense of where the politics of the country were, with Pittsburgh not what it used to be, and more union members marching than cheering them on.

Leaning into Lamb, concerned, he observed, "There used to be a lot more people than this."

The route ended at the United Steelworkers' building. In 2015, Biden had slipped inside for a private reception, in his rush to build not-so-secret support. This time he hopped in his small motorcade and went across town to a big reception at the Electrical Workers' hall. Switching his sweaty navy polo for one with the Beau Biden Foundation logo, he gave a short speech. Mostly, he just stood in the middle of the room, taking in every person he could, holding babies, taking selfies.

A woman approached him cautiously. In her fifties, wearing a black union hat and a REPUBLICANS FOR CONOR LAMB button, she was the picture of the Biden-could-win-back-Pennsylvania voter. She spotted two of his aides and asked them to tell Biden something for her: what happened to his son, everything that he'd been through—maybe it was all destiny for him to be the one to be president in this moment, given what the country was going through. They told her she could say it directly to him, and should, but she protested that she was shy and started to edge away. They later found her in the crowd and waited until they could see a break in Biden's tunneling among people for stories.

She wanted to tell him, she needed to tell him, but she was shaking. He came in close. She said it again: maybe losing his son, losing so much, was what had to happen to make him the president right now, for this moment. "God," she said, "has a strange sense of humor."

He kissed her on the cheek, hugged her. Then he held her hand tightly and kissed it. Whispered in her ear.

Biden thought about conversations like that in the car between events, up at night. He thought about fate.

———

Biden traveled all around the country over the next two months, racking up what would turn out to be the busiest, and ultimately, the most successful record of the midterms. Obama got more attention, but he made fewer stops, and had fewer wins to show for it. Trump was unavoidable, but more consumed by spite crusades like trying to take out Montana senator Jon Tester, who had gone after the White House physician who had suspiciously certified the president's health. The three Republicans who flipped Senate seats did so almost despite Trump's efforts to do what he insisted was helping. Tester ended up winning by 18,000 votes.

Many of Biden's appearances had the feel of a retired ballplayer waving to the crowd before the national anthem. He'd aged, but hey, he still looked good. He obviously wasn't ready to play, but it was nice to see him in a cap, like in the old days.

For a day, one week before the midterms, Biden was more than that. Real. In his prime. On a morning in Madison, Wisconsin, more than a thousand people packed into the top floor of a cafeteria building on the day before Halloween. His presence in Wisconsin wasn't lost on him. Seeing all the young people in the audience wasn't lost on him. Getting this reception in the most famous little liberal city in America wasn't lost on him. Watching the state that had turned on Hillary Clinton now being on the verge of electing a boring old white guy, who'd beaten a diverse primary field and was in a position to beat a Trump ally for governor, wasn't lost on him.

"I'm sick and tired of this administration," he said. "I am sick and tired of what's going on. I'm sick and tired of being sick and tired, and I hope you are too." There were huge cheers all through the speech, then a rush to try to grab a piece of him afterward.

Biden headed for Milwaukee, but the anticipation that day was for his trip to Cedar Rapids that evening. Earlier that fall, Biden's aides had insisted that he would avoid Iowa and New Hampshire as he did his midterm campaigning, specifically *because* they didn't want all the speculators to start speculating— which is precisely what they had done once the trip was announced. It was hard not to, even though the Biden team insisted he was there only because Abby Finkenauer, a young state legislator who had been an even younger Biden 2008 volunteer, had told his office that his validation could truly be the difference in winning. The smile that took over his face as soon as he saw the crowd was of a man who had been told, and could see, that he'd drawn more people than any of the other likely Democratic candidates who had already been in before him. It was also about seventy-five times the size of those he'd spoken to while finishing off his 2008 presidential campaign, en route to getting 1 percent in the Iowa caucuses and dropping out the night of that vote.

He came out to Obama's 2012 music, Bruce Springsteen's "We Take Care of Our Own," because he didn't have his own song (and didn't get one for the rest of the campaign). He did all the Biden happy-at-a-rally moves: both arms out, then both arms out with a mouthed *Wow!*, then another *Wow!*; hand over his eyes looking out into the distance and pointing; then both arms out again, with his lips pulled up over his teeth; a salute to no one in particular.

"Hello, Iowa! Hello, Cedar Rapids! It's been a long time!"

He spoke about stress levels spiking in young people, moral equivalence for racists, the importance of unity, mocked China for not being able to get its own act together. "Folks—competition? Remember who the hell we are," and then was off again into the stump speech that he insisted wasn't a stump speech. "The only thing that's strong enough to tear America apart is America itself— and we've seen it start, and we must make it stop," he said. "We have to make it clear as Democrats: We choose hope over fear! We choose unity over division! We choose allies over enemies! We choose truth over lies! We choose a brighter future over the desperate grip that the darkest elements of our past have on our ankles!"

He was so into what he was saying, and what he was getting back from the crowd—"It's good to see you again!"—that he forgot to say anything about the candidates he was ostensibly there to campaign for, and had to stop the applause to read their names from a piece of paper in his jacket and call them back onstage. Like that morning in Madison, this event was bigger and more enthusiastic than any event he would do in Iowa once he started actually running. His staff had intentionally planned the trip so that he wouldn't sleep the night in Iowa, to keep more ideas from forming in anyone else's head, or his own. He now had a former Secret Service agent standing nearby, after two packages from the Trump-supporting mail bomber in Florida, who had targeted several Democrats and news organizations, were found addressed to him. He stayed over an hour working the crowd, long after the candidates themselves had left.

He never drew a crowd in Iowa half as large again.

Biden would Hamlet around with the idea of running for president for the next six months, but flying back to DC from the Midwest trip on a small private plane, he was already thinking ahead.

"There are a lot of great women out there," Biden told his political aide, and later his first campaign manager, Greg Schultz. "A lot of them could be a good vice president."

That wasn't the only sign.

"He's definitely running!" Harry Reid had told a confidante, after watching Biden on TV in the fall of 2018. "He got new plugs!"

CHAPTER FIVE

NOT FRIENDS

One of the things I do worry about sometimes among progressives in the United States is a certain kind of rigidity where we say, 'Uh, I'm sorry, this is how it's going to be' and then we start sometimes creating what's called a circular firing squad where you start shooting at your allies because one of them has strayed from purity on the issues. When that happens, typically the overall effort and movement weakens.

—BARACK OBAMA, APRIL 2019

September 2017–November 2018

What he needed, Bernie Sanders knew, was Elizabeth Warren. And he knew she couldn't refuse.

For a year, Sanders's policy aides had been tweaking and tightening his plan for Medicare for All. He had transformed the conversation around health care in his 2016 run, mainstreaming the concept of national socialized medicine among Democrats. Now he was determined to prove it was more than just a slogan.

His political aides saw a bigger opportunity. Maybe he was going to run again, maybe he wasn't. If he did, they had to assume he'd face a bigger field of candidates, many of whom would be trying to prove themselves to the left. So start with a health care proposal that at least seemed passable, even if it was never explained how it would be paid for, and that would make him look like a seasoned, reasonable legislator. Then try to get every senator who might run against him to sign on as a cosponsor. Theoretically, that would make the legislation stronger. Realistically, that would prevent his opponents from ever being able to attack what would likely be the central idea of his campaign. If Sanders introduced the bill on his own, which used to be his style when he was a lefty looney loner during his days in the House, then he'd be out on his own. But if he got his colleagues to back him up, he would be viewed as a thought leader insulated by the party he still wouldn't join. And they knew the catch: if he did run, he would be the only one who would get the credit from the activists for backing Medicare for All. Everyone else would come off as followers, neither as pure nor as original. Once the other senators signed on, Sanders's aides calculated, they had essentially signed with blood. Getting senators signed on would be self-reinforcing. They might try to reason that they were cosponsoring the bill because they believed broadly in any sort of health care reform, or that they'd claim that they didn't agree with all the specifics but liked the general idea. They could tell themselves whatever stories they wanted.

The original plan had been to introduce Medicare for All in the spring of 2017, when the period after the Obamacare fight would give them time to build up working groups to loop in more and more senators. They started with what they thought was an ambitious goal of five targets. There was never much conversation about protecting private insurance. The only sticking point was the transition time. Kirsten Gillibrand, an unexpected early ally, wrote the language for a speedy one. Al Franken tried to push a transition period that would take decades.

Sanders kept his requirements simple: covering everyone means covering *everyone*. Not just preexisting conditions, or poor people, but undocumented immigrants, felons—everyone. They debated within his office whether to include co-pays. Sanders said no. Once a fee was involved, even a small one, he argued, health care would be viewed as a service, not a right.

They prepped for a September rollout. They never realized Kamala Harris was interested until she informed them that she wanted to be the first cosponsor. This was all politics. Just a few months into her time in the Senate, Harris and her consultants were already looking at polling that showed that her best chance to build support in a presidential run was on the left, that if she was in a race with Sanders and Biden, she could pull more of Sanders's voters than

Biden's. Like pretty much everyone else, Harris and her aides misjudged how durable Sanders would be, assuming there would only be an upside to going into his space. *Sign onto his bill first to get the credit for taking a bold stand,* Harris thought, and make the announcement as a surprise at the end of August in a church back home in Oakland. Aides realized afterward that she had so thin a grasp of the policy that she'd said she was backing "Medicaid for All" in the church. Almost as soon as she finished, she was stressing about now being signed on to ending private insurance, kicking off a two-year-long hokeypokey that would help end her campaign.

She started a stampede. Within weeks of Harris's announcement, Sanders had sixteen cosponsors, including all the other senators already looking at 2020 runs—Gillibrand, Cory Booker, Jeff Merkley from Oregon.

Warren was the holdout. She and her staff hadn't come to any of the official working group meetings, but they had stayed engaged, getting into the weeds on questions. She didn't believe Medicare for All was realistic, or good policy, and though she had a general principle of supporting any legislation to expand health care, this one troubled her. Sanders worried. His staff worried. It was easy enough to get the lefty health care groups to back the bill, but Sanders wanted Medicare for All to become central to the progressive agenda. Warren, queen of the intellectual left, was the key. With her backing, the rest would come along. This was the canniness of the Sanders move, so blinkingly obvious it was never said: What was she going to do, run for president as a progressive and not back Medicare for All, when every liberal was on the bill?

Sanders invited her to his office in the Dirksen Building on Capitol Hill. They sat for an hour, just the two of them. She was clear with her concerns, getting across that she was signing on out of respect for him. This is not the kind of argument that Sanders really registers, or would be so hot on if he did. He saw them as having a policy discussion, working through the ideas. As soon as she left, he told his Senate staff that it was done. He had her.

On September 13, Sanders was standing behind her at the official rollout. As she drew a line from FDR to LBJ to Obama to that press conference, he looked as if he were waiting for her to say the words "Medicare for All" and smiled when she finally did. "Thank you, Bernie, for all that you have done. I am honored to be part of this fight," she said. He patted her twice on the back as she finished, leaned in, and said, "Good job."

Medicare for All was no longer a fringe idea. Before that bill, there wasn't anything nearly as notable that would have identified Gillibrand or Booker or Harris as more "progressive" than say, their eventual competition in Amy Klobuchar or Michael Bennet, neither of whom was then preparing to run and neither of whom was much interested in what they saw as pipe-dream legislation. It didn't matter that Sanders's bill didn't include anything about how to actually make it happen, or that it could never pass the Senate. Now the people who supported it were progressives, and the people who didn't were moderates, whatever else they stood for.

Warren, like Harris, came to regret signing on.

A progressive could have won the 2020 primary. Arguably, with the energy in the party where it was, one probably should have. "It's a big deal that the left didn't win this primary," a person close to Warren said, looking back on the race months later. "Medicare for All is a major reason why the left did not."

If progressivism in 2020 had been defined around another debate, like Warren's wealth tax proposal—two cents off of every dollar of net worth over $50 million, which her campaign argued would provide trillions in revenue to knit a whole new social safety net—the whole shape of the race might have been different. That idea also probably could never have passed Congress or the courts, but strategically, at least it wasn't opposed by a big chunk of the party and every Republican. In a country where feeling screwed by the rich was a bipartisan pursuit, a little class warfare might have even gotten further.

"To light a match on us, he really just lit a match on the whole wing of the party. And he and his people are too stupid to get that," the Warren person said. Medicare for All gave Sanders his power. His bulk of support. It also helped make sure that he couldn't get any further.

———————

Sanders's favorite restaurant is Outback Steakhouse. He likes watching old boxing videos and '70s-era *Saturday Night Live* clips online. He doesn't engage online himself, but he has lurker Facebook and Twitter accounts so he can monitor what his aides are putting out in his name. He's a little shy, and very uninterested in the lives or feelings of most of the people around him. After his sudden success in 2016 after a long life of being written off by the smarter people in politics, he became insistent that he should be taken seriously, given respect.

He has been a successful, continually elected politician for forty years, so he can turn on the warmth when he needs to, but outside of his grandchildren, Sanders tends to think more in terms of people than about any one person.

Warren and Sanders have known each other for years, having appeared together back before either was a national figure. They agree on many issues. They mostly get along. They are not friends. He used to believe they were, as much as he believes anyone is. She never saw him as one and doesn't have many actual friends. They don't hang out together after work or on the weekends. They are both socially awkward. They don't have much to say to each other.

She sees herself as always trying to be inclusive, while he is curmudgeonly. This defines their personal relationship too. He sees himself as the one who's spent his life committed to the cause, and that her tourist-with-a-guidebook approach explains why she never gets the politics quite right. He's not a deep thinker, she believes, while he finds her delusional for being convinced that the answers will come from cracking a code. He's been crucial to the movement, she thinks, but she also thinks he could never see his own limitations. She's more the person who's read *The Motorcycle Diaries*, he thinks, but he's the one who really gets Che.

Sanders had gone into the 2016 race telling the advisers who urged him in, "I just don't want to be like Dennis Kucinich. I want this to be a serious candidacy." He had enjoyed becoming a star, being listened to. He liked that CNN kept inviting him on to be part of primetime policy debates. He liked the way Schumer had tapped him to lead rallies to save Obamacare at the beginning of 2017. And he had come to like the new lifestyle that came with his new prominence. Before he ran for president, Sanders moved around Washington without anyone caring who he was, proudly sitting in the middle seat on JetBlue flights home to Burlington. Charter flights were a revelation to him. He would always be a little embarrassed pulling into the private terminals, but boy, did he get a kick out of not worrying about being late for a flight that couldn't take off without him. By the beginning of 2017, his staff had put together a document laying out his minimum requirements for the kind of aircraft he'd require if asked to go on trips beyond his regular route back and forth between Vermont and Washington. Couldn't be too cramped. Couldn't get too bumpy.

Then there was the "Senator Comfort Memo" to account for other Sanders quirks, which had now become demands. It was distributed to anyone involved with logistics around trips he took, and he expected it to be followed to the letter. Hotel rooms had to be away from elevators and from ice machines, so that quiet was guaranteed. He didn't like getting upgrades and would often switch with an aide if he got the nicer room—"If there's a bomb in there, it's yours tonight," he'd joke—but he liked suites, and he liked bathtubs, and he insisted on a king-size bed, which had to have a down comforter or another blanket in the closet. He preferred that the extra blanket be dark blue, and made of cotton. The temperature in the room had to be kept at 60, even if that required having a staffer sit in the room with an open window in the winter to make sure it cooled enough, or calling management in to override the system. There was no bending the rules: once on a stop in California, annoyed that his aides couldn't get the temperature below 65, he had them call the woman from the front desk up to change the thermostat while he sat on the bed, watching. She couldn't get it to work, and nervously humiliated, she apologized. Sanders didn't care. "So, Chloe," he said, annoyed. "You don't want me to sleep tonight?"

All pamphlets and promotional material were to be removed from any room he was in. He also liked there to be a fan—preferably oscillating—at the foot of the bed, to keep him cool and for the white noise to help him sleep. He once sent an aide out to buy one for him while staying on the Strip in Vegas. Another time, he dispatched an aide to buy one in the middle of a blizzard.

For his hotel rooms and backstage at any events, the memo specified the snacks he expected:

- Green tea with honey
- English breakfast tea
- 1 healthy, low-sugar drink (per person per day)
- 1 small bottle of red Gatorade (per person per day)
- 1 bottle of smartwater (per person per day)
- Small can of unsalted cashews/walnuts/almonds, and clementines

It also offered a tip to stressed-out staffers: "When you find mini honey bottles or single honey packs, stock up!" It did not mention that his preferred low-sugar drink, which he expected to find in the rooms, was Naked brand blueberry juice.

Sanders had become the most popular politician in the country after

Obama, but he wasn't sure he should run again, worried that he might not be able to generate the same excitement. Losing Iowa after coming so close would be an embarrassment, but worse, it would be a setback for the movement. What if he couldn't raise the money online? He'd gotten 43 percent of the vote in the 2016 primaries and thought he could start with that. What if his campaign spun around until it sputtered out?

All of that subsumed under the biggest question. "He did not want to be the candidate who ran in the primaries, won the primaries, and then lost to Trump," said Jeff Weaver, his 2016 campaign manager and closest adviser. "If he thought he wasn't the strongest candidate against Trump, he would not have run."

On January 20, 2018—a year exactly since Trump's inauguration—Sanders and his closest advisers sat in the living room of Ari Rabin-Havt's apartment in DC's Adams Morgan neighborhood. Rabin-Havt came onto the team after the 2016 campaign but had quickly burrowed into the senator's trust by presenting himself internally as the dependable progressive who could translate Washington politics, and externally as the gatekeeper who would dole out dollops of information and access. He'd make sure people knew he was a really good poker player. He'd make sure they knew others had said that he and Sanders were basically the same weird, determined-to-be-too-serious-to-laugh person, separated by forty years in age.

Sanders is never really comfortable in meetings like these—PowerPoints and polls and consultants sitting around, consulting. "The way Bernie thinks about campaigns—he calls it 'the magic,'" Rabin-Havt recalled later, by which he meant the intangibles. Sanders tells people not to believe anyone who tries to claim any great genius about organizing or campaign strategy. He was trying to see if he could recapture the magic.

Sanders sat on the couch, under two paintings of a man holding up his fist, more self-conscious and less self-confident than he ever comes off in public. Weaver was there, as was Nina Turner, the former Ohio state senator who had attached herself entirely to him after the 2016 race. Three sets of consultants were in attendance: Tim Tagaris, who had mastered the digital fundraising for the previous run; Mark Longabaugh and Julian Mulvey, who had joined as consultants in 2015 through their partner Tad Devine, though Devine and

Sanders hadn't spoken since a blowup over the senator's holding off on endorsing Clinton in the spring of 2016; and Chuck Rocha, who came to Sanders after years of labor and Latino connections. Arianna Jones, who had started as a junior aide when Sanders had no chance, listened quietly. Ben Jealous, then running for governor of Maryland, sat in. Jane Sanders, his wife, closest adviser, and keeper of his most *screw-everyone-else* instincts, listened in over the phone, as did RoseAnn DeMoro, the former head of National Nurses United, the union that had spent millions backing his 2016 run.

Tagaris presented a fundraising plan: they could exceed what he had brought in over the 2016 race, by so much that the democratic socialist could wind up being the best-funded candidate in the field. Longabaugh tried to center the discussion around a couple of basic slides he'd put together. He had earned his credibility in 2015, when he had accurately projected that Sanders could win the Michigan primary and potentially slingshot that into the nomination. He'd been one of the consultants behind that amazing ad of crowds stepping forward together to the tune of Simon & Garfunkel's "America." He saw himself as the right nexus of true believer and political professional, and made no secret of the fact that he wanted Sanders to run, with himself as campaign manager. Tagaris wanted everyone to recognize that he should be in control, both internally and in the press.

That was exactly why Sanders was wary of him. Jane was the one who was always really in charge. He was also convinced that Longabaugh, who liked to talk to reporters, was behind the leaks out of his first run, which used to drive him crazy.

Longabaugh started his presentation. The second slide read "2020 WILL NOT BE LIKE 2016" with bold emphasis.

1. You will be the frontrunner (or one of two).
2. Intense scrutiny (more than 2016).
3. You will be the fulcrum of the campaign, and thus under constant attack from press and opponents.
4. There will be a large field of candidates.

Sanders had the message, the enthusiasm, and the organization and networks to call on, Longabaugh said. But he was old, refused to become a

Democrat, and he was going to have to compete for progressives. The right progressive challenger could shake him in Iowa, scatter his support in New Hampshire, and that might be the end. They all kept referring to "other progressives," but they all knew they were talking about Warren. With her in the race, Longabaugh figured, it's "mutually assured destruction." If they could somehow keep her out, and have Booker and Harris in the race through South Carolina to split the Black vote—even with Biden strong there—there wasn't just a path to the presidency. There was a highway.

"The race may not be extended like 2008 and 2016—and could be resolved by mid-March," another slide read. "If we have secured the nomination by mid-March—we will need a large move to reassure and consolidate the party."

Sanders loves reading polls but hates the idea of pollsters telling him what to say. He had been convinced late in the 2016 race to hire Ben Tulchin, who remained in the circle. Tulchin had run his own numbers in Iowa. Tulchin knew the field would be big, but he was focused only on three permutations: what would happen if Sanders, Biden, and Warren all ran; what would happen if it was only Sanders and Biden; and what would happen if it was only Sanders and Warren. They were already seeing the split between more blue-collar male support for Sanders and more college-educated female support for Warren.

Tulchin's advice: start thinking forward to naming a more establishment running mate, or cochairs of the campaign. Maybe start thinking about getting lunch, or at least cups of coffee, with members of the Congressional Black Caucus to start building connections that might help down the line. At least make them think a minute before jumping behind another candidate. A more basic move, but a more visceral one for him, was to run for reelection to the Senate in 2018 as a Democrat instead of as the independent he'd been for the last forty years.

What it all came down to was trying to run for the Democratic nomination, instead of trying to stage another hostile takeover. However much Sanders understood that argument, he didn't really feel it in his bones.

They pitched plans. Longabaugh suggested picking off union heads and other establishment leaders. Jones argued against having the headquarters in Washington: not being in Burlington would leach the camaraderie, the sense of movement, the fun of 2016. Weaver wanted an expanded press operation, citing how big and experienced the Clinton team had been by the time she had launched her campaign. Sanders's cakewalk reelection campaign in Vermont in 2018 was the perfect opportunity, he said. Do some planning, train an army of organizers, then have them fan out to the primary states as soon as he won.

"Bernie executed none of it," Longabaugh recalled later.

———

After the 2016 election, Joe Rospars wrote a memo for Warren. It had a simple theme: *You're going to be the president, and here's the plan to get there.* Rospars had helped run Obama's online efforts during his campaigns, which he had parlayed into a successful online campaign consulting business, but he'd turned to Warren early. His first memo to her about running for president was right after the 2014 midterms, hoping to get her into the 2016 race. It's going to be a small primary field, he'd argued, and there's going to be a hunger for change. If nothing else, Rospars said the reason that she should run was to get Clinton weathered more, so that as the nominee, she didn't go up against a Republican with an untested, bloated campaign. All in all the message was: *Don't wait.* Warren mulled the memo for a few days and then declined.

After 2016, Rospars felt Warren's chances were even stronger. Democrats needed to have a candidate who wasn't a white guy. It was Warren. It had to be Warren. This time she was mostly on board, and had a team start to lay the groundwork. There was only a tiny group that Warren trusted: her former law student and always closest aide, Dan Geldon; her college dropout but organizing maven campaign manager, Roger Lau; and her camera-shy but quietly aggressive communications director, Kristen Orthman, whom she had picked up from Harry Reid.

Warren and her closest advisers viewed Sanders as sucked up in his own self-satisfied delusion, refusing to realize how many of his votes in 2016 were the result of his being the binary alternative to Hillary Clinton. That belief was borne out by polls, which showed Sanders's support in the teens, not far ahead of Warren and behind Biden. He had no claim on the nomination, and he certainly couldn't beat Trump.

She, meanwhile, was a woman at a time when women were proving key to the party's future. She had an appeal beyond just Sanders's supporters, drawing from many Clinton voters too. They weren't the same in the eyes of Democratic voters, they said. She was more. And while Sanders was taking his time deciding whether to run, they had to proceed as if they didn't care where he ultimately landed.

"The whole thing that they have the same core of support," a Warren ally said as their collision course was becoming clear in the fall of 2018, "tends to be overstated."

On this point the Sanders circle agreed. "Beer track/wine track," is how Sanders aides came to refer to it internally. She had the fancy progressives, the intellectuals, the Whole Foods crowd. He had the bus drivers, the waiters and fry cooks, the people who wanted to knock down the system not because they wanted to make it work better or that it was the right thing to do, but because they were tired of getting screwed. She might get all the progressive stamps of approval, but within those groups was a solid core of Sanders supporters who would stick with him no matter what.

Sanders felt that he had politely held back on his own plans to get into the 2016 race while waiting for Warren to rule out the campaign into which supporters had tried to draft her. To the Warren Circle, that was one chivalrous moment in what was otherwise a sea of ungraciousness. Because Warren didn't think she or anyone else could have really beaten Clinton that year, vulnerable as she seemed. "Hillary's like a 1929 bank," she'd say. "Everything looks like it's going fine, but then one guy comes asking for his money and the whole thing falls apart."

Still, Warren had been disgusted by the way that Sanders had stayed in the race in 2016, dogging Clinton, slicing at her until the very end. It was only more evidence to her that Sanders shouldn't be the nominee, and probably couldn't be. Behind the scenes, she was conferring with Clinton and John Podesta about how to try easing him out of the race.

Warren is the teacher, is how Sanders's aides would put it, while he's the preacher—and the preacher is the one that most people connect to. She *is* the teacher. That's who she had always been, how she has always thought of herself: the beloved professor whose classes were always packed, helping her bright students unlock what became so obvious in themselves once she gave them the keys. "If you want to understand me," Warren would say later, talk to her former students who had become teachers themselves, "because I worked with them and helped them."

And sure, *while Sanders might be the preacher,* she thought, *it didn't accomplish much to preach if only the true believers were coming to church.* He may have helped introduce a lot of key ideas, but wasn't it better to get somewhere with them than to keep getting nowhere? Not that she would fully give him credit for getting the conversation started.

Sitting backstage at the progressive activist conference Netroots Nation in July 2019, Warren looked around at a big empty room—which she said reminded her of going into a lecture hall up at Harvard once when, because of a computer error at the registrar, she ended up with just one student cleared for the class. She gently downshifted a question about whether Sanders was moving the Democratic Party to the left.

"Oh, I think Bernie deserves enormous credit for making visible to all of America how deeply progressive much of this country is," she said.

"He brought it up. He brought it to the fore." She then immediately pointed to a speech she had given at the AFL-CIO convention in Los Angeles in September 2013, when she was in her first year in the Senate and the big progressive star, and Sanders was still mostly known only to his own email list. She'd walked out onstage in a bright pink blazer to the union president Richard Trumka calling her "an honest to god champion, the real deal," as Diana Ross's "Ain't No Mountain High Enough" blasted on the speakers. "On almost every issue of economic concern, our values are America's values, and our agenda is America's agenda," she said.

Downstairs at Netroots Nation that day, Markos Moulitsas, the lefty blogger-activist who had started the conference and helped catapult Warren into progressive fantasies years earlier, said he'd be shocked if Sanders ended up anywhere near the nomination: "He made it safe for Warren to be Warren. But that doesn't make him the best messenger. And it's clear he lost last time. There's nothing wrong with recalibrating that message to be more inclusive."

Warren's aides turned 2018 into a yearlong boot camp, getting her a spot on the Senate Armed Services Committee and turning her Senate reelection campaign into presidential prep. She traveled the country, banking hundreds of thousands of dollars, stopping in to support a few campaigns, but mostly building up her own network around the country. She invested in state parties and down-ballot candidates. After years of avoiding reporters in Washington, she used town halls back home in Massachusetts to sharpen herself and then started making more media appearances.

Warren's preferred tool is the phone. She makes calls all day long, comes prepared for and enthusiastic about whatever she's going to say, launches right in, and makes her case. All through 2017 and 2018, she was ringing up local leaders and politicians, pledging support or checks, turning around to donors to land the money to write those checks, and building up what quickly became (and still is) by far the largest political staff of anyone in Congress.

She expanded her efforts and embarked on a social tour. After her attack on Obama for his paid speeches blew up, she reached out to have tea with Valerie Jarrett. Pick anyone else around Obama, or among recognized leaders in the Democratic Party, and she probably had dinner with them or invited them to her office at the Senate for a friendly meeting: Denis McDonough. Former health secretary Kathleen Sebelius. Former Michigan governor Jennifer Granholm. Virginia governor Terry McAuliffe. Even former treasury secretary Jack Lew. About a hundred House candidates in 2018 came by, among others. Los Angeles mayor Eric Garcetti left his meeting feeling as if he were being sized up as a potential running mate.

For years, the Congressional Progressive Caucus had essentially been a commiseration society. The dozen or so far left–leaning House Democrats would get together in a private room at Hunan Dynasty, the famous greasy Chinese restaurant a few blocks from the Capitol popular with all sorts of members of Congress, sit around complaining about the Republicans, complaining about the Democratic leadership, complaining about the colleagues who'd say they were in the Progressive Caucus but never show up for the dinners or vote the way they wanted. The group had solidified over the years, with basics like voting as a bloc, cooperating with one another on legislation, and starting to be in contact with the progressive groups that some of their members found annoying. Their strategy for expanding the Progressive Caucus wasn't much more than hoping that candidates they liked won. They argued over whether it was smart to get into fights with the Democratic leadership.

Now, they were sure, one of their members was going to be the next president of the United States. They were way beyond beef and broccoli.

————

Events in 2018 turned out trickier than easy Senate reelection campaigns en route to a presidential run should have been. Our Revolution, the group that had formed out of Sanders's 2016 campaign, was off to a sputtering start. Its candidates were losing primaries. Fundraising was faltering. "Creating a grassroots organization is different from running a presidential campaign," Jane Kleeb, the group's treasurer and the Nebraska Democratic Party chair said that spring. As so often happens with any new movement, internal fights soon broke out over leadership and money. Many involved quietly accused Nina Turner, who had become the president of Our Revolution, of using the group as a vehicle for promoting presidential ambitions of her own. "I hope he runs again. I am right with him," she said that May. "If he doesn't, we'll see what happens with other candidates." But both inside and outside of the group, Sanders fans were worrying that Our Revolution's efforts were only proving his limited appeal.

Warren's problem was courtesy of Trump's racist "Pocahontas" cheerleading. There wasn't much way around it: long before she got into politics, she had been trumpeted as Harvard Law's "first woman of color" professor because she claimed to be part Cherokee. Her later excuses about innocently believing stories her mother had told her about some great-great-great ancestor never quite added up. She had considered doing a DNA test as part of her first Senate campaign in 2012, but decided against it. She won that race in a romp.

Warren knew she'd never get through the presidential election that easily, especially because she was running for reelection against Trump's old campaign cochair in Massachusetts, who knew he was going to lose but also that he could probably generate some problematic debate clips for the greater cause. Her refusal to resolve the issue was getting her hammered from even the people who wanted to like her on the left, and her inner circle was obsessing over Trump's tweets about it.

So they flew Warren to the town where she grew up in Oklahoma to make a video and to take a test. And even though they had carefully plotted the rollout, complete with a fully packaged production in *The Boston Globe*, they managed to screw it all up. They didn't check in with any of the local tribal groups. They tried to hang some claim to her heritage on a test that revealed she had at most 3 percent Native American blood, and not long afterward they had to revise the percentage down. "As a person of color who works with people of color, it felt like it was almost diminishing the role of race in our politics. It really went against the grain with a lot of people. It trivialized race as a factor in so many ways," said Jonathan Westin, the executive director of New York Communities for Change and one of the people involved with the "draft Warren" effort ahead of the 2016 campaign, marveling at the scale of the mistake even then. "She's clearly a white woman." Beyond his offhand racism, Trump's attacks were aimed to undermine Warren's core strength as a truth teller. Her attempts to get around them only ended up damaging her actual core strength of competence.

Her inner circle was distraught. They felt as if they might have blown the whole thing. It seemed too late to turn around. "Nobody wanted to say it out loud, but there was a lot of anxiety," acknowledged one of her advisers a few months later. What surprised them was how little any of that political chatter had penetrated Iowa.

The Sanders team, meanwhile, only laughed, and an adviser on one of their Sunday night conference calls with him said: "She's gone, she's dead, it's over." The supercompetent, savvy behemoth that everyone was supposed to be in awe of had shown itself to be a bunch of dorks who couldn't handle the basics of politics.

He'd been hesitating, wondering if she was strong enough to win, and first, to beat him. So much for that.

Sanders's top advisers felt that she had been trying to muscle him out of the race, though they were less bitter about it than sneering. Did Warren actually think she'd get anywhere with her overtures to people like Nina Turner or RoseAnn DeMoro, who had been a Sanders devotee since the 1980s? "She's engaged in a chess game where she's moving her pawns around and she's trying to demonstrate to many people, including Bernie, that not only is she running, but is fully capable of running, and is so far ahead that you should just give in to her," said one of the main people speaking to Sanders at the time.

Weaver, reflecting on how this was all hitting Sanders, gave that opinion a brush-off that sounded high-minded. "The place where the country is now is so far off, so out of whack, that those kinds of tactical discussions really don't give an appropriate amount of appreciation of the danger that Trump and his kind of politics represent to American politics. That's where Bernie's head is right now," he said then.

Eventually the Sanders conversations turned to encouraging him to sit down and talk to Warren in an effort to sort out their relationship. "I see her in the Senate all the time," he said, and let the conversation roll by.

Warren and her advisers continued building the warship. Some of the support was from progressives and Clinton supporters who came to her because they liked her, some was from moderates who saw her as an acceptable, potentially winning nominee who'd be a pressure valve to stop Sanders from blowing up the party entirely. Over time, they would hear insiders and reporters talk up the idea of some kind of summit to figure out which one would run, and which one would sit it out for the cause. A *conversation*. Warren's circle knew that these suggestions were coming from Sanders. They always thought it was a ridiculous idea, a one-sided benefit. "What was she getting out of that? What's the benefit for her?" argued one person in Warren's orbit at the time. "That she gets to know ahead of time if he's running?"

———

Eventually, on December 11, Warren invited Sanders to her apartment near the National Archives to have a talk.

For two hours they talked around what they were talking about, both of them expecting the other to say something. Neither did. She didn't make it clear she was running. He didn't either. They both explicitly said they hadn't made their minds up yet. This was a circular wink-wink nudge-nudge right out of *Monty Python*. Sanders told her he doubted a woman could win against Trump. Warren heard that as informing her that he doubted she could win, and though he'd deny it when the story went public, she was immediately recounting his remarks to people around her, overcome with offense. She gave up on whatever scraps of friendship they had that night, though Sanders and his aides liked to point out later how often she still referred to Sanders publicly as a friend.

Afterward, Sanders told aides that she'd cooked lasagna for him, though she'd ordered in from a medium-grade local Italian spot. When they asked how the food was, he'd say, "OK."

Ahead of launching her exploratory committee on New Year's Eve, Warren called Sanders to let him know she was running. He wasn't very encouraging or warm about it, and the conversation didn't last very long. "OK," he said.

CHAPTER SIX

THE SPARK

We call BS.

—PARKLAND STUDENT
EMMA GONZALEZ

January 2018–November 2018

Any time that Chuck Schumer had to calm down Bernie Sanders, he'd call Tom Perez.

Over the course of four years, Perez had gone from being one of the country's foremost civil rights lawyers, as the head of that division at the Justice Department in Obama's first term, to inadvertently becoming the center of the stalemate that led to the first blowing up of the filibuster because Republicans held up his nomination as labor secretary over accusations he'd been too deferential to the left. He'd been deemed too progressive to be picked as the sleeper option for Clinton's running mate, but faced constant complaints that he was a corporate establishment shill who was selling out the DNC.

He had barely been chair a week when Schumer started easing him into his new role as Sanders soother. Perez was on his way to one of his first big donor meetings when Schumer called and conferenced in Sanders.

"Let's get right down to business," Schumer said. "The senator and I have had conversations about how we might move beyond 2016—"

"Chuck, Chuck . . ." Sanders interrupted the minority leader and then started running through what was going to happen. He'd been pleased with the rallies he'd led at the beginning of the year to help light up the opposition to repealing Obamacare. Now they needed more. A unity tour.

"We'll split the costs," Sanders said, issuing his decree. "Staff will coordinate."

By the end of April, Sanders and Perez were flying around to Maine, Kentucky, Florida, Texas, Nebraska, Utah, Arizona, and Nevada. They didn't talk much in the air. At each stop, they never knew whether they were going to be greeted by women furious at Sanders for having made Clinton lose, or by screams of "Bernie would have won!" Over just a few days they managed to worsen their own relationship, remind Democrats of all the things they were still mad about, and provide new material to show what a mess the party still was. They even floundered into a new problem, with Sanders pushing support in the Omaha mayor's race for a Nebraska state senator with a record of backing abortion restrictions. By now the conventional wisdom was that Democrats were going to have to accept some compromises if they wanted to win—even as Sanders continued to say he couldn't accept compromises on any of his own core class-based agenda. When Sanders attended a rally for the candidate, DNC staffers quickly put out the word they had nothing to do with it, and Perez made sure to be far away, appearing at a fundraiser for Jon Ossoff, then running for the House special election in the Atlanta suburbs, which was becoming a national cause. "A unity tour that bred disunity," was how Jane Kleeb, the Nebraska Democratic state party chair and a board member of the Sanders-inspired Our Revolution group, looked back on it.

Sanders was on Schumer's mind a lot those days. That summer, amid all the stress about Obamacare, he invited two of Sanders's top aides from the 2016 campaign, Jeff Weaver and Mark Longabaugh, to give a presentation to the weekly lunch of Democratic senators at the Capitol on how to meet progressives where they are. Sanders, now part of the official Democratic leadership team, sat up front, alongside Debbie Stabenow, the Michigan senator up for reelection herself in 2018 and on high alert after Trump's sneaking up to win her state in 2016.

There were slides, and lots of talk, all building to playing two closing ads—one from Clinton, one from Trump. The Clinton ad was two minutes of her looking into the camera, soft lit in an off-white outfit, speaking about core values and against divisiveness, and promising how hard she'd work to achieve those. The Trump ad was two minutes of agitated voiceover, with shots of empty factories; complaints about jobs and unfair trade; attacks against the political establishment, who "don't have your good in mind"; and footage of crowds cheering together as a movement, with a little Clinton corruption thrown in for spice.

"This campaign was lost because we failed to address what went wrong," Longabaugh told the senators. Clinton and Obama had assured America that the country was moving forward, getting better, but that wasn't what many people were actually experiencing. Too many voters felt left out of the economy, they said, and now those voters felt as if they were being left out of politics as well. Where was the anger directed at what had happened to them, or any promise to do something about it besides more talking? Take out the Trump signs and the red hats, and this could have been a Sanders ad, they pointed out, trying to get the Democrats to realize that there wasn't such a mystery about Sanders's strength against Clinton, which most were still burning about.

The Reverend William Barber, the North Carolina activist minister who had just founded a revival of Martin Luther King Jr.'s Poor People's Campaign, was up next for the senators. Watching the Sanders aides' presentation, he had become angry and now lit in with his own questions. Why weren't they talking about race? Poverty? Why were they parroting the same blabber about the white working class and Obama–Trump voters that obsessed the cable pundits? They pushed back: Sanders had talked about racial inequality in 2016 more than anyone, they argued. This wasn't a question of either one or the other issue.

Afterward Schumer made his way over to Weaver and Longabaugh. Like many of the senators in the room, he was worried about Sanders-style primaries— against incumbents, or for seats Democrats were hoping to flip. "We're going to have some of the *most* progressive candidates," Schumer said, trying to prove himself to them. "Great," they said. He seemed to be missing the point. Sanders and his crew weren't the ones who needed to be convinced.

———

On Valentine's Day of 2018, a nineteen-year-old former student walked into Marjory Stoneman Douglas High School outside of Fort Lauderdale, Florida, and started shooting. Within a month, teenagers who had watched their friends and teachers being shot were standing on a stage by the National Gallery of Art in Washington, DC, in front of two hundred thousand people.

This event didn't happen spontaneously. Jimmy Fallon, Lin-Manuel Miranda, Ariana Grande, Cher, and Kevin Bacon didn't just all decide to be backstage meeting with the high schoolers who had become overnight activists, and overnight famous, with Kanye West and Kim Kardashian scooting up on a golf cart even though they weren't on the guest list. The signs in the crowd were handmade—THOUGHTS AND PRAYERS DON'T STOP BULLETS, WHICH KID IS NEXT? with arrows pointing in every direction, THE ONLY GLOCK I WANT IN MY CLASSROOM, with a drawing of a glockenspiel. The response was organic and overwhelming. What happened that Saturday morning in Washington and in companion rallies around the country were signal events in how the new energy, the established politicians in Washington, the big donors, and Hollywood had begun to come together in a new aligned purpose.

Gun control was the great failure of Obama's presidency, and he knew it. He had cried at the White House podium in December 2012, thinking about the twenty children shot dead at Sandy Hook Elementary, and promised in a mesmerizing speech at the prayer vigil that weekend in Connecticut that he would use "whatever power this office holds to engage my fellow citizens." He had just been reelected, the horror of what had taken place had paralyzed the NRA into silence, and all that came of his promise was a commission led by Biden that produced a collection of largely meaningless executive actions. He and Biden couldn't even get a Senate vote for the bare minimum of mandating background checks. "It was the best that could have happened at that time, and even it didn't happen," is how Joe Manchin, the conservative Democratic senator from West Virginia, puts it. Obama effectively gave up. There was no greater example of the disparity between Obama's making Americans want him to lead and his inability to do so.

George Clooney was at home in Los Angeles the day of the shooting, sitting with his parents, watching Anderson Cooper on CNN interview Cameron Kasky and David Hogg, two of the students who quickly became central figures. He was caught up in the moment, struck by how smart and searing they were on camera. He wanted to help, so he called Cooper, asking for their numbers. When Cooper hesitated, Clooney told him to give them his number.

"You guys have lit a fire," he said when he finally reached them, and told them there should be a march—just kids. Put together a small group, start organizing.

Clooney called Obama because that's a thing that can happen between guys who'd been friends dating back to their playing basketball together when Obama was a state senator. "I am full on radioactive," Obama told Clooney. "If I'm near it, it becomes the 'Barack Obama liberal agenda.'" He offered to activate pieces behind the scenes and to keep other politicians away.

Obama saw the spark—but he worried. These kids were his daughters' age, suddenly tumbling through tragedy and celebrity. He worried about their getting thrown into the national spotlight, that there wasn't an infrastructure to protect them, whether when attacked online by gun nuts or when a Hollywood producer called a student demanding rights to a song the school choir sang during a CNN town hall a few days later. He worried about another missed opportunity by not channeling the energy into anything constructive. He worried about the politicians taking over and messing it up.

Clooney started calling more celebrities to pitch in—John Legend, Jimmy Kimmel. Obama called Mark Kelly, the retired astronaut husband of Gabby Giffords, who had become a nexus of his own antigun network in the seven years since his wife had been shot in the head. Kelly pushed back on the idea of a march at first, tried to warn all these suddenly gun-focused celebrities against getting their hopes up. "You're thinking that this is going to be like Sandy Hook," Clooney told him. "It's going to be different." They should have a march.

Clooney called around to Sunday shows, pulling in favors to get the students booked. The shooting had taken place on a Wednesday, and by the following Sunday, they were announcing the plan. Clooney and a television producer named Deena Katz, who had helped organize the Women's March, went looking for a name under which to register a website. They'd call it the March for Our Lives.

"People keep asking us what about the Stoneman Douglas shooting is going to be different. Because this has happened before and change hasn't come. This is it. People are saying that it's not time to talk about gun control. And we can respect that. Here's a time. March 24 in every single city. We are going to be marching together as students begging for our lives," Kasky told Martha Raddatz on ABC. "This isn't about the GOP, this isn't about the Democrats, this is about the adults. We feel neglected and at this point, you're either with us or against us."

Clooney called producer Jeffrey Katzenberg, and together they worked out a plan to have Clooney donate $500,000 on one day, Katzenberg to give on the next day, Steven Spielberg on the next, and then Oprah Winfrey. Walmart gave $1 million, and Warren Buffet's daughter chipped in. In the end they put $22 million in the bank.

First, the students headed to Tallahassee to lobby for new gun restrictions. Kelly flew to Florida, tracked them down eating lunch in a room in the state capitol. The teachers recognized him as soon as he walked in. Most of the kids, who had been in grade school when Giffords was shot, had no idea who he was until he started telling the story of what happened. Horror connected them. Listen to the lesson of that, Kelly warned them: it had been seven years since Giffords had been shot in the head. Making progress was going to be a long, long fight.

Clooney planned another trip for the students, to meet with kids who'd survived gun violence in Chicago. He'd been on the phone with Al Sharpton and other Black leaders, who saw this as yet another time when the country only cared about violence because white kids had been shot. They introduced the kids to one another, videoed them together, invited the Chicago group to be part of the march.

The National Rifle Association was the only major institutional player that invested in Trump's campaign in 2016, and it invested a lot: $50 million that was traceable, and almost certainly more that moved outside the view of campaign finance laws. Trump arrived with full Republican control in Washington, and an NRA wish list that Republican leaders were eager to move: lifting restrictions on silencers, plus a law called "concealed carry reciprocity" that would have allowed gun owners in states without many restrictions to have those laws apply even when they were traveling in more stringent states.

But those efforts ran into a changed mood among Democrats, which crystallized with the sit-in on the floor of the House in 2016 after the shooting at the Pulse nightclub in Orlando. House Speaker Paul Ryan had ordered the lights shut off, but John Lewis had elevated the fight to a civil rights issue, and every Democrat joined in, with a mostly unknown congressman from Texas named Beto O'Rourke livestreaming the whole event because Ryan had also turned off the C-SPAN cameras. The gun safety group founded by Giffords and Kelly had gone into the Trump years with a triage plan titled Resist the Gun Lobby, and by 2018, it had stopped the lifting of silencer restrictions and passage of concealed carry reciprocity, and helped write the language for a law that actually strengthened the background checks system.

Try telling a bunch of teenagers who just had their school shot up that they should be happy with incremental change and the idea that a couple of votes on technicalities could have gone worse. It wasn't just the politicians and the adults who hadn't protected them, they said. If all these antigun groups had been successful, they would have changed the laws and the world already. They hadn't.

Obama wrote a short letter, made public immediately, about how the students' resilience and solidarity had "helped awaken the conscience of the nation," giving them his stamp of approval without saying anything directly, while Clooney kept working his phone. On the day of the march, he kept the event from looking too Hollywood by keeping most of the stars backstage, chatting and taking selfies with the shaken kids. Obama wouldn't speak, dissuading any other politicians from doing so, to keep it from turning into just another gun rally. Kelly and Nancy Pelosi, hoping to make a splash for Democrats going into the midterms, both wanted to speak, but Clooney told them both no. He was helping script speeches and picked music for the event, including having Jennifer Hudson—whose mother, brother, and seven-year-old nephew were shot dead in 2008—close out the rally by leading a gospel choir singing "The Times They Are A-Changin'."

Virginia governor Ralph Northam, standing at the top of the bleachers, where he'd gone to make sure reporters saw him as available to interview, looked out at the crowd. "We were up here a year ago for the Women's March," he said. "We saw a tremendous amount of energy across Virginia after that."

Mike Bloomberg's Everytown for Gun Safety group showed up with money, helping put together logistics—permits for all the companion marches around the country, digital ads to promote the events, the livestreams, the outreach to all the mayors. March volunteers circulated with clipboards and flyers urging people to get into the database by texting "FIGHT." DNC organizers at the marches elsewhere in the country passed out "commit to vote" cards. The Brady: United Against Gun Violence campaign produced "227 Days Until Midterm Elections" stickers. When the students all went onstage together at the end and student Emma Gonzalez grabbed the microphone back from Hudson, she yelled, "Get out there and vote! Get out there and get registered!"

Kelly had the Giffords gun control group move up a voter registration drive that had been planned for the months before the election. They organized a trip for two hundred students and families to Washington for the march, and started them off the day before with a lobbying day on Capitol Hill. To kick things off, they invited just one person to speak—because he had worked in Congress, had pushed for gun control, and knew grief.

"I love you a lot, a lot," Giffords said, hugging Biden as she greeted him waiting in a holding room in one of the Senate office buildings before they walked in together.

"It's mutual, kid," Biden replied. At the microphone he spoke about being in a valley that only those in there with him could see.

"I'm sure a lot of people come up to you and say, 'I know how you feel.' And after about the twentieth time, you want to say, 'You have no idea how I feel.' You know they mean well. But you know they have no idea. *I* know how you feel," Biden said. "I got a phone call, like you got a phone call. I had just been elected to the United States Senate. My wife and my three children were Christmas shopping. A tractor trailer came barreling down a hill and broadsided them. Killed my wife, killed my daughter. And my two sons were very, very badly injured. Not expected to make it."

He wrapped his fingers around the long microphone in the hearing room they'd commandeered.

"People used to come to me and say, 'I know how you feel,'" Biden repeated. "You know they meant well, but after a while you felt like screaming."

The following day Biden was back home in Wilmington, at one of the dozens of companion marches.

"Folks, too many people are dying," he said. "Too many children are being hurt. But here's the deal: You guys talk about how you are going to change things. You are going to change things. What's happening now is you're ripping the Band-Aid off. You're forcing people to look squarely in the eye what they don't want to face."

———

The first big meeting of world leaders after Trump won, the annual Asia-Pacific Economic Cooperation summit, had taken place in Peru less than two weeks after the election. Obama had just returned from Greece and Germany on the trip that had originally been planned as a paean to democracy for his final international swing. Instead, it came off with not just Obama but with America itself as a lame duck. He was met everywhere with grim looks and questions about whether the American century had just ended.

World leaders were walking around Lima quoting Mario Cuomo about campaigning in poetry and governing in prose, hoping that maybe Trump was going to change and pull back once he was in office. ("I didn't notice a lot of poetry," Chilean president Michelle Bachelet observed.) Even China's Xi Jinping was telling his colleagues that he just assumed Trump was mostly bluster, and that he'd settle down now that he'd won. Obama tried to encourage that thinking, while urging Australian prime minister Malcolm Turnbull and other center-right leaders to exert influence to anchor Trump. Trump would believe that *right wing* in their countries meant the same thing as *right wing* in America, Obama told them. Bill Clinton, making his own phone calls after the election, had made a similar point. Trump would listen to them, they'd said, and the whole world was depending on their getting Trump to listen.

Turnbull had been wary of Trump long before even Obama was. He'd come up through Australian politics facing off with Rupert Murdoch, Conrad Black, and others in what he thinks of as his megalomaniac training. As much faith as he had in America, he worried about the appeal Trump was demonstrating. Sitting in the Oval Office in January 2016, discussing a deal between the two countries for taking in refugees, the prime minister asked Obama what he should make of the Republican candidate. "Don't worry, Malcolm," Obama told him, "the American people will never elect a lunatic to sit in this office."

Just over a year later, Trump blew up the refugee deal in a phone call that never got much past his bringing up that both he and Turnbull knew golfer Greg Norman, and then asking, "Who made the deal? Obama?" Didn't Turnbull understand, Trump told him, "I am the world's greatest person that does not want to let people into the country." As anyone can see from a transcript of the call, which leaked months later, Turnbull tried patiently to explain to Trump that he had no idea what he was talking about. Trump told him that their conversation, a week into his presidency and a day after enacting the Muslim ban, was "his most unpleasant call all day." He compared it with his chat with Putin a little while earlier, which was "a pleasant call."

Just over a year after that call, Turnbull walked into the suite on the twenty-ninth floor of the InterContinental Sydney at four p.m. on March 23, during a break from a few well-paid speaking gigs, Obama was long into worrying about what Trump had been doing while sitting in the Oval Office. Observing what was happening to America was starting to seem like watching a good friend drink himself to death, and being powerless to do anything about it. Turnbull had by now seen how Trump behaved around Putin in private meetings—like a new kid in school glomming on to the captain of the football team.

Weathering Trump was proving harder than he expected, Turnbull said. China was asserting itself more, playing into Australian politics. He didn't know how long the world could hold the line, where the international order was going to be on the other side of this.

"Obama and I were absolutely of the same mind that the international system could not stand eight years of Trump," Turnbull recalled, "the damage would be irretrievable." Merkel, Obama said again then, was going to need to stay in power for as long as possible to be a bulwark against Trump and the forces of protectionism.

All right, then, Turnbull wanted to know, could anyone beat him?

Obama wasn't optimistic. The Clintons, he'd said, had run such a concerted effort to eradicate the competition that there wasn't any obvious candidate in the wings, no bench or obvious runner-up. He'd looked at polling. It didn't seem as if America was ready to elect a woman—depressing, he said, but maybe a reality that Democrats were going to have to accept.

That trip stayed with Obama. Maybe it was just a conglomeration of Trump's behavior over the year, hearing concern from foreign leaders and everyone else he talked to on that trip, or his perspective on the state of America from being all the way on the other side of the world and seeing it so clearly. When he got back, he was now repeating Turnbull's assessment all the time—America could withstand four years of Trump, but probably not eight. He seemed to have grown more serious in those days, more on edge. Aides and others who heard him say that remember feeling as if they'd been zapped. Maybe everything wasn't going to be OK.

At the end of June, in a lush backyard in Beverly Hills where the twenty round tables had mini watermelons as centerpieces, he told the rich donors who'd paid big money to get their picture with him that they were doing it all wrong. Sitting in a gray armchair, taking questions from Tom Perez, he urged them to stop dreaming of him. "Don't wait to feel a tingle in your spine because you're expecting politicians to be so inspiring and poetic and moving that somehow, 'OK, I'll get off my couch after all and go spend the fifteen to twenty minutes it takes for me to vote'—because that's part of what happened last election. I heard that too much," Obama said. Instead, they should take note of the brutal pragmatism of Republicans: "They don't worry about inspiration. They worry about winning the seat, and they are very systematic about work not just at the presidential level but at the congressional and state legislative levels."

He said he regretted that, during his presidency, "people were so focused on me and what was happening at the White House and the battles we were having—particularly after we lost the House, that folks stopped paying attention up and down the ballot." He made an almost up-to-date reference. "Christina Aguilera was wonderful, but you don't need to have an amazing singer at every event. Sometimes you're just in a church basement making phone calls and eating cold pizza."

He then tried to summarize his point, which he was making in his typical winding way: "I think it was F. Scott Fitzgerald who said the sign of a sane mind is one that can hold two contradictory ideas at the same time. I'm paraphrasing." He was. The Fitzgerald quote is that holding two opposed ideas is "the test of a first-rate intelligence." But neither sanity nor intelligence was his ultimate point. "Keep what seems to be two contradictory ideas in your mind," he told the donors. "This is a moment of great urgency, and you are right to be concerned. The progress that has been made in this country is not a given. It has to be nurtured and fought for and cultivated."

———

"Don't be so creepy," her husband told her, a few months in.

All her training was to blend in: lie about her job, make it sound so boring that people at parties changed the topic for her. Never be important in any room. Pretend on Girl Scout troop trips that she had trouble with orienteering too. She hadn't realized how much her face was contorting while being honest until her husband told her to stand in front of the mirror practicing.

"Hello," she said, over and over. "My name's Abigail Spanberger, and I worked at the CIA."

She'd been cleared to say as much—but not so cleared that she could discuss many details of what she'd done in the Middle East working contacts and gathering intelligence—about a year before she decided to run. She hadn't been saying it much before that afternoon in May 2017, sitting at her desk in her new job, watching the CNN news alert about the House voting to repeal Obamacare.

"Every crazy-ass circumstance I was ever in was for the purpose of ensuring somebody else could make a good decision. Risks I took, times I traveled away from my family and had an alias and couldn't call home for days—everything I had done was because I had this vision of these policymakers and diplomats, military members, people who really cared and sought out the information. Everything I did was so that those people could make good decisions," Spanberger said, thinking back. "And so there was almost a level of personal offense that here we have people who just wanted, 'Repeal! Repeal ACA!' But for what? And they're hurting real people."

Children on her kids' school buses were crying when the Muslim ban was signed, worried they'd be kicked out of the country, that their parents would. Coming out of a town hall where her congressman, Dave Brat, had talked about why the ban was so good for national security, she'd joked to her husband that she could do a better job. And that was as far as she thought it would go—in this district in Virginia, Brat had shocked politics in Obama's final midterms in 2014 by knocking out Republican majority leader Eric Cantor in a primary, killing any chance of immigration reform.

Then that Obamacare news alert, and a Facebook post from a gay couple with a disabled adopted child she had known for years, asking how much more they were supposed to take. She decided to make good on the joke and run for Congress.

Spanberger became part of a network of veterans, national security experts, and other service alumni who were already starting to reach out to one another over the summer. Pelosi was telling people she knew early on that this was the group that would win enough seats to give Democrats the majority. And she wasn't the only one feeling confident.

"I'm here today because this is one of those pivotal moments when every one of us as citizens of the United States need to determine just who we are, what it is that we stand for," Obama said that September, finally uncorking on Trump.

"As a fellow citizen, not as an ex-president, I'm here to deliver a simple message, which is that you need to vote, because our democracy depends on it."

And what a relief, after two years of holding himself in, to channel the anger burning in every Democrat for two years. "The closer," Perez called him in a rally in Miami the Friday afternoon before the election.

He was very, very happy to talk about health care. Constantly moved it up and expanded it in the speeches his aides would prepare. He always believed it would prove to be a winning message. Finally, it was. No more defense. When Republicans claimed they would protect preexisting conditions, Obama said in Miami, they had "some kind of gall, some kind of chutzpah.

"It's a lie," he stressed. "They're lying to you."

More requests for appearances came in than Obama's team had been expecting. Aides overlaid them with polls and demographics to determine where he was the strongest, then tracked them against the handful of days on his calendar set aside for politics, amid his paid speaking appearances, writing his book, and golf games. They looked for any overlaps with state legislature candidates, adding a couple of races that he should do even though they were probably lost causes, like campaigning in the governors' races in Florida for Andrew Gillum and in Georgia for Stacey Abrams, because that was part of the process of building up future leaders.

Pelosi's staff had been calling three, four times a week, trying to squeeze out more stops. Harry Reid phoned to lean on him to come to Nevada, and Obama knew he couldn't say no. Toward the end of the campaigning, Schumer called Obama armed with stats and data to insist he could be the margin in the Senate race in Indiana they were hoping to save, if he'd just show up in Gary, right across the state line from Chicago, the Sunday before the election. Obama relented, dropping in on the way to his final rally, back home in Chicago.

"What we have not seen before, at least in my lifetime, are politicians who are blatantly, repeatedly, baldly, shamelessly lying," Obama told the crowd at that last rally. "I mean, just no shame."

On the plane between stops, Obama stressed. Were people turning out for him, or for these candidates? "Does me being there in person in this day and age help as much as we think it helps?" He could feel the energy, but those last few days on the trail in 2016 for Clinton were still eating at him. Did anyone care about the Democrats or what they were talking about, or were they just coming to see the celebrity, the way that people kept buying tickets to Bob Dylan shows long after his voice was shot and he mumbled through songs, too arthritic to play guitar anymore?

The question felt resolved on election night.

———

Randi Weingarten had spent most of October on the road. Since Labor Day, she had been to thirty cities in eighteen states. Early on the morning of Election Day, she was kneeling on the floor of a campaign office in Troy, Michigan, hands clasped, joking that this was a strange pose for a union president. She wanted to thank the volunteers for their efforts. "In the last twenty years, there has been a sense of, 'Who cares? Why do we have to vote?'" Weingarten said. "This year feels different. It feels different in Michigan. It feels different around the country, it really feels different in the Midwest. We know part of the reason is Donald Trump, but part of the reason is candidates like Haley Stevens." She looked back at Stevens, then thirty-five, who'd been a member of the Obama administration group that had helped save the auto industry, then moved back home after Trump was elected to start running for a Republican-held House seat herself.

Weingarten was in her blue American Federation of Teachers T-shirt with the slogan they had come up with in those rough days of the transition: "We Care. We Fight. We Show Up. We Vote." "You are the evangelists, who get through that hate, who get through that despair," Weingarten told them. "Do everything you can today, as if our lives depend on it—because frankly, they do."

Weingarten flew back to New York. She likes to vote in person, on the machines. That night she rented a suite at the Hilton in midtown Manhattan. Four different rooms, four different networks on the televisions, friends and other union officials wandering around. The first big race call that came in was Gillum's loss, which felt like a gut punch. The last time a Democrat was elected governor in Florida was 1994, when Jeb Bush lost the first time, but Democrats had shined themselves up to believing that Gillum was going to win. Then the other governors races came in, ones that the teachers union had pushed hard on, for the sake of pushing back on Trump, and for the sake of their own interests in contract negotiations. Pennsylvania. Michigan. New Mexico. Colorado. Kansas. Wisconsin, for an extra gratifying victory over labor-busting Scott Walker. Haley Stevens won, flipping her seat, helping flip the House, becoming her state's first millennial in Congress. In the 2014 midterms, thirty-five million people voted for Democrats. In the 2018 midterms, fifty-nine million people voted for Democrats.

"Politics is not for the faint of heart," Weingarten said, thinking back on that night at what Trump was saying and doing, all the talk of migrant caravans, which magically disappeared from the conversation in the days after the election. "Having a president who is so disassociated with the truth and who doesn't care—this is what autocrats do, this is what demons do, this is not what democratically elected presidents do."

In Michigan, the Democrats held their main party at the MotorCity Casino Hotel in Detroit, in a very different mood than when the state had tipped for Trump by 10,704 votes two years earlier. The women at the top of the ticket had ridden there together in the afternoon on a campaign bus: Gretchen Whitmer, running for governor, was sipping from her red water bottle with the Wonder Woman logo on it. Debbie Stabenow, running for her fourth term as senator, was touching up her lipstick and her puff of red hair. Dana Nessel, who was keeping to herself behind the pile of boxed salads in a seat next to her wife, was finishing off her first-ever run for office in an attorney general campaign that was inspired both as a reaction to MeToo revelations ("Who can you trust most not to show you their penis in a professional setting? Is it the candidate who doesn't have a penis?" she'd said in her first ad) and the president himself. "If Donald Trump can be president of the United States, then I sure as hell can be Michigan attorney general, right? I'm not less qualified for my job than he is for his," she recalled later.

"We need a Democratic fight song we can all agree on," Whitmer said. Stabenow leaned forward in her seat. "This is my fight song," she started to sing, moving her hands with each word of the lyrics that Hillary Clinton's campaign had tried so hard to use to make her look cool. "No!" a bunch of the young aides shouted. Beyoncé came on, but only until Whitmer got her first pick: Lizzo's "Good as Hell." The younger aides were surprised she knew it. "I do my hair toss," Whitmer mouthed and tossed her hair, "Check my nails," and spread her fingers on both hands, looking down at the red polish.

There they were, about to ride a blue tsunami off the Great Lakes: a former state senator with a simple "Fix the Damn Roads" slogan, a woman who should have been ripe for picking off as a proud Queen Bee of the DC establishment, and a lefty Jewish lesbian who had never run for office before.

Whitmer had decided to run on election night 2016, watching the results with her daughters. "Mom," one asked her, "are we going to be OK?" She didn't know how to answer, so she told them she'd do something about it. Her first major appearance as a candidate had been headlining the satellite Women's March in 2017 near the state capitol in Lansing. She started off being made out to be the mini-Clinton, matched up against a thirty-year-old doctor named Abdul El-Sayed, and running a very Sanders-inspired, youth-centric campaign. Sanders and Alexandria Ocasio-Cortez, who had instantly become a progressive sensation from the moment of her upset primary win over a high-ranking incumbent that June in New York, had both come to Michigan to campaign for him. He went on to lose the primary by 22 points and immediately pledged to support her against a Republican candidate who'd started out Trumpish and become fully Trump-y. "All of us learned the lesson of 2016," El-Sayed had said the afternoon of the election.

In Washington that night, Pelosi came out onstage, wearing a purple suit, to chants of, "Speaker! Speaker! Speaker!" She said she wanted to "salute" Perez from the stage, though, at first, he hadn't been invited to the party. "Remember this feeling," she said after introducing all eleven members of her leadership team. "Know the power to win."

The feeling Pelosi wanted them to remember, she said later, was of taking pride in starting to reclaim power from Trump, but also of recognizing that when thirty-one of the forty seats that flipped to give Democrats the majority were in districts that Trump had won in 2016, there was only so much to celebrate.

"What we were winning was fragile, because he wasn't on the ballot and the next time he would be on the ballot," she said. "I never underestimated him at the polls."

This time Obama spent election night at home, in the living room of his new house around the corner from the one Jared Kushner and Ivanka Trump had rented. He read the email updates about each batch of races, emailing back with how the results in some districts compared to how he'd done in his runs in 2008 and 2012. He was watching the House majority projection percentages online, asking why the needles were moving up, moving down.

Democrats took the House. He was thrilled. Was it a wave? Maybe. Hard to tell as they went to sleep that night.

It wasn't hard to tell by morning. Keep focused on the wave, he told a few aides who'd gotten wrapped up in hoping for Abrams and Gillum, chasing the dream of Beto O'Rourke taking out Ted Cruz in Texas. It sucked, he said, that they didn't win, but everyone had known those were stretches.

"Well," Paulette Aniskoff said to him, "we won."

"*That* is right," Obama said. "We won."

The celebration lasted about twenty-four hours.

After Trump fired James Comey from the FBI, Obama's aides had prepared a few drafts of statements they figured they should have a head start on. Better to think about what to say in advance, while they were calm, if Trump did something like fire Bob Mueller, than to start worrying about wording when the American government was already on fire.

Somehow they had never really believed that Trump would fire Jeff Sessions. Obviously, they had seen all of Trump's movie mobster tweets hounding his attorney general. Yet Obama and those closest to him still held out hope, wanting to think that it couldn't actually be this bad. But Trump lashed out after losing. He didn't care that Sessions had been his first and most committed supporter in Congress. All that mattered to him was that Sessions had stopped short of a clear violation of ethics, and potentially the law, by recusing himself in the Russia probe, clearing the way for Mueller's appointment as special counsel.

Sessions's firing began a panic. Trump's Saturday night massacre, it appeared, was starting on a Thursday morning.

Denis McDonough said it was time to pull the trigger on confronting Trump. Put out a statement, the usually even-keeled but dark-minded former White House chief of staff insisted. If they didn't take a stand now, Trump would just keep going, and Mueller would be gone next. "When you see some of those things that you thought were pretty well set in concrete, going back into the post-Watergate world, you definitely go on alert," McDonough remembered, and recalled Obama being as concerned as he was. Other Obama advisers hesitated.

Quietly Obama aides reached out to George W. Bush's office. What if they put out a joint statement, a Republican and a Democrat, two presidents who had both hired Mueller as FBI director—Bush initially, and then Obama when he extended Mueller's term? They could avoid getting directly involved in anything regarding Sessions, but use it as a moment to speak up for Mueller's integrity and the importance of the special counsel, and try to block what was probably coming next.

Bush's aides weren't interested—dismayed as he was with Trump, he was still determined to stay out of politics—so Obama stayed quiet too.

———

Organizing for Action had been flailing since the win preserving Obamacare in 2017, with no clear sense of its mission. OFA's executive director, Katie Hogan, who had worked her way up after starting as a junior press aide in Obama's first campaign, had flown to Washington that spring to meet with him, ask for some guidance figuring out the next step. Obama gave her a capsule version of his argument that Democrats needed to win the House to save America, told her he wanted the group to shift into doing whatever they could to help achieve that—though OFA was a nonprofit, and had been specifically oriented away from campaign politics for its entire existence. Obama left it to OFA to figure out how to proceed, or how to raise money, but he didn't offer to chip in on either front himself.

With the midterms done and the House won, Obama and his advisers knew they didn't want OFA to engage in the issues that would define 2020— the Green New Deal, Medicare for All, and any others that might suggest he was endorsing them in the presidential primary process. They knew if they didn't engage in those fights, OFA would be effectively pointless. Just before Christmas, Obama announced on a call with OFA members that he was pulling the plug. The experiment had failed. He'd fold what was left into Eric Holder's redistricting group and give it a punny new name: All on the Line. "People want commonsense gun safety laws, Congress ignores it. People want comprehensive immigration reform, Congress ignores it," Obama said, trying to persuade his supporters to focus on the much less sexy process of electing state senators.

"If you say, 'The Obama legacy will then be focused on redistricting,'" Holder remarked on the afternoon of the announcement, "that's the mechanism by which the things the Obama presidency were about will be preserved."

———

In mid-March 2018, Biden had gone to Capitol Hill to meet with two dozen members of the Blue Collar Caucus—a group founded after the 2016 election by Brendan Boyle, a congressman from a white working-class district on the edge of Philadelphia, and Marc Veasey, from a largely Black working-class district splotched in a gerrymandered mess between Fort Worth and Dallas. "If we don't win the House, Trump is there for eight years," Biden said. He could see that he got the attention of the members of Congress. "I'm serious," he told them. "So, no pressure."

In December, after the Democrats had indeed won the House, Boyle went to see Biden at his office on the Senate side of the Hill. This time, he was delivering a warning to someone who already agreed with it. "If Donald Trump wins a second term, America won't be the country that your ancestors and my ancestors wanted to come to," Boyle told him. They talked about how many Obama–Trump voters there were in Pennsylvania. He remembers saying, "I urge you to run," and joking, "Sorry for more pressure."

Boyle had been a Biden booster since he ignited a news cycle meltdown in October 2015 by tweeting, "I have a very good source close to Joe that tells me VP Biden will run for Prez." Despite being wrong, he hadn't come back off that limb in the years since. Think about the Blue Collar Caucus pitch, Boyle told Biden. With the exception of Obama, who'd solidified the support of the nonwhite voters, every Democratic nominee had been the candidate to appeal to the white working class, winning the primaries against the candidate of the well-educated, affluent progressive white voter. Walter Mondale beat Gary Hart. Michael Dukakis beat a field of more elite candidates. Bill Clinton beat Paul Tsongas. Al Gore beat Bill Bradley. Even John Kerry turned into Everyman to beat Howard Dean. And Hillary Clinton beat Bernie Sanders.

Ignore the speculation playing out on Twitter, Boyle said: "You know who's not on Twitter? My dad."

Biden listened. He'd just been all over the country campaigning, less buzzy but more in demand than anyone else, and he liked what he'd seen. By now his family was on board. They were excited. He was about 60 percent of the way to yes, he told Boyle.

———

Obama formally celebrated the midterm wins by meeting with the new House freshmen at the home of a big Democratic donor in Washington, DC, at the end of March 2019. By that time, they had been sworn in amid a government shutdown, when Trump, backed into a corner, had asserted a national emergency to seize funding for a border wall that wasn't getting built and that he never ended up following through on. By then, the story of 2018 had already been rewritten, and it wasn't about Spanberger or any of the other Democrats who'd won back the majority, or about protecting Obamacare, or the rise of suburban women as a powerful voting bloc. A week after the election, in DC for freshman orientation, Ocasio-Cortez had joined 150 young activists from the youth climate group Sunrise Movement who were staging a sit-in in Pelosi's office. "What is your plan?" read the plain orange printouts they held up. They were demanding that Pelosi name a select committee on climate change, and when they realized she had already said she would, shifted to demanding that it contain specific conditions.

Ocasio-Cortez was a member of "the Squad," four younger women of color who had won Democratic primaries in heavily Democratic districts and were determined to be the out-front leaders of the new Sanders-style, aggressive progressivism that they were certain most of the country wanted, at least based on what they could see their friends tweeting about. Now, in addition to Medicare for All, there was the Green New Deal for easily sorting who was in and who was out.

"All of a sudden, it was like all the air went to a type of politics that I don't ascribe to. We had just spent literally a year and a half talking about health care and restoring function to our government. And then all of a sudden it was like all of these policies that we hadn't begun to talk about. I certainly talked about environmental issues in my district, but it was green jobs and solar panel installation," said Spanberger, who had been getting more and more annoyed about the wins like hers being eclipsed over those months.

Yet for all this noise, and all the major Democratic presidential campaigns other than Biden's that had already launched by the time Obama arrived to talk to the freshmen members, he was still the one they were excited to see.

"Four more years!" someone in the audience called out when Pelosi, who retained the position of Speaker despite having lost the votes of a few of the freshmen in that room, introduced him.

"Thank you," Obama said with a smile, quieting the joke. "There's one president who believes in the Constitution."

The group he saw before him—diverse, young, new to politics, and already full of stars on the rise—was proof to Obama that his theory of stepping back had proved correct. Few of these people would be there, he figured, if he had listened to the voices complaining he wasn't doing enough and making the last two years a constant cage match between him and Trump.

He had made progressives excited when he had said in that speech kicking off his midterm campaigning in September that some Democrats were "running on good new ideas like Medicare for All, giving workers seats on corporate boards, reversing the most egregious corporate tax cuts to make sure college students graduate debt-free." Don't get him wrong, Obama said. But also don't get the voters wrong. Don't forget, he was not so subtly slipping in, that the freshmen getting the most attention as the big bold progressives had flipped 90 percent Democratic districts. And don't forget that Sanders's Our Revolution group had flopped in almost every race it touched and managed to blow up relationships with potential allies, like refusing to endorse John Fetterman, a committed progressive who looked as if he could be the bouncer at a biker bar, in the race for Pennsylvania lieutenant governor, which he won.

Learn from how voters responded, Obama urged them, frustrating as it might be. "We shouldn't be under illusions about the fact that there is an asymmetry: the other side can get away with just cutting taxes and not paying for it. But actually, the voters in your district, generally, there's something, they don't believe in free lunch, so if there's something that you say you're going to give them, they kind of want to know, 'Well, how are you going to pay for it?' They have a responsibility gene that apparently doesn't apply to the folks who create trillion-dollar deficits," Obama said. "I don't think we should assume that just because somebody professes to believe in being a true progressive, but if you then said, 'Oh, but your taxes are going to go up 20 percent,' that they automatically sign on. So we have to be honest about that."

Two of those new Democrats who had flipped Republican seats—Haley Stevens from Michigan and Colin Allred from Texas—were both alumni of his administration and the elected presidents of their freshman class. (These titles don't mean much beyond granting them the right to ask questions at events like these, which they did.) The world had changed, they told the group. Politics had too. And by the time they were running for reelection for the first time in 2020, "this campaign's going to actually have President Trump on the ballot," Allred reminded them, "and so we'd like to talk to you about your thought about keeping a positive message while trying to deliver on the kind of ideas that you ran off of: change."

Obama admitted that his own 2008 campaign wouldn't have worked in the politics of this new moment. "You know, I'm proud of the speech I gave in 2004 where I talked about there are no red states and blue states—that was an aspirational statement. It wasn't a description of reality," Obama said. "I would not give that speech now because it doesn't speak to our current time and place. People would be like, 'Well, yeah, that's not really true.'"

Watching the presidential race get started, he empathized with how the candidates were struggling to figure out how to campaign against Trump as a Manichaean evil while also acknowledging that he was a rational outgrowth of how thrown Americans were by decades of failing politics. "How do we confront a resurgence of racist or misogynist attitudes? How do we confront things that we thought were no longer acceptable but have been made acceptable again?" Obama asked. "How do we deal with the fact that, despite all of the extraordinary efforts that Nancy and I and others made to make sure that we didn't have a second depression, we weren't able—in part because we only had two years—to deal with some of the structural inequalities that are in the economy, and that have gotten worse since that time?"

He wasn't naive, he pointed out. He also wasn't giving in, even though he felt himself longing for the days when at least he could agree with John McCain that torture was bad and climate change was real.

He didn't feel the same anger, couldn't make sense of the anger, and the anger worried him in some ways more than what was causing the anger.

"It's not going to solve all your problems, but if every time you say something, folks get a sense, 'You know what? That person, I think they care about me and I think they're trying to do the right thing,' they will cut you some slack when your position does not perfectly align with theirs," Obama said. "Now look, I want to make sure that I'm not having all of you go to the front of the Capitol and set yourself on fire."

CHAPTER SEVEN

DEMOCRAT X

It was the best of times, it was the worst of times. I've got an awesome kid, a job I don't hate, and everything is kinda looking up . . . but also the planet is on fire and I've gotta make sure my daughter knows how engines work in case she needs to do some *Mad Max* shit after whatever logical postapocalyptic scenario we've laid out for the next generation plays out.

—UNDECIDED WISCONSIN WOMAN, LISTED AS CAUCASIAN, AGE 18–34, INTERVIEWED IN A DNC SURVEY OF POLITICAL FEELINGS GOING INTO 2020

December 2018–March 2019

The setup was like one of those meeting-of-the-families gatherings from a mob movie, except a cartoon version: early evening at the Four Seasons Hotel in Washington, DC, just at the edge of Georgetown, on December 12, 2018. A room in the back, off the lobby, just outside the good line of sight from the Bourbon Steak restaurant. Invitations had gone out from Bernard Schwartz, a Democratic donor who wrote big enough checks that every Democratic insider takes his call. Each guest arrived separately.

The day before, Nancy Pelosi had sideswiped the president in the Oval Office during their first postmidterms meeting and coined "Trump shutdown" for the budget crisis he was forcing out of pique to get funding for his border wall, then strode confidently out of the office in her instantly iconic red coat, which she'd originally bought for Obama's second inauguration. A few hours before the dinner, Pelosi had formally ended the challenge of a few of her own renegade members, locking up the votes to be Speaker of the House again. They cheered and applauded when she walked into the Four Seasons meeting. She was seated near Chuck Schumer, still minority leader and now with three fewer seats. Terry McAuliffe sat at the other end, though he was no longer governor of Virginia or anything official. Delaware senator Chris Coons, who worked hard to be viewed as Biden's most devoted acolyte, had a seat, as did the heads of all the big Democratic groups: Guy Cecil, who ran the major super PAC Priorities USA. Neera Tanden of the Center for American Progress. Stephanie Schriock, president of EMILY's List. David Rolf from SEIU. Nick Hanauer, the party power player and venture capitalist who'd signed on to economic populism. Mack McLarty, Bill Clinton's first White House chief of staff, and now a lobbyist. Congressman Ted Lieu, a dorky local politician from Los Angeles who had found his voice as a Trump Twitter troll. Congressman Eric Swalwell—also from California, young and making a name for himself by appearing on every cable interview he could to discuss the Russia investigations— was there as the voice of the next generation. So was Pete Buttigieg, before most people in the room even knew who he was.

The topic: How do we put guardrails on the primary?

The subtext might as well have been blocked out in glitter on a banner up on the wall: the donors had brought these people together because they wanted to make sure the party didn't stumble into choosing Bernie Sanders—or almost as bad, Elizabeth Warren—as the nominee.

The more measured version: the organizers said they wanted to talk about Democrats' message for 2020, how to deal with what was clearly going to be a huge primary field, how to learn the lessons from 2018 about how they actually won seats. No one who represented anyone near the progressive wing of the party was put on the guest list. That's who the donors who had organized the dinner wanted to stop.

Schriock, Cecil, and Tanden kept interrupting the conversation. Guardrails? What sort of guardrails were any of them trying to believe in? Who was going to enforce these guardrails? The primary was going to be huge. Anything they tried to do to steer it would probably backfire, and they would probably be found out and embarrassed first.

Maybe, Schumer suggested, they could get the candidates to agree to a pact to not attack one another.

At the far end of the table McAuliffe stood up, as he did every time he spoke, and said, "Good fucking luck with that." (McAuliffe insists he wouldn't curse in front of Pelosi, but others in the room remember distinctly how well he cut through all the bloviating, and how hard everyone laughed when he did.) "No one's going to agree to that, and nor should they, because it's a good thing. You need to be attacked. You want to wait until the fall against Donald Trump to see if your nominee can handle a punch?"

McAuliffe was serious enough about running for president himself at that point that he was doing polling. Buttigieg was five days away from announcing he wasn't running for another term as mayor of South Bend, Indiana, step one of his launching the presidential campaign that everyone thought was nuts. He and Swalwell were both headed to Iowa a few days later.

As tends to happen when Democrats get together to try to set an agenda, they didn't get much of anywhere. Multiple attendees around the table started texting aides and spouses, mockingly reporting what was happening in real time. McAuliffe and Schumer started arguing about trade, McAuliffe insisting that the Democrats had veered too protectionist, had collapsed under progressive talking points without thinking through the consequences. "You have never been in a trade deal. You've never been on the other side of the table," McAuliffe said, rising to his feet again. "Until you guys are actually on the other side of the table, you put up these walls that make it hard for us to do our job." Schumer fired right back at him, his voice hitting a higher pitch. Voters didn't trust the Democrats on this. They needed to adjust, be smart. That was about as deep as the conversation got, and as productive. Then, mistaking Buttigieg for Swalwell, Schumer asked him about a House vote the following day. Pelosi zeroed in on Buttigieg's minipresentation on engaging millennials.

The dinner was long, and eventually everyone had had enough. Shortly after nine p.m. they started to leave individually, the planners swept up in protecting how secret the event was supposed to be.

"That dinner," Cecil recalled years later, "was the last gasp of people who thought they had control, losing it."

———

"Running for president is like having sex," Clinton political strategist James Carville once told *New York Times* columnist Maureen Dowd. "Nobody does it once and forgets about it."

The early 2020 maneuverings were more like a bunch of horny high schoolers counting down to prom night.

Tim Kaine became the rare vice presidential nominee who didn't enter the next presidential race. He was determined that the party shouldn't nominate another white guy, hoping that the nominee would be a woman. There was no obvious next natural nominee.

Everyone who considered getting into the race shared shades of the same four concerns, each soaked in his or her particular brew of ego, self-doubt, ambition, and patriotism. *What if I'm the only one who can beat Trump?* they'd ask themselves. He had to go, America needed him out of the White House, and *maybe*, each one would ask him- or herself, *I'm somehow exactly the candidate who would take him down.* But then—*What if I get in the way of the only person who* can *beat Trump?* What if they finished the election feeling as they imagined Sanders should have felt in 2016? The introspection turned personal: *What hell would Trump and company unleash on me if I run?* Running for president is always hard, but this was going to be much, much worse. Fair play was a fantasy. Above the belt was a joke. This was going to get dirty in every possible way, with collateral damage to family and friends a given, and for what? *How terrible will it be to be faced with cleaning up this mess in 2021, and how destined will I be to fail?*

Two days before Trump's inauguration, Eric Garcetti was in Washington meeting with reporters and national operatives, deliberately churning chatter about how the mayor of Los Angeles might be interested in running for president. He flew back to LA on January 19. He avoided making any TV appearances on Inauguration Day. He was out on the streets back home for the Women's March on January 21.

"I think the rules have changed, absolutely. And these categories are artificial," Garcetti said that April, dismissing the traditional thinking about politics. "Does a governor of a state of three million have more experience than a mayor of a city of four million? I mean, we've got the sixth-largest economy—in California—in the world. We've got the seventeenth-largest in Los Angeles, if it was an independent country.

"It's not an issue of experience. I think, 'What does this country need? Who will they need?' And I trust voters. They respond to the right people at the right moments," he added.

Ambition took on the feeling of philosophical searching. What was America now? How much did Trump expose about its character, how much had he already changed it? How wrong had Democrats been on everything? How should one deal with the Obama legacy—running as the bridge back to sanity, or arguing that his policies hadn't worked?

At a salon-style dinner at a restaurant in midtown Manhattan in September 2017, Andrew Yang, an entrepreneur behind a group called Venture for America, said he wanted to speak. Months of having become obsessed with the idea of universal basic income poured out of him. He'd written a book on the subject and wanted to write another. He'd been studying up on the economy, and was overwhelmed by the devastation he had learned about in the Midwest. He had reached out to Andy Stern, the former Service Employees International Union president, and asked him to lunch at a Chinese restaurant. Did he know anyone who was going to put universal basic income (UBI) into a presidential platform? No, Stern told him. He went to an event hosted by Facebook multimillionaire Chris Hughes on UBI hoping to find a candidate there. He didn't. "If another smart guy published a book, it would have near zero impact," Yang remembers thinking, as his ideas developed. "You can pretend to yourself that publishing a book is going to make a huge difference in the world."

At the restaurant that night, he had all the basics of a pitch he would build up over the next two and a half years. Automation was defining the future. The destruction of the American worker was why Donald Trump won. We were living through the fourth industrial revolution. "And," he announced, "I'm running for president in 2020."

"Of America?" someone asked.

"Of the United States," he said. "As a Democrat."

Zach Graumann was a recent college grad working in corporate giving at a large bank, chasing a dream of being in the circuit of whoever was doing the next big thing. He told Yang he wanted to work on the campaign. Yang had never run a campaign before. How about being his campaign manager? Graumann had never run a campaign before either, so he gave himself a crash course by reading David Plouffe's book about managing Obama's 2008 campaign and Corey Lewandowski's about managing Trump's 2016 campaign. From Plouffe, he took away the lesson of building a campaign that was perfect on branding and mechanics. From Lewandowski, he learned about not getting in the way of the candidate's personality. A reporter who had taken an early interest in Yang suggested that he was the opposite of Trump, and Yang turned that into a joke at a rally that night, saying, "the opposite of Donald Trump is an Asian who likes math." They looked at Trump's signature red MAGA caps and placed their first order for dark blue MATH caps. A staffer spotted a supporter tweet with the #YangGang hashtag. There was concern that this would make them sound like thugs. "We won't have to do Yang Gang if you guys can come up with something better," Graumann told them. No one did. Yang Gang stuck.

Then there was Michael Avenatti, the shaved-bald, wall-toothed trial lawyer who became a cable news fixture for representing Stormy Daniels, the porn star paid hush money by Trump to hide their affair. He had convinced himself that his money and TV time made him a ladies' man, and that his shouting sessions on Fox News over Daniels, and the Twitter following it gave him, made him something of a political Doogie Howser. By September 2018, he was already back from what he promised would be his *first* campaign trip to Iowa, sitting in a Starbucks with a view of the White House around the corner, getting noticed through the window as he showed off all the invitations coming into his phone.

"This is not about nominating the person who would make the best president of the United States and then hoping that person can beat Donald Trump. This is about beating Donald Trump," he said. "This is a new age."

He was mostly caught up in what he was going to say on Tucker Carlson's show on Fox that night, and what he had planned afterward in his room at the luxury Jefferson Hotel up the block. "There's a dearth of leadership in the Democratic Party," he said. "I can't beat John Kasich. This is about matchups."

But yes, Avenatti said, he could totally imagine himself sitting behind the desk in the Oval Office. Obviously.

Tap-dancing dragons would have been less fantastical than what was going on in some corners of the party at that point. Anyone could win! "That's the magic of it," Jeff Merkley, a progressive, awkward senator from Oregon said, with a smirk that was trying to be conviction, sitting at the back of a burger bar near Capitol Hill. Merkley had thought about running in 2016, and regretted that he hadn't, because he would have been the progressive check on Clinton without causing the longer term damage to her campaign. Dragging himself around to New Hampshire, Iowa, and South Carolina through 2018 was part self-imposed penance, part feeling the swoon against reality himself.

"I'm not too junior, but I'm not too senior," said Eric Swalwell, sitting in a different Starbucks, this one down the hill from Union Station, a few weeks later, squinting to imagine his lane in the race. What had started with an exasperated joke two years earlier—"If Donald Trump wins, we're running for president," he'd told his political team in October 2016—had hooked into his brain and started to seem like a good idea, like considering getting a tattoo during a long night of drinking. He had been on Fox News more than anyone else thinking about running. And his family was full of Republicans, though they didn't want him to run. And he was thinking about Watergate, though he hadn't been alive when Watergate happened, and how politics needed to turn to a new generation.

"I don't think it's a winning argument to be Obama's third term—and I think a lot of people will be running for that," Swalwell said. The race should be a "big, bold canvas, to paint something new."

The next morning, at a fancier table with about the same quality coffee at the Hay-Adams Hotel, across Lafayette Park from the White House, Maryland congressman John Delaney was burnishing his own sense of Somehow This Could Work. Delaney had grown up the son of a union electrician in New Jersey, started two companies that had made him enough millions to retire early and run for a seat in Congress, grew bored sitting in the minority, and had announced he was running for president in July 2017 because he still had money to burn. For three years, he would vacillate between grimly acknowledging that what he was doing was absurd and being annoyed that it was being perceived as such.

"What frustrates me is, the media wants to build a narrative about where the Democratic Party is going, because that's the story they want to tell,"

Delaney insisted, arguing, "if I would have announced in January 2019, I would not have a path to viability.

"I'm perfectly suited to do the job," he said. "The challenge I have is to get people to vote for the person who's perfectly suited to do the job."

Being ignored was the great equalizer, even for those who, but for one twist of history, would have been in an entirely different spot.

In 2016, Clinton's campaign had printed four sets of signs for her four prospective vice presidential finalists. Just a few of each, so that they could get a sense of what the potential logos might look like, and to have them ready to wave at the first event, whenever it would come, wherever it would be. Aides secretly laid them out in a room in her Brooklyn headquarters: Clinton–Tim Kaine: the white guy who'd be an able but supple number two. Clinton–Tom Vilsack: the former Iowa governor, and agriculture secretary who was a few notches whiter and more boring than Kaine. Clinton–John Hickenlooper: the Colorado governor, who at best was weird in a completely noninteresting way (once, spotting a dime on the sidewalk, he picked it up and said with genuine enthusiasm, "That's ten times as lucky as finding a penny!"), but could maybe help her lock up a few states she needed. Clinton–Cory Booker: the dynamic young Black senator from New Jersey who could put a crowd on its feet in a way she had always been jealous of, and who could remind people of the bridge back to Obama and that there was more excitement on the horizon.

Booker lived on a low-income block in Newark, New Jersey, up the hill past Martin Luther King Jr. Boulevard with the Manhattan skyline visible just over the rooftops, and talked of love and racial understanding and being friends with Chris Christie. Maybe the perfect antidote to Trump—maybe way too much. He was a vegan who'd have extended conversations about how he couldn't wrap his mind around whether to allow himself to eat eggs, who had stacks of Talmud books in his office on Capitol Hill, who loved *Star Trek* and dated as many women as he could. Eric Garcetti—whom Booker had known since 1993, when he welcomed the future mayor to the dorms at Oxford, a year ahead of him on his Rhodes Scholarship—used to tease him. If he was going to run, Garcetti would say, he'd have to either get married or start eating meat, because he was already asking a lot of America.

He did neither. But he and his closest aide, Matt Klapper, slowly built the groundwork for a campaign they dreamed of as being that of the new Jimmy

Carter, who came in after Nixon and Watergate promising calm and uplift. In 2017 and 2018, he was the most active guest star at political events around the country and giving way too many hours of time to whichever reporter wanted to profile him. The plan for 2019 was to start small and focus on Iowa, then follow Obama's model in 2008, and slingshot a caucus win toward the nomination.

He was supposed to arrive in Des Moines on the first Thursday in October. Then it was moved to Friday. Then Saturday. In a career that's been both ridiculously lucky and orchestrated to the point of seeming contrived, he ended up on the ground about an hour before he was due onstage, straight from the Brett Kavanaugh confirmation vote to the Iowa Democratic Party dinner, courtesy of a flight on a private plane.

"There's nothing I can affect tomorrow. And in the Trump world, I hate to say this, we don't know what next week will look like. I'm staying focused the best I can," Booker said the next morning, sitting at a coffee shop in downtown Des Moines, between being stopped for selfies. A few minutes later, he was heading to a three-hour church service at the old congregation to which his grandmother—a bona fide Des Moines native whose family had come from Alabama to mine coal in nearby Buxton—had once belonged.

Trump, Booker said, is "a variable in this equation that is uncontrollable."

Anthony Kennedy hadn't yet retired when Booker was planning his trip to Iowa. Christine Blasey Ford hadn't yet come forward to delay the confirmation vote that Democrats always knew they were going to lose. Booker didn't know that he was going to be making his presidential debut on Democrats' darkest night since Trump won.

"I heard some laughter, but it wasn't from the Lord," Booker had told the crowd. "I heard a president mock and laugh and jeer at a survivor for telling her story. I heard cheers and joy coming after a vote pushed a nominee forward."

He would have done pretty much the same routine no matter when, because that's what he does: method performances of emotions lived out fresh onstage at each appearance, moments from his life stamped into parables of the New Age-y Gospel of Cory, each one introduced with "I want to tell you a story. . . ."

No one left his speeches with any clue where Booker stood on almost any issue, aside from a riff that talked about the Democratic commitment to

Medicaid, Medicare, voting rights, civil rights, LGBTQ rights. ("The party of people who believe that someone who is nice to you but is not nice to the waiter is not a nice person.") But they did walk out saying things like, "I *so* needed that today."

Everything for Booker goes back to the civil rights movement, John Lewis, and the march across the Edmund Pettus Bridge in Selma. He learned later in life that a lawyer who happened to be watching *Judgment at Nuremberg* that night in 1965 when the broadcast was interrupted to show the troopers attacking the marchers was so inspired by the sight that he got into civil rights work. He wound up being the attorney who helped his own parents prove housing discrimination in a sting operation in which they all took part. In most speeches, Booker just told the part of the story that ended at the bridge. That night in Des Moines, he pulled another quote, from when the marchers got to the Alabama capitol and Martin Luther King Jr. spoke to them.

"How long will justice be crucified, and the truth have to bear it?" he quoted King saying. "How long? Not long. Because the truth, crushed to the earth, will rise again."

Booker turned it on the crowd, mostly white except for the five tables of his cousins and other family that filled out part of the room.

"How long will we respond to their hatred with love? How long will it take? Well, I'm going to tell you, not long now," Booker said, and they were all on their feet, cheering. "How long until we answer the president's hate with our universal love? How long?"

They shouted back, "Not long!" His fourth standing ovation in forty-seven minutes.

———

A few days later, Tom Perez sat in a chair in his office at Democratic National Committee headquarters, where the signs pointing to the restrooms were photocopied shots of former Trump press secretary Sean Spicer's head with arrows drawn on his forehead. As a lawyer, Perez specialized in suing police departments and jurisdictions that attempted voter suppression, but at heart he's a political romantic with a touch of impostor syndrome, despite having been a cabinet secretary and now the chair of the party. Almost any conversation will lead to Perez's recalling something that Ted Kennedy taught him when he was a young Senate aide. He never got over being intimidated by Obama, which meant he wouldn't say anything about how he'd stew privately about the former president's disappearing from the DNC, despite his promises of assistance when he lured Perez into the job.

"We had a fairy dust model of government. All's you had to say was 'Barack Obama,' and the fairy dust would come down, and you'd win elections," Perez said. "That's not how you win elections."

He was clearly annoyed that Alexandria Ocasio-Cortez was getting more attention than Fred Hubbell, running for governor of Iowa that fall, or Tony Evers, running for governor of Wisconsin, or even Stacey Abrams, then running for governor of Georgia. "I look at the aggregate data, and there's a remarkable pragmatism," he said, arguing that primary voters were often choosing candidates based on who they believed could win, rather than ideology.

He couldn't get too excited about who won a primary for a House seat in Queens and the Bronx, when he was supposed to be thinking about the House and Senate majority, and regaining the White House. "This is about arithmetic," he said. They needed to get relevant again. They needed to not get drawn into fights with one another that Republicans were desperate to cheer on—or, in a typical Perez construction that sounded clever in his head and clumsy out of his mouth, they needed to not "confuse unity with unanimity."

He had given in on the Sanders push to get rid of superdelegates at the convention, and had settled on making qualifying for a presidential debate contingent on a Sanders-friendly threshold of attracting online donors. He'd say publicly that his mission was to make the DNC relevant again and privately that it was also to not let the Sanders crowd turn the DNC into a scapegoat for their own failings, and he felt as if he were making progress on handling both the stress of getting blamed, potentially justifiably, for Trump's winning again and the country's collapsing into whatever that would entail. Asked to pick the worst moment of his year and a half as chair so far, he offered, "I can't pick one, because there are so many gut-punch days.

"We could have Donald Trump for four more years," he said, "or we could have Democrat X."

He knew all the Democrats running. He had no idea which one would be

Democrat X, though he had his guesses about who it wouldn't be. All he could come up with to describe that person for certain was whoever had "the best capacity to unite our country."

A few months later, Colorado senator Michael Bennet was sitting on the set of *CBS This Morning*, joking that when he told his mother he was getting into the presidential race, it was because he'd decided it needed a twenty-second candidate, but then he found out he was only the twenty-first. This is the kind of joke that comes out of Bennet, who has a voice that sounds like Bill Murray's and a demeanor more like that of a sedated Chevy Chase. He would never have been on anyone's list of senators likely to run for president. He'd only been appointed to the Senate after Obama had passed him over for education secretary and left a seat open when he'd picked Senator Ken Salazar to be interior secretary. He was smart and personable and came across as finding it great to be a senator. After hearing him speak during his first swing through Iowa, one very active Iowa Democrat said Bennet was like good, hearty pea soup—but still pea soup, when there were sizzling fajitas and cake alongside it on the table. "There's something to that," was Bennet's response. Bennet wasn't deterred by that kind of dismissal, having survived a colon cancer diagnosis that had him on the operating table in the spring. Or by how even several of his colleagues in the Senate didn't realize at first that he was running too.

"Right now, the Democratic Party doesn't stand for very much at the national level with respect to what people think," Bennet said as he announced his run, stretching to make that a justification for why he needed to be in the race. "A process like this is long overdue in the Democratic Party."

The process never really got started. Not once Biden entered the race. Amy Klobuchar would often say in one of her many jokes she'd repeat over and over because she was so proud of them, Biden was like a low-pressure system. "He never rains. He never lifts," she said. "He's always just there."

Kirsten Gillibrand, the New York senator who combined an almost evangelical sense of being called with a sorority president's sense of empowerment and determination that no, they were going to have that party, felt herself being overwhelmed. "She didn't need to see the path to victory to decide to get in," an adviser said early on. "Of course, she would not do it if she thought there was no path." She'd declared her candidacy in January on a set with Stephen Colbert after deciding she wanted to go bigger than a guerrilla announcement by video selfie, but had to rework her plans as other outlets and dates got snapped up by competitors. She was mocked for referring to herself on set as a "young mom" at fifty-two, then drove north to her hometown of Troy, New York, to do whiskey shots at her favorite bar.

By March, Gillibrand was already scrambling for a reset. Her staff came up with what they were convinced was a breakthrough idea: a launch in front of Trump Tower. Except they couldn't get a permit because the building was on Fifth Avenue, surrounded by a constant police blanket. They settled for having the event in front of Trump World Tower, at the southwestern corner of Central Park. Except they couldn't get the permit to put the stage in a place that would allow the actual building to be seen in the background, so they settled for having it off to the side. They were hoping for open TV coverage, by planning it for a Sunday afternoon. Except that the day they picked ended up being the very one that Trump's attorney general, Bill Barr, put out his summary letter of the Mueller report, hoping to preempt its findings of the Russian attack on the 2016 election and the inability to either prove or clear Trump and those close to him from being involved, so she barely got a minute of attention. Gillibrand knew all that; it didn't shake her. Catching sight of Clinton's former communications director Jennifer Palmieri in the crowd at the launch, Gillibrand grabbed her and said how invested she'd felt in her book, *Dear Madame President*, written with the conceit of being an open letter to the first female president about all the challenges she'd face and how to get through them. "It's written to me," she told Palmieri, earnestly.

———

Watching all the contestants struggle was the woman who thought she'd be the first female president, who had beaten Trump by 2.9 million votes, who never got over thinking she'd been robbed. Many of the prospective candidates made their pilgrimages to Hillary Clinton to ask her advice, get her blessing, tick the box. "Remember," she'd joked to Steve Bullock, the governor of Montana at one point, "you can win the whole thing, and still lose the Electoral College." She talked to them, tried to be helpful. Much like Biden, she wasn't convinced any of those who came to see her could get far against Trump.

For a while, this was also giving Clinton a chance to size up herself against the competition. She ordered polling to gauge a 2020 run of her own, routed through another company so that the efforts couldn't be traced back to her. She spoke with a number of Black leaders, concentrated in the South. She wondered if Biden would really be able to pull off a campaign. She talked it over with her husband. They discussed potential campaign staff, especially as other candidates started making hires. They sounded out a few donors, some of whom said they'd support her if she ran. She weighed all that against dividing loyalties among Democrats and doing more damage to her and her husband's reputations. Once the Clintons decided that she and Biden couldn't both run without effectively guaranteeing that Sanders would be the nominee, they backed off.

"It's hard not to come after a loss like that to Donald Trump and not feel you should get back in it again," said one of the people who spoke to her as she was deciding what to do. "It wasn't that she looked around the primary and said, 'Oh my god, I can't beat any of these people,' but more: 'What if I lose to Trump again?'"

Still, the dream lived on. Let's say the whole mess ended with a contested convention, Clinton would muse aloud sometimes. Maybe it's a deadlock, and on the second or third ballot, party leaders decide they need a new option— someone the party might be able to settle on, someone who'd be ready and well enough known to stand up and stand out on short notice.

Well, Clinton said, she would still be available then . . .

CHAPTER EIGHT

WHY NOT?

A man's usefulness depends upon his living up to his ideals insofar as he can.

—TEDDY ROOSEVELT

March 2019–May 2019

M r. Mayor, why did you order the rib tips?"

Chasten Buttigieg was holding out a pen like a microphone, while a cameraman set up the shot in front of the sign for the Elks Lodge. He had the Jif logo tattooed on his arm, because his family was so poor when he was growing up that they knew it was a special treat when his father had enough money to bring home name-brand peanut butter. Chasten had been conflicted about being gay and had ended up connecting over a beer and a South Bend Cubs game with a guy he had met online who happened to be the mayor of their small city, and was now an overnight national political sensation. That afternoon they were about to do a joint interview that would put them on the cover of *Time* as the "First Family."

First MSNBC wanted a live shot, to get the mayor to talk about the latest decision out of the Supreme Court, and about Ro Khanna, the California congressman who'd gone from running as a friend of Silicon Valley in a 2016 primary against an eighteen-year incumbent to being one of Bernie Sanders's national cochairs. Khanna had picked a fight with Buttigieg over how they were talking about income inequality.

On Dyngus Day, a South Bend tradition passed down from the Polish, the city spends the Monday after Easter in social halls, drinking beer and eating sausages. Mostly drinking beer. Also, dancing to music tortured through karaoke machine speakers. The mayor had pulled down the cloth on an honorary street renaming, then headed inside to sign a stack of copies of his *Shortest Way Home* to sign, because suddenly people cared that he had written a book. "Mayor Buttigieg," a local television reporter had asked him as he walked out of the Elks Lodge, "what does it feel like to be back in South Bend?"

In January, when Buttigieg had launched his exploratory committee, there were a dozen reporters in a room on the third floor of the Hyatt Place, two blocks from the White House, a location his campaign had chosen out of concern that otherwise no one would show up. He had almost delayed the launch because he'd spent the week in the ICU with his father, who was dying of cancer, and afterward had made it back to South Bend just before he passed away. When Buttigieg officially launched his presidential campaign a week before Dyngus Day, he packed an old Studebaker factory in South Bend, with a camera on a crane sweeping across the crowd as if he were making a concert movie. On that earlier appearance in January, he'd raised $120,000. That afternoon in April, he raised $1 million in a few hours.

Back in January, he had run into Biden backstage at an event across the street and been greeted with a jokey "Mr. President!" by the former VP. By the time he returned home in April after a conquering tour of New Hampshire, he was drawing crowds bigger than Biden's at every stop.

The following Friday, after he spent a week fundraising in California, Buttigieg pulled his car up to the awning of Ellen DeGeneres's studio. Pete and Chasten tweeted their selfies. They were fans. They were greeted like celebrities.

DeGeneres stops by to greet all her guests in the green room, but this was a more serious conversation. She wanted to talk to Buttigieg. Protect him. She talked to the Buttigiegs about their marriage, and about hers, the stresses that come from being a gay couple in the spotlight. Her eyes were focused, on edge. No jokes. There were things she wished she could go back and tell herself at the time she'd come out, she said, so she was going to tell them to him instead.

She's an introvert, she said, and she could see that Buttigieg was too. Get ready for what's coming, she warned him. They all want a piece of you. It's exhausting. It's corrosive.

"Save some of it for the air!" said Andy Lassner, her executive producer. He'd stopped by the green room to say hello himself and was shocked by what was going down. She never does this, he said. Never. And she was still going. "No," DeGeneres told Lassner, "I'm not going to say this on the air. Let me finish."

Buttigieg told her he could already feel the way people were pulling at him. Maybe it was Emma Thompson coming by the green room and saying, "Is it you? Is this our hero? We have been waiting for you. You give me hope. You give us so much hope." Maybe it was Mike Pence actually taking the bait and saying Buttigieg should know better than to question how Pence could still be a good Christian and discriminate against gays. "I hope that Pete will offer more to the American people than attacks on my Christian faith or attacks on the president as he seeks the highest office in the land," Pence had said, insisting they were friends from working closely together when he had been governor of Indiana, though they barely knew each other.

Buttigieg has a knack for making the carefully planned seem nonchalant, as if he's ambling idly along when in fact he's in the middle of a plié. Every sentence is precisely arranged, the words weighted, the haymakers casually landing as if he'd just thought of them.

"I'm not interested in feuding with the vice president," Buttigieg said once he was on camera, "but if he wanted to clear this up, he could come out today and say he's changed his mind, that it shouldn't be legal to discriminate against anybody in this country for who they are. That's all."

His campaign had set a $1 million goal for his first quarter in the race. He hit $7 million. His conversation with DeGeneres kept worming its way through his head.

"The truth is, some things are very easy to get used to, and some things are not. It's plenty easy to get used to having more attention. It's easy to get used to having more staff. It's easy to get used to your operation growing. What's harder to get used to is the intensity," Buttigieg said, riding in an SUV back to his campaign office in what counts for downtown South Bend. He'd been to the West Side Democratic Club for Dyngus Day nine times, he said, but had never had trouble getting through the door before. "The process of becoming famous has been challenging. It creates a lot of constraints. When you're mayor, you can be very well known in one place and just be some dude everywhere else you go. Now what we're finding is everywhere else we go, you're as visible as in South Bend—and when you're in South Bend, people look at you a little different."

By then, DeGeneres had already talked him up to Oprah Winfrey, who'd anointed Obama "the One" in Iowa in December 2007. Well, DeGeneres said, maybe this is a *different* One. Winfrey was searching, just like Obama, just like everyone else. She'd interviewed O'Rourke onstage at an event in New York in February. She'd recorded a podcast with former New Orleans mayor Mitch Landrieu in the summer of 2018. After her phone call with DeGeneres, she invited Buttigieg over to lunch on his next fundraising trip to California later that month.

———

At the beginning of March 2018, a year before this all got started, Buttigieg had been driving a rental car from the Kansas City airport to Topeka, looking out the windows at the signs for the Eisenhower Presidential Library, quoting from memory Ike's line about how a political party could never survive by attempting to eliminate Social Security, unemployment insurance, labor laws, and farm programs. "There is a tiny splinter group of course that believes you can do these things," Eisenhower said, as Buttigieg remembered near verbatim. "Among them are a few other Texas oil millionaires and an occasional politician or businessman from other areas. Their number is negligible, and they are stupid."

Buttigieg was enough of a novelty then that the Kansas Democrats had booked him for their big annual fundraiser, yet still enough of an unknown to most that earlier in the day, no one had noticed him when he walked around outside the Westboro Baptist Church taking photos on his iPhone of the GODHATESFAGS.COM and FAG MARRIAGE DOOMS NATIONS signs, with the upside-down American and rainbow flags on the poles. He was on his way to visit the rainbow-painted Equality House across the street. Driving over, he had been interested in whether the city had expanded its sidewalks downtown. Inside the building, as he admired its design and the work those in charge were doing to help LGBTQ youth with nowhere else to go, he asked if they had run into any zoning or municipal issues.

Young and smart and gay and clearly talented, Buttigieg had been one of the few politicians that Obama named in a *New Yorker* interview when asked about Democrats' future after Trump won (the others were Kamala Harris, Tim Kaine, and Michael Bennet). And here he was, the marquee guest at the Ramada Topeka Downtown.

"I'm just going to ask, and ask on behalf of the team," the second vice president of the Kansas Young Democrats asked him when he stopped by for a session. "How do you pronounce your name?" For fun, Buttigieg asked a few to try. He smiled. "Close," he said. (It translates, from Maltese, to "lord of the poultry.")

He talked to them about how young people were always going to be viewed in politics as being about technology and innovation and new ideas. There's power in that, he said, but only if connected to something larger. Use that, Buttigieg told them, like the Iranian protesters did when the students took to the streets in the Twitter revolution in 2009.

"To me, actual victory is when Republicans start sounding more like Democrats" in "an emerging national consensus," he told them. "Part of what's on our plate is not just to redeem national policy, but to redeem the idea of politics."

His next session was with labor leaders. The mood was dark—in part because of Trump, but more because the Republican control of the state government had turned Kansas into a years' long experiment in new hard-right government, with funding, labor laws, and farm programs all slashed.

"I don't hear a lot of reasons for hope. What keeps you feeling up?" Buttigieg asked as the conversation wrapped up.

"Antidepressants," said a man from the local Service Employees International Union.

"It kills me when people say we don't have a message," Buttigieg said. "We tie ourselves in knots over it. It doesn't have to be that complicated."

Democrats needed to be able to do better, he said, though at that point he wasn't quite sure what that actually meant. In that big and boring Ramada ballroom, he was starting to sketch out the sounds of what would eventually become a major theme of his presidential campaign: Freedom isn't just freedom *from* what people don't want, but freedom *to* do what they did want. Freedom to be able to leave a job without worrying about health care. Freedom to love and marry whomever they wanted. By the time he spoke, the Westboro Baptist Church crew was onto him, tweeting about protesting him in the parking lot.

After his speech that night, he sat for an interview in front of an old Obama "Hope" poster in the Kansas Democratic Party headquarters, trying to explain how he wasn't crazy to believe that there might be a place for him in the presidential race. "There's no going back. There's no 'again' to be had. Things are going to be different," he said. "There was a liberal era in American politics that lasted thirty or forty years, followed by a conservative era that lasted thirty or forty years. And now, we're on the doorstep of a new era."

Axelrod had continued quietly giving him advice, but his main gift to Buttigieg had been connecting him with Lis Smith, an operative who was the *New York Post* in human form. She had run what's called rapid response—essentially smacking back comments and news of the day on Twitter—for Obama's reelection campaign. Her highest profile splash in presidential politics to that point had been, while working on the never-going-anywhere campaign of Martin O'Malley, beating Hillary Clinton to the one-toilet women's room backstage during a commercial break at a debate in 2015, leaving Clinton to apologize with a wry smile when she made her way back on stage late.

Buttigieg had the bowl haircut, Smith had the leopard-print heels. He had the aw-shucks manner, she made reporters scared of her. He was the one who had signed up to go to Afghanistan in the Navy Reserve, in part because he thought it would be good for a political career; she was the one whose blaring iPhone snooze alarm went off the morning after the Topeka speech, in the car back to the airport before the sun came up, jarring him because it sounded so much like an air-raid siren back on the base.

But to see Buttigieg as a creation of Smith's, a notion that started to become a meme of the Sanders-and-Warren-aligned Twitter militias once his campaign took off—he was an android assembled in Smith's basement, went one—was to miss how much his own carefully guarded instincts matched hers. Buttigieg was always a little unnatural in front of crowds, but in his mind that was his natural habitat. Smith wrote a memo laying out a plan to get him in front of every reporter and donor and tastemaker and cocktail party host in

Washington and New York, so he was all in, because he thought that's precisely where he belonged. They were both so confident in his smarts that they could just let him run loose in whatever room and expected everyone he met to be struck, eager to hear more.

Usually they were. Buttigieg has the kind of intellect that really does dazzle. He sops up information with maddening ease, whether about sewage metrics or Norwegian verb conjugations. When he played the keyboard at an occasional campaign event and put on sunglasses to try to look the part, he could all too often look like a high school English teacher wearing the giveaway shades from a credit card promotion table, but he did hit every note with the same polymathic ease. People became fans of his the same way they consumed *The Wire*, passing him along to their friends in the in-crowd as what everyone just *had* to see. "Perhaps it's unusual, but he's a young, accomplished man," said a former high school teacher named Denise Clark in Manchester, New Hampshire, one night in April 2019, after watching him speak in, naturally, the interior courtyard of the local art museum. "He's my daughter's age. She's accomplished. He's accomplished. Why not?"

Buttigieg's town hall on CNN on March 10, 2019, was as close as the entire 2020 primary campaign came to a true grassroots moment. It was a Sunday night, the third of three hours of the network's box-checking due diligence, with the also-running candidates taped at South by Southwest to give the programming a little flair. John Delaney got the seven p.m. slot; Tulsi Gabbard, eight p.m.; and Buttigieg came last at nine. (Julián Castro had been invited to participate that night too, but declined, deciding he was too big a deal to be lumped in with the crowd). Buttigieg delivered what the type of Democrat who was paying attention to primary campaigns a year out was desperate for: calling for Supreme Court reform and getting rid of the Electoral College, distancing himself from Sanders, landing a pile driver on Pence as he spoke about his own Christian faith. "How could he allow himself to become the cheerleader of the porn star presidency? Is it that he stopped believing in Scripture when he started believing in Donald Trump?"

Buttigieg knew when he got his first meeting with Obama in early 2019 that he was just getting a polite audience, mostly for the sake of not seeming as if Obama had been playing favorites. He knew that most people would have thought he shouldn't have even gotten that. But he kept pushing.

Buttigieg and Smith had envisioned the early stages of the campaign as a series of heats. Biden wanted the field crowded so that he could coast on name ID and be seen as the only adult not in the pig pile, but Buttigieg aimed to be the best in the young candidates lane. With Massachusetts congressman Seth Moulton and Hawaii congresswoman Tulsi Gabbard in the race, he'd also be the best in the veterans candidates lane. He would do any podcast, any interview, anything to get himself out in front of people, bulldozing with an almost manic level of self-confidence through all the rational concerns about a thirty-eight-year-old mayor of the fourth largest city in Indiana breaking the traditions of presidential campaigns in a way inspired by Trump—just subbing smarts for sinister savvy. That interview he gave in Norwegian, marveled one person working with Kirsten Gillibrand's campaign, was "an awakening." Gillibrand herself spoke Mandarin, but had gone into the race thinking that she'd win it by going voter to voter in Iowa, winning them over by the kind of campaign she had always heard was what mattered in the caucuses. Suddenly they were all chasing their own viral moments. "Thinking about that becomes more important than visiting Iowa's ninety-nine counties, all the shoe-leather campaigning," that Gillibrand aide said. "That's a massive change."

———

Beto O'Rourke's implosion worked out better than Buttigieg and Smith could ever have hoped. No one came into the race, or maybe any race, wrapped in more puffery, to the point of being introduced at his Austin kickoff rally to the "Si Se Puede" chants as "the man—not the myth, but the legend."

O'Rourke had lost his Senate race in Texas in 2018, but had since raised more money, created more of a movement, than made any sense—all on his own virtuosic instinct for pioneering politics into livestreaming and unscripted authenticity. "Washington was wrong about Obama and there are many reasons to believe it's wrong about Beto. Not only should Beto run, there is a strong case to make that if he were to do so, he would be one of the strongest candidates in the field," wrote Dan Pfeiffer, who had gotten to know O'Rourke during his Senate race, in a December 2018 column titled THE CASE FOR BETO O'ROURKE. Pfeiffer's partners at *Pod Save America*—the audio outpost of the resistance that had made a collection of Obama Bros niche superstars—had invested as producers in a documentary about the Senate run. Obama, who had been impressed and intrigued with O'Rourke when he came by the office in Washington for a meeting in December, told him to meet with David Plouffe, and had lower-profile adviser Paul Tewes sit with him in his living room in El Paso. Tewes in turn encouraged O'Rourke to meet with Jen O'Malley Dillon, whom he eventually hired as his campaign manager.

The Obama-ite competitiveness with Clinton lingered from 2008, but the interest lasted for longer than that: watching her lose in 2016 proved to their own self-satisfaction that an establishment insider couldn't win, that their own good taste and insight enabled them to key in early to the Next Big Thing, as if they had just laid their hands on an original copy of the first Velvet Underground album. O'Rourke was the punk rocker who'd nannied after college to pay for his pot money and had air-drummed to the Who's "Baba O'Riley" in a viral video from a Whataburger drive-through after finishing a debate with Ted Cruz in the 2018 Texas Senate race. They knew about Buttigieg. He wasn't cool enough for them.

Outside the immediate bubble, intrigue mixed with skepticism. "About the worst comparison you want is everyone says you're like Barack Obama," is how one big Obama donor put it after O'Rourke reached out. Among several of the aides who flocked to him, there was quickly a sense that maybe he was not the magical new Obama they'd imagined. When O'Rourke finally launched his campaign in mid-March on a *Vanity Fair* cover, the butter pats were just melting off the pancakes in the Annie Leibovitz shot of the strangely clean griddle he was using with his son. "Man, I'm just born to be in it, and want to do everything I humanly can for this country at this moment," he said, a line that landed on the cover and in the collective psyche screaming, "White male privilege!"

Still, at the start, there was a cool high school vibe to O'Rourke and his campaign, the effortless charisma of the guy who hopped on a skateboard and knew the lyrics to every Clash song. A bubble inflated around him, his aging hipster talk being taken as epigrams of wisdom. "I'm convinced that we will have to work from as much common ground as possible. No one person and perhaps no one party can force the decision on this. This has to be something that America comes together on," he said on his first day in Iowa, hours after the *Vanity Fair* piece was published. Few noticed or cared that this was the same sentiment that had, to the same crowd, proved that Biden was naive and out of touch for believing, or that it was interchangeable with what many of them had mocked John Hickenlooper for telling George Stephanopoulos a week and a half earlier: "When someone's angry, you don't fight back with them or argue with them. You repeat back their words. I would go to Mitch McConnell, to his office, and I would sit down with him and say, 'Now, what is the issue again?' and we would talk. Sounds silly right? But this works." It just sounded so much more believable in O'Rourke's earnest Keanu Reeves voice.

When it looked as if O'Rourke might take down Cruz, he became a hero that liberals and Cruz-haters didn't have to think hard about to love, making a race happen in a state that hadn't been expecting one. In longer conversations then, O'Rourke tended to come off as thoughtful and well-read. In the spotlight of a presidential campaign, however, he had gone from high school cool kid to the guy at the end of the dorm hall with the Dalí prints on his wall. Swarmed by a big crowd in Waterloo, Iowa, a few days into his campaign, after actually climbing onto the bed of a pickup truck to shout a speech, he was asked by a TV reporter eager to get just a piece of him what his favorite book was. Joseph Campbell's *The Power of Myth*, he said, which he then used to explain what he'd been trying to convey to the *Vanity Fair* reporter. Did he still feel that he was born to be in it? "I feel like this is my purpose, being where people are coming together, with the common purpose of getting things done," he said. "When I say I'm born to do it, I think that's—we were just talking about Joseph Campbell a second ago, and he talks about following your bliss. My bliss is service, is in working with people, is in trying to find the commonality in the midst of great division. I feel like I have something to contribute in this way."

O'Rourke let loose that mess of words on March 16. By then, he'd already muddled his position on impeachment, health care, why he wasn't releasing his early fundraising numbers. He seemed overwhelmed by the basics of running a campaign, insisting on driving himself around in a minivan, insisting on stopping the minivan at one point as he drove past the Mississippi so he could put his feet in the river. He would do things like answer a very Iowa-specific question about what level of ethanol he favored in fuel with a block of words—delivered while standing on a bar in Mount Pleasant, Iowa—that sounded good unless you tried to make sense of them: "How do we free ourselves from a commodity market over which we have no control? We do so by adding value to what we grow at the same time that we meet our energy needs, renewable standards that we have in this country and the crisis of climate change. The farmers in Iowa are able to do that. We visited an ethanol facility today: Fifty jobs in a community that wants to have high-wage, high-skill, high-investment industry in their hometowns—drawing young people back or keeping them there in the first place. Owned not by some gigantic corporation in another place; owned cooperatively by the farmers that are growing the corn there in the first place. In other words, we're addressing not just a fuel standard, not just environmental concerns, but we're reviving rural America in the process. So let's stand behind and with those farmers. Iowa is showing us the way."

"I'm not sure he answered," Mirt Bowers, the retired former vice president of patient services at a local hospital, who had asked the question, observed afterward. But she let him off. He was from Texas, she reasoned, and he probably had to think about his politics back in oil country—even though he had lost the race back in Texas, and was there answering questions because he was running to win in Iowa. He was just so *interesting*.

This was how it went. O'Rourke would give long, vacuous answers, the packed in crowd would applaud, but they'd walk away wondering exactly what they had just seen. He was famous for being famous, a spectacle for being a spectacle. He knew a lot more than Kim Kardashian, but he probably got the same reception she would have, at least for the first few days. His campaign was part postcollege backpacking trip, part midlife crisis. The biggest crowds he ever drew came on that kickoff swing. His own midlife crisis, along with America's—and Democrats' larger obsession with Obama—was less interesting each week.

Buttigieg was building something else entirely.

"Of course we're all going to distinguish ourselves on policy, but the truth is something like 80 percent of the Democratic candidates' messages are going to converge," he said in an interview in Concord a few weeks later. "Other than some differences in degree and a few individual signature programs that might be different, most of what you're going to see is going to align. Even more than usual, I think, some of those intangibles are going to matter.

"The arrival of Trump made some of us question which rules still apply. Some people think there are no rules, which has resulted in some 'Why not?'

candidacies. I don't think that's true, that there are no rules," he said, framed by the fake cowhide upholstered on the back of the booth. He knew that people were insisting that a mayor of South Bend, Indiana, getting a serious look as president was proving that the rules were gone. "I was aware that it might look that way, but hopefully we're proving that wrong."

Buttigieg thought about the letter he'd written to his parents when he was serving in Afghanistan in the Navy Reserve, in case he died. Some of it contained computer passwords. Some of it told them what they'd meant to him. He kept it in his desk, never sent, never opened. He thought about missing his father, the articles about his campaign, or about how the process of running for president was so strange that he caught himself thinking of sticking it in an email. This attention was still crazy, he acknowledged—but he wasn't going to let himself be dismissed. "I hope it's not *completely* crazy," he said.

Before getting back in the car, he stopped to pose for some glamour portraits outside, his knee raised on a stone, hoping that bold expression would give them the shot they would use for the *New York* magazine cover, which was one of about a dozen articles featuring him that week. He had to get to DC for the LGBT Victory Fund brunch the next morning, where they didn't know he was going to give an emotional speech about how desperate he was as a teenager to be straight, and he didn't know that they were going to suddenly greet him like a hero.

O'Rourke, meanwhile, was already chasing a reset, back on Facebook Live for the kind of chats that had first made him a sensation. In mid-May, he went to get a haircut in El Paso, going for authenticity in a red smock. He asked for questions to be submitted online. Aides told him most of what they were getting were suggestions on what kind of cut to get. "Cutting out some of this ear hair that you get when you get older," he said, narrating himself. "It grows out of your ears. If you don't get it cut, can get really nasty." The conversation only got more gripping when another man walked in to get his own haircut and said his name was Robert. O'Rourke said his name was Robert too, but they call him Beto. "You're the guy from TV. Governor? Mayor?" O'Rourke was better looking in person, the man observed.

At the high point, 488 people were watching.

O'Rourke had been the nightmare for the Sanders campaign—the only other candidate they believed had the potential to stir a youth movement, who looked able to knit together outsider cred with insider support. For that reason, they viewed the arrival of Buttigieg as a gift. With the cleverness that sprouts on email chains between campaign aides, a few Sanders aides nicknamed him the Beto Blocker.

They sneered at him quietly to reporters—the mediocre small-town mayor. But they were scared of what he represented. "He's what people wanted Beto to be," a Sanders adviser said that April. "There's only room for one fresh-face alternative." If at this moment, when America seemed ready for a revolution, the voters turned to a candidate who might lock in the idea of youthful moderation instead of to Sanders, that could lead to the worst kind of primary defeat. He annoyed them. He unnerved them. "What Bernie doesn't like is people who aren't principled," Jeff Weaver explained later. "Pete Buttigieg seems like he's willing to move unmoored from principle."

Look at his life: Buttigieg wrote an essay in high school about how much he admired Bernie Sanders, used the award he won from it to help get him into Harvard, and then ended up going straight from finishing at Oxford on his Rhodes Scholarship to a consulting job at McKinsey & Company recommending cost restructurings. (Sanders had been amused to learn about the essay.) To the Buttigieg haters, nothing captured his clever opportunism as much as how he supported Medicare for All before he started running, then backed away from it once he was in the race, and then came up with a plan seemingly born out of wordplay: Medicare for All Who Want It. At best, he could appear to be working his way through the primaries as if he were solving a Rubik's Cube. But what seemed worse than that to the Sanders people was that he wasn't just a sellout but a cipher, a sneak attacker from all the establishment Democrats who had fawned over him at those cocktail parties and who intended to put a calm midwestern face on protecting corporatism. The Manchurian Candidate for late-stage capitalism, as a Sanders aide put it toward the end of the primaries. The millennial traitor. A joke that maybe he was a CIA plant became a mini Twitter obsession.

Buttigieg's real problem wasn't any of this. For all his and Smith's running laps around every other candidate on every other issue, they were never able to figure out how to stop the idea from setting in that Buttigieg had a problem connecting with Black voters—because he did have a problem with Black voters, but then so did every other candidate except Biden. Even Harris and

Booker, the two Black candidates in the race, did. The Black support for the rest of the field combined wasn't half of what Biden had.

Aides insisted that they had ideas for how to change this. Buttigieg was courting Al Sharpton, they were developing an economic empowerment plan for Blacks, he was chasing other endorsements. Then, just as he was becoming a front-runner, a white South Bend cop shot a Black man named Eric Logan without having his body camera on.

Buttigieg's charmed rise seemed all but over. For all the pundits and primary voters who'd been awed by his knack for offering answers that seemed to fit problems as tidily as puzzle pieces, the residents of his own city saw an uncharacteristically unprepared response to the shooting. He met with police for longer than he did with Logan's family. He kept scooting out of South Bend on his charter jet to get to campaign events. "When you're in charge of the city, you know that any given day, things can come up and will come up that you have to answer for, first as mayor and then also in the context of the campaign," he said in an interview one day, pulling up to an event in South Carolina on a Saturday afternoon in late June, before heading back home to face an angry community meeting the following day.

A few hours after Buttigieg landed in South Bend that weekend, there was another shooting. By the time he spoke to reporters after the community meeting, he had tears in his eyes.

CHAPTER NINE

LAUNCHED INTO A VOID

If they don't give you a seat at the table, bring a folding chair.

—SHIRLEY CHISHOLM

August 2018–June 2019

The night Trump won, Kamala Harris was out to dinner with her family. That was her election night tradition. They were three hours behind East Coast time in Los Angeles. By the time the food arrived, Trump was up in both Wisconsin and Michigan.

"Are you seeing this shit?" she texted her campaign manager, Juan Rodriguez, and her close consultant, Sean Clegg, who were at a separate dinner with all the top staff.

Then another text: "Doug"—her husband, Doug Emhoff, known as Dougie to her and her crew—"is freaking out."

Clegg scrambled, checking the prediction needle on *The New York Times* website, starting to think what to do. Over at the nightclub where Harris then headed for her own victory party, she and Clegg huddled backstage. "I can't believe that mothafucka won," she said. She likes that word, likes to correct the pronunciation when people say the *r*'s. "That mothafucka really won?"

Harris and Clegg worked out new lines. It couldn't be the celebration of her victory that they'd planned. She improvised a little more in the moment. "Do not despair. Do not be overwhelmed," she told her supporters. "Do not throw up our hands when it is time to roll up our sleeves and fight for who we are."

Rodriguez and Clegg rushed her out of her party not long afterward. She wanted to stay, enjoy the victory. All that people were now going to want to talk to her about, they told her, was whether she was going to run for president. She had literally just won her Senate seat. Doesn't matter, they said.

Harris's speech went viral overnight. A digital staffer asked for a small budget to do more promotion of it, so aides gave him $25,000 left over in the budget, and the hits kept racking up. By the end of the year, they were raising $10 for every $1 they put into advertising. People who had never even heard Harris's voice or could not have named a single nondemographic fact about her took it as a given that she'd be the nominee in 2020.

Politicians like to come off as humble, unassuming, and insistent that they had never thought about running for president until the moment came upon them. That's what Harris says. That's not what anyone who ever dealt with Harris believes. She was always thinking about running—likely before she squeaked out her win in the 2010 California attorney general race, and definitely as soon as she did. The first step was sorting out that she would run for Senate and that Gavin Newsom, who had been the mayor in San Francisco when she was the district attorney and was now biding his time as the state's lieutenant governor, would run for governor. She assumed there would be eight years of Clinton as president, giving her time to build up her record before she launched her own campaign. She had not been planning on the speculation starting right away.

"Oh, hi . . . Good to meet you. A lot of people seem to be talking about you out there, you know, running some day for president," stammered an older Republican senator one day on the minisubway under the Capitol, about three weeks into her term. He didn't know how to follow up, so he went with, "That would be something."

Harris is smart, and she can give the impression that she's the student who's always hitting the books. She's in fact more of a crammer, but when the time comes, she prepares for every hearing and interview as if she's a prosecutor going through the case file. Part of the reason senators tend to face-plant when running for president is because it's hard to show them doing their jobs. They vote; they make speeches on C-SPAN that no one watches. They're all in

Washington and of Washington, talking about cloakrooms and points of order. They pop up on the Sunday shows and recite talking points.

Through a combination of good committee assignments and luck, Harris found herself facing Jeff Sessions on the Intelligence Committee in June 2017, and within seconds, reduced him to a pile of blinking and blubbering. "I'm not able to be rushed this fast. It makes me nervous," Sessions complained, in a moment that instantly had Harris going viral again. By then, Harris and her team still weren't prepared for that kind of attention, the way people would chase her down afterward, the way the calls flooded her office.

But they were intrigued.

Harris decided she was going to write a book—that is, have a ghostwriter write it for her. Charlottesville changed her thinking too. What was supposed to be a meeting about the book in September 2017 quickly grew into a discussion about Trump, how addressing the damage from his presidency wasn't going to be fixed by electing another white guy. There had to be a full reversal, she told aides. The country needed an antidote, needed a stark and clear statement that Donald Trump didn't represent America.

This is how Harris's sense of higher purpose and her ego, both pumped full by her no-bullshit mother, intertwined: she had deliberately chosen to go to Howard University for college to assert her own Black identity; she had gone into prosecution to be the victim's advocate; she had run for office to represent and give a voice to more people whom she felt were being left out. She was the first woman, the first Black person, the first South Asian person to be San Francisco district attorney; she was the first woman, the first Black person, the first South Asian person to be California attorney general; she was the second Black woman to be a senator. She is always cognizant of what her presence and her wins represent. That she always sees herself as the answer, and reaps the benefits from that—well, she likes that too.

She made the call about how they'd proceed: start putting together what a campaign would look like. Her consultants commissioned focus groups in Iowa, New Hampshire, and Nevada, testing her against Kirsten Gillibrand and Cory Booker for controls on the responses for another woman and another Black candidate. In South Carolina, the question was about the pathway for a Black candidate, so they tested her against Booker and Deval Patrick. Participants were shown short video clips—for Harris and Gillibrand, the clips were pulled from each of their first appearances on Stephen Colbert's show. Women didn't like Gillibrand, said she seemed too perky. They liked Booker, but said they thought Harris came off stronger.

Rodriguez set off on a separate track, but with the same goal in mind. Working the California state legislature and secretary of state Alex Padilla, who just happened to be a new client of the consulting firm where he and Clegg and long-time Harris adviser Ace Smith were partners, he officially made a high-minded argument for moving up the California primary from June, at the end of the calendar, to Super Tuesday in March, the earliest it could be held. The state had 12 percent of the population and the most representative demography of America. As such, it should be more than a coda to the nomination fight.

This was a worse disguise than Clark Kent's glasses. From inception, the plan, which Harris's main consultant, Smith, worked out, had been to follow the Obama model of slingshotting into South Carolina with a strong showing in Iowa—Black voters, they knew, tended to respond to Black candidates only when they saw white voters responding first. Then Harris would weave through a crowded field by picking up a few southern states on Super Tuesday, capped off by a favorite-daughter win that night in California. She would be unstoppable.

In August 2018, the whole team descended on a conference room in the fancy midtown Manhattan apartment building where Harris's sister and most trusted adviser, Maya, lived with her husband, Tony West. They were joined by Clegg, Smith, Rodriguez, pollster David Binder, Democratic power lawyer Marc Elias, her Senate communications director Lily Adams, and a few others. Meetings like this are Harris's weakness, and her strength. She takes in information from the people she trusts, cross-examines, Socratizes. Then she makes a judgment—except when she doesn't, having gotten caught in her own internal web of indecision.

Over the course of two days, aides gave presentations on the focus groups, the status of the primary date–change push. No phones or computers were allowed into the meeting, except for a laptop from which to run all the PowerPoints—"a way to set the tone," they were told, for no leaks during a campaign. They walked Harris through what running would mean for her life, what the process looked like, what the schedule would be. She had never paid attention to the mechanics of a presidential campaign, so this was all new to her, and she interrogated each slide—"What did Barack raise in this quarter?

What did Hillary raise?" she asked about the phase-by-phase fundraising plan. They tested her by running through hypotheticals of how she'd have responded in situations Clinton faced, such as when Trump was stalking behind her in the second debate.

That was easy, Harris said. "I'd turn around and say, 'Why are you being so weird? What's wrong with you?'"

Harris breathed it in, looked across at her sister. Harris's self-psychoanalysis is that being older than Maya always provoked a protective instinct that propelled her to becoming a prosecutor, and then to becoming one who specialized in cases about children and sexual assault. How sad, Harris told the group around that long table, that their mother wasn't around to see that this was what was happening. She would not have believed the conversation they were having, about her daughter actually running for president.

There wasn't any discussion of policy, the *why* she would run. "We launched into a void, without a worldview," one of the people at the meeting griped later. Because Harris is always the lawyer, the session ended with a moot court. Elias took the *Run* side, throwing all the idealism and poetry he could at her, working himself up to the line that stuck with many in the room: "The house of our democracy is on fire, and you're the only one who can put it out."

West, who could be forgiven for going after her because he was family, took the *Don't Run* argument. *You haven't been in the Senate long enough. You're inexperienced.* He tore into her record as a prosecutor. Every question and attack that would ultimately come from a progressive during the campaign, he said right to his sister-in-law's face.

Harris sat for a minute, taking it all in. She cocked her head to the side, looked at West. "Yeah," she said. "I locked up some mothafuckas."

"If you say it just like that," Clegg told her, "you're going to be the president of the United States."

The only decision that came out of that meeting was that she was going to run.

—————

First, she needed to get in for one of those Obama meetings.

Harris and Obama had known each other for years. In 2003, she was running for DA, he was starting to run for Senate, both were on the move. They were connected in the circuit of next-generation young Black leaders. She won first, but he became a big deal first with that convention speech. By the time he was a freshman senator, she was asking for his help by coming to a fundraiser for her reelection. He liked her, and agreed to do it—but told her he was being careful enough with his sudden stardom that he couldn't do anything outside of Illinois or Washington for a few months. He promised her she'd get the first event once he did.

By the time he made it to California, there was so much interest in his appearing that Harris's team had to scramble to find a new spot at the last minute. Instead of a mansion in Pacific Heights, they ended up onstage at a San Francisco nightclub called Bimbo's. The genuine warmth between them was clear. So was Obama's still making sense of his new life, as he stood there talking about opening his desk on the Senate floor, knowing that it had once been Robert Kennedy's, seeing Paul Simon's and Paul Wellstone's names carved inside.

She was in the crowd in the freezing cold that day in February 2007 in front of the old state capitol in Springfield, Illinois, when Obama announced his run, taking a risk going against the Clintons. She became the California cochair of his campaign, flying to Iowa at the end of the year to knock on doors for him. Over the years, Obama got in trouble for joking at a fundraiser back in San Francisco in 2013 that she was the "best-looking attorney general in the country," and checked to see if she would be interested in coming on as Holder's replacement as his attorney general the following year for the nomination that eventually went to Loretta Lynch. (Harris made it clear that she wouldn't be interested, knowing that the job would probably get in the way of her eventually running for his.)

After a year and a half in Washington, though, Harris still hadn't been to see Obama. She'd been putting it off, well aware that the question of running for president would come up. She didn't want to pay a visit to the former president of the United States in the middle of a roiling national crisis and feel as if she were winging it when talking about a possible presidential campaign. "Men do that more often," she'd say. "Women can't come in unprepared for those kinds of conversations."

When she did set up the meeting, Obama welcomed her into the office like a big brother. He talked with her about what running would really be like, what she was probably going to encounter. "Don't do it because you think you can win," Obama advised her, because statistically, it wasn't likely that any of the candidates would win the nomination. "Do it because you have to do it. And if you don't feel that way, don't do it." He saw how the appeal she was counting on might be able to work. She has a path, Obama would tell people afterward.

Harris's first trip to Iowa was in the works before Brett Kavanaugh's Supreme Court nomination hearings—but by the time she landed in Des Moines, the hearings had given her a new reason to feel that she had to do it. Two years after Clinton lost, a year after MeToo ripped through Hollywood and Washington and New York, most men still weren't aware of how fed up most women were. No one was ready for what those hearings became—Harris had expected her big moment to be pinning Kavanaugh into a potential, but ambiguous, conflict with the Mueller report because of his connection to a firm that had briefly represented Trump.

When Kavanaugh returned three weeks later facing the new accusation of sexual assault, Harris was more direct as a cross-examiner. She asked him if he'd take a polygraph. She asked him how he could justify claims of a conspiracy against him. Chin resting on her folded hands, her face set in one of her *Check this guy out* lip holds for him, and for the camera, she asked, "Do you agree that it is possible for men to both be friends with some women and treat other women badly?" Just under the clock, she got Kavanaugh to admit he hadn't watched the testimony of the woman accusing him, whom he was calling a liar.

She only had five minutes questioning him. That was enough.

"Everything that was in my head," Jenny Ostem told Harris a month later in Indianola, "was coming out of your mouth." Ostem was a thirty-five-year-old white insurance consultant—not the obvious Harris demographic. She was gripping Harris's arms, looking right into her eyes at three o'clock on a Monday afternoon, thirty minutes south of Des Moines, on the top floor of a bar that didn't start serving drinks for another hour. A crowd of women had formed around Harris, waiting one by one, hoping to connect.

With Kavanaugh being confirmed on top of everything else since Clinton lost, Ostem told Harris, she felt like giving up.

Harris had been getting a lot of this lately—in Iowa and all the places she had been, and in the airports in between, from women across ages and races.

Crying. Saying thank you. Telling her their own stories. Her Iowa trip was planned as a show of force, with big events all over the northeast corner of the state where, realistically, most of her votes were probably going to come from. She had already worked out her stump speech, going on with a whole architecture around a "let's speak some truth" refrain about confronting injustice and hate and lying. "You give and you receive trust. And one of the most important ingredients in trust is truth," she said, in one of her formulations. "There's a funny thing about truth. Speaking truth can often make people quite uncomfortable."

She had a low-grade Trump impression, mocking his deep voice saying, "The economy is great, the economy is great." Iowans came for the political spectacle, because that's what Iowans do, but they stayed afterward with her on that first trip for moments like these.

Harris put her hands on Ostem's shoulders. "No, no, no," she scolded her. "Keep it going."

"It feels worse than ever," another woman told her.

"We take that feeling and move forward with it," Harris told her.

Ostem's mother, Deb, stood watching. She was looking for hope. She was worrying about a civil war. "I'm tired of the old guard," she said. "For so many of us that are emotionally empty, people like her help me keep the fight up." Harris "is wonderful. But she's going to have a hard time." America, the political forces, the rest of the "they," they weren't going to elect a woman.

"Things will change," Harris insisted to her. "It might be incremental. It's worth the fight."

———

At the end of the swing, Harris sat in a law firm in Ames, Iowa, trying to explain what she saw ahead. What about that "Prosecutor for President" line that her consultants had cooked up? She reacted to that as if she were trying to remember the plot of a book she'd read in college.

She was a politician and prosecutor who had specialized in child sexual assault, saw a society that wasn't grappling with any of its crises. "Nobody wants to have that conversation, and as a result of not having that conversation, we've not dealt with it as an issue. So the absence of conversation about it has had an impact in that we have not improved the situation. So let's speak that truth. It is real. Because guess what? Unless we say it even just that way, people will choose not to believe it is real." Her mother was a cancer researcher and a civil rights agitator who died of cancer. What she saw facing America was the mix of both perspectives.

"It's about diagnosis and then there needs to be treatment, right? That's also speaking truth—the diagnosis: you have cancer. So that is the truth, now let's deal with it: What's the treatment required? To deny it and not speak the truth means to let it fester, means to let it get worse in a way that could be irreparably harmful," she said. "Let's speak these things, because it is a prompt to say, 'Are we all on the same page with this?'"

She pushed back on the idea that she seemed to see the world, make sense of it, as a lawyer. "Being a prosecutor allowed me to be a voice for people who did not have a voice," she explained.

She said that all these questions about her and how she thought about herself and the world made her feel as if she were in therapy. "I think about issues and I want to talk about issues. I think that's what people want, as opposed to people like me, thinking about me."

"Dear Lord," she said when she recognized her face and 2020 on a man's T-shirt after a small rally at the University of Northern Iowa the morning before.

"Well," the man asked, after they posed for a photo, "are you going to run?"

"One day at a time," Harris replied.

⸻

January 20, 2019, marked the halfway point of Trump's presidency. All across the country, just after midnight, there was a supermoon that turned red, a wolf moon—the Earth getting between the sun and the moon, little bits of light glowing around the edges to change its color. In Washington, it was the coldest night of the year.

The following morning was Martin Luther King Jr. Day, and Harris was in New York on *Good Morning America*, announcing her campaign. That wasn't her original plan—her aides had assumed that Cory Booker was going to use a planned trip to South Carolina on the holiday to make his announcement.

Once it became clear he had decided to wait, they grabbed the day for themselves. She went right from the set to the train station back to Washington for a press conference at Howard to take in the national media.

A half Jamaican, half Indian woman from Oakland with a Sanskrit name born to two Berkeley grad students, who went to high school in Montreal, then married a Jewish lawyer later in life, with no biological children of her own— she wasn't like any presidential candidate who'd come before. Being acceptable was very much on her mind. She wasn't going to make herself out to be the candidate of criminal justice or the economy or racial reconciliation or the environment or any other set of issues.

"Nobody is living their life through the lens of one issue," Harris said that day. "Let's not put people in a box, and as they make their decisions, let's give them credit for being smarter than that.

"On the issue of climate change: Every parent wants to know that their child can drink clean water and breathe clean air. And that same parent wants to know that they're able to bring home enough money with one job to pay their bills and pay their rent and put food on the table, instead of having to work two or three jobs," she said. "Every person wants to know that there will be a criminal justice system that is fair to all people, regardless of their race. Every person wants that a mother and father should not have to sit down with their teenage son and have the talk, and tell that child about how they will be stopped or arrested, or profiled and potentially shot because of their race."

This was the closest she came to an argument for her candidacy other than wanting people to look at her and think she should be the president. Her aides also didn't realize how much damage had been done by a *New York Times* op-ed that had run a few days earlier, attacking her for keeping innocent men in prison and not being an ally in changing marijuana and other laws. The headline was a torpedo: KAMALA HARRIS WAS NOT A "PROGRESSIVE PROSECUTOR."

The Harris campaign was focused on her being seen as a progressive. She and her advisers didn't fully appreciate how she was already being shoved away from that side of the party, and didn't think it made sense how they were being played. That the *Times* op-ed wasn't a news story being held to the paper's reportorial or editorial standards was something they obsessed over, but not something that most readers would likely take into consideration. Five months after that moot court at the planning meeting in New York, she was caught in her own head about what to do, how to confront it. The advice was coming in from everywhere. Black leaders were telling her she was coming off like a sell-out. Tom Perez reached out to Tony West, a friend from when they had worked together at the Justice Department, and told him they should be embracing every attack because they differentiated her from the crazy liberals, which would help her when she got to the general election. Harris embodied how the Democratic Party liked to think of itself post-Obama, post-Clinton: a smart, sharp, largely self-made cosmopolitan biracial woman who'd been through liberal ideology and come out demanding actual answers.

Not letting herself get pinned down or pigeonholed initially seemed smart. But in a giant primary race with a new demand every day for answers to questions that she hadn't had time to think through, she came across as appearing unsure of herself and what she stood for. That started looking like a liability. She constantly gave the impression she was searching for what the right reporters and Twitter hounds would approve of—in part because that is precisely what many on her staff did obsess over, and in part because she was herself always stressing about what to say long past when she should have already said *something*.

Her kickoff rally on a bright Sunday in Oakland, a week after the official announcement, was the campaign's attempt to plow through all of that. They believed that the race was all about asserting that she was a big player, there to stake her claim, getting her on as many TV screens at once as possible. Move her into the top tier by *saying* she *was* in the top tier and acting as if that were the case, which would convince the pundits, the big donors, the millions of people they needed to attract online as supporters and grassroots fundraisers.

"Let's speak some truth," she said, over and over. Truth about people drowning in debt. About racism and anti-Semitism and homophobia in America. About climate change. About "foreign powers infecting the White House like malware."

The speech had been massively rewritten in the day before she gave it, then rehearsed and rehearsed and rehearsed again.

"The doubters will say what they always say: It's not your time. The odds are long. It can't be done. But our story has never been written by the doubters or the naysayers," she said. "Robert Kennedy said it best: 'Only those who dare to fail greatly can ever achieve greatly.'"

The helicopters overhead counted twenty-two thousand people crowding the streets. Weeks of effort to ramp up the event, build the stage, order the giant flags felt as if they had paid off. Other campaigns insisted they weren't intimidated, that she was a roman candle who'd burn bright and burn out. They were all watching, sizing themselves up around her now, just as the Harris campaign hoped.

"It's a long fucking game," an adviser on one of the other campaigns said that morning, as the crowd was starting to pack into the square in Oakland. "Do you want to do the nine-inning analogy? Because if you do, we're still in batting practice. The fundamentals are there, but the question is if it can be taken to a next level. Just because you're good at A, AA, AAA, doesn't mean you can make it in the majors. But sometimes you can."

Harris and a few aides left right from the rally for Iowa in another attempt to make a big splash, with a CNN town hall in Des Moines. Did she support Medicare for All? she was asked. Yes, she said. That's why she signed on to the bill in 2017. What about people who liked their insurance? The whole point, Harris said, was getting rid of the insurance system, with all the paperwork and delays and denials of coverage. "Let's eliminate all of that. Let's move on," she said, shooing it away with her hand.

That became an uproar. To be for Medicare for All was by definition to be for ending private insurance, though somehow almost no one in the Democratic Party or the political media seemed to have realized that. Harris thought if she was going to own the politics of being for it, she might as well just say what it actually meant. "If your brand is truth, you can't lie to people," a Harris adviser remarked a few weeks later. "Credibility in saying it straight is more important for Kamala than maybe for any of the other candidates."

By then, though, Harris had already tried to explain that she had really meant something else, and was in fact *for* private insurance, though she was also still for Medicare for All. Or maybe for another plan that she still hadn't come up with yet. Her own position on health care, like most Democrats', never got much clearer than that.

CHAPTER TEN

"GOD KNOWS HOW RUSTY JOE IS"

Thomas Jefferson once said, 'We should never judge a president by his age, only by his works.' And ever since he told me that, I stopped worrying.

—RONALD REAGAN

January 2019–June 2019

Biden had a vision of where his campaign would kick off, the kind of welcome into the race he wanted and thought he deserved. He'd talked about it with his grandkids: the steps of the Philadelphia Museum of Art, to mix the grand with the *Rocky* statue for a little underdog flavor. Lady Gaga and Bruce Springsteen performing. Gaga, because she had worked with him on the "It's On Us" campus sexual assault awareness initiative that he spearheaded; Springsteen, because he was Springsteen.

The grandkids would have to be there too. They were the future. What a show it would be! He was coming to fight for America, and they were going to rock him into the race. The crowd would pack the street along Ben Franklin Parkway, as they do every year for the fireworks on the Fourth of July. He'd seen all the marches. That's what he wanted this to be.

Others whom he ran the plan by weren't so sure. What if the weather doesn't hold? What if the crowd doesn't show? What if it looks as if he were trying for a Clinton-style coronation? Besides, people needed to hear from him, who he was, why he was running.

"But they *know* me," he insisted.

He had spent the last few months haggling with himself over whether to actually run, doling out to potential big donors and supporters his percentage chances of his getting into the race. Most also got a rundown of his memo from John Anzalone, the Democratic pollster who'd started his own career in politics as an organizer for Biden in Iowa in 1987. Anzalone had put together all the publicly available data and prepared a presentation for him, Jill, and his sister, Valerie Biden Owens, at their house in the DC suburbs, laying out how strong and stable the support for him was. Eagerness for his experience was a huge factor in the Biden-friendly polls, but Anzalone was also seeing how much people simply liked Biden, connected with him because of a sense of his compassion and empathy, which had only been reinforced by watching him after Beau died. He was Uncle Joe, and he had lived through a death in the American Family.

Anzalone turned the presentation into a packet for Biden. When he would have people over to the office in Washington to talk about running, he would slide the packet across his desk, urging them to check out the charts. He invited Chris Coons, Tom Carper, and Lisa Blunt Rochester—Delaware's two senators and its only member of Congress, who by virtue of being from his home state got to be his sounding board—and spent two hours with them over a lunch methodically going over the details. Look at what Americans say they want, he told them, and look how perfectly he lined up. He was ahead of Trump nationally. He was ahead of Trump in every battleground state. He'd be crazy not to run.

With staff he'd stress more, driving them crazy. People liked him, they'd assure him. But *why* do they like me? he kept asking. When they showed him how many likes and retweeted pictures of him with Obama they were getting, he wanted to know, was the engagement so high because it was about him? Or because it was about Obama? Or because it was trashing Trump?

Every conversation became an exhausting gut check. He didn't want to look back and say, "I should have." Ted Kaufman, his close friend and longtime chief of staff, who had taken a temporary appointment to Biden's Senate seat after Beau passed on it in 2008, described it in the spring of 2019 as the mirror test. "He knows it's going to be hard. He's been through it. He looks in the mirror and says, 'Am I not going to run because it's going to be hard?' 'Am I not going to run because,' he thinks, 'maybe I'm going to lose?'" Biden didn't want to watch Trump be inaugurated again and think he was the one who could have stopped it. He hated expectations being so high. He hated the race starting this early. He hated that anyone was even talking about how old he was. He wanted to be greeted with the pomp due to a former vice president, but he didn't want to be slammed for falling short.

"People should lower their expectations," a Biden friend said in April, after the news broke that he was going to enter the race. "He's ready to open up the barn door and speak to a half-empty crowd, but the media will kill him if it's a half-empty crowd."

And the venues were half empty. And the media did kill him for it. People on the Biden campaign maintained they were just fine with all of it. When he showed up in Ottumwa for the first stop of his second Iowa tour, the campaign picked a theater with 664 seats for the event, but because they knew he'd never fill that, they had him speak in a hallway outside with 96 folding chairs set out—then made out to be pleasantly surprised when 250 people actually showed. This was good, they said.

He'd ask staff what happened to all the people who had been telling him to run for two years. "Everyone saying, 'Come on, do it'—all right, we're doing it. So where are they?"

By the time Biden landed in Iowa for that trip in June, his campaign had already been through its first two crises. In any other election, probably with any other candidate, either would have been fatal. Instead, both disappeared—but not before leaving a lasting impact on the campaign.

Soon after New Year's, Biden's staff had begun having weekly meetings organized by Schultz, the political aide he'd kept with him from the vice president's office. Every Thursday morning they'd call in—Schultz and Mike Donilon and Kate Bedingfield, and a few other trusted operatives in a few states. Schultz would start, give a rundown of what they knew, whatever could be determined about where Biden's head was. What were the rest of them hearing? How could they get ready for whenever Biden made up his mind? Schultz would ask. Signing up good staff was going to be hard if they didn't get started, they'd warn him. He knew, he said—he just didn't know how to get Biden to see that too, especially because Ricchetti was telling Biden that he could wait to get in, maybe even until after Labor Day.

If Biden didn't launch his campaign, he couldn't start hiring, because he couldn't legally fundraise to pay staff salaries unless he filed the paperwork to run. Maybe, one person suggested, they could get friendly local politicians to put operatives on the payroll to lock them down for whenever Biden hit go. They never got far enough to figure out how they'd explain that to the offices, the operatives, or the Federal Elections Commission.

Sometimes teasing Biden with how many talented, respected operatives were ready to sign up was a way to move him toward a decision. In early February, he even called a woman they were thinking would be perfect to run his campaign in South Carolina. She was young but experienced, well known among insiders but not a celebrity chasing her own promotion. "I'm thinking about it," Biden told her, "and you need to be on our team." The conversation went well. He made no offer. The next day, Harris announced she'd hired the woman to run her own campaign in the state.

Schultz would joke that he could have staffed two full primary campaigns with the number of people who would have accepted offers if they had started five months earlier. In the meantime, Biden was being treated like a presumptive candidate, but didn't yet have the staff to promote or protect him—which meant that even though he had a skeleton crew working for him in a complex of mostly doctors' offices near Dupont Circle, there was no defense ready when, on the last Friday afternoon in March, *New York* magazine published an essay from Lucy Flores, a former Nevada state legislator, saying that Biden had made her uncomfortable a few years earlier with how he had touched her.

Videos of Biden putting his hands on women, of nuzzling in and rubbing shoulders, had worked their way around the internet and newsrooms in the fall of 2017, during the MeToo rush. They were met with a collective shrug: this was just Biden, he didn't mean anything by it, and besides, he didn't matter much anymore. What was the point of beating up on a retiree? A year passed. Attention faded.

Biden's aides, though, expected this chatter to be weaponized once he entered the race. "We always knew that this is one way that opponents would come at us," an aide said a few days after the Flores essay hit. He's the presumed front-runner, the aide argued. He's going to be attacked. This looked like an opposition research dump, designed to scare him out of running, but "there's nothing about this that is giving him second thoughts if he decides to."

Biden is an empathetic person, a caring person, physical with both men and women. He has rubbed. He has nuzzled. He grabs hands, he hugs because he reaches out to people, and because people reach out to him, sensing that they can lay their pain on him, that he wants to take it from them. He may be the world's most complete, purest extrovert, feeding off others' energy, but not in the vampiric way of Bill Clinton. He draws actual personal happiness from making other people happy, like a human golden retriever.

He could never believe that he had made women uncomfortable, and was hurt by the thought that he had—for their sake, not for his own. People connect to him in a unique way, the aide contended. That's a good thing. That's a powerful thing. An asset, not a liability. That's part of why people love him so much.

Flores said she spoke up on her own, but Biden aides saw all these as attacks meant to turn Biden's great strength into a vulnerability. They immediately began coming up with possible suspects. Harris, maybe. Her aides were certainly hoping that the incident would scare him out of running, to spare himself the pain. Sanders's advisers panicked that the Biden campaign would see them behind it—Flores was a former board member of his Our Revolution group, and there was a picture circulating of her smiling with Sanders's hand on her shoulder in a pose not too dissimilar from the one she had accused Biden of violating her with. Jeff Weaver called Tad Devine, the strategist behind Sanders's 2016 run. Devine hadn't spoken to his old client since a blowup in the spring of 2016 when Sanders stayed in the race, attacking Clinton, after the math showed he couldn't win the nomination. None of the Sanders inner circle knew any of the Biden inner circle, but Devine knew Donilon. Weaver pleaded with him to relay the message that they were not behind the story. Biden's aides were not totally convinced.

When new accusations started to appear, the furor caught the attention of a woman in California named Tara Reade, who had worked for Biden in the Senate in the 1990s, and who now added her own story. She claimed Biden had touched her several times inappropriately back then, and that she'd been fired from his office for refusing to serve drinks at an event. Others started speaking up in his defense. Stephanie Carter, star of a viral photo of Biden's hands on her shoulders and leaning into her from behind after her husband was nominated to be Obama's defense secretary, wrote an essay that she said was meant to reclaim the moment for herself, and the truth: Biden "leaned in to tell me 'thank you for letting him do this' and kept his hands on my shoulders as a means of offering his support. But a still shot taken from a video—misleadingly extracted from what was a longer moment between close friends—sent out in a snarky tweet—came to be the lasting image of that day."

The punditry and pretty much every operative not working for Biden agreed: he was going to have to do *something* in response. He and his advisers didn't get how it worked these days, the Washington wisdom went, how quickly opinions set in on Twitter. Biden waited days to respond, and when he did, his iPhone video recording didn't help him seem with it—shot vertically rather than horizontally, he seemed to be riffing off what he'd been told to say. He wanted to be authentic but instead came across as stumbling through: "It's just who I am. I've never thought of politics as cold and antiseptic. I've always thought about it as connecting with people," and then, "Social norms have begun to change and have shifted, and the boundaries of protecting personal space have been reset and I get it. I get it." True to form, Biden started the video with, "In the coming month, I expect to be talking to you about a whole lot of issues," letting the campaign announcement slip.

But he didn't apologize. Reporters' tweets gave away the game for many: they wanted an interview to see and hear his penance, an apology, a full humbling. Usually complaining about "the media" is a convenient and trite way to distract from whatever reporters are or aren't focused on. This was one of those times when "the media" really was moving like a single-brained beast, demanding to be fed. Biden's advisers saw the trap: if he apologized for this, he would have to start apologizing for everything, and after a forty-seven-year-long career of comments and compromises, they'd never get his candidacy to be about anything else.

Biden had to test the way the world worked now, because he had no choice. Stare down Twitter. Take confidence from the fact that of the tens of thousands of women he had put his hands on in his life, less than a dozen spoke out against him, and none accused him of anything more serious than inadvertently making them uncomfortable. The Democrats had forced Al Franken out of the Senate at the end of 2017 over just as few—though slightly more intense and definitely more intentional—incidents, out of a commitment to getting right with the time. "Women voters, like all other voters, are watching. But it's not just women voters," Donna Brazile, the former DNC chair, had said the day Franken resigned. "Millennials are watching. Everyone is watching." The party that had tossed Franken didn't seem to be one that was likely to nominate Biden.

Surviving not by bending to the new reality but by withstanding it became the model for the Biden campaign. He and his aides would get taken by surprise and fumble the initial response. Quietly, they'd reach out for help, but find skepticism from the people who at every point weren't sure that the party hadn't already moved past him. He'd dig in. He'd withstand. He wouldn't do any of the things on cable that the smart talking heads were saying he *had* to do. He wouldn't submit. He'd survive.

Obama was watching this all unfold, getting nervous. He knew Biden's closest advisers, and he didn't think much of them. He worried that they might have pushed him to run because they wanted one last shot at the big time before retirement, that they had no sense of the current state of politics or the party anymore, and they couldn't protect him when he didn't either. "I'm rusty," Obama would say. "God knows how rusty Joe is."

He had a unique position as Biden's friend and political consigliere, as well as the top Democrat and the one who'd been meeting with all the competition, which had given him an inside view of the political landscape. He decided to use his sway. He wanted a briefing. He wanted to know if Biden and the people around him knew what they were doing.

Obama trusted Anita Dunn. She had been a key adviser on his 2008 campaign and was briefly his communications director during his rocky first months in the White House. In the years since, she had remained an informal adviser to both him and Michelle, helping launch his foundation, then guiding the public strategy around both the original plans for the postpresidency and their Trump-win rewriting. Obama knew Dunn had been advising Biden, and that gave him some confidence. Two weeks before Biden's launch in April, he asked Dunn to brief him on the plans.

Obama started the discussion by making it clear that he would be fine if Biden lost. His concern was how ugly politics had gotten, and he didn't want his friend's career and reputation to be destroyed. Don't let them just tear him down, Obama told her. "Joe needs to know what he's in for," he said, pushing, testing. Dunn and Bedingfield, whom she had brought along, went through the plan: when and where they were going to launch the campaign, and what the pitch to voters was going to be: restoring America, battling for the soul of the nation.

He leaned back and crossed his arms. "That looks pretty good to me," he said at one point, and told them to just make sure to protect Biden. He left the meeting more confident than he had been expecting—not convinced that Biden was going to win, perhaps, but reassured that at least he wouldn't embarrass himself.

Staff started to coordinate the wording for what Obama would say when Biden launched. Warm and supportive, the statement sidestepped any mention of an endorsement, tenuously holding to Obama's commitment to remaining neutral. Biden lasted only a few hours after releasing a video officially launching his campaign and made it only as far as the train station in Wilmington before he stomped on that plan. No, no, he insisted, "I asked President Obama *not* to endorse."

Back in Obama's office, they slapped their foreheads. Biden's aides weren't concerned. All they needed was the video of when Obama had given Biden the Medal of Freedom in 2017. "A lion of American history," Obama had said then. "The best part is, he's nowhere close to finished." The Biden campaign released it as an online ad after Obama's office gave the sign-off.

―――――

Biden went back to Scranton to record a campaign launch video in front of where he had grown up, but Donilon scrapped it. Instead of a "Joe from Scranton" feeling to the launch, he subbed in a direct-to-camera speech from a Biden text he had written about the searing horror of Charlottesville—and the battle for the soul of the nation. An initial launch date had been set before the online fundraising system was ready, and before anyone on the campaign realized that it had been scheduled for the same day as a Black women's political forum that the rest of the field would be attending in Houston.

Biden announced not via an event but with a video that had a script written by Donilon. He never got new walk-on music: he came out onto the stage for his first event in Pittsburgh the following week to Bruce Springsteen's "We Take Care of Our Own," just as Obama and he had all through the 2012 campaign. He never got a new array of supporters: the person introducing him in Pittsburgh was Harold Schaitberger, the head of the firefighters union with a mustache older than most voters, making him out as a Cincinnatus out of Wilmington. "We need Joe more than Joe needs to be president," Schaitberger told a six-hundred-person union hall, which was about as big a venue as Biden could fill then. "This country needs Joe."

Even after all that buildup, Biden still wasn't ready. When he went to Los Angeles to fundraise during his first week on the trail, his campaign asked for a suggestion for a spot to get tacos, to appeal to Latinos. Garcetti's top political adviser suggested they also parlay his support from firefighters with an appearance with the Bomberos Association—Latino firefighters, who for the last six years had been running training sessions for their counterparts in Latin America, teaching them how to put out wildfires safely. Firefighting, the human impact of climate change, international cooperation, America leading the world. In other words—it was a perfect opportunity to show Latinos doing something more substantial than making tacos. Can't do it, Biden's team told Garcetti's team. He hadn't been updated on climate change, wouldn't be for at least two more weeks. Stick with the tacos, and the mindless chitchat in front of the cameras.

When the official campaign kickoff rally was finally launched in Philadelphia in mid-May, Biden came running out onto the stage in his aviators, but there was no Lady Gaga, no Springsteen—not even on the playlist. He stood in a patch of grass by the art museum, not on its steps. The *Rocky* statue wasn't in the shot for the TV coverage, but someone had put a blue Biden T-shirt on it. The crowd that the campaign estimated at six thousand (though other estimates put the number closer to four thousand) was bigger than any Biden drew for the rest of the campaign—even before the pandemic ended normalcy— a number well behind those of Harris events, and well behind even what Klobuchar had been able to draw out in a snowstorm in the middle of a Minnesota February. "If you're saying that, you're totally not focused on what's going on here," Kaufman explained in a walking interview as he made his way backstage at the rally. He tried an argument reminiscent of the one Trump's then press secretary, Sean Spicer, used to rationalize calling the skimpy 2017 inauguration crowd the biggest in history: "It's about social media writ large." The counterpoint to crowd enthusiasm, Kaufman argued: "Beto O'Rourke." Just a few weeks into his campaign, that would-be phenomenon had already become a punchline.

Adam Forgie, a forty-one-year-old seventh- and eighth-grade teacher from Pittsburgh, found his mind wandering to Obama. "If I could have voted him four more years, I would have," he said, though he had already absorbed the talking points Biden wanted, with his positive message and standing in the world. "He'll push Trump's buttons without animosity behind it," said William Mead, a sixty-six-year-old former Marine Corps sergeant who'd been injured in Vietnam and spent his career in land use. Tom Brown, a seventy-year-old retired telephone line splicer, says he knew people were worried about Biden's age, but he was overlooking that because he thought Biden could beat Trump. "I am in fear for my children and grandchildren," he said. He looked around and took the measure of the smaller crowd. "Doesn't matter at all," he said. "This is his chance to talk to the country."

It was so much the chance to talk to the country on TV that some in the crowd could barely hear him and kept shouting "Louder!" Yet what Biden said that Saturday featured many of the same things he'd been saying for years, and that he would say over the coming year and a half.

"Some say Democrats don't want to hear about unity. That they are angry and the angrier you are the better. That's what they are saying you have to do to win the Democratic nomination. Well, I don't believe it. I believe Democrats want to unify this nation. That's what we've always been about: "Unity," Biden said. "If the American people want a president to add to our division, to lead with a clenched fist, closed hand and a hard heart, to demonize the opponents and spew hatred, they don't need me. They've got Donald Trump."

Biden talked about climate change, Obamacare, investing in the economy, but the focus throughout: "The single most important thing we have to accomplish to get this done is defeat Donald Trump." He couldn't believe how much was at stake, but really, it was all at stake, bigger than any of the policies or issues they were fighting over. "The only thing that can tear America apart is America itself," Biden said. "Everyone knows who Donald Trump is. We have to let them know who we are."

Jason Miller, a Trump adviser who'd been stopped from joining the White

House in 2016 because he had impregnated a younger Trump aide who wasn't his wife and the mother of his other three children, gleefully welcomed Biden into the race. He had a line he kept using about how Biden was a better Robin than a Batman. He knew he was undercutting Trump's clear anxieties about facing Biden, but Miller declared a few hours before Biden's first official kickoff event in Pittsburgh, "I think Joe Biden is the best possible general election opponent for President Trump of anyone in the field.

"Even though Trump will be the incumbent, Biden being in the race allows him to be the change agent, allows him to be the reformer," Miller insisted the day that Biden got into the race. Trump didn't win in 2016 because he was running against Clinton, Miller argued, but because he was running against what Clinton represented. Biden's forty-seven-year record—forty-eight years if he made it to the general election—was an even better fit against which to rail at the Washington establishment. "Trump can simply point at Joe Biden and say, 'Why would we go back to that?'"

This wasn't just campaigns sniping back and forth. Clinton alumni had sneered at Biden when he was thinking about entering the race in 2015, and as they watched him fumbling instead of dominating, there was a collective sigh of *Good luck*. "Biden possesses many of the downsides of Clinton's attributes with fewer of the upsides," is how a Clinton aide from 2016 put it then. When Clinton was knocked for being establishment, at least she had the endorsements and donors, "whereas Biden is going to be vulnerable to many of the same criticisms without that." Lindsey Graham, the South Carolina senator who'd gone from being a McCain protégé to a Trump suck-up and ditched any suggestion of his old friendship with Biden in the process, said Trump "believes that Joe Biden represents the old way of doing business that was pretty soundly rejected, and that it would be going backwards."

Biden's aides reacted with confidence that seemed overblown at the time. "The notion that Biden is arguing for the status quo is a little hard when the status quo is Donald Trump," was a Biden adviser's response in those early days. "What he's advocating for is a pretty radical change from what we have."

———

Once upon a time, not that long ago, there was room in the Democratic Party for differing views on abortion. Those days are completely over, but Biden had

lived through all of them—from when he said the year after it was decided that
Roe v. Wade had gone "too far," that "I don't think that a woman has the sole
right to say what should happen to her body," to developing a sense of himself
as the biggest male champion for women's rights in government.

Biden's team had been failing to get him to realize how much damage could
come from a straightforward story about his support for the Hyde Amendment, which bans federal funding for abortion procedures. Among all but the
older aides who had been with him for years, there was intense frustration that
he wouldn't change his position or listen to them about why he should. Then
when the story was published and the political world erupted, Biden became
angry at his staff, blaming them for not preparing him. He was defensive about
where he stood, adamant. "Nobody has spoken about it more, or done more,
or changed more than I have," is how Biden put it to a woman who confronted
him about his position on abortion a few days later in Iowa. Didn't everyone
understand how good he was on women's issues? Everyone did not. At best,
many of the advocates and activists were anxious that he had an old white
man's sense of wanting to get credit for what they thought were baseline positions.

Biden believes abortion is wrong. He also doesn't believe in imposing his
personal views on public policy. He is antiabortion, pro-choice. The Hyde
Amendment was designed to be a wedge, and Biden had been wedged for
years. He doesn't think that government should be funding a procedure that
many oppose. He doesn't think his own tax money should be going toward
funding a procedure he personally opposes.

He wanted time to consider, sit, and think through his ideas with Jill, his
advisers, himself. But he didn't have time to do so and pushed back on the
political pressure. He waved away Symone Sanders, the new young aide who
took it as a mission to confront him over his not understanding how his position disproportionately affected poor women and women of color without easy
access to abortion—he barely knew her, and this was an issue that scratched
right at his Catholicism. Alyssa Milano, the actor who had become a major
online presence on issues of women's rights as well as a friend of the Biden
team, called Schultz, telling him that the candidate needed to change his thinking. More calls came in, more tough conversations. He listened as Schultz,
Congressman Cedric Richmond, and his policy director, Don Graves, walked

him through the implications on policy, but more important, the political hits that were quickly piling up from Democrats who weren't concerned with nuances, and were asking if he really was pro-choice.

Aides tried to get him to see that this could easily reverberate into bigger problems that could take down his campaign. "Is this more important than all of the issues you can address as president?" aides pushed him, appealing to his ambition. Then, appealing to his aspiration: "If you are president, we can make a difference on this."

"I'm getting a lot of pressure," Biden confided privately after they spoke.

He was headed to Atlanta to speak at a DNC fundraising dinner. He and his campaign felt the need to address the subject there. This was the first of what became many *Do you actually want to be president?* moments.

Reading what aides wrote for him on the way to the event, Biden settled in. "I signed up to do this to win," he said. "That has to be part of the calculation."

Backstage he was tense, obviously not comfortable with where he had landed. Holding the pages of his prepared statement, he kept to himself, pondering what he was about to do.

"If I believe health care is a right, as I do, I can no longer support an amendment that makes that right dependent on someone's ZIP code," Biden finally said, when he stepped to the microphone. "Folks, times have changed."

＝＝＝

"Embrace of radical left complete," responded the Republican National Committee. Then, from the other Democrats: "'Always' means 'always,'" tweeted Lily Adams, Harris's communications director, attaching a video clip of her boss saying, "I will always fight for a woman's right to make whatever decision she believes." Even Seth Moulton, the Massachusetts congressman who had once chased Biden to be his mentor, and whom Biden had once seen as a politician in the mold of Beau, took a shot as part of a presidential campaign where no one could quite figure out why he was running. "It takes courage to admit when you're wrong, especially when those decisions affect millions of people," Moulton tweeted. "Now do the Iraq War."

The following week, standing at the front of a room at a community college in Mount Pleasant, Iowa, where he'd just given another drab and poorly attended speech, he continued to squirm: "First of all, I still believe if in fact there was a means by which poor women would be able to access their constitutional right and it was able to be paid for without taxpayers' money, it should be done."

He insisted that he had made the decision on his own, that it had grown entirely out of the process of finalizing his own health care plan—not in response to the pressure from the news story, from his own staff, or from exasperated supporters. That part wasn't true. What was true is that he felt as if he were being forced more to the left than he wanted because of how far Republicans were spinning off on their own as they passed new abortion restrictions in the states, including the one that had just passed in Georgia that criminalized abortions if a fetal heartbeat was detected, at about six weeks.

"It's just outrageous," Biden said. "I made a commitment that I would not ever attempt to impose my religious views on anyone else in terms of relating to this most unique question in all of humanity. When is it a human life and being, when does that occur? And so I'm not going to do that. And conversely, I find myself in a position: How do you say—to women who are in poverty that increasingly have no access to women's health care—how do you say, 'Well, guess what: it's gone, it's gone'?"

Trump had tried to make the day about taking on Biden. That morning, because they would both be spending the day in Iowa, he had started in, calling him "weak mentally" and "Sleepy Joe"—the usual fare. Biden was glad to have Trump's help elevating him over the rest of the primary field. He liked being able to attack Trump while insisting he wasn't getting personal, just talking about "why he's doing such damage to the country—that's totally different than attacking his character or lack thereof."

All the other Democrats had just barnstormed through the state over the weekend for the first big Iowa multicandidate event of the campaign, but Biden had skipped it to attend his granddaughter's—Hunter's daughter's—high school graduation. (He made sure to point out to the crowd that he had been at a joint graduation party with the Obamas because Sasha Obama was his granddaughter's classmate and close friend.)

Biden said he wasn't concerned with the competition. "A young woman came up to me, said, 'Why shouldn't I vote for a woman?' You should! You want to vote for a woman, vote for a woman. That's a fine thing to do, they're equally as qualified as any man. The question is, who is best prepared at this moment to handle the issues that are before us? Who's most likely to be able to beat President Trump? Because if that doesn't happen, nothing changes."

But then he got back to how annoyed he was that he kept getting written off.

"You all said I was going to fail from the beginning," Biden said. "You said, 'Biden is going to start off and he's going to plummet.'"

CHAPTER ELEVEN

THAT LITTLE GIRL

When a man hears himself somewhat misrepresented, it provokes him—at least, I find it so with myself; but when misrepresentation becomes very gross and palpable, it is more apt to amuse him.

—ABRAHAM LINCOLN, OPENING OF
THE FIRST LINCOLN–DOUGLAS DEBATE

June 27, 2019–July 5, 2019

Andrew Yang kept running to the bathroom to throw up. The walls weren't thick, and he was so loud that operatives on other campaigns started joking about "Yanging." He'd been having a blast pretending to run for president, but this was the real thing, live, on national television, standing onstage a few podiums down from people who might actually *be* president, and he was sick and nervous. He'd had an IV in him earlier in the day, a massive nosebleed an hour before going onstage. "I was literally thinking, 'Please don't bleed on national TV,'" he said.

Debate night was at Miami's Ziff Ballet Opera House. A big NBC peacock logo sat next to the driveway, right up front on a street that had in recent years begun to flood with ocean water when big storms came in. With so many participants, the DNC scheduled two nights of ten candidates each—and there were still those who didn't make the cut who complained that the rules were too stringent. Round one had been the night before. The luck of the draw meant that the only leading candidate onstage that night was Warren, and the most dramatic moment had been her deflating moderators' hopes for a moment by saying she agreed with Sanders on Medicare for All.

Biden's aides told MSNBC he wasn't going to show up as early as the producers wanted. He didn't need that much time for makeup—he'd done enough of these, even if he hadn't taken part in a debate for eight years—which would give him an extra half hour at the hotel to relax.

Stage managers prepped the candidates, instructing them, "Don't be Ben Carson," reminding them of the infamous moment from one of the 2016 GOP debates when Carson had created a pileup backstage after not hearing his name called. Then, just before airtime, producers were running around, shouting, "Has anyone seen Biden?" into their headsets. They finally found him around a corner, chatting with a few of the crew.

As soon as she walked into the green room, Harris spotted the little metal hand that someone had dropped on the carpet. She recognized the symbol but couldn't remember what it meant. Neither could Lily Adams, the communications director who'd been her first big new hire in December 2016, or Jim Margolis, who'd come on a few months before to run her debate prep, though he'd sworn Clinton would be his last presidential race. She'd watched the first of the debates with Adams the night before. Her lines were prepped, the accompanying Twitter memes keyed up. But this object had thrown her, and she wanted to know what it was. Though Adams wasn't Jewish, she had gone to Brandeis, so had an automatic minor in things like recognizing that it was something Jewish, and she Googled it on her phone to find out that it was a hamsa, a good luck charm. Harris liked the idea. She stuffed it in her pocket.

Harris and her team had been holed up all week in the Fontainebleau—Hillary Clinton's favorite hotel in America, because she'd gotten a "perfect peach" while staying there during the 1972 convention that nominated George McGovern—up in a room around a conference table, running lines. *The Marvelous Mrs. Maisel* was shooting scenes for season three in the lobby, with extras all done up in bright '50s costumes. That choreography was less scripted than what the Harris team was lining up. The only hitch was not to get sidetracked by Sanders, so Ace Smith played him in the mock debates, pulling out every annoying caricature of an old man he could come up with. Ian Sams, her press secretary, played Biden.

They were staring down some hard fundraising math: they had bragged about how well she'd done in the first quarter of the year after her launch, but aides could see she was falling short ahead of the quarterly fundraising deadline on June 30, which would come three days after the debate. She had raised $12 million, and their plan had targeted that number to be at least $15 million. It was also the practical consideration of political math: there was no path to the nomination for Harris—or for pretty much anyone, except for Sanders, and maybe Warren—except through a Biden collapse. She had to make a splash to get her political donations up. She had to take Biden down for any of that money to matter.

Then, nine days before that first debate, at a pricey fundraiser at the Carlyle Hotel in Manhattan, Biden had wandered off in his speech into reminiscing about his early days in Washington, working with the South's last segregation holdouts in the Senate, when "at least there was some civility. We got things done. We didn't agree on much of anything. We got things done." Like good old James O. Eastland, the rabid segregationist. "He never called me 'boy,'" Biden said. "He always called me 'son.'"

That was a gift to the Biden detractors, tied up with an ironic bow: the only reason anyone had heard it was because Biden's campaign had decided from the launch to let reporters into his fundraisers as part of his ploy of acting as if he already was the president, by doing things like moving him around in a faux motorcade and holding to the Obama-era transparency rules of having a "pool" of reporters cover him for nonpublic events.

When an aide told Harris what Biden had said, she winced. "He did *what*?" she asked, with an *oh no* tone that captured the sense of the many people who cared for Biden but felt as if all he was doing was proving he should be out to pasture. When she spoke publicly about his remarks, she went at him with an ax. "If the people he was talking about with such affection had their way, I would never have been able to be a United States senator," she said to reporters two days later in South Carolina.

Booker had really wanted to summon righteous, disappointed anger to destroy Biden. He could hear the lines in his head, thought maybe that a star moment at the debates could bounce him into the contention he wasn't attracting on his own, but he'd been stuck on the first night of the debates, which had so few of the front-runners that it was treated like the JV stage. Booker kept feeling as if he were running up against fate. All during the campaign, he kept getting run over by it.

That left Harris.

Her campaign was prepared. Smith, a wizard of the dark arts of opposition research, had already dug through Eastland's archived papers at the University of Mississippi, and let the letters to him from Biden dribble out in the press. A month earlier, an aide had slipped *The Washington Post* the file on Biden's record on busing. The Harris campaign was armed with video clips and related storylines, like Biden's work with Strom Thurmond on tough-on-crime measures in the 1970s that just reinforced the bad look of the 1994 crime bill (the Violent Crime Control and Law Enforcement Act of 1994). Smith used to tell people that he was like Baskin-Robbins, thirty-one flavors of Biden trouble. He hadn't expected to be able to start with a sundae.

Biden could at times be everyone's inadvertently teeny-bit racist grandpa, Harris thought, but this was 2020. Trump and the Republicans were the throwbacks, not Democrats. Right? Here was a smart, tough woman who was the daughter of two immigrants, neither one white. Obama had embodied all of America's changes in 2008, but she was going to be an avatar of how much more needed to change. "I have my own legacy," Harris said a few weeks earlier, pushing back on the suggestion that she was Obama's heir. "Listen, I was the elected district attorney of San Francisco, I was the elected attorney general of the state of California—twice elected to both positions. And now I'm a United States senator, and only the second Black woman elected to the United States Senate. I think I've earned my own legacy." From her first floor speech in 2017, she had spent her time in the Senate deliberately promoting the causes of immigrants and speaking about race, and she wanted to seize the electricity in the Democratic Party around the latter.

Her team told Harris that she had to land hard on Biden. But Harris knew him personally. She had grown close to Beau while working on the national mortgage settlement in 2011 and 2012, fighting back against an administration to which they both felt loyalty. Her husband still has the voice mail he saved of Joe Biden's calling to congratulate them on their engagement. She didn't like how personal this was getting. She wanted to beat him, but she was searching for some way to condemn him for what he had said and done without attacking the man she liked and respected.

Debate prep sessions are like writers' rooms. Toss out ideas, work them out, shoot them down, build them back in. Adams and Margolis thought she needed to start with a big punch, make sure everyone was paying attention. She'd wait until race inevitably came up in the debate, then claim the floor as the only Black candidate onstage. Certainly the moderators from MSNBC, of all channels, wouldn't stop her. And then, they argued, go right in, starting the shredding with, "I do not believe you are a racist . . ." Make Twitter explode. Become the story of the night.

When Harris asked, "Are you sure this is the right thing to do?" Clegg backed her up. That was like saying a person wasn't a child molester. No, Adams said, she was specifically saying he *wasn't* a racist, because she had to get ahead of the possibility that Biden might respond with, "Are you calling me a racist?" Even if he didn't, that's certainly what the media narrative was going to be when a Black woman took a shot like this at a white man. Adams and Margolis argued their approach would blunt and depersonalize the attack, enable her to do what she needed to do, but allow her to insist that it was just a substantive difference.

They ran it through. Sams, as Biden, anticipated much of the actual response, including how surprised he'd be, how emotional he'd get. Margolis stopped the discussion for a gut check. If she hit Biden like this, he said, and she didn't win and he did, it would probably cost her the VP slot, which most already assumed would be hers in a Biden presidency, or even a cabinet spot as attorney general, if that's what she preferred.

She knew that, Harris said. She thought it was a fair hit. This is a debate, she said, and debates were supposed to be about differences. She wasn't running for VP, despite what so many people—Biden included—assumed. She was running to be president, to beat Biden and everyone else. She wanted everyone to know that.

Onstage, she seized her moment.

"I'm going to now direct this at Vice President Biden: I do not believe you are a racist, and I agree with you when you commit yourself to the importance of finding common ground," she said, looking over at him. "But I also believe, and it's personal—it was hurtful to hear you talk about the reputations of two United States senators who built their reputations and career on the segregation of race in this country. And it was not only that, but you also worked with them to oppose busing. And, you know, there was a little girl in California who was part of the second class to integrate her public schools, and she was bused to school every day. And that little girl was me."

Biden, taken aback, plodded through a response. She was mischaracterizing his position, he said. That's not what he stood for, and she knew that. He found his way to the end of the answer and stopped speaking.

A few minutes later, the moderators paused for a commercial break. Biden leaned over to Buttigieg, at the podium to his right. They barely knew each other, but Biden was looking for someone to share the moment with.

"Well," he said. "That was some fucking bullshit."

———

Biden had been ready for the attack. Or at least, he should have been. His aides could tell that Harris's campaign had been planting the stories about him, they could see that she was going to try to make him out as a man from another era, and they had scripted a thirty-second response that he went over again and again for debate prep back in the hotel conference room in Wilmington. But he couldn't take seriously that all those other people onstage were actually thinking that they could be the nominee, that running was anything but a way to shine up their careers—in a way he supported as a party elder. And he was less ready to feel Beau with him onstage than Harris's consultants had planned for.

Back in Biden headquarters in Philadelphia, Biden's campaign manager and other aides were watching the debate while hand-stuffing bumper stickers into envelopes, as if he were running for state legislature in the 1970s, except they were trying to fulfill a hokey, low-tech promotion they'd done to try to build up their email lists. The Harris attack hit hard, but it didn't seem fatal. "One night," said Schultz, then the campaign manager, in his way that was both fatalistic and resolute, "in a long campaign."

Biden's top press aides had been watching from a hotel room a few blocks from the debate site. Earlier that afternoon they had gathered reporters in a conference room on the top floor of the art museum a few blocks away to try to set their expectations on what was going to happen that night, though the only reason most were there was to get some colorful tidbit about debate prep that they could work into a story. They waved off the idea that Biden would stop by the spin room himself after the debate, like all the candidates had done the night before, insisting that he was holding himself up to the same media standards as the other candidates, that critics should look at the local TV interviews he was sitting for, and taking questions from reporters on the trail—which all the other candidates (except Sanders, who almost never took questions) were doing as a baseline. They wanted credit for Biden's doing the minimum.

That night, doing the bare minimum seemed to have caught up with him. "Even if you're a well-known national figure you have to open yourself up and show that you're willing to be evaluated and not above the fray," said Ben LaBolt, a Biden 2020 skeptic who had been the press secretary for Obama's reelection campaign, watching him implode onstage that night. "Limiting appearances to big rallies and interviews may limit gaffes but has its perils." Or, as another Democratic operative who wasn't working with any of the campaigns put it more succinctly the next morning: "They're trying to run out the clock, and the game hasn't even started."

After the debate, the Biden group began the march over to the spin room to try to put a good face on the night—T. J. Ducklo, his press secretary, and Bedingfield, Dunn, Symone Sanders, Louisiana congressman Cedric Richmond. They didn't talk. They all had the same thought: *This is going to be terrible.* They knew that Harris's attack would be all anyone would want to talk about, and they had worked out the basics of how they were going to respond. They got themselves ready, feeling that the campaign might already be over. The Biden cheering section that had gathered outside was gone, as was the ice-cream truck that had been parked across the street from the theater handing out free Biden ice-cream cones (flavor: extra-sweet vanilla, colored light blue).

They walked into the middle of the black floor of the stage, steeling themselves as the reporters swarmed.

"I think he listened to her story. It was personal. It was heartfelt," Bedingfield tried, taking the lead in responding. "He heard her story. I think she told it very powerfully. He listened. You heard him focus on his message for the American people and what he would do as president."

Symone Sanders jumped in. "I think you guys are looking for Vice President Biden to comment on Senator Harris's experience," she tried. "It's not for anyone to reject or validate what she was saying. Her experience is her experience, and I think we should leave it at that." Dunn kept falling back on the words *energetic* and *forceful* to describe Biden.

They were asked to explain Biden's position on busing. None could.

"He's a front-runner," was what Bedingfield came up with. "People were going to take swings at him, trying to take swings at him, trying to score points. It's a debate. We understand that."

After eleven minutes, they wrapped it up. Faiz Shakir, Bernie Sanders's campaign manager, looked over at where the Biden crew had been standing. "We had an opportunity to finally hear from him, and it was underwhelming as a performance. There were many parts where he was talking, I don't even remember if he made a point or not," Shakir said. He wasn't sure why Biden was even running. "I certainly know he'd like to defeat Donald Trump. As somebody who'd also like to defeat Donald Trump, I'm worried about his ability to do that."

Harris spent a few hours alone in her hotel room, uncoiling. Biden got on a plane for home. Harris's aides spent the night drinking. Biden's aides spent the night in meaningless Twitter fights, projecting and only making the situation worse.

Two days after the debate, Biden's campaign reached out to an opposition researcher and bought all the files on Harris.

Back in Philadelphia, Biden's top advisers rented a conference room at an office space a few blocks from headquarters for an emergency meeting. Everyone felt that they were teetering. No one knew what to do. He was coming off as old, angry, spiteful. His supporters were attacking Harris, saying she just wanted to be president, as if they were not backing a guy who clearly wanted to be president himself.

"Here's the message," Donilon said, repeating the argument they had been making from the start: beat Trump, experience, soul of the nation, working-class jobs. "Don't let him get knocked off balance."

Realistically, no one understood busing policy, because it was 2019 already, and the days of forced integration were fifty years in the past, before most of the operatives on the campaigns and most of the reporters covering the campaigns were born. Biden's argument was that he had just been opposed to federally mandated busing, not voluntary busing, but that's not the way politics works. Suddenly he was made out as a segregationist himself, the Orval Faubus of Wilmington.

The whole subject was confused, convoluted, and almost entirely irrelevant. De jure busing? De facto? Up onstage the candidates had spent half an hour not making any sense about their health care plans other than to raise their hands and agree that they thought illegal immigrants should be covered. Thanks to a ploy of his own by Julián Castro to raise the topic on the first night, most had to guard against being characterized as heartless Latino haters and make a show of saying they were for decriminalizing illegal border crossings. Nearly all made pilgrimages to peer over the fence at the temporary white shelters put up on the Homestead Air Reserve Base, about an hour outside of Miami, for the teens in orange hats who'd been rounded up during Trump's family separation policy.

This was the kind of fight with which they were going to go up against Trump: With twenty bumbling candidates in a low-stakes, low-interest rumble over which one could get the most woke Likes on Twitter? They were going to bash Obama, when he and his wife were the only people Democrats could agree on liking anymore?

There's no one who better embodies the Democratic establishment than Terry McAuliffe, so watching that first debate on TV was the one time he says he regretted running. "People are sitting at home saying, 'Wait a minute, I can't afford my prescription drugs' or 'I'm going into a hospital, and all of a sudden I get home and I've got an $800 anesthesia bill.' Nobody was talking about the issues that matter to people at home," McAuliffe said. Maybe talk about Social Security, drug costs? "They can come in, it's no crime, nothing at all. Now we're going to give them health care? Wait a minute. How about me? I'm sitting home today. I don't have health care. What are you doing for the people who don't have health care in America? And you want to give these folks health care?" Biden's own team had struggled to explain his position afterward, and never quite did. The argument was something about how reporters would have to ask Barack Obama why he didn't cover undocumented immigrants under Obamacare, but that Biden's supporting Obamacare then and supporting covering the undocumented now wasn't a contradiction, retro-rationalizing a position they hoped he wouldn't have to come back and explain in a general election. Follow?

Biden and Harris both headed to Iowa for Fourth of July weekend. Reporters following Harris received phone calls from Biden's press aides with more of a history lesson on busing than they ever could have wanted. The team suggested questions. They suggested wording of the questions. They pushed and pushed until finally a television reporter asked Harris the question they were confident would trip her up: What exactly was her own position on busing? How was it different from Biden's?

First, Harris said she did not support federally mandated busing except as an option when local governments opposed it. Then Biden said that was also his position. So they agreed. Then the next day she said that they *didn't* agree, and didn't understand why Biden had been so unprepared for her attack, and tried to link it back to the segregationist comments. By then, she was the one in a tailspin. A moral challenge became a technical parse. Her team had spent so much time working on the strategy of the attack and the THAT LITTLE GIRL WAS ME T-shirts that they never worked out an answer for what she believed herself. And they were bewildered by how the Biden team was turning this around on her, falling into screaming matches with reporters they thought weren't getting it.

"One of the frustrations of the campaign trail is—we're talking about running for president of the United States. I wish that the issues were covered with more thoughtfulness," Harris had said in May, describing her own comfort level. "This is not a game show where you've got a buzzer, and you should hit the buzzer and you can win some money."

Now she was trying to figure out what her own policy actually was, in between stops on the trail, and whether it would now be what it would have been in the 1970s—and how it differed from her parsing of Biden's policy. She had built up no goodwill. Voters didn't like her. She had spiked in the week after the debate—one poll from CNN had him down 10 points and her up 9 points from the previous set of numbers. After that week, the spike started disappearing. It never came back.

This was the rare moment in the Biden campaign when there was a plan, and a plan that worked. "We had an attitude throughout the primary," said

Bedingfield, "that because we came into the race in this weird place as the underdog front-runner—always leading in the polls, always discounted by the press—that we were always going to have to do some disruption to get the kind of coverage that we needed."

The Biden Burger was just a regular Deluxe Burger, except with American instead of aged white cheddar, and was featured on the menu for one day only at the gourmet fast-food spot in Dearborn where Biden went for lunch with his superfan, Detroit mayor Mike Duggan, and a few local Muslim leaders two weeks later. He'd overlooked it on the menu, and ordered just a regular cheese-burger.

On the way out, he stopped to answer questions from a few reporters who had trailed him there from the NAACP convention downtown, where he'd received a standing ovation. Biden's fundamental liability remained that he was an old white man running in a party increasingly defined by young peo-ple, Black and Latino voters, and women. That boosted Harris. Primary voters liked the idea of a vibrant Black woman, even if they didn't connect with what was coming out of that vibrant Black woman's mouth. A poll from CBS a few weeks later, in the run-up to the second debate, captured that dynamic. Biden was still ahead, but Warren and Harris were given much higher numbers on being stronger and readier to fight.

"My guess," Biden said sarcastically by way of explanation, "is that to the extent that it occurs, I was probably overly polite in the way I didn't respond to an attack, 'You're not a racist'—which is a nice thing to say, really reas-suring."

Jill Biden didn't have to worry about being so politic, and never had. She had watched the debate from her seat in the opera house, ready to jump out of it. She's small and a community college professor who looks the part of the pretty, gracefully aging politician's wife. Most people forget that she's proudly still the Philly girl who likes to tell the story of when she showed up at the door of a boy named Drew who'd been throwing worms at her nine-year-old sister, and "pulled back and punched him in the face." She'd recalled the incident one night in September 2018, her old accent creeping in despite the off-the-shoulder black evening gown she was wearing at a Human Rights Campaign gala. Standing next to her, Biden shook his head as he laughed at the story.

She let her husband play out his decision to no in 2015. She made sure he got to yes in 2019.

Then came Harris's attack. The aides could do the political maneuvering. She was and is the guardian of the Biden honor, the Biden id, and the Biden rage. She couldn't bear to watch a woman who called herself a friend of her son's—although Beau may not have been her biological child, she'd raised him his entire life as if he were—unforgivably try to tear her husband down, to score a point at a debate.

"With what he cares about, what he fights for, what he's committed to, you get up there and call him a racist without basis?" she said on a phone call with close supporters a week later. "Go fuck yourself."

CHAPTER TWELVE

HOW MUCH FUN

If one morning I walked on top of the water across the Potomac River, the headline that afternoon would read: "President Can't Swim."

—LYNDON JOHNSON

June 2019–August 2019

This is how we pick presidents.

Michael Bennet, who was appointed to the Senate from Colorado only because he hadn't gotten the job he wanted as Obama's first secretary of education, was sitting in the basement of a farmhouse in Polk City, Iowa, talking about tariffs and DC legislation that hadn't done anything to address erosion and unsustainable land. "We don't need corn and soybeans. We grow them because we made markets for them," said Wade Dooley, a younger farmer, eleven years in, when his turn came for a question. "We got stuck in the mindset where corn is king. But it doesn't have to be." Bennet's campaign was probably most distinguished for the copies of a Frederick Douglass biography and a book about eviction he tied in a wide blue ribbon and gave to anyone who hosted him. He understood Dooley's logic. "If you're getting paid money to do a stupid thing, you're going to keep doing it, even though you know it's a stupid thing," he observed.

A few hours later, the hotspot of the presidential race was the basement of the Collegiate United Methodist Church, with the rain on that late Saturday afternoon quickly turning into a blizzard. Flights were already canceled for the morning out of Des Moines, so it was packed at the Soup Sipper, which is actually a fancy way to describe folding tables full of different flavors of heartburn boiling in slow cookers. Cream soups. Tomato-based soups. Homemade soups. Soups from a can. Soups from a can with an extra ingredient plopped in for flourish and a personal touch.

John Hickenlooper arrived first. Fresh off a sixteen-year stretch as mayor of Denver and then governor of Colorado—Bennet's first job in government was as his chief of staff at city hall—Hickenlooper filled out his own name tag as he walked in down the entry ramp, because no one in the place had any idea who he was. Well, one person did: a man who pushed through the crowd to shake his hand, as he knew that the candidate had been some kind of scientist. "It just feels," Hickenlooper told the man, "like a calling, like everything in my whole life is coming together for this.

"There's a certain amount of exhilaration, anticipation," Hickenlooper explained a few minutes later. He's odd in a completely not interesting way. "So many different things have come together that seem to make sense. In a lot of ways, it does feel like a calling." When asked exactly what had come together, other than his term as governor conveniently ending a month earlier, he responded, "That and some of the projects that we worked on that people brought to me five years ago, and that struck me, and I really invested myself in, now turn out to have real relevance."

He began weaving his way through the folding chairs toward the front of the room, making certain not to chat with Julián Castro too long so as not to lose his spot next to Harris. That kickoff rally she had in Oakland at the end of January, attended by twenty-two thousand people, really made it hard for everyone else, he told her. She gave him a polite laugh. Up onstage, she talked about "existential threats" in a stump speech that right then still seemed fresh, even with a typical Harris LSAT construction such as, "The nature of a relationship of trust is such that it is a reciprocal relationship." "Speak some truths," she said. "We're at an inflection point."

She told how her mother kept asking her, "What are you going to do about it?" and then deployed her laugh, as she does strategically, to draw people in.

Then Harris slipped into the waiting car, through the snow building up on the highway, to an Iowa Black Caucus dinner, even though the Black Caucus consisted of just four members (which was still more than the number of Black members of the United States Senate). There were trays of meatballs and cookies and a vegetable platter—self-serve—and seats around more long folding tables. She brought out the stump speech again, but with some special additions about disproportionately high maternal mortality rates among Black women. She referenced a Coretta Scott King quote she liked to paraphrase about civil rights gains not being permanent: "Right now, the baton is in our hands, and the ancestors are looking at us and saying, 'What did you do when the baton was in your hands?'"

Then it was back in the car, for a drive to get a head start on the next day's round of more and more of these appearances, a full year before the caucuses. That night Bill de Blasio, the mayor of New York City, had holed up in a Super 8 motel when the snow had forced him off the trail near Sioux City. He was there, in his mind, to help enlighten the people of the Midwest about their progressive solidarity with the causes of the five boroughs. "I come from a city that works, is prosperous, is safe, because we see the opportunity," he said, when he pulled into a union hall on the edge of Des Moines the following afternoon. He told them what working people feel. He told them they needed to listen to Iowa farmers. He told them that they needed to invest in renewable energy, like wind farms, though a higher percentage of energy is produced by windmills in Iowa than in any other state. "We have to show that we're not the party of the elites!" he said.

A little under three dozen people came to see de Blasio that day. More people tended to show up to protest him at rallies back home.

———

The candidates bounced around the country, event after event. With a field this big, it didn't take much to throw together a program with multiple presidential hopefuls, all desperate for any chance at attention, so each week had at least two or three forums or panels or conventions or conversations, each with a critical mass of participants. Campaigns' schedules were defined for them, the candidates giving the same speeches to interlocking and overlapping groups instead of having the time to reach out to the kind of people who don't spend their afternoons and weekends at political events a year and a half before an election. Every day was the same circus and the same audience staging the same show, just with different backdrops and datelines. Yang called all the events they were asked to take part in, all the skills they were supposed to showcase, from flipping burgers to bowling to dancing at senior centers, the "candidate Olympics." By June, Hickenlooper was leaning into that. "My wife calls me the dark horse from the Rockies. If she were here, she'd compare me to Seabiscuit, the dark horse who becomes the legend."

The biggest event was Jim Clyburn's World Famous Fish Fry. "World Famous" because in the world of politics, there is no sense of reality, and because Clyburn is an institution in South Carolina: a member of Congress since 1993, the majority whip in the House, the duke of Democratic politics in the state, his name on a pedestrian bridge on the highway into Columbia. He is proudly, definitively, in control—"I worked hard as hell to get to be part of the establishment," is how he puts it—and he expects the proper deference, and the proper attendance. The "Fish Fry" had started as a cheap alternative for campaign volunteers who couldn't afford the high-priced state Democratic Party dinner traditionally held the same night, with the same candidates speaking first there before they headed over.

Usually the Fish Fry was held in a parking lot. As the first and, in the end, only event to which all the candidates would be coming simultaneously, the night was instead moved to a park that managed to be too crowded for anyone to sit and eat, and too spread out along a narrow redeveloped waterfront for most to be able to see the stage. "Fish Fry" overstates what was happening that night—no stacks of filets were being breaded and prepared by a fry cook. The fish, which organizers bragged weighed a total of 4,400 pounds, was deep-fried in advance and piled into aluminum containers, then dropped into plastic baskets, each containing a slice of white bread. The blue-and-white-checkered paper lining the baskets kept the meal clean and classy. Hot sauce packets were optional.

All the candidates were put in the same big holding room, with few staff allowed in, where they were presented with a pile of bright-blue Clyburn T-shirts they were asked to put on before going out to speak. This made for mash-ups like Beto O'Rourke, Eric Swalwell, and Tulsi Gabbard—who had been friends since their orientation as new members of the House in 2013— trying to squeeze in for a selfie together, and Biden popping over to offer to take it for them. Or Sanders asking de Blasio to give him a play-by-play of who was out speaking onstage, because the New York mayor is six foot five, and can easily see over most crowds.

It also meant two hours of awkward moments trying to put on the T-shirts. Without a bathroom to get to, they were left ducking into corners to change. The women huddled. There had never been more than one female presidential candidate before, so this was new too. The four senators made a pact: either they'd all wear the shirt, or none would wear the shirt. No one wanted to engage in the high school acrobatics of slipping out of and into a shirt in public. Kirsten Gillibrand was in a dress, making for another layer of awkward. Then, at the last minute, Warren headed out to the stage with a shirt on. *Damn it.* They all pulled their shirts on.

That wasn't the only shirt drama. When a staff member handed Sanders his T-shirt, he said he didn't need it, grousing, "I'm not going to be a billboard for Clyburn." When he came offstage, aides showed him tweets pointing out that he hadn't worn it. "Fine," he said. "Give me a shirt."

Onstage was the purest distillation of the presidential primary race: hours of the attendees waiting around for a free show that went on way too long, packed with candidates most people had never heard of before. One by one the candidates rushed onto the stage to give ninety-second speeches, each with a straight-from-the-Comedy-Cellar intro by Clyburn as the emcee, reading off blue note cards. "I give him credit for helping establish the tone for making our comeback possible," he said of the former congressman whose name he pronounced, "Beto O'Rook," citing both his Senate campaign in Texas and the original breakthrough, livestreaming the Democrats' sit-in on the House floor in 2016 to protest Republicans' lack of action on gun laws. Introducing Julián Castro, Clyburn said that Obama's former Housing secretary was "a young man who aspires for another housing program: the White House." Marianne Williamson, the New Age Oprah friend who sounded as if she had inhaled too much patchouli through a crystal and could never explain what she was doing in the race, was "writing a self-help book about running for president."

Biden, in his short speech, nodded to Clyburn as "the highest-ranking African American in the history of the United States of America, other than the guy I worked for, for eight years." Yang came onstage, bent his knees, and leaned back as he said, "Helloooooo South Carolina!" in full wrestler mode, while a small group of very excited supporters screamed his name over and over again in the type of chant that, under any other circumstances, would have seemed frighteningly cultish. Sanders took twice as much time speaking as he was allotted. Jay Inslee, the Washington governor, took a brief break from climate change to be the only candidate who even mentioned the big news of the moment: Trump was rattling around about a military strike on Iran. Harris spoke about the Mother Emanuel shooting, as a reminder of the divisions in the country and how she was running to overcome them. Warren shouted about big structural change and received the biggest, loudest cheers of the night as she ticked through the slogan versions of her main proposals for reworking the economy.

Only Buttigieg was absent that evening, as it fell during the week that a South Bend police officer shot a Black man, and he had decided to spend one night back home as mayor before reappearing on the trail the next afternoon.

All the other candidates stayed until the end, because Clyburn told them to. All the other candidates came back onstage after the last speaker, because Clyburn told them to. They all had on their matching blue T-shirts by then. "Get your head between someone!" Clyburn's daughter called out, as her father arranged the shot with Biden positioned at the center. They waved, applauded for one another, standing around for a whole minute wondering what to do, like confused first graders waving to their parents at the end of a school play. As Clyburn took the microphone to close out the evening, they began to wander off, a few joining in a chant from the crowd: "Beat Trump! Beat Trump! Beat Trump!"

The first Saturday in August, a white nationalist shot forty-six people at a Walmart in El Paso, killing twenty-three. That night in Dayton, Ohio, another man without a clear motive, but with a clear obsession with mass shootings, walked into the nightlife district and shot another twenty-six, killing nine. A few days later, an apocalyptic climate report hit, and ICE started doing mass roundups in Mississippi.

The following weekend, it was time for fried Oreos at the Iowa state fair, along with fried cheese curds, fried PB&J, and giant turkey legs. Harris bought a six-pack of pork chops on a stick. ("We'll know we're getting somewhere when people start pronouncing her name correctly," one of her consultants joked to another as they walked behind the pack of reporters and fans calling out "Ka-MAHL-a," "CAM-el-la," and more.) Steve Bullock put on an apron and grilled his own chop, after riding a potato sack down a three-story slide with his children. Gillibrand got a cone with two scoops of strawberry at the Iowa Dairy Barn booth, then stopped to smell the award-winning roses. Booker took a ride on the Ferris wheel. Bennet and Sanders both chowed down on corn dogs, and Bennet followed his with an intense turn on the bumper cars and a flight on the hang-glider ride with his teenage daughters. Most stopped by to see the sculpted Butter Cow and that year's special exhibit, the butter Big Bird and butter Oscar the Grouch.

"It's harder to smile these days," Castro said, as he walked through. "It's harder to smile because of everything that has happened. There's a darkness that this president has created for a lot of people, and what happened the other day in El Paso was just one more example of the times that we're living in and the lack of leadership that we have that's supposed to try to make it better."

He headed to meet his family at the cow-milking barn. Three dollars per pull. He passed.

Tim Ryan, the Ohio congressman running a hapless campaign, made his way around the fairgrounds with his wife and son. Ryan had just come from a caravan protesting for background checks that had driven through Ohio and into Louisville, Kentucky, to call on Mitch McConnell to order the Senate back into session for legislation.

"There's a general sense of insecurity, and yes, it's guns, but it's also health care, and it's also the economy," Ryan said, his son on his shoulders. "Then they win."

Tom Perez was walking row after row in the livestock barn, making the rounds of the goats and the pigs with the former lieutenant governor of Iowa, who had lost a 2016 Senate race. Democrats had tried to turn that race into a cause back when the biggest Republican outrage was blockading Merrick Garland and the incumbent was the chair of the Judiciary Committee. "This president wants us to be in a crouch," Perez said. "He wants us to be fearful every moment of every day." Back in 2007, Perez noted, Obama showed up at this same fair, despite all that the world was facing then, and he "put hope on the ballot." The cattle rancher to whom he had been talking was getting half as much for beef because of Trump's tariffs, he said. The tweets were exhausting. There seemed to be massive opportunity to organize in new spots. "I don't ask them who they voted for, but there's a lot of folks here who voted for Barack Obama twice and then voted for Donald Trump—" and then a goat on the loose from one of the pens ran by, and Perez was laughing too hard to finish his thought.

"Uh-oh!" he said, the chair of the Democratic National Committee and former labor secretary becoming for a moment just an awkward dad with a goofy laugh banging from the back of his throat as he watched a wrangler slowly corner the animal. "Still not caught! Still at large! Still at large!"

He focused again, complaining that Trump was always coming up with distractions. He knew that one of the most significant distractions was the sheer number of Democrats running, which was only going up. Tom Steyer had shown up at the fair after launching his campaign late. Joe Sestak, a retired admiral and former congressman who had lost two Senate races in Pennsylvania, had an aide handing out buttons as he stood near the soapbox, sketching out his fantasy of a first day as president that started with a town hall somewhere in the Midwest, followed by a visit to a mosque, then a trip to a gun show, then a flight to Paris to meet with European allies, ending with a flight back to meet with union leaders.

"I've been asked periodically to tell candidates A, B, and C that it's time," Perez said. "I was elected DNC chair—I wasn't elected king."

Biden's staff had brought him in by a side entrance and pointed him right to an ice-cream booth, where he'd bought two chocolate-dipped vanillas with sprinkles for a pair of young girls nearby and a chocolate-dipped vanilla for himself, leaving a $5 bill with orders to surprise the next child who ordered with an already paid-for treat. He spent his time on the soapbox giving the same stump speech. Naturally, he mentioned the "I refuse to postpone" quote from JFK's speech about going to the moon, which Biden has been telling audiences for forty years that they might not realize was actually his favorite line. He managed to mangle his standard big close as he shouted, "We choose truth over facts!" He came off the soapbox, worked his way around the building to the exit, and ran smack into a pack of reporters. He tried not to go on too long and blunder into trouble, kept interrupting himself with "the fact is," or "the point of the matter is," to steer himself to fast landings. The question of the day that everyone was baiting all the candidates with was, "Is Trump a white supremacist?" and Biden had his answer primed.

"I believe everything the president says encourages white supremacists, and I'm not sure there's much of a distinction," he said. "As a matter of fact, it may be even worse, in fact, to be out there trying to, in fact, curry the favor of white supremacists, or any group that, in fact, is anathema to everything we believe. Whether he is or is not a white supremacist, he encourages them, everything he does, he speaks to them, he's afraid to take them on."

The reporters were aggressively unimpressed. Would the third time for him be the charm in Iowa? "That's going to be up to Iowans. I feel good about it." How was he supposed to represent change? "I think I represent the change we need." How was he supposed to electrify voters? "Look at the polls. So far so good. I do it by being me."

He looked across the fairgrounds road to the stands at the covered picnic tables. "Hey, Joe, want a turkey leg?" a man called out to him. "Hey, Joe, we'll buy you a beer!" shouted another. Between them was another waiting fifty-reporter scrum of cameras and microphones and digital recorders waiting to shuffle in a mass around him, including a troll from Breitbart News shouting at him about the ridiculous right-wing insistence that Trump hadn't said anything defensive about the neo-Nazis in Charlottesville. How stupid, that this is what Biden had to do. What an incompetent campaign operation he could see he had, no one had mapped out the path he was supposed to take, making him ask the aide in front of him over and over "Where am I going?" or "Where am I headed?"

The state fair was supposed to be fun. This was all supposed to be fun. And now this mess of an appearance in a mess of a campaign—and with the shootings a reminder of how much whatever they were doing was pointless and detached from reality.

Was he having fun?

"So far," Biden said with a sarcastic smile, "you can see how much fun it is."

CHAPTER THIRTEEN

THE LINE FROM KYIV

I would not like to be a Russian leader. They never know when they're being taped.

—RICHARD NIXON

September 2019–December 2019

There might as well be a provision in the Delaware state constitution that if Joe Biden calls you in for a meeting, you have to go. Chris Coons never complained. He grew up revering Biden and had hiked all around Iowa in 2007 when he was a Delaware county official and Biden's second presidential campaign was in the process of never getting off the ground. Then in 2011, when he'd won his first Senate race for Biden's old seat, he'd arrived in Washington with a direct line to the vice president of the United States. Coons's Senate office desk had been Biden's when he was in the Senate and then in the White House. That's the kind of relationship they have.

Biden had called Coons in for a consult on January 8, 2019. His first sign that Biden was serious was that he was almost on time for the meeting. The second was the packet of polls Biden handed him about his popularity and what an appealing message he could deliver out on the trail. He was focused, with none of the usual tangents. Those were the days when Biden was still carrying on about his indecisiveness, such as when he was in a meeting with Larry Fink, the CEO of BlackRock investments, and responded to the rich man's offer to help by saying, "I'm 70 percent there, but I'm not all the way there." Coons didn't get the 70 percent version. He got the full pitch.

Sitting around a small round table in his private office, Biden asked Coons to level with him—not as a hometown cheerleader, but as a guy who'd been living through the last few years in the Senate, with Trump and the Kavanaugh hearings and everything else. The contrast with Trump was full of opportunity, Coons told Biden, so long as he didn't get caught up defending every bill he put his name to in the Senate in the 1970s or trying to run for a third Obama term. America is a country defined by change, Coons said. Recover, restore, rebuild weren't going to work.

Biden's biggest worry, Coons said, should be how Trump would go after him. He would try to turn Biden's family into a vulnerability, because that was Biden's strength, and Coons warned, "You already know how this is going to play out. Donald Trump is the most capable eighth-grade bully this country's ever seen. And he is really, really good at figuring out what holds you together, what's your core, and then going after it over and over."

Think about Ted Cruz, and how Trump had called his wife ugly and claimed his father had been wrapped up in the JFK assassination plot. Think about John Kerry, and how Republicans had turned a Purple Heart winner into a coward who ran from enemy fire. "They are going to Swift Boat your family," Coons told him. "You're going to see congressional hearings. Movies. They're just going to make shit up," Coons said. "Think about the worst possible personal attacks and then really think about whether that's worth it, even if you don't win."

"I know," Biden said. "That's exactly what I'm thinking."

Coons had been invited in by Ted Kaufman, Biden's longest-serving aide, and for two years, Coons's predecessor in Biden's old Senate seat after getting the appointment Beau had passed on. By then, they had already run through a memo for Biden of the specific targets that might come up in the campaign, how Trump would make an issue out of Hunter and whatever else he could. "We decided real early on that this was going to be the campaign from hell," Kaufman said, looking back. "I don't think there's a single thing that happened in the campaign that was a surprise." They also knew the cleanup after a Trump presidency would be intense. Kaufman liked to say the decision reminded him of the famous 1970s bumper sticker, "Life's a bitch and then you die," except in this case, "The campaign's a bitch and then you get to be president."

———

There's no understanding Joe Biden without understanding his relationship with Beau. There's also no understanding Joe Biden without his relationship with Hunter.

Hunter was the second son, just a year and a day younger. His brother got his father's and grandfather's name: Joseph Robinette III. Hunter was his mother's maiden name. They were both in the car that day in 1972, on their way to buy a Christmas tree, when they were hit by a truck. Their mother and baby sister were killed instantly. They survived, barely. Firefighters spent three hours pulling their bodies from the wreck.

Beau, as Hunter remembers it, awoke before him in the hospital room. That's Hunter's first memory: his big brother, all of three and a half to his two and a half, holding his hand and repeating, "I love you, I love you, I love you." As Hunter told it in his eulogy for his brother, the scene was reversed forty-three years later, with Beau dying as Hunter held his hand, repeating, "I love you, I love you, I love you." Joe sat there with them, holding each of his son's other hands. The original circuit.

"Growing up, when I attended political events with my pop, people would ask if I was Beau's daughter or 'Beau's brother's daughter,'" Hunter's daughter Naomi wrote in an emotional series of tweets in September 2020. "He liked it that way. He found his purpose in doing everything in his power to help Beau achieve his dream." She went on: "He and Beau were one. One heart, one soul, one mind. They grew up with the weight of knowing that each day they lived was a day that their sister, my namesake, and their mother lost. But they had each other, and that would be enough. They would make sure it was enough."

Beau was always special, had an ease about him. Hunter had the cool air that covered feeling not quite up to it. "I'm not sure if people put a lot of weight into who my mom and dad are as much as they focus on whether I'm doing the job they elected me to do," Beau said in that 2012 interview in Wilmington, halfway through his second term as Delaware attorney general. "George Bush, who I don't often quote, had a great line. He says he inherited all of his dad's enemies but some of his friends. . . . I've never spent a lot of time worrying about, and I don't think Delawareans spend a lot of time thinking about who my dad is. They judge me on what I'm doing or not doing." He meant this sincerely, though he was also aware of the absurdity of his claim: it was impossible to have run statewide in tiny Delaware in his first race, after his father had already been a senator there for thirty-four years and pretend that being Joe Biden's son didn't help. Beau, though, made an effort to push off on his own. There are more glamorous jobs than being an AUSA in Philadelphia for five years. Or being a member of the Delaware Army National Guard. He declined a gift-wrapped appointment to the Senate after Biden was elected vice president, though he knew his father revered that seat, and dreamed of passing it on to the next generation of the clan he'd built his family into. Joe didn't even try keeping the disappointment—but also grudging admiration—from seeping through the official statement he released in response: "Beau has made it clear from the moment he entered public life, that any office he sought, he would earn on his own."

If Beau didn't need Joe, Hunter had spent his life trading on his father's name. Joe was protective, always stepping in to help him along. When Biden was in the Senate, Hunter got a job at the Commerce Department. He got an appointment to the Amtrak board of directors. He was a lobbyist who managed to attract some heavy-hitter clients who were hoping for help from his sheen.

Joe Biden is a lifelong teetotaler after having grown up in a family full of alcoholics; Hunter was an addict from an early age with a self-destructive streak. And there was always a safety net: Beau famously kept his last name off his uniform when he was deployed to Iraq with his unit while he was attorney general so that he wouldn't get special treatment as the vice president's son; Hunter managed to get a special waiver to join the Navy Reserve at age forty-three and made it a month into his commission as an ensign before testing positive for cocaine. Then he somehow received an administrative, rather than dishonorable, discharge.

Hunter had no background in the natural resources business. Once he was done with the navy, he just happened to be named to the board of an energy company in the one country that had become his father's top foreign policy priority. Joe was aware, but not involved, always ready to again trust his son to do it right *this* time, a la-la-la willful naivete that Biden believed he could, and sort of did, maintain. Hunter raked it in again, while Biden considered selling his house to help Beau's family pay hospital bills.

And so this all became the story of how Trump, after spending his own life trying to impress a father who never trusted him but gave him his fortune, became obsessed that Biden loved his own son but hadn't stepped in directly to help him get rich—a monkey's paw wish that got Trump himself impeached and elevated Biden. And it's the story of how Biden, who defined himself as the guy who could find common ground—"the truth is somewhere between the two poles," he'd told the Wilmington *News Journal* in November 1970 in his first big interview as a prospective Senate candidate—finally began to give in and see himself as part of the resistance.

Biden's campaign was so weak, so broke, so dysfunctional that it might not have survived at all, had it not been for Trump's fear that he was a sleeping giant instead of Sleepy Joe. A direct line can be drawn between Trump's manic call to Kyiv and Biden's hand on the Bible sixteen months later. A year before the election, a Biden adviser was declaring the hearings "a help" to the struggling campaign. "You have people testifying under oath that the vice president did nothing wrong," the adviser said, "and you're fundamentally reminding people every day that Donald Trump doesn't want to face Joe Biden at the ballot box." "It gives him a really unique opportunity, in that it underscores his statesmanlike nature—what this means for the country, what it is for the Constitution," said another Biden adviser at the time. "It's not about Democrats and Republicans. That's his wheelhouse."

That Biden survived long enough to face Trump was almost in spite of Hunter. Hunter kept being sure he knew what he was doing, like the television interview in which he told his side of the Ukraine story in the middle of the House impeachment hearings, which the campaign found out he'd recorded only when they saw a commercial promoting its airing the morning of the October debate. Or when he decided to have a *New York Times* reporter and photographer visit his art studio for a feature that ran right before the South Carolina primary.

A few weeks after the chair set aside for him by the stage at Biden's campaign launch event in Philadelphia had stayed empty, he and his new wife spent the summer of 2019 in meetings with producers about a hazy concept they had for a reality TV show to highlight his charity work, which he said would also help soften his father's image.

He's OK with this? one of the producers remembers asking Hunter.

"I know where the line is," he said. "And my dad is understanding of what I am up to."

=====

By the time Trump dialed the president of Ukraine, demanding an investigation into Joe and Hunter Biden in exchange for releasing the military aid that Congress had already approved, every major presidential candidate except for Biden and Sanders had already called for his impeachment based on the Mueller report.

This wasn't a close call. Democratic primary voters hated Trump. Say terrible things about him, they'd cheer every time. Say he was a criminal, lock *him* up, and their guts would boil with the righteous, sneering hate that became a defining Democratic trait in the Trump era.

Biden wouldn't do it. He is an institutionalist. He didn't believe in impeachment—still doesn't—didn't want to support it, as offended as the former Senate Foreign Relations Committee chair was by this perversion of international affairs, and despite the impeachment being the result of Trump's targeting him and his son.

These were the days when pretty much everyone but Biden could see his campaign was over. Biden's staff hired a fire truck to march with him into the Iowa Steak Fry in September. He needed the boost, needed to see that his campaign wasn't just a humiliation for him and his family. Firefighters were his longest, strongest political supporters. Firefighters had saved his sons. He'd always see them all as heroes.

This had started as another simple fundraiser for Iowa Democrats, a reason to have a picnic, hear a political speech or two. Over the years, the event had become a production just short of featuring Macy's Thanksgiving balloons. Millions of dollars and weeks' worth of planning, all for an afternoon of political performance art for the reporters looking for colorful moments and for another couple hundred actually undecided Iowans.

The O'Rourke campaign had big letters floating in the water that read YOU

BETO BELIEVE IT and supporters banging cowbells—"To all of you boat-building, overnight-camping, sign-holding crazy motherfuckers, I am so proud to lead this campaign of the best people in America," he said coming in. Bennet's campaign had toy gavels "pound some truth into this campaign" and Colorado green chili at his booth. Warren's had people dressed up like pennies (for her two-cent wealth tax). Harris's had a woman dressed like a steak, and she arrived herself at the front of her drum line, clapping and playing air snares. Buttigieg had a five-piece band, including a cello and saxophone, entering to "Hey! Baby" ("I wanna know if you'll be my girl") on horns with his drum line and chanting, "I-O-W-A, Mayor Pete is on the way!" Castro had a mariachi band, dancing in a circle with women in white cowboy hats to "Guadalajara," at his personal request.

When Biden got his turn onstage, he was listless. He was always listless in those days. Still introduced by the same Springsteen song from the Obama rallies, reading the text printed out for him even though he had given the same speech a hundred times by then. Charlottesville. The country could survive four years of Trump, but not eight. America is an idea. The middle class. Unions. Scranton. His dad. Barack. It started raining again while he was talking. He put on a Beau Biden Foundation hat and pulled the microphone from the stand to wind up to his finish. "This is the United States of America—so let's get up! Take it back!"

A couple of people in the audience stood to applaud.

But at least Biden got the fire truck, and an ice-cream truck, and a crowd that came in chanting "Fired up, ready for Joe," before the reporters surrounded him and started to ask if he had ever spoken to Hunter about whatever he was up to in Ukraine. Never, Biden said. Don't look into him, investigate Trump, he said. "He is violating every basic norm of a president. You should be asking him the question, 'Why is he on the phone with a foreign leader, trying to intimidate a foreign leader?' if that's what happened. You should be looking at Trump. Trump's doing this because he knows I'll beat him like a drum."

That last part was the rare Biden riff that didn't leave his campaign depressed. Suddenly everyone on the campaign was tweeting a snare drum emoji. They had a new theme, if not any clue what to do with it.

Biden was still floating when he got in the car to ride off. Then *The Des Moines Register* poll hit. An aide handed it to him displayed on his phone.

Warren had surged; the poll numbers had caught up to the hype. He was falling—just second place so far, but headed down. He made a sound—"Boh"— like Homer Simpson, but with a *B*, as if a little air had been knocked out of him. As if he'd always assumed the ride would end eventually, and here they were.

Everyone in the car started rushing to explain to him why the numbers didn't matter. *Margin of error! It was early! She was too liberal to last!* But Biden was annoyed, angry, miserable. He had watched Warren catching on, and couldn't believe she was doing so well. He just didn't get it, just as he still didn't get why other Democrats were so willing to take him on. He'd been a devoted Democrat his whole life, and all of a sudden he wasn't good enough? And now he thought his terrible team was blowing it for him. Biden spiraled. He wanted explanations. He shot down the ones he got. He wanted solutions. They didn't have any. They kept talking, but he was already off into his own head. He couldn't rely on them. He was going to have to do it himself.

"Look guys," he finally said, cutting off the conversation. "It's fine. I'm not going to freak out over one poll."

In the spring, he had been focused on every detail. He wanted to compare how each twist of the campaign, each stop, compared to when he was running in 2007. By the fall, a sense of resignation had settled in. He wasn't asking those questions anymore.

"Iowa is just a thing to him, a thing in his head," Ricchetti would tell people. "He thinks bad things are going to happen there."

———

This is a constitutional crisis, Biden's advisers told him. He agreed; it was a constitutional crisis. Trump had been the one to politicize Hunter's role. Voters want to see strength, they want to see toughness, they want to see that you're going to duke it out. Biden and his advisers weren't going to make the same mistakes they decided Elizabeth Warren did by letting Trump taunt her by calling her Pocahontas until she got her DNA tested. No giving Trump an inch.

Whatever questions existed about Hunter Biden, they would insist to anxious supporters and skeptical reporters—because even the most on-message Biden aide knew there was no way to pretend Hunter hadn't been trying to trade off his father's name—well, Trump had overshadowed those by committing an impeachable offense.

It's always easier to get angry at someone else than face your own problems. For the Biden campaign, that involved indignantly picking fights over who else should be standing up for him. Biden felt that because he had endorsed Perez in the DNC chair race, and that they were close from being in the Obama administration together when Perez was labor secretary—and anyway, come on, he was going to be the nominee—he should merit a little cover. The Biden campaign asked the DNC, short on cash itself, to drop a few million into an ad campaign on Ukraine defense. DNC aides said no. The Biden campaign wanted Perez to go on the Sunday shows to speak up for Biden. DNC aides were surprised that the Biden campaign thought Perez could get himself booked that easily. Even if he could get on camera, no, they told him, he couldn't step in for one candidate in a big primary field when his whole mission had been to keep the DNC from looking as if it was favoring anyone, especially the non-Sanders candidate, no matter what the president had done.

Biden aides wrote talking points and emailed them to supportive pundits who were booked for TV appearances, trying to seed more suspicion. "This is the same scheme Trump pulled in 2016. He's attempting to hijack an election. He's attempting to pick the Democratic nominee. Voters won't let him. The media shouldn't fall for it again. And the DNC shouldn't let Trump dictate the race either," the document read. "It's clear the RNC will stop at nothing to bolster their president. Will the DNC let them? They've largely been silent on this issue. Will they call out Trump for his abuses of power?" Most of the people who got this email deleted it without ever thinking about it again.

Biden's aides stepped it up, pushing the idea that the DNC was too incompetent and broke to help. Finally the DNC's CEO called Biden's campaign manager, Greg Schultz, to ask them to stop. This wasn't helping anyone, she told him, but Schultz was unapologetic. "It's true," he argued. "You guys aren't pushing back."

Trump had pushed what had already been a slow sinking feeling among Biden devotees into a panic. Two former aides, both of whom had spent years playing up their connections to Biden, announced that they were starting a super PAC "committed to fighting back against Trump, his allies, the Russians, and the Republican Party—all of whom are engaged in unprecedented attacks against Vice President Biden in order to deny him the Democratic nomination." They launched a website, and to them that was a big deal. That looked as if it was about the most they could manage.

This was exactly the kind of small-ball, low-grade politics that appealed to Biden's instincts. For years, his sister had been his campaign manager and one of his brothers his fundraiser, and his newer aides were desperately trying to keep them out of this run. They needed artillery, not BB guns from old buddies.

Biden prided himself on being against super PACs. Again his aides went to him: he was going to lose if he stuck to principle, so he should decide whether he wanted to win—and if he did, he was going to have to do more than rely on old friends who, he might have noticed, had never actually helped him win a campaign. Biden gave the nod. Bedingfield released a statement with the careful wording necessary to abide by the laws about coordination. Schultz made two calls: to Steve Schale, the guy-who-knows-everything Florida strategist who had flung himself into the Biden orbit in 2015 and stayed tight with Schultz; and to Michèle Taylor, a well-connected donor from Atlanta who had attached herself early and fully to Biden shortly after Clinton lost. "You may have heard news reports that a super PAC is forming," Schultz said, reading from a carefully worded legal script. "The Biden campaign of course has no formal affiliation with the super PAC, and is not coordinating—but perhaps you might decide to join it."

Alan Turing was not required to crack this code. They both signed on.

Biden didn't want to address the charges or talk about Hunter, so short of any other tactics, his aides drafted another memo. They couldn't get their boss to go on the air, so at least they could try to get Rudy Giuliani off. It was another long, fulminating *Have you no sense of decency* approach, stretched out over two pages, addressed to the heads of the news divisions at all the big TV networks.

"While you often fact check his statements in real time during your discussions, that is no longer enough. By giving him your airtime, you are allowing him to introduce increasingly unhinged, unfounded, and desperate lies into the national conversation. We write to demand that in service to the facts, you no longer book Rudy Giuliani, a surrogate for Donald Trump who has demonstrated that he will knowingly and willingly lie in order to advance his own narrative." The paragraphs tumbled on. "Giuliani is not a public official, and holds no public office that would entitle him to opine on the nation's airwaves. The decision to legitimize his increasingly outlandish and unhinged charges and behavior—calling it 'news'—rests solely with you."

"We ask," the memo concluded, "that you no longer book him on your air."

The memo worked. Outside of Fox News and for the gleeful propagandists at OAN (One America News Network), Giuliani never appeared on TV again.

And still the conference calls stretched on and went nowhere. Impeachment didn't feel politically savvy, didn't feel as if it advanced Biden's fundamental view of what government should be. He would deflect, resist, delay. He would say he had to think about it a little more. Advisers told Biden he would have to relent, that he needed to be for this. He said no. The polling was obvious, the pressure was enormous. He said no.

Bedingfield had only been with Biden since 2015, coming on as his last communications director when he was in the administration. He connected with her immediately. She became a sounding board. She knew how to calm him. She knew how to poke him. This was the time to poke him.

She tried once, phoning while pacing outside her apartment building in Philadelphia. When that didn't work, she tried again a few days later with Donilon on the line, while taking a break from kicking a soccer ball in Rittenhouse Square with her kids. Cutting short one of his rambles, she told Biden, "This isn't about playing Donald Trump's game. This isn't about getting down in the gutter. Sir! He is coming after your family."

Poked.

On October 9, the campaign set up Biden in front of his preferred multiple-American-flag backdrop in New Hampshire. "To preserve our Constitution, our democracy, our basic integrity," he announced at a town hall, "he should be impeached." Biden invoked Joseph Goebbels, said Trump wanted the country to buy into his big lie. He said Trump needed to be removed because of the offenses he had already committed and the threat he posed to the future of the country if he stayed in office. "His lying," Biden said, "is matched only by his manifest incompetence." Four days later, Biden was at a United Food and Commercial Workers International Union forum in Iowa. "I may be the last guy to publicly call for impeachment," he said, "but I am the only reason why there is impeachment going on." That became the explanation, the roundabout rallying cry.

It wasn't all high road. Andrew Bates, a junior aide the campaign had hired as director of rapid response, got a reporter to give him Giuliani's cell number. Freelancing for his own amusement, Bates would text the former mayor every few days, trolling him directly onto his phone, never identifying himself.

"Hey, saw that you might be going to prison. You give them hell, Mr. Mayor! FWIW, I think you'd look STUNNING in orange," Bates wrote at one point. He kept going, sending him a link to a CNN article about the "shifting answers" he had been giving about which Russian oligarchs he had been meeting with in his crusade for Biden dirt, adding, "Sup? You see this?"

"You are a coward who can't identify himself because you're a liar," Giuliani responded. "You're cut off."

=====

Biden's real problem was that the campaign was broke. While the super PAC could pay for TV ads, he couldn't pay his staff, or for the hotel rooms to stay in on the road, or to keep the lights on at the headquarters in Philadelphia. It wasn't just that the fundraising had basically stopped, though it had. It wasn't just that Biden was burning through millions of dollars on private jets because he refused to take a commercial flight during the entire campaign, though he was. The chief financial officer had made an accounting error that did not include state payroll taxes on paychecks for a staff that had grown bloated, leaving the campaign hundreds of thousands of dollars short of where they thought they were, or where even the skimpy budget needed to be. Events had to be canceled, ads were pulled off the air. A hiring freeze was announced. There was so little money that aides would order extra salads and sandwiches on the tab for the press bus, which was billed back to the news organizations. Longer trips were scheduled to cut down on the money they were spending on planes and other sunk costs, though that led to Biden being more tired and prone to mistakes.

In October, the campaign invited its biggest donors to a special summit in Philadelphia. They knew this was about persuading them not to bolt but wondered how they were supposed to feel reassured when they were brought into a rundown, windowless room stocked with warm cans of Pepsi, the chairs arranged in rows, with a screen up front, like the grandparents in an old sitcom would use to show slides of their family vacation. Every presentation was another version of *Don't worry*. Don't worry, they would make their budget. Don't worry, Biden was going to come close in Iowa, close in New Hampshire, and then dominate beyond that. Don't worry, their analytics showed Biden was probably the only candidate who could count on getting enough delegates to win the nomination at the convention. *Who are these people?* donors started to ask themselves. *How are they in these jobs?* This felt like an event for a candidate running for Congress, not the front-runner former vice president trying to win the White House in an existential election for the nation.

The last item on the agenda was a "special guest," as if anyone hadn't already guessed that it was going to be Biden. He wasn't very reassuring, as he wandered off from the old podium in the corner and walked around the room, saying that he thought the campaign was going fine. He kept ragging Warren, complaining that she wasn't getting a real examination from the press, that the numbers in the plans she was touting didn't add up. He barely mentioned Sanders, waving off a question as it was asked, and spoke even less about the rest of the field.

Sanders, though, was talking about him. A lot. He was convinced that people believed in his message, and he didn't think the attacks on Medicare for All or free college worked. If people could see him as having equal chances of beating Trump, he'd win, and maybe, his aides thought, the way to get there was to chop down Biden's viability through his financial problems, which they sensed but had nowhere near a full understanding of. That fall, Sanders's campaign manager called a meeting of the senior staff and asked, "What can we do to push the gas in public and private to put him in tight spots?"

In the middle of this mess, Biden's Iowa field director asked for five days off for Thanksgiving and the week between Christmas and New Year's, and without asking for approval, emailed her staff to tell them they should all expect the break. No campaign would ever have approved a full week off for the entire staff a month before the caucuses, but there was such disorganization at the Philadelphia headquarters and on the ground in Iowa that the managers didn't realize what was going on until most had bought their nonrefundable plane tickets. When the leadership started coming down to cancel the vacations, the field staffers quickly set up a phone tree to spread the word that anyone who bought tickets before getting a call would have to be grandfathered in.

Frantic, the campaign management offered a compromise: they could have the days for Thanksgiving, but not at the end of the year, and no payments for change fees. Field staffers bombarded human resources with emails to say they were being abused, that their wages were being garnished. The campaign couldn't afford to have the staff leave for other candidates, it couldn't afford the headlines of a labor dispute on the campaign, and it literally couldn't afford to cover the costs. Schultz wrote to about a dozen of the biggest donors, scrambling for cash:

> Some of you are aware that we are trying to quickly hire 15 new field organizers in Iowa by Dec. 1st. The cost of a field organizer from Dec. 1 through Super Tuesday is right around $15,000. So far we have had 6 people step up and commit to raise $15,000 in new donations by the end of December to fund these positions," is how he framed it. Then he went full Sally Struthers: "We need to find 11 more people willing to commit and raise to fund these roles by the end of November. With these new dollars we will keep the hiring going and I will keep you updated with who you have all helped support.

Quietly, Jeff Zients was brought in to review the books. A multimillionaire whose deals included bringing both Major League Baseball and a proper bagel shop back to Washington, Zients had held a variety of budget and economic jobs in the Obama White House, but was mostly known as a fixer—most prominently when he'd come in to sort out exactly how the Obamacare website launch in 2013 had become such a sinkhole of dysfunction.

Zients created an escape plan, building the budget so there would be no debt when Biden pulled out, if and when he had to. They couldn't run a campaign that way, Schultz told him. They were going to have to, Zients said, because they needed to get ready to lose. They should try to win, Schultz said, and that meant blowing through whatever they had to so they could get to South Carolina.

＝＝＝

Every time Biden couldn't figure out how to break through, the answer was to think about naming a running mate. This time, he called Deval Patrick. The former Massachusetts governor was close with Obama, and was the rare politician whose skills the former president actually admired. Patrick had been gearing up to run himself before his wife's cancer diagnosis abruptly scuttled the plan. They kept the diagnosis private even from the Obamas—and though the former president reacted with disappointment but understanding, Michelle Obama was frustrated that he wasn't going through with it, eager to see him pick up where Obama had left off.

"We'd be unbeatable," Biden told him.

Patrick stopped him. This wasn't a conversation Biden should be having with anyone, Patrick said. The last thing voters wanted was presumption, especially presumption of being the nominee. "Why would you want me or anyone else to be portrayed as the person you need to win the primary?" Patrick said. "Go win the primary and then pick your running mate." He might be interested then, Patrick said, but not if he was just being used as a symbolic play for excitement or to give some Obama sheen or to attract Black voters.

Patrick left Biden with some advice, as long as they were on the phone: Stop talking about Obama and going back to Obama times, no matter how much he wanted to remind voters of that connection and to have them think about calmer times with more trust in the White House. "Nostalgia is not the point today," Patrick told him. "A lot of these issues were issues then, and people want to know where we're going, not where we've been."

By then, calls had been coming in for Patrick, asking him to think about jumping in late. The pieces all seemed to line up: His wife had responded well to treatment. Biden was pathetic. Sanders was talking about the right problems, but not the right solutions. Warren was coming off more strident and determined to outsmart everyone than the thoughtful, pragmatic person he knew from Massachusetts. Buttigieg wasn't catching with Black voters. Harris and Booker weren't catching with anybody.

He flew to Chicago for the Obama Foundation annual meeting, the only former politician Obama had invited to be on the board. The size, silliness, and celebrity had been scaled down, though not entirely. Billy Porter came. So did Charles Barkley. Obama closed the event with a warning shot to the Twitterfication of politics: "This idea of purity and you're never compromised and you're always politically 'woke' and all that stuff. You should get over that quickly. The world is messy; there are ambiguities. People who do really good stuff have flaws," he said. "That's not activism. That's not bringing about change."

In an interview that afternoon, foundation CEO David Simas, who had gotten his start working as an aide to Patrick in Massachusetts, tried to describe Obama's mood.

"I would not describe him today as optimistic. That doesn't mean there aren't reasons to make him feel better—the work he's doing through the Obama Foundation and seeing these incredible young people who are having a dramatic impact on the ground," he said. "But is he deeply and profoundly concerned about what's happened over the last few years? You bet."

After the foundation summit ended, Patrick got together with David Axelrod, his political consultant and Obama's. Axelrod spotted Barkley in the lobby. He introduced Patrick. The former NBA star did a riff about how he liked Julián Castro, but that campaign didn't seem to be going anywhere, and he liked Buttigieg, but he didn't think most Americans would go for a gay guy. "You should have run!" Barkley told Patrick. He knew Patrick had gone to Alabama to campaign for Doug Jones in the 2017 special election for Senate. Maybe he would come campaign for him back home in the Alabama primary on Super Tuesday.

Barkley headed out. You know, Axelrod said, he's right. The field was still lacking. The race was completely unsettled. John Lewis, who had also wanted Patrick to run originally, had quietly been telling him the same thing.

———

Harris had kept the little metal hand she'd found in Miami as a good luck charm and brought it with her onstage for the second debate in Detroit. This time it didn't work as well. She stumbled through trying to introduce her own Medicare for All alternative, then flubbed the response when Tulsi Gabbard, the congresswoman from Hawaii who seemed to not exist on quite the same plane of reality, started torching her over her record as a prosecutor. Gabbard had been telegraphing her attack for a week, and Harris had an answer prepared. Her sister, Maya, a former top official at the ACLU and Clinton's policy director for the 2016 campaign, was the main conduit for anxiety among Black supporters about Harris's coming off like a cop, and she was hesitant about going on offense. That night, her top advisers got drunk reminiscing to one another about how great the night would have been if Harris had actually said onstage what they had expected from her.

One of Harris's top advisers liked to compare her high-highs and low-lows candidacy to an EKG. Of someone with an extreme cardiac condition, maybe. Or someone just getting hit with the paddles every month. That second debate had been held at the end of July, and by August, her inner circle knew that the campaign was probably over. She was back at single digits in the polls, and nothing was getting attention. They didn't have any new ideas, so they kept repackaging what had already been planned, hesitating on the mundane. Staff who'd been bred in the Clinton campaign mentality of winning meetings and seeing headquarters as a factional battlefield began knifing one another, selling one another out to Harris, and feeding stories to reporters who were eager for the melodrama. Younger aides remained obsessed with whatever was playing out on Twitter, particularly on Black Twitter, though there weren't many expected Black primary voters on Twitter, and there weren't many Black voters at all in Iowa. Her top staff was privately admitting they didn't see any way she could turn it around. When they weren't spinning, they were admitting that they'd lost patience. "You think I don't know?" an aide said one night, recounting how many reporters were saying she had a problem with consistency. "You think I don't see it?" *This was the candidate whom all the others were supposed to have been so scared of?* one of her struggling rivals said in September, eyes going wide at the thought that anyone would support her. "She has no core."

By the time Harris landed in Atlanta for the November debate, her team was giving her maybe a two on a scale of one to ten for any chance of coming back. When has anyone ever gotten a second look? they'd ask in response to people trying to buck them up. That last stretch had devolved into the press staff, most of them younger, pushing for a blaze of fury against Buttigieg— arguing that was the only way to get attention—and the mostly older consultants trying to steer her to a respectable landing, a mix between fatalism and convincing themselves there was some code that their ingenuity could crack. Priorities bounced around like microwave popcorn—opposition research to immolate everyone else into oblivion, finding the perfect phrase, finding some way to get the press to ignore bad stories and promote good ones. The press staff developed a well-earned reputation for flipping out on reporters and mocking other campaigns for not being better at getting into fights with them on Twitter. No one was thinking about trying to explain why she was running for president. No one had ever been thinking of trying to explain it.

In the end, Harris turned out to be the mascot of the Democratic Party in 2019: unsure how much to stand by her past, both still obsessed with *and* unable to outrun Obama and Clinton, intrigued by the progressive tilt but skeptical it could ever really work, stumbling through figuring out race and identity and the rage of women who weren't going to take it anymore. She was suffocating under wanting to be defined by something more than Trump, yet feeling maybe that's all there was.

There's a difference between *I want to be president* and *I should be president*. Harris always had loads of the former. She never got much of the latter. Maya only reinforced her indecisiveness. She became so caught up in her own self-doubt that she wound up a never-ending mush of compromises and caveats that she knew was coming out as crap.

They, too, were running out of money. This went far beyond missing fundraising goals, as there were days when only a few thousand dollars would come in online, not even enough to cover their travel costs for the day. Harris was still telling people that she was a front-runner presidential candidate, but the response she was getting online was worse than that of a straggler House hopeful.

For a moment, Trump seemed as if he might have stumbled into saving her. He was a criminal; she could be the prosecutor again. "I think we made a big mistake going away from what we started with," she confided to a top aide as she thought about what to do. They decided to recalibrate starting in September at the Blue Jamboree, the Charleston County Democratic Party's big event of the year. Harris worked the small tent, where many of the local organizations and campaigns had set up their material. One table held jars with the candidates' headshots on popsicle sticks for the black-eyed-pea poll. She wasn't doing well.

"Sometimes folks say they can't connect because they've already made a decision," said Dot Scott, watching Harris shake hands and pose for iPhone photos a few feet away. "It's a woman thing, and a Black woman thing," she added. "Will America vote for a Black woman before a white woman?" The look on her face gave the answer. Scott was standing behind the Charleston NAACP table because she was the president of the chapter. No, she said, that didn't make what she was saying about Black women not being able to get ahead ironic. It made what she was saying even harder to deny.

Then, in the distance, a drum line. Twelve snares. Ten bass drums. Ten tubas. Sixteen trombones. Five sets of cymbals. "One, two! One, two three, four! *Impeachment.* Here we come!" And in marched Tom Steyer, the man who had helped mainstream putting Trump on trial with the Need to Impeach group that he bankrolled. Steyer had a big smile on his face from thinking the criminal had finally been caught, and from the high school band that his campaign had hired for his big entrance.

Steyer was first on the program. He hit on term limits and voter suppression and the climate emergency that had persuaded him to get into the race. "I listen to these debates, and I think, 'Wow, it sounds like we're a failed society, it's one crisis after another,'" he said. The crowd cheered more than he could have expected. He pumped his fist and scrunched his face as if he were keeping up with the beat at a family wedding.

Harris was next, serenaded onstage by a local mayor. This was like the first set at the Comedy Store getting a new hour ready. She held a sheet of notes in her hand. "I know, we're all exhausted. Who's exhausted right now? Just with all this stuff," Harris said, waving her hand over her head. "We've been spending the last two and a half years just throwing things at that inanimate object called the TV, going through individual and group therapy about it all, trying to figure out how this is all going to turn out, where we're going to end up. Is this really us? Is this reflective of who we are?"

The wind blew off the marsh. She started by trying to keep her hair under control, whipping it back, but gave up after a few minutes. "Justice is on the ballot in 2020. The fight for justice is on the ballot in 2020," she said, and connected that to people who couldn't afford to have children, children worried about shooting drills because Congress wouldn't move, threats of bigger hurricanes and floods because Republicans were in the pocket of corporations. All building up to: "Justice is on the ballot when we know we have a criminal in the White House who has been trading and attempting to trade our taxpayer dollars, holding them hostage in exchange for what he is trying to get from the head of a foreign government, to manipulate yet again a race for president of the United States," calling Trump "a walking indictment in a red tie" who had sold the workers of America out for tax cuts for the rich.

Harris was the one who had any hope of ending up anywhere near the presidency, but it was Steyer who made a bigger splash that day with the crowd.

In addition to the band, he had an area for his volunteers away from everyone else's lawn chairs with a massive spread of coolers of soda, chicken, Cobb salad, shrimp sandwiches, BLTs, and piles of pimento cheese. She was trying to appreciate the absurdity.

"Did you get my message?" Harris asked, catching up with him. Steyer looked confused, so she repeated what was in her voice mail: "I got nothing but mad respect for that marching band." He laughed, trying to make sense of the joke.

A few days later, Harris was sitting back in Washington, going through the Senate work that had piled up, looking at what had already been reported about the Ukraine call. She said in an interview, "We've got a confession, we have a cover-up—which suggests to me consciousness of guilt. And so I think that when it comes time to think of the impeachment process as leading up to a trial, you know it won't take a lot of time to present the evidence. And I think that there's a lot of evidence that is going to lead people to probably a quick decision."

Her polls didn't move.

=====

You'd think that Trump's zeroing in on him would have given Biden a burst of energy. It didn't. You'd think it would have made supporters more defiant. It didn't.

They could never get him to wake early. He'd have been up late the night before, stressing over every statement that went out under his name, as if each sentence were a policy statement he'd have to stick to. He was reluctant to call big donors, which had never been a major part of his political career when running in Delaware. Teleprompters were put in front, not because he didn't know a speech that stayed the same but to remind him to stay on script. When he'd grab the mic and start pacing around, spinning off script, he'd defend himself afterward to frustrated staff by saying he was "reading the room." A few aides had a running bet on whether he was going to tell the Lee Kuan Yew story—a hard-to-follow tale of the former president of Singapore asking him to locate the "buried black box" of America that explains the country's success. (The answer is a Bidenish pseudoscientific cultural mythology about the combination of challenging orthodoxy and a constant renewal of ambitious immigrant spirit.) Biden had been telling it since he was vice president, and never seemed to care that no one knew who Lee Kuan Yew was—even if he called him "Asia's Henry Kissinger"—or could make sense of what he was saying about the secrets to America's success. Sometimes he'd edge up to the story and aides would get nervous, but the bet only counted if he got all the way to saying Lee's name. They couldn't stop the one about his having dinner with Xi Jinping when he was asked how to define America, and he replied, "One word: possibilities."

Biden would always travel in two cars with staff. Sometimes they were vans with curtains over the windows, sometimes the standard tinted black SUVs. They'd call it the motorcade. He was always the VP, and they'd tense up when people referred to him just as Biden. He kept a collection of old aides around him like a security blanket, constantly briefing him in the car rides, and a printer in the back seat so he could edit minor tweaks into his scripts.

On Halloween, the motorcade pulled, too on the nose, into a "living history" museum in Fort Dodge, Iowa, made out like a preserved frontier town, with an old-town Main Street, a "Colby Bros. Livery," a blacksmith, and a general store. He delivered a stump speech at the front of a fake opera house. The day was getting late, but there were more walkers in that room than people who possibly could have had children young enough to trick-or-treat. By the time he walked over to the red tape his staff had put on the ground to remind him where to stand in front of the cameras, he'd talked to and taken selfies with everyone who wanted, then gone backstage to sign copies of his book and other memorabilia, like the flyer for a speech he'd given in Fort Dodge on that same day back in 2004.

Reporters were all rushing out their advance obituaries. After the event, Biden smiled and gave the half head shake and chuckle that he does when he's not trying too hard to hide that he's annoyed.

He could feel the race slipping away. "He's aware that there are issues with the campaign, especially as it relates to money," one person who'd been talking with him at the time said. Aides had gotten the nagging sense they were spinning one another in meetings about how things weren't actually so bad. Some built angry Potemkin delusions around themselves. "The problem here is the same problem this campaign has had from day one—which is not that the campaign has a problem, or the candidate has a problem, but the coverage, and the way this works is at odds with reality," said one adviser at the time. "If we ran this campaign in order to appease the press corps, we would have been in trouble. We would have had to drop out the first week in April."

Echoing Trump, Biden aides would complain about being beset by media "elites" who didn't get it and wanted to see him fail, and about how everyone said early polls didn't matter when Biden was in first place but insisted that the (not as) early polls mattered when Warren was up. All the smart insiders writing him off now were the same people who'd written off Trump and Sanders, never self-reflective about how wrong they'd been and still convinced that their little bubble of retweets was a good reflection of America.

Meanwhile, all the attention from impeachment tripled Biden's online donations from the summer slump. Three times close to nothing still didn't add up to much.

In the spring, the swing-district national security–minded House Democrats who had helped win the majority were complaining about the new progressives pushing them into becoming activists. By the summer Trump was making them feel as if they had no choice. "I have an Article II where I have the right to do whatever I want as president," he had said in July—two days before he called the president of Ukraine. Recklessness and freneticism were constant. "We're just not there, and when we're there, we'll know it," they would tell themselves in small huddles, or on a group text chain they kept going on Signal, the encryption app that became popular in Washington after all the hacks of Democrats in the 2016 campaign. "When we know it, we'll act."

As soon as the news of the Ukraine call broke, the reaction was, "We might be there."

Politicians facing tough elections don't like to go out on their own. The first week in December, Abigail Spanberger, hoping to hold on to her own seat in Virginia, suggested that the seven "security Democrats" take a position together, in writing. Back home in their districts for the weekend, over a conversation on Saturday night without telling their staffs, they agreed. Spanberger proposed an essay on Medium, so they could take as many words as they wanted to hash out their argument, not fully grasping what they were about to bring on. When a few aides were finally looped in, Spanberger's communications director told them this was the kind of earthquake that needed to be an op-ed in *The Washington Post*.

On Monday morning, Spanberger and Jason Crow, a former army ranger from Colorado, headed to the office of Chrissy Houlahan, an air force vet from Pennsylvania. Sitting on the couches in her private suite, balancing their laptops on their knees, they started pasting drafted paragraphs into a shared Google document. Mikie Sherrill, a former navy helicopter pilot who had flipped a seat in New Jersey, and Elissa Slotkin, another former CIA agent who'd flipped a Republican seat in Michigan, called in with their suggestions. They were all on edge, arguing over sentences, bartering over words. Eventually they landed on a version all could agree on.

"This flagrant disregard for the law cannot stand," they wrote. "To uphold and defend our Constitution, Congress must determine whether the president was indeed willing to use his power and withhold security assistance funds to persuade a foreign country to assist him in an upcoming election."

All they wanted was an investigation to determine whether Trump did what he was being accused of. Feigned innocence: If he didn't do anything wrong, wouldn't *he* want to clear his name? Wouldn't all his supporters in their districts? This was performative. They knew he did it, because by then, Trump had acknowledged that he had done everything he'd been accused of. He just insisted that he could, as part of his broader, very not-Madisonian insistence that the Constitution gave him "the right to do whatever I want as president," as he had put it in a speech two days before trying his call with the Ukrainian president. "If these allegations are true, we believe these actions represent an impeachable offense," they wrote.

Spanberger and a few others headed to the house where Houlahan lives when she's in Washington, waiting for the op-ed to go live on Monday evening. Their phones started going wild.

Pelosi had been planning to announce the impeachment inquiry on Monday morning. Her staff had been reaching out quietly over the past few days, warning a range of members that she was about to move, and that they probably wanted to get out ahead of her so they didn't seem as if they had been bullied by the liberal speaker from California. She announced the impeachment inquiry on Tuesday afternoon, charging that Trump's actions revealed a "betrayal of his oath of office, betrayal of our national security, and betrayal of the integrity of our elections."

They split hairs to explain themselves. Slotkin argued that the difference between the Mueller report and the Ukraine call was that the call was prospective, crimes that the president was still in the process of trying to commit rather than an investigation into what he had already done.

She acknowledged that given the timing of Trump's calling the Ukrainian president—the day after Mueller's testimony to Congress in July—he might have been reacting to how little Democrats had done to stop him.

"Even though many of his cohort are now serving time or in the middle of litigation, the lesson that he clearly took away is that 'I dodged a bullet, and now maybe I'm bulletproof,'" Slotkin said, a few days after the op-ed ran. "He said that he could shoot someone on Fifth Avenue and no one would care, and he clearly is acting that way when it comes to our national security."

Everyone knew Trump had done it. As soon as that op-ed ran, everyone knew that he was going to get impeached. Everyone knew that he was going to be acquitted too. But what a perfect couple of months, as senators got to pretend they were weighing evidence as impartial jurors, and cable news got to cover the performance art, interspersed with trivia about Senate procedure and Andrew Johnson.

Perfect, that is, except for all the presidential candidates who still hadn't broken through and now never would, and the senators in the race who became leashed to Washington just at the moment when the race got hot. The process was plodding but unpredictable, a boa constrictor slowly gulping down one manic mouse after the next.

Cory Booker was standing in a parking lot in Des Moines after spending an hour in a day care center just a few blocks into the lower-income part of town for a roundtable discussion on helping domestic abuse survivors, boosting stay-at-home parents, and addressing gun violence. Responding to a question about the crisis in America, he talked about the terrible burden of child poverty in America.

No, not that. The whole impeachment, the cracking of the Constitution thing.

"Oh, *that* crisis?" Booker asked.

"On some level," Buttigieg said, after an event in Rock Hill, South Carolina, "you could say that the stakes right now, the level of crisis we're facing, is so great that it's almost impossible to speak to it through a traditional political process like a campaign. In many ways, we may yet be underreacting." He would talk about the situation in a very Buttigieg way, explaining that what America was facing was reminiscent of the architecture in Saint Peter's, which placed the pope's seat at such a focal point for the whole structure that the human mind couldn't quite process it.

A few days later, in the middle of a swing through Washington, he stopped himself. How close was America to the brink of a much worse situation? "Closer," he said, "than we think."

The articles of impeachment were passed by the House on December 18, while Biden was in the air on his way to Los Angeles to participate in yet another debate. It was the forty-seventh anniversary of the accident that had killed his wife and daughter and put Beau and Hunter in the hospital.

CHAPTER FOURTEEN

HEART TROUBLE

Mothers all want their sons to grow up to be president, but they don't want them to become politicians in the process.

—JOHN F. KENNEDY

October 2019–January 2020

On another night, Sanders probably would have been at the Triple George Grill, putting away another steak. But in October 2019, he felt weak onstage and asked for a chair, which was out of character. His staff was spooked. In the van driving back from the event, his deputy campaign manager Ari Rabin-Havt prodded him, worried, but also worried that he'd get angry and snap back. "What are you feeling?" Rabin-Havt asked.

"My chest feels tight," Sanders said.

"Can I get you a doctor to your room?"

"You can do that?" Sanders asked, surprised. He was breathing heavily.

Rabin-Havt was done being delicate. Without Sanders seeing, he searched for urgent care facilities on his phone. He told the body man where to drive, in a spot tucked in behind the MGM Grand. "How long until we're there?" Sanders asked a minute later. Panic.

The staff at the facility called 911 almost as soon as they saw him.

The siren was going, the lights were flashing inside the ambulance and outside as they sped out onto the Strip. Sanders wanted to know how much the drivers made per hour. And what did they think about the health care system? Did it make any sense to them?

They pulled into the ER driveway. Rabin-Havt hopped out with Sanders's driver's license to alert the nurses who the patient coming in was. They took him around the back, moved him into a room. Started him with the pain chart, all the smiley faces going from hunky-dory green to crying red. "That's a bullshit question," Sanders said. "I don't feel pain. I just feel tight."

He called Jane to put her on speaker as the doctors gave him the diagnosis: one clogged artery going into his heart, which meant he was going to have to go in for a procedure immediately. The nurses asked him to take off his glasses and his wedding ring. He handed Rabin-Havt the ring, wouldn't give up his glasses. Jane rushed to the airport in Vermont while Rabin-Havt called Jeff Weaver and Faiz Shakir, who himself rushed on a flight to Vegas. The few staff who'd been alerted stayed up all night, thinking through necessities, like making sure all his grandchildren didn't find out about what had happened from a news alert on their phones. They were scared. Rabin-Havt held the ring tight, terrified of dropping it. He slipped it onto his own finger, just in case. They all waited to find out what happened next.

———

Warren's launch back on New Year's Eve had been a flub. The first few weeks of fundraising were terrible. She was still barely holding on to a dream of heading off Sanders from getting in. She had been the top fundraiser in the Democratic Party before she'd started running, but almost as soon as she entered the race, she had to dip into that bank account to backstop the payroll for the enormous staff the campaign had hired to be the dreadnought in the race. At the end of February, she announced that she would stop attending private fundraisers with big donors, which her aides portrayed as a brave stab at campaign finance reform. The subsequent press release spun out political nerd trivia that, for the past few Democratic cycles, whoever had staked out the strongest position on campaign finance reform had surged in the primaries: Howard Dean in 2004, Obama in 2008, Sanders in 2016.

Clever calculations weren't enough. Warren and her aides telling themselves for months that she was the only candidate who knew exactly why she was running had added up to little more than insistent intellectual narcissism.

Every sentence in every story sounded as if she'd practiced it one hundred times in the mirror, and every one of those sentences and stories was repeated in every speech. "She takes what is utterly authentic and makes it sound inauthentic," said David Axelrod, the former Obama political consultant whose great maxim was that campaigns are won by candidates connecting voters to their stories. She'd recorded an episode of his podcast at the end of February. He'd been blown away by how bored he was sitting there with her.

No one was expecting much when Warren showed up at the Sheraton Manhattan Midtown for a speech at Al Sharpton's National Action Network convention at the beginning of April. The national media was mostly focused on one sentence in which she had come out for ending the filibuster. That was news for a few hours. The more significant move for Warren's campaign was a story she'd told a few times before, about how as a young mother she'd broken down, her baby son kicking and screaming, not letting her change his diaper until she was covered with snot and pee and his tears and hers. Her Aunt Bee, sounding as if she'd popped out of Mayberry, called from Oklahoma to check in. Warren started crying and said she was going to quit her job. "I can't get there tomorrow, but I can come on Thursday," she remembers her aunt telling her. And she did, along with her Pekingese named Buddy, staying with the Warrens for the next sixteen years.

Then the revolutionary twist: "Now, if every working mom in the country had an Aunt Bee, we'd all be good. But that's not the case. I know how lucky I was to have Aunt Bee save the day," she said. "Think about all the moms in America who don't have an Aunt Bee." And from there she unrolled the first and most extensive child care proposal of any candidate in the whole campaign. "So," she said, "here's how my plan would work."

She had a plan, it started to seem, for everything. Warren the wonk was reborn as Warren the Wonk. Her momentum built by the week. She had a plan for that. She greeted thousands in a selfie line at every stop, pioneering a new hybrid of free advertising and movement building. She could have been spending time with big donors getting money to buy TV commercials, hoping they'd hit voters. Instead she was spending hours winning over voters personally, then getting each person's entire network lit up from seeing the photos on Facebook, Twitter, Instagram.

Excitement mounted. By June, her campaign was producing I'M A WARREN

DEMOCRAT T-shirts and buttons. By July, while in Milwaukee to speak to a Latino issues conference—where she rolled out her new immigration reform plan—she took an afternoon to go on a walking tour with a community activist and a twenty-two-year-old whose parents were undocumented immigrants. "Talk to me about housing," Warren said, as the reporters tripped on the curbs and banged into fire hydrants, and her videographer team banked the footage. "Where are the teachers drawn from?"

The walk ended in a parking lot, beneath a mural of a bald eagle facing a dove under a rainbow, with an olive branch between their beaks, a lightning bolt striking the section closest to the dove. She stared at it for a few seconds, made sure to have a studious reaction pose.

That night 1,500 people packed a Milwaukee high school gym, cheering and laughing along with Warren through a town hall. She walked out to "9 to 5." She stood in front of an oversize American flag. She finished to "Respect."

Two days later in Philadelphia, at the liberal-activist Netroots Nation conference, the annual gathering where her appearances going all the way back to 2010 had helped launch her into progressives' fantasies, she looked at a photo of the mural. What did she see? "Power, but also change." She moved in close to point to the eagle. "Look at how much power there is. And yet, notice the dove is not afraid. The eagle is static; the dove is more dynamic," she said. "The lightning bolt is not the most prominent, but it is the piece that says, 'It all changes.' And it changes fast and powerfully when the moment comes." She was so on message that even graffiti in a parking lot in Wisconsin slotted right into what was already on her mind.

"Some people think small change, incremental change, is how we will move America in a better direction; I think big change is easier," Warren said, ticking through some of her biggest proposals, from universal child care to canceling student debt. If put into place, she would make for the biggest active restructuring of the American economy in history. "It's easier to get more people into the fight, and it's easier to get more people to pay attention to how it would touch their lives. And that's our path to winning. So this is the 'Ask for big or ask for little.' Ask for big!"

More established Democrats watched the crowds, the coverage, and the monster fundraising numbers she started posting, and they were drawn in too. Maybe Warren *was* the answer, the way to get the Sanders energy without having to take Sanders. Maybe she could pull off all the policy smarts for which Clinton had gotten thrashed. After years of Trump battering, maybe voters didn't want to burn down the building anymore, but wanted some blueprints for what might come next. "It's the planning and the ability to explain it and get things across," Ben Silver, a twenty-nine-year-old, said after a Warren town hall in New Hampshire in July. "It's about telling people exactly what I believe is broken and what we can do to fix it," Warren explained to reporters a few minutes later. "The number one thing I hear afterwards when people come through to do selfies is, 'This gives me hope.' Hope because it really is a path forward. It's not pretend; it's not hand-waving."

Warren knew that being an awkward academic made her seem an odd fit for leading the kind of mass politics beginning to take off under her. "The difference now is, I see the path," she said in that interview at Netroots Nation. "I am an unexpected person to lead this movement. But I know that it's right."

She arrived as the conquering hero when the Democratic National Committee members had their summer meeting in San Francisco at the end of August. The event had less of a political-bosses-in-the-backroom than an insurance-convention sheen, meeting in a drab Hilton ballroom with rows of folding tables covered in white tablecloths and evenly distributed hotel pens.

"To her advantage, it appears as though she did not let the growing pains of the early stage of her campaign sidetrack her from creating an infrastructure," said Trav Robertson, the Democratic Party chair in South Carolina, who was starting to consider that she might win the crucial primary in his state. "Her campaign's been fascinating to watch," he said. "It's a study of 'Steady and slow wins the race.'"

"Most of all, she's smart as shit," said Don Fowler, the then eighty-three-year-old former South Carolina party chair who'd been around the establishment for so long that he wasn't even Bill Clinton's last DNC chair, heading out as the meeting ended on a Saturday afternoon. "You don't want a dumb-ass president."

———

Before the heart attack, Sanders's campaign had been struggling for months. The early front-runner energy had evaporated; events that had been like rock concerts had become small liberal arts professor seminars.

In 2016, the most serious that Sanders and his aides got to considering actually winning the presidency was joking about appointing Weaver, then his campaign manager, as ambassador to the Vatican. In 2019, he entered as the front-runner. "There's a three-out-of-four chance we are not the nominee," Shakir told the senator as they got ready to launch, "but that one-in-four chance is better than anyone else in the field."

Those first few months of his 2020 run, Sanders was Eddie Murphy in *Trading Places*, suddenly flush with money and status that transformed him overnight: $10 million raised online in five days, blowing past the goal of 1 million people signing up on his website to support his campaign (including 324,000 new ones who hadn't been part of 2016). Aides started out identifying three weaknesses—that Sanders was too old, that "socialism" was scary, that voters would hold Sanders's not being registered as a Democrat against him. They hoped those could all be conquered by a well-run campaign, but they knew they only needed to peel off so many voters from other candidates, because no one in the field had a core of supporters anywhere near as big or as passionate. Take their 20 percent, build it out to maybe 30 percent, knock Warren out along the way. In a big, divided primary, that's about all Sanders would need to hitch a plurality to the nomination.

The plan was to prove their case through a tour of the industrial Midwest, the blue wall that Democrats needed back, and that most had convinced themselves only a moderate could win. The Sanders campaign would fight back by showing he could draw big crowds, and end at a Fox News town hall in Bethlehem, Pennsylvania, with old steel blast furnaces visible out the window behind the camera shot, where the audience applauded him talking wealth redistribution, to the visible discomfort of the anchors. (Other ideas that had been bounced around included having the actor and chief Hollywood Bernie bro John Cusack suggesting the senator give a speech at a convent.) But by Memorial Day, Sanders was the one chasing a quiet reboot in New Hampshire, aides picking a small room for a weeknight rally in Manchester, then not coming close to filling it. They attempted to claim this was all part of the plan—the *new* plan. The plan they always figured they'd have to rely on, because that's just how it goes in a long race for the nomination.

"It certainly would be *cool* to become president of the United States, and that public housing they have there in Washington is pretty good for the president," Sanders had said at one of the earlier stops in the swing, trying to reboot the insurgent spirit, with backyard fundraisers where Ben Cohen and Jerry Greenfield themselves came to scoop ice cream, now needing more flair than he could generate on his own. "I'm not running just to occupy the White House. It would be cool, but I've got a good job now. I am running because I think the time is now to transform this country. I don't want to win and bring us back to the status quo."

He jokingly threatened to sing ("Nah, that would be a disaster") and played what one aide called "Professor Bernie" as he turned the microphone around at town halls and quizzed people on how well they knew the Sanders diagnosis for what's wrong with America. Staff who had gotten tired of swearing to reporters that Sanders was really much warmer in private than his Larry David persona were amazed to see him start asking people to line up at the end of events to take selfies, Warren-style. Among those who took up his offer in New Hampshire was a woman holding a pet she introduced as Bunny Sanders.

Convinced that part of why he fell short in 2016 was a staff that on most days seemed as if they were working at an adult summer camp, Sanders ordered a more professionalized operation for this run. They all felt the burden: in the first, out-of-nowhere campaign, any impact they made was a success; in the second campaign, every day was another chance to disappoint the expectations for him. There wasn't much long-term planning or set budgets for particular departments. Instead of managing from headquarters, Shakir was often on the road with Sanders to build up his own relationship and trust with the candidate. Dysfunction piled onto dysfunction. Because the initial spark came from not being the establishment, professionalizing meant losing what made the first Sanders campaign feel exciting and powerful. Sanders became the first live experiment in a well-funded, unionized campaign workforce, and top aides acknowledged the irony of grating at the pushback from junior staff who saw the campaign as a fight for their values, and so didn't understand why they should have to work long hours or not be paid more.

Feeling the lack of his magic, Sanders focused on logistics. By the summer, he was demanding daily reports of how much cash the campaign had on hand. He would count the number of staffers with special security access pins backstage. He'd ask advance staffers where they'd come from, as if he cared to get to know them, when he was really just spitballing airfare estimates in his head.

A new policy was whispered around: "If the senator asks where you're from, just say the city where you're based." Sanders got wise to it, started asking deeper questions to test if they were telling the truth. He would try to count the crowds onstage, then ask for the official count as soon as he walked off-stage. They'd puff him up with white lies to keep him on track, stop him from getting caught up in what was going wrong.

A fatalistic martyrdom set in: "2016 was understanding the mission. This race is about understanding why the man pushes so hard for the mission," said Nina Turner, the former Ohio state senator and campaign cochair who elevated her defensiveness of Sanders into a capoeira of sermonizing and activist-speak, on a conference call that the campaign organized in the middle of August to insist that everything was fine. "Polling is one thing, but the energy on the ground," Turner said, was more important. To demonstrate her point, she claimed that Sanders had drawn the largest crowd at the Iowa State Fair the previous week. That had visibly not been true. Warren's crowd had clearly taken up more of the fairgrounds.

"It's not that polling doesn't reflect our strength in Iowa—it's that bad polling doesn't reflect our strength in Iowa," Weaver chimed in. Turner turned the phrasing around another way: "This is about what we see with our eyes and hear with our ears." Campaign aides and supporters were thrashing around in their own bubble, tweeting photos of Sanders's crowd at anyone who noted that Warren's had been bigger, without ever sending photos of Warren's as a comparison. They were sensitive, edgy, insisting that the campaign was going great but that no one else recognized it, or that they were victims of one scheme or another to refuse to recognize it: The polls were part of the effort to stop him. The reporters were part of the effort to stop him. Everyone was part of the effort to stop Sanders, to stop Medicare for All, or to stop . . . it was hard to keep track.

When Sanders gave his speech in San Francisco at the DNC meeting at the end of August, he was less combative than he'd ever been at a party function. Perez had succeeded in his efforts to keep Sanders from perceiving the DNC as his enemy, through all the outreach and all the concessions and building debate qualifications around what suited the man attempting a hostile take-over. There was some applause when he mentioned Medicare for All.

"Let us be honest with one another as we head into the 2020 election," Sanders told them in that ballroom. "Playing it safe, according to the old rules, is the most dangerous course of all, and a course of action that could cost us the election.

"This is our time. This is our time to stand up for the working families of this country and bring the transformative change that has been so long ignored. This is our moment to invite working people and young people into the Democratic Party to create that grassroots movement we need to sweep Trump and his friends out of office," Sanders went on. "This is the moment in this crucial, unprecedented time."

Sanders's high-minded talk didn't reflect how his supporters were internalizing the fact that Warren was starting to overtake him. At events, they'd call her a poser. Bring up the Cherokee DNA scandal, say she couldn't be trusted. Warren's top aides started keeping track, with Dan Geldon compiling a long document listing the tweets of Sanders's aides attacking her. "The whole idea of a neutrality pact, a nonaggression pact, didn't exist," said a Warren adviser of that period. "It was us not responding to constant provocation."

Eventually Warren had heard enough. In September, she called Sanders and told him things were getting a little hot. "I know this is a campaign," she said, "but I'm worried we won't be able to unify in the spring because of this."

Sanders started badgering back. He'd heard stories of progressive groups being pressured to back Warren, and that was compounding his bitterness at being eclipsed, his frustration at seeing his own campaign flag. She was the one who had drawn twenty thousand people to Washington Square Park. She was the one who had just won the endorsement of the Working Families Party, a group that bills itself as the home of grassroots progressives, though it is controlled by union leaders who had helped secure the vote for Warren. "I keep hearing that *your* people are going after *me*," he said.

Warren's campaign wouldn't make job offers without reviewing every prospective hire's tweets, then monitored staff accounts throughout the campaign to keep them in line. Sanders's campaign was proud of its adept Twitter trolls, which were part of his business model. Sanders never took responsibility for his supporters. That's just the way they were, he would say. He couldn't control them. What was the point of telling them to stop? And anyway, everyone had their own people acting terribly online—his just got more attention because he had more supporters, and more supporters online, and because those who were out to get him liked to tag him with that.

As long as she'd known him, Warren was still taken aback at his response. That much unwillingness to acknowledge a problem, or to even see that there was a problem, poisoned what was left of their relationship. She told herself— and then relayed to her top aides—that she wasn't going to deal with him the same way anymore.

━━━━

Two weeks after that call, Warren was phoning Sanders in the hospital.

Jill Biden had called Jane Sanders. Harris reached out, asking to stop by, but Sanders aides pushed that off. Harry Reid called, said he already knew which hospital to go to, had spoken with the doctor and was coming by for a visit that Sanders's aides quickly decided to take advantage of as a signal to anxious Sanders staffers and the larger political world alike that Sanders was OK.

The call that changed the race came through on Shakir's phone. Sanders's was still off, and Alexandria Ocasio-Cortez was determined to get through. Shakir held up his iPhone. She was in, she said. She was ready to endorse.

Warren had been chasing Ocasio-Cortez the way she chased everyone— Energizer Bunnying in phone call after phone call to talk issues, to talk politics, to push and check in and push again. Ocasio-Cortez listened to Warren's pitches about reinvigorating progressivism, showing it could win and work. The power of women. It was interesting. But Sanders was a hero who had become a mentor. She was never going to turn on him.

Sanders hadn't endorsed Ocasio-Cortez in her 2018 primary run, though it would have made sense to: he had inspired her into politics when she'd knocked on doors for his 2016 campaign, she talked about Medicare for All and free college because he'd set the way, and his Our Revolution group supported her. The day after she won, Sanders called to congratulate her, and they'd clicked immediately. He asked her to come along to Kansas to campaign for two House candidates who both went on to lose. Sanders is forty-eight years older than Ocasio-Cortez and he's not much for new friends, but he was fascinated by her savant understanding of how to get the progressive message out.

Sanders left it to aides to lean on her for an endorsement. Not even for her would he get too involved in the chase. She put them off for months. She didn't want to get into the presidential race too early in her first year in office, and, cautiously guarding her own reputation, waited to see how serious Sanders's campaign became. They kept after her, and a week before the heart attack, they arranged for her to fly secretly to Burlington, with covert hotel reservations and surreptitious airport pickup, for dinner in his backyard. When they went for buckwheat blueberry pancakes the next morning at a well-known café in Burlington, they were quickly spotted. Sanders assumed that this must have all been part of her social media savvy. It wasn't.

Far from Vegas, Sanders's aides were in tears, distraught that the man they'd fallen for way beyond politics might die, terrified that the movement might be over. What was meant to be a caring gesture—a cart of catered desserts sent to Sanders headquarters with a note, "From your friends at Team Warren"—was taken as gloating by Sanders staffers, who wanted to respond, "We're not out of the way yet." That wasn't the intention of the aides who'd placed the order—though at that moment, several of Warren's senior advisers were looking at Sanders's flagging campaign, poll numbers which showed she could beat Biden in a head-to-head race but that Sanders couldn't, and hoping he might use the health scare to make a graceful exit.

Sanders himself was adamant: if he was healthy enough to run, the voters should get to decide what happened to him. That wouldn't have amounted to much if not for Ocasio-Cortez. Twelve days after telling doctors that he thought their smiley-face pain chart was stupid and then recovering back home in Vermont, Sanders showed up on the debate stage in Westerville, Ohio. Just as the debate was hitting its dragging point an hour in, the news leaked that the heart attack had pushed Ocasio-Cortez over the edge to back him, and she was going to harness as much of the new progressive energy to Sanders as she could. With Warren peaking and reporters instinctively turning to taking her down a few pegs, here was the perfect new political story to chase: the battle for the progressive lane.

The debate itself was an even bigger problem.

Over the summer, Buttigieg's pollster Katie Connolly—a one-time *Newsweek* reporter who tended to surprise people when she piped up with insight into American politics in her native Brisbane accent—tried to make sense of what was going on with health care. Buttigieg's "Medicare for All Who Want It" proposal seemed like a semantic ship in a bottle, assembled like the clever first slide in a McKinsey PowerPoint presentation, because it was. His campaign's job was to make an actual policy out of a turn of phrase. Sanders and Warren were the only ones who seemed keyed into where the voters were, according to

Connolly's numbers: 41 percent said they strongly supported and 37 percent said they somewhat supported Medicare for All. There wasn't much sense in Buttigieg's running against an idea that had a combined 78 percent support.

Suspicious, Connolly asked the next question. What did they think Medicare for All meant? She read them two options. First: "The best way to fix our health care system would be to offer an affordable, comprehensive Medicare-type plan to anyone who wants to buy into it so that people could leave the private insurance system if they want," essentially tweaking and expanding Obamacare. Second: "The best way to fix our health care system is to move every person in this country to a completely different system like Medicare that is run by the government and not private companies." The first was Buttigieg's proposal, and Biden's. The second was the logical outgrowth of Sanders's plan, which had gotten Harris into so much trouble when, in that first January 2019 town hall in Iowa, she'd acknowledged that Medicare for All did mean the end of private insurance.

The results weren't close, on almost any breakdown. Overall, 67 percent picked the first, 32 percent picked the second. Among Iowa and New Hampshire voters, 56 percent picked the first, 41 percent picked the second. Buttigieg was looking to grab moderate voters from Biden, so it mattered that 80 percent of identified Biden voters liked the keep-private insurance route, but he was also looking to appeal to Warren's college-educated liberals, so it was even more important that 60 percent of her voters said they wanted to keep private insurance too.

In other words, when voters said they wanted Medicare for All, they were confused. They definitely hated their insurance companies. Most believed everyone should be covered. Beyond the fundamental fact that America both pays more for and overall has worse health care than pretty much anywhere, Sanders's argument was purely theoretical—the closest he ever came to detailing how he'd actually implement Medicare for All was a speech in July when he'd said Lyndon Johnson had pulled off the much smaller Medicare transition in four years, and technology had gotten better since then.

Sanders wasn't the one with the problem. Though Warren had caved in to Sanders on backing the Medicare for All bill in 2017, reporters still looked for differences between them once they were both in the race. She had ended that speculation by declaring, "I'm with Bernie on Medicare for All" onstage at the first debate in June. Her "I have a plan for that" branding was catching up with her. She'd been trying to keep two sets of plates spinning: hoping the Sanders progressives would be satisfied that she supported Medicare for All, and that everyone else would be satisfied that she wasn't getting pinned down into admitting that Medicare for All meant raising taxes across the board, including on the middle class. The straight talker was talking in circles. The way Warren had sold herself, everything she said was supposed to have an elegant, doable solution, but Medicare for All as legislation rather than aspiration was too much of a fantasy for that. She was undercutting her own authenticity and highlighting Sanders's.

Buttigieg had been hoping to take his shot at Warren in the September debate, but he'd gotten so sick with a cold that he'd had to have a booster shot a few hours before walking out onstage in Houston, and he was too hazy to come up with a good way to get around the moderators not teeing him up with the question. On that night in October, he was ready to go. "Your signature, Senator, is to have a plan for everything. Except this," he said, going in for the kill. "No plan has been laid out to explain how a multi-trillion-dollar hole in this Medicare for All plan that Senator Warren is putting forward is supposed to get filled in."

"Whenever someone hears the term 'Medicare for all who want it,' understand what that really means. It's Medicare for all who can afford it," Warren tried in response, but she was caught.

Sanders pulled the booby trap he'd laid two years earlier when he made the competition dance for him on Medicare for All to prove their bona fides on the left. One by one, they had collapsed under the weight of trying to prove that the idea could be real in a way he was never expected to, while he retained the sense of purity. "As somebody who wrote the damn bill," he began, cutting into Warren's answer, well, it would do all sorts of wonderful things, like get rid of premiums, co-payments, deductibles, and out-of-pocket expenses, in a program better than Canada's. He said out loud that taxes would go up, and got away with it because everyone assumed he was talking in concepts, not real plans. He was preaching, which worked better than teaching. She was the one being held responsible by her opponents and the press for there being no realistic way for Medicare for All to pass the Senate or become law. He was the one who got to mop all the progressive excitement for setting the agenda.

Standing in the spin room afterward, a gleeful Weaver wouldn't answer a question asking whether Warren was the one being dishonest. He was, though, eager to argue that Sanders was the one being "straightforward" in saying that raising taxes would help pay for Medicare for All. "That's the honest answer; that's the only answer," he said. It didn't matter that this far in, Sanders still hadn't released more than a worksheet for what he would do. They were feeling self-righteous.

O'Rourke, for all his own troubles giving straight answers and by now riding the final fumes of his celebrity, eagerly joined the pile-on himself, accusing Warren of not telling the truth. "She failed to do that tonight, and she's failed to do that in previous debates," he said. "And I think on an issue as important as health care, and an issue as important as taxes on the middle class, this country deserves to hear the truth."

Warren's staff left Westerville that night insisting that the problem had been contained. There *was* a plan, they said; they were getting ready to release it. But there was no plan. If she had released her plan in July, maybe it would have undercut her from the beginning and she never would have peaked at all. If she had tried to define her campaign around her own idea of a wealth tax, maybe that could have become the progressives' litmus test. She tried to beat Sanders at his own game. Only Sanders won when that happened.

———

The Sanders campaign was already busy planning the Ocasio-Cortez public rollout. Weaver's big idea was to have Sanders come out onstage to *Back in Black*: "Forget the hearse, 'cause I'll never die." He liked that line. Sanders always gets a little sentimental about events in New York, as if he's still showing off in his hometown for his mother—whose own mother's heart problems were part of why he cared so much about health care.

In fact, his team had worried about the risk. What if not enough people showed? What if it didn't match up to Warren's rally in Washington Square Park the month before? Then the story would be that the people abandoned him in his moment of weakness, that he was chasing the last smoke rings lingering from 2016. He already had to answer constantly for being an old man, they thought, and now here might be the textbook example of something that happens to an old man. What if that's how the world responded, and they were left on those baseball fields in Queens with the superfans and no one else?

As it happened, the twenty-five thousand people in Queens didn't need help getting excited. They were packed onto the dusty field, defiantly across the river from the Manhattan skyline, four smokestacks from a power plant rising up behind the stage. It was the biggest event of the entire election cycle, all of them feeling the same feeling and chanting, "We will win! We will win!"

The heart attack "got everyone rallied," said Erik Pye, a forty-five-year-old army veteran and store owner from Brooklyn. "It gave everyone a sense of urgency." "It's either going to be him or it's going to be Trump," said Casey McDaniel, who'd driven in from Harrisburg. His friend, Sam Emami, said Warren was a second choice he could live with. "I wouldn't say she stirs my heart. She's palatable."

Backstage, aides who hadn't been with him for a while were seeing the man they'd been hearing reports of from the road. Before the heart attack, he was getting tired, crankier. The scare had shaken him too. He felt revived, was suddenly more interested in running, and more energetic and more pleasant to be around. They were all going through their own versions of feeling as if maybe they'd taken him for granted, that they could have lost him. And now, looking out from around the corner, they could see the movement in front of them. This was it. This captured what progressives had been trying so hard to say.

There's a word that's central to how Sanders supporters describe him: *only.* Ilhan Omar, endorsing him a few days before, called him "the only candidate that has built a movement and continues to build a movement that transcends gender, ethnicity, religion." At the rally, his provocative campaign cochair Nina Turner said of the other candidates, "there are many copies, but there is only one original."

"No one wanted to question the system, and in 2016, he fundamentally changed politics in America," Ocasio-Cortez said when she went to the microphone, explaining why her endorsement was always foregone. "We right now have one of the best Democratic presidential primary fields in a generation and much of that is thanks to the work that Bernie Sanders has done throughout his entire life."

"I am happy to report to you that I am more than ready—more ready than ever—to carry on with you on the epic struggle that we face today," Sanders said after she brought him onstage. "I am more than ready to assume the office of president of the United States." He flicked back to the debate, accusing the "Democratic establishment" of being just like the "Republican establishment": "They want us to believe that the only reality we can live under is the status quo."

He built up to his challenge, tweet and meme ready. "Are you willing to fight for that person who you don't even know as much as you're willing to fight for yourself?" he asked. "Are you willing to fight for young people drowning in student debt even if you are not? Are you willing to fight to ensure that every American has health care as a human right even if you have good health care? Are you willing to fight for frightened immigrant neighbors even if you are native born?"

That was the moment when he seemed as if he could win. When he could feel the old magic from 2016, but when it meant so much more now, in the age of Trump, and arriving right at the moment when Warren almost snatched it away.

"They shouldn't write him off yet," said Sabrina Gover, thirty-eight, who'd driven in from Philadelphia. "There's more of us than they think."

———

Late at night in November 2007, onstage in Des Moines, Obama gave a good speech. Not a great speech. Not one with any memorable lines or innovative turns of phrase. Politics can be defined by the way stories get written, and stories are often redefined for dramatic effect by those looking to assert their own great insight. Obama's twenty minutes onstage at the Jefferson-Jackson Dinner are often talked about as the moment that set him on the path to winning Iowa, the nomination, the White House. He was brought onstage that night to an announcer bellowing that he was "a 6'2" force for change!" and his speech played well in the moment. But it was in the hours that followed that it was turned into a sensation by the coverage in print and on TV. In reality Obama's poll numbers had started to trend upward before that speech, and his operations on the ground in Iowa were stronger than most had yet realized. But mythology is important to presidential campaigns, and Obama mythology is gospel to Democrats.

The entire 2019 campaign year had been building up to Iowa's big dinner— now renamed the Liberty and Justice Dinner to keep up with political correctness but not stray too far from its original initials. Smoke machines surrounded the stage in the big arena. Andrew Yang hosted a free concert with half the members of Weezer. Warren's campaign put up a Thanksgiving parade-size balloon of her dog, Bailey, complete with two giant pennies on his collar to represent her wealth tax. The speaking order became such high drama that Klobuchar had spent a week streaming texts and emails to the state Democratic Party chairman about how terrible he was because the polling formulation he'd used put her in the second half of the program—and when he wouldn't change it, she refused to say hello to him backstage, with a fight then following over whether one of her staff had pushed him out of the way, or one of his staff had pushed her.

Campaigns sank thousands of dollars into buying tickets, then thousands more dollars into getting volunteers to the site to sit in the seats, then thousands more dollars on top of that to put on shows for them, with glow sticks and foam boots and bullhorns and matching jumpsuits in greens and yellows and blacks to match each campaign's logo. Think summer camp color war, on a huge budget, with the prize being amorphous bragging rights and a supposed leg up toward fighting to preserve American democracy and being leader of the free world.

O'Rourke couldn't bring himself to be part of the spectacle. After his raw response to the anti-immigrant shooting in El Paso over the summer, his campaign had a brief moment when they thought he might be able to break back into the national consciousness. Channeling a greater exasperation with process and the press and the minimization into partisanship that his candidacy was supposed to have been all about blowing apart, he went viral again with a video of his letting loose on a reporter who'd asked if Trump could make things better. "What do you think? You know the shit he's been saying. He's been calling Mexican immigrants rapists and criminals. I don't know, like, members of the press, what the fuck? Hold on a second. It's these questions that you know the answers to. I mean, connect the dots about what he's been doing in this country. He's not tolerating racism. He's not tolerating violence— he's inciting racism and violence in this country. I just—I don't know what kind of question that is."

Within weeks O'Rourke's campaign manager told him that all the attention and stunts like calling for the government to seize assault rifles or making a trip to the mass-shooting site in Newtown hadn't helped with bringing in the money needed to keep his campaign going without beginning layoffs. He had raised more on his first days in the race in March than he had over the rest of his campaign combined. His supporters had gathered in a park across the street from the arena for a rally to send him in hot to his speech. Instead, they got word that he was going to drop out, and they watched him say one final goodbye, "Gracias" with hugs and distraught faces, as if they were listening to the Beatles announce their breakup live.

Inside, Buttigieg was preparing to go onstage. With the luck of the draw that was part of his charmed rise, he was up first. He started out his speech recalling how he had first come to Iowa in 2007 "to knock on doors for a young man with a funny name." The rest of his Obama references throughout were just as subtle. "America, our moment is now. Our moment is now. I don't want to spend the next year or the next four years refighting the same fights that we had in the 1990s. I don't want to pit Red America against Blue America, I want to be the president of the United States of America," Obama had said in his 2007 speech. "Iowa, are you ready to bring this country together? Iowa, are you ready to turn the page to a new era together?" was Buttigieg's version.

Biden was up next, giving the rare speech in which he didn't mention Obama at all, stumbling as he looked up at hundreds of empty seats in the sections of the arena that had been set aside for his fans. He had dreamed again about getting Lady Gaga to come, this time to perform as his musical act before the dinner, as if that had any chance of happening. Months of money problems and dribbling enthusiasm caught up to him all at once that night. His self-doubting, self-conscious suspicions that he didn't have a good campaign operation were playing out in front of him. Trump's going after Hunter was enraging, but expected. Being failed by his own team sunk Biden into weeks of despondency.

Harris's talk became a window into what might have been. Her new "justice is on the ballot" stump speech was a hit, and she was dramatic and powerful, and her volunteers were energizing the room, to the point of getting operatives working for other campaigns on their feet, applauding. "That was the best speech no one's ever going to remember," Pete Giangreco, the top consultant for Klobuchar's campaign said, leaning into Buttigieg's adviser Lis Smith. "She just killed it, but no one cares." Not that it mattered. Harris had just announced she was slashing staff in New Hampshire, the first clear sign that her campaign was withering.

Backstage, Booker watched the other candidates, waiting for his turn as the speaking order worked further and further down in poll positions. As the crowd leaped up for Buttigieg, he told aides he hadn't been impressed and said that he could give a better speech than that—simmering as always with the maddening jealousy of never getting the credit for also having been a Rhodes scholar who had been elected mayor, and the mayor of a bigger and more complicated city, who had then been elected senator. Booker's own speech was fine, not as well received, though that might have been a function of how many people in the audience had left by then as the night stretched on.

"I still have this instinct in my heart that we are going to emerge on top," Booker said, as he walked through the hallway of the arena afterward. He stopped to lead a group of excited volunteers, jumping up and down in their red Cory Booker T-shirts, in what had become his campaign's Iowa chant: "Hope! Hype! Hustle!" pointing his finger up to the ceiling along with the rhythm. He spotted a Booker cardboard cutout and took a picture of himself and his girlfriend, the actress Rosario Dawson, hugging it along with his chief of staff, Matt Klapper. He tried to explain getting washed over in the night.

"If we can win an election based on our highest ideals, our highest principles—not more partisanship, not more tearing each other down—I think that wins. The rest of this stuff I have no control over. I am who I am. I'm some Black dude, Christian, from Jersey. I am who I am. As Gandhi said: honor your incarnation. And as a person of faith, the idea of honoring your incarnation means everything is happening that I can't control, as it should. The only thing I control is how much I fight on, what kind of energy I bring to not just each stage, but to every hand I shake."

Warren tried to take advantage of all the attention on the dinner to move past Medicare for All.

"Let's put it out," Warren told her top aides of the plan they came up with. "Let's defend it." She still regretted not having swung back at Buttigieg harder. She'd underestimated how much the candidates would be piling on her at the debate. She told her top advisers to rush out the ideas they had been kicking around.

The result was intricate and clunky and brilliant and basic, the way NASA engineers rigged a new air filter out of socks and spare parts for the broken Apollo 13 command module on no notice. She'd raise $20.5 trillion, she said, off new corporate and stock transfer taxes, without having to follow Sanders's route of middle-class tax hikes, which he insisted would be more than made up for by households not having to pay premiums anymore. Her whole candidacy was pitching herself as a more thought-through, viable version of Sanders.

Warren's campaign was hoping to grab control of the conversation and pull out of what was starting to feel like a tailspin. But the Biden team worked over reporters again, as they had after the debate with Harris. Warren's team had sent around a copy of its plan to a small group of journalists under what is known as an embargo, an early look for the sake of getting coverage prepared, with a promise not to publish or share it until agreed to. Instead, one of those reporters forwarded the document to a Biden aide, enabling his campaign to jump ahead of Warren's planned rollout by a day with a bazooka shot across the bow: a statement accusing Warren of dishonesty, detachment, and broken promises, citing "mathematical gymnastics" in one sentence and "sleight of hand" in the next.

Warren was so taken aback by the disruption and the statement that she stumbled, as she almost never does. Asked on the day she released her plan what was supposed to happen to all the people who worked for health care companies, she laid out the kind of logic that comes from not really having thought through real-world consequences. "No one gets left behind," she said. "Some of the people currently working in health insurance will work in other parts of insurance. In life insurance, in auto insurance, in car insurance." Warren aides burned about that statement and the stumble it caused for weeks.

Now Warren was getting smacked everywhere, as the Biden gambit gave the Medicare for All story new blood. The press was all over her: the perfect professor who didn't do her own homework, the front-runner with the fatal flaw. To those who felt Warren had always been a little too smarmy—"Your idea is not the only idea," Klobuchar had snapped at her in that October debate, capturing her mood perfectly—the debacle pointed to deeper concerns.

Because Warren herself was always so anxious about making mistakes—she would sit with staff for hours on the phone, line-editing speeches and doing dry runs of every word she ever said publicly—this misstep was bewildering. "It was a rare moment in the campaign where we weren't creating our own weather," one person close to her said at the time. They told themselves the whole episode was less about Medicare for All than a proxy for questioning her electability, for questioning whether a woman could win. They insisted that she wasn't getting the leeway that the political world had given to Harris or Buttigieg.

Sanders purists saw their own suspicions confirmed: She wasn't *really* with Bernie on Medicare for All, as she had claimed in that first debate. She was just performing for the pundits. Here was their proof that she was indeed the capitalist Trojan horse they'd feared all along. It snowballed quickly. If Warren was really so much like Sanders, then why was she even running? Why didn't she just support him? And speaking of that, if she was really with him all the time, why didn't she endorse him when he was running against Clinton in 2016, instead of staying neutral until the primary race ended?

Larry Cohen, the former union leader and Sanders's old friend, who had stayed off the 2020 campaign staff to continue running Our Revolution, started putting feelers out to Warren supporters, particularly in the leadership of the Working Families Party. The way Cohen could see the math shaping up, he didn't think either candidate could get enough delegates to secure the nomination on the first ballot at the Democratic convention the following summer. That was crucial because the DNC rules changes (which Cohen had helped negotiate with Perez on Sanders's behalf) kept party elders from being superdelegates on a first ballot—but they got their votes back if the nomination took more than one ballot. Almost certainly, one was likely to be in a position to stop Biden. They should make a pact, Cohen was urging, for whoever had fewer votes to back the one who had more votes, which meant keeping the relationships amicable. "We need to stay on the issues that unite us, not things that divide us," he stressed.

Sanders and his top aides stayed focused on getting 30 percent of delegates, which would form a plurality in a crowded field. Cohen's calculus seemed remote. But they were happy to have Warren continue her hold on the punditry, while they worked to undercut her on the ground.

"Warren was—is—a difficult opponent. He doesn't want to go after her hard," Weaver said, assessing the situation that November. He liked the dynamics, though. "The best thing for us is Elizabeth coming in first place in some of these polls. My sense is that not a lot of folks over there know how to do hard-nosed politics."

———

After the heart attack—especially facing questions of why his campaign had initially referred to it as a myocardial infarction—Sanders's campaign said he would release "comprehensive" medical records by the end of the year. The furthest that he ended up going was a note from his doctors. It wasn't just that he and his advisers felt the health danger had passed; they believed the political danger had too. While Warren kept trying to appeal to voters' sensibilities, like by responding to the impeachment process by touting her proposal to bar donors from being appointed ambassadors, Sanders kept going for their guts.

They came because they were angry. Because they'd had enough of feeling powerless. Not thinking about left or moderate or progressive, but desperation and pain and knowing they weren't really being heard at all. In 2015, at the beginning of his first race, Sanders would tell aides he was running "because I want people to know someone gives a shit." In late 2019, he finally persuaded them to believe it again.

There were still the pop-up vendors selling T-shirts with the black-and-white shot of Sanders getting arrested in college and those with him done up like a mix of Bert and Ernie from *Sesame Street*; the bros inside showing up with Bernie dolls for him to sign (still in the original packaging, to preserve value); events that were slow to start because everyone had to go around the room and introduce themselves with their preferred pronouns. But there were also people like Jack Reardon, his voice squeezed as he told a room of volunteers being trained to knock on doors in Des Moines about going to see to his mother in the emergency room in the middle of the night. "When I should have been worrying about, 'Is my mom OK?' I was thinking about, 'Is this hospital going to break us?'"

"He hears these stories of people dying, of people going bankrupt, of families being forced into huge debt, not having a place to live, and it fuels him," said Ro Khanna, the California congressman and another of Sanders's campaign cochairs. "He's moved by it. Sometimes he'll be at a loss for words. Sometimes he'll try to comfort them, in his way. He'll certainly comment about it afterward. He feels a real burden that people have put so much of their hopes in him, that when you talk to people they really believe that maybe if Bernie Sanders becomes president, that maybe their lives will improve—that it's not just another politician with another rhetorical promise."

Sanders still believed that political journalists were either actively working against him or had to act biased against him because they were chasing favor with management. They weren't entirely wrong: journalists did regularly skip past Sanders, and he received none of the ooh-aah coverage accorded to candidates with nowhere near his chances at the nomination. That had its upsides: as he looked to sneak up on the political establishment, few were paying attention to crowds that were showing up consistently larger than for anyone except Buttigieg; the money kept pouring in online; supporters were fanning out to knock on doors in Iowa for free; and his staff had studied the process well enough to apply for satellite Iowa caucus locations at Latino and Muslim community centers. Sanders was the only presidential candidate who was met with cheers from teenagers at the Sunrise Movement's protest in front of the Iowa state capitol on a freezing Friday morning in December, the only candidate who got a standing ovation at a Teamsters forum the following afternoon.

Suddenly he was talking about luck and stars aligning. Biden's support of trade deals and the Iraq War, he predicted, would be huge vulnerabilities in the election. He liked Biden personally and thought they shared a respect for the working class, but he would say that Hillary Clinton was five times as politically talented. He'd muse privately that he didn't think Warren could take a punch, that she wouldn't be able to compete with Trump politically. She was too thin-skinned, too worried about *The New York Times* editorial board. He saw Buttigieg as a chameleon of convenience, and that galled him—but it also spooked him because he thought the young mayor could wheedle his way into fooling people that they didn't really need Sanders's revolution. But Sanders also wanted Buttigieg to remain strong because that cut into Warren's numbers, and discouraged allies from going after him too much.

He remained fascinated with the Obama–Trump voters. The disaffected white working class who flipped Republican in 2016 and the young people who sat out the race, he believed, would show up only for him. When they did, they would be his ticket to the White House. This was a race between him and Biden, he concluded, and if he could just persuade everyone to believe he had the same chances of beating Trump, they'd be tied. His campaign handed out BERNIE BEATS TRUMP buttons, hoping they could assert that into inception.

His own people, at least, started to believe it. "In 2016, I thought it was a dream too good to be true—and I was right. For 2020, it feels like a real possibility and probability," said Caitlin Weyant, a preschool teacher on her way out of the Sanders speech in a middle school gym in Cedar Rapids. "We've just been pushed down so low and so far, there's not really much further we can go without a revolution."

"This is when political life becomes interesting," Sanders said at the end of the rally, working through a perfectly reasonable scenario. "Win here, win New Hampshire, win Nevada, we're going to win California, we're going to do well in South Carolina."

"There has never been a peaceful left-wing political revolution in an advanced industrial state," Weaver added later. Was that what this campaign was meant to be? "We hope!" he replied.

———

The orbit around Obama, meanwhile, had been reconciling itself to Warren. Obama had too—his daughters were into her, and he'd been listening to them. Not so shocking that well-educated, liberal young women were Warren fans, but he had been impressed by how she was connecting with the young voters whom he always considered *his* people. Maybe there was more to her than the woman who'd annoyed him throughout her time in the administration, and then through her time in the Senate, and then through the beginning of his postpresidency.

But Obama could feel the race needed a circuit breaker. Two weeks after the Liberty and Justice Dinner, he sat down at the Democracy Alliance—the group of big liberal donors that had been engaged in backing up the activist efforts since that dinner at Podesta's house two and a half years earlier—for a "fireside chat" with Stacey Abrams. There wasn't a fire, and it wasn't so much a chat as Abrams's teeing up Obama for what he wanted to say.

He bragged about the movie his new production company got on Netflix. He did a riff about being an empty nester. Then he got to the point: a "robust primary" wasn't what worried him. A debate that became disconnected from people's lives did.

Take, for example, health care. Sanders supporters were still taking prissy satisfaction in Obama's mentioning Medicare for All in his September 2018 midterm campaigning kickoff speech. Calm down, Obama said, explaining, "I wouldn't run the same campaign today in this environment as I ran in 2008 in part because we made enough progress since 2008, of which I am very proud, that it moved what's possible. So I don't want people to just revert to what's safe. I want them to push out and try." As he often does, he called Obamacare a starter home. He said he hoped the law would be extended.

Sanders's sudden surge had caught him unprepared, and he pushed back in public in much the way he had in their meeting at his office. As for the candidates who had been attacking his record, Obama said, he could take care of defending himself. He saw his role as standing up for the Democrats who weren't the ultraengaged, who had by now zoned out after four rounds of debates harping on technicalities around a Medicare for All bill that barely existed and would never pass.

"How do we win?" Abrams asked him.

"My one cautionary note is I think it is very important for all the candidates who are running at every level to pay some attention to where voters actually are and how they can actually think about their lives, and I don't think we should be deluded into thinking that the resistance to certain approaches to things is simply because voters haven't heard a bold enough proposal—and if they hear something as bold as possible then immediately that's going to activate them. Because it turns out you know what, people rightly are cautious because they don't have a lot of margin for error," Obama said. "When we tried to get the Affordable Care Act passed—and we did get it passed—one of the reasons we didn't get a health care bill passed before is because 85 percent of the country has health care. They may not love it, but it roughly works for them. Eighty-five percent is a large number, and they are going to be very sensitive to the possibility that even if, in the abstract, there might be a better system out there, changing this now might lead me to be worse off, or 'I just don't know.'

That's not false consciousness. That's people being concerned about their health care because they want to make sure it's there."

———

Warren was leaking support by the day, and she could feel it. A *Des Moines Register* poll in mid-November that showed Buttigieg rocketing over her into first place had left her sitting on a staircase in Iowa, taking in the quickly changing world. Maybe she could still outhustle everyone, her aides would tell themselves. Seeing the enthusiasm out on the trail, especially among young women, refueled her. The unmistakable excuse-making of a campaign in trouble started to seep out. She will see it as a win even if she loses, aides would say, not for moving the party to the left, but for changing the sense of what was possible. What really upset her, they'd add, is thinking about letting down the people who believed her when she said change was possible. She was more than a movement leader, they contended; she was a thought leader, not the center of a cult of personality, like Sanders.

Except she wasn't. On Thanksgiving weekend, she emailed her top aides, still determined but already plaintive.

"As we sat around the table this evening, we talked about what we were thankful for. I'm thankful that I'm in a fight for the future, a fight that has already changed America, a fight that will change it even more. I wouldn't be in this fight without you. We wouldn't be doing so well if we didn't share a common vision of a better America and a commitment to making that vision a reality."

CHAPTER FIFTEEN

THIS SYSTEM IS CRAZY

If you look at the world and look at the problems, it's usually old people, usually old men, not getting out of the way.

—BARACK OBAMA, DECEMBER 2019

January 2020–February 3, 2020

Tom Perez was trying to be diplomatic, ease them into the discussion. But it wasn't long after sitting down in Perez's suite at the Hilton off Union Square in San Francisco in August 2019 that Troy Price spotted the words on the prepared notes. This was exactly what he'd been worried about: no virtual caucuses.

Price hadn't become the Iowa Democratic Party chairman by glad-handing his way through running for office or by making big donations. He was an operative. He had been executive director of the state party four years earlier, left to become Clinton's political director for the 2016 caucuses against Sanders, and then been elected by the members to lead a party that barely measured up even to the rundown office space it occupied in a hut across from the Des Moines airport. Constantly pulling on his vape pen, he had been trying to keep the peace between the proudly parochial Iowans holding on to their process and a DNC that was eager to start moving beyond a method of voting by standing around in rooms and shouting at one another to form little huddles of candidate support. Or, in the words of an Israeli reporter observing what ended up going down in a West Des Moines Holiday Inn ballroom that February: "This system is crazy. It's like the Middle Ages. But they seem to enjoy it."

There had to be some way to participate online. Workers on shifts, young parents, anyone else who might find it inconvenient to get locked in a room at a hotel or a middle school for two hours on a Monday night at the beginning of February, they still deserved to have a voice. The DNC wanted remote voting in place. This wouldn't seem to be so hard: corporations count virtual shareholder votes all the time. The combination of security concerns and incompetence made it impossible. They hadn't even been able to get electronic voting to work for the DNC meeting in February 2017 when Perez was elected, and that was just 435 DNC members *all in the same room* at the convention center in Atlanta trying to use clickers. That attempt had to be scrapped at the last minute. Then a few members were confused by the paper ballots handed out and it took two rounds to make Perez the chair.

Price had said his mission in becoming state party chair was to make the caucuses work better than they had so that there was more confidence in the results than in 2016, when Clinton barely scraped out a win. He promised to secure the results and get them out more quickly. And he thought the easiest solution to the accessibility problem was to have some people piped in by telephone, like mystery bidders in a Sotheby's auction. Or to design some kind of secure app that tallied first and second choices ahead of time.

The problem was that Price had no idea how to make that happen, or how to do so while fulfilling the transparency and accessibility requirements the DNC had put in place. Or how to roll out a reliable new system involving significant changes that never would have been used before the one big night, with the entire country watching. He issued a request for proposals from prospective companies, without much explanation of how the security or technology was supposed to work. Each proposal was sent to a clandestine team of Silicon Valley software engineers that had been selected by the DNC—few knew their names in order to duck issues about confidentiality and noncompete agreements with the big tech companies for whom they all worked. Days would go by as the Iowans waited for responses. The DNC didn't approve any of the proposals.

The primary process is full of idiotic idiosyncrasies. Iowa held caucuses so it could go first, because New Hampshire had declared by state law decades earlier that it would have the first *primary*. Longtime New Hampshire secretary of state Bill Gardner—known for his cardigans and delivering soliloquies about the history of the primary to every candidate who came to his office to register for the ballot—jealously guarded that distinction. When Iowa Republicans had pushed to move their caucus to earlier in January in the run-up to the 2012 race, he threatened to hold the 2012 Republican primary in 2011 if that was needed to stay first.

Perez was on a break from overseeing a meeting in San Francisco where the news was dominated by candidates polling at 0 percent, complaining that he'd sold out to corporate interests by not putting enough of them onstage for the debates. Then the activists from the Sunrise Movement accused him of selling the party out by not having a debate completely committed to climate change and staged a walkout of the meeting, videoing one another as they chanted their way out the door. He didn't have much patience for another fight where he was made out to be the bad guy just for trying to keep the party from going off the rails.

They were running out of time, Perez said. They weren't taking the security concerns seriously, the way the DNC had been ever since the 2016 hacking. Perez and his team thought Price was acting like a parochial local political organization, and he had to understand that the whole party, the country, and the world would be depending on Iowa's getting this right. There was a lot to screw up, and there were a lot of people who were going to be hoping that happened.

They were behind, Price snapped back, because the DNC had wasted months wrangling over the effort. All the leaking about the problems didn't help.

Perez was pulling the plug: no more virtual caucuses. It wasn't going to work. Maybe they could try mail-in ballots. "How in the flying fuck do you expect me to do mail-in ballots?" Price asked, thinking that was exactly the kind of technical change that would light up Gardner in New Hampshire to complain that Iowa was becoming a formal primary, and make him leapfrog backward to protect his first-in-the-nation status. "How in the fuck do I do that without blowing up the calendar?"

Jim Roosevelt, a longtime DNC member from Massachusetts and the co-chair of its Rules and Bylaws Committee—and one of FDR's grandsons—chimed in. "If New Hampshire has a problem with it, they will have to suffer the penalties—including not getting delegates to the convention," he said. The idea was to dare Gardner: let Iowa finagle this technical way through the caucus, or risk the New Hampshire primary being taken away entirely.

Price said he wouldn't sell out Iowa or mess with New Hampshire. No mail-in votes. They'd stick with just the standard caucus system, with satellite caucuses at a few locations outside the state, like Florida and California and, for some reason, Paris, where enough Iowans happened to be for the winter. "Does this mean no technology at all?" he asked.

They all looked around at one another. Someone suggested an app called Shadow to at least help with reporting the results.

"We've got five months," Price said. "I don't have enough time to get all this shit done. The only way we're going to get this done is if we're working together."

In the room, everyone agreed.

The first Monday in February they went into caucus night promising that this was all going to come together in the smoothest Iowa caucus ever. Officials had already missed the deadline in December to send the app around to start testing. When the app did arrive in mid-January, it came with a convoluted log-on process, bugs, and complaints from local poohbahs who didn't at all like having to change their habits by using technology. Worried that so much was going wrong, the DNC asked for access to the raw data being put into the app as a backstop. Trying to make that happen inadvertently triggered more problems.

Price was walking back from having a smoke in the cold, passing the time while the caucuses were under way, to find panicked staff chasing him down, telling him the app hadn't worked at all. Results should have been streaming in. But there was a problem with the input. There was conflicting information about the backup system. No one knew what had gone wrong, or how. They'd sort it out in fifteen minutes, the DNC tech team promised. Then another fifteen. Then they said they needed another thirty. That passed too. There was a basic error in the software, with results that were being entered into the wrong spot in a spreadsheet, and with the cascading algorithms, they couldn't identify or isolate it.

The quickly spreading news of the meltdown managed to make the situation even worse. Caucusgoers and reporters were calling the hotline to keep letting them know that there was a problem. Then campaign aides rushing to document the vote totals to prove their candidates had won sites started tweeting photos of the official sheets. At least one shot that included the state party hotline made it to a person posting on 4chan, the QAnon and nationalist-friendly reactionary message board. The state party had built a capacity to take two thousand calls that night. They received eight thousand. State senators were grabbing phone lines. Back in Washington, Perez started fielding calls himself. Some had been placed to jam the lines and just keeping operators talking as long as possible. Others were reporting deliberately fake results. When officials realized this, they had to scramble to call back each person in charge of a caucus to check. No one built a backup plan for the app. The state party team was tumbling into a panic spiral. Price kept popping out to nervously tug on his vape. The DNC had sent staffers to be on the ground as emergency backup, but they didn't have the details of what had gone on before they quickly moved to take over the counting.

There had been Iowa caucuses since long before there were apps, and Iowa caucuses with higher turnout. The failure that night was of a system that both outsmarted and out-stupided itself. Combined, campaigns and news organizations had spent over a year and hundreds of millions of dollars on a process that was over in two hours, couldn't manage to report results, produced a muddle of winners—and, along the way, undermined faith in both the process and the field. Republicans were already leaping: *This* was the party that wanted to talk about voter fraud? *This* was the party that thought it should get more involved in running Americans' health care? *This* was the party that was supposed to be running on doing a better job managing the government?

Campaigns kept calling, pressuring Price for answers. He didn't have any. He kept asking the DNC staff for the updates on the vote count so he could announce who was ahead. That wasn't the point, the DNC told him. They needed to finish counting.

At two a.m., Price held a press conference by conference call. The entire political world and every reporter was looking to him to explain a disaster that he couldn't understand himself. "This is a reporting issue—not a hack or an intrusion," he read from a short statement, his voice shaking, "and it's exactly why we have a paper trail."

In high school, Price had lost a million dollar–winning McDonald's Monopoly piece somewhere in an outlet mall. This was worse. He headed back to his room at the AC Hotel, down in the funky-for-Iowa section of town, which insisted on calling itself the East Village. He got into bed. For two hours he stared at the ceiling. Then he gave up and headed back to the office to start assessing the damage.

———

"This shit would really be interesting if we weren't right in the middle of it," David Axelrod remembers Obama saying to him during one of the long drives around Iowa in the 2008 campaign. Being in the middle of it is terrible. The state is full of amateur pundits and political experts who've seen all the candidates and listened to all the speeches, and have a confidence in their own insight and ability to measure up anyone, wrapped in a haughty self-serious sense of duty to the nation. Imagine trying to get a room full of five-year-olds to agree on the best ice-cream flavor ever. Andrew Yang had a joke about doing the math and each Iowan voter being worth a thousand Californians—"In any other state in the country, I'd be lying to you if I said your vote could make a big difference, but here, it can. You only need about forty thousand Iowans to change the future of this country." He wasn't arguing this was good for democracy. He was appealing to the state's collective political ego.

Now throw in an impeachment trial in a race full of senators being forced to spend long and ultimately pointless days listening to the pomp and the proceedings as if the verdict hadn't been set since before Pelosi approved the House vote.

Cory Booker tried to hold on until caucus night. Sitting in the front seat of an SUV at the end of the first week in January, he headed back to the airport after his second day trip to Iowa in three days, rubbing his fingers up and down his nose and trying to make the case for staying in. He couldn't. "If we get folks to hear my message and feel my spirit, we will win this election," he was saying. If he had been able to campaign full time in Iowa, "we would have run away with this."

Booker was riding toward Cedar Rapids from a town called Mount Vernon, at what turned out to be the final event of his campaign. It was held in a library down the street from the piano bar where, ten months earlier, O'Rourke had stood on a counter, waving his arms around, managing to get praised for ducking a question on ethanol. A woman at the library had given Booker an original Jimmy Carter 1976 campaign button, and he showed it off as if it were a talisman that could ward off the inevitable.

Booker's last hope had been to get on the debate stage in January in Des Moines, for what would be the first time that the audience was more than just reporters and diehards whose minds were already made up. In December, Perez had decided that the contestants needed more than one moderate and more than one woman, and retrofitted the thresholds to allow Amy Klobuchar to qualify. He did not make the same accommodation for Booker, who was the last of the Black or Latino candidates running—Harris dropped out, her campaign completely broke, the week after one last plaintive and puttering trip to Iowa over Thanksgiving. Booker was realistic that he probably couldn't survive without the attention and fundraising boost he would get from being onstage. Then had come the scheduling of the impeachment trial, then Trump's ordering a missile strike on an Iranian general, which for a moment looked as if the president were strutting his way into World War III. No one was paying attention to the candidates who were doing well, let alone the ones they'd never seriously considered.

Every morning Booker and his top advisers had a call or a meeting to ask themselves if he could still win. Each time, often with some impressive conceptual acrobatics, they worked themselves to yes. When he got back from Iowa, he held one last meeting in his living room in Newark. The answer was no. In any other presidential race Booker probably would have been a leading candidate. In this one, he never broke 2 percent in the polls.

On breaks from the impeachment proceedings, the senators still in the race rushed back to the cloakroom to make calls back to Iowa. They chartered private planes to take them back and forth across the country for an event or two at a time, sleeping in the air. They were crazed. They were exhausted. This was no grand contest of ideas or a cinematic barnstorming of the heartland. This was feral survival. Trump news had swamped the race again, and the senators were left betting on whatever they already had going for them by then, unable to build more.

Biden, meanwhile, was stumbling, spending more of his time off the trail than anyone would have recommended for an underdog campaign. That left Buttigieg, who had the time and the energy to be full time on the trail, with the state mostly to himself for a month.

Everything seemed set—until the morning before that last debate in Des Moines, when CNN published a story about that 2018 dinner when Warren had invited Sanders over to discuss whether they would both run. Warren had told the story privately a few times since, saying how taken aback she had been. She carried the insult with her the whole time, every encounter they had. Sanders hadn't registered the conversation at all. He never told even his closest aides about what he had said, because to him he hadn't said anything beyond a straightforward assessment of the dynamics of the race, and hadn't meant her to take it anything else.

Sanders was in debate prep when the team's phone started buzzing with the news. His eyes went wide. He felt betrayed, as if Warren had deliberately misinterpreted what he had told her. His aides raged, accusing her of leaking the story to embarrass him at the debate. His campaign manager went on TV and called her a liar. Warren's aides fired back, claiming they hadn't leaked the account, but the account was accurate, and Sanders should have to answer for it.

Sanders was rattled. Warren stuck by her story at the debate, and the moderator stuck with her, taking her version of the encounter as fact. "Why did you say that?" the moderator asked Sanders.

Sanders supporters treated this as if it were the big reveal in a movie, that Warren had been a double agent all along. On Twitter and Facebook, #Never Warren and #WarrenIsASnake started circulating with photos of her head pasted on a snake's body, the Sanders superfans swarming like pigeons at the feet of an old man tossing breadcrumbs.

"I think you called me a liar on national TV," she was caught saying indignantly on a hot mic, refusing to shake his hand when he walked over after the debate.

"You called me a liar," Sanders responded, before heading offstage.

They saw each other a week later, at a Martin Luther King Jr. Day event in Columbia, South Carolina. They made a point of linking arms and chitchatting as they marched a few blocks to the state capitol, where the Confederate flag had flown until after the Mother Emanuel shooting, in that flash of a moment when America was supposedly confronting its racism and looking forward, Republicans and Democrats together. The senators were acting, both well aware that they needed the shot of them getting along, and so they made sure the photographers got it.

Later that week, with Sanders stuck back in Washington for the impeachment trial, Ocasio-Cortez kicked off a swing of rallies in his place. "The system is not fine," she said in Iowa City, telling a story of how, just eighteen months earlier, she was on Obamacare but was not able to afford a blood test her doctor said she needed. "We have to demand a radical new vision aligned with the century we're actually living in," she said. She related how as soon as she arrived in Washington, Democratic colleagues were admitting to her that when they said goals were "unrealistic," what they really meant was that they were scared that embracing them would lose them their seats. There wasn't much sense, she said, to arguing that America could afford wars but couldn't afford Medicare for All. What she demanded was "a transcendent intersectional movement that is rooted in justice," and the crowd applauded as if anyone could understand what that meant.

Sanders came so close to beating Clinton in the Iowa caucuses in 2016 that he may very well have actually won them, if not for party insiders hedging numbers and resorting to coin tosses to break ties in precincts. (Really, this is how the system works.) She won 49.84 percent of the vote, he won 49.59 percent. She called that a win. He called it a tie. In the years since, Sanders aides had used the 2016 funkiness to push for transparency and changes, which led to the revamping and digitizing of the system, intended to make the caucuses work better . . . or maybe to blow them up forever. Sanders went into the race at an advantage, and as his post–heart attack surge showed up in Iowa, he was coming into first place in polls right at the moment his aides had been hoping for. A majority of Democratic caucusgoers said they were socialists themselves or fine with a socialist as the nominee. Democrats who hated Sanders began to reconcile themselves to the idea that he was winning, that maybe he had always been on the path to winning. Democrats who weren't sure and hadn't been paying attention started moving toward him because he was in first place, in the self-fulfilling momentum that always shapes races toward the end. Democrats who loved him started to get drunk on the first grapes of winning.

Clinton has not moved on from not being president, nor forgiven those she believes stopped her. She greeted Sanders's arriving at the cusp of winning by saying in an interview that his supporters were obnoxious and responsible for the lack of party unity behind her in 2016. The comments shot across the internet. At an event on the Saturday night before the caucuses in a town called Clive, with Sanders still on his way back from the impeachment trial in Washington, a moderator asked Rashida Tlaib—the Michigan congresswoman who was the most belligerent member of the group known as the Squad—what she made of Clinton's comments. The crowd started to boo, and the moderator asked them to stop. "No, no, I'll boo," Tlaib said, leading more to join in. Fellow Squad member Ilhan Omar from Minnesota and Pramila Jayapal, a Washington congresswoman who was the cochair of the Progressive Caucus, onstage with Tlaib, started laughing. "You all know I can't be quiet. No, we're going to boo," Tlaib said. "That's all right. The haters will shut up on Monday when we win."

By the next morning, Tlaib had apologized on Twitter—"I am so incredibly in love with the movement that our campaign of #NotMeUs has created. This makes me protective over it and frustrated by attempts to dismiss the strength and diversity of our movement," she wrote, hashtagging Sanders's slogan. "In this instance, I allowed my disappointment with Secretary Clinton's latest comments about Senator Sanders and his supporters [to] get the best of me. You all, my sisters-in-service onstage, and our movement deserve better."

Conciliation was not the mood of the moment. "Rashida, you're all good. We love your passion and conviction," Sanders's campaign manager tweeted back. "Don't change."

The final projections from Sanders's pollster Ben Tulchin were full of good news. Assuming the high turnout that everyone expected, given so much attention to the race, Sanders was at 29 percent; Biden at 20; Warren at 15; and Buttigieg at 12 percent. Given the Iowa caucus rules of people moving over to their second choices over two rounds, Tulchin predicted Sanders would win with 43 percent of the vote, with Warren at 37 percent, Biden at 33, and Buttigieg at 24 percent.

With the caucuses coming on Monday night, Tulchin had stopped polling for the final weekend. His numbers didn't account for the changes that had taken place coming into the homestretch. Looking back, he would say the Tlaib comments hurt Sanders more than they realized in the moment, as she seemed to be demonstrating a smarminess that backfired with stuffy Iowa caucusgoers who so revered themselves and their power, leaving some asking if they should give their votes to a candidate who behaved so brashly. Biden, meanwhile, was weak. Voters went looking for a different home.

━━━

Warren landed in Des Moines late on the final Thursday before the caucuses, squeezing in one of her selfie lines in front of the old barrels at a brewery. She was more upbeat than her poll numbers would suggest. "How will you keep people engaged?" a woman in a pom-pom hat asked her—"I love your puff-balls!" Warren said—and she leaped right into it. "Oh, and you asked it in the right way," Warren said, as her staffer clicked the iPhone photo. "God, I'm feeling good about this," she said. A young boy came up to her, asked her what she'd do if she could change Medicare for All. She smiled. "Medicare for All, and maybe kitties and puppies?"

Over the weekend in Indianola, a half hour outside of Des Moines, she headed to the same theater at a community college where Sanders had been the day before. He drew most of the major TV anchors and other big-name journalists parachuting in for the final days, out to see the winner in action for themselves, as if by being there, they were the ones making it real. She drew an overflow crowd, living it up as she told a long story about the possibility of changing work in America when she explained, in answer to a question, why FDR's labor secretary, Frances Perkins, was the historical figure who inspired her most.

She reflected on being stuck in Washington for the impeachment trial. She compared the experience to going to Trump's inauguration. "I come from a witnessing tradition," she said. "It's now burned in the back of my eyes. If I ever get tired, it's there, and it's like, 'Let's go.'"

Warren went into those final days talking up her two-cent wealth tax, "the head and the heart," she would say, as the way to pay for universal child care and education and enable more people to get closer to living the lives they wanted to lead. And, she explained, she wanted to lean in on talking about why nominating a woman would be better, because women tended to be voting and winning these days. "I always start with what the numbers show," she said that weekend, linking herself to the Women's March and Democratic wins across state legislative races since, "and that is that the world changed when Donald Trump got elected." But her massive operation on the ground, so long the envy of every other campaign, was falling further short than they knew. Her campaign's decision not to spend much money on television advertising, in the belief that she was breaking through in her own way online, and then to make her final ad before the caucuses entirely about her plan to bar major donors from being appointed ambassadors—a leftover from one part of the impeachment testimony against Trump—wasn't doing much for voters looking for a connection to their own lives.

On the night of February 3, as caucusgoers were driving to their sites, two Warren-supporting Democratic operatives settled in at Fong's, an absurdly famous Des Moines restaurant, where egg rolls can be ordered as appetizers before pizza, and the pizza comes with toppings that often seem ill-advised for the Midwest. They ordered the Crab Rangoon Pizza and proposed a toast—no matter what happened that night, they thought, Sanders or Warren were going to win.

"To the rise," one said, clinking glasses, "of the new left!"

Exactly a month before the caucuses, January 3, Biden was in a farm equipment museum in a town called Independence. There was a display of old canned-hog products. There was a LEGO map of Iowa with blocky cornfields and the never impressive skyline of Des Moines. It smelled exactly like what metal and wood left without climate control on a concrete floor for years should smell like. Snow was getting thicker outside. It was a Friday night, and a few dozen people had come to see the former vice president of the United States.

Sanders was clearly rising in the polls, but Biden still wouldn't engage—"You guys expect me to take Bernie's comments seriously? Come on," he had said at a campaign office opening at Cedar Rapids on the way over, when a reporter tried to wind him up about the senator's knocking his vote for the Iraq War. "I don't respond to Bernie's ridiculous comments."

Biden wouldn't deviate from the schedule. He wouldn't deviate from the stump speech. The campaign was down to an old man going through the motions and an ever smaller crew of press gathering material for the inevitable stories about his collapse, timed for whenever he stopped fighting and dropped out. The youngest person there that night who wasn't a journalist was Abby Finkenauer, the congresswoman for whom he'd come to campaign in 2018, who had flipped a Republican seat in the midterms but had been annoyed when Ocasio-Cortez's primary win meant she would no longer be the youngest woman ever elected to Congress.

Wandering around the front of the folding chairs, Biden said out loud a thought he had been bouncing around. "If the perfect president had ten great attributes or talents or qualities, none of us ever have more than five. And sometimes the qualities needed at the moment are different than the qualities needed at the previous election or the future election," he said. He rambled off, hitting his line about how Putin didn't want him to win, how he had already withstood so many attacks from Republicans. That Biden blend of self-doubt and self-assurance eventually pulled him back to what he had been trying to say.

"There's two ways people get inspired, in my view: one, by the John Kennedys of the world who genuinely inspire and lift us up, Abraham Lincolns, who appeal to our better angels. And another way is we have a really bad president—no, I'm not being facetious. A president who, in fact, when you learn what they've done and how they've done it, we say, 'No, no, enough of that,'" he said. Obama was Obama. He could never be Obama, shining on his own. He could be what stopped the backlash Obama had set off, if only he could get a chance. "We have such an enormous opportunity," he said. "My Lord. My Lord."

Biden aides who were being honest with themselves had known for months that they were in trouble. Some didn't want to believe it; some couldn't. Others felt as if they'd gotten into a taxi with a driver who was swerving all over the road, and they were just holding on and hoping they made it to the end.

Whatever big ideas they seemed to have were mostly swiped from previous campaigns, like identifying veterans by pulling county-by-county records of who'd qualified for a special state tax credit (pilfered from John Kerry in 2004). They deployed Jill Biden to appeal to teachers. They sought out independents and disaffected Republicans, targeting them with messages that portrayed Biden as a statesman, in contrast to Trump. They chased Catholics. ("Consistent with the highest traditions of Catholicism, Joe Biden has demonstrated his belief that we have a shared obligation," the former ambassador to Ireland declared in a handwritten letter that was copied and mailed to thousands of homes.) They turned to paid workers, rather than relying on volunteers, to knock on the doors of African American and Latino voters—although they did bring in hundreds of volunteers for the final few weeks (though with logistical stumbles, such as failing to tell some of the people who'd agreed to house those volunteers when their guests would be arriving). They emphasized Biden's character. They insisted everything was fine.

The Thursday night before the caucuses, Biden's campaign bus pulled into the parking lot of an American Legion hall in Ottumwa, across the river from the theater where he hadn't filled the hallway the previous June. This time about two dozen Iowans showed up, settling into that limbo between drowsy and nodding off. Biden was also clearly tired. His skin looked like parchment. His hair looked like yarn woven through the parchment. He was so washed out that from a distance it seemed as if he were wearing makeup. The walls were covered with Biden signs, except for the spot where the bingo rules had been left up.

No one was under the impression that the Biden campaign was going well. The reporter rubbernecking seemed cruel. What had been the point of putting himself and his family through all this misery for a year, to go from the heights of that Medal of Freedom, Obama's holding him up as America's hero, to ending like this?

Two weeks earlier, Sanders had been shamed into apologizing for an op-ed by a prominent supporter that accused Biden of corruption for issues that had nothing to do with Hunter. Driving between events, Sanders had been furious to see that the op-ed had been featured in a newsletter that was privately owned by an aide but masqueraded as an official campaign document, though as was his usual response, he wasn't going to say anything publicly about it. While his aides engaged in a long round of internal finger-pointing, Anita Dunn called Weaver to tell him that Sanders needed to disavow the attack. Weaver went to find Sanders and explained the situation. Sanders agreed, first telling Biden directly that he didn't stand by the op-ed, then having aides steer him toward a reporter so he could go on camera and say the same.

Sanders had no similar qualms about sticking by an attack on Biden for his record of supporting cuts to Social Security. A video, tweeted by the same aide who owned the newsletter, took a 2018 clip of Biden speaking sarcastically about going after Social Security and Medicare to make ends meet in budget negotiations, and made that look as if Biden were stating his own position. The video was misleading, but it was true that Biden had backed Social Security cuts over his career. For Sanders, that was enough.

In Ottumwa that snowy Thursday night, Biden was so annoyed by the charges while being so tired of the back-and-forth of campaigning that when a reporter asked him about the video, he reached into his jacket pocket and handed him a printed index card with his response, under the header BERNIE FALSE ATTACK ON SOCIAL SECURITY, with selections from a speech he had given, which, he argued, more accurately represented his position. To his traveling press corps, this was viewed as absurd. He wouldn't answer questions. He wouldn't engage in the race. He and his closest advisers kept repeating to themselves that he just had to survive Iowa and get himself to South Carolina. To anyone outside that circle, this felt as delusional as when he'd been insisting that the ploy could have worked in 2015.

The night after Ottumwa, the final Friday before the caucuses, John Kerry stopped by Biden's campaign headquarters in Des Moines to try to buck up the volunteers and workers who were still pushing, along with his old Senate buddy Chris Dodd; firefighters union president Harold Schaitberger; and Iowa attorney general Tom Miller (who had originally backed Steve Bullock in the race)—the old white guys carrying the flame for the old white guy they had known for years. Kerry had been musing about running again himself through the spring of 2019, eventually pulling back in deference to Biden, but that night he was reminding workers and volunteers how he had surged in the 2004 Iowa caucuses, and that fast turnaround had sprung him to the nomination.

Was Biden too old? Kerry asked himself. "How many of you wouldn't want Nancy Pelosi where she is? Nancy Pelosi is seventy-nine!" Kerry said, pedantic and adamant. "I'm over seventy." He was seventy-six. Dodd was seventy-five. Schaitberger was seventy-three. Miller was seventy-five. "Seventy is the new fifty!"

Could Biden win? Kerry asked himself. "Everything they're throwing at him is Donald Trump's paralysis and fear of Joe Biden. Make sure people understand that. The minute he was a candidate, they started going after Joe Biden. Three years prior, Trump never mentioned Hunter Biden," he said. "We can't be a place where truth cannot be discerned."

Standing outside a few minutes later in his bomber jacket and a periwinkle scarf, Kerry said he didn't understand why people never put the same premium on experience for politicians as they did for, say, heart surgeons. "I think in this case, some people have been torn between the idea of new, fresh, whatever versus somebody with experience, and they're trying to wrestle with it," he said, predicting that Biden was going to win Iowa by suddenly convincing the 50 percent of caucusgoers who told pollsters that they were still undecided going into the final days—though he was saying privately that he could tell Biden was worn out and not catching.

"If we come in first, this is over. If we come in second, one more punch and it's over," Mike Donilon had said in one of their planning calls for the caucuses. "If we come in third, we're still alive."

"If we come in fourth," his Iowa director, Jake Braun, responded, "we're all fucked anyway and going home."

Biden came in fourth, so unprepared and disorganized that Atlanta mayor Keisha Lance Bottoms had flown in to monitor a caucus site because there weren't enough volunteers from Iowa, and when she called in to alert the state headquarters to the meltdown over the app, no one was around to pick up her call. No amount of complaining about the caucus meltdown was going to change how badly he did, though his aides decided to try. An official complaint letter addressed to Price was quickly written up and signed by campaign counsel Dana Remus, in which she cited the "considerable flaws" in the system and "acute failures" in producing results. In the letter—which was, naturally, immediately emailed to reporters—Remus framed this as a legal issue, and not a desperate political play to try to undermine faith in the results, which had so clearly not gone Biden's way.

Meanwhile, Biden's press aides were rushing him to get out and speak. With a distant fourth-place finish, he could either speak first while the cable networks were waiting on everything else, or risk not being covered at all. Biden and his top aides had sensed the loss was coming, but now it was real and more frightening than they had expected. Tom Vilsack, the former governor who'd been through every caucus since 1976, told Biden he'd be all right, which made the loss sting even more. Biden meandered at the hotel, saying he was waiting for one of his grandchildren. Schultz, the campaign manager, called in: *Get him there.*

In the boiler room that Klobuchar's team had set up at the Des Moines Marriott, the staff could see she was coming in fifth, behind Biden—the kind of result that, in any other cycle with a functioning caucus, probably would have spelled the end of her campaign. They talked themselves into seeing a wisp of hope. Assuming that the caucus app problem would be fixed within an hour or two at the latest, they went back and forth about whether it made sense to say anything without knowing the results. Her campaign manager stepped out to take a call from her. "OK," he said, when he came back into the room, "Amy's on her way."

"You probably heard we don't know the results," she said when she arrived, prompting a little chuckle from a crowd of supporters still trying to figure out what was happening as they waved her bright-green campaign signs at her. "We know there's delays, but we know one thing: we are punching above our weight."

When Biden's aides saw her on camera, they told him he couldn't wait any longer. They got him onstage while Klobuchar was still speaking, trying to grab back the attention. "We feel good about where we are," he said, and then, almost pleading, "We're going to do this, I promise you. I promise you we're going to get this done. God willing, we'll do it together. On to New Hampshire!"

Ever since 2008, when *The Des Moines Register*'s final poll before the caucuses predicted Obama out ahead, it's been an institution in the Iowa process. The last poll of the 2020 race was scheduled for the final weekend before the Monday night caucuses.

Buttigieg's charmed political career got one last boost on Saturday morning, when a lower-level campaign worker called one of the mayor's top advisers to relay the odd experience of getting a call from an operator conducting the poll. The worker had been read a list of candidates and asked to pick a top choice. The worker pointed out that Buttigieg was not one of the options offered. The operator put the worker on hold. The operator came back and said that there had seemed to be an error. There was no more explanation.

Lis Smith went to work. She didn't know what the poll results were, but assumed they weren't great for Buttigieg, and she leaped on the chance to clear the way for a last-minute surge. She worked contacts at CNN and *The Des Moines Register*, which were cosponsoring the poll, setting off an internal review. She kept grinding them as they conducted the review, ramping up pressure as she heard that the pollster had known of a problem but hadn't informed the news organizations—the pollster claimed that the issue was as simple as a font-size error limited to one terminal and the order of the names had been randomized, but couldn't prove that. Smith alerted a few national reporters, getting them primed to jump on the story if the review didn't go as she wanted.

The results were never released, but eventually they leaked. Sanders was at 22 percent, Warren at 18, Buttigieg at 16, and Biden at 13. These numbers were off too.

Buttigieg didn't get involved with the machinations. He spent Saturday night getting ready for a full round of interviews on the Sunday talk shows, finishing up the primary campaign the way he had gotten in, counting on the national press to float him.

On that final Sunday afternoon in Des Moines, he walked into the gym of Lincoln High School, home of the Railsplitters, and looked up at the ceiling, taking in the moment but not quite focusing on the crowd. He had a riff in his stump speeches about how when he had first started, "literally dozens of people" showed up, curious about what he was up to. Now he was looking out at a crowd that the police put at 2,030.

Maybe they should have asked a couple of people to leave, one aide joked, and they could have had the crowd at 2,020. Or maybe, said another, they could have knocked on a few more doors to get to 2,054—which would have matched the year, as Buttigieg used to point out in his stump speeches, that he would be the same age that Trump was then. An hour later, five miles away, in a middle-school gym that was smaller but more tightly packed, Biden had eight people and three different videos to introduce him, and a crowd of just 1,108—including, Kerry, Dodd, and two other former Senate colleagues whose gray heads easily blended in with the crowd.

———

Americans, Buttigieg's deputy campaign manager Hari Sevugan had said a few days before the caucuses at a breakfast hosted by Bloomberg News, "are exhausted. They are exhausted over the division, they are exhausted over the dysfunction," and "this notion of lanes, progressive, left, center left—Pete does not fit in that." Buttigieg's campaign just had to figure out how to get enough Iowans to believe in an operation that a few months earlier had no money, no presence on the ground, and no real clue about how presidential campaigns worked. His campaign manager had never worked on a presidential campaign before. He spent the final week before the caucuses on a tour of their thirty-three field offices in the state. Some were packed; one had just a single organizer making his way around. Buttigieg's top person in Iowa, who had moved in from Indiana, had to get a new cell phone because the company he had his personal phone with didn't get service in much of the state.

Those final days before the caucuses were odd for the Buttigieg inner circle. They knew that the data wasn't predicting the kind of surge he needed to do well, which is what he needed in order to be taken seriously past the caucuses, but they also had internalized the charm and energy that had carried them this far. Maybe it would take him a little further. Buttigieg had begun taking implicit and explicit swings at Biden's age and entrenched ways, and at Bernie Sanders for being a risky choice that could sink Democrats. Their best bet, Smith said, was trying to showcase what Buttigieg was, not what he stood for.

"Everything is fatiguing and polarizing, even just going to dinner with your family," Smith said. "And there's something to be said for someone who doesn't wake up in the morning just looking to punch someone in the face."

Buttigieg was always fighting the sense that he was a fake—a criticism eagerly promoted by the Warren campaign, and by Weaver and Nina Turner, who mocked his high-priced fundraiser habit by showing up at the December debate wearing T-shirts printed with PETESWINECAVE.COM, a reference to the Napa vineyard cellar where he'd had dinner with a bunch of billionaires a few days earlier. The Biden campaign got in too, with two aides tracking down a Black South Bend city councilman who'd been taking swings at Buttigieg over the Logan police shooting, persuading him to endorse Biden just for the sake of a zinging press release.

Buttigieg never escaped his problems attracting Black support, or the legacy of that police shooting in the spring of 2019. He was the great hope of the new generation with an infection at the root.

A week before the caucuses, Buttigieg's strengths and vulnerabilities were exposed together at a pricey Chicago fundraiser at the Standard Club. He was beginning to attract significant support in Obama's hometown from the kind of donors who give to serious candidates, not causes, when a few protesters forced their way in, holding QUEERS AGAINST PETE signs. "How would you advise a transgender, queer, or nonbinary teen who is disowned by their wealthy homophobic parents and therefore cannot afford college, because you oppose universal free public education?" one shouted at him.

Only in 2020 could there be the sense of entitlement that would allow someone to demand that a presidential candidate have a policy tailored to this specific situation. Only in 2020 could a candidate go in a matter of months from being protested by the Westboro Baptist Church to being attacked for being a gay sellout. This had been a running theme of Buttigieg's campaign. In July 2019, *The New Republic* had published an op-ed from a gay literary critic repeatedly referring to "Mary Pete" as "the gay equivalent of Uncle Tom." (There was enough confusion and outrage over that piece that the magazine took it down within a day.)

"I have great news for you," Buttigieg said, deciding to engage the protester. "That person will get free college under my plan, because what we are doing is basing it on somebody's ability to pay. Now, if you are in the top 10 percent by income, I am going to have to ask you to pay your own tuition," he said. "None other than Bernie Sanders thought this was the right thing to do a couple years ago, so I think it's a great area for us to come together with a commonsense solution that targets our dollars on those who most need it."

When that didn't work, he went into full Buttigieg mode: "I respect your activism, but sometimes love is not expressed by interruption. Sometimes love is expressed in a different way." The crowd clapped. "Even though you're supporting another candidate, I respect your belonging, I respect your rights, I respect your activism."

"If I write down my question, will you answer it?" the protester shouted.

Buttigieg: "You know what? Just go ahead. Let's do this."

The protester clearly wasn't ready to do anything but shout. "Mayor Pete, as somebody who says you want to unify communities, as someone who says they want to follow the rules of the road, there are police officers in South Bend who kill people. What's his name, Logan . . ."

Buttigieg tensed up. "Not 'What's his name.' His name is Eric Logan."

"There's so many I can't keep track anymore."

"That's false. Please state your question so I can respond to it." Still as if he were in high school debate club.

"Eric Logan was murdered in your community," the protester said. "How can we trust you will show up for queer and trans people and people of color when there were eight community meetings in South Bend about a police officer who killed someone in your community and you did not go to them?"

"So your question is whether queer people and people of color can trust me if I did not go to community meetings on policing?" Buttigieg said, failing to hold his frustration and condescension in. "Right . . ."

Days later, up on the thirty-first floor of the Des Moines Marriott in the penthouse suite a few minutes before the caucuses began, Buttigieg reflected on the moment and what it meant about his campaign, about politics.

"On one level, it's a great sign of progress, that one of the problems you're confronted with is a gay candidate being asked by a hostile queer activist about whether you've contemplated whether your plan for free college for most Americans has contemplated the situation of disowned trans kids who grew up wealthy," he said, sarcasm mixing with bitterness.

"I know Eric Logan's family. And I know what some of them think about total strangers invoking his name for a political purpose, regardless of what they think of me politically or as relates to what happened to him. Those moments are jarring," he said.

Buttigieg ticked through some of the other mania about his work at McKinsey that had set in.

"It's so over the top. I'm a CIA agent? Cleverly disguised as an intelligence officer, I guess. I took down Blue Cross Blue Shield of Michigan?" he said. "It's the cognitive style of Twitter. That's what it lends itself to."

It was quite a night for a first-time presidential candidate whose previous election consisted of crushing a Republican opponent when he received 8,515 votes running for reelection as mayor, to her 2,074. Buttigieg insisted he'd always assumed he would end up here, on the verge of winning the Iowa caucuses. "You don't do this unless you think you can win," he said. "Doesn't mean you think the odds are on your side. It means you think you can win."

Buttigieg haters found this kind of cockiness enraging. For his fans, his assuredness in his own unnerving intelligence was his superpower. He wanted to learn Norwegian to read a book, so he studied Norwegian on a lark. He saw how to make a presidential run happen, what role he could play in it, and what he could represent, so he clicked the tumblers into place on that too. Buttigieg was always analyzing, the chess piece and the chess book at once. His analysis that night: "There's not a scenario where we win quickly. There are scenarios where we win slowly—and then there are the downside scenarios."

Push him a bit, and he could be knocked back into himself: a thirty-eight-year-old mayor of a city smaller than Cedar Rapids who knew how nuts it was to be sitting at one of the highest points in Iowa, let alone on the verge of maybe winning the most famous contest in American politics.

"We are bracing for a muddle," he admitted. "Although for us to be in a muddle, if you just zoom out for a second, is fucking amazing."

Going into the night, Buttigieg's aides had prepared two versions of his speech, knowing that he needed a first- or second-place finish to continue, while trying to come up with some way to argue that there was a way forward if he came in third or fourth—the "Alamo draft," they called that one. The "entrance polls" CNN conducted of caucusgoers had shocked them, as they revealed that Buttigieg and Sanders were neck and neck across demographics, regions, ages. As the precinct data started to come in from their captains and aides across the state, they only got more excited. They took another swing through the speech. "Make sure the faith part doesn't drop out," Buttigieg had told them. A few minutes in, Smith, always eyes on her phone, saw the tweets coming across. "What do you think about this app thing?" she asked. He went to change into his suit, anxious about when he should get onstage for the event they had put together, carefully orchestrated for the camera shots that would in themselves credential him as a top contender.

He came back and asked his advisers to make a case on what to do. They had a flight to New Hampshire to catch to get there by morning and wanted to get footage and photos out for the news. They were unanimous: give the speech. "Yeah," Buttigieg said, "let's go out there." The stage, the giant American flag, the lights, his first sentence declaring "an improbable hope became an undeniable reality" were all about invoking Obama. They hedged phrases in the victory speech—he was originally set to say, "We leave here with a victory," but it became, "By all indications, we are going on to New Hampshire victorious." Buttigieg was "one step closer to becoming the next president of the United States," mostly, at that point, because he said so.

Usually it takes a victory to give a victory speech, and in the days leading up to the caucus, it had been Buttigieg's aides who were warning reporters not to fall for the Sanders campaign's attempt to claim victory from the early results. Now Sanders staff and supporters were nailing Buttigieg for claiming early victory, calling it the ultimate white male privilege moment in a campaign that they insisted was about little else. Buttigieg and his inner circle didn't realize that night just how much he'd been screwed by what happened. They assumed the results would be cleared up in a few hours, not that they would drag out over the course of a week.

Four months later, when the first butchering haircut he had given himself during the pandemic had finally started to grow back, Buttigieg reflected on that night. On the could-have-been of history, his life, his career, all sucked into back-end app mismanagement. What might have been? "We'll never know," he said.

Imagine the headlines: MEET IOWA CAUCUS WINNER PETE BUTTIGIEG. FIRST GAY CANDIDATE TO WIN A DELEGATE. THE SMALL TOWN MAYOR WHO ROCKED THE POLITICAL WORLD. Instead, he was at best a secondary mention under accounts of the disaster and confusion and finger-pointing. Hoping for a shoot-the-moon victory, his campaign optimistically budgeted a $10 to $15 million fundraising bump from the attention and notoriety of making history. Instead, he was treated as a haughty jerk for having declared a victory that he knew was his, and raised only about $2 million.

"We had a fundamental need to do well outside of the places we did best— Iowa, New Hampshire. And that would have been the same. But I think just the seriousness with which we would've been taken. . . . I could feel it, especially with Black Southern voters. There was a sense of 'OK, but who are you?' that I think would have been different if we were propelled by an unambiguous Iowa win. You could play all these games, right? If Iowa were more decisive, it actually could have made New Hampshire a little more contrarian—although I think that's less likely, just given what Iowa would have done to the other candidates if it became a clear quicker result," he said.

Hard to process then, hard to process still. "We still would have had a real mountain to climb in Nevada and in South Carolina. Put it this way: there's no way to imagine I could have been worse off if we got the results that night. The question is only: How much better off would I have been?"

Sanders, Warren, and Klobuchar flew to New Hampshire for a few hours before heading back to Washington again. The caucuses were Monday night, the impeachment vote was Wednesday afternoon. Pure party lines, with the exception of Mitt Romney defecting on one of the counts. No suspense. Trump wasn't going anywhere.

CHAPTER SIXTEEN

WHAT WAS THE PLAN?

The alternate domination of one faction over another, sharpened by the spirit of revenge, natural to party dissension, which in different ages and countries has perpetrated the most horrid enormities, is itself a frightful despotism.

—GEORGE WASHINGTON

February 4, 2020–February 22, 2020

On the Tuesday and Wednesday nights before New Hampshire, Sanders kept a comfortable lead in the daily polling his campaign was running there, though Buttigieg had been rising since he claimed victory for himself in Des Moines. On Thursday afternoon, the official call came in for Buttigieg in Iowa. Ben Tulchin, the campaign pollster, saw the effect immediately. Buttigieg was taking the lead in the state that was supposed to be Sanders's stronghold. That wasn't the only problem: Biden's apparent collapse and the chaos that was benefiting Sanders was driving more and more energy to Mike Bloomberg, who was spending millions per hour to take advantage of the situation.

Tulchin called a few of Sanders's top aides to raise the alarm. Usually he sent a summary of the daily poll numbers in the morning, but there was no time to waste to get Sanders worried. Tulchin emailed the numbers straight to

Sanders that night so he'd read them right away, up late and scrolling through his iPad.

"Urgent situation," the subject line read:

The bottom line is Buttigieg is surging and has serious momentum. As a result, the race is now essentially tied over the last 2 nights (25% for you to 24% for Buttigieg and tied in tonight's data). Even more troubling is that ***Buttigieg now has higher very favorable ratings than you by a statistically significant margin, which means he is the most popular candidate in the race.*** That plus his rising vote share means ***Buttigieg now has real momentum and will likely win the NH primary unless he is stopped.***

If you win the NH primary, you will likely win the nomination. (538 has given you the best odds of winning the nomination of anyone, but it is predicated on you winning NH.) However, if Buttigieg wins the NH primary and you do not, then he will carry that momentum to NV and will be VERY difficult to stop from winning NV and then winning the nomination.

Therefore, the nomination hangs in the balance in NH and Buttigieg now has the momentum and upper hand on us right now so we MUST stop his momentum. The good news is we have an excellent opportunity at Friday night's debate to draw a sharp contrast with him on multiple issues.

Freed up from the impeachment show trial, Sanders, Warren, and Klobuchar rushed back to the campaign trail. Sanders's first stop on Friday morning would be Saint Anselm College, a small Catholic school on the outskirts of Manchester that had been able to turn itself into a destination on the presidential campaign trail by being in the right state with a gimmick called Politics & Eggs. Candidates came through to give short speeches while breakfast was served. Then, as tradition dictated, each one signed with a marker all the souvenir polished wooden eggs in a basket.

Before sending the email, Tulchin reached out to David Sirota for a consult. Sirota had been a press secretary for Sanders during his early years in the

House, then transmuted that experience into becoming an advocate journalist to support what always seemed to be his true passion: trolling anyone on Twitter whom he deemed to be a sell-out Democrat and their journalistic enablers. He was the epitome of the Bernie bro: self-righteously tearing into anyone who wasn't on the team with a fury that didn't quite match a veganism so strict he would sometimes serve peaches as the main course at dinner. Sirota had been hired as the speechwriter for the 2020 run, but Sanders doesn't even like sending out emails with his name on them that he hasn't written himself, and often called staffers to yell if he read a quote he didn't like that was attributed to him. Sidelined, Sirota had spent months once again picking fights on Twitter with reporters and other campaigns and anyone else he could find. Most of his interactions internally were relegated to sending around links to his own tweets in the campaign's Slack chat system, to the point that it became a running joke for others to respond by pasting in a photo of Sirota from an old publicity shoot in which he's leaning in a shower while wearing a shirt and tie, looking forlorn as water runs over him.

Tulchin and Sirota had become their own mini unit of aggression within the campaign, riling each other up, pitching ideas like having Sanders take advantage of being stuck in Washington for the impeachment trial to give a takedown speech in front of the Trump International Hotel. These were dismissed, especially given Sanders's aversion to anything coming from Tulchin, because, he would always say, he didn't need a pollster or anyone else to tell him what to say.

Here they had their moment. Tulchin advised in the email:

> **_You should very explicitly declare that the race is clearly our grassroots_**
> **_movement supported by working people versus 1) the billionaire's_**
> **_candidate, Pete 2) a media/Wall Street billionaire, Bloomberg 3) a_**
> **_billionaire reality TV show president, Trump._** To be clear, to make this
> really travel as a story, you would have to say that EXPLICITLY, not just
> implicitly. You would have to actually name these candidates (Buttigieg
> especially, but also Bloomberg and Trump) and frame the New Hampshire
> race as a battle against allowing this triumvirate of billionaire forces to
> buy the election. And to make it zing, you could invoke the phrase "wine
> cave"—which would bring that meme back up. (Perhaps we bring back
> those t-shirts for this debate.)

Tulchin ended it with a list of links to articles that Sirota had collected. He didn't hear back from Sanders until he saw the senator pick up a printout and start reading the headlines at Politics & Eggs the next morning. Trump had made the system worse. Bloomberg's wealth and the millions he was spending showed he wasn't interested in making it better. Buttigieg's donations meant he'd never dare truly upset the system. Sanders's aides were giddy. They could never stand Buttigieg. They had been eager for Sanders to go on the attack for months. This was perfect.

"We are in a moment where billionaires control not only our economy, but our political life," Sanders said. "This campaign is about which side are you on." Like Woody Guthrie, he said. "He wrote a song which I *will not* sing for you," he said, putting his hands up, a little jowl shake. "You would not want to hear it."

———

That night all the candidates were back at Saint Anselm for another debate. Biden wrote himself out of the story early by declaring he'd probably lose the state badly, just as he'd lost Iowa. Depressed and veering well off his talking points, he'd been so down when he got to New Hampshire that the campaign had made sure to have him meet with Brayden Harrington, a young boy with a stutter like the one Biden used to have, just to steady him. It's not as if many other people in the state were rushing to see him.

Klobuchar was the one who emerged as the story of the night, slashing Sanders and Warren for sticking to Medicare for All—"I keep listening to this same debate, and it is not real," she said—then turning around to maul Buttigieg every chance she got. Keying into voters' anxiety about actually nominating a thirty-eight-year-old small-town mayor, she hit him for his immaturity in calling the impeachment process tiring, then hit him for an old tweet of his from before he was in the race, calling Medicare for All a *good* idea.

The next morning, as Biden wandered through a speech at the front of an old theater in Manchester, his press secretary, T. J. Ducklo, worked his way to the reporters shoved in a back corner. It was surprising to see him there—he'd announced in December that he'd been diagnosed with Stage 4 lung cancer, at age thirty-one with no history of smoking. But he'd pushed himself back onto the trail for Iowa and New Hampshire. Some reporters asked one another whether, at this point, his return was worth it.

Ducklo sidled up to each of the reporters with the same mischievous smile. "Have you seen the video?" he'd ask. "You gotta watch the video." And then he'd stand and wait for each reporter to pull it up on his or her phone: a one-minute-and-forty-second-long ad snarkily comparing Biden's record with Buttigieg's. "Both Vice President Biden and former Mayor Buttigieg have taken on tough fights: Under threat of a nuclear Iran, Joe Biden helped to negotiate the Iran deal," the narrator says. "Under threat of disappearing pets, Buttigieg negotiated lighter licensing regulations on pet-chip scanners."

The ad was harsh and petty, and Biden hadn't wanted to run it. After what happened in Iowa and what was going to happen in New Hampshire, his closest aides told him, they had no choice. This was another *Do you actually want to be president?* moment. Still, the campaign didn't have money to put the ad anywhere but on Twitter, which was why Ducklo was making sure it was loaded one by one on reporters' phones. Buttigieg's aides initially dismissed the attack—Biden was desperate, and he was making the case for them that Washington insiders looked down on the rest of America. By the time Buttigieg did his rounds on the Sunday shows the next morning, he was being asked about his experience at every turn. "This video," Biden's digital director Rob Flaherty tweeted with pride that afternoon, "now has more views than the population of South Bend."

New Hampshire primary voters pride themselves on following their own idiosyncrasies, but it was getting a little much that final weekend. That afternoon, Colorado senator Michael Bennet drew more people than Biden had at both of his events combined, for an event that ended with James Carville and Bennet's wife tossing Mardi Gras beads into the crowd. A joke candidate who wore a boot on his head and called himself Vermin Supreme trudged up and down Elm Street with two ponies and a few supporters. And by evening, the political world descended on the arena where Trump had, the previous summer, made a big deal out of selling more tickets than Elton John had in 2001, and where all the candidates had already performed once, for the state Democratic convention the previous September.

This was the last big multicandidate circus event of the cycle, and the campaigns went wild one more time. Flashing lights, waving signs, plastic clapping-hand noisemakers with the candidates' names on them. Buttigieg walked onstage and observed that South Bend was a lot like Manchester.

(Manchester is actually slightly bigger.) He contrasted himself to Trump. He said Sanders was wrong to say the only choices were revolution and the status quo, which prompted the Sanders section to chant, "Wall Street Pete! Wall Street Pete!" A few waved light-up signs reading SHUT UP. His own fans responded by chanting "U-S-A! Boot-edge-edge!"

When Buttigieg finished, he made his way up to his skybox, full of supporters and junk food, for hugs and handshakes. An aide handed him a can of Rebel IPA, and he walked out to watch the competition. Biden was by now onstage, speaking from a podium that had been rolled out for him. He was doing a version of one of his most common speech bits, of the "longest walk" a father has to take, to tell a child that he's lost his job and they were going to have to move. Buttigieg's hand moved up to his mouth over the course of it, evaluating the performance.

"One of the great political figures of our time," he said with a shoulder-shrugging sadness, "and he's running on autopilot—his hand in his pocket, wandering around."

"I'll be damned!" Biden said, as he tried to summon some anger to grab the crowd.

"That's good," Buttigieg said, still grading.

"I'll be damned if I'm going to lose the country," Biden said, discovering a little more energy.

"That's better," Buttigieg said.

Biden's aides were already planning when to pull him out of the state.

———

Biden's campaign wasn't known for innovation, but during debate prep a few days earlier, he had asked Anita Dunn, who lives by a "here's to those who wish us well, and all the rest can go to hell" sensibility, to fully take command of his campaign. She had been consolidating control since the disaster at the Liberty and Justice Dinner back in Iowa, but now she started giving orders directly. Without much money, the only intel aides had was the public polling and what they could see happening—and they could see not a lot was happening. What picture would they rather have on TV that night, Dunn asked: a half-empty ballroom with a dispirited crowd in New Hampshire, or an upbeat, diverse crowd in South Carolina with a gospel choir singing "All in His Hands," with Biden leaning in to talking about how he wasn't going to let Black voters be ignored just because Iowa and New Hampshire, white and tiny as saltines, had voted?

Biden called former governor John Lynch, asking for permission to abandon his supporters in the state. That was one of the upsides of flying private: the plane could be fueled and headed for Columbia so quickly that cable news hosts would be left rebooking segments minutes ahead of going on air. Before Biden left the arena, an aide came and found Chris Coons, who was pitching in. Biden wanted to see him backstage.

Coons had never seen Biden so distraught, except for after Beau died, his face clearly feeling that the race had slipped away, that it was over.

"I believed that they knew what the hell they were doing," Biden was saying about his campaign team. "You know what a candidate does. You go and go and go and give the speeches, you go to the places, you can talk to people."

His voice trailed off. His eyes too. Reality was crashing down on him. "Dammit!" he said, his teeth gritted.

Coons has always admired how his wife, Annie, gives pep talks. She can really make people feel better, make herself believe what she's saying too. For his part, he isn't a politician who's good at saying it'll all be OK. He put his hands on Biden's shoulders, telling himself, *Channel Annie.*

"It's going to happen," Coons told him. "It's going to work. South Carolina is going to turn this around."

Biden made one last stop on his way to the airport, to guiltily deliver a box of donuts to a campaign office.

———

In 2016, Sanders had carried New Hampshire by 23 percent and 57,000 votes. In 2020, he won by fewer than 4,000 votes or 1.3 percent, just ahead of Buttigieg. Without the Sanders-Klobuchar-Biden pile-on over the weekend, without Klobuchar still in the race as a distant third, pulling all the votes she did, it's hard not to see how Buttigieg wouldn't have won there too. Warren, who everyone had once assumed would win the state, was fourth. Biden was fifth, with a third of the votes that Sanders and Buttigieg received.

Yang dropped out that night—"I don't want to take people's money and time and support if I genuinely don't think that we can contend and win," he explained. Bennet dropped out, with a year on the trail having yielded all of 984 votes. Deval Patrick, who had been hoping his years as the governor next door in Massachusetts would give him a leg up to prove himself ahead of South Carolina, finished with 1,258 votes, and he was soon gone too.

That was it for dropouts. The melee moved forward again.

Talk to Tom Steyer for two minutes and all you'll get is goofball. Donald Trump is a working-class guy's fantasy of being rich—the hot wives, the gold-plated everything, eating a bucket of Kentucky Fried Chicken on his private jet. Steyer tends to come across more like an eight-year-old boy's fantasy of being rich. Not Richie Rich, but like Macaulay Culkin in *Home Alone* if he were alone because his parents died and left him $1 billion.

Most people, if they registered Steyer at all in the presidential race, knew him for the ratty tartan ties that he wore as if he were still slipping past dress code in prep school, or the beaded belt he picked up on the kind of trip to Africa that rich people take where they stay in ritzy hotels at night and are driven to impoverished settlements during the day. His big moments in the race were stumbling awkwardly into Sanders and Warren yelling at each other after their debate showdown in Iowa because he wanted to shake Sanders's hand, or the video which shot around Twitter of the sixty-three-year-old white man dancing to Juvenile's "Back That Azz Up" at a party he threw for himself in South Carolina. He'd flown in the rapper to perform the classic live.

Steyer is also one of the most successful investors in history, a hedge fund master before most people had even heard of hedge funds. His father was the editor of the *Yale Law Review* and a junior prosecutor at Nuremberg who did well for himself, but Steyer had pioneered hedge funds for the kind of fortune that enabled him to retire in his fifties. He bought a whole building in down-town San Francisco for a foundation that funded a bank for smaller nonprofits, became the biggest donor in Democratic politics, started an enormous youth activism political organization of his own, started another group devoted to impeaching Trump, and still had more than enough to self-fund hundreds of millions of dollars into a presidential campaign he launched with a video shot at his regenerative agriculture ranch in Pescadero, California.

Talk to Steyer for more than two minutes, though, and what starts to emerge is the clueless sincerity born of innocence and the sheltered life of the mostly good-hearted ultrarich. It wasn't hard for him to have watched the first two presidential debates in the spring and imagined how easy it would be for him to do better. He was having a late midlife crisis. His marriage with his wife, who had become what she called an "Episcopagan," was on the rocks. He had hundreds of millions of dollars sitting around. So why not? Steyer showed up at the Iowa State Fair in August with campaign buttons and a staff quickly booking millions in TV ads.

By then everyone could see the game that the DNC debate requirements had become, and Steyer was eager to play. Cory Booker's staff burst into tears at headquarters when the DNC announced the doubling of the minimum number of donors required, from 65,000 to 130,000. Steyer's staff shrugged and spent a couple million on Facebook ads and on buying an email list from his Need to Impeach group. He quickly hit the threshold. By the time he went to his first debate, 166,000 people were giving a total of $2 million to a self-funded billionaire. He easily cleared the other threshold—hitting 2 percent in four different polls—with millions more in television ads, and was onstage by October, to stammer through a few answers while the rest of the field pounced on Warren over Medicare for All. Absurd, maybe, how easy it was to qualify for a presidential debate. Also absurd, maybe, how few established politicians were able to get that far.

What was Steyer's plan, in what was essentially presidential campaign fantasy camp for him? That was never clear. He and his aides would insist that this was for real, though *real* had a special definition in the 2020 campaign. He was spending real money, and his campaign had real internal polling (there was lots of money to pay for this too) showing that he was in second place in Nevada and third in South Carolina from the advertising he was doing. This made him a potential chaos factor, capable of bumping a more "real" candidate out in those two states. If he ate into Biden's numbers in those states, as he seemed to have been doing for months, he alone could have ended that campaign.

On the final Friday before the Nevada caucuses, Steyer started the day at a Culinary Workers Union medical center on the outskirts of Vegas, touring around like a real politician, as if they are ever actually absorbing information behind the interested expressions cycling through their faces as they walk from room to room. In the car back to his hotel on the Strip, he said he couldn't get over a stat he had just heard about Black girls disappearing from their homes. He was dismissing the idea that he could be thought of as a spoiler. He was trying, still, to justify his existence in the race. He'd be the only one who could take on Trump because he was an actual billionaire who had built an actual business, he said, and Democrats should be much more worried than they seemed to be about the lack of faith they were inspiring in the economy. Put someone up who didn't know business, and the voters would punish Democrats, buy into all Trump's fluffing about the stock market.

As for the panic that none of this was going to matter because Sanders was about to run away with the race—Steyer laughed as he pointed to Mike Bloomberg's debate debut collapse two nights earlier. "Everybody's jumping to conclusions about what's going to happen. Everybody is way too ahead of themselves. They're assuming they know how this is going to play out, and we don't. I understand that there are probabilities of the way it will play out, and I understand that the things that people are worried about can happen, they're not sure to happen," Steyer said. "There are a lot of other things that can happen and that will happen, that no one understands yet. Once they've happened, everyone will assume they always would have happened. But until they do, there are going to be big surprises."

———

Compared to the other early voting states, Nevada is huge, but it's mostly two sprawling metropolitan areas at different corners of its borders, without much in between. The population averages younger, and more Latino, than most of the country. With so much of the state's economy hooked into casinos, Democratic politics revolves largely around the Culinary Workers Union, which had sixty thousand members. In all, one hundred thousand people ended up voting in the caucuses in 2020.

"Education" time was built in around lunch breaks and shift changes for union leaders to tell members whom to vote for. The approach wasn't subtle. A sheet handed out to members listed only six candidates and three policy areas: health care, good jobs, and immigration. The only difference among the candidates with respect to the bullet-pointed, standard Democratic positions on good jobs and immigration was that Klobuchar wanted to "work with unions about regulations about technology at work." Under health care, they were all listed as wanting to lower drug prices, while Biden, Buttigieg, Klobuchar, and Steyer were listed as wanting to "Protect Culinary Health Care" and "Expand Obamacare with public option." Warren's position was a mushy mishmash of "Medicare for All" and "Replace Culinary health care after three-year transition or at end of collective bargaining agreements."

Sanders was listed as wanting to "End Culinary health care" and "Require 'Medicare for All.'" In August 2019, when his campaign was nose-diving, Sanders had in fact announced an ambiguous proposal that would have allowed unions to negotiate for additional benefits on top of Medicare for All, so the flyer was technically accurate. Yet Sanders supporters insisted it was an attack meant to undermine his campaign, which it was. As always seemed to happen when Sanders supporters were upset, part of how that manifested was with some jumping on Twitter to call a union official a whore and claim that the union was embarrassing itself.

It was yet another instance of the Democratic Party collapsing into more of its own cracks, with Medicare for All still haunting every moment. The union decided not to endorse. Sanders anguished over the attacks in his name on a labor leader, and became suspicious that these people on Twitter might actually be part of a plot to undermine him, make him look worse, make his supporters seem unacceptable so that their politics couldn't get through. Sanders aides wanted to portray him suffering over the matter, but the furthest he'd go in public was to release a statement broadly condemning bullying, and in an email sent out under his name rather than words that came directly out of his mouth.

Losing Iowa (though Sanders's aides insisted then, and still do, that he won) and his close win in New Hampshire (though his aides insisted then, and still do, that this had occurred only because the field was more fragmented than it had been in 2016) left Sanders anxious about his ability to beat Trump, and about being seen by primary voters as being able to do so. He knew he had a problem in that, so far, his movement and the young people hadn't turned out as he'd predicted. But Sanders's strength in Nevada, diligently built up over the four years since he'd nearly beaten Clinton there in 2016, was never in question. Nevada was where the magic and the tactics came together for him, the epitome of what his campaign could have been. Latinos, especially younger Latinos, were connecting and activated. Progressives were engaged. Before most of the first-time campaigns realized how much they had to learn about the Iowa caucus process, the Sanders campaign had already been getting ready for the Nevada caucuses.

At the February 19 debate, held down the hall from the slot machine pit at the Paris Casino, Sanders was the only candidate to insist that whoever had the most delegates going into the convention be given the nomination—saying out loud what his campaign's strategy had been all along. With the looming Democratic disaster, the waking nightmare of a contested convention, apparently already set, he was attempting a hostile takeover by trying to hook the nomination of a party he didn't belong to with 30 percent of the vote. He was going to dare Democrats to stop him this time, give them the choice of submitting to him as the plurality nominee or watch him blow the whole party up because he didn't get his way.

"It was the worst thing he ever said," remarked Sanders's friend Larry Cohen. "It was an insane, stupid thing. He couldn't get the words out of his mouth. He should have said, 'My goal is to work with you, and build the party, and beat Donald Trump.' It was terrible." On that night in Vegas, it was the only moment of the debate that mattered outside of Warren's clotheslining of Mike Bloomberg.

"Bernie Sanders has about 25 percent of the vote, that leaves about three-quarters against him," said Joaquin Castro in Vegas the night of the debate. The Texas congressman had chaired his twin brother's presidential campaign and then followed him into endorsing Warren. If the anti-Sanders forces couldn't stop him before the convention, Castro argued, they would take advantage of the contested convention rules themselves to stop him there by coalescing behind another candidate. "Remember," Castro said, "the full primary process *includes* the convention."

A few feet away in the spin room that night, Nina Turner was already planning her convention speech. "Every Democrat on that stage said they were going to support the winner," she said, confident in who that winner was going to be. Bloomberg just had the most spectacular flameout in the history of presidential debates, Biden was clearly finished, Warren was going nowhere, Buttigieg wouldn't be able to make it past Super Tuesday, the rest were afterthoughts. Not that Turner expected resistant Democrats to give in easily. Just as much as she was looking forward to Sanders being the nominee, she was anticipating taunting them into accepting him. "If it is true that the Democrats on that stage are unified in defeating President Trump, then they're going to support him when we win."

Tom Perez was thinking ahead to asking Nancy Pelosi to take over chairing the convention, so at least there would be a strong, known hand on the gavel when the screaming started. Chuck Schumer was telling Democratic colleagues that Sanders at the top of the ticket would lose the White House and more Senate seats, but that he didn't feel he could assert that publicly.

Sanders doesn't write his own tweets, but the Friday night before the caucuses, his account summed up his feelings: "I've got news for the Republican establishment. I've got news for the Democratic establishment. They can't stop us." He was right that there were forces trying to stop him. He didn't realize, though, how much help he provided those forces when that tweet shot around the internet.

———

Right around the time that the Sanders tweet posted, Buttigieg was onstage at a middle school in southwest Las Vegas. Michael J. Fox had just introduced him, called him "magical," compared him again to Obama, said that he liked how calm Buttigieg was compared to the rest of the field. "Bernie, why are you yelling at me?" he asked. Fox is one of the few famous men whom Buttigieg towers over, and they shared an awkward hug when the mayor joined him onstage. While he was driving to the event, Buttigieg's campaign had popped on his latest ad—big surprise, a direct attack on Sanders over Medicare for All. Airing in South Carolina, the ad highlighted words like *choose* and featured a peppy female narrator saying, "Instead of polarization, progress," as a yellow line crossed through the word *polarization*. Weaver texted Lis Smith, mocking the ad, and quoted their polling that showed that Sanders wasn't the candidate he should be worried about.

This was missing the point. Buttigieg was just as convinced that Biden and Bloomberg and Warren were over. He was getting ready to consolidate as the only anti-Sanders candidate with staying power. "It just feels like we're in a groove now. We've reached this point where we just know exactly what the center of gravity of this campaign is, and what is really exciting here is you can tell that there's a lot of enthusiasm there, but it was also a lot of new faces," he said backstage after the event.

After a year of trying to become a local sensation, he felt how much the speed of the campaign was picking up under him. South Bend had a population of 100,000, the Iowa caucuses had a total of 150,000 voters, New Hampshire had about 250,000, and in a week and a half he was going to be up in front of the whole country on Super Tuesday. Of that crowd at the middle school, he said, "I think this is what broadening the coalition feels like. When you go to one place for a year, you have your diehards. This is a lot of folks who clearly are pretty new to this and still have that energy."

Buttigieg was worried about the Russian intelligence report, about Democrats being turned against one another. He was more worried about how Sanders had responded to it. "I don't know that he's figured out what to do with the position that he's in, because of all this," Buttigieg said.

Because of the particular type of dork Buttigieg is, and despite his success in politics, he approaches most people as if he's an amateur anthropologist and psychologist. One of the ways he likes to get to know someone is asking what his or her useful skill would be in a postapocalyptic world. At times in the past, he'd said his own would be survival. That night, he changed it up. "Probably running," he said, but he did not mean running for office. "I could run down a deer."

At other times, the answer he'd given was that he was a good shot, and that he could be persuasive. He smiled when reminded of that. "Yeah," he said. "Persuasion."

―――

The Sanders wave peaked the next morning in East Las Vegas, at a community center that filled with multiple different precincts caucusing. "This caucus process will proceed in a uniquely Nevada way," the governor had written in a note with instructions that was read out at the beginning of each vote. That meant using an iPad to tabulate the votes, and a deck of cards to draw the high card in the event of a tie. There were no ties. There and throughout the state, Biden had a couple of votes, Buttigieg had a couple of votes, but Sanders was completely dominant, including drawing significant support from the Culinary Workers Union, even with that attack on Medicare for All.

And Warren was fully left behind.

Renee Bedoui, a mom and a hairstylist who had just spoken on behalf of Sanders to urge support among her caucus group was hopped up on deeper connections. "This may sound ridiculous, but I could tell that the establishment started backing her," she said, launching into an explanation in what she'd been able to find on YouTube and other sources, "if you're really paying attention." Warren had apparently clearly sold out Sanders with the story of what happened at that dinner "because somebody put her up to it." Warren should have endorsed Sanders in 2016. She shouldn't have run against him then. Bedoui eased right into talking about "Pocahontas," explaining that she was more receptive to Trump's attacks on Warren than his attacks on Sanders. "'Pocahontas' is different than 'socialist.' When he says things like that, he's really talking about her character and integrity."

DNC staff had flown directly from Des Moines to Las Vegas to head off another potential caucus disaster. As was the case in Iowa, the results were coming in slowly. Unlike Iowa, the winner was so clear that Sanders had already left for Texas, campaigning for Super Tuesday, where he gave his victory speech. "We have just brought together a multigenerational, multiracial coalition which is not only going to win in Nevada, it's going to sweep this country."

Twenty points back and still in Vegas, Biden and his staff were driving to the electrical workers union hall when they spotted a rainbow in the distance. They decided to take that as a good omen, because most in the motorcade thought they were probably on their way to a concession speech if Biden came in third.

Dunn's first move after taking over Biden's campaign had been to pull all the staff in Super Tuesday states and send them to Nevada and South Carolina. If he didn't do well in Nevada, she decided, the money and the support would dry up, and even if he did go on to squeak by in South Carolina, it would probably be perceived as something like a gold watch to give the old man on his way to retirement. Months of trying to persuade Jen O'Malley Dillon to take over as campaign manager hadn't worked—she had just finished running O'Rourke's campaign and was wiped, plus Biden obviously wasn't going to win, and her father was sick. Dunn did persuade her to at least come into Nevada and run the state like a one-week Senate race. Scrap the big events, because no one was coming anyway. Go nuts on media access, give all the TV anchors exclusive in-person interviews for five minutes so at least they'd cover him. The "battle for the soul of the nation" line had always played more weakly than Biden imagined, especially with Latinos, who tended to feel as if this were a proposition that left them out, so they dropped it. With the couple of dollars left, Biden's pollster John Anzalone dug into what might work better. Biden started talking up his record on gun control and climate change.

On Saturday afternoon, aides were scrambling to get reports in from around the state to counter the Buttigieg campaign's claims that he was coming in second. Biden kept saying, so his staff kept repeating to reassure themselves, that he just had to make it to South Carolina. If he could get there, he could win. He repeated it like a daily affirmation.

Sanders won 40.5 percent of the vote. Biden had to be convinced that what turned out to be his 18.9 percent in a distant second place was somehow good news. That's not a win, he said. That's not close. It was Dunn who talked him into being happy about it.

He took the stage to an unusually current and peppy Carrie Underwood song: "I'm a fighter like Rocky," then, "I was made for this, I was born to win / I am the champion," as if he'd really won. Obama's "Fired up, ready to go!" had now become "Fired up, ready for Joe!" A man in the crowd screamed "Comeback kid!" and he smiled. "You all did it for me."

Biden spent almost as long shaking hands after the speech as he had giving the speech. As he walked backstage, he was talking about the people who'd stuck by him—the aides who had flown in to work caucus sites, and Chris Dodd, who had paid his own way because the campaign couldn't afford a ticket for him. Family. He stopped himself. With Biden, the grief is always part of him, so when it comes, it comes quickly. He was crying. Collapsing into himself. He didn't say Beau's name, but the small cluster around him knew he was thinking about Beau. "Where's Finny?" he said. "Where's Finny?" An aide rushed to get his granddaughter Finnegan, Hunter's middle daughter, who had been onstage with him, but had already gone to the car. She steadied him. He breathed. He headed home for a few days before throwing himself into chasing his South Carolina resurrection.

In the end, Biden edged out Buttigieg by a point and a half, the latest twist against what, in any other race, might have been the beginning of a march to the nomination. Buttigieg had come from nowhere to win Iowa, he'd been a guy from Indiana who almost won New Hampshire and beat much more powerful politicians to get there, and now the difference between Biden's revival and his getting left behind in the race came down to being all of 3,000 votes behind Biden.

As for Warren, there was nothing respectable about her 11.5 percent, giving her a second fourth-place finish in a row, after placing third in Iowa. The rest of the candidates were so far behind that they were afterthoughts at best. Warren was still talking about being the Sanders alternative, but those dreams were over. Steyer was still talking about doing well enough to matter in South Carolina, but that was over too.

Really, the only candidate anyone was talking about was Sanders.

———

"Emergency time," a panicked operative texted Rahm Emanuel a few hours after the caucuses wrapped.

Obama's former chief of staff wrote back quickly: "Yes."

To all the smart people in politics, Sanders was now obviously the nominee. There were frantic texts and phone calls, another round of *Can't Obama do something?* but mostly there was a sense of resignation. Maybe he was always going to be the nominee, they told themselves. Maybe this could work out? Or maybe—probably—oh, forget it, just move on and treat the election the way the mainstream Republicans had once they'd thrown their hands up at the prospect of Trump in the spring of 2016: he'd never win, but let the diehards get this out of their systems, and hope there would be something left to redeem by 2024.

Nevada was February 22. South Carolina was February 29. Sanders had to keep it together for only a week, and he'd probably be the nominee. He and his team needed a plan to undercut the importance of South Carolina and Biden's strength there, then glide on to Super Tuesday, when his own and the other campaigns' projections showed him racking up an insurmountable delegate lead. What needed to be done that week was completely predictable, obviously crucial. Sanders and his advisers managed to screw it up anyway. They had help.

The whole point of Sanders's campaign was that he was running against conventional wisdom. That didn't go over well in most newsrooms, which tend to be oriented around a defense of the status quo that masquerades as middle-of-the-road centrism. There's often more interest for understanding what's coming out of the fringes on the right, both as guilty compensation for the left lean of most of the editors and reporters, and to provide anthropological coverage for readers and viewers who think they don't know anyone who would vote for Trump.

Sanders found the most trouble with MSNBC, which often featured Clinton alumni commenting about his campaign in a dismissive "Here's the gadfly!" tone. In August 2019, when Sanders was at the low point, his campaign manager had arranged for an off-the-record town hall meeting in New York with MSNBC staff, hoping that this could open them up to him or at least shame them into changing their attitude. Ahead of the debate in Las Vegas, hosted by MSNBC, Sanders had confronted network president Phil Griffin in a hallway and demanded to be treated fairly. Neither conversation made much of a dent.

As the Nevada caucus results were still coming in that Saturday afternoon, MSNBC anchor Brian Williams interviewed James Carville, in his capacity as the last knight of the Clinton Templar, who called Sanders a disaster for the general election. Then Williams turned to Chris Matthews, whose time as an aide to House Speaker Tip O'Neill and years hosting MSNBC's flagship show *Hardball* meant that he was treated as an oracle of Democratic wisdom, despite how increasingly disconnected his analysis had become in recent years.

"What is going on here, and is this any way to pick a nominee?" Williams asked, a perfectly reasonable question, but with a tone that made clear what he thought of Sanders's starting to run away with the race.

"It's a little late to stop him," Matthews said. He had his analogy primed: "I was reading last night about the fall of France in the summer of 1940 and the general, Reynaud, calls up Churchill and says, 'It's over.' And Churchill says, 'How can that be? You've got the greatest army in Europe. How can it be over?' He said, 'It's over,'" Matthews said. "So I had that suppressed feeling."

The Sanders mob descended, raging with offense at Matthews having compared the most successful Jewish candidate for president ever to Nazis. Even if Sanders hadn't been Jewish, invoking Hitler's army rolling up the Champs-Élysées was a little much. It reflected, though, the mood throughout the media that Sanders and his supporters were overrunning the people who *should* be in charge. There's no question that any other candidate in the field who had nearly won Iowa and then won New Hampshire and Nevada would have received more favorable coverage.

"We were always pushing the boulder uphill," said Tulchin. "We were stronger than in 2016, but we were still pushing the boulder up the hill."

The campaign knew Sanders had a problem with older voters, so the plan going into that week was to book him on a *60 Minutes* interview to air the Sunday after Nevada, so that he could show how inoffensive and presidential he could be. Instead, the interview blew up after Sanders refused to distance himself from old comments he had made defending Cuba, played off a grainy 1980s video featuring his same Brooklyn accent and his uncombed hair before he'd gotten a statesman trim for the 2020 run. "We're very opposed to the authoritarian nature of Cuba," he told Anderson Cooper, "but, you know, it's unfair to simply say everything is bad." He cited an example: "When Castro came into office, you know what he did? He had a massive literacy program—is that a bad thing, even though Fidel Castro did it?" The reaction focused on how Sanders was essentially writing off Florida in a general election, given the number of Cuban expats in the state, but the problem was deeper: rather than succeeding in mainstreaming Sanders, the interview reinforced his connection to and pride in his more radical roots.

Publicly, Sanders aides tried to blame the media for this. Privately, they knew he'd hurt himself more than Matthews or any of their other media boogeymen could have. They discussed scheduling another big speech to reach out—Obama had to give his famous speech on race in the middle of the 2008 primaries, explaining that he wasn't a scary Black guy, so maybe Sanders had to try to show he wasn't a scary radical. Maybe emphasize more the part about completing FDR's fourth term, Ro Khanna suggested, play down the democratic socialism stuff. "Very good," Sanders told him, in his favorite way of dismissing an idea. "We have won the ideas battle," he kept repeating, as an insistent salve. He didn't need to do more.

In August, Tulchin and Sirota had ambushed a Sanders debate prep session at a Boulder, Colorado, hotel, waiting in the lobby until they were invited in to present a memo with a list of contrasts to Biden that they were convinced would destroy him: trade, the Iraq War, the 1994 crime bill, Social Security. Sanders had to move quickly, they insisted, because at that point Warren had been about to overtake him completely in the polls, and if he slipped to third and it became a two-person race between Biden and Warren, then by attacking Biden he'd only be helping her. Sanders was skeptical. He'd snap back at anyone who attacked him—"Fuck me? No fuck *you*," is how an aide once described it—but he didn't like throwing the first punch. He won his first House race in 1990 because one of his opponents went harshly negative and drove Vermonters away, and he was haunted by that past as well as his dreams of the future. "It's always been his view that he wanted to be elected on his agenda. He knows that if he were president, it would be a brawl, and if you're not elected on your agenda, it's harder to claim a mandate," Weaver said. Plus, Sanders liked Biden, as he felt that Biden had always treated him with the respect that is his baseline demand.

Sanders had turned to Weaver, who had put his name on the memo, as had Nina Turner. "Do you think we have to do this?" he'd asked. "Absolutely, senator," Weaver said. "We have to do this."

Weaver turned the memo into an opening statement for the September debate in Houston. Sanders rehearsed it. Before he went onstage, his wife interceded, urging him against going negative. Onstage he listened to the other opening statements, all upbeat and positive. Yang had used his to announce a lottery for ten families to receive a pilot $1,000-per-month check for a year, based on sign-ups to his website. When Sanders's turn came, he rocked on his feet, looked around, the thought process regarding scrapping what he had prepared playing out on his face, and he landed instead on his usual rhetoric, talking about taking on the oligarchy. Unlike with Buttigieg in New Hampshire, he never saw Biden as an immediate threat—and certainly didn't in that week after Nevada.

Sanders's biggest problem was that Warren was still in the race. Her campaign premise of being the Sanders alternative, the happy medium between committed progressives and the more establishment voters, might have been proved out by the weeklong freak-out over Sanders, if not for how deeply she had become the devil to the Sanders devotees. Sanders himself hoped she would drop out after New Hampshire. He was apoplectic that she didn't do so after Nevada.

"At every turn in the campaign where the Warren infrastructure had an opportunity to weigh in to help the progressive who was in the lead to win, versus sabotaging that person, they chose the latter course. After New Hampshire, it was over," Weaver said. "If Elizabeth wins Iowa and New Hampshire, and Bernie is in fourth, the drumbeat for him to get out of the race would have been so loud. 'For the good of the movement!' 'For the good of progressive politics!' 'You're being selfish!' 'It's all about you!' It would have been deafening. Where was that?"

Sanders aides toyed with other tactics. The grabbiest was committing to having a female running mate. Sanders nixed that, arguing that he was trying to build up credibility in voters' minds. That tactic would be read as a presumptuous move, as if he had already won the nomination, and it would backfire.

What might have been a bump in the road for Sanders in South Carolina became a pothole. "We knew the bar was higher," Weaver said. "But we didn't realize how high that bar was."

CHAPTER SEVENTEEN

A BILLION DOLLARS
FOR SAMOA

My wants are many and, if told,
Would muster many a score;
And were each wish a mint of gold,
I still should long for more.

—JOHN QUINCY ADAMS

October 2019–March 3, 2020

Billionaires get to keep people like Kevin Sheekey around. For twenty years, he's been Mike Bloomberg's top political adviser, getting paid enormously well to be a little involved in everything and not fully responsible for anything, using his elusiveness to build up the sense of his genius and power. There are two stories that Sheekey likes to tell about Bloomberg's first run for mayor in 2001. The first is about Colin Powell calling Bloomberg and telling him not to run unless he was ready to give a concession speech. The second is about Bloomberg coming to him one day during the campaign and asking—because Sheekey had told him that most people made up their minds based on TV advertising and that most people didn't make up their minds until the final two weeks before an election—why they didn't just buy all the TV ad time in the final two weeks. Sheekey stopped him short of that, but not by much. He spent $74 million on that race. That was a record—which he broke four years later with his first reelection campaign.

Bloomberg had been daydreaming about running for president since at least 1997, when he slipped the idea into his ghostwritten autobiography, in the same sentence where he first teased that he might run for mayor. Sheekey had been floating a Bloomberg-for-president campaign publicly since the day after Bloomberg won his second (and at that time, term-limited) term. "Don't you think the mayor should run for president next with his unique view on how to solve the problems in urban America?" Sheekey had asked the host on the local channel NY1, smiling coyly.

Each time, Sheekey would seed the idea with a few well-known reporters eager for the buzz, who he knew would take him seriously, even if they shouldn't have. Each time, he'd ask: Can you *imagine* how much money Bloomberg would be able to spend? Once, when he was mayor, Bloomberg got Sheekey a gag gift of a stack of business cards that listed his job as Covert Operations.

The magic of the Bloomberg for President talk was that it always seemed like the right idea, in concept, for people who thought about political ideas in concept, most of them from inside offices in Manhattan or DC, or over chardonnay at parties in Manhattan or DC. So many reporters in the national political press corps had covered his campaigns, and his ultracompetent reimagining of the corrupt bureaucracy of city government, or had just tried to shimmy their way into the always way-too-lavish afterparties he threw with *Vanity Fair* for the White House Correspondents' Dinners, where yes, that *was* Paul Rudd over next to Jack Lew.

Each cycle the concept shifted slightly. Bloomberg for President in 2008 was that the country was tired of partisanship; they wanted someone who wasn't caught up in Washington but had some experience—and look at the turnaround he'd managed in New York after September 11! He made it as far as switching his registration to independent, and dispatching an aide to travel around the country putting together the battle plan for how to get on the ballot. Bloomberg for President 2012 was a thought that passed quickly, as it was predicated on Obama's complete collapse, but never one that got serious. Bloomberg for President 2016 was that America couldn't stand Hillary Clinton, and Trump was a cartoon, and nobody wanted either of them. His aides cooked up an intricate and extensive *Federalist Papers* fan fiction scheme with Oprah in the cabinet and former chairman of the Joint Chiefs of Staff Admiral Mike Mullen as his running mate, hinging on no one's hitting 270 votes in the

Electoral College and the election being thrown to the House of Representatives to decide. The aides most sold on this one insist that the only real problem was not being able to guarantee that he'd be able to sway (read: entice with promises of money to overcome their political exhaustion) enough House delegations to actually win the White House. "It weighed on him," one person talking to him said after he pulled out in 2016, "but at the end of the day, the fact that this was probably the last shot wasn't enough to make him want to do it."

Being a bored billionaire with a dream led Elon Musk to shoot his convertible into space. For Bloomberg, it meant that the last shot wasn't the last shot. (Not that he was a *Hamilton* fan: Bloomberg would tell people he thought the show was "silly," because there wasn't a good tune to hum along to, and because everyone knows George Washington wasn't Black.)

Bloomberg for President 2020 was premised on the notion that Trump had to go, and that the Democrats were a bunch of jokers who were being lemmings on the left—and by the way, did you know he had run a government and had endless billions of dollars to spend? When Bloomberg started toying with the idea in the fall of 2018, all he had to do was get word out that he'd changed his registration back to Democrat—what it had been before he was an independent and before he'd become a Republican to run for mayor the first time—and make a couple of trips, a couple of comments. Was he actually serious about running, about believing that a rich, white, by then seventy-eight-year-old defender of Wall Street who had been sued by women and African Americans would be the right fit for the Democratic Party at that point? "He is serious enough to let Kevin run with it, and he's having fun on the stump," an adviser said at the time. As for how much he'd spend, no reason to put a cap on what would be his "most significant competitive advantage," the adviser said. "There's no difference between five hundred million, one billion, or two billion dollars."

That didn't mean there was a strategy. Or even the beginnings of one. "It's much more ad hoc than you'd think," the adviser said. But that was the special, unique advantage of Bloomberg: With that amount of money, with that much ability to make news just by showing up, they didn't need much of a plan. If he decided to make it real, he could make it real almost overnight.

On Martin Luther King Jr. Day of 2019, Bloomberg and Biden sat together at a table in a ballroom of the Mayflower Hotel in Washington. They were nominally both there for Al Sharpton's annual National Action Network breakfast, though they were really both there to use the time in the fancy room as a way to chase forgiveness for their parts in gutting Black communities with police policies that were no longer in fashion in Democratic politics. Biden told Sharpton backstage that he was thinking of running, asked what he thought. Sharpton told him he had to deal with his role in the 1994 crime bill first, and that, in any case, he figured a Biden run would be a long shot, what with all the other candidates already moving.

Biden's speech that morning was the first time he started to distance himself publicly from the crime bill. Bloomberg's speech was less direct. "I can't stand up here and tell you every decision I have made as mayor was perfect," he said, hinting that he was talking about his legacy promoting and defending the institutionalized harassment policy known as stop-and-frisk. He never went so far as actually saying the words.

Sharpton was less impressed. So were the rest of the people there that morning.

Bloomberg also offered this: "Whatever the next year brings for Joe and me, I know we'll both keep our eyes on the real prize, which is a Democrat winning the White House."

The data that Bloomberg was getting back from the political machine he'd built was coming in pretty clear: Biden was strong, and primary voters weren't too interested in an old, white, former Republican New Yorker billionaire who lauded the financial industry and questioned the MeToo accusations against Charlie Rose. Bloomberg could nonetheless get pretty far surfing the networks of eager mayors, environmental groups, and gun control activists that his money had paid for.

He couldn't get far enough though. One morning at the beginning of March, Bloomberg announced to his inner circle that he wasn't going to do it, and they rushed to write a column for him to be published on the *Bloomberg* news website arguing that he could have beaten Trump, but he just couldn't get through the primary field. An event that was being put together in New Hampshire for later that week was scrapped. He went back to his job at the company, back to long weekends in Bermuda playing golf.

There was always a wink to the aides who knew him best. *We could always come back to this. This doesn't have to be the end.*

———

Bloomberg likes rich people. He had even warmed to Jared Kushner, when the wannabe wunderkind devoted himself to getting invited to high-priced Manhattan charity dinners in his pre-Trump life. That's the Bloomberg bubble, where the price of admission is a nine-figure net worth, where they all assume that making so much money is proof of their genius. There, they are sure they understand what the world needs and wants as their planes fly them to their vacation homes. Everyone they know has Bloomberg Terminals in their offices and thinks Bloomberg was a fantastic mayor. Of course they believed Bloomberg would be a fantastic president. And of course they were flipping out that Warren or Sanders was going to be the nominee and hand Trump the election. The thought that Warren or Sanders might win was almost as bad.

They called him. He called them. The idea was hard to resist.

He thought about climate change—not because he hikes or snorkels, or cares all that much about what happens to any individual human. He thinks in statistics, considers pushing up life expectancy in New York his greatest accomplishment as mayor. That was the impetus for the smoking ban and restaurant cleanliness grades and all the other nanny-state regulations, even if he himself always pours extra salt on his popcorn. Pushed once at a press briefing in Gracie Mansion when he was still mayor to explain how his sustainability initiatives weren't tackling how unaffordable the city was becoming, he shrugged that higher rents were the inevitable consequence of keeping crime low, improving the schools, cleaning up the parks, investing in the arts. Supply and demand, he said. OK, the reporter replied, but a New York built around luxury apartments for foreign oligarchs to sink stolen fortunes into didn't seem *sustainable*. Well, Bloomberg answered, which would you have him do? Let crime go up? Stop helping the schools?

He thought about Charlottesville, synagogues being attacked, the responsibility he felt he had as a Jew. For his entire life he had been more of a stop-by-services-on-Rosh-Hashana kind of observant, but what was going through his head those days was deeper, etched in him from conversations around the family table in Medford, Massachusetts, and the images of the Holocaust on newsreels. Now, to see Nazis marching in America? It was terrifying, he would tell people.

Bloomberg kept paying for polls all through the year. Through impeachment, Biden kept going down while he kept going up. That's when his old engineer's brain kicked in. He wanted to be president, but if he couldn't be president, running didn't make sense. But if he *could* be the president, he'd run. He was seventy-eight. His bank account made more interest in a day than what all of the candidates were raising in their campaigns in total. There was nothing else in business to accomplish—his company ran fine without him when he was mayor, and it didn't really need him around now. "You don't make the ask, you'll never get the ticket," he'd always say, as if he'd been a salesman in a Dashiell Hammett novel, not at Salomon Brothers in the 1970s.

Then he talked to Chuck Schumer. The Senate minority leader was panicked too, and for many of the same reasons: Biden was a disaster, the rest of the field was a mess, Warren would lose to Trump, Sanders would *definitely* lose to Trump. And, Schumer said, they'd both take the Senate Democrats down with them. Bloodbath. Michigan gone, Virginia gone, any hopes of what were already looking like easy pickups in Arizona and Colorado gone. They could lose the House again. Imagine, Schumer said, if Trump won a second term, the Senate would have a bigger Republican majority, the House too, maybe.

Bloomberg walked away from the conversation believing that Schumer was going to endorse him, despite there being five Democratic senators still in the race. Schumer hinted at promises, Bloomberg would tell aides. Schumer thought that Bloomberg understood that while he'd be rooting for him, he couldn't actually say so publicly. Twenty years of dealing with each other, and they still were having separate conversations within the same meeting.

On November 4, Bloomberg called a meeting with Sheekey and his two other closest advisers, Patti Harris and Howard Wolfson, to go over the numbers at the converted Upper East Side mansion he had bought for his private offices and foundation, a block and a half from the expanded townhouse where he lived. They met again the next day, Election Day for state races in Kentucky and Virginia, where Bloomberg had put some money behind pro–gun control causes, and it seemed as if they'd be getting good news.

They thought that they were humoring him, having the meetings because he paid them well to have the meetings, but that he would hear how hard winning was going to be, how slim his chances were. Bloomberg looked at the date his aides flagged for him: November 8, the deadline to file to get on the ballot in Alabama—the earliest of the states after the first four. He said he would think overnight about running. They all left assuming that the only thing to think about was what he'd do when he ruled it out again—maybe endorse Biden, but probably just sit it out for a while.

With all that Bloomberg had accomplished in his life, this remained the one thing he wanted to do that he had not done. He saw the opportunity, understood the chances were slim, but concluded that there wasn't a downside in trying. He had the money. He had the time. Several people who talked to him after he decided said he seemed to have a "fuck-it moment." The burden of the self-made billionaire is to always believe everyone else is wrong and you are right.

To Bloomberg, days in the office begin at seven a.m. Those who have succeeded get paid well by him and have learned to beat him to their desks. Sheekey was at his by quarter to seven that morning. Right after seven, Bloomberg rang his extension. "So I thought about it, and we're going to run," he said. "Talk later." He hung up. Sheekey scrambled to make calls, turn on a campaign overnight. He started with Harris and Wolfson. "Game on," he told them.

Bloomberg made a few calls of his own: Obama, Harry Reid. He left it to Sheekey to call Steve Ricchetti, instead of giving Biden a heads-up directly. He called Hillary Clinton and made a joke about how he might be heading to a contested Democratic convention, hoping to emerge as the consensus choice by promising to spend billions to help heal the breaks and bruises that kind of fight might leave. "Hope I'm not stepping on any toes," he told Clinton, knowing she might still be nursing a contested convention consensus dream herself.

Aides were dispatched to Alabama to oversee the paperwork. He got his own plane ready to fly to Arkansas for the filing deadline a few days later. He called *The New York Times* to say it was really, seriously, actually happening this time, and then headed out for a small dinner at a French bistro on the Upper East Side where a plate of french fries goes for $10.

===

Bloomberg's campaign proved that money can buy a shot at the presidency— as Steyer had been showing on a smaller scale, with just a few hundred million dollars. According to his own internal polling, he went from 5 percent as a potential choice before he started advertising to 18 percent when he dropped out. His favorable opinion rating went from 31 percent to 59 percent. His campaign, however, proved that, ultimately, the candidate matters.

Going into the Iowa caucuses, insiders thought Democrats were headed to a Sanders versus Bloomberg contested convention: the socialist versus the billionaire, the independent versus the former Republican, the man with undying commitment from his fans versus the man with the bottomless bank account to keep boosting support. Also: two old Jewish men, neither of whom could ever have brought the other's supporters in.

With the Iowa caucus meltdown, Bloomberg looked smarter for having just ignored the state, his competence standing out in a party that clearly didn't have much.

First, though, he had to get through a debate. All the Democratic candidates made big shows of how offended they were that Bloomberg qualified for the debate in mid-February. They complained that there had to have been a backroom deal between Bloomberg and the DNC to grant a big-spending donor a spot. The truth was, all the Democratic candidates were salivating over the chance to smack him around.

No one who works for Bloomberg is under any delusion that he's particularly good at politics. He's definitely not good at debating, and the only debates he had ever done before now were with local politicians who had been the chum tossed in against his hundred-million-dollar mayoral campaigns. Sheekey toyed with skipping the debate, to make the argument that he was bringing his case directly to the voters. Bloomberg is a traditionalist. If he qualified for the debates, he said, he had to do the debates.

Pretty much everyone on the campaign ended up wishing he'd listened to Sheekey. "It was like putting him in the middle of the Royal Shakespeare Company, and he'd done community theater," an adviser said.

Prep was a struggle from the start. Bloomberg wouldn't accept that a presidential debate was different from anything else in politics, no matter how much his staff tried to make him see it. He spent hours studying issues and facts that were new to him, and was already talking about how he'd reorganize management at the U.S. Postal Service. They could never get him interested in doing the mock sessions, which they knew he desperately needed.

They also could never get him to accept how much of a problem he had regarding the women bound by nondisclosure agreements (NDAs) as part of sexual harassment lawsuits naming him while he was running his namesake company. One had alleged he'd told a pregnant woman to "kill it"—and when the woman asked if she'd heard him correctly, he repeated, "Kill it." But, he insisted, these stories had been floating around for years when he was mayor and that had never stopped him. Anyway, he had to make a decision based on what was good company policy. Plus he took a circa Lee Iacocca–era view of the situation: he'd only been named in three lawsuits, and considering how long he'd been in business and how many women he'd interacted with, by the standards he knew, that was almost batting a thousand.

Everyone involved knew Bloomberg didn't have good answers for serious problems. There was only so far that aides were willing to go, aware they might be risking years of high six-figure salaries and consulting contracts ahead, once the campaign inevitably collapsed.

Warren had been whipping shot puts at him from the day he got in, eager for the distraction from her own Medicare for All tailspin. Bloomberg didn't want to respond. She wasn't a threat, he would insist in debate prep, wasn't in his path to the nomination. And he didn't want to get into a head-to-head with a woman, especially not on accusations of sexual harassment. He knew enough to avoid that.

When the podium order came out with Bloomberg placed next to Warren, aides thought about the camera angle, how everyone would see Bloomberg's scrunched Kermitlike facial reactions when she teed off on him. The assessment: "Oh fuck."

A former city hall press aide had played Warren in the mock sessions. She hit on almost every attack the senator herself ended up launching onstage—but Wood was nowhere near good enough to anticipate how Warren would blitz him. First: "I'd like to talk about who we're running against: a billionaire who calls women 'fat broads' and 'horse-faced lesbians.' And, no, I'm not talking about Donald Trump. I'm talking about Mayor Bloomberg." Then more: "Democrats are not going to win if we have a nominee who has a history of hiding his tax returns, of harassing women, and of supporting racist policies like redlining and stop-and-frisk." More: "Look, I'll support whoever the Democratic nominee is. But understand this: Democrats take a huge risk if we just substitute one arrogant billionaire for another." Warren had already started churning out policy on responding to the just-emerging coronavirus, antici-pating difficult times but imagining nowhere near the terrible scale of what was to come. She had thought about making it the centerpiece of her debate performance that night. She went after Bloomberg instead.

Biden jumped in. He had always thought he and Bloomberg got along— he'd considered hiring Sheekey to be his first chief of staff as vice president, and they'd become allies on gun control and other issues. He knew Bloom-berg's candidacy was meant to effectively declare his own over, and he'd been waiting to let rip for months: "The mayor says that he has a great record, that he's done these wonderful things. Well, the fact of the matter is, he has not managed his city very, very well when he was there. He didn't get a whole lot done." Then he went right after stop-and-frisk. Buttigieg took a swing. Warren went right at Bloomberg again. Fifteen minutes later, Bloomberg pointed out how many women had been in leadership roles at city hall, at his company, at his foundation, and how he was committed to equal pay. Warren hadn't been expecting to get another opening. She didn't have lines prepared but listened to what he said, cocked her head in theatric professor mode, and took off.

"I hope you heard what his defense was: 'I've been nice to some women.' That just doesn't cut it," she said, jumping on what he didn't actually say. "What we need to know is exactly what's lurking out there. He has gotten some number of women, dozens, who knows, to sign nondisclosure agreements both for sexual harassment and for gender discrimination in the workplace. So, Mr. Mayor, are you willing to release all of those women from those non-disclosure agreements, so we can hear their side of the story?"

"We have a very few nondisclosure agreements," Bloomberg responded. "How many is that?" Warren asked. He squirmed through another line. "How many is that?" she repeated. Now Biden was jumping in. "Come on," he kept saying. Then Buttigieg took a swing. Then Sanders. The Democrats had finally found something to agree on: Bloomberg should go to hell.

Bloomberg's inner circle was watching in a hotel suite. "He's nervous," one had said out loud, watching him walk out. He came in flat and he got worse.

Wolfson plodded into the spin room and let the reporters swarm around him. Everything went fine, he insisted. They were very pleased with how he did. He was looking forward to another debate. "I think it was clear that there were a lot of folks coming in loaded for bear," Wolfson said. "He did not lose his cool. No one got under his skin. And I think he very clearly established a two-person race between him and Bernie Sanders."

In fact they had seen in their tracking polls that Bloomberg had been bleeding support for days before the debate, dropping each time attention was drawn to a problematic remark in an old video or other revelations of his record. They didn't realize how many were being planted with reporters by Biden campaign staffers who, with their candidate collapsing, suddenly had a lot of time and spite on their hands, and had essentially transformed themselves into a tiny anti-Bloomberg super PAC to make sure that if Biden didn't get the nomination, neither would he.

Bloomberg left early the morning after the debate to campaign in Utah. It was on to Super Tuesday, but not really. He was upset, well aware that he'd blown the basic argument that he could take on Trump. His campaign had spent millions paying social media influencers to generate memes about how cool he was, but these and the free T-shirts they'd hand out at events were just a flaming pile of money for a guy who'd tanked himself. Wolfson started telling reporters it was all his fault, he'd failed to prepare the boss adequately, trying to please him. That made Bloomberg angrier. He appreciated prostration, but it only rubbed in how bad the performance had been.

Back at Bloomberg headquarters, the instant data showed he was a projected 150 delegates down within twelve hours. Very quickly top advisers were consulting one another about how to talk him into quitting. If he got out before Super Tuesday, he would save some money, and more important, save face. Even for an aging billionaire, drawing out the loss would be embarrassing, and put him in a weaker position for having influence in the rest of the race. Who would bring the idea to him? Again, no one wanted to risk his or her own big checks by being the one to take a stand against the guy writing them. College tuitions and summer homes have been paid for by those multimillion Bloomberg pseudopensions.

The difference between creativity and magical thinking in politics is often about what works. Sheekey reached out to Andrew Yang. Maybe they could come to an understanding—an endorsement, in exchange for helping line up some pieces for him if he wanted to run for mayor of New York himself in 2021, as he'd been making a little noise about? Interesting. Yang made a counter-offer: How about Bloomberg puts $1 billion into a universal basic income pilot program? Sheekey's own counter: How about $1 billion for a UBI pilot program *once Bloomberg was already president*? No deal.

A Yang endorsement would have been fun but irrelevant past a few hours of play on Twitter. The real hope for a shake-up was brewing in a conference room back at headquarters, where a lawyer named Gary Ginsberg sat with stacks of research and polling to match against vetting files the Bloomberg team had put together. He was in charge of picking a running mate.

In the end, Ginsberg's job came down to a very easy calculation by the end of January: debate prep was still not going well. The polling was showing that Super Tuesday would narrow the field but not produce a nominee, and that there wasn't a clear path to beating Sanders. The campaign needed a jolt. What if instead of just skipping the debate, Bloomberg counterprogrammed it with a big announcement and a day of campaigning?

Bloomberg needed to neutralize how much of a problem stop-and-frisk was still proving to be with Black voters, and he needed some way of hamstringing Biden's win going into South Carolina—which meant cutting him down with Black voters. There was an initial phone call to Klobuchar to tease the running mate idea, who mulled the idea for about six hours before saying she wasn't interested. The thinking quickly zeroed in on Harris, Booker, Stacey Abrams, and Florida congresswoman Val Demings. Bloomberg himself added Muriel Bowser, the mayor of Washington, DC, to the list.

For halfway plausible deniability, aides handled the conversations with the prospects rather than having Bloomberg talk to them directly. They walked through why a ticket would be such a good match, why each should want to sign on, what the path to victory would look like. The strong implication was made that Bloomberg was turning seventy-nine a few weeks after Inauguration Day, so his running mate could probably count on being the nominee by 2024.

Bloomberg had always been intrigued by Harris, whom he had first met when she was attorney general. The polling made Sheekey and Ginsberg like her even more. She would help in the California primary, she would help nationally. She cautiously listened to their pitch and said she wanted to hear more, but pushed off meeting with Bloomberg directly. First, she said, she wanted to see him debate. Then, after the massacre had taken place, she said she wanted to see what the results were out of Nevada. Then she said she wanted to see what happened in South Carolina. The weeklong flirtation fizzled into Harris's usual caution. She knew she had a good chance of being Biden's running mate, and she knew that jumping on with Bloomberg would put an end to that.

Booker had been an early acolyte of Bloomberg's from when he was first elected in Newark. He'd once called Bloomberg the Papa Smurf of the new generation of pragmatic mayors (with Bloomberg, naturally, paying for lots of smurfberries for them to use on projects in their cities). They agreed on charter schools and education reform. Bloomberg had bungled by calling Booker "well-spoken" in an interview during the primary, and Booker had said the comment certainly smelled a lot like racism, which annoyed Bloomberg. Booker didn't like how Bloomberg had bought his way into the race, thought it undermined the process, all those days in Iowa and New Hampshire he'd spent hustling for himself.

As much as he didn't want Bloomberg to be the president, he *did* still want to be president himself. And he knew there was a pretty good chance a match with him would work, especially if he signed on early enough to head to South Carolina to campaign ahead of the primary and undercut Biden. The morning after the debate, Ginsberg went to see Booker at home in Newark and walked through the pitch. Booker polled well, they told him. They would give him a plane and unlimited resources, let him loose on the stump all over the country. Booker agonized. Booker didn't believe Bloomberg should get to buy the presidency, or that he and his record were what Democrats should stand for in this moment. He also knew there was a pretty good chance he'd never get to be president if he didn't take this lifeline. A few days later, he said no.

Bloomberg's Everytown for Gun Safety group had been a big backer of Stacey Abrams's run for governor in Georgia in 2018, and had kept putting money into the voting rights group she founded after she lost. In January, he announced a $5 million check to the group, and his aides went after her, laying out all the reasons she should say yes, how her lack of national or executive experience would be less of an issue with Bloomberg at the top of the ticket than with anyone else. She'd help him with women. She'd help him with Black voters. She'd give him a beachhead in the Super Tuesday states in the South, where he was hoping his spending could make for an unlikely foothold for a short Jewish billionaire from New York. She wouldn't walk away from her voting group before the Georgia primary in June, and that was going to be too late.

Demings was a Black woman, a former police chief from Florida—Bloomberg had poured money into a group backing her first run for Congress, and stayed interested. She had impressed many as one of the House managers of the impeachment trial, presenting the case. Maybe she would be the right fit, and she was definitely interested, though they worried her police past might draw even more attention to his vulnerability over stop-and-frisk. Bowser was a harder sell among the top advisers, but Bloomberg had always liked her. And he liked that she had endorsed him as soon as he got in the race. That wasn't enough, though, for them to ever get serious about considering her.

"The idea was essentially: if we're breaking all the rules, why not break the rules of saying we can't run as a ticket and bring that to the dance?" Sheekey said, looking back.

———

Bloomberg kept flying around and buying more ads. The crowds were still showing up, and he liked the applause. Sometimes he'd walk to the back of the 747 he'd chartered to talk up reporters, but by the final week, they were done asking the kinds of questions they'd pose if he were a real contender, and focused more on why he was running, whether he'd back Biden, and whether his campaign was going to hurt Democrats' hopes of beating Trump.

The most animated Bloomberg became was when he was talking about the variety and levels of private planes and whether his jet was nicer than Trump's. "There are planes with full bedrooms," he noted. However punchy he seemed, he wasn't trying to tell them they were crazy for not seeing how he was still going to win.

The Sunday morning after Biden won South Carolina, Bloomberg flew into Selma. He sat in the front pew of Brown Memorial Chapel for two hours, the only candidate to be there from the start of the service through the end. He passed around a tin of Altoids (original flavor) to the people sitting next to him. He stood for the hymns, just listening. The pastor introduced him from the altar by telling a story about how Bloomberg initially didn't want to come. About ten people waited until Bloomberg started speaking, stood up, and turned their backs in silent protest.

Bloomberg walked up to the lectern and laid the narrow notecards he likes to speak from atop an open Bible. He talked about his record as mayor, and about working with Sharpton, who preaches at the Selma church every Bloody Sunday anniversary. At the time, Sharpton was out with Biden for a private tour of a memorial nearby, and the only time he spoke publicly about Bloomberg that day was when he got to the service late, to rib him to put some money for church renovations into the collection basket. Bloomberg chuckled. He'd already pulled two bills from his wallet and put them in the basket—another couple of bucks toward the record for the largest amount of money spent in the shortest amount of time with the least to show for it.

That night, Bloomberg flew to San Antonio to appear at an old airplane hangar that had been turned into an event space. There was a six-piece mariachi band onstage. There were three food trucks (barbecue, tacos, and hamburgers) that had been paid well enough to hand out everything for free. On the open bar was a bowl of Texas-specific Bloomberg campaign buttons. And there was Bloomberg, giving the kind of no-frills speech he's best at. "Mike! Mike! Mike!" the crowd chanted. At one point, when he mentioned Trump's impeachment, a few yelled "Lock him up!" and Bloomberg laughed, almost giggling. He said he'd flip Texas. "Blue! Blue! Blue!" they shouted. He was having a good time. Never much of a handshaker, he did one round of working the crowd, then turned before heading out the door to do another.

No one woke up on Super Tuesday thinking they were going to do well. They were full into might-as-well-see-this-through mode. Maybe there'd be some fluke. Maybe Biden's rapid consolidation would miss. Bloomberg went through the motions, skipping ahead to Florida, where the primary was two weeks later. He ordered a coffee in Little Havana in his Massachusetts-accented gringo Spanish. ("*No azucar, pero poco leche.*") He told a person waiting to sit with him that he couldn't believe how crazy people were already being about the coronavirus, refusing to go out to Chinese restaurants. He snapped at a few reporters pushing him on hurting Biden's chances, which had turned around overnight after South Carolina—"Joe's taking votes away from me," he said. "It goes in both directions. Have you asked Joe if he's going to drop out?" He took a shot at Sanders for saying nice things about Fidel Castro. He flew to Orlando to lay a white rose wreath at the site of the Pulse nightclub shooting.

Then he got on the plane again and flew to West Palm Beach for the final stop.

The evening had been conceived in a different reality, when it might have been a bigger deal that Bloomberg was taunting Trump by hosting his party just across the water from Mar-a-Lago. Expat New Yorkers and curious Floridians stuffed themselves full of free sandwiches and mini cupcakes as they waited to go into the blue-lit ballroom, with giant MIKE WILL GET IT DONE signs above and to the side of the stage. A camera on a crane prepared for sweeping shots once he got onstage. Judge Judy was set to come out and give a speech. Bloomberg was in a hotel suite waiting to see just how bad the returns were, and Sheekey popped out to do a little more spinning.

The reporters' impatience spilled out. So, one asked, is Bloomberg a spoiler or a kingmaker? Sheekey sped right past acknowledging that the question already took as a given that Bloomberg wasn't going to be the nominee. "He's certainly not a spoiler. He's on the ballot for the first time tonight," Sheekey said. "Mike Bloomberg is either the candidate for the party or the single most important person helping that candidate defeat Donald Trump."

That was not true. Not then. Not in the fall.

———

Bloomberg dropped out the next morning.

After he had given the obligatory speech, he called a meeting of his top aides to talk through closing down the campaign. What about, he was asked, the talk of paying staff all through the year?

This was news to him. "I never made this promise. Did you promise this?" Bloomberg asked, looking right at Sheekey.

"No," Sheekey said, which was true, except that it wasn't. Sheekey hadn't said it openly, but it was also well known that he'd floated the idea anonymously to a few reporters, then leaned in to his man-of-mystery routine when other reporters tried to nail him down on it, never shooting the idea down, as wacky and unprecedented as it would have been to pay workers for months after the campaign ended. Everyone in the room knew that, and he knew that everyone in the room knew that. "This is crazy," Wolfson said. They had made the promises in Bloomberg's name, and the damage from holding out on this wasn't worth whatever it was going to cost. They were talking about $14 million, maybe $17 million. Relative to a normal person, it's a lot of money. Relative to a guy worth $60 billion on a bad day who had just spent a billion dollars on his campaign, it's nothing. Relative to the hundreds of thousands Sheekey had spent just on catering and outfitting the headquarters, it was idiotic, especially as the pandemic started to cripple the economy. They could even have found the money in the existing budget if they'd wanted to. Sheekey could have built the costs into the budget earlier. He hadn't. Bloomberg could have written the check to cover it anyway and literally never noticed however many millions it would be. He didn't want to. He's generally a pretty rational person, but in the funk of losing, he was impervious to rational arguments.

Instead of paying the staffers, Bloomberg aides calculated how much paying the salaries and benefits for a fully funded staff of organizers in the six closest swing states would be, then threw in some extra to cover infrastructure and operational costs. Obama had left the DNC $24 million in debt from his 2012 campaign, which he won, as the sitting president. Bloomberg gave the DNC $18 million after a campaign that he lost in the primaries.

Part of why rich people start philanthropies is to shine up their images as generous. Bloomberg has given more money away than nearly anyone in the history of America. That short meeting helped redefine thirty years of image building. He was living up to the worst caricature of himself: the self-centered Scrooge whose own middle-of-the-night epiphany was to get more bitter, tighter with his money, less willing to help. He stewed in his own well-appointed COVID lockdown, flying between one of his mansions and the other. He put up several hundred million to help fight the disease and support organizations facing shortfalls—but nowhere near the amount, or with a specific target, that could have made him a national leader.

"Suddenly, the music stops. He doesn't go back to the Senate. He doesn't go back to a governor's office," said one of the people who worked on the campaign. "He goes back to puttering around his house with his golf simulator."

In the months after Bloomberg quit, his loyalists insisted that he said the campaign had been a good use of time and a good use of money. It's hard to see how that's true. He blew a billion dollars to win one primary, in American Samoa, and with the four delegates he won plus those in a few other states, wound up spending about $30 million per delegate. He probably could have bought American Samoa for less.

If Bloomberg hadn't run and sucked up attention, Biden probably wouldn't have had the space to recover after Iowa and New Hampshire. Warren wouldn't have had a last burst of oxygen, which gave her the attention and money to stay in a few more weeks. Sanders wouldn't have had a foil to prove that the billionaires were out to stop him. Outside of the politics, the only lasting impact Bloomberg's campaign had was the $100 million his foundation later gave for medical school scholarships set up for Black students, inspired by Bloomberg's trip to the Tulsa race-massacre memorial in January, where he said he wouldn't have made his fortune if he'd been Black. That trip, and the plan he'd put together to improve Black economic standing, were the highlight of his campaign. Most people didn't even know they had happened.

"We had an almost perfect understanding of this race: The country was tired about being tired, angry about being angry, wanted to go back to not thinking about the president all the time. The stakes were so high that the left, the centrists, and Republicans who are skeptical about Trump came together behind someone who's about decency and fairness and intelligence," said Stu Loeser, Bloomberg's press secretary when he was mayor and one of the first staff to show up for the presidential campaign. "That is what happened—just with a different guy."

CHAPTER EIGHTEEN

SEVENTY-TWO HOURS THAT CHANGED HISTORY

In every presidential election, Democrats want to fall in love—
Republicans just fall in line.

—BILL CLINTON

February 23, 2020–March 3, 2020

The way Jim Clyburn tells the story, American history pivoted on a chance encounter at a small funeral, on the Friday eight days before the South Carolina primary.

The congressman had known Joe Biden for decades. Clyburn had been pulling for Biden since all the way back in 2015 when he was looking at running against Clinton—until a comment from Clyburn that fall had helped convince Biden that it might be too late to get in. He had urged Biden to be active in campaigning in the midterms, pointing out that he had a unique ability to attract working-class white voters, African Americans, and suburban women. Clyburn and his wife had talked about backing him for months before she died in September, in the middle of the impeachment furor—Biden came off the campaign trail to attend the funeral—and Clyburn expected to stick to their plan.

Clyburn's preference wasn't a secret. Two weeks before the Iowa caucuses, the action was briefly back in South Carolina. The night before Martin Luther

King Jr. Day, with all the major candidates headed to Columbia the next day, Biden hosted an oyster roast in Orangeburg. Clyburn was onstage. "Nobody needs to make this country great again! This country *is* great!" Clyburn said, repeating a turn of phrase he said so often he turned it into a billboard. "Our challenge is to make the country's greatness accessible and affordable to all its citizens."

"I'm not trying to take America back to some place that never existed," Biden said, picking up the thread. "I'm trying to take it to somewhere it's never, ever been."

The mood felt closer to that of a front-runner event than any of the others he'd been doing anywhere else those days: the sour fishiness of the oyster grease in the air, big barn doors that had opened for Biden to make a grand entrance, a crowd that was so eager to see him that it stuck with him even when he stumbled through a section about Charlottesville.

Then came Iowa, New Hampshire. The internal Biden confidence that the first three states weren't reflective of his strength wasn't translating to the world. The Friday before Nevada, Clyburn was in church in a town called Hopkins to pay his respects to his accountant, when a woman grabbed him and asked whom he was with. She told him to whisper it in her ear, because she thought that might make him more honest. *Biden*, he said. She snapped back. People needed to hear him say that. This, he says, is why he decided to endorse.

This isn't the full story. There was a funeral, and a woman did grab Clyburn's arm. He didn't endorse Biden because of her, though, and wouldn't have done so if not for that second-place finish in Nevada.

Everyone knew how critical Clyburn's backing would be for Biden. He would consolidate Black support. He would run up the count in Biden's must-win state. Biden chased him. Aides chased him. The super PAC supporting Biden chased him to the point of sending him videos and mail flyers for his approval so that they'd be ready to go as soon as he gave the word. Back and forth. He was ready—but then came the fourth- and fifth-place finishes, and word came back to the PAC from one of the people working with Clyburn: "He's not going to try to rehab a corpse." Clyburn was sensitive to race dynamics in South Carolina and nationally, and wasn't going to go public as long as there was still a Black candidate running, so even Deval Patrick had been holding him back until quitting the morning after New Hampshire. Still, Clyburn wondered: Could Biden actually win minority votes? Could he actually win *any* votes?

Clyburn was determined, in any case, to make sure Sanders didn't win the nomination. They had collaborated to get funding for community health centers written into Obamacare—arguably, Sanders's biggest actual legislative accomplishment in his thirty years in Washington. But Clyburn never liked Sanders's socialist politics and was convinced that if he were to become the nominee, he would tank Democrats around the country. It didn't help that Sanders had no patience for all the genuflecting and outreach that politicians like Clyburn thrive on. Once, when shaking hands with a big crowd on the way into an event in South Carolina, he was told that Clyburn was stuck behind and trying to get to the front. Sanders said, "He can wait." At the big Fish Fry event in June 2019, he brushed off one of Clyburn's daughters when she asked him not to create a traffic jam by working the crowd. He'd make his way to where he was supposed to be eventually, Sanders told her, then muttered, "Little does she know, 'eventually' is when this event is over."

Convinced that there was no chance of landing Clyburn's endorsement, he was advised by aides that he might be able to keep the congressman neutral, or at least tempered, but he didn't call Clyburn once over the entire race.

Clyburn got the message. When Biden was tailspinning after New Hampshire, Clyburn's top political aide, Antjuan Seawright, headed to New York for a meeting at Mike Bloomberg's campaign headquarters. "We're trying to get my guy to endorse your guy," Seawright told an aide, explaining his presence, as he made his way out of the meeting. After Bloomberg's belly flop in the Las Vegas debate and the Nevada results a few days later, Clyburn was back leaning toward Biden.

The night after Nevada, Biden flew to Charleston. Clyburn was at a reception on the USS *Yorktown*, docked just outside of town. Biden arrived toward the end of the event and pulled him aside for a private meeting. He hadn't called Clyburn since he'd lost Iowa, and though the congressman hadn't felt that he needed the call, it was now time for him to unload. Talk less, he told Biden. Get focused. Chop every meandering answer down to, "Here is what this answer means for you, here is what it means for your family, and here's what it means for your community. And then stop talking." Biden listened, like a scolded kid stuck in detention. That wasn't all. Clyburn told him to promise to put a Black woman on the Supreme Court. Done, Biden said.

Biden didn't ask for an endorsement outright. That was implied.

＝＝＝＝＝

Winning the South Carolina primary is about running strong with Black voters. Biden had spent years on golfing vacations there. He had gotten close with one of the state's long-serving senators, Fritz Hollings. When Hollings died, Biden had been relieved that it was before his delayed campaign launch, so that when he gave a eulogy at the old man's funeral in April, he could be there without busking for votes.

Another twist of fate. If a Black candidate had survived in the race until South Carolina, the primary would have almost certainly shaped up differently. Booker, Harris, and Patrick had all been banking on exactly that. They were all long gone by the time the race arrived in the state.

After 2016, Sanders had promised he would build up his appeal to Black voters, make inroads in South Carolina. He made the motions for a bit. Then, apart from a few appearances, he gave up. Aides talked wistfully to one another about skipping the state entirely because they knew that for all his attempts to improve with Black voters, he was never going to win the state. They couldn't figure out how to make that not look as if they were giving the finger to Black voters overall. A series of *Atlantic* stories detailing how far Sanders had gone in considering running a primary challenge against Obama when he was up for reelection only deepened his problems. Biden was running on his loyalty to Obama because that's who he was, but also because that connected with Black voters who were already looking to him as the best chance of beating Trump, and there was little appetite for taking chances. Sanders's aides, after a year of either catering to friendly media sources or being largely written off by the mainstream press, kept scuttling to undercut the story, but their efforts kept coming up short.

Buttigieg landed in South Carolina without having much improved his standing with Black voters. Nothing he did had worked: not his ham-handed "listening" events, not a detailed plan for Black empowerment that went deeper into detail than any of Biden's or Sanders's proposals. Buttigieg's record on police and housing policies as mayor was torqued by skeptical Black leaders and fanned by progressives and many reporters who saw him as the epitome of white male privilege—or just didn't like that he was competition for Sanders and Warren. He looks back with regret at not having hired more senior Black staff, and not having made the overtures before Buttigieg's Problem with Black Voters became a shorthand he couldn't escape. "Some of this took on a life of its own," Buttigieg observed. "I could have found my voice in a different way or made different choices. But I think, like anything else, it's a mix. I don't think the way it was told is quite right. But I also don't want to be defensive about things that we really could have or should have done differently."

Buttigieg was, typically, all computation, analysis. He'd built up his relationships with Obama and Sharpton, and he turned to them for advice coming out of Iowa. Obama called during debate prep in New Hampshire, and Buttigieg stepped out to talk to him. Obama saw the call as starting to talk Buttigieg down, pushing him to consider that as impressive as his caucus wins had been, he should still be thinking ahead to how to be in a good position when he lost. This was another case of Obama's inflated sense of his own Jedi powers: he was trying to guide Buttigieg toward thinking about dropping out, but that's not the message Buttigieg heard.

Clyburn sat in the audience of the debate that Tuesday night in Charleston. Biden was doing better, he thought, keeping the answers shorter. Clambering to stop Sanders's momentum, each candidate came at him with a different attack—Biden on gun control, Buttigieg on Medicare for All, Warren on his ability to competently do the job, Bloomberg on the Russian support for him. "I'm hearing my name mentioned a little bit tonight," Sanders said. "I wonder why." Mostly, though, the evening was defined by the pimento cheese platter in the media spin room and the candidates' clear exhaustion with the race and one another and a month of almost weekly debates.

During the last commercial break, Clyburn hurried backstage. Remember to promise to appoint a Black woman to the Supreme Court, he urged the candidate. Biden, who was trying so hard to get his footing in the debate that he let slip that he'd just called Obama for a pep talk, was frightened of forgetting it again. The first question he was asked when the feed went live was to name the biggest misconception about himself and to identify a motto for himself to match South Carolina's "While I breathe, I hope." This was his answer: "When you get knocked down, get up. And everyone is entitled to be treated with dignity, no matter what, no matter who they are. My—also, that everyone should be represented. Everyone—and no one's better than me and I'm no better than anyone else. The fact is, what we should be doing—we talked about the Supreme Court. I'm looking forward to making sure there's a Black woman on the Supreme Court, to make sure we in fact get every representation." The crowd applauded. Then he added another motto from his mother, and when pushed about the biggest misconception about himself, joked, "I have more hair than I think I do."

Clyburn had seen enough to convince him. He'd already recorded an ad for the super PAC that afternoon. It would start airing as soon as he went public with the endorsement.

Ro Khanna and Nina Turner had been chasing Jesse Jackson for months. They hoped to get him to endorse Sanders two weeks before the South Carolina primary, to give him a boost out of Iowa and have him on the trail to at least blunt Biden's lead, if not compensate for a campaign operation that had relied on young white liberals knocking on doors in Black neighborhoods, hoping to sell them on socialism. Sanders had endorsed Jackson in 1984 and 1988, back when he was mayor of Burlington. Sanders sees himself as connected to Jackson's vision of a rainbow coalition fighting economic injustice. That Jackson never forgave Biden for briefly running against him in the 1988 primary and had taken shots at Biden over the 2020 race seemed to strengthen the case for an endorsement. They laid that out to Jackson's staff. They couldn't get an answer.

Khanna couldn't believe his luck when he got on his flight to go stump in South Carolina and discovered Jackson in the seat next to him. Khanna pitched him hard the whole time in the air, explaining what a difference he could make. Jackson's age had caught up with him and he had Parkinson's, but he was clear: he couldn't get involved while Warren was still in the race. He wouldn't choose between the progressives.

Early on the morning after the debate in Charleston, Sharpton hosted a ministers breakfast at a church on the north side of town. All of the candidates came. None received an introduction like the one Sharpton gave Sanders. "The civil rights movement always was targeted by those who would use the 'red scare,'" Sharpton said. "If socialism's on your mind, read about what they said about Martin Luther King and others." Sanders gave him a hug as he took the microphone in the church's gym, then delivered a civil rights–tailored version of his stump speech, mentioning his own arrest at a protest in college and the civil rights leaders he had met over the years. He made a special point of noting that he supported Obama in his reelection campaign. He quoted King: "We all too often have socialism for the rich and rugged free enterprise capitalism for the poor." This was a line Sanders had adopted, charging often on the trail that Trump "believes in corporate socialism for the rich and powerful, I believe in a democratic socialism that works for the working families of this country."

Backstage, Sharpton had given Sanders the good news. He was going to endorse. "I have to talk to someone on my board," Sharpton said. "I'll call you back."

A Sharpton endorsement would upend the race. Sanders hoped to come in second in the primary with about 30 percent of the vote, showing improvement from 2016 as he headed into Super Tuesday. Sharpton could bring the Black votes in South Carolina and beyond. He could create an entire news cycle. They waited for the call. It never came. They phoned him. They couldn't get through.

Clyburn had been at the breakfast too. Sharpton had named an award after the congressman's late wife, and surprised Clyburn by making him the first recipient. As Sharpton was leaving the event, Clyburn told him what was about to happen. "I'm endorsing Joe. Joe has repented for the crime bill and done everything you asked. If you can't help him, don't hurt him," he said. Sharpton deferred. "For you, Jim, I'm going to say that he's off probation and we'll just see where it goes."

Across the road at another event, Clyburn made his Biden endorsement official in an emotional speech about his late wife and the connection she felt to Biden, and how fearful for the future of America he had become. He looked out at his two youngest daughters in the audience, the empty chair they had left between them, and imagined his wife sitting there, remembered what she had said to him the night when he had gotten home from the Fish Fry in June with twenty-three candidates onstage. "Well, I know it's a big crowd, and I know we've got good friends running," Emily told him, "but our best hope for defeating Trump is Joe Biden."

Clyburn was tearing up by the time he brought up Biden. Biden was tearing up by time he shook his hand, stood as close to him as two men of that generation can be without going all the way in for a hug.

Clyburn's endorsement had huge ripples. They campaigned together the following afternoon, and suddenly the media coverage was of Biden with the wind at his back, which was an appealing counternarrative to all the coverage of how Sanders might be unstoppable. Two days later, Buttigieg's campaign abruptly canceled a meeting he was supposed to have at a soul food restaurant with nine Black mayors, none of whom wanted to come anymore, out of respect to Clyburn. "I thought the endorsement would be meaningful," Clyburn said, looking back. "I had no idea it would be that consequential."

That Friday night, Biden made an appearance at yet another gym, this one at Wofford College in Spartanburg. "Joe Biden has suffered great loss," said Fletcher Smith, a former state representative, introducing him, "but he is not a tragic figure."

Biden spoke for a long time. He was energized that night, as he had been throughout South Carolina, feeding off the energy of crowds that, unlike those who had been showing up in Iowa and New Hampshire for him, were not dominated by old white people dozing off before he started speaking. He told his stories about coming into the Senate, learning how to work across the aisle. He told a story about his son, punctuated by "I miss Beau." Watching him work, Smith said he could feel Biden's momentum. "When you connect as a white guy with Black people, it convinces white people that you're good too," he said with a smile on his face. "All over America, this same kind of conversation is going to help him punch through."

As Biden worked one of his last prepandemic rope lines after he finished, a woman handed him a piece of paper, tears in her eyes already, checking the message she wrote out for him because she was worried she wouldn't be able to keep herself together to talk to him. "Don't be nervous," a junior staffer urged her on, "this is what you've been waiting for." He held the piece of paper stretched tight in his hands. Her thirteen-year-old daughter had a rare disease. They wanted to send her to a center known for excellence in treatment, but

Medicaid wouldn't cover it. Biden looked at her. "Give me a number," he said, "because I might be able to help."

He looked up and saw another familiar face. How did it feel to be winning this election, for once?

"Well, it's not there yet," he said. "Don't want to jinx myself."

========

Biden woke up early the next morning to stop by a polling place in Greenville. Leap Day. Virus news was coming quickly. The night before, Trump had called it the latest Democratic hoax.

"He said *what*?" Biden asked. "Some of the stuff he says is so bizarre that you can laugh at it. When he says things like that, it just so diminishes the faith that people around the world have in the United States. Even for him, it's hard to believe."

He'd heard that Trump was already calling the coronavirus a conspiracy to hurt his chances in the election. "It's hard to know what to say," Biden said.

Biden flew to North Carolina during the day to get a jump on Super Tuesday with an event there, then was back in Columbia for the victory speech. This night was completely different. Happier. Earlier, with polls closing at seven.

Sanders took just under 20 percent of the vote. He'd done worse than in 2016 against Clinton, and hadn't blunted Biden, who came in with a whopping 48 percent. Steyer, for the millions he spent and the dreams of having an impact on the race, finished with 11 percent, and dropped out that night. The rest of the field pulled about as many votes as they would have if they hadn't bothered campaigning in South Carolina at all.

Just as the polls were closing, Biden's aides got word that the networks were going to call the race for him immediately. Dunn got Biden on the line, and delivered the news. For a moment, he was silent. His whole career in politics, his whole life dreaming of this, and he had never won a primary before.

When Biden walked out onto the stage, this time he fumbled a bro hug with Clyburn, wiped away another tear. "For all those of you who've been knocked down, counted out, left behind—this is your campaign," Biden told the crowd.

Most of the staff was back in headquarters in Philadelphia, gathered around four TVs, already drinking. At the second debate back in July, Biden had been mocked for stumbling through his online fundraising pitch, with the pure grandpa "Go to Joe 30330," saying each number as if it were the first time he had pronounced the words. This time he got it right. The money started coming in. He headed back to his hotel, and the staff headed out to a bar, calling friends drunkenly, urging them to contribute to keep pushing up their numbers.

In the twenty-four hours after his win, Biden raised as much as he'd been raising in the course of a month during the fourth quarter of 2019, which still didn't add up to much.

Since the beginning of the year, Biden had been calling Obama multiple times a week, venting. Obama tried to ground him, act as a political therapist. That night, though, Biden made a point of saying privately that he'd pulled off the win himself.

———

Add up the lessons Democrats were supposed to have learned from their loss in 2016 and their victories in 2016, and the answer would seem to be Amy Klobuchar. A moderate from the Midwest, a woman, a record of getting things done with Republicans and Democrats. A mom, a good debater, a prosecutor, a legislator with a large and bipartisan record, she represented both cities and farmers. But politics isn't about propositions, and presidential elections don't happen in political science labs.

Until the Brett Kavanaugh confirmation hearings, Klobuchar was only Washington famous, if that. Two minutes at Kavanaugh's second turn in front of the Judiciary Committee elevated her national profile. She started by mentioning how her ninety-year-old father still went to AA meetings at his nursing home, then calmly cross-examined the Supreme Court nominee. He responded like a full-on prep school dude, with his sniffing and his snapbacks. "So you're saying, there's never been a case where you drank so much that you didn't remember what happened the night before—or part of what happened?" she asked. "Have *you*?" he replied. "Could you answer the question, judge? So that's not happened? Is that your answer?" Kavanaugh leaned back as she was posing the question, then leaned forward with puckered indignance. "Yeah, and I'm curious if *you* have," he said. "I have no drinking problem," she responded. "Yeah," he said, with a grunt. "Nor do I."

Kavanaugh came back from a short break in the hearing and apologized. Klobuchar used that as another opportunity to call for the FBI to look into the allegations against him. She had been earlier toying with a presidential run, with a thought of being able to make a play for Iowa as a neighboring state to Minnesota, and New Hampshire as having similar politics as those she was accustomed to. With her profile now raised, she spoke with Clinton, with Obama, and met with pollsters. Her political infrastructure was what would be expected from having only run sleepy races for the Senate, but aides pushed her on to TV as much as possible to prepare for her campaign kickoff in Minneapolis. A blizzard came in that day, and the temperature dropped below freezing, and an aide rushed out to buy a binder with plastic page holders so the ink wouldn't run through the paper. Even with that, nine thousand people showed up—including some on cross-country skis—and Klobuchar got the perfect TV shot of snow caked in her hair. Watching back at the White House, Trump became confused about science as he mocked her on Twitter for "talking proudly of fighting global warming while standing in a virtual blizzard of snow, ice, and freezing temperatures. Bad timing. By the end of her speech she looked like a Snowman(woman)!" In one of the cutting but groaner mom jokes she'd become known for on the trail, she tweeted back at him, "Looking forward to debating you about climate change (and many other issues). And I wonder how your hair would fare in a blizzard?"

And Klobuchar was off, in a campaign that at first seemed only slightly less confusing than Marianne Williamson's soft-focus guru-empowerment speak, talking up "heartland economics" and repeating the same routine over and over about how she had launched her campaign next to bridges over the Mississippi because *she* wanted to be a bridge. Klobuchar became infamous for her smackdown of Buttigieg for getting away with running for president as a young small-town mayor, in a way a woman never would have been able to. She dismissed him on the debate stage and yelled at the TV when she would see him getting more airtime than she did. Her campaign was like *The Little Engine That Could*, if the engine had kept a running enemies list, made a point of making reporters agree with her that she kept getting better at town halls, and sometimes got lost in talking about antitrust regulations.

By December 2019, she was clearly taking satisfaction just in having survived longer than anyone would have guessed. Like Elton John, she said, sitting backstage at a Teamsters forum in Cedar Rapids, not singing, but pacing out the words "I'm . . . still . . . standing."

Klobuchar's whole campaign was premised on being able to win. Then she came in fifth in Iowa. If not for the caucus meltdown, she might have been forced to drop out that night. The chaos convinced her that she had a chance—no longer stuck in the impeachment hearings, she could change the race by her hustle on the campaign trail in New Hampshire. While Buttigieg was up in his penthouse suite at the Des Moines Marriott that night waiting to claim victory, she rushed out to a small ballroom downstairs to be the first to give a speech. By that Friday, she was quoting her newspaper endorsements from memory onstage in New Hampshire, suddenly becoming a weekend phenomenon, as fire marshals had to start capping attendance at her events. "We better not screw this up!" she kept telling voters. Teresa Gladstone, a sixty-five-year-old woman from Concord who had voted for Trump in 2016 because she felt as if she were choosing between the lesser of two evils then, said she was waiting forty minutes in line for a photo because she thought Klobuchar was smart and knew the answers to questions, unlike Sanders and Warren, and "this is not good language from a Christian woman, but she has balls—or as a friend of mine said, ovaries of steel."

There were a few hours when Klobuchar and her top aides believed she could win New Hampshire, or come in second. She tried to make the best of a far-back third, but campaign donations quickly dried up. Then she was sixth in Nevada and sixth in South Carolina. She landed in Selma, Alabama, the following morning for the fifty-fifth anniversary of the Bloody Sunday march, back in reality.

She heard that Buttigieg's charter plane was supposed to be landing soon. After his own fourth-place finish in South Carolina, she figured he would be in a similar spot, so she waited in a conference room at the terminal, hoping to talk through what to do next, make a decision together. But he was late coming in, and Klobuchar didn't want to miss the church service ahead of the memorial march.

Presidential campaigns don't leave much time for thinking. Give a speech, shake some hands, get prepped on the next speech on the car ride over, record an ad, do an interview, do another interview, give the next speech, take questions from a huddle of reporters, call a donor, call a potential endorser, stop for a short photo shoot, approve a statement, do another speech, shake some more hands, hope to have a human interaction or two along the way. The last few weeks, Klobuchar was taking her role as a juror in Trump's impeachment trial seriously, taking detailed notes during the day while flying back and forth to Iowa for trips that usually took more time in the air than she spent on the ground.

She didn't have a speech in Selma and didn't have to do anything other than walk across the bridge and have an interview that afternoon with Al Sharpton, after the event was over. She sat in the back of the Brown Memorial Chapel, her first moment on her own in weeks. She thought about herself, the race. This obviously wasn't going to work. She was going to win the Minnesota primary on Super Tuesday, but what a sour sense of weakness it would display to have to drop out after that. She had never become more than a proposition, but she still wanted to be important.

Anyone who lived through the shelter-in-place isolation of 2020 would not believe what it was like that Sunday in Selma, just a week and a half before the pandemic panic began. The streets were packed. The sidewalks were packed. There was supposed to be an official procession to the Edmund Pettus Bridge, led by the presidential candidates. Sanders had never been scheduled to appear, Biden left as soon as the service was over, Buttigieg arrived just as they were getting ready to march, Bloomberg's security moved him ahead of what was supposed to be the front of the march, until a woman chased them down, telling him he had to turn around. One man was shouting parts of directions into a bullhorn, and another man was using his own bullhorn for an uncanny impersonation of Martin Luther King Jr. delivering the "I Have a Dream" speech. The organizers had planned for Klobuchar and Warren, as the female candidates, to lead the procession, but there was no real front to what became a giant, stumbling mass of people. *Whatever*, Klobuchar thought, for one of the rare times in her driven, ambitious life. She had already made her decision.

They were almost across the bridge when everything stopped. John Lewis had arrived for a surprise appearance. "We still have many bridges to cross," he'd said in December 2019 when he announced he had Stage 4 pancreatic cancer, and he had come to Selma to cross this bridge one more time. He stood on a stool, steadied himself. The day was hot and sunny, but he was thin and wearing a red sweater that hung on him.

His voice hadn't changed. He was still the impish preacher, who swung his hips to "Happy" but always spoke as a moral voice for the nation. "We must go out and vote like we've never voted before," he said. "Go out there! Speak up! Speak out! Get in the way! Get in good trouble! Necessary trouble, to help redeem the soul of America," Lewis said. "I'm not going to give up. I'm not going to give in."

Buttigieg was crying. Klobuchar was dazzled. Warren made sure to be the first one to shake Lewis's hand as soon as he was done. Biden's campaign was frustrated, watching from afar—if they had known Lewis was coming, he would have stayed for the march. Stacey Abrams helped him climb down from the stool and began leading him back to a waiting car. He waved one last time before he closed the door. In 1965, Lewis couldn't remember how he had gotten off the bridge and back to the church after the state troopers attacked and cracked his head. This time, he sat in the back of a car, waiting for the crowd to part so he could make his way across.

Klobuchar called her husband to tell him what she'd decided. He was in Maine, stumping for her for Super Tuesday.

"I just spent forty-five minutes talking to a lobster fisherman," he said. "He's going to support you!"

"I know he's going to be OK supporting Joe Biden," she told him.

To others, she went right back to politicking, amazed that Warren was staying in and claiming that her own bad showing was due to sexism.

"Can you believe that?" she'd asked, shivving her colleague through the end.

———

Buttigieg was late landing in Selma because his breakfast with Jimmy Carter had run long. Seeing how badly South Carolina was going to go, Lis Smith had cooked up the trip to elbow Buttigieg into the news ahead of Super Tuesday, chase some scrap of sustained credibility from being the only one to meet with a former president, another out-of-nowhere politician who'd surprised the world by winning the Iowa caucuses. By the time they landed in Plains, Georgia, the night before, Buttigieg had told staff he was going to sleep on a final decision while they started planning an exit event back home, but he made a show of asking Carter for advice. The former president, still recovering from a series of bad falls and fighting brain cancer, listened genially, in that beatified air he'd grown into since leaving office a year before Buttigieg was born. Then he weighed in gently: "You know it's over now," he said. "You should get out."

Buttigieg kept up the show for the march across the bridge. Traveling reporters were loaded onto the campaign plane, expecting to go to their next stop. In the air they were told that they were rerouting to South Bend. He was dropping out.

Pretty much every involved Democrat who wasn't a Sanders supporter had been having some kind of "Save Us, Barack" conversation over those weeks. A surprise endorsement, an interview where Obama dropped some pointedly encouraging words for one candidate in particular, or gave a brushback warning about Sanders. Some nursed dreams of a backroom deal at Obama's office with Chuck Schumer and Nancy Pelosi and representatives of each of the campaigns to figure out who should quit to consolidate the opposition. Obama and his advisers had always thought he couldn't have done much, and that now it was too late to do even that. What if no one listened? What if it backfired? He was worried about Sanders as the nominee too—not only that he'd lose to Trump, but also what he might do if he somehow won—but wouldn't he make it worse by trying to stop it? He didn't want to trigger Trump, didn't want to violate his insistence that Democrats move past him. In attempting-to-be-more-positive moments, he would muse about how he'd never be where he was if someone had intervened to stop his 2008 run.

"People want an act of God—and short of that, they're looking to President Obama," said one person talking to him at the time.

After South Carolina, Perez reached out to see if he was ready yet.

Obama called Buttigieg the night he dropped out to congratulate him on his run and ask what he was going to do next, politically. Buttigieg said he was thinking about endorsing Biden. That would be a good idea, Obama told him, gently nudging, as he was doing a lot of those days. Buttigieg said he would sleep on the decision. Biden called too, to check in, tell him he ran a hell of a race. Buttigieg said he'd probably be endorsing. Sanders didn't reach out to try to get him.

"There never was a moment where I thought we've got this," Buttigieg said later, looking back. "Just as there was never a moment that I thought we were out of the game until we were just about out of the game."

Smith started negotiating with Biden's team while Buttigieg headed to

Dallas, where Biden had a rally planned. Before Buttigieg's endorsement went public, Klobuchar had announced hers—Klobuchar's still-competitive aides like to believe that she scored one last one-upping by beating Buttigieg to it. That's only true about the decision being public. She would appear at the rally with Biden, though there was still enough disorganization that Klobuchar's staff had to search online for where Biden was going to be that night so they could buy plane tickets for her. Buttigieg wanted his own event, before the rally. Back in the fall, in the heat bubbling toward impeachment, Buttigieg had defended Hunter Biden onstage in a debate, and Biden had called him from the car afterward to thank him. Biden never forgot that. They spent a few minutes together before walking out to the cameras in the backyard of a bar and fried chicken shop in West Dallas. Biden had been twenty-nine when he was elected to the Senate, he reflected, the same age as Buttigieg when he'd been elected mayor. He wanted to be a bridge to that next generation, he said, to help bring politicians like Buttigieg forward.

"I'm looking for a leader, I'm looking for a president who will draw out what is best in each of us," Buttigieg said, announcing his endorsement. "We have found that leader." It was four weeks since he had won the Iowa caucuses. It was twenty-three days since he'd watched Biden from the skybox in New Hampshire, shaking his head at how Biden seemed on autopilot. It was the first time in modern political history that a candidate with more primary delegates endorsed a candidate with fewer delegates.

Biden put his hands on Buttigieg's shoulders, leaned his head into him when the mayor said the words of the endorsement. Stepping up to the microphone, Biden said, "I don't think I've ever done this before, but he reminds me of my son Beau. I know that may not mean much to most people, but to me it's the highest compliment I can give any man or woman."

Buttigieg didn't come with him to the rally. That was Klobuchar's moment, who got to drop out with a long private meeting with Biden and their spouses backstage, then a raucous rally cheering her on. Concession speeches usually include supporters calling out "No!" This one was all cheers. Buttigieg and Klobuchar each turned on their political operations and social media presences for Biden, who didn't have much of either, and Klobuchar walked him through interviews with the Minnesota press. Beto O'Rourke, a late addition to the evening, came onstage for a wave, then took Biden out for a livestreamed dinner at Whataburger, the Texas chain he had made famous in that viral video of him air-drumming to "Baba O'Riley" after the debate in his 2018 Senate race.

⸺

Bloomberg was onstage in suburban Virginia at a Fox News town hall as the Biden rally went down, getting yelled at by a man in an orange Guns Save Lives hat; four gay rights protesters waving homemade flags and demanding that he release the NDAs; a woman who shouted "Thank you for saving our children's lives!" with his gun control efforts; and another woman who yelled back, "What are you talking about? He's for infanticide! He's for full-term abortion!"

In Minnesota, Ilhan Omar—the Somali refugee who had been elected to Keith Ellison's old House seat—was onstage with Sanders, who was trying to push back on the flabbergasting rush of momentum for Biden. She danced out, blue-and-white Sanders signs waving behind her, and picked up the line from the Queens heart attack comeback rally with Ocasio-Cortez: "While others are gathered tonight to fight our movement, we're gathered to fight for someone we don't know."

Sanders and Klobuchar have an odd but genuine friendship, and he had been certain that she would stay in the race through Super Tuesday to win her home state. He wanted to place second, because that would come with a runner-up stash of delegates to add to his total. Saturday afternoon, a few hours before the polls closed in South Carolina, he had held a rally in Boston, which Warren's campaign saw as insulting her by coming to her home state— and which Sanders's campaign saw as doing her the grace of not coming to campaign in a competitive state earlier. Larry Cohen, the old Sanders friend who had been laying the groundwork for a unity effort to get him the nomination at the convention, called to beg him not to needlessly provoke her.

Warren saw this as demonstrating how completely incapable he was of expanding his coalition, more proof to her that he had already lost, though he hadn't realized it yet.

Sanders and his top aides can still instantly rattle off all the states they believe he would have won if Warren had done as Buttigieg and Klobuchar had done for Biden and dropped out of the race to support him: Maine, Massachusetts, Texas, North Carolina, Oklahoma. Their whole campaign plan had been premised on a big field of candidates staying in and splitting up the Super Tuesday votes. "We ran a campaign positioned for that moment," said a top aide on his campaign. "That moment didn't come."

———

Biden was in California when the Super Tuesday results started coming in. "You know you've got to be a dull person when you're known after all these years for Ray-Bans and ice cream, man," he said, as he leaned over the counter for his order in East Los Angeles. Riding with him to the next stop, Eric Garcetti—the mayor who had endorsed Biden a day after Bloomberg came asking for support in January, back when that seemed like cannonballing onto a sinking ship—quoted Robert Browning's "Andrea del Sarto": "A man's reach should exceed his grasp, / Or what's a heaven for?" Biden thinks in Irish poetry, but he took the point. The night was going to go well, but there would still be much to do.

They were working the tables at Roscoe's Chicken and Waffles when the first results came in from the East Coast: Massachusetts, Warren's home state, called for Biden as soon as the polls closed. After Massachusetts came Maine, Virginia, North Carolina, Tennessee, Alabama, Arkansas, Minnesota, Texas. He won almost as many delegates in California as Sanders.

Biden's campaign was out of money. (They were all out of money, except Sanders.) He hadn't won because of ads. His campaign hadn't mounted an amazing overnight operation across the country—the staff that had been pulled back from Super Tuesday states and into Nevada and South Carolina hadn't been redeployed. He hadn't changed his schedule to appear at more events. He hadn't stopped making gaffes. He hadn't even appeared in most of the states he won, as he didn't have the cash to fly his charter jet there. This was pure momentum, the fastest turnaround from flub to front-runner in the history of American politics.

Going into a Super Tuesday, which no one expected to produce a clear nominee, Biden planned to round out the night with a small speech. He took in the news of his romp sitting in a classroom in a rec center in Baldwin Hills, a predominantly Black upper-middle-class neighborhood, two blocks over from Barack Obama Boulevard, having a small dinner with his wife, a few staff coming in and out of the room. Two doors down, a children's karate class went on as scheduled. They didn't have TVs set up to watch the results come in because they couldn't afford that kind of setup. They had to keep up by checking Twitter and news sites on their phones.

Hunter Biden lives a few miles from the site, but they knew he couldn't join them. The grandkids hadn't come, because no one had anticipated quite how big a deal the night was going to be. His sister, Val, his closest adviser, was there, as was his daughter, Ashley. He was processing the night, knowing his family would never be complete.

"It's hard for anyone who hasn't been on his journey to know the spectrum that he measures light on," said Eric Ortner, a well-connected entertainment industry adviser who had grown close to Biden over the years, and was with him backstage at the school that night.

When Biden went out to give his speech, he was rushed by two women who for some reason had chosen that as the venue to protest against dairy, but were knocked back by Jill Biden, showing off her old Philly girl moves again, then pulled offstage by two aides. Biden wasn't thrown. "They don't call it Super Tuesday for nothing," Biden said, ticking off all the wins.

"Just a few days ago, the press and the pundits declared the campaign dead," he said. "And then came South Carolina. They had something to say about it."

Backstage after the speech, Ortner gave Biden a souvenir, a red die he had picked up years earlier at the Trump Plaza casino—the one that went bankrupt in Atlantic City and was eventually imploded—with a keychain attached certifying that the piece had been used on a gaming table for one shift before being removed from play.

Biden laughed. He started to walk back to the waiting motorcade. Then he told Ortner to wait.

"You know what, champ?" he said, tossing back the die. "I don't want to choke on this."

CHAPTER NINETEEN

TAKE HIM SERIOUSLY

> My great concern is not whether you have failed, but whether you
> are content with your failure.
>
> —ABRAHAM LINCOLN

March 4, 2020–April 8, 2020

The first time they met was in early 2006, when Sanders came asking Obama for a favor. Obama was an overnight political superstar, the hottest in-demand campaigner in the country. Sanders was Vermont's disheveled loner congressman who now wanted Vermont's open Senate seat. He was a democratic socialist hoping Obama would come to Burlington to give him a stamp of approval in the Democratic primary race.

All the new senator asked in return was access to Sanders's email list, the standard request staff made of any politician who came looking for a favor, so they could build up Obama's presence in preparation for the presidential run he was swearing at the time he wasn't going to make. Sanders's email list then was nowhere near the millions it would become, but it was enough to get Obama to the University of Vermont in March. Sanders called Obama a great leader of the Senate. Obama called Sanders a force against cynicism and said the state should elect him and the man running to succeed him in the House to "keep on stirring up some trouble."

Sanders sat out the 2008 presidential primaries, arguing he shouldn't get in the middle of a presidential race. Over three months after Obama won the Vermont primary and two days before Clinton dropped out but when Obama had already clinched the nomination, Sanders endorsed him, promising to "do everything I can to see that he is elected president." Everything he could do turned out to be giving a few speeches during the year.

"It's not to say they had a bad relationship when Obama got to the White House, it's just that they didn't have a relationship at all," as one of the people who worked in Obama's West Wing put it. They barely spoke over the next eight years. Sanders is exactly the kind of liberal Obama always mocks, who carries on about purist principles and never compromising with Republicans, and never gets much of anything actually done. Obama, meanwhile, is exactly the kind of Democrat that Sanders always decries, who rides in promising big help but never offers anything up but piddling middle-ground mushes that leave everyone disappointed.

Sanders came up with the idea for staging a primary challenge against Obama ahead of his 2012 reelection run, in the same way his essay writing when he was unemployed in Burlington in the 1970s led to his running for Senate as the Liberty Union candidate—someone should do something, and why not him? "One of the reasons the president has been able to move so far to the right is that there is no primary opposition to him," Sanders said on a liberal radio show in July 2011. His comment was quickly noticed in the Chicago headquarters by the Obama aides, who were already worrying about getting hit from the left and were a lot less confident about Obama's reelection chances than they were projecting at the time, saying he might be able to win Georgia and Arizona that year. Sanders and his closest aides argue that he just wanted to goose Obama, get him to back off his plans to cut Social Security and other programs, and that's how they try to write off the fact that he then started showing up in New Hampshire for events.

Politicians don't just wander into New Hampshire. "Check out the special guest," an Obama aide wrote on an internal chain on August 2 that year, pointing to Sanders's name on the invitation for the Merrimack County Democrats barbecue. Half an hour later, another wrote back, "The Cheshire County Democrats are in the process of lining him up, too."

Patrick Leahy, Vermont's other senator, reached out to Obama's reelection campaign manager, Jim Messina. Sanders wasn't messing around, Leahy said.

Take him seriously. Flustered, Messina called Harry Reid, then the Senate majority leader and a man whose approach to protecting Obama was like a father standing up for his kid through every call at a Little League game. Reid had also made a point of building up a good relationship with Sanders, welcoming him into the Democratic caucus in a way he'd never been in the House. Reid is blunt, and his conversations in 2011 with Sanders to get him to back off—he had to have two of them—were harsh: *What are you thinking?*

Obama didn't hold much of a grudge, if only because nothing ever came of the challenge. To Obama, this was just Bernie being Bernie. He wasn't a player; he wasn't serious. Obama gave Sanders a courtesy meeting in 2014 when the senator came to tell him that he was probably going to run for president, and then another annoying, longer meeting in January in a show of faux neutrality after using a podcast interview to pull one of his standard sly maneuvers: he heaped praise on Clinton, and only Clinton, just a few weeks before the Iowa caucuses, with the deniability of never actually saying he was endorsing her.

After watching Sanders knocking Clinton around for months while the Republican field was somehow coalescing around Trump, Obama had enough. Sanders had just lost the California primary. He didn't have the delegates to win the nomination, but he had enough to tear the convention apart for the sake of making a point.

"Bernie," Obama said, calling him from the golf course in Florida. "The math no longer works. You've got to end it."

"No, no, no," Sanders said. "I want to keep going."

"I'll give you to Wednesday," Obama said, "and then I'm putting out a statement."

Sanders instead scheduled the meeting for Thursday. The minutes ticked by, and he was a no-show. Obama's aides, confused, realized they didn't have his cell number, even this far into a primary campaign, even after eight years in the White House while Sanders was in the Senate. Someone finally tracked down the number for Weaver and called him, but got the voice mail for the comic-book store he owns in Virginia. Finally, Sanders appeared, bringing Jane with him. White House staff didn't know what to do with her, because she certainly wasn't going to be joining them in the Oval Office. Sanders brought his own coffee and his own scone, and they didn't know what to do with that either, because who brings their own breakfast to the White House? They weren't going to have him walk in to meet Obama with a cup and paper bag in his hand. Sanders's lateness bumped into another meeting, and he and Jane were led into the Cabinet Room, next door to the Oval Office. She was chatty with the White House aide left to mind them, but he sat off to the side, nibbling the scone. He said he'd need a podium when he went to talk to reporters afterward, and when he was told that the White House didn't have any podiums but could offer a music stand, he said fine.

The scone and coffee cup were shuffled off. Jane was escorted to the West Wing lobby to wait. The doors opened, and Obama welcomed him, asked him to take a seat, then got down to business. Time to wrap it up. "You got beat by a lot," he told Sanders. "Hillary got way closer to me than you did to her. You're not that special." They spent forty-five minutes together, counting the photo-op Obama gave him of them walking together in the White House colonnade by the Rose Garden. The air was out of his run, but he kept pushing, and didn't endorse Clinton until a month and a half later, when he lost at the convention.

They didn't talk again for two years, until Sanders came asking for his postpresidency meeting in the spring of 2018.

Everything about Democrats not letting 2020 be a repeat of 2016 started with Sanders. And Obama knew that meant it started with his own gritting through dealing with a guy whom he found exhausting and whom he blamed in part for bringing about the Muslim ban and the children in cages and America collapsing in front of the world. Now his job, Obama thought, was keeping Sanders from helping Trump win again. That started with regular calls to Sanders, to make sure he felt the respect he wanted.

———

The day after Super Tuesday, Warren spoke with both Sanders and Biden. She wasn't sure what to do. "We fell well short of viability goals and projections, and we are disappointed in the results," her campaign manager wrote in an email to staff, which was obviously intended to leak immediately. An aide who asked not to be attributed by name, to keep up the illusion, added in a comment to a reporter: "Elizabeth is talking to her team to assess the path forward," as if any candidate ever assesses the path forward and concludes there *is* a path forward.

On Thursday morning, Warren made the news official. Standing outside her house, as she had after being the first to jump into the race on New Year's Eve fourteen months earlier, she replied to a reporter who asked what guidance she would give to supporters who didn't know whom to support now: "Well, let's take a deep breath and spend a little time on that. We don't have to decide that this minute." What went wrong, when she couldn't even win her home state? "I was told at the beginning of this whole undertaking that there are two lanes, a progressive lane that Bernie Sanders is the incumbent for, and a moderate lane that Joe Biden is the incumbent for, and there's no room for anyone else in this. I felt that wasn't right," she said, "but evidently, I was wrong."

She was flustered, and Obama called for his standard end-of-campaign check-in. They started talking through what she should do. "All I want is for Joe to win," she'd say, and then disappear into weighing painstaking pros and cons. Was the right approach to endorse Biden right away, to help suck the oxygen out of Sanders? Or endorse Sanders, so that she'd have the credibility and connection to help push the senator out of the race a few weeks later? Or hold off, let the race play out on its own, so she could then take on the role of a uniter? Obama listened. And listened. And listened. Confident that she wasn't going to land on endorsing Sanders, he didn't push her. Whatever sequence she landed on was going to be fine, he told her, just make a decision.

Sanders called again. "Do you regret not dropping out sooner in 2016?" When he told her no, she asked, "What's your plan if you don't win? What's your exit strategy?" He didn't have one. He was still running, that was the point. He was annoyed by the questions, annoyed that he had to be on the phone begging her for support at all. She was confident he was going to lose the primaries, and didn't want to be on the hook for defending him a few weeks later, anxious about putting her name on another Sanders kamikaze. He was wondering where all her commitment to progressive politics and unity behind the cause seemed to have gone. They talked and talked. They got nowhere. She was frustrated; he was exasperated. He could tell that nothing was coming.

Warren's take on what happened is a very generous spin. "I believe," she said months later, "it was important that Bernie had the space he needed to make the decision about his campaign."

Each up and down of the race, each time a candidate got hot, Obama would say the same thing to whoever came at him, stressing: "You've got to be all in—this is going to be hard, but we're all going to be all in." Going into the week, he had started to envision how he'd make the case for Sanders—not by embracing democratic socialism, or pretending they were close friends, but with a broader "You might not agree with all his positions, but he respects the rule of law," as one person who talked with him then put it, and that Sanders would run "a government that people can believe in and be proud of." Biden, obviously, wouldn't take that much threading. He would start from the same existential need to get rid of Trump and reinstate norms, but center also on his vice president's character and how to "build on the success of our eight years."

Now, with the melee mostly over, Obama's anxieties turned to Biden. Like most Democrats, Obama wasn't sure about the decision they'd all just made. Biden was the compromise candidate, the collective consensus about who could actually beat Trump, but who wasn't exactly inspiring. The chariot could turn back into a pumpkin at any point. His campaign was in the same terrible shape as when he hadn't had any delegates. He had barely raised any money, and Trump was flush. Biden's online presence was terrible. The pandemic was starting, no one knew what to do, and Sanders was pushing ahead.

"How do we accelerate this?" Obama started asking his small clutch of informal advisers. Democrats couldn't afford to waste any more time on being divided. The fastest way, he suggested, was to put Sanders or Warren on the ticket right away. Probably Warren. Advisers were used to how calm Obama always was, how good his instincts always seemed to be. David Plouffe, his first presidential campaign manager and still close adviser told him his instincts were off this time—but not before he called Dunn and sounded her out on Obama's anxiety.

At so many other points when he'd been trying to juice his presidential prospects, Biden had toyed with naming a surprise running mate. Now that he had the nomination, he wasn't going for the gimmick.

———

The crash came quickly. The Monday night after Super Tuesday, Biden's campaign planned a big rally for Detroit. The Michigan primary was the next day, and Biden wanted a big win. Governor Gretchen Whitmer was going to endorse him. Booker and Harris were too. They had both been waiting until the race was cleared of Warren, committed not to get out ahead of a female Senate colleague still running.

They were packed in tight on the line. There were Biden supporters having a calm back-and-forth with six young Sanders supporters holding a DETROIT LABOR FOR BERNIE sign. "They can go for Biden. But they're not going to go for Bernie," one man said, in pundit mode. "Who was the last moderate Democrat to win? Wasn't Kerry, wasn't Hillary, wasn't Mondale. Obama won as a progressive, that's how he *won*," a Sanders supporter with a nasal northern Michigan accent responded. They kept talking but weren't able to come to a resolution.

Inside, members of the high school marching band, the night's preentertainment, were in their spots in the bleachers, instruments down, leading the dance to the "Cha-Cha Slide" as the gym slowly filled. "There's a movement out there," said Jackie Jerome Marks, a fifty-five-year-old social worker from Detroit in a natty suit and feathered fedora. "Don't take voters for granted." He'd been stunned by Super Tuesday, Marks said, but he'd always been a Biden supporter. "It's Uncle Joe," he said. "He reminds me of my father and uncle who taught me work ethic." He mentioned Obamacare. He mentioned Biden's "decency."

A few weeks later, Whitmer would be saying that if she'd known what was coming and not been getting "inconsistent messaging" from the federal government, she would have canceled the rally. That night, though, she was packed in onstage, saying she "felt better in the last ten days than I have in ten months." The crowd cheered when she mentioned Buttigieg, Klobuchar, Warren. The crowd held quiet when she said she'd been thinking about how the "brain tumor that took my mother is the same one that took Beau." Booker came next, with an effortlessly inspiring speech, connecting the campaign to the high school's phoenix mascot, calling the candidate "the best one to heal the soul of America, he is the best one to bring dignity back to that office, he is the best one to stand up for all of us in America," and introducing Harris as "a rising star in America—she is lightning bringing the light." Harris warned the crowd of what she said was a conscious effort out of Trump's Washington to undermine faith in American democracy and their own power, "trying to convince us that we are alone." Then she told them how she'd first met Biden, through working with Beau. "You've never seen, it's a rare thing, to see such a special relationship between a father and his son. It was an extraordinary relationship they had," she said. "Beau showed courage all the time, and conviction, and he spoke with so much love about the father who raised the man that he was."

Biden's stump speech that night, after watching those introductions, had a few new twists. He turned to Whitmer. "When I hear that line you say, 'Just fix the damn roads'—well, let's fix the country," he said. Then, as he worked up to his finish: "Look, I view myself as a bridge, not as anything else. There's an entire generation of new leaders standing behind me. They are the future of this country."

The president who wrote the Emancipation Proclamation ran on a platform of not expanding slavery to the territories. The Four Freedoms came from a boarding school alum. A racist from Texas fought for and signed more civil rights legislation than anyone in history. Trust him, Biden was saying. An old white guy was going to get America to its future.

The night after the rally, the first two coronavirus cases were reported in Michigan. Biden spent the night at the MotorCity Casino Hotel, where the Democrats had hosted their party on the night of the 2018 midterms. He woke up to some of the once-abandoned, now-reclaimed buildings of the Detroit skyline under a gray sky and headed out for his final, almost normal day on the trail.

———

Jesse Jackson finally endorsed Sanders that weekend in Grand Rapids. They sat by themselves talking backstage. Sanders was overwhelmed by Jackson's endorsement in a way he rarely is about anything. Michigan was the state that had almost tipped the Democratic nomination to Jackson in 1988, that had led the then Burlington mayor to participate in a Democratic caucus for the first time in support of Jackson, setting off a familiar sense of panic among the establishment about a popular movement that seemed about to seize power from the party leaders. Ocasio-Cortez then came for a rally in the college town of Ann Arbor, connecting the generations through supporting Sanders's campaign as "a rainbow coalition to fight for racial justice, for economic justice, for human rights, and politics like that has always been deemed unelectable in this country."

Biden and Sanders were both supposed to finish the night of March 10 in Cleveland, pitching ahead to the primary there the following week, with rallies only blocks apart. Mike DeWine, the Ohio governor who was out ahead of most of the country and all of his fellow Republican leaders in taking the pandemic seriously, told the campaigns he didn't want crowds at the events. There had already been three confirmed cases in Cuyahoga County, and he was trying to head off the spread. Biden's plane landed in Cleveland, and he paced around the terminal waiting for his wife to arrive. Anita Dunn and Jeff Weaver coordinated the decision to cancel both events.

Flying home from Michigan, Sanders could feel that the campaign wasn't working. Four years earlier his win in Michigan had been such a surprise that he'd ended up addressing the results live on TV from the outdoor shower stall at a Miami hotel where aides had taped up a few campaign signs to make it look pseudo-official. As much as he was hoping for more magic, he couldn't get there in his own head, even when his campaign manager ran him through all the reasons to be optimistic about their operation in the state. Maybe it could still work, Faiz Shakir told him.

"And so," Sanders said, "what happens if it doesn't?"

Biden won every county in Michigan that night.

<hr/>

Another debate was scheduled for that weekend, and Dunn tried to get the DNC to cancel it entirely. Nine months and ten debates in, she had the same take on these events as she had had at the start: they were pointless, a waste of time, theatrics and performance art good only for revealing more problems and vulnerabilities that they'd have to spend days cleaning up. Few voters were watching other than reporters and people who knew which candidate they were voting for and were just tuned in for sport and self-confirmation, even at this stage. The virus was a good excuse to pull the plug. No way, the DNC replied. Perez had been doing everything possible to prevent giving Sanders the opening to blame the DNC for losing the nomination, and he wasn't about to end the campaigns by giving him a whopper of a reason to complain.

Suddenly they had to think about social distancing, aerosols, surface contamination? The virus was terrifying and unknown, and both candidates were men in their late seventies. First the DNC canceled the spin room, told the reporters and all the supporters not to come. Then it canceled the debate in Arizona and replaced it with one to be held in a closed studio at CNN headquarters in Washington.

Without giving a heads-up to colleagues or the campaign, a reporter who had been covering Biden in the traveling press corps announced on Twitter that he might have symptoms. Biden's advisers were rattled, unsure in those early days how concerned to be. Dunn had been near the reporter, so she took herself out of the room for the final debate prep, wary of posing any threat to Biden, and turned to format negotiations. She wanted the candidates seated at a table. Enough already with making the old guys stand for two hours. That setup might also facilitate an actual discussion, rather than have the two of them going at each other from podiums that must now be even farther apart to keep to the six-foot rule. Rabin-Havt is a good and committed enough poker player that he has to report his winnings on his taxes, and he was ready with his hand. "Bernie would like to stress he will stand up," he texted the CNN producer. That was how Sanders always debated, whatever kind of chair was onstage—the first sign that something was wrong when he'd had the heart attack was asking Rabin-Havt to get him a chair in the middle of the event. Give him a chair, Rabin-Havt warned, and he won't go long before getting up and walking around. That would make for completely unmanageable television, the producer explained, given camera angles and lighting. If Biden stayed seated while Sanders wandered off from the table, it would all look ridiculous.

Dunn was dug in, until she wasn't. The race was over, she knew, and Biden was going to be the nominee. This could be the perfect way to start ramping down, start bringing Sanders in. Let them have the win. Biden could deal with one more debate.

Sanders said going into the debate that he wanted to press Biden for answers on issues that mattered to him, but the only moment anyone remembered from the debate was Biden's dropping the news that he was committing to naming a woman as his running mate, which also served to conveniently short-circuit any talk of a forced unity ticket with Sanders in a way that no progressive could credibly complain about.

Sanders was caught off guard. When asked to respond, he started off by attacking Biden's position on the Hyde Amendment and abortion until the moderator pressed him again on whether he would make the same commitment. "In all likelihood, I will. For me, it's not just nominating a woman. It is making sure that we have a progressive woman, and there are progressive women out there," he said, "so my very strong tendency is to move in that direction." If there had been a studio audience, the groans and the boos would have been audible, '80s sitcom style.

Going into that night, Sanders advisers had been holding out one last hope, that maybe Biden would stumble and be incoherent, live up to the "senile" chatter that was all over the Bernie-friendly Twitter accounts they followed (and even more popular with Trump and his own supporters on Facebook and Twitter). "Speaking of cognitive decline, I was disappointed that Joe Biden won Super Tuesday. I was even more disappointed that he *thought* he won Super Thursday," as one Sanders supporter put it as he livestreamed pirating the Biden campaign's online phone-banking tool to call supporters and accuse the candidate of having dementia.

Biden had been a mess in the bigger debates, unable to keep up with the questions coming at him from multiple directions, frustrated with not having enough time to make a long point. That night, one-on-one with Sanders and on top of every topic, he didn't give the conspiracy theorists much to work with.

Afterward, Dunn held a conference call with reporters to express the campaign's annoyance with Sanders for having gone in for the kind of attacks he had claimed he wanted to avoid. "I think it's fair to say," she said, "that Vice President Biden showed up to a debate tonight and for two hours graciously dealt with the kind of protester who often shows up at campaign events, on live television."

Behind the scenes, Tom Perez was also working the phones, calling governors and other state officials. With COVID shutdowns tumbling through the states, he wanted to hold them off long enough for the race to be sealed up on March 17 with the big primaries in Ohio, Florida, Arizona, and Illinois, which if Biden won would give him enough delegates to take a definitive lead.

Only Ohio shut down. After the votes came in from the rest, Biden was well ahead.

———

Sanders and his closest advisers knew the race had slipped out of their fingers over the course of just ten days. Hard to believe. Maddening. He woke up on Super Tuesday thinking that he was on track to be the nominee. He had a big rally planned back in Burlington that was supposed to be a celebration but became a living wake. Internal polling showed the roof caving in. The public perception was worse.

"We knew that the establishment at some point would do everything to knock Bernie down," said Ro Khanna, the California congressman and Sanders campaign cochair. "The surprise was not that we were in a drag-out fight with

Joe Biden post-Super Tuesday. The surprise was that we were in a drag-out fight as the underdog, as opposed to the drag-out fight as the favorite."

Beating Trump weighed on Sanders. When he first began running in April 2015, Trump was still using presidential noisemaking as leverage in his contract negotiations with NBC. When he kept chipping at Clinton all through the spring of 2016, it seemed obvious that Trump would lose, and his candidacy presented a perfect opportunity to concentrate the attention on how much more the rising left could do.

Now Sanders, despite his dreams of a new progressive America and of having gone from outcast rabbler-rouser to presidential front-runner in just a few months at the age of seventy-five, worried Trump was going to win again. "I know what this could lead to," he would sometimes confide to close advisers. He didn't like to talk about his childhood, because he didn't like to talk about himself much at all. He would get caught up remembering the refugees and Holocaust survivors he knew back in Brooklyn while growing up. The numbers on their arms. The trip he quietly took to Poland years later with his brother, Larry, to see the site of the house their father lived in before fleeing ahead of the war, and to stand at the family graves. He would cry when he spoke about it, so he would avoid speaking about it beyond occasionally mentioning "my family's experience" on staff calls and a brief mention in his campaign kickoff speech back in Brooklyn in 2019.

As much as he fought against the more corporate wing of the Democratic Party, Sanders saw Trump as representing a much different kind of danger. In his conversations in 2018 and 2019 about running, this haunted him: If he had thought he would lose to Trump, or that his running would make another candidate lose to Trump, he wouldn't have run. He believed Trump and Trumpism posed a deep danger to Americans, one that he felt personally. He believed what came after Trump could be even worse.

After Super Tuesday, Sanders and his small inner circle sat around his living room in Burlington, discussing the options. They were loyal to him, they said, and if he wanted to remain in the race, they would be all in. But staying in, they warned, meant that he would have to be all the way in himself. He would have to raise money. He would have to go up on TV. He would have to figure out how to campaign in the face of the new coronavirus restrictions coming down by the day. He would have to attack Biden, tear apart his record, try to bring him down.

Sanders made it clear that he didn't want to do that to Biden. He didn't want to risk making him more vulnerable to Trump in November. But he wouldn't pull the plug.

Obama worried Sanders was now punting. "I've been knee-deep in COVID," Sanders told him. "Let me talk to my team" or "Let me just get back to Vermont." Weeks passed. It's getting to be time, Obama would say. On calls with his own top aides, Sanders was being just as indecisive, talking about how what he wanted was a platform to keep talking about his ideas, pushing back when they told him that he wasn't going to able to do that without running a real campaign—because if he didn't do so, he'd only hurt the movement by staying in and looking feckless, weak. Sanders didn't want to do that, but he also didn't want to disappear. He was seventy-eight, he had gotten so close, and it was gone more quickly than an early morning dream.

Sanders kept telling Obama how worried he was about what would become of his movement once he quit. "I have these millions and millions of people, we're about to pull out the oxygen from this—what do we do?" he asked. Hard question, Obama told him. He hadn't been able to keep his own folks together even when he was in his second term in the White House. His vision of Organizing for Action as a permanent part of politics hadn't worked, and he was still figuring out what the hell he meant when he said his foundation's mission was empowering the next generation of young leaders. And look, Obama reminded him, some of this was simply chance, with a pandemic hitting right at the moment when Sanders had been hoping to change the dynamics of the race. No one could be expected to have a plan for that, but sometimes that's how politics is.

Another week went by, and then another. Wisconsin held its primary in the middle of the pandemic and a rainstorm, voters wrapped in their own homemade protective gear and under umbrellas. Turnout surged, and in another state Sanders had won in 2016, Biden crushed him with 63 percent of the vote.

Like everyone else in his party, Obama was getting antsy. He then pitched Sanders on an idea: task forces. He knew that sounded blue-ribbony, the usual political bullshit. But hold on, he said: He was proposing a series of committees, each addressing a different issue area, with Sanders representatives and Biden representatives hammering out ideas and recommendations. It would be a party platform committee long before the convention, aimed at coming up with proposals that might actually have some bearing on reality. Biden didn't have many set ideas anyway, Obama said, so Sanders could embed his legacy into the framework for Biden's presidency in a way that would live beyond his candidacy.

Sanders agreed. The matches that were arranged were meaningful. Pramila Jayapal, a Washington state congresswoman and head of Congressional Progressive Caucus, was paired with Biden's top pandemic adviser, Vivek Murthy, to chair the health task force. Sara Nelson, the flight attendants' union president and prominent progressive labor leader, was paired with California congresswoman Karen Bass to chair the economy task force. Alexandria Ocasio-Cortez was paired with John Kerry to chair the climate task force.

Sanders finally endorsed Biden on April 13. "Not in a million years would we have believed that we would be talking to each other in our respective homes, that we could not do rallies, that we could not get out of the house," Sanders said as he appeared on a livestream. Nor, he said, would anyone have ever conceived of the loss of life and jobs the virus had already claimed. Sanders called on people to come together "to make certain that we defeat somebody who I believe is the most dangerous president in the modern history of this country." Biden spotted a chessboard behind Sanders in the shot and joked about playing a game. "We'll bore everybody for a few hours," Sanders replied.

Obama endorsed Biden the following day in a carefully constructed video message. He spoke about his former vice president at length, and then spoke about Sanders at length. Then he talked about the scale of the response that the pandemic was already demanding.

"We need to do more than just tinker around the edges with tax credits or underfunded programs," Obama said. "We need Americans of goodwill to unite in a great awakening against a politics that too often has been characterized by corruption, carelessness, self-dealing, disinformation, ignorance, and just plain meanness, and to change that, we need Americans of all political stripes to get involved in our politics and our public life like never before."

Biden was the nominee.

"He's like a rowboat with seven holes in it," a top Democratic operative said as he clinched the nomination, "but we've all just got to hold on tight and hope he gets across the ocean."

CHAPTER TWENTY

TIC TOC

Please scream inside your heart.

—JAPANESE AMUSEMENT PARK
CORONAVIRUS GUIDELINES

April 2020–May 2020

A few days before Trump's inauguration, Susan Rice invited reporters into her office in the West Wing for a final chat as national security adviser. "What keeps you up at night?" one of them asked her toward the end of the meeting. Her answer: a pandemic that spirals out of control. She had been through the Ebola meetings in 2014. She had overseen the creation afterward of the pandemic response office, which Trump eventually eliminated.

Looking back, how did what was happening in America in 2020 compare to what she had feared? "This is about in the realm of my worst nightmare. The only thing that would be worse, potentially, is a very deadly flu virus that's as transmissible as COVID, but much more deadly. Some of the avian flus have a mortality rate of 50 percent. So think about that. But in terms of the number of infections, the number of deaths, the economic implications, the complete disruption to our domestic and global economy, this is exactly what I worried about," she said, a few months into COVID. "This is entirely foreseeable, which is why we tried to put in place plans, offices, equipment, preparatory briefings to help the incoming administration be ready for such a scenario, because we knew it was going to happen. We just couldn't know when."

Bandanna masks. Disinfecting vegetables. Fights about who would get the vaccine months before vaccines were developed. The world divided between people Instagramming sourdough starters and the supply-chain essential workers keeping the shelves stocked at the grocery stores and those waiting for hours in their cars in food bank lines. The Javits Center had been where Clinton was going to declare victory. Now it had been transformed into a field hospital in anticipation of an infection surge. "Stronger Together" had been the Clinton campaign slogan that had been made fun of through 2016. In the pandemic, suddenly "stronger together" was everywhere—PSAs on bus stops, selling Pepsi. "I've noticed that, as you might guess," Clinton said, with the bitter sarcasm that often runs through her told-ya-so way of talking about Trump.

And Biden was stuck in his basement. At his final rally in Detroit, he had been warned to be careful about getting too close or shaking any hands, but he just couldn't stop. Even on his way out, he leaned in for a few selfies, autographs, a few force-of-habit handshakes. Every moment of exposure was a reminder that the Democrats had nominated the oldest candidate ever—who would be older on Inauguration Day than Ronald Reagan, the previous record holder, had been when he gave his farewell address. He couldn't go out and campaign. He was too high-risk even to go to the grocery store.

Biden's real joy in campaigning, though, is connecting with people, talking with them, listening to them, making them feel that connection. When he was vice president, the Secret Service would often cover over windows at events so that he wouldn't see crowds outside and complicate agents' lives by wanting to go out and greet them. When he was running for president, he was kissing old ladies, grabbing both arms of students, leaning in with moist eyes while men and women alike poured their grief and their hopes onto him. "There's something that happens there," said his old friend Chris Dodd, who served with Biden for years in the Senate and bounced around Iowa with him all through 2007 as they watched both their presidential campaigns go nowhere. "I know he walks away from those and what happens stays with him."

Then, just when the campaign began to click, when the retail politics virtuoso was becoming the superstar he always dreamed of being, it was over almost literally overnight. Thirteen days after he'd stared into the eyes of that woman in Spartanburg, South Carolina, holding up her letter, telling her he wanted to help her daughter, he was in lockdown with no clue when it might end. "Can you imagine?" said an aide who was talking to him then. "You're revved up to run for president, you're on a roll. And then you're told to stay at home."

Biden's days were not particularly full at first. A pair of *New York Times* stories about his early life in lockdown were both fed the same set of factoids, noting that he was usually up before eight a.m., as if that were particularly early. His briefings started almost immediately. Fortuitously Biden's longtime aide and debate coach, Ron Klain, had been the Ebola czar under Obama (a job that was a consolation prize for not getting picked for his dream job as White House chief of staff). Klain brought both actual knowledge to the job and the helpful public relations twist of having been the one to recommend starting the pandemic response office. Vivek Murthy, who had been Obama's surgeon general, joined as health adviser during the time he wasn't working on the unity task force. Jake Sullivan—a former Biden aide who had become one of Clinton's close advisers during the 2016 campaign and who would tear up in headquarters in the final week before Trump won, thinking about how a pivotal presidential race for history might be lost over a faux obsession with an email server—stepped in to coordinate.

Biden was never the smartest kid in class or the most brilliant man in the Senate. Part of what impressed him about Obama was the ease of his intellect. Part of what annoyed him about the Obama inner circle, though, was not being taken as seriously himself. He always has a chip on his shoulder, sensitive to those who want to write him off, determined not to let them. He likes binders and long calls and meetings. He likes to make sure people know he's read policy papers. In those early weeks of the pandemic, he plunged himself in, trying to catch up on public health and economics. "There's never been any doubt this will be difficult. I must admit that we didn't figure on COVID-19 and the economy," his friend and former chief of staff Ted Kaufman said over that summer. Being isolated made it worse for Biden. He could see the tragedy on cable news and on the charts he was given. He wanted to be with the people the charts were tracking.

"That crushes him every day. It frustrates him. He's been in the arena and wants to be right now," an aide talking with him then said. "As he looks to the presidency, he sees a genuine opportunity to see something bigger and better after this."

Biden had always considered himself the great compromiser, the great uniter. "I've always viewed my role, what I've done best in the Senate, as one of the guys who kept the pendulum in the middle," he said in an interview in 1986, and that is who he remained for thirty years. The inequities, the structural errors that the pandemic exposed had hit him hard. Nearly every time he appeared in public, he used the line "We've had the blinders taken off." He spoke as if he had finally been freed to be the great liberal he'd always wanted to be, as if something had been holding him back over the years.

=====

"Timing . . . wait for it. . . . tic toc."

That was Tara Reade's tweet, sent late at night on Super Tuesday, responding to a Sanders-friendly reporter at the Sanders-inclined website *The Intercept*, eager for Biden to get the scrutiny of a one-on-one matchup with his preferred candidate.

In 2019, when the "touching" accusations were blowing up for Biden, Reade told a story about his putting his hands on her a few times in a way that made her feel uncomfortable, and then being fired for refusing to serve drinks at a political event. She had tweeted often in support of Biden in 2017, liking posts about Obama's giving him the Medal of Freedom, backing him up as he talked about cancer or praised Lady Gaga for joining him in combating campus sexual assault. Her feelings had clearly shifted.

Her 2019 blog posts seemed to provide a window into more current thinking. "Why would a liberal democrat support Vladimir Vladimirovich Putin? Maybe it is because I believe he has saved the world from a large conflict on more than one occasion," she wrote in one post. The Russian president was "a compassionate, caring, visionary leader," she wrote in another, dreaming. "To President Putin, I say keep your eyes to the beautiful future and maybe, just maybe America will come to see Russia as I do, with eyes of love." She illustrated the posts with drawings of a tiger in the grass.

Quickly, a group of Sanders supporters—including some at *The Intercept*—leaped to her, and Putin's, defense. What made the Russian president so bad anyway? Why did the specter of Russia manage to get raised so often these days? Among them was the aspiring podcast host Katie Halper, who had been raised upper middle class in Manhattan and had been leaning increasingly over the years into the network of Sanders-style aggressive progressive reactionaryism. "When will Putin stop sending time-traveling Russian women to force Biden to touch them inappropriately on camera and video?" she wrote.

Reade, who had used several other names over the years, had been mostly forgotten as the presidential race moved on through the rest of 2019, through Iowa and New Hampshire and Nevada and Biden's surprise turnaround. But, but she was still paying attention. "How about Bernie Sanders and Elizabeth Warren Presidential ticket rather than the Biden/Harris ticket that the DNC is trying to shove down Democrat voters throats," Reade had written in a January 2020 blog post, a week before the Iowa caucuses. Two days after Super Tuesday she went a little further in a tweet. "Biden is a misogynist pred. I worked for him," she wrote. "I support a Bernie/Warren ticket and found Bernie supporters kind and inclusive."

As Sanders prepared to launch his 2020 run, several reporters reached out about joining the campaign, being part of the cause. Sanders's aides waved off most of them, telling them they'd be more useful to the cause staying where they were, allies on the inside, where they could counter everyone else in the media whom Sanders saw as aligned against him.

Exceptions were made. The first was David Sirota, who had been Sanders's former press secretary when he was in the House and remained friendly with Weaver. Then came Briahna Joy Gray, a writer who was called Sanders's press secretary despite rarely actually interacting with reporters. Her focus was instead spearheading the Sanders campaign's in-house production of videos and other content to sidestep the media they hated.

Neither was happy about Sanders's decision to disarm after Super Tuesday. They didn't like their guy losing and couldn't wrap their heads around the nominee being Biden, who couldn't have been more an avatar of the traditional Democratic Party if he had been an anthropomorphic donkey. If this was who won the nomination and the presidency, it undermined the argument that Democrats desperately needed to change to win. "If you think that everything the Democratic Party does is the stupidest thing in the world, Joe Biden is an existential threat to your entire thinking" is how progressive pollster Sean McElwee put it that spring.

Not long after her ominous "wait for it" tweet, Reade was helped to connect with Halper. A few days before a podcast went live in which Reade dramatically changed her story about Biden—now accusing him of throwing her against a wall in a Senate hallway and shoving his hand up her skirt—Sirota called two top Sanders aides to alert them that the podcast was coming. Sirota contacted two more reporters with whom he was friendly to give them a heads-up too, and encourage them to start writing about Reade. The reporter whose tweet Reade had sent the "tic toc" tweet to got an exclusive, and was then invited on the podcast to discuss that reporting.

The podcast itself had no editorial standards or platform, but that didn't matter in the world of the internet. Reade's story was incendiary, fitting right into all the lingering creepiness around Biden from the touching stories that had surfaced a year earlier, mirroring precisely what Trump bragged about doing in the *Access Hollywood* tape that rocked the 2016 election. There was no evidence, but there was no evidence for many of the claims that had become causes on the newly enlightened left, where "Believe All Women" had quickly gone from slogan to edict.

By then, MeToo had been burning through American culture for two and a half years, but there was no set process for weighing or examining claims. Was there a way to be exonerated, or just accused? Was there a way to come back? Who made the rules? Did "Believe Women" mean believe all women, no matter what, about everything? Harvey Weinstein appeared to be a serial predator and Brett Kavanaugh was obviously an aggressive frat boy, but were they equal?

When Hillary Clinton endorsed Biden in late April, neither addressed the accusation, but they spoke at length about the heavier burden on women during the pandemic, with the campaign placing the number for the National Domestic Violence Hotline at the bottom of the screen. Bill Clinton, meanwhile, complained privately that he couldn't be featured in an endorsement event of his own, aware that his own past would bring Biden a problem the campaign wouldn't want to have to answer for.

For reporters the questions were existentially tough. In no other situation in journalism could a claim be treated as fact based on the account of one person without evidence. In any other situation in journalism, the holes in Reade's story and the ways it kept changing would have ended the conversation.

But in newsrooms rushing to prove their wokeness, staffed by mostly younger, more liberal, adamant-about-being-vocal reporters, to question Reade's story was to be complicit in Biden's cover-up. Did it help that in many newsrooms there had been the same inclination in favor of Warren's candidacy that there had been everywhere else among well-educated liberals, and a fundamental flabbergasting that this most diverse field ever landed on an old white guy? Did it help that the chattering classes were happy to feed worried quotes about Biden into stories? Of course it did.

Reade, though, failed even the unofficial standards that had emerged. What made her different from Kavanaugh's accuser Christine Blasey Ford, the argument from the loyalists and the skeptics went, was that Ford's story hadn't changed, that she had been telling it privately for years before going public, and that there was a pattern of behavior for the man being accused. Reporters kept calling. That ended up working against Reade, though, since she seemed to give a different version of what happened in almost every interview she did. New witnesses materialized, then evaporated almost as quickly. Tantalizing clues were dropped—Reade said that she thought her mother had called in to Larry King's old CNN show to talk about the alleged assault not long after it would have happened. The reporter who had been propelling the story mentioned it in an interview with the podcast host who had done the original interview, and a listener emerged with what appeared to be a transcript of the call. King had taken a call from a woman from the same town as Reade describing a problem her daughter had with a senator, and Reade said she definitely recognized that as her mother's voice on the call. But . . . the caller was not actually describing sexual assault. "What the emergence of the call shows is that even if Reade's memory is off on timing or details, the substance of her claims—in this case, that her mother called Larry King and discussed her situation—can still be true," was the accommodating argument made on her behalf in print. In other words, the call proved nothing. But maybe it *could* prove *something*?

A fantasy began to circulate: Biden would be forced to withdraw, the nomination would be up for grabs again, and Sanders would make a play. Sirota, Gray, and John Cusack all tweeted warmly about the idea. Nina Turner tried to start the conversation internally but didn't get far, and not because they hadn't thought it through. Biden didn't seem as if he were dropping out, and they couldn't do anything to force him out. Even if he did withdraw, Weaver and others assumed, Democratic leaders would not hand the nomination over to Sanders. There would be a fight. Some progressives began to believe that Andrew Cuomo, the New York governor and star of his own pandemic briefings, would be subbed in. And though they would wage that fight, they would probably lose. And then what?

Sanders himself wouldn't engage in these conversations.

"Bernie will only come back in if something were to happen to Biden or with Biden. Unless that happens, I don't think it is a path forward. It's late," RoseAnn DeMoro, the former nurses union head and early member of the Sanders kitchen cabinet, said in mid-May. "Biden made a huge mistake in not taking Bernie for VP. He could have generated enthusiasm and given hope." DeMoro had been devoted to Sanders for forty years, since she wrote to him in June 1981, right after he was first elected mayor of Burlington, to see if he actually agreed with her. "If you truly are a socialist, I am shocked and delighted by your nomination. If you are in fact a liberal, than [sic] in reality, it doesn't make any difference."

She wasn't ready to give up now after having gotten so close. DeMoro was complaining publicly that Sanders had dropped out prematurely, and on Twitter was floating the idea that he should use the Reade situation as the pretext for getting back in. "Reade is a very serious issue," she wrote in a text, explaining herself. "But the DNC will never act. That leaves us in a very bad place."

———

Unlike the previous scandals that were supposed to have been apocalyptic for the Biden campaign and ended up passing, this one lingered. Every night for weeks, Reade was the most discussed topic on the nine p.m. calls of top aides. Every night was spent trying to track what more was coming and whether they would survive the day until the next call. How could they respond? What were the pitfalls? They knew, or thought they knew, the story was false. They were convinced that Reade must be getting paid by someone—a Trump ally, or maybe as part of a Russian op. Was Reade going to be like Paula Jones was for Clinton, and haunt Biden forever, or would her accusations run their course?

A plan was set: Publicly repeat that the story wasn't true, but say nothing about Reade, beyond that she had a right to tell her story. Don't respond to

"Believe All Women"—there was no winning in that. Privately, feed research to reporters on Reade to help them chase down the tales, and cite her unreliability and the contradictions in her accusations against Biden.

Central to those efforts was a long call with *The New York Times* editorial board. Biden's endorsement interview at the beginning of the year, recorded as part of a documentary TV series about the newspaper, had become legendary in the primary: elite journalists who were literally stroking their chins on camera had written off Biden as having an agenda that "tinkers at the edges," carried by a man who clearly didn't inspire them. They dismissed his lead in the polls because "that may be a measure of familiarity as much as voter intention." (When he was dismissively asked about his place in the polls in the interview, Biden snapped back, "I've been consistently leading in the polls, after taking all the hits. I go down, and everybody who's hit me is out—you all declared me dead, and guess what? I ain't dead and I'm not going to die!") Meanwhile, the Black female elevator operator who had brought Biden up to the office in New York was captured on the cameras gushing in excitement about how much she loved him.

The editorial board was preparing to weigh in on the Reade situation with the seriousness of a cloud over Mount Moriah, and Kate Bedingfield, and campaign lawyer, Bob Bauer, wanted to lay out the facts that they knew, the contradictions in Reade's story they saw, hoping to blunt the decree. The conversation grew heated, with Biden's aides feeling disrespected and dismissed, particularly by James Bennet, the editorial page editor at the time. The entire conversation felt very holier-than-thou to them, offended that they were being held to a standard by a newspaper that had never transparently addressed its own sexual harassment scandals even as its reporters continued to take the lead in MeToo exposés. Bedingfield and Bauer were convinced that the editorial board's lingering bias against Biden in the endorsement process (which resulted in the incoherent decision in January to back both Warren *and* Klobuchar) was clouding the judgment about what to believe.

Biden himself remained silent on the matter publicly, and for the most part privately, as well. This was another pure Biden moment—an unprocessed, emotional mix of shock that anyone would think he'd done anything wrong, anger about being mistreated, frustration with the people who wouldn't just see it his way and stop warping it, guilt about the prospect of attacking an accuser. "He was outraged. Indignant. It hurt him deeply," said one of his top advisers. "It is such an atrocious lie. It's such an atrocious lie for someone to tell about you. It's such an atrocious lie for someone to tell at all. And it was particularly hurtful because he's worked on these issues." Putting him on live TV, when all of this might spill out, was an enormous risk.

But Biden was going to have to do just that, said the representatives from the leading women's political groups whom the Biden campaign invited onto what became a long and awkward call. Suspicious and edgy, Biden's top advisers felt as if they were trying to flush out their enemies, who believed Reade and were ready to dump Biden. Why hadn't they come to his defense yet? They wanted to know. Several of the women on the call were inclined toward Reade. Others tried to explain their discomfort. Yes, they acknowledged, Reade's allegations were contorted, and definitely seemed suspicious. Yes, they agreed, there were no clear standards for accusations like these. But they also didn't want to be leaders of women's groups dismissing a woman making such a serious charge. They weren't going to defend him before he defended himself.

They hated the position they were in. They didn't want to stand up for Biden, but they didn't want to leave him to be pulled apart either.

"I saw the claims as a way to undermine the guy who was our best chance to get rid of Donald Trump, which was a political imperative," said one of the women on the call, "not to mention the fact that our president was a known serial sexual predator and had never been called to account for it."

—————

Gretchen Whitmer had first met Biden when he called her over the summer of 2018 and said he'd like to come campaign for her. Driving between stops, they got to talking. She wanted him to know that her mother had died of glioblastoma multiforme, which had killed Beau. She wanted to tell him about being a sexual assault survivor herself, how much the work he had done on the Violence Against Women Act and campus sexual assault meant to her. They hit it off immediately, connecting over their families, their dogs, their insistent centrist mentality. He liked that she'd started out local and gotten to be a player in a state that wasn't a traditional national power center. She liked that he was a big-time politician who didn't act like one. She was like the younger, female version of Biden. They saw themselves in each other.

Trump had been interested in Whitmer too, fascinated that she'd won in a state where he'd pulled off his own surprise in 2016, and she'd found herself seated at his table when she'd come to the White House in February 2019 for a dinner with all the governors. "You know," he said solicitously, "I handpick who sits at my table." She smiled. "I would expect nothing less, Mr. President."

Trump's small talk involved pointing out various people around the room, like Rick Perry, his energy secretary and the former governor of Texas, whose 2012 presidential run had famously unraveled when he said in a debate that he wanted to eliminate three departments of the federal government and, when he got to listing them, couldn't remember the third. "He's a great guy. He's just a fantastic guy," Trump said, adding after a beat, "but you wouldn't want him on your debate team."

Energy was the department Perry had forgotten; education was one of the ones Perry had remembered, which got Trump going. "What would you governors think if I abolished the Department of Education and just sent the money to the states?" he asked. Whitmer had a glass of champagne in her, and was feeling loose. "I'd be fine with that," she said, "but would that mean you'd be sending Betsy DeVos home to Michigan?"

"You're not a fan, huh?" Trump asked. No, Whitmer said, "she's not an expert in education." Trump didn't engage on that. He was still thinking about an interview that had aired almost a year earlier. "Did you see her on *60 Minutes*? She was terrible." His steak came, easily twice the size of everyone else's. Well done. Ketchup.

A year later, Trump went to war with Whitmer after she became the first governor to go on TV to say loudly that the White House had no national pandemic strategy, and that her state was in desperate need of protective equipment and testing supplies that she wasn't getting from the federal government. A woman complaining about him all over cable news set off all of Trump's triggers.

"Don't call the woman in Michigan," Trump had publicly told Pence, insisting that he wanted more gratitude shown to him. He tweeted about "half-Whitmer," but she didn't back down. Recording an appearance on *The Daily Show*, she mischievously wore a blue T-shirt printed with THAT WOMAN FROM MICHIGAN ("Someone sent me that shirt, and I thought it kind of said, 'This is not something that was going to hold me back,'" she explained a few days later), but she did begin to worry that Trump might punish her by trying to stop supplies from being sent to her state.

Biden was impressed by her strength. He called to tell her that, and they got to talking more. When Biden's staff launched a podcast for him as a way to speak out during the pandemic, Ron Klain was his first guest, to talk about virus response. Biden said he wanted Whitmer to be his second guest. As soon as that appearance was announced, she was catapulted into the kind of running-mate talk for which she wasn't prepared, leaving her anxious about becoming even more of a target for Trump.

Sexual assault survivors are forced to relive their hardest moments more often than they should. Whitmer had relived hers during the Kavanaugh hearings. She had relived them again as she listened to Reade's accusations. Because she was a prominent—now more prominent, thanks to Trump—woman supporting Biden, because of the political chatter around her, and especially because she was public about being a survivor, Whitmer kept getting asked about Reade. There were so many problems with Reade's story that Whitmer didn't believe her, felt she wasn't behaving how a survivor would. She also felt confident from having gotten to know him that Biden was innocent.

Whitmer didn't want to cast judgment against Reade publicly, but she wanted Biden, in the depths of that moment, to know that she believed him. He was grateful she called. "If you don't want to do any interviews, don't do any interviews," he told her.

No, Whitmer said, she was going to talk. She told him as a survivor what she would want to hear from him. Don't attack Reade. Be straightforward. Make sure to remind people the kind of person he was.

"Believe All Women" was the wrong slogan to use, Whitmer said, when she went public a few days later in an interview. She liked "Listen to All Women" more, and in a television interview that aired April 30, she argued, "We have a duty to vet [the accusations]. I'll add that in doing an investigation, it has appeared as though there has not been, you know, much beyond that, the story."

———

Biden started the next morning, May 1, with an interview with Mika Brzezinski on MSNBC. "It is not true," he told her. "I am saying unequivocally: it never, never happened, and it didn't. It never happened."

Reade had said that she had filed a complaint and wanted Biden's archives at the University of Delaware to be opened to look for it, but Biden's campaign pointed out that any personnel paperwork would be housed at the National Archives or the secretary of the Senate's office, and asked both to search their own records. Wasn't this a different standard from what Biden had demanded during the Kavanaugh hearings? Brzezinski asked.

Biden had his answer ready: "What I said during the Kavanaugh hearings was that she had a right to be heard, and the fact that she came forward, the presumption would be that she's telling the truth, unless it's clear from the facts surrounding it it's not the truth."

The search for the records had become the MacGuffin in the case. *The New York Times* published its editorial that day, calling for the creation of "an unbiased, apolitical panel, put together by the DNC"—though that was an oxymoron—to review the entire Biden archives in search of a slip of paper that Reade had claimed to remember might exist only a month into her accusations, and even then kept changing her story of where it was. This was an extreme position, the editorial board acknowledged, dismissing those concerns with an imperious, "the question at hand is no less than Mr. Biden's fitness for the presidency. No relevant memo should be left unexamined."

Shortly after Biden's interview, Ilyse Hogue of the abortion rights–focused group NARAL and Stephanie Schriock of the women's political action–focused EMILY's List, who had both been on the call of women's group leaders with the Biden campaign, released a joint statement: "Voters deserve the chance to hear from Biden, especially given how much is at stake in this election, and today they did," the statement read. They were satisfied. "Just as Biden has listened and led in the past on the Violence Against Women Act, we now need him to lead us forward to create the sort of systems where survivors' claims are taken seriously and justice and healing are possible."

Although Biden had stumbled at times during his cable interview, at a virtual fundraiser that afternoon with hundreds of Obama alumni, he got out more of what he wanted to say. Valerie Jarrett kicked off the event by not at all subtly noting that during Obama's 2008 running-mate selection process, after the "necessary background checks and vetting . . . guess who was at the top of that list at the end of it? Vice President Joe Biden."

"Unequivocally," Biden said, "this claim is simply not true. It did not happen.

Now, my knowledge that it isn't true does nothing to shake my belief that women have to be able to be heard and that all the claims be taken seriously. It isn't enough just to simply take my word for it and to dismiss it out of hand. Frankly, that shouldn't be enough for anyone, because we know that this sort of approach is exactly how the culture of abuse has been allowed to fester for so long."

By then, America had grown accustomed to a president who had been accused by dozens of women of assault, and who responded by calling them liars and threatening to sue. Biden was welcoming journalists to look into the charge against him. "I know that this claim has no merit. But as a candidate for president, I'm accountable to the American people," he said. "And I welcome that accountability and the scrutiny of the press as well."

Once Biden said his piece on that matter, he moved on to another topic. A week earlier, Trump had called off his daily pandemic press conferences at the White House after wandering through an incoherent ramble about using ultraviolet light or injecting disinfectant as a COVID treatment.

"Trump is—can I say politely?—just about the worst possible person to handle a crisis like this," Biden observed. "He seemed completely overwhelmed by it. He doesn't have a team, the temperament, or, quite frankly, the moral authority to take it on. And frankly, he doesn't put a high enough value on American lives to make this fight and make the right calculations, the right choices. To tell the truth, his priorities are elsewhere, and it shows."

This was the strategy, on Reade and in every other circumstance, that came up during the general election campaign: turn it back to the pandemic, don't get sucked into all the Democratic anxiety that he wasn't doing enough to respond to Trump's daily briefings and constant noise. "Those of us who had worked in the White House, and Joe Biden, who had been vice president of the United States, had a much better understanding of why the Trump strategy that everyone was panicked about, the daily press conferences, would not work unless they actually did something," Dunn, who set that strategy, said later, explaining an approach that was either going to make her out as a wise Buddha or as an ostrich wandering around train tracks. "All those people who were saying, 'Oh my gosh, he's doing daily press briefings. He's all over. He's dominating,' were missing the bigger point, which is unless he actually does something to deal with what is a genuine catastrophe, then it doesn't matter how many press briefings he does."

That's precisely what Biden did on that fundraising call. "When I announced, I said I'm running to restore the soul of America. Well, let me tell you, we're seeing the soul of America. Look at all those people. Look at all those ordinary people risking their lives," Biden said, "stepping up and doing it in circumstances where they know they're putting their lives at risk because they don't have a proper protective gear."

He mentioned the antilockdown protests in Michigan, militants with assault rifles who had filled the state capitol to intimidate Whitmer, protesting her COVID response. He had seen a swastika in one of the photos, which reminded him of Charlottesville. "Can you imagine any former president not condemning those that try to intimidate a governor, the legislature? The responsibility of meeting that threat falls to us."

That day Reade canceled an interview she was scheduled to record on Fox News, and then told the Associated Press that she had never actually filed a sexual harassment complaint, let alone a sexual assault complaint. The Biden campaign counted this as a win, convinced that calling for the records to be released had spooked her. It was another case of the campaign surviving through perseverance: Biden had only waited this long to talk because he couldn't get focused enough to speak, and because he and his aides believed it would go away on its own.

———

After three years of trying to duck out of politics and the news, the pandemic had Obama trying to sort out his own spot. Biden's online presence was terrible, he thought, and he told that to Biden directly. Then he told that to Biden's top advisers when he realized that Biden wasn't really registering his complaints or why they mattered.

He put together a COVID working group at his foundation, but he knew he wanted to hold back from getting too involved in the pandemic, even with all the opinions and suggestions he had. "I don't want to be out there that much. I don't want to be a second president," he would tell donors asking him to share publicly the ideas he'd start rattling off for the response on Zoom calls. He hated those anyway, with everyone able to see him. He missed the phone calls when he could half listen while playing Words with Friends on his iPad, and he could tell that even in smaller calls with staff he made people nervous when they could see him on-screen. "Maybe I'm the old guy now," he'd say. Mostly he missed golf, but he knew he'd been lucky not to get slammed more for hitting the courses in March and April during the early days of lockdown. All the time at home was supposed to give him more time to focus on finishing his memoir, but that was just grating on him. He was looking forward to Martha's Vineyard over the summer, where he could get away with hitting the links without having to worry about appearances.

Biden kept calling, stressing. Obama kept up his role as therapist. Listen to Dunn, he told Biden, listen to O'Malley Dillon. Step up the campaign's presence online. Friends kept calling, stressing. He listened, agreeing that Biden wasn't a great candidate, but versus Trump, it would be an easy choice. Everyone needed to stop sniping and get on board. Reelection campaigns are always referenda on the incumbent, Obama would say, and the pandemic was heightening that—and the more 2020 was a referendum on Trump, the more likely Trump would lose the vote. As he made those arguments, his confidence in Biden began to grow.

Donors to the foundation were still reaching out, looking to trade their checks for a little face time with him. Hurry up and call now, Obama would tell them: "I won't be able to talk to you because part of my job is going to be to save democracy in the fall."

CHAPTER TWENTY-ONE

A KNEE ON THE NECK

A riot is the language of the unheard.

—MARTIN LUTHER KING JR.

May 26, 2020–June 2020

Keith Ellison tends to wake up early. On May 26, he was on his phone right around six a.m. He watched the video. He watched it again. Eight minutes, forty-six seconds. He reloaded, watched it again while he took notes on a napkin. How many times did George Floyd say he couldn't breathe? Ellison had left Congress and the DNC deputy chair job in 2018 when he was elected attorney general in Minnesota. Floyd had lived and been killed in Ellison's old House district. For thirty years, he tried cases, marched in protests, worked constituent case files. Police violence wasn't new to him. The video still shocked him—Floyd's pleading, the officer with his knee on Floyd's neck, the other officers standing by, the crowd yelling at them to stop.

His wife came into the room. He asked her if she wanted to see the video. She'd grown up in Medellín. Gang wars and state-sponsored killings on the streets were part of life in Colombia in those days. She said she didn't need to see this one.

Ellison had run constituent services in these neighborhoods for twelve years and knew the streets. He got in his car and drove down to orient himself around the spot where Floyd had been killed. A crowd had gathered. He watched without getting out of the car.

Ellison hadn't noticed Floyd repeatedly calling for his mother until someone in the office pointed it out to him. That count went on the napkin too.

Every time the terms of the 2020 election seemed set, the world changed again. The most intense crisis for the federal government was impeachment. The most intense crisis for public health was the pandemic. Now the most intense racial and civil rights crisis in a generation was playing out on the streets of Minneapolis and quickly spreading around the country, around the world.

Would these protests be marches or riots? Trump clearly knew which he wanted, blaming Floyd's death on failures in Democratic-run cities, summoning that same 1980s-era nostalgia for the 1950s that defined Make America Great Again as he appealed to the fears of what he called the "suburban housewife." Never mind that most women in the suburbs weren't housewives anymore, and most suburbs weren't the black-and-white version that Trump had in his head, in which the white people lived in the neighborhood with nice homes and the Black people were off camera in the other part of town. Trump's greatest skill in real estate and then in politics had always been playing off racial divisions he aggravated, and he knew exactly how to stoke the situation. Democrats, after years of their own failures and attrition of faith from Black voters, gave him a new opening with a slogan that started spreading around progressive circles more quickly than the coronavirus: Defund the Police.

Slogans are supposed to be helpful, boil down complicated ideas into easily understandable arguments to advance the cause. Defund the Police was the opposite. The people chanting it meant that too many public welfare and public health needs were being handled by bloated police forces, which tended to function only by criminalizing behavior. They were trying to say that taking some of the money going into enforcement and incarceration might be better spent on community engagement and drug rehabilitation programs. Anyone but the already indoctrinated—and that went for most elected Democrats around the country—was left asking if liberals were calling for police stations to be closed down.

"This is the word of activists. It's the language of streets," Alexandra Ocasio-Cortez would tell fellow House Democrats, insisting they adopt the term. Karen Bass, the California congresswoman and Congressional Black Caucus chair who had started working on police reform in 1973, the year Floyd was born, would urge colleagues to turn the slogan around and instead phrase it "Refund the Communities."

Years of anger boiled up at police shooting and choking other Black men, or at killing a woman named Breonna Taylor in a botched raid on her apartment in Louisville, Kentucky, in March. Like the footage from the Edmund Pettus Bridge in Selma fifty-five years earlier, the Floyd video, playing on phones and TVs across a nation in lockdown, seized the national psyche. In demonstrations across the country, a coalition of Black and white, young and old, middle and working and upper class stepped forward. They were bigger and stronger than the small but self-righteous group of progressives adamant that rephrasing Defund the Police would itself be a concession, or than the more anarchically minded group who sensed an opportunity to turn the early days of summer into a pandemic chaos rumspringa.

The Republican Party was born from abolitionism and Abraham Lincoln's fighting a war to keep the country together, with an Emancipation Proclamation rooted in "the considerate judgment of mankind, and the gracious favor of Almighty God." In 2020, the Republican Party was led by a man who had peaceful protesters in front of the White House teargassed so that he could walk across a park to hold up a spare Bible in front of a church, scowling while saying nothing. Military helicopters, meanwhile, were buzzing protesters in the streets of Washington, and unidentified troops were knocking down citizens.

Just as his misogyny had helped spark MeToo, Trump's racism and xenophobia pushed the Black Lives Matter movement into the mainstream. Democrats had been part of the problem too, said Jumaane Williams, who called himself an activist elected official and had been arrested several times before being elected public advocate of New York City—a position that essentially amounted to a city council president with stripped-down powers. "Democrats have now risked the entire country on Joe Biden, on more of the same, who has said that we want to go back to a time before Donald Trump. And most of us are saying, 'No, the hell we don't.' Because that time didn't work for a lot of folks," Williams said.

Democrats had their defenders, like Obama's former attorney general, Eric

Holder. "I don't think it's the failure of the Democratic Party that brought us to this point. I would say it's the failure of the American system that got us to this point," he said. To many that kind of defensiveness was the problem. The pandemic had already exposed the abyss between those who had enough room for offices in their homes and those who couldn't pay their rent, those who tipped heavily to keep their favorite restaurants in business and those who didn't know when they'd find a job again. It had already revealed racial disparities in the number of COVID-19 deaths, in health care, in public education. Yet until Floyd was killed, race was the context, not the crux.

For Ellison, Sanders's earliest ally in Congress and a man proud to be an opponent of the free-market fundamentalism that he believed too many in his party adhered to, Floyd was the reminder of the old Lyndon Johnson quote: "If you can convince the lowest white man he's better than the best colored man, he won't notice you're picking his pocket. Hell, give him somebody to look down on, and he'll empty his pockets for you."

Fifty years after Johnson made that statement, Ellison said Republicans and Democrats had collaborated to allow for much worse, with talk of racial equality countered by winking phrases like Hillary Clinton's "super predators," or the crime bill that Biden had helped write, or fetishizing chasing the *white* working class after the 2016 election.

"America has always been at least two things. It's been that Donald Trump strain. And it's also been MLK, LBJ, Shirley Chisholm. A lot of us thought the Donald Trump version of America was passé," Ellison said. "I don't think anybody really was quite ready for how much it really wasn't, how much it really is part of what's going on. The tug of war that is America rages on."

———

On Super Tuesday 2016, when Hillary Clinton was essentially locking up the nomination and when Trump was too (despite being dismissed as a joke to most) Biden was hosting a packed reception for Black History Month at his official residence at the Naval Observatory. He reflected on his own history of being inspired by the civil rights movement, and shared a story he likes to tell of standing with his sons on the train platform in Wilmington, where he had once seen the city rioting after Martin Luther King's assassination, waiting to be picked up on the route he'd commuted along for decades by a train carrying the first Black president, en route to their inauguration.

"I want to thank Donald Trump," Biden said, and the crowd immediately started laughing. No, Biden stopped them; he was trying to make a serious point. After watching the early Republican primary returns come in on television upstairs, he saw that Trump's candidacy, what he was saying and doing out on the trail, could help America confront and combat its institutional racism. "He's making the American people look in the mirror. And the American people are honest. And they look in the mirror and see what's looking back at them," Biden said. "Maybe the divisiveness, particularly with the other team right now, maybe it's a good thing, to awaken the American people about the subtle and not-so-subtle deals going on."

The Biden campaign contained a fundamental division: those who were with him from before he was clearly going to be the nominee, and those who came on after. Those who believed in Biden only after Super Tuesday had almost all worked for candidates who had been trying to beat him and assumed they could. This included his new campaign manager, Jen O'Malley Dillon, who had previously moved her family to El Paso to be the manager for Beto O'Rourke's run.

COVID-19 entrenched those divisions. When O'Malley Dillon was introduced to the staff, it was by conference call, with people already scattered and, in some cases, rushing through pandemic shopping runs for soup and toilet paper while listening on mute. There were no staff happy hours to be had amid social distancing, no happenstance friendships struck up from trips to the break room or running into a new office mate in line at a favorite lunch spot. Most of the people who were added into the campaign's senior leadership were never in the same actual room for the entire race. Building a wider sense of team and community was close to impossible—except for the shared, almost religious mission of beating Trump. At the beginning of June, when Biden officially clinched the nomination because there had been votes in enough no-longer-competitive primaries to give him the delegate count he technically needed for the convention, O'Malley Dillon led a phone call to celebrate their shared success, while aides who had been with Biden from the start grumbled to one another via text messages about how *they* were the ones who had done the hard work. When O'Malley Dillon attempted to install a new communications director, she ran into a fight with Bedingfield, who was protected by her ability to center Biden. He called her multiple times a day. Some of these divisions were ironed out during the Tara Reade crisis, as holding together against a common enemy inevitably built trust.

After Floyd's killing, though, the divisions blew up beyond just (remote) office politics. Biden *needed* to come out for Defund the Police, many of the newer crew felt. That was where the progressive energy was, they insisted, and he was making a potentially fatal error by not going with it. Pressure was coming in from Hollywood and from activists, demanding phone calls, demanding a sense of reassurance that Biden hadn't just fallen asleep in his basement in Wilmington, oblivious to what was happening in the country. "Sometimes you want to scream, 'All you motherfuckers lost. You worked for campaigns that lost. The guy who got all the votes was Joe Biden, because that's where the country is, that's where the party is,'" said one of the aides pushing back on the new crew. "There's an effort in the campaign to drag him to the left, or drag him away from what got us here—listening to Twitter, letting Beltway narratives knock us off message. We're already fighting Donald Trump. We don't need to be fighting each other."

Biden had seen a lot in his life, he told aides, but the Floyd video had been particularly unnerving to watch. He said he understood the outrage, the protests. From the start, though, he had been worried that the responses wouldn't remain peaceful, and would give Trump exactly what he wanted to make the moment about chaos in the suburbs. And whatever the slogan actually meant, Biden wasn't into "Defund the Police." "I actually want to *increase* funding," he said in internal meetings. "Don't say *that!*" they told him. Those who knew him best also knew he wasn't going to be convinced by what a group of voters who had never supported him in the primaries might want him to say now that he had won the primaries without them.

"It actually isn't where the bulk of voters are, as the primaries had just proved, and also it's not authentic to him," said one of Biden's top advisers. "Forcing things on him never works out well. If he disagrees, or doesn't believe it, he won't do it."

Biden stressed about what to say instead. He didn't have the language. He had gotten into trouble by falsely claiming to have marched in civil rights protests and participated in sit-ins in the 1960s. Just a few months before Floyd was killed, he'd boasted about "the great honor of being arrested with our U.N. ambassador on the streets of Soweto" while going to see Nelson Mandela in prison on Robben Island, when in fact he'd been temporarily delayed at the airport as part of a congressional delegation in 1977 after he refused to let local officials separate him from the Black members. He was also the white guy who had helped write the 1994 crime bill that had expanded and empowered local police to create a legacy of overreach and incarceration, the old white guy who had emerged from the most diverse primary field ever.

The country was cracking, there was a desperation for an answer to Trump, and Biden could sense that. Late on the night of May 30, he sat on the phone with Bedingfield, trying to work out a statement, insistent that he had to get his voice out. He tried to keep it short. He couldn't. "These last few days have laid bare that we are a nation furious at injustice. Every person of conscience can understand the rawness of the trauma people of color experience in this country, from the daily indignities to the extreme violence, like the horrific killing of George Floyd," he said in a statement issued via press release. "Protesting such brutality is right and necessary. It's an utterly American response. But burning down communities and needless destruction is not. Violence that endangers lives is not. Violence that guts and shutters businesses that serve the community is not."

He knew how to talk about mourning, and linked the suffering of racial injustice to the suffering from COVID-19 and the suffering from the collapsed economy. "I know that a grief that dark and deep may at times feel too heavy to bear. I know," he said. "We are a nation in pain, but we must not allow this pain to destroy us. We are a nation enraged, but we cannot allow our rage to consume us. We are a nation exhausted, but we will not allow our exhaustion to defeat us."

Two days later, after Trump gassed Lafayette Square to clear the way for him to wave a Bible that wasn't his in front of a church that had been damaged by agitators in the crowd of protesters, Biden decided to say more. Mike Donilon wrote the speech, connecting again the battle for the soul of the nation rhetoric that he'd written for the launch video over a year earlier, before there was a coronavirus and when Floyd was going about his life in Minnesota.

"When peaceful protestors are dispersed by the order of the president from the doorstep of the people's house, the White House—using tear gas and flash grenades—in order to stage a photo op at a noble church, we can be forgiven for believing that the president is more interested in power than in principle. More interested in serving the passions of his base than the needs of the people in his care," Biden said, with his campaign attempting to give the speech a nonpandemic feel by putting him in front of flags and a small group of supporters in a room at Philadelphia City Hall. "A president of the United States must be part of the solution, not the problem. But this president today is part of the problem."

The speech didn't break through much into the news, but online it was huge. For a campaign that had been struggling for attention and to raise money, that night became Biden's biggest single day of online fundraising to that point. Biden had shown his core, and people across the country responded in the only way they could from pandemic lockdown.

———

Obama hadn't wanted to speak out after Charlottesville—he had always been reluctant to come across as The Black President while in the White House, and he was even less inclined once he was no longer there. He knew that taking a public stance would give Trump another excuse to pick a partisan fight rather than flounder in his rejection by America. Now he had the added factor of not wanting to distract or subtract from Biden.

Obama had tried to address Floyd's killing and the subsequent violence in a written statement he put on Twitter a few days earlier, but he couldn't ignore Lafayette Square, and Trump's trying more directly than ever to split America apart. He was concerned with what he was seeing. His office was in contact with the other former presidents' offices, as they all tried to sort out how to respond. George W. Bush put out a video statement. Obama put out one of his own. They quickly decided he should do more. Obama aides rushed to prepare a speech for him to deliver on a Zoom call that cable news could carry live. "We are in a political season, but our country that he loves is also at a critical inflection point," explained Jarrett that afternoon.

As another curfew notice went out from the Washington mayor's office and men with military equipment began massing outside the White House again, Obama was on TV. He thanked the protesters and praised those police who he said were committed to making policing better. He then addressed the young people watching.

"I want you to know that you matter. I want you to know that your lives matter. That your dreams matter. You should be able to learn and make mistakes and live a life of joy without having to worry about what's going to happen when you walk to the store or go for a jog or are driving down the street or looking at some birds in a park."

Overall the speech was deliberately upbeat, as Obama pointed out that the protests drew together Black and white, young and old, male and female— "a far more representative cross section of America out on the streets, peacefully protesting, who felt moved to do something because of the injustices that they have seen. That didn't exist back in the 1960s, that kind of broad coalition."

He included a warning. "I hope that you also feel hopeful even as you may feel angry," he said. "You have communicated a sense of urgency that is as powerful and transformative as anything I have seen in recent years."

He was clearly gratified by what he saw, taking his own piece of credit for what was taking place. "These are the kids that grew up under his presidency, this is the first flourishing of the Obama generation, acting as community organizers," observed David Simas.

The following afternoon, Obama sat at home on another Zoom call, fiddling with a Rubik's Cube, waiting for John Lewis to log on to a video town hall for the Obama Foundation. The civil rights leader and Georgia congressman was in a red sweater again, as he'd been on the bridge in Selma in March. He'd lost more weight from the pancreatic cancer that was slowly killing him.

Despite the cancer and COVID-19 and another Black man having been choked to death, Lewis said he still had hope: "We cannot give up, cannot give in, become bitter or hostile." He linked what was happening directly to the civil rights marches as he and only a few others still alive were entitled to do. "To see all of the young people, all of the young men—not just men of color— but Black, white, Latino, Asian American, Native American, all of the young women, standing up, speaking up, being prepared to march" inspired him. "They're going to help redeem the soul of America, and save our country, and maybe help save the planet."

Early Sunday morning, Lewis made a surprise visit to the street in front of

Lafayette Square that the DC mayor had renamed Black Lives Matter Plaza, the slogan painted in yellow on the asphalt in giant rounded letters. He was wearing a mask and a heavier sweater, standing for just a few minutes in the middle of the *B*, his arms crossed. "I think the people in DC and around the nation are sending a mightily powerful and strong message to the rest of the world that we will get there," he said. It was his last public appearance.

A few hours later, an impromptu street festival had settled in. There was a stand handing out free water bottles, a tent with chicken and kale sandwiches, an ice-cream truck. Michael Jackson songs played on a speaker, while two young men did a freestyle rap about Trump. The black chain-link fence that had been quickly erected around Lafayette Square since Trump's walk had already been covered over with signs—SILENCE IS NOT THE ANSWER, read one sign; MY SKIN COLOR IS NOT A CRIME! read another; and JUSTICE was spray-painted on a wall. In front of the P. J. Clarke's, members of the New Black Panther Party were speaking. As at all the demonstrations in those few weeks, masks were on, but social distancing had conveniently dropped out of fashion.

Biden's only trip out of his house since March had been a visit to lay a wreath at a veterans park on Memorial Day. The only reason anyone paid attention was that even so short a public appearance by the Democratic nominee for president was remarkable by that point, and because Trump mocked him for the big black mask he wore under his aviators.

Floyd's funeral, meanwhile, was quickly becoming a major political event. Biden's staff was too anxious about the virus to have him attend. They were concerned about alienating the police unions, whose endorsements Biden's 1970s-brewed sense of politics made him eager to get. The compromise was to have him fly to Houston and meet with Floyd's family privately.

Biden came with Cedric Richmond, the Louisiana congressman who had, from Biden's early days of considering getting into the race, positioned himself as the conduit for Biden to current Black politics. Al Sharpton and civil rights attorney Ben Crump were also along to facilitate what they were worried might be an awkward conversation. Biden spoke with all of Floyd's family who were present, but the conversation that stayed with him was the one he had had with Floyd's six-year-old daughter, Gianna.

"He really began to understand the pain because he'd gone through the loss of his son—that this was not just political, that we all hurt," Sharpton said.

Biden had watched the first Floyd funeral in Minneapolis. He was struck by Sharpton's eulogy, that this was a shared Black experience: "The reason we could never be who we wanted and dreamed to be is you kept your knee on our neck," the reverend said.

"I never looked at it that way," Biden said. "No matter who you are, it seems like it's never enough."

If he wasn't going to go to the funeral, Crump suggested, maybe he could record a video for it. Biden agreed and the next morning filmed it in his converted basement, with the folded flag from Beau's funeral in its case on a shelf behind him. He started by addressing Floyd's family—"Jill and I know the deep hole in your hearts when you bury a piece of your soul deep in this earth," he said. The burden of grieving in public meant finding a purpose in the pain, he told them. With soft piano music playing under him, Biden turned to everyone else watching. "When there is justice for George Floyd, we will truly be on our way to racial justice in America, and then, as you said, Gianna, your daddy will have changed the world."

A few days later, after protests had turned violent in Minneapolis and the storyline was slipping into the opportunistic kids busting into shop windows in Manhattan, Sharpton called to follow up. When Biden called back, he thanked Sharpton for speaking out against the looting. "That will help our cause," he told Sharpton.

That conversation stuck with Sharpton. "He went from where we were like coexistent," Sharpton said, "to where he started seeing himself as part of the cause, saying 'our cause.'"

Late at night on a hot Friday in July, when Ruth Bader Ginsburg announced she had cancer again, John Lewis died. Any other president would have issued a statement about his passing and likely ordered a state funeral, but Lewis had called Trump an "illegitimate president" because of the Russian involvement in the 2016 campaign and had boycotted the inauguration. This was just the latest instance of the usual functions of the government becoming refractions of Trump, precisely as he wanted. He was a president who had interrupted the

State of the Union a few months earlier to give the Medal of Freedom to Rush Limbaugh, but went golfing on the morning after Lewis died before ordering flags lowered through the end of the day and issuing a perfunctory tweet that he was "saddened to hear" the news. America under Trump had become a country where most people reasonably thought anything he might have said would have been worse than saying nothing at all.

On the night that Lewis died, Trump called in to a telerally in Wisconsin a lot like the ones that he spent the past few months making fun of Biden for being relegated to. By now, 140,000 Americans had died, at a rate of two times the number of September 11 fatalities per week. The standard that a Trump campaign official had privately joked about earlier in the pandemic—that it was hitting mostly blue states, and those weren't their voters anyway—was no longer true. Infections were surging. Three months had passed since Jared Kushner had predicted that the country was about to come back "rocking," a month since Mike Pence had written, "While talk of an increase in cases dominates cable news coverage, more than half of states are actually seeing cases decline or remain stable," in an op-ed meant to shame the media and tout Trump's supposed success.

Biden spoke with Lewis a few days before he died. They had known each other for years, but their relationship had never been deep. Though they knew that it would be their last conversation, it remained focused on the campaign, on healing the country, on beating Trump.

The Sunday night after Lewis died, Obama appeared from his house at Martha's Vineyard on a prescheduled Zoom fundraiser for the House Democrats, joining Nancy Pelosi. The Chicks (the "Dixie" part newly dropped when they started to promote their new album in the wake of the Floyd protests) patched in from separate studios, waiting to perform. Pelosi mentioned how much pride was beaming on Lewis's face on the day of Obama's inauguration, and Obama spoke about how much Lewis had inspired his own career. It was witnessing the civil rights movement, Obama said, that explained "why I became a community organizer, as opposed to a congressional intern."

Obama had been struggling with the death of Lewis, who had been both a hero and a friend. To lose him now was several types of pain. He kept saying how much he missed him, told a story about C. T. Vivian, the civil rights leader who had died only a few hours before Lewis, sitting with him in the Roosevelt

Room steps from the Oval Office and starting to cry, then Lewis starting to cry, at "how they couldn't have imagined all of us being there with an African American president who was essentially their spiritual son."

Obama worried that the lessons of Lewis and the movement had been lost. "We live in a much more cynical time," Obama said. "There's a sense now that, well, nonviolence may or may not work, politics may or may not work, structural racism is so deeply embedded that things never really change."

You're the hope guy, said John Legend, moderating the conversation with Obama. What gave him hope anymore?

Obama said he had been thinking about that 2004 convention speech again—that audacity of hope was about holding out when there's no reason to.

"Now," Obama said, "is not a good time."

The hope, Obama said, is that people seemed as if they actually wanted to do something about it. His hope was that they would follow through.

"This is one of those forks in the road in history that don't always come back," Obama said. "The stakes in this one—I don't have to tell you, are higher than you think they are."

CHAPTER TWENTY-TWO

A HORRIBLE,
HORRIBLE PROCESS

"Vice president" has such a nice ring to it.

—GERALDINE FERRARO

July 2020–August 12, 2020

The Friday before she was picked as Biden's running mate, Harris was sitting in her apartment in Washington. It was another day of pandemic living, another day of waiting for what seemed inevitable, yet couldn't seem real. Either she was hours away from her political career being made, and probably having the 2024 nomination laid out for her, or from being humiliated and tossed into what some supporters worried could be a difficult 2022 primary back in California to hold on to her Senate seat.

When Harris gets interested in topics, she has her staff give her stats and articles to back up her outrage. Filtering her indignation through the data, her sincerity can at times come out sounding like talking points: "Let's all just be thankful for the blessings that we have—you know, when one in five mothers is describing her children under twelve as being hungry in America, right?"

She had plugged in on the pandemic. "Unless you have somebody you know—and I actually know a number of people who have someone they know, and thank god, I don't have anyone I know yet—but there's been no mourning, right? The ceremonies that we have around death, including 9/11 or war, seeing the caskets, seeing the funerals. There's been nothing, no evidence. You want to talk about carnage, like this guy talks about, right? He predicted carnage: look what he's done."

No pause. "And then the other piece of it is, people are standing in food lines all over America," and whole pieces of the country going about their lives in their "cozy homes," she said. "They'll see what they want to see, based on their choice of the night on Netflix, but people are being given, through the circumstances, an immunity to really see what is actually happening. And unless you're curious or interested or just aware, you can go on with your happy life. Meanwhile, millions of people in our country are suffering."

Part of Harris's mind is forever in the DA's office, and part of it is always trying to remember her Politician 101 training to keep introducing herself to voters. "I used to specialize in child sexual assault cases," she said, flipping back. "I was a prosecutor, and I predicted at the very beginning, this is going to be disastrous for those children. Because the safe place is to go to school. The vast majority of the cases that are reported get reported because someone who was not a family member suspects something is going on. And now these children, and you can talk about domestic violence, there's no safe place for them. And it just breaks my heart."

That afternoon, though, Harris was thinking back on the multibank, multistate mortgage settlement that had defined her first year as California attorney general in 2011. It wasn't her first job in politics, but it was her first time thinking about the law beyond prosecuting criminals. Given the size of the companies, this involved more than finding the one person responsible, and more than just trying to throw anyone in jail. And it was a learning curve. She'd sit behind the big wooden desk in her office in Los Angeles, cross-examining her staff until they stammered through their answers, trying to explain to her why she should take a deal. She wanted to know how to explain the deal to California homeowners who weren't going to be helped much by a few thousand dollars in payouts when their entire mortgages were underwater. She stressed about staving off the pressure coming from the left via demonstrations and behind-the-scenes trouble being stirred up by her supposed ally, the then New York attorney general, Eric Schneiderman.

The banks came back with a settlement that included $20 billion to California, ten times what had been in their original offer. The episode defined her,

her particular sense of politics and practicality and progressivism, of facing critics who had begun to accuse her of compromising and caving to corporate moderates. It's also how she got to know Beau Biden.

Beau was the Delaware attorney general then, chief law enforcement officer of a state where sucking up bank incorporation fees is a local industry. The predatory lending that had precipitated the housing crisis had upset him, though. He liked being the underdog, standing with the other underdogs. "Beau was not about gestures. It was literally—he meant it. He was there. He was in the foxhole," Harris remembered. On a personal level, he liked Harris. Part of that was having connected over feeling uncomfortable going up against the Obama administration when they pushed back on a deal the White House clearly wanted done. Harris felt her kinship to Obama, a loyalty from being younger and Black in politics that went deeper than any endorsement or fundraiser appearance. Her brother-in-law, Tony West, was high up in the Justice Department. Beau was, of course, the vice president's son. They talked about trying to outshine parents who had helped define them—her mother, his father. They were close in age, eager to be part of their own generation in politics. They talked about all of that—sometimes multiple times a day.

The depth of their relationship often gets overstated, but they did connect as much as two high-profile politicians on opposite sides of the country could. A year after the mortgage settlement was done, Biden spoke at the National Association of Attorneys General meeting. Beau led his father around the room, having him meet one AG at a time. When they got to Harris, Beau introduced her with "This is Kamala!" putting a face to the new friend he had clearly been telling his dad about. An aide snapped a cell phone picture of the future running mates—already holding both of each other's hands as they spoke. She flew by herself to Beau's funeral in 2015. In 2016, Biden endorsed her in her Senate race, citing Beau: "I saw them take on big banks, lift up the voices of working people, and protect women and children from abuse and violence."

That was the relationship Biden felt Harris had used to sucker punch him in that first debate a year earlier. She didn't want to mess this up again. She worried that anything she'd say about Beau at that point would sound "opportunistic." "I just feel like the process will take its place. And that's definitely, as we all know, a real soft spot for Joe," she said. She paused. "We were really friends."

―――――

The choice of Kamala Harris as Biden's running mate can seem like the longest, most drawn-out lead-up to an obvious conclusion in the history of modern presidential politics. They ran into each other on an Amtrak train two weeks after she'd launched her campaign, two months before he'd launched his. "Come on in, the water's warm," Harris joked to him, as she stood up at her seat chatting with him, introducing him to her sister, Maya, the whole scene captured in a photo tweeted by an aide that quickly went viral because it already looked to many people then as if they were the ticket.

Like Biden's own path to the nomination, it almost didn't happen, over and over and over again. A few weeks after that encounter on the train, when Biden's plans were already pretty obvious, but he was still officially more coquette than candidate, his staff reached out to Stacey Abrams to arrange a lunch on her next trip to Washington. Fresh off her close loss in the Georgia governor's race in 2018 and being picked by Schumer to deliver the Democrats' official State of the Union response to Trump, Abrams was making out as if she were thinking about running for president herself. This was a way of building her profile to stoke fundraising for her voting expansion efforts to help her in the 2022 rematch for governor, which she was actually planning for. She sat for glowing magazine stories. She had lunch with all the presidential contenders who called. With her name constantly in the news, she watched the dollars pour in. So as she prepared to announce she wasn't going to run, she was interested in one last burst, courtesy of the biggest name in the race.

Conveniently for both, Biden and Abrams got together on the day O'Rourke jumped into the race with his trip to Iowa. They got to make a little distraction from the wild rumpus that could benefit them both. Within a day, the chatter began that Biden had talked to Abrams about being his vice president. Abrams was confused. They had a nice lunch. Biden spoke about how he wanted her in his world, but didn't explicitly ask her about being his running mate. She didn't tell anyone about the conversation, then watched, surprised with her staff, waiting to hear from anyone on the Biden campaign, as the rumors picked up and started to spill out in unattributed items in the press. They were hoping that they could clear up what was going on, and figure out how they were supposed to respond publicly without calling anyone a liar. They didn't want to hurt her relationship with Biden, but they knew she needed to come up with something, because otherwise she would appear to be scheming and evasive. Still, no one called. Confusion shifted to frustration, especially as Abrams and top advisers realized how familiar the shape of the whole play was from 2015, when Biden had his lunch with Warren at the Naval Observatory and suddenly a similar running-mate-offer storyline started to circulate right at the moment when Biden needed to generate some excitement.

Finally, Biden's campaign manager phoned Abrams's closest aide to say he had nothing to do with the rumors. Abrams decided to publicly shut down the story in a way that boosted both herself and Biden, with a brushback at whoever on his campaign was trying to use her. "We talked about whether I was thinking about running. We talked about whether he was thinking about running. But we did not have that conversation and everything else is pure speculation made up by somebody else," she said.

As soon as Sanders officially dropped out, the campaign began what had been meant from the start to be a much more formal process. Four official cochairs were named—Biden's old buddy and former Connecticut senator, Chris Dodd; his home-state congresswoman, Lisa Blunt Rochester; his former high-ranking aide, Cynthia Hogan; and his crucial endorser, Los Angeles mayor Eric Garcetti. They split into pairs (Dodd with Blunt Rochester, Hogan with Garcetti) to divide up the work, though the real decisions were always being driven by Biden and his inner circle. The chairs asked if they were supposed to come up with the list of options. Nope. Anita Dunn gave them a list of eighteen potential women. Most were obvious; a few were not. "There are some people whose names will be mentioned," Dunn had cautioned as she introduced the list to the committee, "who will never go anywhere." The committee's assignment, they came to realize, included vetting at least a few options for the sake of the politics of saying they were considered.

The campaign didn't have enough money to pay for much polling to guide their thinking, but Dunn gave them a few pointers from what they could already see. "We have a path to victory here. This doesn't sound good, but we actually might win just because we're not the other guy," she'd said. "Our biggest weakness is his age. People are really worried about that—we have to be able to counter that." Stuck at home on his pandemic briefing calls every morning, Biden was firm on the contrast he wanted to make to what was coming out of the Trump administration those days—the incoherent coronavirus briefings and frantic fights over supplies. No amateurs. Competence.

The final direction from Dunn: no leaks. The last direction from Biden, relayed by Dunn: make as many of the women look better at the end of the process, once he pulled their names into it.

Initially the process moved quickly, thanks to everyone's sheltering at home. The first round of interviews was completed in the first week in May, and the chairs were so far ahead of Biden's own schedule that Dunn asked them to speak to each prospect again, this time with all four cochairs on the line. If nothing else, Dodd said, this was a way to insulate them from future criticism that one set of cochairs or the other had more influence.

More time, more conversations, more requests meant more rumors started to leak. Six references—three personal and three political—came off as a bit intense to a few of the contenders, on top of the documents they had to submit and phone calls they had to sit through. Garcetti downloaded a Venn diagram maker and plugged in categories: executive experience, COVID-19 experience, person of color. He sent around the results. The only person who hit all three was New Mexico governor Michelle Lujan Grisham. She was never one of the prospects the team spent much time considering.

━━━

Warren started campaigning for the spot right away. She had Biden's cell number and called him to start pitching.

Officially, Warren wanted to discuss pandemic ideas. This suddenly seemed like her moment—if COVID-19 had hit a few months earlier, people close to her couldn't help thinking, she might have been the obvious presidential nominee. Instead, she might be able to get back toward power by pitching herself as the running mate who could lead the thinking about what was suddenly the biggest, most complex, most expensive government response to the biggest nonwar crisis in American history.

Wrapped up in that initial flush of coronavirus panic was a battered survivor's optimism that the pandemic would force America to reconceive the entire economy, schools, health care, and all the other underlying structures of society. The "I have a plan for that" candidate suddenly seemed an appealing contrast to a government failing at such simple things as not forcing nurses to wrap themselves in trash bags to stay safe while treating patients. Warren would be Lisa Simpson, joked one Biden donor, referring to the classic 2000 *Simpsons* episode that imagines a future where Lisa is the president and has a line about how she "inherited quite a budget crunch from President Trump." She'd be the opposite of Selina Meyer on *Veep*, those close to her started to joke, ready to throw herself completely into the work without obsessing about her own political future, as some of the other options would. "She put it all out there. She knows she lost. She knows Biden won," one of those people said at the time.

Biden's inner circle remained suspicious. Warren could be a pain who rarely saw a line between right and self-righteousness, and the notion of a vice president who would be forever on a mission and who carefully studied how to lean on levers of power gave them nightmares of late nights in the West Wing, wondering what she might be up to over in her office. Could they trust her? But given the scope of what they would be facing, could they trust anyone else? Biden kept talking about the blinders being off, and Warren kept talking about a new New Deal moment, so maybe the pandemic meant they both now agreed on big government spending and massive overhauls. Maybe their senses of what was necessary were being brought together by the pandemic. Dick Cheney was the vice president in a national security crisis. Warren could be the vice president for this crisis.

"Joe Biden describes this as the battle for the soul of the nation. He's right," Warren said, back home in Boston at the end of April. "But there's more. It's the battle for the survival of a nation that works for most of its people, or only for a thin elite at the top."

In her phone calls with the vetting committee, Warren kept stressing how much she had studied up on the job, how much she understood that Biden would be in charge, how much more flexible she was than her presidential campaign might have led them to believe. She tried to reflect that publicly as well. "I'm a team player. I want to get things done," she said in April, pushing her case. She talked about setting up the Consumer Financial Protection Bureau, how she had managed to benefit Obama on policy and politics, and insisted that she had "never crossed swords with anyone in the administration," though that was not true. She circled back around and said "team player" two more times in her answer. She knew she had a reputation for being a sometimes frustrating colleague in the Senate, she said. "That's the structure of the separation of powers. And I know that can sometimes be a bumpy relationship. That is my job. And I am a team player because I want to get things done."

Obama was intrigued. He was one of the people in his administration with whom she had, in fact, crossed swords. He hadn't forgotten that Warren had taken a shot at him in that 2017 blowup over his paid speeches, and Michelle Obama hadn't forgiven her for it.

When he thought about Biden possibly becoming president with this much ahead of him, the idea of Warren there as a more focused backstop made him feel relaxed. He called her to talk through ideas himself, then—because he doesn't tweet himself—told his staff to tweet supportively about what she was proposing.

Warren and Valerie Jarrett had always had a good relationship. "You have to understand, you have the hottest brand in Democratic politics," the Obama adviser had told Warren in a 2009 meeting in her office in the West Wing. "Anyone would want your brand." Jarrett was one of the earliest to encourage her to run for Senate. They'd continued to speak regularly, over the phone and over meals. That paid dividends, as Jarrett knew that her willingness to praise Warren publicly lent the air of Obama support. "She's done her homework," Jarrett said. "She clearly understands how to get her arms around a pandemic—as best one can."

While Warren was pitching Biden, they got to talking, because Biden always gets to talking with pretty much whoever he's on the phone with. She confided in him more than she'd been expecting to, as many people often tend to do. Her oldest brother, Don, was in a hospital room back in Oklahoma with COVID-19, and she couldn't be with him as she'd been with her mother and her Aunt Bee as they slowly slipped away. She could only call him on the phone, but "it's not the same. You need to touch people. We have to hug. We have to be with each other," she said, a few weeks after Don died at eighty-six. "It's something none of us were prepared for. It's always hard to lose someone you love. But to lose someone when you have to wonder: What were their last days like? Were they afraid? Were they cold? Were they lonely? That is a kind of grief that is new to all of us. And my brothers won't get over this. They just won't. None of us will."

Connections formed in grief tend to stay with Biden. This one remained with Warren long after he phoned her the day after her brother died. "One person who'd lost loved ones trying to console another person who just lost her beloved brother," she recalled a few weeks later, her voice wavering. "We talked about the crisis and he talked about what we do individually, about my other brothers, but also what we need to do as a nation." That connection to each death, Warren said, "that's what Donald Trump can't manage. And that's what Joe Biden feels in his bones."

Activists who wanted Warren circulated a more pointed argument: Biden needed her to win the left. In the spring of 2016, when Warren had tried to position herself as the mediator at the end of those primaries, Clinton would complain to her on the phone that if only Sanders would cooperate, everything else would work out. "I'm worried about what antics Bernie will be up to," Clinton told her, convinced he'd try to mess up her convention. "I'm not at all worried about his people. They'll all come around because Donald Trump is on the ballot." Now, Warren and her confidants believed, Biden was heading into the fall with the same challenge of convincing progressives to stick with him.

Warren's problem was Sanders. She knew that was how it was going to be. Warren had a plan to be the unity pick, but Sanders wasn't feeling very unified as he sulked in lockdown in Burlington. She shouldn't have run, he thought. She shouldn't have leaked that conversation from their dinner in 2018. She shouldn't have stayed in the race after New Hampshire. She shouldn't have sat out endorsing him when she dropped out.

Sanders could have called Biden and said that he liked Warren. He knew that. He made a point of not saying her name or even bringing up the topic when they spoke. Aides, meanwhile, made their own point of spreading the notion that she lacked any "legitimacy" on the left.

＝＝＝

"So sad to watch what is happening in our country," Dodd wrote in a group chat to Garcetti and Blunt Rochester late on May 30, as the Floyd protests got violent. "Thinking about the two of you at this hour. Wish you and your city and state to return to calm and peace."

Blunt Rochester wrote back a few minutes later to say she'd spoken to Biden that night after the state police were called out in Wilmington. "Things must change," she wrote. "Praying for our country."

Biden's pick was always going to come down to choosing between unifying the party on race or ideology. Now the choice was unavoidable—and clearly tilted in one direction.

Amid those first few manic, soul-crunching days after George Floyd was killed, Klobuchar could see that Trump was wheedling in on how he was the one who could keep people safe and how Biden hadn't done enough for Black communities. She knew her chances of being picked were evaporating by the hour. She was white and a moderate. Whatever nervous Midwest math was going on in the Biden campaign's Electoral College calculations wasn't going to be enough to overcome the likely backlash. Weeks earlier, Klobuchar had been telling people in her joke-maybe-not-joke sarcasm that her husband having been hospitalized with COVID-19 (and recovering) helped her chances, but that was negated too. Then the biggest civil rights moment of the twenty-first century exploded out of her own home county. The controversy around her spiked when the officer who knelt on Floyd's neck was found to have not been charged in another incident, which went through the Hennepin County prosecutor's office. Klobuchar had run that office before getting elected to the Senate. There wasn't much interest in the important nuance that she had already been in Washington by the time that decision had been made, and she herself hadn't made it. "Everyone realized what a problem it was. It put it in all caps, underlined, in bold. It would have been very hard in that moment to go through with that—and what a distraction it would be," observed one of the people working with Klobuchar at the time.

Everything about Klobuchar is intensity and ambition. Mention a line from a *Saturday Night Live* sketch to her, and she'll one-up that one by giving a full rundown of two others she liked more. Mention writing a book to her, and she'll talk about writing her own book. Klobuchar had gotten into politics because she'd been kicked out of the hospital twenty-four hours after giving birth—despite her only daughter having been born with a condition that required her to be on a feeding tube for the first three years of her life—and had joined an effort to change the state law on hospital stays. Three months after dropping out of her presidential campaign, she took herself out of contention again. No press conference, she decided. There wasn't much to get into. There was only one question to answer, and she knew what she wanted to say.

Earlier that day, she had learned that her father had contracted COVID-19. She assumed he wouldn't make it through. The man she cited at the Kavanaugh hearings and who became a familiar character from her stump speeches in Iowa when she talked about his time as a sportswriter covering the Vikings was ninety-two by then, living in a nursing home. She knew if she mentioned his condition on air that she'd break down completely. Besides, she was making enough news for one night, her chief of staff advised. Inhale, wait for the feed to go live. Remind herself one more time: don't cry. The feed went live, and she told Lawrence O'Donnell on MSNBC what she had told Biden over the phone the night before about why she was pulling out. Exhale, accept that it was over. Keep telling herself the John McCain line, "Nothing in life is more liberating than to fight for a cause larger than yourself." Know that by saying she thought the moment was right for Biden to pick a woman of color, she had helped seal Biden's choice before he realized it himself.

Never before has a prospective running-mate pick shaped the process that much by publicly stepping out of it. Klobuchar headed home from the studio. Her daughter had just driven in from New York with her boyfriend. Pizza was waiting for their first lockdown dinner together. Harris, whom she'd grown close to when they spent the previous Thanksgiving together in Iowa with their husbands, chasing hopes of a late surge, called the following day. Tammy Duckworth called shortly afterward. Then Susan Rice.

The day before Klobuchar dropped out, one name was added to the vetting group: Karen Bass, the soft-spoken congresswoman from Los Angeles. Biden barely knew her. They'd only had one real conversation, when she had accompanied him to the packed chicken-and-waffles spot in her district as the Super Tuesday results started coming. She told him then about her only daughter being killed in a car crash, how she'd been literally knocked out of her chair watching him speak at the 2008 convention and telling the story of the collision that had killed his wife and daughter. "We both just shared that you learn how to get up in the morning," is how she remembered the conversation. "You learn how to live, but your life is fundamentally changed, dramatically changed."

Dodd knew Bass from her having helped him out on a problem when he was the head of the Motion Picture Association. He urged his friend to include her. Garcetti knew her from their overlapping in LA. Blunt Rochester knew her from serving together in the House and Bass's leadership of the Congressional Black Caucus. Suddenly she had become the center of attention in the House for actually moving a police reform bill in the weeks after Floyd was killed, getting support from moderates, the new progressives, the older Black members recoiling from activists saying "Defund the Police," and from Ilhan Omar's declaring that she "achieves big goals without compromising her values." Only with Biden as the nominee, reluctant to be upstaged as he finally started to see himself in the job he'd been chasing his whole life, looking for some way to find a woman who was Black and was liked by the Sanders orbit, could a low-key sixty-six-year-old with pointy glasses get any kind of look.

For a brief moment, she got a brief look. "She could be the one," Blunt Rochester told the group, and the committee pushed her forward. Dunn agreed to consider her. Bass told the vetting committee on her first call about her multiple trips to Cuba in the 1970s as part of a group of young wannabe revolutionaries known as the Venceremos Brigade, and how she'd gone to see Fidel Castro speak in Havana. Although she didn't speak Spanish and couldn't understand him, she found him "extremely charismatic," she recalled in the summer of 2020. That could be disqualifying, she knew. On the other hand, Garcetti argued at one point, if Biden needed Florida to win, he would have already lost.

Campaign aides were apoplectic. That Bass was even being considered— "Fairly or unfairly," said Florida-based, Cuban American Democratic consultant and pollster Fernand Amandi, her "history on this subject makes Bernie Sanders look like Ronald Reagan"—opened Biden up to the very argument about communism in Florida that Trump had been hoping for.

———

A sense that Harris's chances were narrowing, that Biden was looking for an alternative, started to spread. Donna Brazile, who served as the interim chair of the DNC when it nearly fell apart in 2016 after the first big Russian hack of that campaign, and the rest of the group who called themselves the Colored Girls—other longtime party operatives Minyon Moore, Leah Daughtry, and Yolanda Caraway—reached out, saying they wanted to share their perspective. The committee assumed they wanted to push for a Black woman, and the only

Black woman they talked about was Harris. Some on the vetting committee felt that the call was so over the top that they were put off a little.

They weren't the only ones thrown. Bass heard about the call and reached out to say she would have appreciated the Colored Girls saying something nice about her too. "We didn't realize you were in consideration," she was told.

Still bruised by how her presidential run had collapsed, determined to come off steadier, and aware that close Biden aides and the larger political world felt she still had atoning to do for her attacks at that first debate, Harris was being careful. The police reform bill was an amazing opportunity: she could reclaim her law enforcement experience as a strength rather than the liability that helped sink her presidential campaign, and she could use it to get herself on TV so Biden and the vetting committee could see how she performed, how she grabbed attention on the Senate floor, and the reaction she could generate from a calibrated tweet. Harris knew that she was the odds-on favorite to be the pick. She needed to appear as if she were the one person in the country who didn't know that to be the case, so Biden wouldn't worry about looking over his shoulder on the morning after the inauguration, wondering how she might be trying to position herself to run in 2024.

"You and I both know at the end of the day it's going to be a group of guys in a room going over polls," Harris said to one of her political allies early out. "They know I'm here. It won't help to have people in the media organizing a pressure campaign."

Behind the scenes was a different story. Aides reached out to reporters to tick through the details of her poll numbers: She was strong with African Americans, especially women, and particularly strong with white suburban women, including progressives; she had an appeal among millennials, particularly those of color. The focus groups, an adviser said, called her "smart," "tough," "strong." Women were impressed that she had risen to the level she had. The whole "she's a cop" line was nowhere near as big in reality as it had been when Harris's very online aides had obsessed over how many tweets it inspired in the primary. "We understand that Joe Biden's the nominee, but the party is so much different than a septuagenarian white male," one adviser said in early May. "There is a sense that the party needs to be more reflective of who its voters are."

Al Sharpton had been very proudly out front in saying that he thought the choice should be a Black woman. Then he went a step further, telling a reporter that he was thinking of making the unusual move of endorsing in the running-mate process—and that he was thinking of endorsing Abrams. Maya Harris called, pressuring him to hold off. They'd known each other since Harris was San Francisco DA, the senator's sister reminded him, so he shouldn't turn away from her now. *That was part of the problem*, Sharpton thought, as he was looking for a more head-on discussion of race and inequity: "Kamala was more like Barack. She felt it, but didn't feel it was her role to be the advocate," he'd observe later. Abrams seemed to Sharpton more comfortable being out front on the issues, and he'd been talking her up publicly since they were together with Biden in church in Selma in March, when he joked from the pulpit that he said he was glad to see "our vice president" in the congregation. ("I'm talking about Stacey, not you, Joe," Sharpton said, to which Biden mouthed, "I know.")

But Maya leaned hard on Sharpton, stressing how good her sister's chances were, warning him how much damage he could do by going out on a limb for Abrams, whom everyone knew would be a stretch for Biden to pick. He agreed to hold off.

The war was on. Warren backers prepared and circulated opposition research, hoping to instigate stories about Harris that would scare the Biden team off. One document, sourced mostly to left-wing outlets, ran for more than nineteen pages, covering everything from direct-mail pieces in Harris's 2003 district attorney campaign to details of her controversial cases as attorney general. Early on, it suggested that Harris was a hypocrite for having condemned Jeffrey Epstein, citing what was an absurd stretch of a connection: that her husband had appeared at a fundraiser at a law firm that represented the infamous pedophile. On its final page, the document hit Harris for all the different positions she had taken on Medicare for All over the years.

In June, sensing that the Floyd protests were shifting the attention away from the pandemic response that had seemed like Warren's most effective way to edge out Harris, one hundred of her supporters went more public—including Jane Fonda; the historian Rick Perlstein; Warren's former Harvard Law colleague Larry Tribe; and Sunrise Movement cofounder Evan Weber—with an open letter in *The Washington Post* detailing all the reasons why Biden should pick her. Then Tribe followed up with an interview in which he was more explicit: "I think African Americans above all would be the first to say they are more interested in results than cosmetics." Tribe later apologized for using the word "cosmetics," which felt dismissive of skin color, given what was happening.

The attacks on Harris were now coming from California too. Dianne Feinstein, the other state senator, had never liked Harris, and was taking shots at her, as was Barbara Boxer, whose retirement opened the seat that Harris now occupied, to the point that Biden was left asking around how she could be so unpopular in her own state.

Right as the process was peaking at the end of June, still-bitter Biden aides texted around to one another to mark the one-year anniversary of the hell Harris had brought down on them in the first debate. One sarcastically announced that morning on a phone call, "You know what today is? It's the one year anniversary of 'That Little Girl Was Me.'" The vetting committee leaned in hard during their interviews with her, remembering what a mess her presidential campaign had been. None of her presidential campaign aides would be allowed to join her staff, they told her. There would be no role for her family. They'd set the schedule. They'd set the parameters. All this was conveyed to her with an edge.

The process dragged on for so long that a *Politico* story broke about a donor's blabbing that Dodd had been upset when Harris waved off her run-in with Biden at the first debate as just politics. Harris's advisers had been trying to get her not to say that, in public or private, ever since her preparation for an appearance with Stephen Colbert in June. She kept doing it. "It was a debate!" Harris told Colbert, deploying her laugh. What she was supposed to say was a more sober, "We were all fighting for the same thing."

Her supporters went on alert. Eleni Kounalakis, the daughter of a wealthy developer and now the lieutenant governor of California, rustled up every prominent Californian she could get, convinced that they could each do two minutes in a video conference with the committee to pressure them to understand the *real* Kamala. Kounalakis said that Harris endorsed her in a crowded field, helped make her the first female lieutenant governor of California. Robert Garcia, the mayor of Long Beach, said that Harris had been the first person to call him after his mother died of COVID-19. London Breed, the mayor of San Francisco, talked about how it was the job of DAs to put bad guys in jail. The call went on for so long that members of the committee started looking for excuses to get off.

They and the others who'd reached out were convinced they'd saved Harris. The people on the campaign and the vetting committee were annoyed that it had come to this. Biden didn't like being cornered or the extra drama that seemed to come with Harris.

"They didn't save Kamala. She didn't need saving," said one person who talked to members of the vetting committee about the call. "It was thought of as amateurish and kind of silly."

———

None of the prospects were knocked out by the opposition research dives overseen by the campaign's main lawyer, Bob Bauer. The biggest surprise was discovering that Bass owned two handguns. The Biden campaign and the vetting committee couldn't help but notice that, given they were examining a group of women, there wasn't much by way of political scandal—financial or personal—beyond Harris's well-known 1990s relationship with former San Francisco mayor Willie Brown. Brown was jealously talking and writing about her in his local newspaper column, but then, after realizing that he hadn't sunk her, wrote a column with his oh-so-friendly advice that she shouldn't say yes if Biden offered her the job.

The timeline was set, and almost immediately started to slip. Biden, because he's Biden, kept pushing off the decision, and went on having more conversations. More interviews. More staff check-ins. More document requests. Accepting more invitations to appear at virtual fundraisers, to see how many people signed up, how much money they brought in. Biden's vision had been to use the vetting process to elevate as many women as possible, boost their careers. Because it dragged on so long, with political reporters stuck in lockdown with nothing else to do and no other story to chase, many of the women were left feeling the veepstakes were more like a pageant. "This is a horrible, horrible process," Warren said to Harris, when they ran into each other at the Capitol, where John Lewis laid in state a few weeks before Biden made the pick.

Tammy Duckworth, the punchy senator from Illinois who'd lost both her legs in a helicopter crash while in Iraq with the National Guard (it was Duckworth who came up with the infamous Trump nickname Cadet Bone Spurs), shot up in consideration for a moment when Trump responded to the Floyd protests by trying to make the area around the White House a secret police state. But the Biden campaign couldn't get around that she was born in Thailand, not America. Maybe if Trump wasn't the birtherism maestro, the prospect of the inevitable lawsuits wouldn't have felt so overwhelming. Given his past history and his hold on the Republican Party, they feared every GOP secretary of state in the country would have sued, Trump lawyers and everyone on Fox claiming the whole ballot was invalid. They were going to have enough problems as it was.

Biden had recently been falling more and more for Gretchen Whitmer. He liked how she'd been handling the pandemic. He appreciated the way she reached out during the Tara Reade trouble. He was impressed by how firmly she'd been standing up to Trump's bullying. Biden felt confident that he could win back Michigan and Wisconsin—realistically, this was the core of why he was running—but putting Whitmer on the ticket would solidify it.

Being part of the public speculation made Whitmer nervous. She had seen up close how petty Trump was at the White House dinner a year earlier when he'd been making fun of Rick Perry, and she worried he might cancel orders for masks and gloves and testing supplies just to stick it to her if she was picked. Every time her name was mentioned, her office was tracking spikes in smears online against her and her family. Death threats came in. Security was stepped up. She called Pence to ask him to help bring down the heat. She called the Republican leaders of the state legislature in Michigan too, hoping they might be able to get through to the president on a pure *this-could-hurt-your-reelection-chances* appeal. Nothing changed. Biden wanted to help, but any comment he made only left her a bigger target for Trump, and for the crazies.

Not long after Whitmer had driven to the state emergency operations center for a COVID-19 briefing, Biden called to ask her to be vetted. At first, she thought he was asking her to be on the vetting committee, and she was going to turn him down, given all the work she had to do. She didn't feel as if she could refuse when he asked for the vetting, but she was firm with the vetting committee what her parameters were: "I'm interested—but I need to have you make a decision quickly. I don't want this to linger. I've got a job to do in Michigan." Her staff started turning over every floor speech she had ever given in the state legislature, every statement. They put together twenty years of tax returns, including having to go to her first husband to help fill in some of the gaps.

On May 20, five days before George Floyd was killed, flooding burst the dams in Midland County, northwest of Saginaw. It was too much for Whitmer. COVID-19 was ravaging her state. The situation with the White House had cooled but not improved. Now ten thousand people were being evacuated. She was on her way to a helicopter to survey the damage and decided to call Biden and ask to be pulled out. "I've got my hands full here," she told him. Biden listened and said he wanted her to stay in, but he'd accept her decision, urging her to just take the night to think about it and call him tomorrow.

Whitmer hashed out what to do with a few close advisers. "Your winning is the most important thing," she told Biden when she returned the call. "If you think I'm the one that you want by your side, I'll do it." Biden thanked her for agreeing to stick in it.

Susan Rice started out as more of a theoretical discussion, a reflection in part of how few prominent Black women there were in the party other than Harris. She didn't believe the interest in her was serious at first, but the pandemic changed that. Since the spring, Biden had been getting darker and darker about what was ahead. Hundreds of thousands dead. An economic crisis that would further destabilize an already teetering country. White nationalists and rioters, and who knows what Trump would do if he lost? If America was going to be burning throughout his presidency, Biden thought, then Rice's national security experience and her famous toughness, which often got her in trouble with the thinner skinned, might be exactly what he'd need. He knew her, liked her, knew how to work with her, knew she had the executive branch experience to back him up.

Biden's advisers started out dismissing Rice's chance of getting picked as nothing more than media noise—until the responses from the focus groups started coming in. Clips of Rice speaking and information presented about her were testing better than those of any of the other options for being ready to do the job, being ready to step in as president. Not really registering was the Republican mania over her supposed role in the 2012 Benghazi embassy attack—a lingering legacy from when, to preserve her own political future, Clinton refused to make a round of Sunday show appearances to discuss the attack and Rice had been sent in her place. Rice's mother told her it felt like a setup, but Rice didn't have the luxury of turning down an assignment from the White House.

Each round of interviews made Rice more interested, until the point that she wanted it. In those final days before the choice was named, she was very much in *bring it* mode. It was a perfect chance to turn the games Republicans had been playing back on them, she thought. If, after so many Americans were dead of COVID-19 "because of this president's ineptitude and incompetence and disregard for human life, putting his own political interests above the health and well-being and the economy of the United States and the ability to educate our kids," she said on the Friday afternoon before Biden made his decision, "they're going to talk about Benghazi? I say fine, let them."

Warren allies became worried enough that they started circulating dissections of Rice's finances, pulled from public disclosures still on the internet from her eight years of working for Obama. The money her husband had inherited made her the wealthiest of the potential picks. There were too many stocks in too many questionable companies to pass the progressive purity test, they insisted. Other stories started to circulate among reporters, coming after her for her "temperament," for her record in Africa when she was at the State Department in Bill Clinton's second term. Everyone involved worried about how much of a distraction these and more would prove if she was picked.

Rice is unusual for having spent so much time in the thick of politics without ever having been considered as a potential candidate herself. With what she had been through so far, she felt ready for Republicans to attack her. She assumed the Sanders wing would take shots at her because she wasn't one of theirs. But she started to suspect that some of the attacks had their roots in Harris's longtime consultants back in San Francisco. Rice knew Harris, liked her, had donated to her presidential campaign, had talked her through a couple of foreign policy issues that came up along the way. This felt like betrayal, but even deeper, more disappointing.

Rice is a pretty direct person. She called Harris to complain. Cut it out. Call him off. Harris said she would, that she hadn't known anything about it. She never followed up with Smith.

———

Up in Martha's Vineyard for a long, weird pandemic summer, Obama kept landing on a formulation: if Biden could count on winning, Rice would probably be prepared for the job. She knew national security, she knew the White House, she knew Biden—and she almost definitely wasn't going to run for president herself. That was the catch, Obama would explain: Biden couldn't count on winning, and Harris knew how to campaign, knew how to debate, and all the problematic stories about her had come out already.

Rice, Duckworth, Harris, and Warren all called Obama to check in, rationalizing that they knew him already, so he might not think they were trying to work him. "What else can I be doing?" they'd ask, as if Obama were keeping track of the cable news schedules and volunteer shifts to know who needed to be plugged in where. Sanders called too, though he avoided the running-mate topic specifically, instead focusing on his worries that Biden was losing the left and Latinos, and that Trump wouldn't leave office if he lost.

Biden kept calling. Over and over he'd go on to Obama about re-creating what they had—the partnership, the family friendship, where he was the trusted adviser and their wives were close, and Obama's children and Biden's grandchildren had sleepovers together. Yes, but they hadn't started out that way, Obama reminded him. That took time. Biden had idealized it into some kind of bromantic courtship. Obama had been impressed by some of his primary debate performances in their race, but his aides spent the summer of 2008 cross-referencing polls and focus group readouts against electoral map math to conclude he was a smart political matchup. Biden was fine with forgiving Harris for going after him in the debate—"He's the only Irishman who doesn't hold a grudge," Dunn said of him—but he worried that their past would get in the way of forming the intimate relationship he wanted to re-create. Obama tried not to have a choice of his own, but he nudged Biden to move on. "You called me unqualified to be president," Obama reminded him. Being aggressive on the debate stage didn't define relationships. That was a skill set of its own, he said, and maybe one he'd like to have come the fall.

"Only you can decide on the chemistry," Garcetti told Biden in one of their calls. "But if you can work out the chemistry, she seems like a great choice. She's vetted. She meets the moment, you have a relationship with her deeper than most."

Biden and Harris found more reasons to connect. He had been inspired into politics by the civil rights movement; she was a child of parents who marched with her in civil rights protests. He had been a single father; she was raised by a single mother. His father had all sorts of sayings he quoted all the time; her mother had all sorts of sayings she quoted all the time. They both felt the injustices of Trump's America acutely, in different, complementary ways.

Still, everyone waited. A small team on Biden's campaign put together full rollout plans for eleven options—logos, spreadsheets with a combined hundreds of names of references they could point reporters to, talking points prewritten for what they assumed would be the first set of attacks each woman might face, videos to post online as soon as Biden picked. A more in-depth version was prepared for just six: Harris, Whitmer, Warren, Rice, Bass, and Abrams, with the understanding that some of those names were included as subterfuge, in case a process that had once again proven almost completely leak-free started to burst. The real finalists were just the first four. And really, just the first two. Warren didn't make the final cut because Biden's aides were worried she didn't create enough of a contrast to how old Biden was, and were concerned that if she was selected, Democrats might lose her Senate seat. Rice was ruled out because they were worried about just how much they were willing to risk on a first-time candidate, given how uncertain everything about the next few months was going to be.

Abrams and her inner circle were a little surprised when she learned that she wasn't the pick. "If you look at what we were able to accomplish in Georgia, the growth of the numbers and the composition of the voters," she said in April, referring to her 2018 run for governor, "I would put my capacity to win an election as the VP running mate alongside anyone's."

Biden invited Harris and Whitmer one last time to Delaware, the only prospects he met with in person twice. At his home by the beach in Rehoboth—"the house that Beau paid for," Biden calls it, because the money came from the advance for the book he wrote about the years when his son was dying—he started the conversation with Whitmer by turning to his wife. "Jilly," he said, "the governor's mom died of the same brain tumor that killed Beau."

Two days before Biden announced Harris, he called Clyburn. A decision that he originally said would be made the first week in August had drifted already well into the second week. He knew, he knew, Biden told Clyburn, and though he was almost there, he was struggling. "I'm torn," he said, "between my head and my heart." Go spend a little time by yourself, Clyburn suggested, and see if you can reconcile the two.

His head—all the advice, all the input from his advisers, all the data from the polls and the focus groups—was clearly with Harris. Her friendship with Beau finally helped him connect her to his heart.

"There's something very poetic, but also very resolving about it," Garcetti said. "He was at peace with his decision, he was reconnected to the reason that his campaign existed, in his mind."

Biden called Clyburn again. He was going with Harris.

The power failed in the high school gym while Harris was practicing her speech. Part of her tendency for overpreparation is rehearsing big speeches while standing at a model podium, repeating the lines over and over. When the lights went off, she was only halfway through the text written for her, getting comfortable with the phrases, shifting some around to make them her own. No time to finish. As soon as the power came back, they'd have to get started. She couldn't make Biden late, they told her. They had to check her makeup.

Her husband, Doug Emhoff, forever the goofy cheerleader for his wife and never quite believing the world of politics he'd stumbled into after marrying her when she was already attorney general and he was already fifty, with two kids from his first marriage and a successful career as an entertainment lawyer in LA, began taking photos on his phone and immediately started tweeting, just as he'd done when she was running for president. Biden aides told him to stop—there was an official photographer. The Biden campaign would decide what to release.

Just before they went out, the two couples had a congratulatory huddle, not holding to the social distancing they kept to on the other side of the curtain. The few staff who came for the moment stayed backstage. No family was allowed in the room.

As expected as the choice of Harris was, she clearly rattled the brains of Trump and many around him. Immediately, Trump attacked her as being a "radical liberal," which was news to all the Sanders supporters, who two years earlier had seen her presidential campaign as a threat. Trump and his acolytes

launched low-grade attacks of mispronouncing her first name and the nou-
veau birtherism of suggesting maybe she wasn't eligible to run for president
because her parents were both immigrants.

That was the noise on the outside. Inside the school, a few reporters were
positioned in the white paper social-distancing circles the campaign laid out
at every event. There were no Biden–Harris signs—the only place the new logo
appeared other than its official unveiling at the podium was on photocopied
signs pointing to the bathroom. The Pointer Sisters' "Yes We Can Can" played
as they waited to come out: "I know we can make it. / I know darn well we can
work it out." All the state flags were set up behind them, freshly steamed, except for Mississippi's—the state legislature was in the process of picking a
new one after having decided, amid the George Floyd protests, to replace its
Reconstruction-era design with the Confederate battle flag in the corner.

With Harris seated on a chair behind him, Biden read out her record. He
talked about climate change. He talked about Charlottesville. He integrated a
phrase that had been central to her old stump speeches, that America was at
"an inflection point."

Just before he brought her up to the microphone, he talked about what went
deeper.

"Kamala, you've been an honorary Biden for quite some time," he said, and
she put her hand briefly over her heart. "I came first to know who Kamala was
through our son Beau Biden. They were friends. They served as attorneys general at the same time. They took on the same big fights together. I know how
much Beau respected Kamala and her work. And that mattered a lot to me, to
be honest with you, as I made this decision."

She took a big breath as he introduced her and broke out in a smile. A production assistant placed a stool behind the podium for her to stand on.

Harris spoke about the ambitious women who had come before her, including her mother. She talked about being a prosecutor, said "the case against
Donald Trump and Mike Pence is open and shut. Just look where they've gotten us."

"Let me just tell you about Beau Biden," Harris said. She described the
mortgage settlement, the money they'd won, getting to know him on all those
phone calls. Biden stared down in thought, arms crossed. "He really was the

best of us. And when I would ask him where'd you get that, where did this come from? He'd always talk about his dad."

Backstage, aides watched on the TVs. It was the first time in the campaign that all the cable networks were taking Biden live. They applauded from behind the curtains, so that at least the candidates heard some support. After all that time in the basement, all that time stuck in the limbo of a pseudocampaign, *Holy shit*, they told each other, *this is real*.

"This is the end of what was a long speculation game," is how one of the aides involved in the process on the Biden campaign described it. "The visualization of Biden and her together was a way for people to envision what would be possible, and to envision the contrast to Trump–Pence even more starkly."

CHAPTER TWENTY-THREE

YOU HAVE GOT TO BE KIDDING

I'm willing to give a nod to divine providence here. There is such a confluence of issues, so many crises that are landing in one time, certainly the economic fallout that has come about because of a brand of fear and a response to a virus that has already killed close to two hundred thousand Americans, and many more around the world. We have this great reckoning that is going on as far as who we are as a people, about our diversity. That there is an election that's going on here in 2020 is almost like, that's when you got to give a nod of the head that something bigger might be at work right here, and there is a chance for a reckoning. Every election comes along, and you can always make the argument, "This is the most important election of our lives." *This* is the most important election in the history of America.

—TOM HANKS, BIDEN FUNDRAISER, AUGUST 2020

August 2020–September 2020

For a tiny, tiny moment, when he'd gotten lost in the fireworks, standing in a parking lot with a mask on, holding his wife's hand, Biden was happy. He finally had the presidential nomination he'd been chasing for forty years, across three campaigns he ran and three more he almost ran. When he won, it was without all the cheering at a convention center. Without a balloon drop, and instead, watching his grandchildren running around him with party poppers in an isolated high school library, waiting to be told which camera to smile into when he accepted. The prize without the ceremony. The acclamation without the acclaim. Shrouded in a sense of mourning. Incomplete. Imperfect. A Biden nomination.

For Harris's speech the night before, the organizers had set up the floor in front of her like a model ghost convention, placards for each state delegation in what might have been the right spots, if they had all been in an arena, if there had been anyone from the actual delegations there. They showed up on the Twitter accounts of the handful of reporters who were allowed into the room for her speech, after three days of COVID-19 tests, temperature checks, mask requirements, pledges to keep isolated from anyone else. Ahead of Biden's speech, staff had moved the placards to the room next door for a TV-ready shot, spacing them along a corridor of state flags that the two candidates could walk down together, now friends again, and into the parking lot full of cars for the drive-in convention and fireworks show on a little stage, set off from everyone.

At least he got to bring the whole country home to Delaware. After a few minutes standing on the stage, he couldn't resist savoring having the crowd. He crouched down and briefly pulled down his mask, talking to the reporters because they were the only Americans he could get close enough to talk to anymore.

"Welcome to Wilmington!" he said, with a smile.

The real upside for Biden was that the virtual convention left no room for protests or demonstrations or even any of the scheduled speakers veering off script. Warren's staff subtly spelling out BLM in toy letters on a shelf behind her at the school where she had recorded her own speech was the biggest deviation from the script. The DNC had spent months planning for how to head off a showdown with Sanders before the pandemic hit—locking down the procedures around a floor fight for the nomination, lining up managers like Denis McDonough to head off the contested convention methadone of a platform fight. They didn't need to activate any of those plans. And for all the candidates like John Delaney, who came asking when to expect the speaking slot they assumed they would get, organizers had the perfect excuse to say no: hey, there were only two hours of programming. Rather than being a problem or a public presence, Sanders kept quietly working with Anita Dunn and Ron Klain behind the scenes, advising them on where he saw them failing to connect with young people and Latinos.

Democrats had more to work out about bigger issues than they ever had during the primary campaign, more questions about what America's future was supposed to look like and how Biden was going to guide his party through. None of that came up at the convention. No walkouts. No real conversations. Even the platform fight never extended beyond a few hundred delegates announcing they wouldn't support a document that didn't include Medicare for All, but it was easily passed anyway. Nothing about restricting aid to Israel went in. Or legalizing marijuana. Or about addressing police funding. Party platforms are pure symbolism, never read and certainly not binding—but as a symbol, this was one of Biden, whom the loudest activists in the party never wanted, getting exactly what he wanted.

"Can any of you here truly stand up and say, 'My party is the party of the principles?'" Black Lives Matter cofounder Patrisse Cullors said into her computer camera at the end of July, in one of the virtual meetings leading up to the convention. "The Democratic Party of today will be remembered as the party of complicity. The party that refused to sacrifice its own creature comforts and material securities to ensure it walked the walk."

Even this sentiment had dissipated by the time the convention got started. That first night, in a pretaped address, Michelle Obama set the tone: Obama nostalgia stood in contrast to "whenever we look to this White House for some leadership or consolation or any semblance of steadiness, what we get instead is chaos, division, and a total and utter lack of empathy." She did a turn on her optimistic urging in 2016, "When they go low, we go high," to say, "Let's be clear: going high does not mean putting on a smile and saying nice things when confronted by viciousness and cruelty." At the core of her speech was a learned bitterness, a thought-by-thought rebuttal of her husband's 2004 convention talk. "There's not a liberal America and a conservative America," he had said. "There's not a black America and white America and Latino America and Asian America; there's the United States of America. The pundits like to slice and dice our country into red states and blue states: red states for Republicans, blue states for Democrats." He was in a roaring convention hall in Boston. She sat alone in a socially distanced room after a summer of COVID-19 fatalities and police shooting deaths. "I understand that my message won't be heard by some people," she said. "We live in a nation that is deeply divided, and I am a Black woman speaking at the Democratic Convention."

Obama's speech two nights later jolted all but the few who knew how concerned he'd become. He stood by himself at the Museum of the American Revolution in Philadelphia, a few blocks from where he had been the night before the 2016 election. Then, with thirty thousand people and Clinton and Springsteen, he said he still believed what he'd said in his 2004 convention speech, that "I'm still as optimistic as ever about our future." Four years later, he placed himself in front of an exhibit about the Constitution—he helped frame the camera angles himself so that "We the People" would be above his shoulder—and lamented, "None of this should be controversial. These shouldn't be Republican principles or Democratic principles. They're American principles. But at this moment, this president and those who enable him, have shown they don't believe in these things." Obama was dark. He was somber. "That's what's at stake right now," he said. "Our democracy."

Overall the convention went smoothly, months of production stress coming together in flashy video packages. The biggest hiccup of the week was on the third night, when Kerry Washington's remote emcee duties were almost canceled because someone at the studio in Los Angeles tested positive for COVID-19, and the whole place had to be shut down for a few hours. A very un-Hollywood Tom Perez prepped for last-minute fill-in duties from Milwaukee until they finished a full clean. The big drama revolved around Julián Castro complaining about the party having forgotten about Latinos, mostly because they hadn't given him a speaking spot. In fact, Anita Dunn had ruled him out because he waited until June to endorse Biden, and he responded by claiming that he didn't have the time on his schedule to participate in group videos with the other losing candidates.

The more-popular-on-Twitter drama, though, was focused on Linda Sarsour. A hijab-wearing Arab American activist who'd first gotten attention while supporting Sanders in 2016, she then cochaired the Women's March in 2017, but was forced out after her anti-Israel comments earned her a reputation as an anti-Semite. On a Zoom call for the Muslim Delegates and Allies Coalition— a minor event which probably would have passed by if not for the controversy— Sarsour said that Trump had driven her to Biden and the Democrats, even though she wanted to be a Sanders hold-out. "It is absolutely our party in this moment," she said. The Trump allies leaped, trying to make it sound as if she had been given a primetime speaking slot, and the Biden campaign panicked with a statement from rapid-response director Andrew Bates disavowing Sarsour and everything she stood for: "She has no role in the Biden campaign whatsoever." The statement almost never went out. *Don't you know how many Twitter followers she has?* asked some of the staff who'd joined after the primary. The concerns were overruled, and the statement was released. Fringe supporters who needed to be answered for and living in fear of Twitter were largely avoided by the Biden campaign during the primaries. Just as in the internal fights over his support for defunding the police, too many people who had never wanted Biden to be the nominee were trying to make him into the nominee they wanted.

But the rest of the Democratic convention had worked: the Billie Eilish music video, the video roll call of the state delegations with the guy from Rhode Island standing silently wearing a mask and holding a plate of calamari, the minidocumentaries that humanized Biden and humanized climate change, gun control, and DACA.

The Republican convention, meanwhile, was a predictable stream of hysterics, actual yelling, outright lies, a Möbius slogan offered first by Pence, then Trump—"Make America great again, again"—and an acceptance speech by the president that dragged and rambled and for some reason mentioned Buffalo Bill. He delivered it to a packed crowd on the White House lawn in a demonstration that he didn't care about exposing his own supporters to COVID-19 and certainly didn't care about any of the laws meant to prevent the White House and its resources from being used as a political prop. In 2016, Trump was the ultimate outsider who was promising "I alone can fix it." In 2020, he was sitting inside the White House gates, the country spiraling out of control, and complaining about what everyone else was doing.

Biden and his aides felt confident that his own theory of the election was right, that he was appealing to voters, breaking through. His headier and headier advisers loved taking advantage of that contrast. Donors complaining? Their response: Did they really want to risk Trump's winning again by holding back their money because they couldn't get a phone call from the candidate, or some basic competence in a thank-you? Reporters complaining? Their response: Did they really want to think about what would happen to press freedom if Trump won again by being mad that Biden refused to sit for an interview? When politicians complained about something he wasn't doing, their response was: Did they want to risk the decimation of the party and the country by not turning out whatever constituents they could just because they weren't getting enough attention? Many days, the slogan might as well have been "Joe Biden: Deal with It."

Biden was up 7 points before the conventions, and up around 7 points after the conventions. He was at a 50 percent approval rating. Trump couldn't seem to break 43 percent. Trump was running out of chances to change the trajectory of the election.

———

Mandela Barnes was sitting out by a lake in Wisconsin reading a book, trying to get centered for the week ahead. He was thirty-three, Black, the lieutenant governor whose spot on the ticket had helped drive turnout in Milwaukee to elect the bland, white, former schools superintendent Tony Evers as governor in the 2018 midterms—knocking out Democrats' bête rouge Scott Walker, whose 2010 election and the union busting that followed were a harbinger of Trump's turning of the Midwest.

Barnes hadn't supported Biden in the primaries. During the Floyd protests, he had tried to reconcile himself to journalists expecting him to be a spokesman for all Black people in the Midwest because he was a Black man with a title. He put the book down, scanned Twitter on his phone. Kenosha was trending. Kenosha was never trending. He tapped through and watched the video of Jacob Blake being shot seven times. *You have got to be kidding*, he thought. *This did not just happen.* "The audacity that I saw in that video, for an officer to shoot a person in the back seven times—after all of this, after all the marches, after all the demonstrations, after all the protests," Barnes said a few days later. "Everybody seemingly coming together to acknowledge that this is a crisis that we face and have faced for some time, that this could still happen."

Trump saw a new opening to shout "law and order" and rev up fears. This, he started to say, was what America would be like under Biden—never mind the pretzel logic, because this was what America *was already* like under Trump.

Biden told his advisers that Trump was onto something. Biden dismissed polls showing that Kenosha wasn't making an impact. Biden was seeing all these things through the eyes of the guys he'd grown up knowing in Scranton and the conservative voters in Delaware he'd been catering to when he opposed busing. "He had real concerns that there was a potentially persuasive argument in what Trump was saying," said Bedingfield. "It was disingenuous and racist—but it could work." Once again, Biden was stuck trying to navigate running for president while also being the voice that the country needed to hear.

Biden called Harris. This was the first crisis since she had joined the ticket, and he wanted to bring her into the decision about what to do, the way he had dreamed their partnership would work. That this was a crisis about race, and that she had been picked in part because she was Black, made him even more eager to hear from her.

Harris launched into a speech about how the campaign needed to start knocking on doors, doing more outreach in the field, even with the pandemic. Black voters in Milwaukee and Detroit weren't seeing the online advertising the campaign was running, she said. They needed to hear from the campaign.

Biden was confused, a little annoyed. He wasn't focused on campaign mechanics. He was trying to talk to his running mate about how to keep the country from coming apart, from Trump pulling off his greatest misdirection yet and beating them by making a race that should have been about hundreds of thousands of Americans dead from a mismanaged pandemic instead about scattered violence in the streets.

Harris's caution and uneven self-confidence often manifest when a prominent squeaky wheel sends her a nervous text or email that sets her off with a new obsession, asking staff to follow up with more information, bringing up whatever the question is with whomever she is talking to. She will get sent an article by a donor and go down a rabbit hole for days. She's especially prone to this on issues related to race. From the moment Harris was picked, even before Blake was shot, her phone was filling up with worries and imperative suggestions—from Jay-Z, from the national head of the Alpha Kappa Alpha Black female sorority, of which she had been a proud member since her time at Howard. Many were still coming to terms themselves with Biden being the nominee. Did Biden need to do more to disavow his work on the crime bill? Harris wondered. Should she call for a Department of Justice investigation into the killing of Breonna Taylor?

Because Biden had asked Harris to be his running mate by video call, she had only spent a few socially distanced hours with him since having been picked. Concerns about how she managed her own presidential campaign meant that she was assigned staff by the Biden team rather than having a circle she trusted, and the pandemic complicated getting close with the new crew. She felt isolated, convinced she had to solve the campaign's issues with Black voters by herself, that part of her role was to be that bridge to problems that the operatives in charge couldn't see.

Harris wasn't the only one worried—Sanders, who told aides he thought Harris was a smart political choice, reached out to Dunn and Ron Klain to say he was worried that Biden wasn't connecting with progressives, young voters, or Latinos.

Biden and his top aides were confident that questions about the crime bill had been settled in the primary. Harris was not. Biden believed he had demonstrated his Black support. Harris was convinced that, outside of those committed primary voters, he had not—and she was reluctant to accept that he continued polling higher with Black voters than she was.

She had only ever run in California, and then in her presidential primary flop. She didn't have a sense of how to appeal to a broader, less left-leaning electorate, or a frame of reference for what a large general election campaign looked like. She came in thinking Biden's team didn't have a plan. Biden's team bucked, telling her to trust them, that she didn't know the full extent of what was happening.

O'Malley Dillon set up briefings for Harris with top staff and their consultants to walk her through the campaign's thinking and plans already under way, attempting to calm the tension through reassurance. Harris never fully got past feeling as if she were being boxed in and controlled, and she continued to push Biden further left than he wanted to go—such as on questions of how much to restrict police from using force—but she did eventually begin to adjust. She and Biden started speaking daily. She grew to be fiercely protective of him. She was still concerned about the campaign operations. Into the final weeks, she was chipping in with her own thoughts on election protection, based on her own first race for attorney general in 2010. That one had stretched on for weeks as the mail-in votes caught up to early returns that initially favored her opponent so much that the race was briefly called for him.

First, though, Biden had to figure out what to do about Kenosha. The voices in Harris's ear were urging her to go, to make the stand for the campaign, be the face of it. No, she was told. Biden was the one running for president. He couldn't let Harris be the answer to Trump's visit there. He couldn't let it look as if the white guy just sent his new Black running mate.

Evers seemed overwhelmed by the events in Kenosha. He told Trump not to come, and told Biden the same. The governor was coming off like a deer in headlights, Biden started saying, so he called the lieutenant governor. "You should come," Barnes told him. Trump was clearly out to stir up anger, he said, and "I think there's an opportunity to be the adult in the room."

"Who can you get in the room for me?" Biden asked. He wanted an interfaith event. Barnes said he'd come up with a list of representatives from the community, including a Black Lives Matter activist, and made a few suggestions about faith leaders who could come together at the Grace Lutheran Church. Biden was adamant that they include a Catholic priest. "You see where I'm going with this?"

Yeah, Barnes said, he saw. There weren't many Black Catholics in Wisconsin.

Every day that Biden didn't speak was a day Trump could force his vision deeper into the country's psyche. There wasn't time to wait for a Kenosha trip to be arranged, so Biden and his top advisers rushed a speech. *The obvious place to do it,* Biden thought, *was Pittsburgh, always back to Pittsburgh.* The city had the white working class he knew, the Black voters he connected with. He thought he could speak to both.

In front of a collection of American flags at an empty steel mill on the outskirts of the city, Biden tumbled through a long speech that tied Charlottesville to Minneapolis to Kenosha: "This president long ago forfeited any moral leadership in this country. He can't stop the violence—because for years he has fomented it. He may believe mouthing the words 'law and order' makes him strong, but his failure to call on his own supporters to stop acting as an armed militia in this country shows you how weak he is," he said. "Does anyone believe there will be less violence in America if Donald Trump is re-elected?"

The speech was deliberately built around one central thought: "You know my heart, and you know my story, my family's story. Ask yourself: Do I look to you like a radical socialist with a soft spot for rioters? Really?"

This was the argument, Democrats began to realize, that only Biden could have made, as the old white man who was so well known that this made it clear what he stood for. "In the primaries, the attack was 'Joe Biden is milquetoast, he's boring, he's safe,'" said a top campaign aide. "That ends up being the narrative that ends up countering in the most beautiful way Trump's attacks that Biden is owned by socialists and cozying up to Antifa. It didn't make any sense."

Voters were now saying that they trusted Biden more on who wouldn't be a radical, and who could manage law and order. "The irony," Biden's top strategist Mike Donilon said of Trump at the time, "is even inside the definition he would like to set for this race, he is losing."

━━━━━

The Kenosha speech on Monday resonated as deeply as aides had hoped. Biden was now back on the attack, pushing Trump on the pandemic, on the economy. On Friday, he scheduled a press conference in Wilmington to discuss what was now looking like a "K-shaped" recovery, "a fancy phrase for what's wrong with everything about Trump's presidency," where the rich got richer and everyone else got more frantic.

Biden got distracted while shaving that morning by shots of John McCain on MSNBC, and of Trump claiming that he'd never said anything like "suckers" and "losers" about dead marines, as had been reported in an *Atlantic* article.

Sucker. Loser. He looked over at Beau's gold star. It was not an actual Gold Star—Beau had died in a hospital bed, not the battlefield—but one that the Delaware National Guard made as a special honor after his funeral. Most days Biden kept it in his pocket, Beau always with him on the trail, running this race with him. He didn't trust himself with it today. *Sucker. Loser.* The campaign had set him up to speak at a community center downtown as the pointed backdrop to talk about the jobs numbers, but he knew it was also where his daughter had worked for a bit as a social worker, had seen in his briefing prep that Beau had come through for an event when he was attorney general. Biden had been in that gym before it was the only room in the building that was pandemic-safe, walked up the same stairs from the street, and had probably stood in that very spot on the stage.

A sign from the community center's track team read: ABOVE EXPECTATIONS. That was not the mood. "I'm always cautioned not to lose my temper. This may be as close as I've come in this campaign," Biden said into the camera. The script in the teleprompter read: "Another crisis that President Trump continues to ignore." Biden was usually very careful about addressing Trump as "president," a way of holding respect and holding himself back. This time he skipped it: "Another crisis that *Trump* continues to ignore."

When Biden made the battle for the soul of America the theme of his campaign, most of the other Democratic campaigns laughed about it. Soul? This was about real things, real policy changes, digging in with the kind of attention that Biden-style gauzy Democrats had been flopping on for years, promising a "Bridge to the 21st Century" and "Hope" and "Love Trumps Hate," while Republicans drilled into a deliberative, decisive rewiring of the system in DC and the state capitals. Khizr Khan, the immigrant Gold Star father whose son had been killed in the Iraq War and who had become a surprise Democratic celebrity by waving a copy of his pocket Constitution at Trump in a speech at Clinton's convention in 2016, was who the Biden campaign tapped to respond the morning after *The Atlantic* story hit. On a phone call that morning with reporters, he charged that Trump had "the soul of a coward."

Of his own assessment of Trump's soul, Biden said, "I'm going to try to be measured in my response. If it's true, and based on other things he said I believe the article is true, I'd ask you all the rhetorical question: How do you feel? How would you feel if you had a kid in Afghanistan right now? How would you feel if you lost a son, daughter, husband, wife? How would you feel, for real?"

With the plagiarism scandal that hit him in 1987 and the comments he'd made about Obama's being "articulate and bright and clean" in 2007, Biden could blame at least part of the demise of his two presidential campaigns on the press. He had grown accustomed to being beaten up by decades of reporters. Still, he liked reporters, viewing them as members of the elite, educated ranks that he'd always wanted to impress, and respected them as a vital part of the way politics worked when it worked the way it was supposed to. They were the check on standards. They could see this wasn't a presidential race, but a choice between fumbling fascism and not.

Trump was insulting the military, Biden was saying, as if he were just talking to the people in front of him and not in a nationally televised press conference. Even the fair-minded reporters in the room could agree with him that was wrong.

"I know that's not your job to express that feeling, but you know in your heart, you know in your gut, it's deplorable. As I've said many times, I'll say again, these folks are the backbone of America. They're the heart, the soul, the grit, that's what patriotism is about," Biden said. "I've just never been as disappointed in my whole career with a leader that I've worked with, president or otherwise," he went on, calling Trump "absolutely damnable."

He was appalled by a president behaving like this, or bucking up the QAnon conspiracy cult because he didn't know or care to recognize the potential danger of hateful, violent delusions about the deep state and a coven of elites running a pedophile ring. Biden's edge came out with a sharp joke about how anyone who believed in that should get mental health help while they still could under Obamacare. He appealed to the press again to back him up on the absurdity of what he was facing. And then he centered himself again.

"What in God's name are we doing? Look at how it makes us look around the world, it's mortifying, it's embarrassing, and it's dangerous. If the president doesn't know better, which I . . . He has to know better, and my Lord we're in much more trouble than I ever thought we were. It's bizarre," he said. "This can't go on, I mean, this cannot go on. It's a deconstruction of a democratic system, they know it."

———

Most people don't know what the pancreas does—it's not the lungs, the heart, the brain, the stomach, the kidneys. It has a simple, secondary job: to produce the enzymes that break down food, help the rest of the body survive. Technically you can live without it, though without a pancreas, everything becomes an unregulated mess.

Cancer in the pancreas, though, tends to kill. That's what took John Lewis.

By mid-September the cognitive dissonance of the pandemic and the state of the nation in 2020 had set in: America was going to pass two hundred thousand deaths from COVID-19 over the weekend, fires were turning more of the West into a hellscape of burned-down houses and melted playgrounds, and so many storms had hit already that the weather service had dipped into the Greek alphabet for extra names. Amid all that, the country was trying to stay calm, adjusting to new routines of life and work and school that months before would have been unbelievable. Early voting started in a few states, and people were feeling relief that the election was finally taking place, their spirits boosted by the lines around the block at polling places in Virginia. Many were sitting down for Rosh Hashanah dinners. Maybe a weekend on pause from existential crisis.

Neera Tanden, who had contracted and then recovered from COVID-19 months before, even decided to throw herself a little socially distanced birthday party in her backyard. She had turned fifty a week and a half earlier, and it felt like time for a celebration with some of the women who had long ago fuzzed the lines of work and politics and friendship. Stephanie Schriock from EMILY's List came, Vanita Gupta from the Leadership Conference on Civil and Human Rights, Stephanie Cutter, Dunn.

Suddenly messages were buzzing everywhere. Within minutes, Tanden's backyard became the makeshift war room. *She couldn't have held on for just four more months?* Ruth Bader Ginsburg had died of pancreatic cancer, forty-six days before the election. Without John Lewis, who had passed from the same condition, Black Americans wouldn't have the right to vote. Without Ginsburg, women in America wouldn't have the right to get a mortgage or a credit card separate from men. And now, after four years of racism and misogyny—and what felt like the rattled older white men like Trump trying one last time to hold off the movements that Lewis and Ginsburg had helped start, the Democratic Party was forced to move forward without either.

A few miles away, Ezra Levin had invited a few of his own friends over to hang out in front of the Indivisible cofounder's house in Petworth. The Domino's delivery had just arrived when his phone rang with a staffer giving him the news. Months earlier, Indivisible had gamed out a late-stage Supreme Court vacancy, but it was based on what would happen if Clarence Thomas suddenly stepped down to give Trump a boost and a chance to secure that spot for another generation. They knew they would fight. They assumed they would lose. Levin's friends quickly gathered up to leave. Leah Greenberg, eight months pregnant, was already sitting inside, at work on her laptop. They lit up their network, trying to make sense of what to do next.

Biden got the news while he was in the air, returning home after he and Trump scheduled events in Minnesota for the same day. With cameras waiting for him in the private air terminal back in New Castle, he sat on his plane for half an hour with the shades drawn, working through what his aides wanted him to say. When he stepped out to speak, he was reflective, remembering how he had been the chairman of the Judiciary Committee in 1993 when Ginsburg was confirmed. He called for the Senate to hold off on confirming her replacement, not with the passion of a believer, but with calculation: "There is no doubt that the voters should pick the president, and the president should pick the justice for the Senate to consider."

Biden finished quickly. Again, it was on Obama to lay out the terms—not just of how to eulogize Ginsburg, but of how to take on this fight. With Merrick Garland, Republicans "invented the principle" that they were now eager to violate, Obama said, in a statement that was both angry and insistent. In 2016, he had pleaded with the few Republican senators he dreamed of appealing to in the weeks after nominating Garland: *Don't stop confirmation.* Blowing up the politics would harm both the Senate and the courts, he warned, but more important, the basic social studies sense that Americans have of how things are supposed to work. This would be a break in norms from which America could not return. Some Republican senators, like Arizona's Jeff Flake, privately told him they were wary of this obstructionism. Publicly, they said nothing.

"A basic principle of the law—and of everyday fairness—is that we apply rules with consistency, and not based on what's convenient or advantageous in the moment," was the florid official text of his statement mourning Ginsburg's death, but the argument was blunt: *Don't confirm.* The institutionalist was saying that institutionalism wouldn't work. The break was done. Working through the final stages of what became the first volume of his memoir, griping about how the writing was taking him away from his golf game, Obama had been reconsidering his presidency, questioning why all the promise he rode in on hadn't ushered in the great new era of twenty-first-century practical progressivism that he'd envisioned. He'd known that Ginsburg was ill, just as he had known about Lewis's condition. He decided long before his aides hit send on the emailed statement that he would call out the predictable Republican hypocrisy, just as he had decided that he would use his speech at Lewis's funeral to call the filibuster a Jim Crow relic. Obama was trying to send a message—in public, so Biden would have to deal with it—that he was going to have to break with his reverence for the past and tradition if he wanted to achieve anything beyond being a ball of yarn for the Republicans to bat around. Part of the question of building the future was always going to be how much Biden was willing to blow up the past. Obama knew he was going to need the push.

The disrupter politician with the establishment sensibility liked having the power to now decide what would be considered mainstream.

No longer putting itself forward as America's moral guardian, the Republican Party was defining itself as the check against America's changing. After winning the popular vote only once since 1988, with a majority of senators who didn't represent anywhere near a majority of the American population, Mitch McConnell was eager to quickly shove in a sixth justice to cement the conservative majority on the court for at least a generation.

Most senators agreed that Trump was petty and mean and not fit for the job. They agreed that he had twisted the presidency into a cult of personality, for his own benefit, and for his own profit. They agreed that he had been promoted by a Russian disinformation campaign to attack American democracy in 2016 and 2020, with his own cheerleading and Rudy Giuliani's hate-driven, self-righteous assistance. They agreed that he stoked xenophobia, racism, and authoritarianism. They agreed his botched and incurious response to the pandemic cost hundreds of thousands of American lives, tanked the economy, and left lasting scars on the people who were hospitalized and on the psyches of the children forced out of schools. They agreed he had unraveled international alliances they once held sacred and had undercut Americans' faith in themselves and in their country. They agreed he fundamentally debased political discourse.

They agreed that America was an unhappy, anxious, coarsened, sick and dying, more hateful, undermined, broken country because of Trump. They also knew this was a chance to fill a Supreme Court seat, to keep their jobs, to get another tax cut. And they accepted that bargain, most of them acknowledging that they never actually wanted to overturn *Roe v. Wade*—they had just wanted to campaign against it for as long as they could.

Powerlessness and fury were a tough mix for Democrats. "Mitch McConnell thinks this fight is over," Warren said on the steps of the Supreme Court the following night. "What he does not understand is that this fight has just begun. She was staring out at thousands of energized Democrats, desperate to feel part of a cause. They had their signs and their costumes and their candles. They were waiting to feel someone grab their energy.

Biden didn't go. He stayed home all day in Wilmington, on the phone with Ginsburg's daughter and granddaughter—again, he was talking about cancer. Harris didn't come. She had taken an impromptu long walk through miles of Washington to the Supreme Court that morning with her husband, not even telling staff that she was going to pay respects. Officially the campaign had decided to keep its distance, separate from the activists, from the anger and passion.

Five and a half years earlier, the steps of the court had been where progressives first read out the decisions on Obamacare and gay marriage, both of which seemed to lock in the promise of Obama. Four and a half years earlier, Ginsburg herself stood on the steps seeing off the casket of her friend Antonin Scalia as Democrats believed for a moment that *they* would be the ones to flip the balance of power with an iconic justice's unexpected death, before they ran up against the wall of McConnell's intransigence. Three and a half years earlier, the morning after Trump's inauguration, that stretch of First Street between Constitution and Independence avenues was packed with signs and pussy hats, so large a crowd that it could barely move. Now it was scattered with tea lights and bouquets of flowers and another set of signs: WE MISS YOU RBG, RUTH LIFE MATTERS, LET THIS RADICALIZE YOU RATHER THAN LEAD YOU TO DESPAIR. A hellish present seemed to forebode a darker future, where America spun backward into evangelical fervor and reactionary antiprogressivism, owning the libs just for the sake of it.

"We take no joy in being right. But we called this from day one," said Rachel O'Leary Carmona, who had become executive director of the Women's March. "We said that it was coming, and we've been preparing for it to come."

By the time Biden arrived at the National Constitution Center in Philadelphia the following afternoon, the party's energy was slipping out from under him. Leading Democrats were past talking about getting rid of the filibuster and were into calling for packing the courts, assuming the battle with McConnell was already over. When Schumer made his own first public comments about next steps, he invited Ocasio-Cortez to stand next to him at a press conference in front of James Madison High School in Brooklyn, which Ginsburg attended (as had Schumer, Bernie Sanders, Chris Rock, and all sorts of other famous alums).

The position Biden took followed Obama's in 2020, but his language mirrored Obama in 2016: "If we go down this path, it would cause irreversible damage"—more irreversible than what already couldn't be reversed. "The infection this president has unleashed on our democracy can be fatal," Biden warned, clearing his throat over and over, scratching at his face. "Enough. We must come together as a nation. Democrat, Republican, Independent, liberal, conservative. Everybody."

Don't be this country, he told America. Don't be this party, he told the Democrats. Have a conscience, he appealed to the Republican senators thinking past Trump, though he knew he was talking more to the voters who wanted to believe that Republican senators existed who weren't either in thrall to Trump or determined to take a conservative majority on the Supreme Court as a consolation prize for having had to deal with him.

"Action and reaction. Anger and more anger. Sorrow and frustration at the way things are. That's the cycle that Republican senators will continue to perpetuate if they go down this dangerous path they have put us on," he said. "We need to de-escalate—not escalate.

"Our country faces a choice," Biden said, "a choice about whether we can come back from the brink."

Democrats were moving harder and faster than they ever had around a fight like this. They weren't going to stop the nomination, but activist leaders saw that they had about one week to shape the sentiment in the country and the party, and within Biden's head.

Biden won the nomination by fighting off just the kinds of progressive demands for institutional change that were now building around adding justices to the Supreme Court, and though he was saying in interviews that court packing (or what the progressives were now calling "court balancing") was an idea worth considering, the words he kept coming back to in private conversations, even then, were "slippery slope."

But he was finally seeing reason to bend on the filibuster. As an aide said a few days after Ginsburg's death, Biden was going to have to take a fundamental look at what was achievable. He knew it had taken only two years for Obamacare to end up in front of the Supreme Court, where it was almost struck down. All the big dreams he was having weren't going to matter if whatever they passed in the first two years was struck down before the end of his term. Trump, through the majorities voted on by his judges, would hang over him long after losing. He was going to keep defining America for even longer.

This only heightened Democrats' determination to fight back, with or without Biden. "The Republican effort to enshrine the rule of a shrinking minority over the majority must be met by overwhelming action, which—ironically will accelerate the very changes that people like McConnell are trying to prevent," tweeted Ben Rhodes.

Four days after Ginsburg died, Harris pulled into the parking lot of the Headliners Barbershop on Seven Mile Road in Detroit.

Four barber chairs had been moved onto the asphalt for Harris to have as much of a community conversation as the campaign could configure in a pandemic. The first question she was asked was about racial disparities in arrests and in COVID-19 rates. Her time as a prosecutor, which was twisted through the primaries by opponents on the left trying to stop her and which she'd never figured out how to run on herself, was now the argument she always hoped it could be.

"You know, I was a prosecutor in my career, and I'm going to tell you, one of the problems—one—of the problems with the criminal justice system is that there's a phrase that is often used, 'accountability and consequence.' There needs to be accountability and consequence. But the term is always used in connection with the person who was arrested, and never in the context of the system itself and the actors within the system," she said, answering with a comfort never there in her presidential campaign. "There has not been consequence and accountability for police officers who break the rules and break the law."

CHAPTER TWENTY-FOUR

WHITE HOUSE PETRI DISH

There's no question I did not adequately explain what I was thinking.

—GERALD FORD, ON HIS 1976 DEBATE PERFORMANCE

September 2020–October 2020

Thirty-five seconds. A whole debate, all the buildup throughout the year, an hour and a half onstage, and in the end, it was thirty-five seconds that mattered. Not Biden saying, "The party is me. Right now, I am the Democratic Party," when Trump started out by attacking Biden for other Democrats supporting Medicare for All. Not Chris Wallace giving up on trying to control a sweaty, agitated Trump. Just one short exchange, sparked by Biden pivoting in the middle of a thought about COVID-19 to talking about Trump's calling the military suckers and losers.

"Are you talking about Hunter?"

"I'm talking about my son, Beau Biden—you're talking about Hunter?" Biden said.

"I don't know Beau. I know Hunter. Hunter got thrown out of the military. He was thrown out, dishonorably discharged," Trump sneered.

"That's not true," Biden snapped back, unable to contain himself. "He was not dishonorably discharged."

"For cocaine use. And he didn't have a job until you became vice president."

"None of that is true."

"Once you became vice president, he made a fortune in Ukraine, in China, in Moscow, and various other places."

"That is simply not true. My son—"

"He made a fortune—"

"My son—"

"—and he didn't have a job."

"My son, like a lot of people at home, had a drug problem. He's overtaking it. He's fixed it. He's worked on it. And I'm proud of him, I'm proud of my son."

Most of the time on the trail, when Biden would say "my son," he was referring to Beau. Not that night. He'd never spoken about Hunter's addiction so openly. Biden and his aides knew that Trump would come after Hunter again. Biden told them he wanted to say he was proud of his son, and they practiced the lines, how he would address the addiction, what he'd say about how much Hunter had struggled. Aides told him to fight his competitive instinct and not indulge Trump at all. They went into the night unprepared for the intensity of what took place in that moment, not realizing quite how much Biden was still burning over the suckers and losers article, and over Bob Woodward's reporting that Trump had admitted deliberately downplaying the pandemic despite knowing how dangerous it was. He shifted from thinking Trump was criminally incompetent to believing that he had knowingly killed Americans. Not to mention Trump's refusal to condemn his angry white supremacist supporters. "Proud Boys," he'd said ominously when Biden offered up one of the more notorious groups to distance himself from, "stand back and stand by."

Biden was upset about the entire night. "That was embarrassing," was the first thing he said to the aides waiting for him backstage. He didn't like being part of the historic moment of a presidential debate that Trump had debased with his ranting and interrupting. Aides showed him Dana Bash on CNN calling the night "a shit show." He had to be convinced that he was not the target of the criticism, that all the coverage was landing on Trump.

Still, he felt as if he had been run over. "I couldn't get a word in," he said. "The whole thing went off the rails." Ron Klain and Mike Donilon assured him he'd delivered the punches they'd wanted him to. Bedingfield and Symone Sanders read through the immediate press reaction on Twitter. Dunn had been watching with a group of people recording instant reactions on dial meters, and she called Biden with the results. She knew he felt that Trump had pushed him around, but the voters didn't like what they had seen. Her theory of the election was strengthening the connection voters felt to Biden so that they turned out for him in November, and he had done that, she told him.

In the end, eleven million fewer people tuned in at all, as compared to the first debate between Trump and Clinton in 2016, even with everyone stuck at home on their couches. Americans were tired. They knew by now whom they were voting for. Enough, was the collective reaction. Hold the election already.

The spectacle did have some impact, however. Run for Something clocked three hundred people reaching out to sign up during and immediately after the debate, clearly eager for a different kind of politics than what they were seeing onstage. "If we did not exist," said Amanda Litman, looking at those numbers, "what would those people have done?"

Another conspiracy theory began circulating on the morning of the debate, claiming that Biden wanted to wear an earpiece. That night it was that he was wearing, for some reason, a wire up his sleeve. What the QAnon nuts and Twitter sleuths had actually spotted were Beau's rosary beads, which Biden had been wearing around his wrist for five years.

———

On Friday morning, Bedingfield woke up, rolled over, and looked at her phone. With the number of texts and phone calls she'd missed, her first thought was that Trump had been shot. Reality was both more absurd and more completely predictable. Up in the middle of the night, a few Biden aides spent hours texting one another, trying to make sense of the news alerts, waiting for everyone else to wake up. Because how could this not end with Trump getting coronavirus? The October surprise had been on everyone's minds for seven months.

Medieval morality plays were more subtle. The spreader event emerged as the tightly packed, sparsely masked Rose Garden announcement of the nomination of Amy Coney Barrett, in the rush for the Senate to pretend it was providing time to do due diligence, squeezing the nomination in before Trump flew off to a campaign rally in Pennsylvania. Here he was in the middle of a pandemic, choosing a justice who would strike down Obamacare, while probably already infected himself or about to be. Mike Lee, a former Supreme Court clerk and Utah senator who had been put on Trump's fake list of possible nominees a few weeks earlier when the president had tried to make an issue over whom Biden *might* pick if a vacancy were theoretically to come up, was on video chatting and hugging and holding a mask in his hand, and he was infected. Chris Christie, slumped in a seat in the briefing room the next day after a debate prep session at the White House, had it. The president of Notre Dame, where Barrett had been a professor, had it. White House aides had it. Reporters whom Trump seems to have breathed on during an off-the-record chat in the press cabin on Air Force One soon had it too.

Biden wasn't surprised when he heard Trump had tested positive. It was fate, once again. Everyone on staff had been chattering with concern and disbelief that Trump's family had been sitting in the theater in Ohio without their masks on. "Why is the Trump family allowed to not wear masks in the debate hall while everyone else follows the rules?" Naomi Biden had wondered on Twitter, sitting in the audience. Two days later, the family and aides ran through their own contact tracing, looking for connections to anyone who had been near Hope Hicks, the Trump aide whose leaked diagnosis tipped off the wider White House outbreak. Biden did his own check with the campaign's public health advisers and doctors. They told him he had been far enough away. A rumor went around that Melania Trump tried to pop in to say hi to Jill Biden backstage, but that was quickly shot down. All year long this was what the campaign had been terrified of, and Trump had exposed Biden in the most reckless, selfish way possible. He was supposed to have taken a test when he arrived at the site, but he was running late, so they'd waved him through on what the moderator, Fox News anchor Chris Wallace, later called "the honor system."

No one knew what was really happening with Trump. In his West Wing, the standard procedure was to lie about what they knew and to cover for being in the dark about what they didn't by bluffing and shoveling misinformation as part of their own constant undermining and bickering with one another, while Trump sat back and watched the show. Aides spread conflicting accounts of how much supplemental oxygen Trump needed to be on, or whether he was on oxygen at all. The Biden campaign started hearing from reporters that Trump was seriously ill, a lot worse than he'd been making it appear.

Critical condition? On a ventilator? The president getting sick was bad for America's standing in the world, Biden told aides. Embarrassing. Bad for the American psyche. When Trump abruptly headed to Walter Reed hospital that Friday afternoon and a panic set in about just how much danger he was in, Biden was firm on a call with advisers: no pointing out the carelessness which had led to this, no mention of how he was on government-run health care now, no normal attacks at all. "He's the president," Biden said. "I need to change my speeches." They put a hold on their negative ads and told the DNC to do the same.

By that Sunday afternoon, Trump had packed Secret Service agents into his limo for a hunched joyride to wave at the supporters who had gathered outside the hospital; Biden told aides to end the cease-fire. If Trump was going to play the role of being healthy, they'd respond accordingly and go back on the attack.

But Biden's aides feared that Trump would come out of the hospital claiming he'd had an epiphany, and was now a changed man, one who'd learned to take the coronavirus seriously, and would turn his careless behavior into a brilliantly written story line of awakening and redemption. The campaign fed friendly pundits talking points to preemptively stress how little Trump's approach to the overall crisis had changed, no matter what he might start trying to say whenever he left the hospital.

In fact, while Americans were dying by the hundreds every day, Trump had been fantasizing about a stunt right out of *Willy Wonka*, where he'd leave the hospital, pretend to still be suffering, then rip open his shirt to reveal the Superman logo. The problem was that he wasn't invulnerable, and instead was clearly struggling to walk from the helicopter after he'd rushed himself back to the White House from the hospital, and was visibly heaving as he stood on the balcony for a staged salute meant to show how healthy he was. Within a few days, he and his staff quickly gave up on masks again, though the White House was itself clocking a higher infection rate than some more responsible countries.

———

In the spring and summer, some Democratic operatives working with the Biden campaign would grimly joke that its only mission was keeping the candidate alive. After Trump's diagnosis, keeping him and everyone attending his events virus-free became even more pressing. A deputy campaign manager was appointed as COVID-19 sheriff, reviewing data about infection rates in every state where the campaign had trips planned. Any event deemed not necessary was scrapped. Anyone involved with the campaign, they decided, needed to start flying private. Trips for surrogates were paused until the final few weeks, while the campaign sorted out new protocols and reallocated money to pay for them.

Back in the long months when Biden was making his pick, the conventional wisdom was that imagining the vice presidential debate with Mike Pence would be a defining factor in the decision. Despite her debate experience, Harris had been nervous throughout the prep, confounding aides with her stressing that Pence would go after *her* record. She had to be reminded to say Biden's name as much as possible. And she was constantly calibrating her lines, arguing that the team wasn't sensitive enough to the standards she would be judged on as a woman, and as a Black woman. That last factor struck Buttigieg—the stand-in for Pence in debate prep, whose impression was so thorough it involved mimicking the vice president's eyebrow straining. Buttigieg had thought that, as a gay man up onstage, he understood the different standards of presentation that candidates could be judged on. This was eye-opening.

In the end, the debate was almost irrelevant amid the mania surrounding Trump's diagnosis, apart from a fight over plexiglass separations on the stage, which Pence's staff pushed back on; a fly that lingered on Pence's head partway through the debate, which Harris noticed but held herself in from reacting to; and a moment that supporters tried to make another T-shirt out of when she sharply stopped an early interruption from Pence with, "I'm speaking." Harris didn't even get to deliver what was supposed to be her big zinger: "You know what, Vice President Pence, you have a hard job. You have to sit up here and defend Donald Trump."

In the last weeks before the election, the country settled into a new rhythm: lockdowns had become normal, hundreds were going to keep dying every day, and Biden looked as if he'd be riding a Democratic wave into a new age. He continued to campaign, speaking at drive-in rallies, hoping he could draw a connection from the honking.

"It's going to take all four years to get us to somewhat where we were before. I'm not saying it was completely right. But at least we had some semblance," said Reid Shaffer, an engineer from Durham leaning on the passenger side door of his Subaru at a drive-in rally in Durham, North Carolina, in mid-October, waiting for Biden to come onstage. He mentioned Trump's abandoning the Kurds. He mentioned his daughter, in London, having a much saner lockdown. He said there were going to have to be prosecutions, to not make the mistake Obama did by leaving George W. Bush to retirement. "They can't be timid—otherwise it'll come back. All they need is someone more polished than Trump."

═══

With their summer vacation on Martha's Vineyard having extended into October, Michelle Obama was lost in her own despondency and anger. She'd never gotten over Trump's election. She hadn't really gotten over what had happened in Obama's presidency, when she felt that Democrats had too often abandoned her husband, left him to the racism she always sensed pulsing in America. They were happy to show up at his rallies, and always desperate to have him show up at theirs, she would say, but there was no loyalty, no sympathy, no defense. People who would hear from her would come away saying she was depressed, in the emotional if not the clinical sense, too angry at America for being a place where Trump was possible to say yes to any campaign requests, too weighed down by her sadness to make any appearances if she had wanted to.

This was an all-hands-on-deck election, Democrats kept insisting, and she had proved again with her convention speech her distinct power to break through. Biden was heading into November knowing he'd have to lean on the types of Black and white female voters to whom she appealed most. While she just couldn't bring herself to do it, her husband was raring to go—just as soon as the dysfunction of the Biden team was able to come up with any kind of plan for what to have him do.

When Obama finally made his debut on the campaign trail for Biden, it was in the gym of a recreational center in Northeast Philadelphia, where folding tables and a set of bleachers had been arranged for a socially distanced roundtable. Over and over, he referred back to his time as a community organizer. Over and over, he talked about how slow progress can be. Over and over, he said people needed to vote.

Malcolm Kenyatta—a young, Black, gay assemblyman who had been a Biden supporter from the launch—stood up to ask the question everyone was asking Obama: "The last four years have been a lot of sadness and destruction—what still gives you hope?"

Obama went right back to talking about the 2004 keynote, the audacity of hope, the belief that things could get better. "So I've never lost hope over these last four years. I've been mad. I've been frustrated. But I haven't lost hope, and the reason is because I never expected progress to move directly, in a straight line. If you look at the history of this country, you make progress, then there's some backpedaling, and backlash. You consolidate some victories, and then there's some slippage, and then you get a renewed surge of energy, then you make some more progress, then there's a little bit of backstopping, then you push again," Obama said. "What we saw over the last four years was with my election, I think we had probably gotten overoptimistic about how much change could happen in the country. But that change was real. There was some pushback. And that was real too. But when we started seeing all these young people across the country demonstrating this summer, it reminded you that they internalized that sense of optimism and change and possibility."

Obama stopped briefly a few blocks away to rile up a group of volunteers, generate some buzz. A few mothers pushed their children to get up close, get in the frame for an iPhone photo.

In the parking lot next to the basketball and hockey arena—where, at Clinton's Democratic convention in 2016, he warned America about Trump and Trumpism and predicted that he'd lose—they were waiting for him like it was still 2008. And the man who hadn't spoken at a rally since his last midterms speech two years earlier hopped onstage and dove right back in, still better at this than Biden or anyone who'd been campaigning over the time since. He channeled how maddening every Democrat had found those weeks with the debate, the COVID-19 diagnosis, Trump's continuing attacks. He had a script. He wanted to riff.

"Donald Trump isn't going to protect us. He can barely take the basic steps to protect himself," Obama said. He joked that the pandemic playbook that his administration had prepared was probably being used to prop up a "wobbly table" in Trump's West Wing. "He's got a secret Chinese bank account. How is that possible? Can you imagine if I had had a secret Chinese bank account when I was running for reelection? You think Fox News might have been a little concerned about that. They would have called me 'Beijing Barry,'" he joked. Americans wouldn't tolerate Trump's behavior from a crazy uncle, he said—just look at his tweets "about secret cabals running the world or that Navy SEALs didn't kill bin Laden. Think about that. The president of the United States retweeted that. Imagine that. What? What?" That exasperated "What? What?" became Obama's signature turn those last few weeks.

"It's funny to say this, given his relative youth, but he's the elder statesman," said Josh Shapiro, the Pennsylvania attorney general and an early Obama supporter in 2007 when he was still a county official, standing in the parking lot as the clouds and the sunset began to frame the shot for Obama's speech. "He's grounding to us. He's comforting to us. He's the dad that looks at you when he's disappointed that you might have done something wrong or disappointed that you're not, maybe, working hard enough. He's the one that steps up."

Hazel Diaz, a retired marine on staff with Veterans for Peace, said she'd driven an hour and a half in from Lebanon, Pennsylvania, to see Obama. She'd been part of the Run Bernie Run effort to get Sanders into the 2016 race. She'd worked on Clinton's campaign. In 2020, she'd wavered between Booker and Harris, but was fine with how the race had landed. "For a lot of people, the Biden campaign is a pause on the chaos," she said, and those people were going to demand more than a pause if he won.

"Maybe Joe Biden didn't win his other two elections because he was too complicit in the system," Diaz said. "Now the people will hold him accountable for change."

CHAPTER TWENTY-FIVE

THE OTHER SIDE
OF THE DESK

Think of what would have happened if he'd have gone out and
said, "This is awful. We should all be afraid. We don't have a plan."

—REPUBLICAN NATIONAL COMMITTEE CHAIR RONNA ROMNEY
McDANIEL, ON TRUMP'S RESPONSE TO THE PANDEMIC

November 1, 2020–November 7, 2020

The year 2020 was the one when people couldn't breathe. From COVID-19.
From police chokeholds. From wildfire smoke. From our constant collective anxiety about all that and everything else.

Even the people who weren't woke were exhausted. It was all just too much.
Trump had pushed too far. He seemed as if he were determined to blow up
everything—and he had. People will usually shrug off government officials
doing a little lying, lining their pockets, being obnoxious, but Trump was so
corrupt, so racist, so incompetent, so self-serving that it was hard for most
Americans to let slip all of that happening all day, every day, while he proudly
bragged about it on Twitter and TV. They let slide voter ID laws that everybody
knew targeted specific—that is, Black—voters, but literally pulling machines
out of post offices and closing down polling places?

Trump has always viewed the world as being populated by winners or losers, and he could see all too clearly that he was about to lose to a man who was
not only Obama's vice president, but who had until November 3 been the most

failed presidential candidate ever. He had gone from having nothing to lose in 2016 to being defeated on the biggest stage possible. He could console himself with whatever fantasyland excuses he wanted, but he was soon going to have to look in the mirror at his face without the makeup, with the bags under his eyes, the cheeks that he knew had gotten fatter and droopier, and see a loser. He already could, because what was he doing, eighteen days before the election, playing defense at a rally in Macon, Georgia? "Running against the worst candidate in the history of presidential politics puts pressure on me," Trump told the crowd. "Could you imagine if I lose? My whole life, what am I going to do? I'm going to say: 'I lost to the worst candidate in the history of politics.' I'm not going to feel so good. Maybe I'll have to leave the country—I don't know."

Trump's attempts at power moves collapsed into manic, self-defeating nincompoopery. He wouldn't wear masks because he thought it was better for his politics, then his numbers tanked because he caught COVID-19. He canceled taking part in a second debate with Biden because he thought he would benefit from making a stink out of not bowing to the demands to appear by satellite in case he was still infectious, then lost an opportunity to be seen by tens of millions of voters in the final weeks. He worked out a televised town hall instead, then ended up confirming that he had paid only $750 in income taxes and was $421 million in debt and said he wasn't sure that QAnon believed anything about satanic cults, but he liked that it was opposed to pedophilia.

"Joe Biden and the democrat socialists will kill your jobs, dismantle your police departments, dissolve your borders, release criminal aliens, raise your taxes, confiscate your guns, end fracking, destroy your suburbs, and drive God from the public square" is how Trump summed up his opponent in a tweet two weeks from the election. "Is that all?" shot back David Plouffe, the former Obama adviser. It wasn't. When the FBI announced that a militia group had been planning to kidnap the governor of Michigan in retaliation for her coronavirus restrictions, Trump responded that Whitmer hadn't been grateful enough to him for stopping the plot, and also that the terrorists had a point. His campaign never released details of his own illness or treatment from COVID-19, but brought in former presidential physician and new House candidate Ronny Jackson on a call to discuss Biden's fitness for office, which he tried to cover by saying, "I've not accused him of having Alzheimer's. I have not made that statement." While he was recuperating, Trump invited thousands of supporters over to the White House for a political rally on the lawn. For at least a few hours on a Saturday afternoon, America became a place where an angry leader shouted about his political enemies from a balcony to a crowd of supporters in matching shirts and hats.

By then, Biden's campaign already knew that one last attack was coming. They knew that Steve Bannon and Rudy Giuliani were involved, that Fox News had passed on the story, and that the *New York Post* had bitten. They weren't exactly sure what was involved, but they knew it concerned Hunter and Ukraine again. Days before the *Post* story ran, purporting to have the contents of a laptop belonging to Hunter full of incriminating personal information, press aides had already met with campaign lawyers to prepare potential responses, depending on what might come.

There was, according to the *Post* headline, a "smoking gun" letter, purporting to be a thank-you from a Ukrainian businessman to Hunter for introducing him to the vice president, printed on what looked like the letterhead of the energy company at the heart of the supposed scandal. Was that real? It didn't seem to be. Was the laptop real, or the story of its having supposedly been dropped off at a Wilmington computer repair shop, with an easily identifiable Beau Biden Foundation sticker? All of it seemed fake. Biden's campaign was leaning on a year's worth of preparation and groundwork: of discrediting Giuliani, of reporters' learning the lessons of how their 2016 coverage had failed (or at least being shamed enough to pretend they had learned the lessons), of greater literacy about Russian and other disinformation, of building Americans' trust in Biden's relationship with his son through that moment talking about his addiction onstage. A year earlier, when Hunter set up his own interview in the middle of impeachment, aides made clear they couldn't tolerate him doing that again, and they were now also leaning on that negotiated relationship with him. They promised Hunter to respond only in ways he was comfortable with and give him visibility into the decision-making process. He promised to leave all the responding to them.

This wasn't easy, especially as the *Post* kept chopping, publishing photos of Hunter getting high and a long text message exchange purporting to be between Biden and Hunter that revealed an angry son snapping back at a father struggling to be loving. The texts were real: Hunter writing from rehab in

February 2019 that he was a "fucked up addict that can't be trusted, relied upon nor defended," then adding, "if you don't run ill never have a chance at redemption," and Biden responding, "I'll run but I need you . . . only focus is recovery, nothing else," then:

> Can I come to see you
> Need to talk to you about the 2020 announcement and what you think
> I love you
> Dad

Their pain and grief were splayed in a tabloid spread. Biden tried to keep himself steeled against it, repeat to himself and to his advisers that this was the cost of running against Trump, that he'd been through much worse, that he was still proud of his son. Giuliani said the texts were more proof of the nefarious scheme he was concocting, but to most, this never became more than yet another storyline in the Trump-friendly media's Comic Con–style universe of inside jokes and obscure references that made sense only to obsessive superfans.

"We were able to put it in a box and have the media treat it like it deserved to be treated—which was like a conspiracy theory, and not like it was Clinton's emails or the crazy parade of accusers at the St. Louis debate," said a Biden aide, referencing Trump's sneaky counterpunch on Clinton in 2016, when he showed up with four women who'd made claims against her husband, mere days after the *Access Hollywood* tape was revealed. "We had been preparing the whole ecosystem to respond to some crazy Trump October surprise. And it responded responsibly. That doesn't happen by accident. This all stems from the way we responded on Ukraine."

———

Biden doesn't have any Election Day rituals. He doesn't go to the movies, or eat a special sandwich. Before 2020, he had been running for a Senate seat in a tiny state, and then was subsumed to Obama as the one making history. But feeling the win that all their data was showing was coming, Biden had his staff build a *This Is Your Life* tour for his final days on the trail.

He started on Monday morning, holding up an index finger as he got out of his car on the tarmac. "One more day," he said, expectant, hopeful. The first stop was Ohio, to pretend that the race was competitive there, but not enough to stay for longer than a car rally in a hangar at the Cleveland airport.

The memories of how this Election Day had been ripped away from them four years earlier had Democrats shaking with the nightmare that Trump was going to win again.

"Oh my god. I feel devastated to even think about it. I know what it's like up close serving for the last four years—I can't imagine another four years of what we've had," said Congresswoman Joyce Beatty that day in the hangar in Cleveland. A puff of gray hair, seventy years old, she'd been pepper-sprayed in Columbus at a George Floyd protest the day before Trump's walk across Lafayette Square to wave the Bible. "Today is emotional. It's the emotion of hope and change. It's the emotion of what if, and we don't want to think about the what if."

Sherrod Brown, the Ohio senator who had urged Biden to campaign in the state, was a few feet away, predicting that Ohio was going blue. Because of the rules about counting ballots, it would even go blue early, to seal Biden's win before they had to wait on Pennsylvania or the other slow-results states.

Biden flew into Beaver County, Pennsylvania, for a rally with Congressman Conor Lamb and a crowd wearing T-shirts from the steamfitters union, the firefighters union, the painters union, the electrical workers union. "Time and your history mean something to these people," Lamb said, arguing that no other Democrat would have been able to turn them out. "This is like home," Biden said in his short speech and then, when the exit music started playing, he came back to the microphone to bring his grandchildren onto the stage: "That son I told you about, who I lost, I want his two children to come up. Come here," he said, and he showed them off to the small crowd.

The motorcade took him for one final trip to Pittsburgh, and at another drive-in rally, he smiled over at legendary '70s Steelers star Franco Harris, who was up on stage introducing him. He got caught up in the memory of Harris and Rocky Bleier visiting Beau and Hunter in the hospital room after the crash in 1972. The team owner heard about the tragedy and flew them in, and though Biden had missed seeing them then—he'd slipped out to buy a plastic Christmas tree for their hospital room, to cheer it up—he was still as grateful forty-eight years later.

On his last stop that night, Biden finally got his Lady Gaga concert, in front of the Steelers' stadium. She had other candidates she'd been interested in during the primaries. Her father was a Trump supporter. That night, she was alone on a platform, urging everyone there to make sure Biden won and then belting out "Shallow" from *A Star Is Born* on a white piano, in a white JOE sweatshirt.

Tell me something, boy
Aren't you tired trying to fill that void?

Biden stood holding Jill's hand backstage, mouthing along what words he could remember: "We're far from the shallow now."

Morgan Overton, a twenty-six-year-old Black social worker from the city, stood with her friends in the lot, watching with a locked-in, hopeful look on her face. She had volunteered for Obama's campaigns, and had supported Sanders in the past two primaries. "It is absolutely weird" to put her hopes in an older white man, she acknowledged, but she had. "I'm sure most of us would rather see Kamala Harris or someone closer to our lived experience" as president, she said. "But it takes an interesting person like Joe Biden to pull us to the other side."

The next morning back in Wilmington, Biden was up early. His motorcade drove him to the cemetery where he'd spent so many hours, standing with his son. Running across the top of the large, gray headstone is BIDEN, in plain letters, a Celtic cross on either side, while below it, much smaller, is JOSEPH "BEAU" ROBINETTE III and FATHER, HUSBAND, BROTHER, SON. Mementos had been left there by others looking to connect with Biden through Beau, putting their hopes on him by leaving a stack of coins, a few stones, a medallion from the 2017 Run for Child Protection and another from the National Guard chaplain's office, a green-beaded rosary. Three American flags had been stuck in the ground, and four bouquets. A Biden–Harris sticker was attached to the bottom right. On the back of the headstone was a little porcelain figurine holding a wreath to be the O in JOY. The J had broken off, askew at her feet.

After the cemetery, Biden drove to the airport because, of course, he was making one more stop in Scranton. Biden went into the house he'd grown up in. In 2008, he visited there and signed "I am home" on a wall. In 2016, he took

Hillary Clinton there after endorsing her, crammed into the kitchen with staff and press to show her where his grandfather had sat at the table, spinning out wisdom and stressing about the bills. This time, he moved a picture to write a new message on the wall behind it: "From this house to the White House, with the grace of God."

———

"Prosecute Trump's presidency on outcomes and effectiveness, not just character. Make Trump's character (erratic, distracted, insults, etc.) the reason he's failed to deliver for working people. Washington is working worse (for working people), not better," was the advice Democratic National Committee operatives gave all the primary candidates, based on interviews they had conducted all around the country long before the pandemic hit. Victory, they predicted, would depend on winning over voters who picked Trump in 2016 but would go into 2020 undecided. Calling the president a racist or an idiot wasn't going to make the difference.

"Trump as a human being . . . ass, schmuck, and other adjectives along those lines," a North Carolina man, identified as white and age fifty to sixty-four, said in one of the interviews when asked to name characteristics that described the president. "Trump as a candidate and then president: different, bold, leader, gets things done. There is a real dichotomy here. Personally, I can't stand him. As a president, I think he is doing a good job for the country in spite of the Democrats' 'resistance.'"

"While he may not have been my ideal president, the economy is doing much better than I expected and he is actually doing more good than harm right now. I think his worst has been in speech and his words that spark division," said a North Carolina woman, identified as Latina and age eighteen to thirty-four.

"Yes, he's that cranky, old uncle of ours, but he's our uncle and we're sticking with him because the economy is rolling," said a Florida voter.

Going into 2020, those undecided voters were complaining that the Democrats were moving too far left and might undo Trump's benefit to the economy. They seemed receptive, though, to sharing their concerns about health care costs and gridlock in Washington, and the sense that Trump was enriching himself and wealthy rich friends at the expense of working people.

Democratic operatives went into the closing weeks stressing over what they were learning from focus groups made up of the still-vaunted Obama–Trump voters. They'd say they hated Trump, but if it weren't for COVID-19, they would argue, the economy would be in decent shape, and Trump deserved credit for that. He'd probably be the better positioned to get the economy rolling again once COVID-19 was gone. That was the problem for Trump: They didn't trust him to beat the pandemic. He'd been inept, chaotic, talking hoaxes and injecting bleach, making false promises of when things were going to get better, landing in the hospital himself.

Biden, they would say, well, he was fine. He was a good man—not scary. He'd probably raise their taxes, and that was a problem. They weren't sure he could handle the economy, and Obama's "I got this" confidence definitely hadn't carried through to him. The politics and the people on the "crazy left" were frightening, at least from what they'd seen with Defund the Police and Black Lives Matter, and they weren't sure if Biden would be in charge, or if it'd really be Harris or Ocasio-Cortez. But he did seem to take COVID-19 seriously. He did seem to be the one who could get everyone back to work and able to go back to restaurants, and to visit their parents or grandparents or children again.

Those voters ended up tilting toward Biden. He won because of the pandemic. The future of democracy—any hope for any kind of progressive or even centrist policy, the prospect of addressing climate change and structural racism—hinged on a virus making the reality TV presidency undeniable reality.

If Trump had brought a genuine businessman's approach to handling the shortage of personal protective equipment (PPE), that might have changed history. If he had delivered some basics—big stimulus checks with his name on them coming every month, maybe wrapping himself in a committee of former presidents to advise him on dealing with COVID-19 or the Floyd protests, enlisting them in a way that none would have been able to refuse. If he had led the country by what he said in the March 11 Oval Office address, when there were toilet paper shortages and canned-bean shopping sprees and everything seemed to be playing out as a precredits scene in an apocalypse movie: "We are all in this together. We must put politics aside, stop the partisanship, and unify together as one nation and one family. As history has proven time and time again, Americans always rise to the challenge and overcome adversity."

"What are the real core elements of Trump? Anti-science, narcissistic/cares about himself and not others, bigoted, bully. Those four that are really true to who he is. This pandemic is right at the intersection of, if you could design the worst traits for a leader to have when facing a challenge like this," said Tim Kaine. "He was outrunning the consequences of his actions for a while. But this one went right at his weak spots."

The Biden campaign's projections had him winning bigger, maybe even in a landslide. They counted on a surge of Trump voters on Election Day, but not at the levels that ultimately turned out. In the end, Ohio was nowhere near close: Trump won the state by 9 points in 2016, and won by 8 points in 2020. The dreams of carrying Florida and North Carolina disappeared quickly, and the thinking retrenched the essence of Biden's argument from the start: beating Trump would require winning Michigan, Wisconsin, and Pennsylvania, and he had the best chance of doing that—but winning that way, they had always known, meant a long wait as the ballots were counted.

There was no great moral realignment. Biden ended up winning more votes than anyone in history, a bigger margin than Obama's reelection in 2012. Still, seven million more people voted for Trump than in 2016—after all the tweets, the racism, the family separations, the recklessness in everything from his meetings with foreign leaders to his refusal to do even the basics of putting on a mask. The blue wave didn't come to sweep in a huge majority in the Senate, or wash over the state legislatures so that Democrats could redistrict themselves back to parity, or even dominance. Madison Cawthorn, the newest, youngest member of the House, and enough of a Hitler fanboy that he took a trip to the führer's vacation home in 2017, made his first statement after his victory via a tweet that read "Cry more, lib."

Standing in the lobby of the Wilmington Westin as he realized the wave wasn't coming, Delaware senator Chris Coons was struggling to understand how this could be. "That may be the hardest question for me to answer," he said.

———

The Biden jukebox plays a lot of standards. Many revolve around his father, who comes across as the homespun Mark Twain of midcentury Delaware. None is as core to him as the one that aides and reporters who have spent the most time listening to him know as "the longest walk."

"You saw too many people here in Pittsburgh, and all around, make what I call the longest walk a parent has to make, up a short flight of stairs to say to their kids, 'Honey, I'm sorry, Mom lost her job, Dad lost his job,'" he said at the Labor Day Parade in Pittsburgh in 2015, before the run that almost happened. "You can't go back to the same school. You can't play in the same basketball team in church. You can't play in the same little league team. We've got to move. My dad made that walk in Scranton, Pennsylvania."

A week before the election, standing in Warm Springs, Georgia, Biden told the story again—not in old Democratic territory, but new territory that the party was trying to win.

"Growing up, I watched my father struggle to find work. He made what I call the longest walk any parent can make: up a short flight of stairs to tell their child, 'You can't play on that little league team anymore. You can't go back to your school. We can't stay here in Scranton anymore,'" he said. This time, it ended with a 2020 twist. "My father always said that a job is about a lot more than a paycheck. It's about your dignity, your respect, your place in the community. Right now, on this autumn afternoon—millions of Americans all across this country feel they have lost all that. A season of protest has broken out all across the nation. Some of it is just senseless burning and looting and violence that can't be tolerated, and it won't. But much of it is a cry for justice from communities that have long had the knee of injustice on their neck."

Biden won by giving the same speeches, and telling literally the same stories, that he had for years. This time, though, what he was offering fit the moment. He won because he was a reaction to Trump, but also because he was a white guy who could connect with white guys even as his association with Obama created a deep bond with many Black voters—"To me, this is about loyalty, when Joe Biden stood by Barack Obama's side, now we've got to stand by Joe Biden" is how the rapper Fat Joe neatly put it at a rally in Miami three days before the election.

The pandemic didn't just expose Trump's weaknesses. It covered over Biden's. He would never have been up to doing as much on the trail as Trump did, and he would have been seen as not being able to keep up. He would never have been able to draw the crowds that Trump did, and he would have looked like a failure. He would never have been able to go so long without making a stumble if he hadn't been as well rested. He would never have gotten the leeway from progressives on policy that wasn't about the pandemic, and he would have looked as if he couldn't wrangle his own party. COVID-19 was the perfect distraction for all of it.

If Biden was going to win, he was going to win battered and uncertain, steeling himself and the country for what was ahead. "The way the last four years have been, no way was this going to be easy," Tom Perez observed after Biden arrived past midnight on election night to give a speech urging everyone to be patient.

But a win is a win, and by the time Biden woke up Wednesday morning, everyone but the conspiracy theorists could tell that he was going to win, or already had. He waited to claim victory before the race was called for him, so he passed the time checking in with staff, calling friends, reaching for connections, as he wrapped his head around actually having achieved his lifelong dream, Beau's mission, the battle for the soul of the nation.

"You can think about it a lot—and then it happens," said Chris Dodd, his old friend, thinking back on their conversation that Wednesday morning. "The distance between being in the chair behind the desk and standing in front of the desk is beyond measurement. To know, all of a sudden, that seat is yours now—he's been in the Oval Office numerous times, with numerous presidents, but now he was going to be the president."

The absentee ballots were counted all day Wednesday, and Michigan and Wisconsin moved out of reach for Trump. Every few hours another batch of ballots would dump in from Pennsylvania, and Trump's lead from in-person voting ticked further down. The sun came up, the sun went down. Biden had won even more clearly by the morning after, but the days passed in limbo waiting for the networks to call the race, all the networks hoping that Fox would go first, Fox waiting on Rupert Murdoch to abandon Trump, America becoming one extended panic attack. Two days in, a Biden campaign aide grimly joked that it was as if the country were struggling to get out of a relationship with an abusive boyfriend.

On Friday morning, the website Decision Desk HQ made the first official call of the race for Biden. Bedingfield sat down on the sofa in her Westin Hotel suite and cried. The day after the 2016 election, she'd wept at her desk at the vice president's office, trying to recount for him Clinton's concession speech, which he'd missed when he went to join Obama in the Oval Office for a buck-up speech to the West Wing staff. He'd comforted her. Jill Biden had given her a handkerchief. "It's a little surreal," she said that afternoon. "It's funny to say 'surreal,' because it's a thing that I fervently believed should and could happen for five years. And yet somehow, it's still surreal."

Biden's victory speech had been locked in before election night. He had decided what he wanted to say, what he was going to say no matter how he won—because he only considered winning, and aides hadn't even bothered to set up a contact to call if he had to concede to Trump. Through all the emotional ups and downs, Biden remained calmer than aides had become accustomed to. There were no calls to Obama.

Sitting at home with his family, Biden methodically went through the numbers coming in from his staff. He saw that he wasn't the one out of sync with his party so much as the party wasn't as popular as he was. He saw how many more millions had turned out for Trump this time than had in 2016. He also saw that Republican leaders he'd promised he could work with were now standing with Trump in undercutting democracy and the legitimacy of his victory. "He always had a clear understanding that if he won, he was going to be governing a country where a large number of people have voted for Donald Trump," Bedingfield said.

But that night passed without any of the networks calling the race, and Biden instead had to give a speech indoors, to just the two dozen reporters who'd been cleared with COVID-19 tests and the TV cameras to say again, *It was really looking good, but just hang on.* "What I am enjoying is that the most famously anti-science, anti-factual president of my lifetime is now being slowly taught mathematics, and the inescapable consequences of mathematics," remarked Coons that night, back at the hotel, still waiting like everyone else.

On Saturday morning, Biden and Jill were by themselves down at the lake on their property in Wilmington when the race was called, first by one network and then rapidly by the rest within a few minutes. They knew he was now the president-elect by the shouting of their grandchildren at the top of the hill.

Trump was golfing, tweet after tweet blocked that morning as he fulminated further from reality. He arrived back at a White House that had become a block party in front of the extra fence erected before the election on top of the one left there from the aftermath of the Floyd protests. Horns were honking, pots were banging all over the country, surprising even Biden and his inner circle with just how much of a cause he'd become, or at least how much of a cause beating Trump had become. "Ding dong, the witch is dead," texted Sanders's closest aide, Jeff Weaver. Tom Carper, the Delaware senator and old Biden friend had been out for a run, looking up at the sun shining, the trees blowing as he took in the news. He started thinking about Ronald Reagan. "Morning in America," Carper said. Arnold Schwarzenegger spent the day sending around a video clip a friend had sent him from *True Lies*, a classic look right into the camera for a ridiculous catchphrase: "You're fired," years before it was Trump's *Apprentice* catchphrase, as he shot a missle, which a terrorist was caught hanging on, into a building.

Nancy Pelosi was at her home in Washington, calling each of the year's Democratic House candidates, winners and losers—more losers than she had been counting on—thanking them for running. She heard the noise on the streets and began crying. "It was like the giant anvil that was taken off the back of the country," she said. "Everybody was crying. The Statue of Liberty had tears. Abraham Lincoln had tears. Smokey the Bear had tears." One of her children sent her a text message she loved showing off: "Live your life so that when you lose your job, people are not dancing in the streets all over the world."

Obama had considered that he might have to pressure other leaders into accepting the results by being the first to make a congratulatory phone call, and then announcing that he had done so. As it turned out, he wasn't needed.

"I'm proud of you," Obama told Biden.

Obama had stressed around the big moments, especially ahead of the debates. He had wondered about the wisdom of risking Biden's health by sending him out for more rallies as the weather got colder. Obama would push back: Did they really need him to go back to Florida, or make a trip to campaign in Georgia at the end? He asked for briefings from the campaign lawyers in the final weeks about their preparations if Trump messed with the ballots or if Republican governors tried to depress turnout by using COVID-19 as justification to close polling places. He got the rundown of what the plans were if Trump tried to change electors.

Biden is not a precise instrument, Obama would say. But he was impressed with the campaign, and with Biden, and how they had worked their way through a pandemic and the racial justice summer without coming apart.

"Wouldn't have guessed it," he told several people, "but it worked."

———

Crowds started showing up around the security gate in Wilmington immediately that Saturday afternoon, looking at the stage from election night still set up in the distance. One woman sat on a bench off to the side, closing her eyes as she listened to "Glory" on a loop playing on her phone. Biden aides slipped out to Macy's to bulk up their wardrobe options for the night. "Now we don't have to say we're near Philadelphia anymore, said a man behind the desk at the Westin, talking to another hotel employee. "No more, 'Where's Delaware?'"

One step at a time.

An hour before Biden's motorcade pulled in, Perez was standing in the Westin lobby, feeling the reality himself. He'd been in the parking lot on election night, his SUV pulled into a spot amid the red, white, and blue prop cars that had been assembled in front of the stage, but for that night, he and his family had tickets to stand on the flatbed of a blue pickup truck.

"I've known for days that Biden was going to be the president, but when you get the Biden-on-the-cusp to Biden the president-elect, it's a numbing moment—numbing in a wonderful sense," he said.

He thought back to the state of the DNC when he'd come on the job, the mess-ups and flare-ups along the way, all the times and all the reasons people had called for his resignation. Democrats were four for four on elections after Trump, he pointed out, even with the setbacks. The Virginia and New Jersey governors races in 2017, taking the House in 2018, turning Virginia all the way blue in 2019, and now Biden, even if they hadn't done as well in the Senate races as they had hoped.

"The election was a referendum to a certain extent on Trump. To a very large extent, it was a referendum on common decency," Perez said.

"Common decency is all over the Democratic platform, because when you have health care for people, that enables you to live a fair life. When you treat Dreamers like the citizens they should become, that's the decency of the moment," he said.

Before heading out to watch the speeches, Jennifer Palmieri called John

Podesta so that they could take a moment together. Trump beat Clinton on November 8, and the two of them had been in the van back from the Javits Center when they found out she had conceded. This was November 7, four years later. They took it all in, quietly.

In the lobby, Palmieri ran into Biden adviser Steve Ricchetti, whom she'd known from back in the days when they were both working in the Clinton White House. "Stevie!" she called out to him, excited. He introduced her to his children, now adults, whom she'd first gotten to know when they were kids. They smiled, tried to get in the mood of the evening.

"You've given America a fighting chance" is what Palmieri came up with as he and the family headed toward the door.

"There was an assumption that because Trump was so unconventional, his victory was a fluke, and any other Democrat would be in a position to beat him," she said, reflecting on how the race turned out. "I did not experience the last four years thinking that the problem was the Democratic campaign—it was that there are a lot of people in America who are drawn to this man."

Bill Clinton, talking over the results from his home in Chappaqua, kept making almost the same point in conversations throughout the previous week. Biden's overall popular vote margin was big, but Hillary Clinton's had been pretty big too, even if it was just half as much.

A combined 44,000 votes between Georgia, Arizona, and Wisconsin going to Trump instead of Biden and the Electoral College would have been a tie, the Constitution would have booted the decision to the House, and Trump probably would have won a second term. Throw in another 33,000 votes in Nevada, and Trump would have won outright, despite being seven million votes behind in the popular vote. Biden's win wasn't much different from Clinton's loss, Bill Clinton said. And he had the whole party united behind him, no Russian interference in the election on the same scale, none of the extra drama and agendas the Clintons always believed their perceived enemies came up with to try to stop them.

In terms of statistics, at least, Bill Clinton was right.

Cedric Richmond was up front in Wilmington for Biden's speech. He'd been working two years for free, he joked, but looking at these election results, he felt as if he made the right call pushing Biden, then pushing Harris. "He was the man for the season and she was the woman for the season. They were both the only ticket for this season. As I look at the numbers and I look at the race that Donald Trump ran, I personally don't believe that there was another combination that would have beat him," Richmond said.

He was wearing a black mask with GOOD TROUBLE in rounded letters running across its front. "I think John Lewis is in heaven, looking down and ecstatic. One of his CBC members broke the glass ceiling for women all across this country in terms of the vice presidency. African Americans in Georgia showed up. Democrats in Georgia. Georgia came out and voted, and that's what he always fought for," Richmond said. He tried to think of an appropriate Lewis quote for the occasion. He came up with one from Martin Luther King Jr. instead. "When he gave the speech 'Give Us the Ballot,' he said give us the ballot so we can put judges on the benches of the South who will do justice and love mercy. And so this is not about judges. But we just elected a man who will do justice and love mercy. And so that's what this country needs right now."

A Biden aide had a simpler formulation. This was like "Dayenu," from the Passover Seder, she said. *It would be enough* if Biden made vaccine distribution work. *It would be enough* if he ended family separation. *It would be enough* if he just got the party and the country through this mess and to whatever was on the other side.

Harris spoke, a deliberate smile on her face as she said, "While I may be the first in this office, I will not be the last." Biden spoke, with words that hadn't much changed over the five-day waiting period, "Let this grim era of demonization in America begin to end here and now. Refusal of Democrats and Republicans to cooperate with one another, it's not some mysterious force beyond our control. It's a decision."

He mentioned Obama, linked him in a tradition of presidential greatness at American inflection points, from Lincoln to FDR to JFK. Then he, too, hearkened back to the 2004 convention speech: "I pledge to be a president who seeks not to divide but unify," he said, "who doesn't see red states and blue states, only sees the United States."

Then, as the fireworks started and the carefully arranged drones overhead put on a wizardry light show forming words and pictures in the sky over the parking lot, he reached out to wrap Hunter Biden in a hug when he came onstage. He was making a statement: he hadn't let Trump tear his family apart, as he said he wouldn't let Trump tear the country apart.

Even before he hugged Hunter, though, he kissed the forehead of Hunter's baby son, Beau, the child from his new marriage and life out in Los Angeles. Biden held him close throughout the show, pointing up at the sky, pumping his fist in excitement with the grandchild, whom he'd never appeared in public with before. After the confetti canons started popping, the reverb piano beat of Coldplay's "Sky Full of Stars" came on, the blue and green stars lit up in the sky for a moment, so they could feel the original Beau there with them too.

YOU KEPT YOUR PROMISE TO BEAU, Jill Freddell had written in blue marker on a sign she held, pacing around the lot after driving in from New Castle. "I know he made that promise to his son that he would run. He not only ran, but he won," Freddell said, "and I know he's thinking of him tonight." Mary Ann Kelly MacDonald, who explained that, by definition as a fourth-generation Delawarean, she knew Joe and had known Beau, overheard Freddell speaking. The highlight of the victory speech, she said, was when Biden quoted "On Eagles Wings," one of the hymns played at Beau's funeral. This felt like kismet, like sad Irish poetry.

"Beau lived to be forty-six," she said. "And now he's the forty-sixth president."

CHAPTER TWENTY-SIX

WHAT IF IT WASN'T?

If we are to have another contest in the near future of our national existence, I predict that the dividing line will not be Mason and Dixon's, but between patriotism and intelligence on the one side, and superstition, ambition, and ignorance on the other.

—ULYSSES S. GRANT

November 8, 2020–January 6, 2021

The morning after Trump won in 2016, Obama gathered as many distraught aides as he could cram into the Oval Office for a pep talk. For many, he reminded them, this was their "first rodeo." They were in shock, in grief, sleep deprived, in awe of the man who had defined not just their careers, but their lives and their psyches, who they had spent a decade of their lives chasing around Cedar Rapids and Manchester and Charleston and then London and Lima and Riyadh and Beijing.

Obama looked through the window to see that the morning rain had cleared, tried to buck up the staff with a line about how, see, "the sun came out." For election night he recorded a video, assuming he would be talking to anti-Clinton Americans who were wrapping their heads around the fact that she'd actually be the president: "Remember, no matter what happens, the sun will rise in the morning, and America will still be the greatest nation on Earth." When he walked out into the Rose Garden after speaking to the staff, he riffed on that theme. None of the other predictions had been right, but "that is one bit of prognosticating that actually came true: the sun is up."

Few of the Obama devotees who were in the Oval Office that day in 2016 remember that Biden spoke too. "We will recover," he assured them. "Your generation will make it so. You're the most inclusive, open-minded generation . . ." his voice trailing off.

Trump, even through the end of his reelection campaign, could never stop thinking about Obama. Late at night at a Florida rally two days before the 2020 election, his red cap pulled down low over his head, he summed up his four years in the White House: "I said, 'What did Obama dooooo?' And then I did the opposite, and it worked."

Trump never figured out what to do with Biden, in 2016 or over the whole 2020 campaign. Biden was actually the guy Trump pretended to be, with the working-class sensibility and the close family, and by being an older, white, straight man, he didn't give Trump any of the usual openings he used for his bullying. Trump liked Biden, he said in a 2016 interview. When Pence came to see Biden for a visit in the vice president's office two days after Trump won, a few Biden aides asked Pence's aides why Trump had never gone after their boss. "He was worried about waking up the bear," one of the Pence team said. "He didn't want the bear to come after him."

Biden asked the same question of Pence himself when they sat down in the office. "Trump has a level of respect for you," Pence told him.

Fast-forward four years, after all the racism and sexism, the manic decisions, the tweets, the pandemic, every well-appointed essay about how terrible Trump was, and every Hollywood celebrity other than Jon Voight, James Woods, and Scott Baio saying that the country needed to stand up. The daily chaos and infighting that was so disheartening and frightening to many was also proof to Trump's voters that he was taking on Washington and the status quo. Anchors on cable news speechifying on how unprecedented and shocking they found that day's Trump news were missing the point: unprecedented and shocking were exactly what many Trump voters had wanted. And many others were willing to hold their noses and squeeze their eyes shut through the Muslim bans and NATO blowups and the Kim Jong-un courtship as long as they got their tax cuts and regulation rollbacks and lifetime judicial appointments. Millions more voted for Trump in 2020 than 2016, because they were still angry that the government wasn't working for them, and he was still angry, and they still wanted to say *Fuck you* to everyone telling them they shouldn't connect with that anger.

Trump's presidency was the greatest voting motivator in history: 128 million Americans voted in 2016, and 155 million voted in 2020. Literally every poll underestimated Trump's strength, which means they also almost certainly didn't get right how popular he was or how much support there was for any of the issues that defined the election.

But a loss is a loss, and Trump was, on the biggest stage of his life, a loser.

And Obama reveled in it. Bleak as he had gotten over the year, like so many other Democrats, he just felt relief. The nightmare was over. Trump was gone, Biden was going to be president, America could move forward. He was happy about the part he played but was now looking forward to stepping back, becoming a Jiminy Cricket adviser for Biden, who was now a real president himself. He could get back to his own plans to transcend politics and become a thought leader of the world. No more stress about democracy collapsing, or more parochial concerns like how to schedule the groundbreaking for his library without having to be concerned about Trump showing up. He even finished the first volume of the memoir. It didn't sell as well as his wife's had, but he was upbeat. Corporations were no longer worried about the Trump White House coming after them for giving to the Obama Foundation, and the money started pouring in. The Obamas expanded their Netflix production deal for more millions for themselves. Staff relaxed too, no longer worried about the Justice Department possibly coming after them on vendetta marching orders.

"He feels amazing," said Robert Wolf, a major donor who had become a friend, "that he's passed the torch."

———

Trump and most of his devotees in Washington responded to his loss like heroin addicts chasing just one last high, shooting themselves up with attempts to undercut the election they all knew he lost. This is what the Grand Old Party had become.

In the 1980s and 1990s, Rudy Giuliani broke the Mafia's hold on New York and saved a city teetering on collapse. He finished 2020 ranting into his computer camera like a QAnon YouTuber about Hunter Biden's ties to Whitey

Bulger, getting pranked by mischievous Biden supporters into holding a press conference on election fraud at Philadelphia's Four Seasons Total Landscaping between a strip mall dildo shop and a crematorium, sweating beads of hair dye down his cheeks at a Republican National Committee press conference that blamed Trump's loss on Hugo Chavez and the CIA.

Ted Cruz, the self-styled great moralizer who brought intellectual imperiousness to his labored Elmer Gantry impression, started by defending the sensationalism of the *New York Post* and pretending to find a constitutional basis for the manic conspiracy theories of Trump, who had spent part of 2016 suggesting Cruz's father was part of the JFK assassination plot.

Trump himself kicked off 2021, during his final days in office, with one more tin-pot tough-guy phone call. "I just want to find 11,780 votes, which is one more than we have," he said on a phone call with the Georgia secretary of state, Brad Raffensperger, who released a recording he made of their conversation after seeing Trump misrepresent what happened on other calls when he'd been trying to get election results changed.

Just like in the 2018 elections, Trump's voters demonstrated that they turned out for him, not for anyone else. He knew it, bragging when he popped in to Georgia the night before the election for a rally ostensibly to help the two Republicans running for Senate, "I don't do rallies for other people. I do them for me," and bashing the governor because he, too, refused to change the election results for Trump.

So much of the 2020 campaign was out of an airport paperback, and the epilogue didn't disappoint.

After years of Democrats rethinking what they were and a campaign in which they had lost John Lewis and Ruth Bader Ginsburg, Biden got Democratic control over his agenda by way of a Black preacher and a Jewish documentarian who flipped both of the Senate seats of a state that hadn't been blue since Biden passed the crime bill. Raphael Warnock was Lewis's preacher, Jon Ossoff had been Lewis's intern. They were the first elected Black and Jewish senators from the southern state, winning a week after Trump became one of the few presidents to have a veto overridden, after he refused to sign the defense funding bill, with one of his main complaints being that it stripped the names of Confederate generals from military bases. Warnock went to the Senate straight from Martin Luther King Jr.'s pulpit; Ossoff became the youngest senator since a guy named Joe Biden. Neither started out as a recruited candidate of the smart Democrats in Washington, who fancy themselves arbiters of what works and what doesn't; neither had ever held office before; neither would have had a chance if not for Trump, and if not for Biden. Warnock grew up in housing projects, and his mother grew up picking cotton; Ossoff was descended from a family that fled pogroms, and he had come up short in the June 2017 special election that became the first national cause and fundraising sensation for Democrats in the Trump years. It was for the House seat that had belonged to Health and Human Services Secretary Tom Price, whom Trump had hired to dismantle Obamacare, but instead had to quit the administration over massive corruption. Warnock beat a senator appointed because she was a top donor who got richer in the pandemic while styling herself a QAnon-friendly populist; Ossoff beat a portrait of the traditional Grand Old Party white businessman who had turned himself entirely over to Trump and Trumpism. They brought in votes for each other, helping each other win. Their wins wouldn't have been so defining if the Democrats had been as successful as expected beating back Trump in November. Neither would have happened without the groundwork of Stacey Abrams.

Obama was reluctant to get involved in the Georgia races at all, skeptical that Democrats were going to win, but his statement the morning after they were victorious—the first time that he made a specific comment on an election since he was in the White House—reflected the party's jubilation. "My friend John Lewis," Obama said, "is surely smiling down on his beloved Georgia this morning, as people across the state carried forward the baton that he and so many others passed down to them." Biden went from almost being laughed out of the primaries to having no shot against Trump to becoming a conquering hero to being a battered victor and now ended with full Democratic control of Washington.

The change in the Senate was a revolution in itself—most notably for Bernie Sanders, who had started his career in politics writing weird essays in local Vermont newspapers and had run two presidential campaigns popularizing democratic socialism. Now, because of Ossoff (whom he had undermined in the 2017 special House race by saying, "I don't know" when asked if Ossoff was a progressive), Sanders became the chairman of the Senate Budget Committee. Between that and the work in the final few weeks of 2020 leading an unsuccessful charge to increase the COVID-19 relief payments to $2,000, which became a rallying cry for Democrats and a wedge issue in the Georgia races, he was now able to flex power in ways that hadn't seemed possible when he pulled the plug on his own campaign and endorsed Biden.

In the spring of 2020, progressives were talking about Sanders as their own Barry Goldwater, who helped inspire the next generation but was mostly in the past tense. "I always bristle at the 'progressives post-Bernie,'" said Jeff Weaver. "Post-Bernie? Where's Bernie gone? Bernie's still here. Still the most influential voice on the left in America, and will continue to be." Sanders, Weaver insisted, would have beaten Trump too.

Biden's presidency will be defined by those wins. With a Republican Senate, he would have been a placeholder president, at best a circuit breaker from the Trump mania, with maybe one hard-fought piece of legislation like an infrastructure bill to show for his time in office. Now he could have an agenda, and he could have cabinet appointments and judges confirmed.

He started the morning after Georgia upbeat. He'd gotten Lady Gaga to agree to sing the national anthem at his inauguration. He'd chosen Merrick Garland as his attorney general, in a little poetic payback for Democrats from the 2016 Supreme Court blockade, but also to have the armor of a respected, nonpartisan judge making the decisions about Trump prosecutions and the inquiry into Hunter's taxes, which leaked after the election. There were going to have to be decisions about who to prosecute.

Trump's push to overturn the election results was expected to be just a performance-art first event of the 2024 Republican primaries, a showcase for ambitious senators cynically throwing up their own objections so that Trump would look kindly upon them from behind his ravings of narcissistic injury. Biden's plan was to counterprogram with a short, boring speech about small-business investment, to show that he was focused on the real world, looking forward. Instead Trump became the first president of the United States to declare war on his own country. He riled up a rally near the White House, told his followers he was going to march with them to the Capitol, and then rode in his limo back home so that he could watch their progress on TV, pleased to see his red caps and other merchandise in the crowd, amid the paramilitary.

Backstage at the refurbished theater in downtown Wilmington that he'd been using as his event space since he started making appearances outside the home, Biden watched Trump's insurrectionists break down the doors of the Capitol and assault police, wander around his sacred Senate floor as if it were a bus station, some of them riffling through desks, wearing Trump flags as capes, some wandering around with zip ties and Kevlar vests with the clear hopes of finding a chamber that hadn't been cleared. One paced about with a homemade sign printed with a warped and invented version of the Ben Franklin quote: WE HAVE A REPUBLIC IF WE CAN KEEP IT. LET'S MAKE SURE WE KEEP IT!

Participants in the Women's March weren't allowed to have wooden sticks on their signs. Trump's crowd showed up with metal rods to smash the windows, with many of the Proud Boys—whom Trump had told to "stand by" at the debate—in tactical formation amid the crowd. What everyone wanted to believe was just a group of keyboard warriors angrily mashing their retweet buttons had now manifested in real life, in the form of thousands of people streaming down the Mall. As with so much of his coup coquettishness in those final weeks—installing apparatchiks in leveraged spots and entertaining conspiracy theorists who fed his ego with tales of stolen glory that he wanted to believe—Trump made out as if he were hosting *Authoritarian Apprentice*. His followers knocked over police officers and climbed into the Capitol, screaming "Hang Mike Pence!" and "Where's Nancy?"

For hours, the most anyone heard from Trump was via his oldest son and namesake, Donald Trump Jr., pretending that they weren't the ones looking in a mirror. "Don't start acting like the other side. We have a country to save and this doesn't help anyone," he tweeted from his phone, already boarding the shuttle back to New York after speaking at the rally and ducking out on the actual march to the Capitol.

Trump's "very fine people on both sides" after Charlottesville was the line that had persuaded Biden to run. Nazi flags, the "Jews will not replace us" chants, all inspired by an attempt to take down statues of secessionist generals. Three years later, it was a crowd with zip ties instead of tiki torches, CAMP AUSCHWITZ T-shirts, and a Confederate flag being marched through the Capitol for the first time ever. Trump bookended the event in what would be one of his final tweets before being suspended (and later banned) from Twitter: the insurrectionists, he wrote, were "great patriots who have been badly & unfairly treated for so long."

Onstage in Wilmington the next morning, Biden quoted one of Lincoln's messages to Congress from the last civil war: "We shall nobly save or meanly lose, the last best hope of Earth," he said. "The way is plain, peaceful, generous, just—a way which, if followed, the world will forever applaud, and God must forever bless."

A fundamental tenet of QAnon mythology is the notion of the Great Awakening, The Storm: the day of mass arrests and public executions for politicians who have finally been exposed and will face judgment for their supposed crimes. The difference of a few minutes, a few turns around a few corners, and the crazed internet message boards would have been playing out on live television.

Maxine Waters had been trying for days to get answers from the Capitol Police chief about the precautions that were being taken for the crowd expected to protest the certification. The longtime Los Angeles congresswoman had images in her head from 2010, when the Tea Party was on the rise, marketing racial anxiety about the first Black president under the label of resisting government overreach via Obamacare. John Lewis walked past the crowd that day, and they weren't shouting about co-pays and deductibles. They were spitting—in one case, literally—racist slurs at him.

Lisa Blunt Rochester, the Delaware congresswoman, was in the House gallery, waiting to see her friend's election certified. She signed up with Pelosi's office for one of the socially distanced spots in the COVID-19 rotation. When the shooting started, she dove to the ground, fumbled with a gas mask, followed the crawl of colleagues to the Republican side of the chamber in the hope that was safer. Her friend Val Demings grabbed her arm. Neither remembers the exact words in the moment, but Demings said something like, "Lisa—we know God is bigger than this." They started praying, louder and louder, until an officer knocked on the door to lead them out. "Don't open it, don't open it!" one of her terrified colleagues shouted. A Capitol Police officer inside the room shouted, "Show your hands! Identify yourself!" Jason Crow, the former army ranger and Colorado congressman who had signed the op-ed that helped prompt Trump's first impeachment and then been an impeachment manager in that trial, showed terrified colleagues in the gallery what to do.

Rushing through the hallways to their secure location, someone called out for the members to remove their official congressional pins, terrified that the rioters were coming to target them. Which was worse, Blunt Rochester asked herself in the panic of that moment, being identified as a member of Congress by crazed domestic terrorists, or risking law enforcement refusing to protect her because she was an unidentified Black woman? This was the America of Trump in 2021, when a woman who'd been a member of Congress for a decade had to face choosing which was the least likely way to die in the United States Capitol. *Take off the pin, hold it in your hand, don't put it anywhere, in case you have to show it*, she told herself.

In the secure location, as members milled around and tried to get staff and family on the phone, Blunt Rochester was laughed at by Republican colleagues when she tried to get them to put on face masks. "We had just literally escaped bullets, and I just wanted to make sure that we were not in a superspreader situation," she said.

As the panic ebbed, Blunt Rochester thought back to the day in 2019 when Biden told her he was going to run. He wasn't home when she knocked on the door, then she saw him pull up in his car with a bag of Dunkin' Donuts bagels and coffee. "I thought you might want something to eat," he explained. "When we sat down to talk, I could see the pain in his eyes from Charlottesville, this sense that he was called to do this at this time and that he did not want to see our country torn apart any longer," she said. "This is pre-COVID, this is pre–George Floyd. This is pre–January sixth."

Cory Booker noticed that the Secret Service was rushing Mike Pence off the Senate floor before he heard the noise of the mob. When he had been mayor of Newark, he was known for chasing down muggers, rescuing a freezing dog, carrying a woman out of a burning house. He started scanning the doors of the chamber, taking stock of the other senators on the floor, assessing which ones could help in a fight and which were the elderly ones they'd need to protect. When they evacuated, he was the last on the floor, protecting the flank.

In 2018, Booker led the fight, along with Harris, to pass a law banning lynching. The bill was mostly symbolic, signaling the country's breaking with its terrible past, and it passed the Senate, then was forgotten about when the House Republicans didn't take it up before handing over the majority after the midterms. Now there were lynch mobs roaming the halls of the Senate.

Had there not been cameras on the bridge in Selma on Bloody Sunday, the civil rights movement might not have broken through as powerfully as it did. That was the broadcast that the lawyer who helped Booker's parents had seen, to get them the house he grew up in. Without the eight minutes and forty-six seconds of George Floyd's death being captured on that cell phone camera, the summer of protests might never have erupted in a country forced to confront how little had changed, how many Black men were being killed. Those shots of rabid Trump supporters crawling the walls, beating police officers with the poles from American flags, and screaming in all their anger and absurdity and racism were a living portrait of what America had become over the four years of the Trump presidency, and especially during the past few months. Repeatedly, Trump said Booker was going to take over some undefined housing program which would overrun the suburbs, in another thread of his scare-mongering, bigoted campaign.

"There is a tragic validation that happens with regularity, the sort of punctuating of human life where you see this flare up—whether it's in a Black church, a Pittsburgh synagogue or an unarmed individual being shot or George Floyd being murdered or marchers savagely beaten on the Edmund Pettus Bridge or girls dying in a church bombing—that somehow then seems to trigger the best of who we are for those people who don't live with that haunting reality every day. For me, it's never that far away," Booker said, reflecting on the riot a few days later. "There are militias and organized groups and a whole stream, dark, dark stream of the internet where these people are activated. These are the people that were activated when Obama became president, when gun sales went through the roof."

The afternoon of the riot, Klobuchar and several of the other senators watched Biden's speech in their secure location. When he finished, they applauded.

Almost two years to the day from when he'd been literally anointed with oil and prayed over on the altar of a Newark church the night before launching his campaign, which might have taken off if not for Biden, Booker watched the speech back in his Senate office. He felt validation in what he heard for his own talk on the trail of pushing for unity and inclusiveness, but he also sensed that, in the end, he couldn't have had the same effect as President-elect Biden was now having, or that Sanders or Buttigieg or Warren or Harris could have had either.

"My hopes have actually expanded for Biden's ability to be a president that people don't expect, whether it was the trustbusting of Roosevelt or Nixon goes to China, that maybe this elderly white man from an older generation can deliver this message with a certain level of effectiveness," Booker said. "He is a guy in this moment that actually could make significant advances not just for racial equality and justice, but also for a lot of America that feels resentful or suspicious or fearful about their own relevance and their own inclusion in a multiracial America."

In Wilmington at the end of that tough week, Biden introduced the last of his cabinet choices: Gina Raimondo, the Rhode Island governor who said endorsing Bloomberg two days after the Iowa caucuses was an "easy call" and then briefly emerged as a dark horse in Biden's running-mate vetting process, was going to be the commerce secretary. Marty Walsh, the Irish working-class Boston mayor who chose Biden to preside over the oath of office at his own second inauguration in 2018, would be his labor secretary. The speculation that Sanders might get the labor job—an idea that Sanders spread around because he was bored with the Senate—finally ended. They discussed it, Biden said, and agreed that with the Senate majority so precarious after the Georgia races, they couldn't gamble with putting his seat up in a special election.

Trying to explain what happened—to the country, to the world, to himself—Biden landed back on the argument he started making in Iowa as the race was falling away from him in 2019. Then he was speaking out of desperation. Now he was speaking out of conviction.

"There's two ways people are inspired," Biden said, "by inspirational leaders and by terrible leaders. What this president has done is rip the Band-Aid all the way off to let the country know who he is and what he's about and how thoroughly unfit for office he is."

———————

Seth Waxman, the solicitor general in Bill Clinton's second term, had already been on edge by the spring. Once Biden wrapped up the nomination in April, Waxman reached out to Bob Bauer, the Biden campaign's legal adviser and one of the more experienced political lawyers around—he served as Obama's second White House counsel. As Bauer's wife, Anita Dunn, became more involved as a Biden adviser, he did too.

Like the rest of America's institutions, the election law landscape depended more than anyone had wanted to admit on conventions and unwritten rules. Like the rest of America's institutions, it was more vulnerable to Trump than anyone wanted to admit. They needed to get ready, Waxman said. Bauer brought in Don Verrilli Jr., a solicitor general under Obama. Waxman added Walter Dellinger, another former Clinton solicitor general. They became known as the Three Amigos, reporting to Bauer. They began talking about what they called Doomsday Plans. Soon they split Doomsday into two phases.

Doomsday Phase One was total election system collapse. Bauer had been on a 2013 commission about the voting systems and was deeply aware of how shaky the infrastructure was already, even before the pandemic. The Wisconsin primary in April was a disaster, with voters left standing for hours in the rain wrapped in garbage bags and other homemade personal protective equipment, and five polling places were open in all of Milwaukee. Combined with the Georgia primary in June, with voters left standing in line for four hours, Bauer saw a catastrophe brewing. Poll workers were resigning around the country, terrified about getting sick. States that were quickly ramping up voting didn't even have the paper ordered for what they needed, let alone the funding or procedures to count the ballots when they arrived. Bauer and his team began vetting groups that were stepping up to see which procedural problems were more serious, coordinating resources and experts, and directing donors who came to the campaign asking how they could help. In the end, the Biden campaign was the nexus for a more than $250 million, six-month nationwide project. By November, there were no notable voting problems anywhere in the country, cutting off any real openings for Trump's lawyers to object to the process or results.

Doomsday Phase Two was assuming Trump's lawyers would object anyway. Nearly six hundred lawyers around the country were quietly recruited into what began as a massive research project covering every eventuality they could conceive of for interference, from Trump sending the military to close down polling places in urban areas on the pretense of keeping the peace (among the scenarios Bauer rated highly improbable) to stationing immigration enforcement officers outside of polling places in Maricopa County, Arizona, under the pretense of stopping illegal voting (among the scenarios Bauer rated unlikely, but possible). A compendium running hundreds of pages was compiled, filled with template briefs and prewritten memos, ready to be filed within an hour of a challenge.

The team became versed in an obscure law called the Electoral Count Act of 1887, passed in the aftermath of the 1876 disputed presidential election, which had stretched on for months and resulted in a deal ending Reconstruction. The law had been meant to clarify the Electoral College rules, because that election was decided by 19 electoral votes from four states that were in dispute. Bauer's team immediately saw that this could be an opening for Trump lawyers, not just to dispute results but to overturn them, with enough insidiously creative maneuvering to raise doubts and force delays. The law requires electors to be chosen no more than forty-one days after Election Day, which they knew could be susceptible to pandemic voting problems—whether late-arriving absentee ballots, disputes over which of those ballots were valid, overwhelmed state election systems, or recounts.

Without clear results in each state, Bauer and the other lawyers worried, there could be a dispute over the electors. Cause enough mischief, and Trump's campaign could have triggered the provision in the law that would grant state legislatures the ability to step in and pick electors themselves—and it just so happened that Republicans controlled the state legislatures in the key states of Wisconsin, Michigan, Pennsylvania, Ohio, Georgia, and Arizona.

Doomsday planning went apocalyptic in April, as the lawyers watched men with machine guns storm the Michigan state capitol, protesting Governor Whitmer's COVID-19 restrictions. "The Governor of Michigan should give a little, and put out the fire," Trump tweeted. "These are very good people, but they are angry. They want their lives back again, safely! See them, talk to them, make a deal."

According to the Electoral Count Act, a challenge to the Electoral College results required at least one senator and one member of the House to object, and the objections are, after review, subject to a majority vote. In 2001 and 2005, a few Democrats in Congress made theatrical objections, which were not supported by either Al Gore or John Kerry.

If the Democrats had taken the Senate majority in November, then they could have voted down the objections. If Democrats hadn't held on to the majority in the House—and with all the losses in November, Pelosi had just a 10-vote margin—then Republicans seemed open to overturning the election.

Many suggested as much, after Senators Josh Hawley and Ted Cruz hatched their plan. "For their theory to work, Nancy Pelosi and House Democrats would have to elect Donald Trump president rather than Joe Biden. That is not going to happen, not today or any other day," was South Carolina senator Tim Scott's reasoning in a statement issued to appease the Trump supporters he was letting down.

If Trump and the Republicans would not recognize the election, backup plans were made to rely on world leaders to start turning to Biden as president. Lists of business, civic, military, and political figures were assembled, hoping they could help stand up against any domestic opposition. Aides would tell allies that what happened after Trump's Bible waving in Lafayette Square gave them faith that clearly there was a line that Trump couldn't cross without the country speaking up. They ran plans by Obama, who again asked to be briefed to be sure that they were taking the possibilities seriously.

Over the weeks leading up to the ceremonial acceptance of the Electoral College, Bauer and fellow campaign lawyer Dana Remus had gone over plans with the counsels in Pelosi's and Schumer's offices, running through all the eventualities. Every time Trump made a move—like replacing top officials at the Pentagon—waves of anxiety would arise about whether he was planning to declare martial law or invoke the Insurrection Act. Democratic attorneys general in Pennsylvania, Wisconsin, Michigan, and North Carolina urged their staffs to be ready to stop the Justice Department from seizing ballots and other material from the states. As January 6 neared, the Zoom calls centered more and more on assuming Pence would try to interrupt the certification of the vote, how to raise the objections if Pence tried to recognize speakers, because the presiding officer for the certification didn't have the right to. They went as far as planning how to respond if Pence literally reached into his jacket pocket and pulled out separate slates of electors and attempted to enter them to be put up for a vote.

By law, the vote has to be certified on January 6. But what would the consequences be if it wasn't? What if the senators, through their speechifying—or the mob, through its terrorizing—had to delay the vote by a few hours, or a day, or more? In that case, there might be an opening in the law. If the official votes weren't there to be certified because they had been destroyed, Republicans might be able to insist that the states would have to vote again, causing more delays. If Congress couldn't get its business done in time—the process was supposed to start at one p.m., and the Republicans had plans to object to five states, each of which would entail two hours of debate—they'd pass midnight.

To the more paranoid on the team who worried Trump might try to get a Supreme Court majority spearheaded by Amy Coney Barrett and Brett Kavanaugh, who'd spat "What goes around comes around" at Democrats after he came under attack at his confirmation hearings, Bauer would quote the scene from *The Godfather* when Sal Tessio, caught on his way to murder Michael, appeals to Tom Hagen to save him. "Tom, can you get me off the hook? For old time's sake?" Tessio asks. "Can't do it, Sally," Hagen says, before telling the gang to finish him off. Barrett had gotten the appointment she wanted out of Trump, he'd tell them. She wasn't going to jeopardize thirty years of conservative rulings ahead just to buy Trump a few days.

For all the planning for every eventuality, neither Bauer's team nor Pelosi's or Schumer ever considered the possibility of actual violence in the Capitol. As the rioters poured into the building, Trump's goading tweet about Michigan from April echoed in the heads of some Democrats: *Give a little, make a deal.*

Evacuated together in their secure location off site as police were still clearing the Capitol, Pelosi, Schumer, and Mitch McConnell talked directly, with no staff present. This had to end. They'd stay however late into the night to get the certification done, so as not to give the rioters or the lawyers another day. Kevin McCarthy, the House Republican leader who had thrown himself in completely for Trump and would end up voting against certifying the election results even after the riot, wasn't part of the conversation.

After the rioters were forced out and Washington was under curfew, Congressman Conor Lamb stood up on the House floor. Cautious by nature, and extra cautious in a district that he had narrowly won again on the strength of Biden's showing in Pennsylvania, he had planned to give a speech of bipartisan embrace, praising the Republicans in the Pennsylvania state legislature, which passed laws to facilitate voting, and the administrators in his home county who worked together to count the ballots. On a phone call with staff after the violence, Lamb told his brother, who is his communications director, "Start typing," and he dictated a furious statement.

Lamb had the text in front of him on the floor, but he didn't look at the notes. Behind him in a mostly empty chamber were his colleagues Eric Swalwell, whose brief presidential run in 2019 had already been completely forgotten, and Brendan Boyle, who had gone to see Biden after the 2018 midterms and pleaded with him to run.

"We know that that attack today didn't materialize out of nowhere," Lamb said. "It was inspired by lies: the same lies that you're hearing in this room tonight. And the members who are repeating those lies should be ashamed of themselves. Their constituents should be ashamed of them."

This, and not the events of earlier in the day, was what got the Republicans in the chamber upset. They demanded to have his words stricken from the record. They started shouting, Pelosi banged the gavel, and a Republican congressman ended up nose to nose with a Democratic congressman, trying to provoke him into a fistfight, while several other Democrats—including Colin Allred, a former NFL lineman—rushed in to stop them.

"It's sad, but it's true," Lamb shouted above the noise. "The truth hurts. It hurts. It hurts them. It hurts this country. It hurts all of us."

When the joint session reconvened that night, Boyle made his way over to Rhode Island senator Sheldon Whitehouse to tell him to call his daughter. She had been worried and hadn't been able to reach him. Chris Van Hollen, the senator from Maryland who ran the Senate Democrats' campaign arm in the 2018 midterms, asked how Boyle knew her. They were working together back in Philadelphia, where she was planning America's 250th birthday celebrations set for July 4, 2026, at Independence Hall.

"It just occurred to me," Boyle told Van Hollen, mostly joking, "we might have been presumptuous."

Biden's win was certified just before four a.m. More than half of the Republicans in the House and six Republicans in the Senate stuck to voting against accepting the results.

That night, America hit a new record: 4,110 dead in a single day of COVID-19.

———

Clinton, Bush, and Obama released coordinated statements decrying what happened, all spreading the blame of complicity wider than Trump alone.

Obama's echoed the Gettysburg Address: "History will rightly remember today's violence at the Capitol, incited by a sitting president who has continued to baselessly lie about the outcome of a lawful election, as a moment of great dishonor and shame for our nation. But we'd be kidding ourselves if we treated it as a total surprise."

At the Queen Theater the day after the riot, formally introducing Merrick Garland as his attorney general nominee and several other officials headed to the Justice Department, Biden made his own statement on the attack on the Capitol: "I wish we could say we couldn't see it coming. But that isn't true. We could. For the past four years we've had a president who has made his contempt for our democracy, our Constitution, and the rule of law clear in everything he has done. He has unleashed an all-out assault on the institutions of our democracy. And yesterday was but the culmination of that unrelenting attack."

If there was a silver lining, Biden said, it was in America's eyes being opened yet again, as they had been being opened all year long. He mentioned a tweet his granddaughter Finnegan sent him, of a picture of unmarked, unidentified troops with machine guns who had been ordered to the steps of the Lincoln Memorial during the George Floyd protests over the summer, protecting against an imagined threat.

"No one can tell me that if it had been a group of Black Lives Matter protestors yesterday that they wouldn't have been treated very differently than the mob that stormed the Capitol," Biden said. "We all know that's true. And that is totally unacceptable. And the American people saw it in plain view and I hope it sensitized them to what we have to do."

—————

The Saturday before the election, before an event at a community college not far from Mar-a-Lago, Harris knocked away a question about what would happen if Trump tried to declare victory even if he lost.

"I really do believe that the American people have a line that they will be unwilling to cross," she said, "and that line is, whoever they vote for, that there will be a respect for the election and the outcome, and they want a peaceful transfer of power, and they will stand for our democracy, whoever they vote for." She had tried to sustain that confidence two days before Washington erupted, answering a few questions after picking up dinner from a local Italian restaurant as part of an effort to highlight how the administration would take care of small businesses. Were the president and the congressional Republicans supporting him engaged in an attempted coup? "Let me just tell you something," she said, "we're going to be inaugurated. Period."

After Biden and Garland gave their remarks on the day after the riot—Biden pointed out that the Department of Justice was created in the aftermath of the Civil War, to combat groups like the Ku Klux Klan, and Garland had added, "The rule of law is not just some lawyer's turn of phrase, it is the essence of our democracy"—Harris stepped to the microphone.

"I believe we must ask ourselves two questions about what happened yesterday: what went wrong, and how do we make it right?" she said. "The challenge we're facing in our country is about more than the actions of the few we watched yesterday. It's about how to reform, how to transform a justice system that does not work equally for all." And with that, Harris was delivering what could have been her kickoff speech in Oakland in January 2019, or at the Iowa Liberty and Justice Dinner in November 2019. Justice had always been on the ballot. She'd almost gotten the race right. She just couldn't get out of her own way and figure out how to convince primary voters she believed in any of it.

Harris had been correct that Biden had a problem with Black turnout—even after the summer of the Floyd protests, the overall numbers were low across major cities, and Trump ran stronger than Democrats wanted to believe with Black men. She had been right when she asked for a briefing with Bauer's team about the legal planning around recounts and contested elections, scarred from her own drawn-out first election as attorney general in 2010. As soon as she was put on the ticket, she pushed Biden's top advisers to consider what would happen if Trump announced a vaccine by October, warning them that he would win if they didn't know how to get out ahead of it. She campaigned around Miami the last weekend before the election repeating at the beginning of each speech a line that she'd been fed—"Let me just be clear: Joe Biden and I are proud patriotic Americans"—which was supposed to subtly cut back against Trump's "socialism" attacks, which had been resonating with Latinos more than anticipated, but she didn't think that was enough. She was working off paranoid instinct, assumptions, and occasionally bad information, feeling as if Biden's aides weren't thinking through the plan. Aides would push back: they *had* thought through the plan, and she needed to learn to listen to them.

They were all wrong.

The week of Georgia and the riot transformed Harris's vice presidency too. Through the first briefings after Biden won, she made a point of piping in with a comment or question, making sure to assert herself. She was overwhelmed, realizing how little she knew about the job. She'd only ever been in the White House once before. She never considered that living at the Naval Observatory meant that her home would be staffed by personnel from the navy. She hadn't taken into account that her husband was going to have to quit his job at his law firm.

Now she was going to be the tiebreaking vote in a chamber that had multiple members who, at a minimum, goaded an attempt to overthrow the government. She wouldn't just be an adviser and a president-in-training for Biden, but now a central figure in his legislative strategy, helping run his beloved Senate with an external platform and an internal perch. That meant more profile, more experience, more opportunity to press for her own priorities, she and advisers started thinking. She could be the deciding vote on getting rid of the filibuster. She could be the deciding vote on delivering COVID-19 relief and infrastructure. She'd managed to make people see her doing her job as senator. Maybe she could pull off the same as vice president with a divided Senate.

One more indirect victory before the inauguration: Friday evening at the end of the week of the riot, Twitter announced Trump's permanent suspension—yet another example of an institution doing something about what it had previously said it couldn't or wouldn't do—and just in time, as the Democrats had gained full oversight power via the Senate wins. Again, Harris had been ahead on the concept, but flopped on the execution. All the way back in the October 2019 presidential primary debate, she and her aides came up with another gimmick to grab attention, and grab it without slamming Biden again: she was going to call for Trump to be banned from Twitter.

The idea was pitched in another tortured debate prep session with her aides, Harris wrangling more over how she was going to say it than what she was actually going to say. She was supposed to cut down Warren for giving another wonky rundown about splitting up big tech companies, a give-me-a-break call from planet Earth, Harris the one focused on what a normal person could make sense of while Warren spun out big talk of taking on tech that didn't seem as if it would actually go anywhere. Instead, flustered onstage, Harris posed it as a proposition to Warren: "Join me in saying that his Twitter account should be shut down." Warren responded, "No," and kept going—and that debate quickly snapped back to piling on her for her position on Medicare for All.

Harris's suggestion was dismissed as a desperate move by a flailing campaign—which it was. "Kamala Harris going after Elizabeth Warren on banning Trump from Twitter is one of the more pathetic stunts I've seen in a debate," tweeted Jon Lovett, one of the former Obama aides who became a cohost of *Pod Save America*. By then, O'Rourke's belly flop in the race had the hosts moving on from their early obsession with him, and toward Warren. Biden wasn't an option, because they were exactly the type of Obama aides who had always looked down on Biden for not being brainy or cool enough. (Biden, sensitive to anyone he knows not thinking he's smart, made clear to those aides that he didn't like talking to them either.)

In a country teetering so close to the edge, where the Capitol had to be turned into a Green Zone to keep the Trump-crazed terrorists from blowing up the inauguration, Harris's future seemed to simultaneously be a glide path to the Oval Office and a route that might crash into a mountain on the way there. As the vice president for an administration with the potential to turn around the country under a president starting out at seventy-eight years old, she couldn't be better positioned to be the next commander in chief. Yet she was also a bundle of potential liabilities, as a half Jamaican, half Indian female Democrat who enraged Trump supporters and inflamed Sanders-style progressives. Her inner circle went into the term determined that she establish herself, but worried about her looking like she was trying to overstep Biden, wanting to be seen as an important presence because of who and what she represented, but as one adviser would sometimes put it in conversations, not be seen just as "Blackety-Black-Black-Black."

She looked like America's future, but the election results showed that America wasn't so sure about what it wanted the future to be.

"With all the emotion and trauma of 2019, I thank God that we didn't win the primary and lose the general to Trump," a longtime friend of Harris's said, after watching the riot unfold. "That's what would have happened. And I would have had to jump off the Golden Gate Bridge."

========

Marco Rubio's plan in 2016 had been to be the Republican Obama, moving his party into a new, multiethnic generation by beating the other party's leader from the last generation. Then came Trump. Rubio was left making fun of the size of Trump's penis—and then when that didn't work, repeatedly calling Trump a dangerous con man. "No matter what happens in this election, for years to come there are many people on the right, in the media, and voters at large that are going to be having to explain and justify how they fell into this trap of supporting Donald Trump—because this is not going to end well one way or the other," he said in a CNN interview as the wheels were coming off. "He's going to be the nominee and he's going to lose. Or he'll have thrown this party into its most chaotic and divisive period, and that's unfortunate, because the Republican Party is the home of the limited government, free enterprise movement in America. And if it crumbles or divides or it splits apart, it will be very difficult to elect candidates that hold those views at any level of the government until we can bring the party back together."

Rubio warned of violence all the way back in March 2016, after a Trump rally in Chicago descended into a near riot, while Trump sat backstage, gawking at the violence on TV. "There are people out there that are not completely in control of themselves and they hear something like from a leader, you don't know what they're going to do next." We could lose the republic, he said. The Republicans who stood with Trump, Rubio said, "are people that—whether it's now or five years from now or two years from now or six months from now—are going to be explaining for a long time how they fell into this." A few months after inveighing with his predictions, Rubio used the massacre at the Pulse nightclub in Orlando as the faux predicate for reversing his pledge not to run for reelection to his Florida Senate seat, arguing that he felt a new calling to be in Washington to work on gun legislation to prevent another mass shooting.

Five years of not working on any gun legislation and ceasing to criticize Trump later, Rubio tweeted his response to the Capitol riot the next morning: "Some misled you that the VP could reject ballots, that objections could pass or be used as leverage to force an audit. They knew the truth but thought it was a great way to get attention & raise money." He added to that thought a few days later: "Biden has a historic opportunity to unify America behind the sentiment that our political divisions have gone too far, but instead he decided to promote the left's efforts to use this terrible national tragedy to try and crush conservatives or anyone not anti-Trump enough."

Rubio's complaint succinctly captured the mood in the Republican Party in the aftermath of the Capitol riot: Blameless. Misdirecting. Pretending that no one could have seen the steamroller running them down, despite having hired the driver and fueled up the tank. And then turning it around on Biden as if he were supposed to be the responsible sorcerer who would have to mop up the floor and put away the dancing brooms. Prominent Trump-supporting politicians turned to whining about losing followers after Twitter followed up banning Trump by suspending seventy thousand accounts with links to violence. They kept using the word *Orwellian* to describe what they insisted was them being silenced. They didn't realize that they might have been better off giving *Animal Farm* a read to see what happened to that revolution.

A few weeks after Trump won in 2016, Connecticut senator Chris Murphy was sitting in his office on Capitol Hill, trying to reconcile the world ahead as the sun went down on a December day. "We've never had to have a conversation about reselling democracy," he said. "Liberals scoffed at his talk of jailing journalists and throwing out major portions of the Constitution, because we just sort of assumed that everybody's on board with this thing called American democracy."

A few days after the riot, Murphy looked back on that conversation. He had turned the thinking into a speech about democracy being unnatural, which he gave often over the Trump years. "We shouldn't take it for granted. We run nothing else in our lives by democratic vote—our workplace, our kids' sports teams—none of it runs by democratic vote," he said. "It's ridiculous that it's lasted as long as it did. And I believed the speech that I was giving. Hopefully I'll live another forty years, and I feel like I'll be lucky if it's still here when I'm gone."

———

Back at the end of November, when most were writing off Trump's response to losing as the harmless grumpiness of a man who had also once complained that the Emmys were rigged against him, Briahna Joy Gray posted her response to a Trump tweet complaining that Biden couldn't handle vaccine delivery: "He might generate enough goodwill to pull off a coup if he started mailing everyone $2,000 checks right now and promised to continue them if he stayed in office."

Sanders distanced himself from his former national press secretary shortly after his campaign ended. She didn't speak for him anymore, he said. He wasn't responsible for her.

Gray wasn't the only one who, even after Biden's win, refused to accept that he represented where the party and country stood. That fight had already been going on for years.

In February 2019, Pelosi called Ed Markey the night before he was scheduled to help roll out the Green New Deal. She asked him to hold off. She wanted more substantive policy. The politics weren't good right then. Don't give the platform to Ocasio-Cortez, she urged, anxious about the new congresswoman's notoriety becoming actual power.

Markey had already been in the Senate for six years by then, but still had impostor syndrome. He had no real friends among the other senators. He served in the House for a full forty years, never thinking about crossing leaders, let alone being one. Markey had been a prominent voice on environmental and energy issues over the years, but had mostly faded into the Washington furniture. The last earmark to ever move through Congress had been millions he'd gotten through for the Kennedy Center in Washington, where he liked to spend nights out. He voted for John Kelly to be Trump's homeland security secretary because, he reasoned, Kelly was from Boston, so had to be all right. He voted, like most Democrats of his generation who'd been in Congress, in favor of the 1994 crime bill and the Iraq War. He was, essentially, Joe Biden without the personality, but with a history of dating Carole King and trying to rub tuxedo elbows as a Washington-society lifer. "Is this guy really the best we can do?" asked a *Boston* magazine article in October 2017 that had left him shattered. He was sorry he left the House, would wistfully talk to staff about how if he'd stayed, he could have been a committee chair.

Throughout most of his career, Markey would have been thrilled just to get a phone call from Pelosi. But that night, he told her no. He was sticking with the plan.

When Ocasio-Cortez arrived in Washington, joining a Green New Deal stunt sit-in organized by the Sunrise Movement at Pelosi's office on her first day in Washington, Markey saw an opportunity. He was close to Joe Crowley, the fellow Irish American congressman whom Ocasio-Cortez defeated in her primary, but Crowley was gone, and she had the energy now. She would need a Sherpa in Washington, someone to prove she had some establishment foothold and wasn't just the bomb thrower she was being made out to be. While Biden, despite how much time he spent talking about reaching out to the next generation of Democrats, never called Ocasio-Cortez until after he wrapped up the nomination, Markey invited her to meet in the Senate Dining Room, because that in itself bestowed institutional credibility, all the way to having its not tasty but still revered bean soup. For her part, she saw a guy who had a record on climate change that was intriguing—the failed 2009 carbon emissions bill known popularly as cap-and-trade was, officially, the Waxman–Markey bill. He arrived late, but they sat talking for hours. Markey came back to his office energized, buzzing to his staff about how great he felt working with her.

The Green New Deal isn't actually a bill. It's a resolution, which means that Congress can vote on it, and then issue press releases about how good or bad voting on it makes them feel. It's like making a promise after the holidays to lose weight without setting a diet or exercise routine. The actual text lays out that "it is the duty of the Federal Government to create a Green New Deal," and then adds that said Green New Deal be transparently constructed and built around a ten-year plan to deal with the enormous climate emergency facing the country and the world.

Trump helped bring climate change into focus in as stark a way as he had the underlying issues of MeToo. Every day since he announced he intended to pull out of the Paris climate accord or let his administration blow through regulations was another reminder of the existential threat of his presidency. At one point when mounting a partially self-interested effort to get the DNC to host a debate focused purely on climate change, Jay Inslee's campaign pointed out that the topic mattered more than all the rest, because immigration and health care and taxes would all be defined by how much the planet was burning.

The idea of the Green New Deal was electric, and immediately became a litmus test along with Medicare for All in proving progressive bona fides. To many in the base, and most reporters looking for easy shorthand, this is what Democratic politics had been for the last two years of Trump's presidency, and beyond: pledging allegiance to a nonbinding resolution and a bill that couldn't pass and being viewed as a true progressive, or holding off and being dismissed as an apostate, a—spit out like turned mayonnaise—centrist. Nothing else mattered.

Markey leaped all the way in, inviting the Sunrise Movement's cofounder to be his guest at the 2019 State of the Union, talking to staff constantly about how he felt invigorated by being around young people. Still, he was turning seventy-four in 2020, which would have been a fine time to retire from pretty much any job but the gerontocracy of Washington. When Joe Kennedy III started nosing around about running in a primary against him, Markey got his back up—and Ocasio-Cortez and the Green New Deal orbit saw a cause in protecting one of its own, with the added benefit of taking out a young, rich white guy. It didn't matter that when they attacked him for being part of a dynasty, that dynasty stretched back to his grandfather, Robert Kennedy, the godfather of modern progressivism. It didn't matter that Kennedy himself had a strong left-wing record in Congress, had distinguished himself as a leader on trans rights and an idea he called moral capitalism. It didn't matter that he had been a law student of Elizabeth Warren's. It didn't matter that turning Kennedy into a symbol of class, race, and entitlement was an odd attack strategy from another white man with decades in the establishment.

Kennedy had briefly considered running for president, sensing that his last name might have given him the familiarity powering Biden and that his young face and bright red hair could give him the new-generation vibe that powered Buttigieg. He went to meet with the consultant who had orchestrated Sanders's 2016 run, and before that, had helped run campaigns for his great-uncle Teddy. He decided against it, but the Senate race was a fallback political calculation: if he didn't move quickly, being a white guy with aspirations in Democratic politics might become a liability.

A theory on exercising power was being decided: It wasn't about bringing in allies who might be there for decades, as Ocasio-Cortez could have done by affiliating with the most famous brand in Democratic politics, and one who could have been a senator for forty more years. It was about leveraging power and brandishing that power as a warning to others to get on board while they could.

Ocasio-Cortez wasn't alone. Kennedy was given no credit for quickly signing on to the Green New Deal himself, long before he launched his Senate run. "It matters when the movement came. By all means, Joe Kennedy, evolve," said Ezra Levin, the Indivisible cofounder, with chapters that lit up for Markey. "It doesn't pass the smell test if you do it in the middle of a campaign."

For most of the campaign, Kennedy didn't realize how much of a problem he had. After so many football games and dinners at Hyannis Port, he still managed to often be a political naïf, so folded into the perfectly reasonable conclusion that no one would vote for Markey that he didn't see all the people who were suddenly ready to do just that. As Kennedy prepared to announce his campaign in the summer of 2019, Markey headed to Boston to attend the local Climate Strike, as the demonstrations were known. Staff purposely didn't schedule him to speak, but left him working the crowd for two hours. He was already famous among the very online Sunrise crowd as Ocasio-Cortez's friend, and was called out repeatedly from the stage, to cheers. Markey cribbed the idea of a climate change debate for himself, challenging Kennedy to one on the night before he made his campaign announcement.

Warren backed Markey, her collegial courtesy outstripping loyalty to her old student, though she started the year saying she hoped Kennedy would eventually run for president. Sanders, who hadn't ever thought of Markey as a progressive ally, stayed out.

"I didn't think that anybody could plausibly make that argument, looking at my record, looking at his record and think that this was going to come down to a referendum on progressivism," Kennedy said, looking back. "We are both by any objective measure pretty darn strong progressives."

Kennedy had spent two and a half years as an entry-level assistant district attorney before easily winning his House seat, but he was made out to be a racist for having worked as a prosecutor. Markey, who early in his career voted against a measure that would have given the IRS power to exert over colleges that banned interracial dating and opposed busing to integrate Boston public schools, was given a pass. Kennedy got knocked for not having a clear reason for running other than wanting to be a senator, and he didn't. Markey didn't either, and that was taken as fine. This whole strain of progressive thinking was premised on the concept of running primary races against disappointing incumbents who were in safe Democratic areas—that is, after all, the path Ocasio-Cortez took to Congress. For Kennedy, running a primary against an incumbent was treated like an original sin he could never get past.

As with Sanders, the politics quickly became personal. Discombobulated and smoldering over Sanders coming up short and Tara Reade's not turning out to be the magical savior to burn Biden down, many Bernie bro Twitter warriors and podcasters redirected their furor toward Kennedy. By the spring, some were raving about how they wanted Lee Harvey Oswald or Sirhan Sirhan to have a grandson to come and kill him. Except for a speech at a local Democratic fundraising dinner in Miami that happened to have already been on the schedule for two weeks after the Parkland shooting in 2018, when he talked about sharing a history of gun violence with millions of other Americans, Kennedy avoided mentioning his own family tragedies. Now, suddenly, the great uncle and grandfather he never knew were being used to mock him. "The glorification of the deaths of my family members, the vitriol directed at my wife online. Not that any of that's ever OK, but to see that coming from folks that are so clearly on the same team, that was surprising," Kennedy said.

Kennedy had been planning on outworking Markey in a heavy retail campaign, taking advantage of his youth and charm and a family whose picture could have come with the frame. The pandemic ended any of that. Kennedy somehow didn't realize the race was slipping away from him until June. After getting smoked in fundraising for months, Markey became a sensation online.

Statewide primaries in Massachusetts are as pure a distillation of Democratic politics as exists. This one was the last competitive race of the cycle, all the way in September, after Biden's winning the nomination and the Floyd protests and the dreams of a new society brought on by the pandemic had been processed in. Kennedy did better in Black and poorer areas of the state, Markey in more educated parts. Kennedy supporters saw those who didn't support him as falling for inanity. Markey supporters saw those who didn't vote for him as ignorant of what was genuinely good for them, voting only on a name. Markey won with 55 percent of the vote. It was the first time in seventy years that a Kennedy lost a race in Massachusetts. The politics turned so much that, by the final days, Markey raised $600,000 from Pelosi's endorsing Kennedy, and just before primary day, liberal members of the House started reaching out to hop on the train and endorse Markey.

The lesson for future Democrats hoping to run, Kennedy said months after the race was over, was to "think very carefully about what the key constituencies for a Democratic primary electorate would be, and to understand that you're not actually asking the question of, 'Can you appeal to the most amount of voters and motivate those voters?' It's a question of, 'How are you able to navigate through the increasingly passionate constituencies that are motivated to vote in those primaries? And that's a very different constituency that you need to be able to talk to and reach."

It began even before Biden gave his victory speech that night in Wilmington. On a postelection call for House Democrats in the middle of that week of waiting for the official call of the presidential race, Abigail Spanberger let loose. They had been led to believe, by public predictions and the private information coming out of their own political operations, that the Democrats were going to have a huge year, expand their majority, come into a new Democratic age. Instead, the Virginia freshman had barely survived her reelection, and many of her colleagues who had helped Democrats win the majority now lost—yet Pelosi had kicked off the call with an enthusiastic line about the election being a success, because despite the battles lost in House races, they won the war in defeating Trump. No, Spanberger said. They needed to talk about what went wrong, what they should have been doing, she said. Socialism, Defund the Police, Green New Deal, Medicare for All: if those were the issues that were going to define the next two years, they'd accomplish nothing other than losing the majority in Biden's midterms in 2022.

Texts came in from frustrated moderate colleagues. "Fuck yeah!" "Keep going!"

"Everyone's walking around saying, 'We're going to crush it,' and then we barely maintain the majority. With my background coming from the Agency, you do a postmortem on everything," Spanberger recalled a few weeks later, referring to her time in the CIA. "The inability that some in my caucus have to actually challenge ourselves to say what can be done better is antithetical to how I think. What comes next will depend on whether or not we're willing to have a conversation about the fact that it wasn't great, the fact that we didn't do as well as we thought we would do—or certainly as well as we wanted to do."

Pelosi wasn't having any of that. Spanberger and other members like her were missing the point. "She said, 'We have to do a postmortem!' Nobody died. We can have our after-action review. We always do, when we win or we don't. But we won," Pelosi said later. Democrats had the majority. She had her gavel as speaker, and 132 committee and subcommittee chairs had their gavels too. Democratic candidates combined won three million more votes than Trump, and ran up the count in districts that helped power Biden's Electoral College win. They had the power. Their losses, to Pelosi, were the simple matter of not being able to overcome Trump's appeal, as she'd been warning about since the night they won the majority in 2018.

"He is grotesque in every way: personally, politically, especially presidentially. He is really grotesque. But he's popular in their districts. He's got charisma," she said. "He's a snake oil salesman, and that has a market."

Ocasio-Cortez was not on the call. But she was in front of the Democratic National Committee headquarters a week and a half later, leading a protest for the Green New Deal. There was no one inside in the building, which had been closed since the pandemic hit, though the protestors acted like someone could hear what was going on. The Sunrise Movement's yellow standard flags were printed with THE PEOPLE HAVE SPOKEN. They were pushing for Biden to agree to a commitment to climate change he already agreed to, but that they didn't trust would hold.

Standing with an expanded version of the Squad, featuring two new members who also took out calcified older Democrats in primaries, Ocasio-Cortez made the moral and political case for tackling climate change, a topic "intersectional with every one of our needs and demands": bridging racial inequity, wealth inequality, Black Lives Matter, indigenous rights, reproductive rights, youth demands, and the creation of more dignified jobs. That, she said, is why climate had so quickly become a top-three issue for voters. What she didn't say is that she believed that Biden was a fluke, who didn't represent where the Democratic Party stood better than she did, and could only have been elected in this particular moment. The movement, Ocasio-Cortez went on, is why she won. She wasn't the one who was a fluke, she believed, even though she'd slipped by in a low-turnout primary, and then become a star by plotting her public presence with savant calculus to make sure she only appeared in ways that promoted her. "The movement," she said, "is why Ed Markey was protected this year!"

Markey nodded along as the crowd clapped and whooped. When it was his turn to speak, he repeated the same statistic he frequently turned to in talking about the election: that eighteen-to-thirty-four-year-olds were 12 percent of the total vote in Massachusetts in 2018 and 19 percent in 2020. "There's an IOU," he said, adding a turn of phrase as if he'd just thought of it: "This isn't a matter of moving to the left—this is about doing what's right."

Thanks to Trump, Ilhan Omar—the Minnesota congresswoman about whom he would lead "Send her back!" chants at his rallies because he didn't like that she was Black and liberal and a Somali refugee who wore a head covering—arrived with a police escort, just in case.

Omar had her own theory of what had happened in the election, with her and Ocasio-Cortez and Michigan's Rashida Tlaib. "We have seen the pundits and some of the leaders within the Democratic Party, or even some of our colleagues, who are freshmen, talk about us getting back to basics. Saying the Squad—Ilhan, Alex, Rashida—all of you have to stop talking about everything you talk about, because we need to get back to basics. So I was confused, because I thought, 'What is more basic than fighting for clean water? What is more basic than fighting for a breathable planet? What is more basic than trying to make sure we get health care for people? What is more basic than fighting for the people you represent, knowing that you represent districts where there are pockets within that community where the children have the third highest asthma rate?'" she asked, her voice quavering at points as she ticked through disproportionate maternal mortality rates, sustainable transportation, standing up for indigenous rights over corporate interests. "People will talk about kitchen tables—and everything we fight for is what my family discusses at the kitchen table. It's what your family discusses at the kitchen table."

Omar pointed to the 88 percent voter turnout in her district, the district where George Floyd was killed, and said she kept getting asked what the secret was to hitting those heights. "For generations, people have tried to get people to come out and participate in our democracy," she said. "For me, it's very simple. It's about the invitation we put out to people and why they needed to participate. Because the invitation was about electing someone who was going to help our country build back better."

But it wasn't just Omar's invitation to which they were responding, but the man and the politics she was there to protest: her heavily Democratic congressional district had the sharpest difference from support for Biden to support for a House candidate in the country, with Omar pulling 64 percent of the vote to Biden's 80 percent—despite all the doors she had knocked on in the final weeks of the campaign, despite all the voters she said she was inspiring when Democrats had failed to.

Facts don't tend to go far in politics. Already, the infighting wasn't just between progressives and moderates, but between progressives who thought the pragmatic, realistic approach was to temper expectations by not expecting Biden to arrive like socialist Santa Claus, handing out priorities for everyone, and those who thought the pragmatic, realistic approach was to deliver major results quickly so that voters could see they were responding.

Ben Wessel, a young operative who took over Steyer's NextGen America after the crew in charge left to work on his presidential campaign, thought back to his days as a Middlebury freshman, squeezing in volunteer calls to New Hampshire voters to try to get them to believe in Obama with a piece of the devotion he felt himself. "I would have jumped off a bridge for him," Wessel said. "There's not a single nineteen-year-old in the world who has the same feeling about Joe Biden. They will hold his feet to the fire."

"I don't think that he should be a bystander, just trying to calm people down, while other Democrats decide what it is we stand for," said Deval Patrick, trying to look forward. "And I don't think he will be."

CHAPTER TWENTY-SEVEN

THE DOG THAT CAUGHT THE BUS

No man who ever held the office of president would congratulate a friend on obtaining it.

—JOHN ADAMS

January 7, 2021–February 2021

Biden's plan was to leave Delaware for his inauguration via Amtrak—from the station he'd gone in and out of every day for years to be at home with his boys after each workday in Washington; the station where he stood with Beau and Hunter in 2009, waiting for the train carrying Obama to pick him up to go to their inauguration together; the station that was already named after him by the time he arrived back at it after Trump's inauguration in 2017. Security concerns after the riot forced the cancellation of that plan. He left instead from the airbase a few miles away in New Castle, delivering a farewell address at the Beau Biden National Guard Center, tears streaming down his cheeks. He flew private one last time, as Trump's petulance through the end stopped a government plane from going to get him.

While he was in the air en route to Washington, America passed four hundred thousand COVID-19 deaths.

Trump's presidency wasn't the only ending of his final week in the White House: Sheldon Adelson, the casino mogul who had invested millions into knitting together Republican and right-wing Israeli politics and had gone from being a Trump opponent to becoming a bankroller, died at eighty-seven. The National Rifle Association, which seemed a forever factor of American politics and in 2016 was the prime funnel for untraceable money backing Trump, filed for bankruptcy in an attempt to avoid prosecution. After weeks of being downplayed by the Trump administration, the Kremlin was clearly identified as orchestrating the massive hack of the federal government revealed at the end of 2020, an attack that reached far beyond the Russian election interference in 2016. Within days of Trump being booted off Facebook and Twitter, the level of overall disinformation online dropped measurably.

And a week before Biden's inauguration, Trump was impeached again for his role in inciting the riot—the only president to be impeached twice, meaning that half the impeachment trials in 244 years of American history were about him. The case the Democrats laid out was not so much focused on punishing him, because they knew nowhere near enough Republicans would dare to become Trump apostates, but on trying to make sure that voters never forgot who stood with him through the end.

"They are going to have some explaining to do to their children and their grandchildren and history for their betrayal of their oath of office and their lack of patriotism for the country," Pelosi said of her Republican colleagues who had denied the election results. "The sad part of it is not them—they're weaklings, they're cowards, they're pathetic. The sad part of it is these people in the country have their own insecurity, whether it's globalization, immigration, automation, women, diversity, the threat of climate issues. They don't see a role for themselves or their families in the future. So they're attracted to that. But we have to show them a path for them in the future."

———

Without focusing on the cement barriers and the concertina wire fences and the troops with machine guns marching by and the checkpoints at which to present the green bracelets proving negative COVID-19 tests, the inauguration had an almost intimate feel. A few hundred people who mostly hadn't seen each other in person for months gathered, greeting one another and settling into their folding chairs for a ceremony that was a national, international, and historical event, the changing of power in the midst of the biggest collection of crises in American history.

Milling in the cabinet section as Biden's car pulled up to the other side of the Capitol, Pete Buttigieg alternated between meeting some of his new colleagues for the first time and being interrupted for selfies by the few non-officials who scored tickets.

"This is that sunrise—or at least that day I'd been talking about, thinking about, for a long time. Who could have guessed when we got into this campaign, everything that would have come—including what happened right here two weeks ago? We didn't know we'd be holding onto continuity itself, in addition to everything else we're up against," he said. "But the day has come."

He turned to point to the American flags planted in the Mall in place of the crowds who weren't there, because of safety precautions given the pandemic and the potential threat of more rioting. "It's stirring, and it's poetic, and it's moving to look out and see those flags," he said. "And it's also reassuring."

Biden and Harris and their spouses arrived at the other side of the Capitol, and could be seen waving on one of the giant TV screens to the side of the stage. Buttigieg had wanted that shot to be of him. He hadn't wanted to be a member of the audience as the transportation secretary nominee, his husband trying to wrap his head around how much more expensive the rent was in DC than in South Bend. Buttigieg had hoped to parlay his all-in stumping for Biden into being picked as United Nations ambassador, to bulk up his résumé for his next run. Instead here he was, headed into a position that has never been a path to political greatness but would now make him a central player in attempting the greatest rebuilding and infrastructure investment since the New Deal.

"Lots of things about this particular future would not have computed to me a couple of years ago," Buttigieg said. "But in the end, this is a good day."

Biden's inaugural address didn't mention Trump, but he didn't have to. Every element of the scene—the security, the masks, the anxiety until the moment he took the oath (ten minutes early, maybe the first time in his professional life he's ever been ahead of schedule), the fact that he was the president and Harris was the vice president—was a function of Trump.

"In my first act as president, I would like to ask you to join me in a moment of silent prayer to remember all those we lost this past year to the pandemic. To those four hundred thousand fellow Americans—mothers and fathers, husbands and wives, sons and daughters, friends, neighbors, and coworkers. We will honor them by becoming the people and nation we know we can and should be," he said. "Let us say a silent prayer for those who lost their lives, for those they left behind, and for our country."

A moment of reflection, of prayer, not for the sake of brandishing a Bible or Beau's rosary. A moment of, for the first time in five years in politics, quiet and calm.

Garth Brooks came out to sing "Amazing Grace," asking the crowd, in person and watching on TV, to join him in the last verse. Harris mouthed the words from under her mask. "Amen!" Obama called out as Brooks finished, and then the singer bowed his head to Harris, shook Biden's hand, shook Pence's, shook Harris's, shook Obama's, hugged Michelle Obama, hugged Bill Clinton, hugged Hillary Clinton, and then, in a moment of slapstick relief, ran back to hug George W. Bush and Laura Bush as the crowd started to laugh.

"It's hard not to be reminded," said Roy Blunt, a Republican senator from Missouri who partnered with Klobuchar to be the emcee of the program, "of President Obama's singing that same song at the Mother Emanuel church—the song that in our culture is as close to both poetry and prayer as you could possibly come."

Bush leaned in to make a joke to Obama, and they both started laughing. When Bush saw Clyburn, he told him that he was the "savior," and that Biden wouldn't have been there without him. When Bill and Hillary Clinton leaned in to give him credit too, Clyburn replied, "I'm taking all the credit because my late wife is not here to take it."

Across the street from the Capitol afterward, Mitt Romney stood in his overcoat on the corner in front of a Senate office building named after a seg-regationist, looking relieved. It was Romney who laundered Trump into the Republican mainstream in 2012, chasing down his endorsement to edge out Newt Gingrich in the primaries to take on Obama, then flying to Las Vegas for a joint appearance making it official. "There are some things that you just can't imagine happening in your life," Romney said then at the Trump casino. "This is one of them."

In the years since, Romney lost to Obama, warned his party against nom-inating Trump in 2016, interviewed to be Trump's secretary of state once he won, moved to Utah to run for Senate in 2018, said he wouldn't accept Trump's endorsement and then thanked Trump for the endorsement when it came, voted for one of the counts of Trump's first impeachment, was mocked by Trump for potentially being exposed to COVID-19 in the spring, marched in a Black Lives Matter protest over the summer of 2020, voted for Amy Coney Barrett in the fall, said he hadn't voted for Trump in November, ran in fear from the rioters in the Capitol in January, and said he would vote to convict Trump over inciting the attack almost as soon as the second impeachment was announced.

"Well," Romney said, looking back toward the people still streaming out of the ceremony, and ready to move past all of that, "I think it was Churchill who said: you can count on Americans to get things right after they've exhausted all the alternatives. And we've struggled, particularly with regards to our response to the pandemic, and the economy struggles as well. And so we're mourning, at the same time we have hope that a new leader that's called on all of us to draw to our better angels, that that can bring a brighter day."

When Biden walked up to the front door of the White House with Jill that afternoon, they paused after the band finished playing "God Bless America." He was, for a moment, lost in thought. He hugged her; she steadied him. Then they looked back and waited for the family to join them as they poured in together.

That night, an immense fireworks show lit the sky over the White House, matching for a brief moment the colors that were projected on the building in 2015 after the gay marriage legalization decision. Lady Gaga sang "The Star-Spangled Banner" that morning, wearing a giant golden dove brooch. Springsteen kicked off the concert that night on the steps of the Lincoln Memorial. At the pandemic-safe, family-only inaugural ball at the White House, Biden held Hunter Biden's baby son, Beau, as he bounced to "Lovely Day," watching on a TV set up on a stand in one of the ornate rooms.

The next morning was the one-year anniversary of the first documented COVID-19 case in America.

—————

Walking out of a bar late at night in Burlington, Iowa, in January 2020, a few weeks before the caucuses, Andrew Yang spoke hopefully about how his core idea of a universal basic income might be written into the Democratic platform by 2028, maybe even by 2024. Three months later, Democrats and Republicans were approving checks as part of the COVID-19 relief—making him the rare candidate whose 2020 campaign had any lasting impact. The pandemic overwhelmed most other policy talk, but Yang kept pushing. "The trends we're living now are things that people were forecasting—malls closing, distance learning, tele-health, robot janitors in Sam's Club," he said. "The vision of the future I was pointing to—everyone can see it now, and it's pretty terrible. And most Americans see it the same way."

Yang had preliminary conversations with Biden's transition team about possibly being named labor secretary. When those didn't pan out, he launched a campaign for mayor of New York City instead.

Because the Georgia Senate wins put Democrats in the majority, all the senators who ran for president came into the Biden era with more power. Many of them had a new profile and new stature—Klobuchar, perhaps, most of all, having been transformed from a DC insider into a national voice. Sanders became perhaps the most influential inside player in determining how Biden's agenda would move forward, an august Senate power broker and a man who became a meme at the inauguration because of his cross-legged slouch and custom Vermont-made mittens.

Even campaigns that lasted only a few months helped build up new party leaders. Jay Inslee won reelection back home in Washington State to be one of just two third-term governors in the country and, after decades of talking about climate change, was transformed into a national voice on environmental issues through a presidential campaign that lasted only a few months. Swalwell—who still laughed about when Biden had whispered to him, "That was a good one, wise guy," after he'd said his "pass the torch line" at the first debate—looked up at the inauguration stage. "I ran making the generational case, but I get why the country right now feels like it needs experience and seasoning," he said. Then Swalwell was on to speculating about his chances prosecuting Trump for inciting the riot—terrified on the House floor that day himself, he had texted his wife, "I love you and the babies, please hug them for me." Pelosi had just named him an impeachment manager for the second trial.

Running didn't boost everyone. O'Rourke had spent the last stretch of the race complaining publicly that Biden wasn't coming to Texas—annoying Biden's aides, who felt that all he was accomplishing was making Latinos doubt the candidate's commitment to winning them over. Two years after exciting so many hopes and expectations, O'Rourke had neither a job nor a clear future in politics.

Like most billionaires, Bloomberg saw his net worth balloon during the pandemic. He spent a fraction of his new money on the election: $100 million against Trump in Florida, $60 million for House candidates, $2.6 million on a Texas railroad commission race. He funded a political data company through the election. His team found extra money in the budget, so threw another $15 million into ads for Biden in Ohio and Texas, because that is effectively a rounding error to Bloomberg despite his refusal to spend less than that paying off the salaries of his campaign workers. His aides coordinated with the original Biden super PAC on spending while funneling millions of dollars into the Priorities super PAC. It wasn't the billion dollars he'd flirted with spending on behalf of any candidate who might win the nomination back when he was defending his own massive campaign spending. But the quarter of a billion Bloomberg spent on Democratic campaigns in 2020 alone is more than anyone else had ever donated to the Democratic Party in a single election cycle.

Was Bloomberg the most important person other than the nominee, as his top aide Kevin Sheekey promised in West Palm Beach as the votes came in on Super Tuesday? "You want to argue Mike should have done more? You want to argue that Mike should have done things differently?" Sheekey asked after the election, conceding that maybe he could have. "But you can't argue that there is anyone who did more than he did." That might have indeed been true—except for the Senate races. Bloomberg didn't forget that conversation with Schumer about getting in, and the betrayal he felt for not getting support. He didn't give a cent to a single Senate campaign.

Amid all this, Perez succeeded in doing what no one thought anyone could achieve when he reluctantly took over the DNC: it was now flush with cash, had won four years of retrenchment election cycles in a row, oversaw taking back both chambers of Congress and the White House, and for the first time in decades (if not ever) was an actually functional institution. "I guess this is where I'm supposed to offer some parting wisdom," Perez wrote in a letter attached to a detailed transition report delivered to the new chair, failed 2020 South Carolina Senate candidate and Clyburn's pick, Jaime Harrison. "This is the kind of job where some days feel like years. But don't let those define your time in this office. Don't allow one bad day or one bad week to set the tone of the year. And whatever you do, don't type your name in on Twitter. It's never good for mental health." All that matters "is whether you stay true to our party's values and help elect more Democrats up and down the ballot." Meanwhile, Perez was taking another look at making that run for governor of Maryland, the dream he'd put off when Obama pushed him into the DNC job, which had been so full of cheap shots aimed at him and bad days for his own mental health.

In 2017, Warren had made a point of attending Trump's inauguration. She didn't agree with all the Democrats who boycotted it, following John Lewis's lead when he said he would skip the ceremony because, given the Russian interference with the election, he didn't consider Trump a legitimate president. Warren comes from a witnessing tradition, she'd explain when she told the story on the trail, and she wanted the image of that day "burned in my eyes." Four years later, on the day of the riot, she was in a car pulling up to the Senate when the attack on the Capitol started, and she immediately left. Being there to watch Biden take the oath, she said a few days afterward, was about witnessing what came next.

"It was witnessing on behalf of our democracy, that the vote of the people is still paramount. Donald Trump tried to take that away from us, and I feel like even now we haven't absorbed the magnitude of what he tried to do," she said. "Everyone tries to do historical references—but there's been nothing like this, nothing."

Warren insisted she was well past any envy or remorse as she watched her former opponent—who she had said in November 2019 was "running in the wrong presidential primary" for not backing Medicare for All—take the oath of office. She made a point of saying how excited she was about what Harris as vice president would mean to little girls across the country. On January 20, 2020, Warren marched arm-in-arm with Sanders for Martin Luther King Jr. Day in Columbia, South Carolina, making a deliberately public show of underplaying how much their relationship—and the progressive coalition—had collapsed after their fight at that debate in Iowa. On January 20, 2021, Warren was looking out over the empty grass on the Mall and the National Guardsmen surrounding the ceremony and thinking about how much was lost under Trump, but also about all the executive actions she was urging Biden's team to have him sign, like a $15-per-hour minimum wage for federal workers and racial equity provisions in COVID-19 relief. Also in her thoughts was the Senate majority, when the new vice president came back to the Capitol to swear in two new colleagues from Georgia and her own replacement from California. "Compare it to, say, a year earlier, when none of that was anywhere on the horizon," Warren observed. "We should burst into a chorus of 'To dream the impossible dream.' Sitting on that dais, I knew they were all within reach."

Wrapping up her stump speech during the primaries, Warren would build to a line meant to electrify supporters with a sense of calling. "This is our moment in history," she'd say, "and this moment will not come our way again!" While her moment hadn't come, still, she argued, "It's like the laws of physics. An object at rest tends to stay at rest. So the question is: When do you get change? And the answer is partly: you get change when the current circumstances become so uncomfortable that people demand it. The pandemic, the follow-on economic crisis, and the racial reckoning that all occurred in 2020 opened the door to change wider than it has been open in generations. Our job now is to lower our shoulders and run straight out that door, knock it open and make real change."

Over the course of 2020, Warren went from running for president, then aiming to be a powerful COVID-focused vice president, then briefly featuring in a progressive fantasy as a possible pick to be Biden's treasury secretary. Now she said she was "pusher-in-chief," staying in the Senate, working the phones, taking solace in the smaller victories she could win. With more spots for Democrats in the majority, she nabbed a seat on the Senate Finance Committee. Her first act, she said, would be introducing her campaign's two-cent wealth tax as a new bill.

"I'm happy where I am now," Warren said. "I'm happy because I have access to a lot of tools to make change, and that's what matters to me."

―――――――

Biden was behind the desk in the Oval Office. It was Groundhog Day, two weeks into the job, the day before the anniversary of the Iowa caucuses and what would have been Beau's fifty-second birthday. In a few minutes, he would sign a pile of executive actions wiping out much of Trump's immigration policy. It was his first interview as president, and he took the opportunity to consider the long road that had gotten him there and what he wanted to happen next.

Being in that room, Biden said, wasn't an adjustment. "It's hard to get used to waking up upstairs, though. I've been in the Oval lots of times. I'd been there every single morning for eight years, so it's familiar. It's hard finding my clothes—the thing I didn't realize, you've got to bring all your stuff, you've got to move, I tell you, man."

In between searching for his socks, he was glad to have the job he'd chased for so long. "I remember someone saying, 'Joe, now you caught the car.' I said, 'No, I think I got the bus.' I'm the dog that caught the bus."

Biden thought back to that night on Super Tuesday in 2016 when he told a crowd celebrating Black History Month that he was glad that Trump was holding, he thought, a mirror up to the country. He thought about his confidence back then that Americans would be inspired to reject him based on what they saw reflected.

He was wrong, he admitted.

"When I ran this time—and back when I was contemplating running—I decided for real that the job wasn't worth it unless I could say what I really believed in my gut: how much was at stake for the country. I really believed way back then—I know I got the living hell kicked out of me. Everybody in the press thought that the party had moved, that I was from another era, that it wasn't relevant, 'What the hell are you talking about, the soul of America? For Christ's sake, Joe, talk about global warming,' or whatever the hell they wanted me to talk about," he said. "But back then, what I saw with Trump was he didn't understand anything about who we are as a people. I really mean it. I think his transparent selfishness, his willingness to say anything, his overwhelming appeal to prejudice and division. He didn't have any social redeeming value, as far as I can see. But I underestimated his ability to take the big lie and turn it into something that was salable."

By then Biden's repeated use of "big lie"—coined by Hitler in *Mein Kampf* and popularized by Goebbels—had made its way into the political vernacular among Trump critics. His supporters complained, arguing that the term implied they were Nazis. Biden, now that he was president and Trump had clearly proved that he would have overturned the election if he could have—and that most Republicans in Congress would have stood by him—wasn't being even that subtle in discussing the private conversations he said he was having in 2016. "The really bad guys in America and world history have been the guys who've been elected legitimately and then tore down the guardrails to turn things into a semidictatorship, moving in a direction of autocratic rule," he said.

He looked up, over the Oval Office fireplace, at the portrait of Franklin Roosevelt he chose for the most prominent spot, flanked by smaller paintings of George Washington and Abraham Lincoln on one side and Alexander Hamilton and Thomas Jefferson on the other. Roosevelt had been told to call Congress illegitimate for opposing him. He toyed with packing the Supreme Court when it struck down parts of the New Deal. He broke precedent to run for four terms.

Biden's Oval Office decor features a color scheme similar to the one Bill Clinton used, and he has kept the bust of Martin Luther King Jr. first brought in by Obama, added one of Robert F. Kennedy and another of César Chávez (the original "Yes, We Can" guy). A painting of Philadelphia's own Ben Franklin hangs in the spot where Trump had had a portrait of Andrew Jackson. There is, naturally, a table full of framed pictures of the family. One of Pope Francis. The room is now distinctly his. But as the new president talked about where Democrats went wrong, he slipped into speaking of Obama's presidency as "our administration," when it was his administration that he was now leading.

"How many times did you hear us, even in parts of our administration, talking about the middle class?" he asked. So much of the Democratic conversation had been about helping the poor, he said, and though he had shifted over the course of the campaign to backing a $15-per-hour minimum wage and building up more social welfare programs, he felt that there was not enough attention to what he considers the base of the Democratic Party: "hard-working folks, ethnics, and Blacks."

Was the Democratic Party prepared for the 2020 campaign? "No. I don't think it was. I'm not trying to make myself be some kind of clairvoyant here," he said, and started rattling off all the wins he racked up among the candidates for whom he campaigned in the 2018 midterms, how he told each one to explain again the benefits of Obamacare and hit their Republican opponents with the point that they were against protecting care for people with preexisting conditions. When other Democrats veered away from that message and toward Medicare for All or other issues he considered to be more about abstract principles than about having a real effect on people's lives, Biden said he became confused and frustrated. "I think they lost faith. Some of the party sort of became a little bit elitist.

"It's not that I don't think that I am educated and bright, presumptuous of me to say, but it is that the people who built the country are the people who are all being left behind. When that happens, and you don't have a counter-voice to 'the reason you lost your job is because of an immigrant, the reason you lost that job is because those Black folks are taking your job,'" Biden said, "it opens up the door to the Charlottesvilles of the world. It opens up the door to what happened in El Paso. It opens up the door to 'we're being invaded' and the like, and the pure, unadulterated white supremacy. It's not cut through at all: it's pure, pure white supremacy. That's the engine behind everything Trump was doing.

"There's a direct line," he added, "between Charlottesville and January sixth."

Almost a year earlier, at the outset of life with COVID-19, Neera Tanden—who would end up having her minor cabinet nomination pulled, incoherently, because Republican senators and Sanders were upset about her tweets being too mean—had sounded out how she saw him fitting into this moment in history. "His power in a pandemic is that this country is going to feel like it experienced a lot of loss, and he's a person who can be a grieving, empathetic figure for a country that is going through a deep psychological loss," she said. "He can draw upon his personal loss in a way that few can. And the Democratic Party chose the polar opposite to Donald Trump on empathy as the country deals with the pandemic."

Biden described his run as a kind of electoral zen, where he got what he wanted only because he stopped trying so hard to get it.

"Everybody thought when I ran that I've been waiting for ninety-nine years to run, I was salivating to be president. I give you my word. I did not want to run. I give you my word as a Biden, I did not want to run," he insisted. Not after Beau died, when he felt that he couldn't put the whole of himself into the job. "This is the one time that I've run, of all the times I've run for office, that I felt—this is going to sound awful, I shouldn't say this—I felt an obligation to run, because I felt that I could beat this fella." The disdain in his voice was so un-Bidenlike, and as the conversation went on, he stopped himself on a few occasions from saying Trump's name. (After "fella," substitutes included "the last president" and "this guy.")

In those first two weeks, he left the White House only to go to church, and that night he headed out late to the Capitol to pay respects at the coffin of one of the police officers killed in the riot, lying in honor in the Rotunda that had been ransacked by the insurrectionists. The black chain-link fence that had been erected around Lafayette Park after Trump's Bible photo op during the George Floyd protests was still up, its perimeter now effectively expanded by new pandemic precautions that had been put in place. He had gotten both doses of the vaccine while still president-elect, but he was still having as many interactions like this one as he could by phone. Still he connected, as he always does, by talking about kids, throwing in over-the-top compliments, thinking about the future, weaving between hope and pathos in the quality he has that makes people unload their grief and stories onto him.

His old friend and chief of staff back in the Senate, Ted Kaufman, often calls Biden the luckiest and unluckiest man in the world. So many things had gone his way: the spectacular come-from-behind Senate win at twenty-nine; two wives with whom he fell completely in love; the Senate career that put him at the center of history; the unexpected second act as vice president, an offer from Obama that he had at first turned down; and achieving his lifelong dream of being elected president toward the end of a long life. But there was also all the heartbreak—the car crash that took his wife and baby daughter, the aneurysms that almost killed him, Hunter's struggles, Beau's death. Rarely in history does a person dream of achieving something for five decades, and then have that dream come true. Rarely in life does a dream come true with this many sacrifices and sorrows along the way.

"Here's a guy, at his age, he's done what he's done—and if he doesn't run against Trump and Trump wins, he'd think, if he had run, he could have beaten Trump," Kaufman said during the transition. "What is the rest of his life like?"

What was the rest of his life like now? On the one hand: amazing, because Biden was president and Democrats were in full control of Washington and the big legislative question seemed less *Could he get anything done?* and more *When would he come out for ending the Senate filibuster so he could maybe get more done?* Progressives started out his presidency excited that he was sticking to big action on COVID-19 relief and climate, trying hard to overlook the internal divisions that hadn't gone anywhere and were ready to crack open. Mounting a liberal agenda amid the pandemic and economic crises "is kind of like saying you're going to go play tennis with concrete tennis shoes and a spoon as your racket," said Mark Pocan, the Wisconsin congressman and Congressional Progressive Caucus chair who had been a Sanders supporter, explaining his own measured expectations. Still, Pocan was hoping for more once Biden got through the immediate triage. "Biden doesn't have much of a career after being president. He doesn't have to plan for a lot of things that other presidents have to plan for. That's our opening." Moderates believed Biden would hold off the revolution on the left that frightened them, would just get the country on track again. Republicans were so flabbergasted about how to take him on that their initial response was to insist his strings were being pulled by conniving aides yanking him to the left. Democratic leaders were already working toward the John Lewis Voting Rights Act, hoping to set the congressman's legacy with new protections that would fight the voter suppression efforts that Republican state legislators had started rushing to pass to make sure that Democrats could never again do what they did in 2020.

On the other hand, there was so much on the bus that Biden had caught: the wreckage from the pandemic, the economy, societal and individual psychology, education, and disparities of nearly every kind. Despondency almost immediately set in among Democrats who had convinced themselves that everything would immediately change after Trump was sent back to Mar-a-Lago, as if a new world would magically blossom the moment Biden lifted his hand from the Bible after taking the oath. By virtue of gerrymandering alone, Republicans were in strong shape to win the House majority in 2022—because there wasn't the anticipated big blue wave in November, Obama's and Holder's efforts had fallen short of flipping enough state legislatures in 2020 to reverse the redistricting legacy of 2010. Republicans were disavowing neither Trump nor QAnon nor their attempt to overthrow the election, mocking Biden for talking about unity, then pretending that the violence at the Capitol had just been a raucous rally. And the defeated president was determined not to let the party out of his grip. Mar-a-Lago wasn't Elba. It was the new GOP Golden Temple for pilgrimages.

It was hard to take people seriously in negotiations over the budget or voting rights or anything else after they had voted to overturn his election even after the riot, Biden acknowledged. Republicans, he said, were "in a really tough spot" coming out of the Trump years. His mind turned to 1972, when Democrats were being pulled relatively to the left with George McGovern at the top of the ticket, and a close poll in his own first Senate race got him invited to an ACLU forum in a high school gym where he felt ambushed by the organizer, demanding he announce his support for amnesty for draft dodgers. Biden refused, and in his telling, assumed at that moment that he was throwing away any hope of getting the left to support him or winning the Senate, but he stuck to his position because he knew it was the right thing to do. Those were different times, Biden said, not as polarized between the parties, not as polarized within the parties because of primaries. And, Biden said, McGovern wasn't vindictive, as Trump was, scaring Republicans into submission. "You expect people to be willing to get into the second edition of *Profiles in Courage*, but it's awful hard," he said.

The day before this conversation, Biden had invited a group of Republican senators into the Oval Office to discuss the $1.9 trillion COVID relief package that would help define his presidency. He'd shared a moment with Romney, chatting about taking his sons skiing in Park City. The newer senators in the group whom he hadn't served with before seemed to feel "like, *holy mackerel*," he was serious about actually reaching out to them, Biden said. To him, that represented so much of what he was trying to accomplish as president: to prove he wasn't lost in nostalgia of the good old days of the Senate in the 1970s and '80s, that they could disagree without inciting lynch mobs.

In October 2019, when Biden's primary campaign was pinballing between pathetic failures and embarrassing shortfalls, a major donor voiced the desperation of so many frantic, panicked Biden supporters and staffers at the time. "This isn't Obama. No one's saying this is going to be a transformational president," the donor pleaded. The point was to be *transitional*. Just give him a chance. He'd be the one who could beat Trump.

That had been Biden's own pitch, from the speech in Philadelphia at his official campaign launch, when he promised dramatic change on climate, education, infrastructure, and health care and said, "The single most important thing we have to do to accomplish these things is defeat Donald Trump." He had imagined his presidency more as an emergency reboot than an innovation, but he'd been reading FDR books during the transition and seeing the opportunities created by the COVID-19 crisis. Biden knows he'll always be seen as a function of Obama and Trump. He is determined not to let that alone define his place in history.

Biden usually can't get through a speech without quoting a saying that he attributes to his father—often his grandfather and grandmother and mother pop up too. His favorite is "A job is about a lot more than a paycheck," and that's the one that came to him sitting in the Oval Office that afternoon. Now as president, he connected that to a sweep of history he argued begins with 2000 and the rise of the internet.

"This is one of the things that, if I get out of here, I'm going to write a book about: the fourth industrial revolution. I think that there is a fundamental shift taking place in moral society. It's not a surprise that this phony populism has taken hold in Poland, in Bulgaria, in other parts of the world. You wonder why. I think it's because people are wondering what their place in the world is, what are they going to do? And I think a lot of it has to do with this whole notion of people feeling that they are worthwhile, that what they're doing matters, being able to look their kid in their eye, look their husband or wife in the eye, and say, 'What I'm doing matters. I'm doing my job.' And I think it's really frightening," he said.

Biden didn't want to be seen as a necessary compromise. He wanted everyone to remember that, well, he *won*. "I'm going to say something outrageous, well, not outrageous—I have the most progressive platform any Democrat who's ever been president has run on," he said. He was still trying to convince progressives that he could help them achieve what they wanted, if they'd just let him. He knew there wasn't much patience, that many of the Democrats who hadn't wanted him to be the nominee were still suspicious of him as president. He knew the younger generation agreed with David Hogg, the most prominent of the Parkland shooting survivors, who'd spent the pandemic at home from college and would end up taking a leave from the March for Our Lives group after the election, under stress. "A great way to make sure that the Democratic Party can lose our generation would be to work with white supremacists, compromise with them, and say, essentially, 'This slightly lesser form of genocide is OK,'" Hogg said. "We're not going to take that. If there's anyone Biden needs to work with, it's progressives and young people of color who turned out to vote for him."

Biden knew that attitude was out there, and he was pushing against it. "The problem is that, like with the environmentalists, the duck hat guys, if you don't do it their way *exactly*, it doesn't matter," he said. Climate had become Biden's great cause over the course of the campaign, though he still wasn't buying the Green New Deal. He had come so far from the spring of 2019, when his campaign had turned down the offer to meet with the Latino firefighters in LA because he hadn't yet come up with a climate plan. To him, the failure to get real environmental progress encapsulated what he thought the left wing of his party got so wrong in its absolutism over the years. It gave him the chance to make sure his presidency made history. It reflected both his overriding insistence that people talking to one another in government could really solve problems and his approach to the presidency as a trust for his and everyone else's grandchildren.

His plan was net-zero carbon emissions by 2050. The people who responded to the rising oceans and freak weather by insisting that he had to get there by 2030 weren't being realistic or smart, he said. Before announcing his climate plan, he talked to union leaders, making them see why there was more opportunity in supporting his proposals. He also wanted to modulate the environmentalists. Think about the miners and the oil riggers and everyone connected to them and their towns who had drifted toward Trump, feeling that Democrats were done talking to them. Biden wasn't. "In order to be able to get to net zero, your jobs are going to be eliminated. Your job. And nobody is willing to talk to you about what your alternative is," he said, and then mimicked the response he imagined from those he considered the never-satisfied progressives: "'Well, you're just for unions and all those prejudiced white guys with blue collars.' Come on. I think a lot of people feel so disaffected by the way society's functioning now, and it just gets further and further and further apart."

Biden told another story he tells occasionally, of how both his sons would be present in the greenroom before every debate he ever took part in, in every race he ran, until the 2020 campaign, when neither was there with him.

"The last thing Beau would say to me, he'd grab me by the lapel and say,

'Dad, remember: Home base. Home base, Dad. Home base.' What he meant by that was, 'It ain't worth it, Dad, if you're not sticking with what you believe. It's just not worth it.' That's what home base was," Biden said.

Beau was a better politician than him, Biden acknowledged. More modern, he said. As president, he was still in awe of the son he had thought would be president himself one day instead of him. He stopped to consider what Beau would have made of everything that had happened since his death over Memorial Day weekend in 2015, three weeks before Trump came down that escalator with his grin and thumbs-up flashing to start his own run.

"Beau knew how to operate—like, I'd be in a rope line, someone would shout a question, I'd answer the question, it'd be taken out of context. Beau knew better. Beau was more like Barack. As Barack said in Beau's eulogy, he was Joe 2.0," Biden said. "And so I think Beau would have been proud—I pray he would have—that I never walked away from what I believed. Not a joke, I get up in the morning, go to bed at night, thinking, 'I hope he's proud of me today. I hope he's proud.'"

ACKNOWLEDGMENTS

One hot day during the summer between seventh and eighth grade, I complained to my mom that I was bored, and she told me to go try to write a book. I'm only twenty-seven or twenty-eight years past deadline.

That's not the only debt I owe to the woman who took the impossible and made life workable. The road was never easy, but eventually we got there. Thank you for teaching me love and perseverance and how there's always a way to get through.

Writing is always a lonely experience, and writing a book even more so. Writing a book during a pandemic was sort of like being a monk marooned on a mountain, just with cell service and access to ice cream supplies. In a year that was robbed from all of us and a campaign that seemed intent on constantly producing new, more absurd chapters, I am indebted to the people who helped me keep sane while I was trying to keep track: That starts with my wife, who took on way beyond her half of everything the past three years that was not related to writing this book. And it includes my two boys, who dealt with many days when, even during a pandemic, I still managed to not be around. But it's also Josh and Jaime, Dan and Jackie, and Ari. Hopefully the phone calls and dinners, as these thoughts were forming, didn't ramble on for too long. Mark, as always, kept me grounded, and I was boosted throughout by the support of Mike and Bonnie (my most excitable fan).

This work was done in concert with reporting at *Politico* and *The Atlantic*. Thanks to John Harris, for believing I could make sense of Washington when he first brought me down, and to David Blum for getting me in his head. Also to Carrie Budoff Brown, who suggested I write one of the original articles that helped form the first foundation of what was to come, and to Blake Hounshell for editing it. Jeff Goldberg, Adrienne LaFrance, Vernon Loeb, Scott Stossel, and Nick Baumann all had hands in the articles that followed. Thanks to SiriusXM for all the guest-hosting invitations, which included working out some of these themes on air.

A few weeks after Donald Trump's inauguration, in the days when the new White House was the only story and the Democrats were too pathetic to seem like they could ever come back, Lauren Sharp began what has become four years of guidance, prodding, and enthusiastic interest. Also patience, as I worked through all the strands and stray thoughts that eventually coalesced. There are many factors that came together to make this book possible, but it would not actually exist in this form without her insight as an agent, and all the help she, with the team at Aevitas, provided.

Back when we started working on this in 2018, Rick Kot could never have realized how much events were going to make him live up to his promise of being an expert in crash edits. He was all that and more, gently guiding me before the words arrived and then masterfully chiseling them into shape once they did. His notes were incisive and generous, the editor that any author (especially this first-time author) hopes for. He helped bring both the facts and the spirit of this book to life, and saved me from myself more than a few times.

I'm indebted to Camille Leblanc for keeping us both on point, as well as the whole team at Viking quarterbacked by Brian Tart, whose enthusiasm was heartening and essential. Also to Andrea Schulz, Lindsay Prevette, Carolyn Coleburn, Bridget Gilleran, Mary Stone, Kate Stark, and everyone else involved in helping get this to as many readers as possible.

If you want to be a political reporter, you want to cover a presidential campaign. If you want to cover a presidential campaign, you wanted to cover this one—even when that meant lying in a gravel road in the middle of a field in northeastern Iowa late one night, trying to figure out how to reattach part of the front bumper to a rental car. There were many helpful customer service employees and gate agents and late-night check-in clerks along the way who made all that time on the road passable. My colleagues on the road who were there with a beer or a backup of a recording helped to make it enjoyable too.

The readers and listeners who kept up with the articles and podcasts along the way provided important insight and feedback. Whether you were there for those or started with this book, thanks for letting me be part of your guide to what was going on.

This book, of course, wouldn't exist without the hundreds of voters, operatives, and politicians who let me into their lives and helped illuminate what was happening in the politics of our country during this defining moment. Many people with lots to do were willing to find time for just one more phone call or another fifteen minutes to stretch past what we'd agreed on. I hope that these pages do justice to those conversations and the motivations behind them, whether that's a shy nurse standing at the back of a small rally in Milwaukee or a new president sitting at his desk in the Oval Office.

NOTE ON SOURCES

My first official reporting trip to cover the 2020 campaign was in Des Moines with Cory Booker on October 6, 2018. My first unofficial trip to cover the 2020 campaign was in Manchester with Joe Biden on April 30, 2017. Much was already under way by then. This book is the product of more than four years of daily reporting on Washington, DC, Democratic politics, and the presidential campaign—including two and a half years on the ground in twenty-nine states (much of that in Iowa, New Hampshire, Nevada, and South Carolina). The reporting draws on more than four hundred interviews with politicians, their aides, operatives, and voters across the country, in person and during pandemic times over Zoom chats and phone calls. With the exception of internal meetings that are re-created within, any quotes not marked otherwise were said at public events or directly to me in interviews.

Though some of this information was public at the time and appeared in articles over the course of the campaign, most interviews were on the condition that they be held until the publication of this book. They were conducted in a combination of on the record and background, in which case I was able to report the information even if not attributing it directly to the sources. All documents and emails cited within were obtained over the course of the reporting and are drawn directly from the originals.

INDEX